MBE Released
Answers & Explanations

Explanations for
Released MBE Questions

AmeriBar
Phone (800) 529-2651 • Fax (800) 529-2652

MBE Released Answers & Explanations

Revised 2011

Copyright 2011 AmeriBar

ISBN 1-44046-976-8

NCBE COPYRIGHT NOTICE

Table of Contents

MBE ANSWERS

MBE PRACTICE EXAM 1

Question # 1 – Evidence
Answer: D

(A)   Incorrect. The majority common law rule, which is followed by Rule 301 of the Federal Rules of Evidence, adopts the "bursting bubble" view under which a presumption disappears when sufficient counterproof is offered about the presumed fact. Here the testimony of the witness, although not conclusive, is sufficient to rebut the presumption that neither spouse survived the other and to support a jury finding that the wife outlived the husband. Therefore, the presumption is no longer controlling, and the witness's testimony is admissible.

(B)   Incorrect. The testimony is not "too speculative." A witness need not be absolutely certain of matters about which the witness testifies. Here the testimony is based on the perception and memory of the witness and thus satisfies Rule 701 of the Federal Rules of Evidence.

(C)   Incorrect. The statement by the woman is not hearsay, because it is not being offered to prove the truth of the matter asserted. It is being offered to prove that the woman was alive at the time she made the statement and hence is relevant on the issue of whether she survived her husband, even if by only a few minutes.

(D)   Correct. The testimony is not barred by the hearsay rule or any other rule and is relevant on the issue of whether the wife survived the husband.

Question # 2 - Criminal Law and Procedure
Answer: A

(A)   Correct. The defendant properly could be required to utter the words spoken by the bank robber. The privilege against self-incrimination extends only to compelled "testimonial" communications; "[t]hus, even though the act may provide incriminating evidence, a criminal suspect may be compelled . . . to make a recording of his voice." *United States v. Hubbell*, 530 U.S. 27, 34–35 (2000) (citing *United States v. Wade*, 388 U.S. 218 (1967)).

(B)   Incorrect. This explanation for why the defendant's suppression motion should be denied is overbroad and therefore incorrect because testimony based on firsthand observation may be suppressed in certain cases if the testimony derived from an unconstitutional identification procedure. *See, e.g., Manson v. Brathwaite*, 432 U.S. 98 (1977); *United States v. Wade*, 388 U.S. 218 (1967).

(C)   Incorrect. Requiring the defendant to utter the words spoken by the bank robber did not violate his constitutional rights. The privilege against self-incrimination extends only to compelled "testimonial" communications; "[t]hus, even though the act may provide incriminating evidence, a criminal suspect may be compelled . . . to make a recording of his voice." *United States v. Hubbell*, 530 U.S. 27, 34–35 (2000) (citing *United States v. Wade*, 388 U.S. 218 (1967)).

(D)   Incorrect. Requiring the defendant to utter the words spoken by the bank robber was not a compelled "testimonial" communication. *United States v. Hubbell*, 530 U.S. 27, 34–35 (2000) (citing *United States v. Wade*, 388 U.S. 218 (1967)). Accordingly, it was not necessary to provide *Miranda* warnings, which are designed to protect the privilege against self-incrimination. *See generally Pennsylvania v. Muniz*, 496 U.S. 582 (1990).

Question # 3 - Constitutional Law
Answer: C

(A) Incorrect. The space on city buses used for the posting of placards qualifies as a designated public forum because it is public property that the city has decided to open for an expressive use. The organization's placard was consistent with the city's designated use of the forum. The city administrator's denial of space to the organization was based on the content of the placard and therefore triggered strict scrutiny, which requires that the denial be necessary to serve a compelling government interest. The mere reasonableness of the administrator's denial is insufficient justification to satisfy strict scrutiny.

(B) Incorrect. Because the placard is neither commercial speech nor defamation, the truth or falsity of the message has no bearing on whether it qualifies as protected speech. The space on city buses used for the posting of placards qualifies as a designated public forum because it is public property that the city has decided to open for an expressive use. The organization's placard was consistent with the city's designated use of the forum. The city administrator's denial of space to the organization was based on the content of the placard and therefore triggered strict scrutiny, which requires that the denial be necessary to serve a compelling government interest. The reasons cited for the city's denial of the organization's request do not implicate compelling government interests that would justify a content-based speech restriction.

(C) Correct. The space on city buses used for the posting of placards qualifies as a designated public forum because it is public property that the city has decided to open for an expressive use. The organization's placard was consistent with the city's designated use of the forum. The city administrator's denial of space to the organization was based on the content of the placard and therefore triggered strict scrutiny, which requires that the denial be

(D) Incorrect. This choice overstates First Amendment protection of the expressive uses of public property in two respects. First, not all public property qualifies as a public forum, and government custodians have broad discretion to disallow the expressive use of non-forum property. Second, government custodians also have considerable discretion to enforce content-neutral restrictions of the expressive use of property that qualifies as a public forum.

The space on city buses used for the posting of placards qualifies as a designated public forum because it is public property that the city has decided to open for an expressive use. The organization's placard was consistent with the city's designated use of the forum. The city administrator's denial of space to the organization was based on the content of the placard and therefore triggered strict scrutiny, which requires that the denial be necessary to serve a compelling government interest. The reasons cited for the city's denial of the organization's request do not implicate compelling government interests that would justify a content-based speech restriction.

Question # 4 – Torts
Answer: D

(A) Incorrect. Although barbed wire did cause death in this case, it is not considered to be "deadly force." The statement is true but not applicable to these facts. *See* Restatement (Second) of Torts §§ 63 cmts. b & c, 84 & cmt. c.

(B) Incorrect. The landowner had a property interest in the land, and she was entitled to protect that interest even if her motive was primarily to protect the deer. *See* Restatement (Second) of Torts § 77.

(C) Incorrect. The landowner's refusal to permit others to enter her land was established both before and after she turned down the photographer's request for an exemption. The photographer would have been a trespasser whether or not the landowner had specifically told him not to enter. *See* Restatement (Second) of Torts § 77.

(D) Correct. The landowner is privileged to protect her property from intrusion by a means not intended or likely to cause death or serious bodily harm. The fact that the barbed wire presents its own warning and is not a hidden trap makes it a reasonable device for discouraging trespassers. *See* Restatement (Second) of Torts § 84 & cmt. c.

Question # 5 – Torts
Answer: D

(A) Incorrect. The plaintiff in a battery action must establish that the defendant intended to inflict a contact on the plaintiff. Restatement (Second) of Torts § 13.

(B) Incorrect. The plaintiff in a battery action must establish that some sort of bodily contact occurred. It is debatable whether smoke is sufficiently physical to create the necessary touching.

(C) Incorrect. The defendant may argue that the legislative determination to allow restaurants to retain some space where patrons may smoke is evidence that this sort of touching is not offensive in context. See Restatement (Second) of Torts §§ 20, 286.

(D) Correct. Whether the defendant's conduct was reasonable under the circumstances is irrelevant if in fact the defendant intended to make a harmful or offensive contact with the plaintiff. It would be relevant in a negligence action, but not in a battery action.

Question # 6 - Criminal Law and Procedure
Answer: A

(A) Correct. The Fourth Amendment protects the woman's expectation of privacy in her dwelling, including her temporary hotel room dwelling. Absent exigent circumstances, which were not present in this fact pattern, the Fourth Amendment would require the officer to have obtained a warrant before entering the hotel room. See Minnesota v. Olson, 495 U.S. 91 (1990).

(B) Incorrect. The result is correct but the reasoning is wrong. Admitting the diary would not violate the woman's self-incrimination privilege because the woman was not compelled to write (or to produce) the diary. See United States v. Hubbell, 530 U.S. 27, 35–36 (2000).

(C) Incorrect. The hotel manager did not have authority to allow the officer to enter the woman's hotel room. Stoner v. California, 376 U.S. 483 (1964).

(D) Incorrect. The hotel manager did not have actual authority to allow the entry, Stoner v.

California, 376 U.S. 483 (1964), and any reliance by the officer upon the manager's unauthorized consent would not have been reasonable. Illinois v. Rodriguez, 497 U.S. 177, 187–89 (1990) (discussing Stoner).

Question # 7 - Real Property
Answer: A

(A) Correct. The conveyance to the church created a fee simple determinable. The future interest retained by the grantor is a possibility of reverter. The church's right to possession ended automatically when the church stopped using the land as the site for its principal religious edifice. The heir inherited the possibility of reverter retained by the landowner and is entitled to possession.

(B) Incorrect. Although this option correctly concludes that the landowner's heir will prevail, it misstates the rationale. The church's right to possession ended automatically when the church stopped using the land as the site for its principal religious edifice. The church did not attempt to convey any assets. The church received a fee simple determinable which ended, and the heir inherited the possibility of reverter retained by the landowner and is entitled to possession.

(C) Incorrect. The church received a fee simple determinable and the grantor retained a right of reverter, which was inherited by the heir. The church's right to possession ended automatically when the church stopped using the land as the site for its principal religious edifice. The doctrine of *cy pres* may be used when there is a general charitable intent but not when the terms of the conveyance state a limitation that must be complied with for the charity to avoid automatic termination of its possessory interest in the property.

(D) Incorrect. The landowner conveyed a fee simple determinable to the church. The landowner retained a future interest known as a possibility of reverter, which was inherited by the heir. A possibility of reverter is not subject to the Rule Against Perpetuities.

Question # 8 - Constitutional Law
Answer: C

(A) Incorrect. It is true that the district court lacks diversity jurisdiction because the parties are citizens of the same state. But the court nevertheless has federal question jurisdiction over the case because it "arises under" a treaty of the United States, as provided for by Article III of the Constitution.

(B) Incorrect. The relationship of a matter to interstate commerce is relevant to the legislative power of Congress pursuant to Article I, but not to the jurisdiction of federal courts pursuant to Article III. The court has federal question jurisdiction over the case because it "arises under" a treaty of the United States, as provided for by Article III of the Constitution.

(C) Correct. The court has federal question jurisdiction over the case because it "arises under" a treaty of the United States, as provided for by Article III of the Constitution.

(D) Incorrect. The scope of the President's power to enter into treaties with the advice and consent of the Senate is quite broad, but it is irrelevant to this item, which concerns the power of a federal court to hear a case. The court has federal question jurisdiction over the case because it "arises under" a treaty of the United States, as provided for by Article III of the Constitution.

Question # 9 – Contracts
Answer: D

(A) Incorrect. In an offer for a unilateral contract, an offeree who accepts by rendering the requested performance is required to give notice only if the offeree has reason to know that the offeror would not learn of the requested performance with reasonable certainty and promptness. Such is not the case here since the offeror learned of the performance when the detective took the fugitive to the authorities. Restatement (Second) of Contracts § 54(2).

(B) Incorrect. The general rule is that a party's performance does not become due until all express conditions to it have occurred or are excused. In this case, the detective's entitlement to the award was subject to two conditions—the arrest and conviction of the fugitive. The failure of the latter condition—conviction—is excused under the doctrine of prevention, which requires that a party refrain from conduct that prevents or hinders the occurrence of a condition, because the authorities themselves prevented the conviction from occurring. Restatement (Second) of Contracts §§ 178, 225, 245 cmt. a.

(C) Incorrect. This answer is nonresponsive because it relates to the enforceability of the agreement between the fugitive and the authorities rather than the enforcement of the purported contract between the authorities and the detective. The dispositive issue is the effect of the nonoccurrence of an express condition. In this case, the detective's entitlement to the award was subject to two conditions—the arrest and conviction of the fugitive. The failure of the latter condition—conviction—is excused under the doctrine of prevention, which requires that a party refrain from conduct that prevents or hinders the occurrence of a condition, because the authorities themselves prevented the conviction from occurring. Restatement (Second) of Contracts §§ 225, 245 cmt. a.

(D) Correct. A performance that is subject to an express condition cannot become due unless the condition occurs or its nonoccurrence is excused. The detective's entitlement to the award was subject to two conditions—the arrest and conviction of the fugitive. The first, the arrest, was satisfied when the detective delivered the fugitive to the authorities. The second, the conviction, did not occur. Its nonoccurrence is excused, however, under the doctrine of prevention, which requires that a party refrain from conduct that prevents or hinders the occurrence of a condition. Restatement (Second) of Contracts §§ 225, 245 cmt. a.

Question # 10 – Evidence
Answer: A

(A) Correct. Miranda warnings must be given before a confession made by a person under arrest can be admitted. Since the defendant contends that no Miranda warnings were given, she is entitled to a hearing on the issue. Under Rule 104(c) of the Federal Rules of Evidence, the hearing must be conducted outside the presence of the jury.

(B) Incorrect. Rule 104(c) of the Federal Rules of Evidence provides that "[h]earings on the admissibility of a confession shall in all cases be conducted out of the hearing of the jury."

(C) Incorrect. Oral confessions are also admissible in criminal cases.

(D) Incorrect. A confession of a criminal defendant is indeed a statement of a party-opponent, which is admissible under Rule 801(d)(2)(A) of the Federal Rules of Evidence. But the rules of evidence cannot alter the constitutional requirement that Miranda warnings must be given before a confession made by a person under arrest is admissible.

Question # 11 – Torts
Answer: C

(A) Incorrect. Res ipsa loquitur applies only to situations in which a lay jury could say that the accident would not ordinarily occur in the absence of the defendant's negligence. This is not such a situation because it involves complex machinery beyond the ordinary experience of a lay jury. Also, another potential defendant is involved, and the findings of the jury are inconsistent with a conclusion that this is the sort of accident that would not ordinarily occur in the absence of the government's negligence. See Restatement (Second) of Torts § 328D & cmt. d.

(B) Incorrect. This is the principle of Rylands v. Fletcher, a case based on strict liability rather than on negligence, and the Federal Tort Claims Act only permits actions based on negligence. See Rylands v. Fletcher, [1868] All E.R. 1.

(C) Correct. The trier of fact has found no evidence of negligence on the part of the defendant. The defendant selected a reliable manufacturer for the component part and could not have anticipated or prevented the malfunction. See Restatement (Second) of Torts § 298.

(D) Incorrect. Proximate cause is necessary to establish liability in negligence, but it is not sufficient. Given the findings of the trier of fact, the plaintiff has not established breach of a duty by the defendant. See Dan B. Dobbs, The Law of Torts § 114 (2000).

Question # 12 - Criminal Law and Procedure
Answer: D

(A) Incorrect. The state statute includes lack of consent as an element of the offense. Accordingly, the statute cannot shift the burden of proving this element to the defense, by a preponderance of the evidence or any other standard. Due process "protects the accused against conviction except upon proof beyond a reasonable doubt of every fact necessary to prove beyond a reasonable doubt all of the elements included in the definition of the offense of which the defendant is charged." Patterson v. New York, 432 U.S. 197 (1977); see also Mullaney v. Wilbur, 421 U.S. 684 (1975).

(B) Incorrect. The state statute includes lack of consent as an element of the offense. Accordingly, the statute cannot shift the burden of proving this element to the defense, by clear and convincing evidence or any other standard. Due process "protects the accused against conviction except upon proof beyond a reasonable doubt of every fact necessary to prove beyond a reasonable doubt all of the elements included in the definition of the offense of which the defendant is charged." Patterson v. New York, 432 U.S. 197 (1977); see also Mullaney v. Wilbur, 421 U.S. 684 (1975).

(C) Incorrect. The state statute includes lack of consent as an element of the offense. Accordingly, the statute cannot shift the burden of proving this element to the defense, beyond a reasonable doubt or by any other standard. Due process "protects the accused against conviction except upon proof beyond a reasonable doubt of every fact necessary to prove beyond a reasonable doubt all of the elements included in the definition of the offense of which the defendant is charged." Patterson v. New York, 432 U.S. 197 (1977); see also Mullaney v. Wilbur, 421 U.S. 684 (1975).

(D) Correct. The state statute includes lack of consent as an element of the offense. Accordingly, due process "protects the accused against conviction except upon proof beyond a reasonable doubt of every fact necessary to prove beyond a reasonable doubt all of the elements included in the definition of the offense of which the defendant is charged." Patterson v. New York, 432 U.S. 197 (1977); see also Mullaney v. Wilbur, 421 U.S. 684 (1975).

Question # 13 – Contracts
Answer: C

(A) Incorrect. UCC § 2-509(1)(a) and (b) together refute the notion that the risk of loss passes from the seller to the buyer at the time of contract formation.

(B) Incorrect. UCC § 2-501 defines the concept of identification but does not articulate the standard for determining when the risk of loss passes under the circumstances present here. UCC § 2-509(1) governs the passing of the risk of loss under these circumstances.

(C) Correct. Under UCC § 2-509(1), a contract that requires the seller to ship goods to the buyer by a third-party carrier is either a shipment or a destination contract. Comment 5 to UCC § 2-503 provides that where the contract is otherwise silent, a shipment contract is presumed where the contract requires shipment by a third-party carrier. Since this is a shipment contract, the risk of loss would pass from the seller to the buyer when the seller duly delivered the goods to the third-party carrier.

(D) Incorrect. As stated in UCC § 2-509(1)(b), under a destination contract, the risk of loss shifts from the seller to the buyer when the goods are duly tendered to the buyer rather than when the goods are unloaded. More importantly, however, this is not a destination contract. Comment 5 to UCC § 2-503 provides that where the contract is otherwise silent, a shipment contract is presumed where the contract requires shipment by a third-party carrier. Since this is a shipment contract, the risk of loss would pass from the seller to the buyer when the seller duly delivered the goods to the third-party carrier.

Question # 14 - Constitutional Law
Answer: C

(A) Incorrect. Although the law regulates only commercial speech and the First Amendment does not protect commercial speech that is misleading, the facts state that the phone calls only "occasionally" were misleading. The First Amendment protects truthful commercial speech subject to the law.

(B) Incorrect. Although the law regulates only commercial speech, the First Amendment invalidates any law regulating such speech unless the law is narrowly tailored to serve a substantial government interest. The rational relationship between the restrictions imposed by the law and a legitimate state interest is not sufficient to satisfy this standard.

(C) Correct. The law regulates only commercial speech, and the First Amendment invalidates any law regulating such speech unless the law is narrowly tailored to serve a substantial government interest. The U.S. Supreme Court has held that a law barring the solicitation of accident victims within a limited time period following an accident was narrowly tailored to serve the state's substantial interest in protecting the privacy of the victims.

(D) Incorrect. The law at issue is not a time, place, and manner regulation because it restricts speech based on its content. Because the law is a content-based regulation of commercial speech, it is valid only if it is narrowly tailored to serve a substantial government interest.

Question # 15 – Evidence
Answer: D

(A) Incorrect. The statement is the admission of a party-opponent and would be otherwise admissible under Rule 801(d)(2)(A) of the Federal Rules of Evidence. However, under Rule 605, the admission may not be proven by the testimony of the presiding judge.

(B) Incorrect. Although it is true that reasonable efforts were not made by the defendant and his attorney to preserve confidentiality, this means only that the communication was not privileged. It does not mean the statement is necessarily admissible. The problem here is that under Rule 605, the statement cannot be proven through the testimony of the presiding judge. The defendant's statement probably would be admissible if someone other than the presiding judge had heard it.

(C) Incorrect. The statement would not be privileged because reasonable efforts were not made by the defendant and his attorney to preserve confidentiality. The statement was made in a public place in a voice loud enough to be overheard.

(D) Correct. Rule 605 of the Federal Rules of Evidence provides that a "judge presiding at the trial may not testify in that trial as a witness."

Question # 16 - Real Property
Answer: C

(A) Incorrect. An assumption of a mortgage makes the buyer primarily liable for any deficiency. The buyer is primarily liable. Absent a release by the bank, the man also is liable, although the man is secondarily liable. This situation can be contrasted to one in which the buyer purchased "subject to the mortgage," in which case only the man would be liable for any deficiency.

(B) Incorrect. The agreement in the contract to assume the mortgage created the primary liability for the deficiency in the buyer. The buyer did not have to sign the promissory note to become liable. The buyer is primarily liable. Absent a release by the bank, the man also is liable, although the man is secondarily liable for any deficiency.

(C)   Correct. With a mortgage assumption, the buyer who assumes the mortgage debt becomes primarily liable. The man, absent a release by the bank, also is liable, although the man is secondarily liable. This situation can be contrasted with one in which the buyer purchased "subject to the mortgage," in which case only the man would be liable for any deficiency.

(D)   Incorrect. A novation occurs when the bank agrees to substitute the personal liability of the buyer for that of the original debtor, who is then released. In that case there would be an assumption with novation. Here there was no agreement by the bank to release the man from liability and to substitute the buyer as being solely liable for the debt.

Question # 17 – Contracts
Answer: C

(A)   Incorrect. The rule of *Foakes v. Beer*, which is a specific application of the pre-existing duty rule, provides that part payment of a liquidated debt is invalid for a lack of consideration. The rule does not apply, however, where there is a compromise of a claim disputed in good faith. This exception applies even if it later becomes apparent that the reason for disputing the claim was invalid. Restatement (Second) of Contracts § 74; E. Allen Farnsworth, Contracts § 4.23 (4th ed. 2004).

(B)   Incorrect. The statute of frauds is removed as a defense when an oral agreement is fully performed. Moreover, the dispositive issue is whether consideration exists to enforce the agreement to settle the claim. Restatement (Second) of Contracts §§ 74, 145.

(C)   Correct. The architect's agreement to accept a payment for less than the amount due constituted an effective accord, supported by consideration, which was satisfied with the payment of $7,500. Consideration is present because of the good faith dispute as to the amount owed. By compromising, each party surrenders its respective claim as to how much is owed. Restatement (Second) of Contracts § 74.

(D)   Incorrect. A novation arises where either one or both of the parties to a contract is replaced by a third party. The architect's acceptance of payment does not constitute a novation since neither the client nor the architect was replaced by a third party. Restatement (Second) of Contracts § 280; E. Allen Farnsworth, Contracts, § 4.24 (4th ed. 2004).

Question # 18 – Evidence
Answer: C

(A)   Incorrect. Although the probative value of this evidence on the issue of whether defendant intentionally burned her house down is not particularly strong, the evidence is relevant to the issue of possible motive. Rule 403 of the Federal Rules of Evidence provides that relevant evidence should be admitted unless its probative value is "substantially outweighed" by the dangers of unfair prejudice or confusion. Here, the evidence of insurance is neither unfairly prejudicial nor particularly confusing.

(B)   Incorrect. Under Rule 411 of the Federal Rules of Evidence it is true that evidence that a person was insured is generally not admissible to prove that the person acted negligently or otherwise wrongfully. However, such evidence may be received for other purposes, and proof of motive is such a purpose. In this respect, Rule 411 is similar to Rule 404(b), under which evidence of past conduct cannot be admitted to prove a propensity to engage in such conduct but can be admitted on the issue of motive.

(C)   Correct. Although this evidence is certainly not conclusive that the defendant committed arson (many people fully insure their houses), it is relevant to the issue of whether the defendant would have had a financial incentive to commit the arson. The defendant might be able to generate cash more quickly by burning down the house and collecting insurance proceeds than by attempting to sell the house. To be relevant under Rule 401 of the Federal Rules of Evidence, the evidence need only have "any tendency to make the existence of a fact that is of consequence to the determination of the action more probable or less probable than it would be without the evidence." Therefore, evidence that has only the slightest probative value can be admitted under this rule.

(D)   Incorrect. There is no such broad rule that any conduct of a party may be admitted against that party.

Question # 19 – Torts
Answer: D

(A)   Incorrect. There are limits on the ability of employers to circumvent respondeat superior liability through the use of independent contractors. Work in public places often gives rise to a nondelegable duty on the part of the landowner.

(B)   Incorrect. Proof that prior accidents have occurred is neither necessary nor sufficient to establish negligence or the existence of a nondelegable duty. Dan B. Dobbs, The Law of Torts §§ 151, 337 (2000).

(C)   Incorrect. The status of the injured plaintiff is irrelevant to whether the duty is nondelegable. Also, when a business is open to the public generally, members of the public are typically treated as invitees whether or not they intend to make a purchase on any particular visit. Dan B. Dobbs, The Law of Torts §§ 234, 337 (2000).

(D)   Correct. Although employers are not usually liable for the negligence of independent contractors, there are limits on the ability of employers to circumvent liability in this way. Work in public places often gives rise to a nondelegable duty on the part of the landowner.

Question # 20 – Contracts
Answer: A

(A)   Correct. UCC § 2-613 provides that where goods, identified at the time the contract was made, are totally destroyed before the risk of their loss has passed to the buyer and without the fault of either party, the contract is avoided and each party is relieved of its respective obligation to perform. Under UCC § 2-501, the goods were identified at the time of contract formation since the parties agreed to the delivery of a specific automobile. In addition, the facts state that the car was destroyed without the fault of either party and before the risk of loss had passed. Therefore the contract is avoided. Since each party's performance is discharged, neither party can assert a valid claim against the other.

(B)   Incorrect. UCC § 2-613 provides that where goods, identified (UCC § 2-501) at the time the contract was made, are totally destroyed before the risk of their loss has passed to the buyer and without the fault of either party, the contract is avoided and each party is relieved of its respective obligation to perform. The avoidance of the contract excused both parties' performance obligation. Consequently neither party has a claim against the other.

(C)   Incorrect. UCC § 2-613 provides that where goods, identified (UCC § 2-501) at the time the contract was made, are totally destroyed before the risk of their loss has passed to the buyer and without the fault of either party, the contract is avoided and each party is relieved of its respective obligation to perform. The avoidance of the contract excused both parties' performance obligation. Consequently neither party has a claim against the other.

(D)   Incorrect. UCC § 2-613 provides that where goods, identified (UCC § 2-501) at the time the contract was made, are totally destroyed before the risk of their loss has passed to the buyer and without the fault of either party, the contract is avoided and each party is relieved of its respective obligation to perform. Consequently neither party has a claim against the other.

Question # 21 - Constitutional Law
Answer: A

(A)   Correct. A bill of attainder is a legislative act that singles out particular individuals for punishment without a trial; bills of attainder are explicitly prohibited by the Constitution. The U.S. Supreme Court held, in *United States v. Lovett*, 328 U.S. 303 (1946), that a statute barring particular individuals from government employment qualified as punishment within the meaning of the constitutional provision prohibiting bills of attainder.

(B)   Incorrect. Although due process entitles an individual to notice and hearing before being deprived of an interest in liberty or property, these requirements do not apply to legislative acts. It is the bill of attainder clause that imposes these requirements on Congress. The U.S. Supreme Court held, in *United States v. Lovett*, 328 U.S. 303 (1946), that a statute barring particular individuals from government employment qualified as punishment within the meaning of the constitutional provision prohibiting bills of attainder.

(C)   Incorrect. Although the statute at issue punishes individuals for past conduct, the *ex post facto* clause applies only to criminal or penal measures. The statute at issue does not impose a criminal penalty on the targeted individuals. It simply bars them from government employment. The U.S. Supreme Court held in *United States v. Lovett*, 328 U.S. 303 (1946), that a statute barring particular individuals from government employment qualified as punishment within the meaning of the constitutional provision prohibiting bills of attainder.

(D)   Incorrect. The takings clause prohibits the government from taking an individual's property without paying just compensation. The statute at issue does not take property owned by the targeted individuals. It simply bars the individuals from government employment. The U.S. Supreme Court held, in *United States v. Lovett*, 328 U.S. 303 (1946), that a statute barring particular individuals from government employment qualified as punishment within the meaning of the constitutional provision prohibiting bills of attainder.

Question # 22 - Real Property
Answer: D

(A)   Incorrect. It is not relevant who drafted the contract. The contract was silent regarding any risk of loss. If there is no statute, the Uniform Vendor and Purchaser Act, which places the risk of loss on the one in possession, is not applicable. The court found for the seller, and thus the minority common law rule, which places the risk on the seller under these facts, is inapplicable. Under the majority common law rule of equitable conversion, the individual with the equitable interest bears the risk of loss. The equitable title passed to the buyer when the seller signed the contract because the contract was unconditional and was silent regarding the risk of loss.

(B)   Incorrect. There were no conditions in the contract of sale. The contract became binding when the seller signed the acceptance. The buyer would have been obligated to purchase even if the buyer had not received a loan commitment. If there is no statute, the Uniform Vendor and Purchaser Act, which places the risk of loss on the one in possession, is not applicable. The court found for the seller, and thus the minority common law rule, which places the risk on the seller under these facts, is inapplicable. Under the majority common law rule of equitable conversion, the individual with the equitable interest bears the risk of loss. The equitable title passed to the buyer when the seller signed the contract because the contract was unconditional and was silent regarding the risk of loss.

(C)   Incorrect. Possession does not pass to the buyer until closing absent a contrary provision in the contract of sale. If a jurisdiction has adopted the Uniform Vendor and Purchaser Act, the risk of loss is on the party in possession if the contract is silent regarding the risk of loss. The question notes that there is no applicable statute. The court found for the seller and thus the minority common law rule, which places the risk on the seller under these facts, is inapplicable. Under the majority common law rule of equitable conversion, the individual with the equitable interest bears the risk of loss. The equitable title passed to the buyer when the seller signed the contract because the contract was unconditional and was silent regarding the risk of loss.

(D)   Correct. Under the doctrine of equitable conversion, the risk of loss goes to the party with the equitable title if the contract is silent. Equitable conversion occurs when the contract is capable of specific performance. This contract was silent regarding the risk of loss and there were no conditions to be met. The buyer thus had the equitable title at the time of the loss. If there is no statute, the Uniform Vendor and Purchaser Act, which places the risk of loss on the one in possession, is not applicable. The court found for the seller, and thus the minority common law rule, which places the risk on the seller under these facts, is inapplicable.

Question # 23 - Criminal Law and Procedure
Answer: D

(A)   Incorrect. A grand jury witness does not have a constitutional right to counsel inside a grand jury room. *See Conn v. Gabbert*, 526 U.S. 286, 292 (1999) (citing *United States v. Mandujano*, 425 U.S. 564 (1976)).

(B)   Incorrect. The Fourth Amendment exclusionary rule does not apply to federal grand juries and is not a basis upon which a federal indictment can be dismissed. *United States v. Calandra*, 414 U.S. 338 (1974).

(C) Incorrect. The issue here does not turn on waiver, nor does the fact pattern demonstrate a waiver of any constitutional rights. Rather, wholly apart from any waiver, none of defendant's constitutional rights were violated: a grand jury witness does not have a constitutional right to counsel inside a grand jury room (*see Conn v. Gabbert*, 526 U.S. 286, 292 (1999) (citing *United States v. Mandujano*, 425 U.S. 564 (1976)), and the Fourth Amendment exclusionary rule does not apply to federal grand juries. *United States v. Calandra*, 414 U.S. 338 (1974).

(D) Correct. A grand jury witness does not have a constitutional right to counsel inside a grand jury room. *See Conn v. Gabbert*, 526 U.S. 286, 292 (1999) (citing *United States v. Mandujano*, 425 U.S. 564 (1976)). The Fourth Amendment exclusionary rule does not apply to federal grand juries and is not a basis upon which a federal indictment can be dismissed. *United States v. Calandra*, 414 U.S. 338 (1974).

Question # 24 – Torts
Answer: B

(A) Incorrect. Nothing in the fact situation suggests that the weakness of the limb could not have been discovered by the exercise of reasonable care. If the property owner had owed a duty to take reasonable care to protect the hiker, he might have been required to make regular inspections of the conditions on his land. *See* Dan B. Dobbs, The Law of Torts § 235 (2000).

(B) Correct. A possessor of land is not required to exercise reasonable care to make his land safe for trespassers. Restatement (Second) of Torts § 333.

(C) Incorrect. A possessor of land is not required to exercise reasonable care to make his land safe for trespassers. Restatement (Second) of Torts § 333.

(D) Incorrect. A property owner is liable only for artificial conditions highly dangerous to trespassers and only when he knows about the trespasser or has some reason to anticipate the trespasser's presence. Restatement (Second) of Torts §§ 334–336.

Question # 25 - Criminal Law and Procedure
Answer: A

(A) Correct. The warrant was valid, but its validity was triggered by and limited to the delivered package. *See United States v. Grubbs*, 547 U.S. 90 (2006). Accordingly, once the only object of that search was discovered, the warrant did not authorize a further exploratory search of the house. *See Horton v. California*, 496 U.S. 128 (1990).

(B) Incorrect. Probable cause was not required for the customs officers' search of international mail. *See United States v. Ramsey*, 431 U.S. 606 (1977).

(C) Incorrect. The warrant was valid, but its validity was triggered by and limited to the delivered package. *See United States v. Grubbs*, 547 U.S. 90 (2006). Accordingly, once the only object of that search—the package—was discovered, the warrant did not authorize a further exploratory search of the house. *See Horton v. California*, 496 U.S. 128 (1990).

(D)   Incorrect. Officers may conduct a "protective sweep" of a home only if they have reason to believe others inside the home may pose a danger to them. *Maryland v. Buie*, 494 U.S. 325 (1990). The facts in this scenario would not seem to justify such a protective sweep, but even assuming a protective sweep was authorized, *Buie* limits such a sweep "to a cursory visual inspection of those places in which a person might be hiding." Thus, even an authorized sweep would not extend to the footlocker.

Question # 26 – Contracts
Answer: C

(A)   Incorrect. The $40,000 figure is an attempt to calculate the contractor's restitution recovery, measured by the benefit conferred on the owner, which will yield the smallest amount of recovery. The restitutionary measure would not allow the contractor to recover damages related to the benefit of the bargain. Circumstances are not present that would cause the contractor to seek damages based on the restitution principle and forgo his expectation measure of recovery. In addition, the $40,000 amount is incorrect as a restitution amount since it fails to deduct the $5,000 worth of oak flooring the contractor used on another job. Restatement (Second) of Contracts §§ 371, 347.

(B)   Incorrect. $40,000 represents the contractor's reliance measure of recovery and fails to take into account the contractor's benefit of the bargain, the profit the contractor anticipated making on the project. Reliance damages are measured based on the contractor's unreimbursed expenses for labor and materials, $45,000, less the salvage value of the oak flooring, $5,000, which equals $40,000. Circumstances are not present that would cause the contractor to seek damages based on the reliance principle and forgo his expectation measure of recovery. Restatement (Second) of Contracts §§ 349, 347.

(C)   Correct. $50,000 represents the contractor's expectation measure of recovery and gives the contractor the benefit of the bargain—this amount would place the contractor in the position he would have been in but for the breach. It is also the greatest amount the contractor is able to recover. The general expectation formula permits the contractor to recover $50,000 and can be computed as follows:
General expectation formula = loss in value + other loss – cost avoided – loss avoided:
LIV = the difference between the performance the nonbreaching party should have received under the contract and what was actually received, if anything, in this case, $300,000 less $0
OL = consequential and incidental damages, if any, in this case, $0
CA = the additional costs the nonbreaching party can avoid by rightfully discontinuing performance under the contract as a result of the other party's breach, in this case, $290,000 less $45,000
LA = the beneficial effects of the breach due to the nonbreaching party's ability to salvage or reallocate resources that otherwise would have been devoted to performing under the contract, in this case, $5,000
So $300,000 + $0 – $245,000 – $5,000 = $50,000.
Restatement (Second) of Contracts § 347; E. Allen Farnsworth, Contracts § 12.9 (4th ed. 2004).

(D)   Incorrect. A $55,000 damages recovery will place the contractor in a better position than he would have been in but for the breach because it fails to take into account the loss avoided—the beneficial effects of the breach due to the contractor's ability to salvage or reallocate resources that otherwise would have been devoted to performing under the contract. Here the loss avoided is the $5,000 worth of oak flooring that the contractor used on another job. Restatement (Second) of Contracts § 347; E. Allen Farnsworth, Contracts § 12.9 (4th ed. 2004).

Question # 27 - Real Property
Answer: B

(A) Incorrect. This option correctly concludes that the charity will prevail but misstates the reasoning. Ademption occurs when a specific gift of property in the will is no longer in the estate at the time of death of the testator. The man made a specific gift of the residence to the friend. At the time of the man's death, the man still owned the residence, and thus there was no ademption. Still, a deceased person cannot take and hold title to property. The specific gift of the residence to the friend, now deceased, lapsed and should pass by way of the residuary clause in the will.

(B) Correct. A deceased person cannot take and hold title to property. If a named beneficiary predeceases the testator, the gift to that beneficiary lapses. In this case, the gift to the friend lapsed because the friend predeceased the man. The gift of the residence was a specific gift, and the lapse of this specific gift passes the residence through the residuary clause of the will. The charity is the residuary taker. There is no applicable anti-lapse statute which might have substituted the friend's child as the beneficiary of the bequest if the friend were a protected beneficiary under the statute.

(C) Incorrect. The gift of the residence in the will was to the friend, who was specifically identified in the will. Nothing was said in the will as to who should receive the residence if the friend predeceased the man, and thus the gift lapsed and passes by the residuary clause to the residuary beneficiary, the charity. The will's meaning is clear. Extrinsic evidence cannot be used to rewrite the will. The will contains no ambiguities which might allow in extrinsic evidence.

(D) Incorrect. A deceased person cannot take and hold title to property. The specific gift of the residence to the deceased person lapsed and should pass by way of the residuary clause in the will. The man could have noted in the will who would have taken the property in the event the friend did not survive and thus have prevented the lapse from occurring. But because the man did not state what would happen if the friend did not survive him, the gift lapsed.

Question # 28 - Constitutional Law
Answer: D

(A) Incorrect. The discriminatory impact of government action on a religious practice is insufficient to establish a violation of the free exercise clause. In order to establish a free exercise violation, the challenger must show that the government action targeted the religious practice in question.

(B) Incorrect. A simple benefit-burden balance of the government action at issue does not establish a violation of the free exercise clause. In order to establish a free exercise violation, the challenger must show that the government action targeted the religious practice in question.

(C) Incorrect. The government is required to select the least burdensome alternative only if a court exercises strict scrutiny to evaluate the action at issue. The court will exercise strict scrutiny only if the challenger can show that the government action targeted the religious practice in question.

(D)   Correct. The court will exercise strict scrutiny only if the challenger can show that the government action targeted the religious practice in question. A court typically invalidates government action at strict scrutiny.

Question # 29 – Evidence
Answer: B

(A)   Incorrect. The evidence as to peacefulness is admissible as a pertinent trait of character under Rule 404(a)(1) of the Federal Rules of Evidence. Truthfulness is not a pertinent trait of character in a prosecution for battery, which is a crime of violence. Under Rule 608(a), truthfulness is a relevant trait to rehabilitate a witness whose character for truthfulness has been attacked, but there is no indication that such an attack has taken place here.

(B)   Correct. The defendant's character for peacefulness is a pertinent trait of character under Rule 404(a)(1) of the Federal Rules of Evidence. Rule 405 allows the defendant to offer evidence of his reputation for peacefulness. The evidence of the defendant's truthfulness must be excluded, because there is no indication that the defendant's character for truthfulness while testifying has been attacked.

(C)   Incorrect. Peacefulness is a pertinent trait of character in a prosecution for battery, and evidence of a defendant's reputation for peacefulness is admissible under Rule 404(a)(1) of the Federal Rules of Evidence. Truthfulness is not a pertinent trait of character, and hence evidence of the defendant's truthfulness is inadmissible. The evidence of truthfulness would be admissible to rehabilitate under Rule 608(a), but only if the defendant's character for truthfulness as a witness had been attacked.

(D)   Incorrect. Peacefulness is a pertinent trait of character in a prosecution for battery, and evidence of the defendant's reputation for peacefulness is admissible under Rule 404(a)(1) of the Federal Rules of Evidence. Truthfulness is not a pertinent trait of character, and hence evidence of the defendant's truthfulness is inadmissible.

Question # 30 – Torts
Answer: A

(A)   Correct. A common law right of publicity can be violated when an advertisement, viewed as a whole, leaves little doubt that the ad is intended to depict a specific celebrity who has not consented to the use of his identity.

(B)   Incorrect. The fact that a celebrity is a "public figure" is irrelevant to whether he is owed compensation for the use of his identity. In fact, his celebrity may increase the value of the identity that has been misappropriated.

(C)   Incorrect. The person whose identity has been misappropriated need not be identified by name so long as it is clear that the ad is meant to depict that person.

(D) Incorrect. The injury in a right of publicity case is based on the commercial exploitation of someone's name or likeness. The plaintiff need not prove that he or she suffered any emotional or dignitary loss. Dan B. Dobbs, The Law of Torts § 425 (2000).

Question # 31 - Criminal Law and Procedure
Answer: D

(A) Incorrect. There was neither a Fourth Amendment violation nor a *Miranda* violation. There was no Fourth Amendment violation because the stop, frisk, and questioning were permissible, under *Terry v. Ohio*, 392 U.S. 1 (1968), based on reasonable suspicion. There was no *Miranda* violation because warnings are not required for *Terry* stops. *See Berkemer v. McCarty*, 468 U.S. 420, 439–40 (1984).

(B) Incorrect. There was neither a Fourth Amendment violation nor a *Miranda* violation. There was no Fourth Amendment violation because the stop, frisk, and questioning were permissible, under *Terry v. Ohio*, 392 U.S. 1 (1968), based on reasonable suspicion. There was no *Miranda* violation because warnings are not required for *Terry* stops. *See Berkemer v. McCarty*, 468 U.S. 420, 439–40 (1984).

(C) Incorrect. There was neither a Fourth Amendment violation nor a *Miranda* violation. There was no Fourth Amendment violation because the stop, frisk, and questioning were permissible, under *Terry v. Ohio*, 392 U.S. 1 (1968), based on reasonable suspicion. There was no *Miranda* violation because warnings are not required for *Terry* stops. *See Berkemer v. McCarty*, 468 U.S. 420, 439–40 (1984).

(D) Correct. There was neither a Fourth Amendment violation nor a *Miranda* violation. There was no Fourth Amendment violation because the stop, frisk, and questioning were permissible, under *Terry v. Ohio*, 392 U.S. 1 (1968), based on reasonable suspicion. There was no *Miranda* violation because warnings are not required for *Terry* stops. *See Berkemer v. McCarty*, 468 U.S. 420, 439–40 (1984).

Question # 32 - Real Property
Answer: D

(A) Incorrect. If the man recovers title to the property, it would be because the jurisdiction provides a statutory right of redemption. A statutory right of redemption allows redemption after there has been a valid foreclosure of the equitable right of redemption. As is implied by its name, this right is provided by statute. If the jurisdiction provides a statutory right of redemption, it does not matter whether the property being redeemed is residential, commercial, or another type of property, unless the statute so notes.

(B) Incorrect. The foreclosure was of the equitable right of redemption, a right which arises prior to foreclosure. The equitable right of redemption gave the man the right to pay what was due or otherwise perform his obligations after default and have his title restored to him. The foreclosure of the mortgage ended the equitable right of redemption. The foreclosure sale occurred and the man lost his ability to redeem under the equitable right of redemption.

(C) Incorrect. The common law doctrine of exoneration arises when a testator has died and the testator's will devises property which is subject to a mortgage debt for which the testator was personally liable. Exoneration would then direct that the mortgage debt be paid from the assets in the residuary clause. In this case, the man did not die. The property was sold by way of foreclosure.

(D) Correct. A jurisdiction may, by statute, provide a statutory right of redemption, which sets out an additional time period after the foreclosure sale during which the prior mortgagor and perhaps others have the option to pay a certain sum of money and redeem the title to the property. The right arises only by statute and only after there has been a foreclosure of the mortgage.

Question # 33 - Real Property
Answer: C

(A) Incorrect. The doctrine of estoppel by deed arises when a person executes a deed purporting to convey an estate which either the person does not have or is larger than what the person has. If that person later acquires that estate, then the subsequently acquired estate passes to the grantee. The farmer owned the farm at the time when she executed both mortgages. The mortgages were liens on the property. The first bank properly foreclosed its mortgage, after having given notice to the second bank. The second bank, as a necessary party to the foreclosure action, was given notice. The buyer at the sale acquired the title that the farmer had at the time the mortgage was given to the first bank, which was a title free of any other mortgage, and the buyer then conveyed that title when he sold the property back to the farmer.

(B) Incorrect. The first bank had priority. The second bank was a necessary party to the foreclosure proceeding and was given notice of the sale. When the second bank failed to appear at the foreclosure proceeding, or to take any other action, the buyer at the sale received the title the farmer had at the time the mortgage was given to the first bank. The buyer had title which could be conveyed to anyone, including the original owner. The farmer and the buyer were not acting in collusion, so there could be no claim of fraud when the farmer reacquired her original interest in the farm.

(C) Correct. The first bank had priority. The second bank was a necessary party to the foreclosure proceeding and was given notice of the sale. When the second bank failed to appear at the foreclosure proceeding, or to take any other action, the buyer at the sale received the title the farmer had at the time the mortgage was given to the first bank, which was free of any mortgage liens. The buyer and the farmer did not act in collusion, so there could be no claim of fraud when the farmer reacquired her original interest in the farm.

(D) Incorrect. This option correctly concludes that the second bank does not have a valid mortgage on the farm but misstates the rationale. The due-on-sale clause allowed the first bank to accelerate the debt in the event the farmer sold the farm without first seeking the permission of the first bank. The farmer never sold the property and thus the due-on-sale clause was not involved. The property was sold at a foreclosure sale after the farmer went into default. The first bank had priority. The second bank was a necessary party to the foreclosure proceeding and was given notice of the sale. When the second bank failed to appear at the foreclosure proceeding or to take any other action, the buyer at the sale received the title the farmer had at the time the mortgage was given to the first bank, which was free of any mortgage liens.

Question # 34 – Evidence
Answer: A

(A)   Correct. What the defendant said to the plaintiff, even in a private conversation, is an admission of a party-opponent and is admissible under Rule 801(d)(2)(A) of the Federal Rules of Evidence. The plaintiff has personal knowledge of what the defendant said and can testify about it. The fact that the audiotape might be better evidence of what the defendant actually said makes no difference. The Best Evidence Rule applies only when a witness testifies about the content of a writing or recording. Here the plaintiff would not be testifying about the content of the audiotape but rather about what she personally heard.

(B)   Incorrect. The testimony is admissible because the plaintiff will testify to what she heard directly from the defendant, not about what she heard on the audiotape. Therefore, she would not be attempting to prove the content of the audiotape and there would be no violation of the original document rule. The answer is incorrect in stating that the original document rule does not apply to audiotapes. The original document rule, Rule 1002 of the Federal Rules of Evidence, applies to writings, recordings, and photographs.

(C)   Incorrect. Rule 1002 of the Federal Rules of Evidence requires a recording to be introduced only when its contents are being proved. Here the plaintiff is offering to testify about what she heard directly from the defendant, not about what she heard on the audiotape. The fact that an audiotape was contemporaneously made does not mean that the tape has to be produced, since the plaintiff has independent knowledge of what the defendant said. If the problem were changed so that the plaintiff only learned of the defendant's statements by listening to an audiotape, then the audiotape would have to be produced.

(D)   Incorrect. There is no rule automatically barring evidence obtained by deception. Moreover, the evidence obtained by deception (the secretly recorded audiotape) was not in fact offered. Some state and federal statutes do regulate secret recordings of conversations, and violation of such statutes sometimes means that recordings obtained in violation thereof must be excluded. But the recording was not offered in evidence in this problem. Only the statements made by the defendant were offered, and they would be admissible whether or not a contemporaneous recording was made.

Question # 35 – Torts
Answer: A

(A)   Correct. Although the manufacture of explosives may be an abnormally dangerous activity, strict liability for injuries caused by such activities is limited to the kind of harm that makes the activity abnormally dangerous. This accident could have occurred when a roof tile fell from a building that housed a perfectly safe and ordinary activity. The owner may, however, be liable for negligence. *See* Restatement (Second) of Torts § 519(2).

(B)   Incorrect. The fact that the windstorm was unusually severe may be relevant to whether the owner took reasonable precautions to prevent the accident, but it is not relevant to a claim of strict liability where the risk that materialized was not of the sort that makes the activity abnormally dangerous. *See* Restatement (Second) of Torts § 519(2).

(C)   Incorrect. Although the manufacture of explosives may be an abnormally dangerous activity, strict liability for injuries caused by such activities is limited to the kind of harm that makes the activity abnormally dangerous. This accident could have occurred when a roof tile fell from a building that housed a perfectly safe and ordinary activity. The owner, however, may be liable for negligence. *See* Restatement (Second) of Torts § 519.

(D)   Incorrect. Strict liability is based on the abnormally dangerous nature of the activity and is limited to the realization of the kind of harm that makes the activity abnormally dangerous. The inappropriateness of the activity to the place where it is carried on may be one factor in deciding whether the activity is abnormally dangerous, but it is not the only factor, and in this case, the harm that occurred was not related to the dangerous nature of the explosives plant. *See* Restatement (Second) of Torts § 519.

Question # 36 – Contracts
Answer: C

(A)   Incorrect. Restatement (Second) of Contracts § 45 prevents an offeror from withdrawing its offer for a unilateral contract once the offeree has begun to perform.

(B)   Incorrect. The consideration required for an enforceable contract is present. The bank's promise to pay the customer $25 and the customer's standing in line constituted a bargained-for exchange. Restatement (Second) of Contracts § 71; *see* Restatement (Second) of Contracts § 45.

(C)   Correct. Restatement (Second) of Contracts § 45 provides that where an offer invites acceptance by performance, the offeree's beginning of performance creates an option contract which precludes the offeror from revoking its offer.

(D)   Incorrect. The customer's mere presence in line constituted the beginning of performance but not the requested acceptance—standing in line for more than five minutes. Restatement (Second) of Contracts § 45.

Question # 37 - Constitutional Law
Answer: A

(A)   Correct. The statute satisfies the commerce clause because it regulates a commercial activity (the purchase of cars) that, when aggregated, has a substantial effect on interstate commerce. The statute does not violate the Tenth Amendment as applied to the city because it does not commandeer the city to regulate the conduct of others pursuant to congressional direction. Instead, it directly regulates the city on the same terms as other entities engaged in the same conduct, which is permissible under the Tenth Amendment.

(B)   Incorrect. Although the federal government does enjoy sovereign immunity from suit, this immunity applies only to suits seeking compensatory monetary relief and not to suits seeking only prospective injunctive relief. The suit at issue seeks only prospective injunctive relief.

The statute satisfies the commerce clause because it regulates a commercial activity (the purchase of cars) that, when aggregated, has a substantial effect on interstate commerce. The statute does not violate the Tenth Amendment as applied to the city because it does not commandeer the city to regulate the conduct of others pursuant to congressional direction. Instead, it directly regulates the city on the same terms as other entities engaged in the same conduct, which is permissible under the Tenth Amendment.

(C) Incorrect. The statute does not violate the Tenth Amendment as applied to the city because it does not commandeer the city to regulate the conduct of others pursuant to congressional direction. Instead, it directly regulates the city's conduct on the same terms as other entities engaged in the same conduct, which is permissible under the Tenth Amendment. The statute satisfies the commerce clause because it regulates a commercial activity (the purchase of cars) that, when aggregated, has a substantial effect on interstate commerce.

(D) Incorrect. The statute satisfies the commerce clause because it regulates a commercial activity (the purchase of cars) that, when aggregated, has a substantial effect on interstate commerce. The statute does not violate the Tenth Amendment as applied to the city because it does not commandeer the city to regulate the conduct of others pursuant to congressional direction. Instead, it directly regulates the city on the same terms as other entities engaged in the same conduct, which is permissible under the Tenth Amendment.

Question # 38 - Criminal Law and Procedure
Answer: A

(A) Correct. The movement in the neighboring state would constitute sufficient "asportation" for a kidnapping conviction, and was more than incidental to the robbery. *See* 3 Wayne R. LaFave, Substantive Criminal Law § 18.1(b) (discussing Model Penal Code § 212.1).

(B) Incorrect. It is hard to characterize the proceeds of the robbery as "ransom," but, in any event, the propriety of a kidnapping conviction does not turn on whether ransom was paid. The stranger properly could be convicted of kidnapping because the movement in the neighboring state was more than incidental to the robbery. *See* 3 Wayne R. LaFave, Substantive Criminal Law § 18.1(b) (discussing Model Penal Code § 212.1).

(C) Incorrect. The stranger properly could be convicted of kidnapping in both states. The movement in the neighboring state was more than incidental to the robbery and would constitute kidnapping there as well as in the driver's home state. *See* 3 Wayne R. LaFave, Substantive Criminal Law § 18.1(b) (discussing Model Penal Code § 212.1).

(D) Incorrect. The movement in the neighboring state was more than incidental to the robbery and would constitute kidnapping. *See* 3 Wayne R. LaFave, Substantive Criminal Law § 18.1(b) (discussing Model Penal Code § 212.1).

Question # 39 – Contracts
Answer: A

(A) Correct. UCC § 2-206(1)(b) provides that a seller's shipment of conforming goods with a notice of accommodation does not constitute an acceptance and breach, but rather a counteroffer, which the buyer is free to either accept or reject. Section 2-206(1)(b) also provides, however, that a contract calling for prompt shipment can be accepted by either a prompt promise to ship or by the prompt shipment of goods. The seller accepted the buyer's offer by a promise to ship when he mailed his June 2 letter. UCC § 2-601 allows a buyer to accept or reject nonconforming goods and in either event recover damages. The buyer has an action for breach since the computer shipped on June 3 failed to conform to the contract formed on June 2 when the seller mailed his letter of acceptance.

(B)   Incorrect. Because the seller's June 2 letter constituted an acceptance, the seller tendered nonconforming goods that the buyer can either accept or reject. UCC § 2-711 states that upon a buyer's rightful rejection, certain remedies are also available to the buyer.

(C)   Incorrect. The seller's shipment of the different computer model did not constitute an acceptance since the seller accepted the buyer's original offer when he mailed his June 2 letter. UCC § 2-206(1).

(D)   Incorrect. The mailing of the notice of accommodation was irrelevant since the seller accepted the buyer's offer by promising, in his June 2 letter, to ship the computer. UCC § 2-206.

Question # 40 – Evidence
Answer: B

(A)   Incorrect. The statement is an admissible statement for purposes of medical diagnosis or treatment under Rule 803(4) of the Federal Rules of Evidence. While it is true that the plaintiff is present and presumably could be cross-examined about the statement, the rule does not require his presence. The statement would be admissible even if the plaintiff were not present for cross-examination.

(B)   Correct. This statement fits Rule 803(4) of the Federal Rules of Evidence as a statement made for the purpose of medical diagnosis. This rule allows not only statements made to treating physicians, but also statements made to other doctors for evaluation or diagnosis.

(C)   Incorrect. Rule 803(4) of the Federal Rules of Evidence does not require that the statement be made to a treating physician. It also admits statements made to a doctor for purposes of diagnosis. It is specifically designed to admit statements such as this, where an injured party is seeking a diagnosis and opinion from a medical specialist.

(D)   Incorrect. The information the plaintiff related to the doctor, although it does relate to the cause of the injury, is pertinent to diagnosis or treatment and hence is admissible under Rule 803(4) of the Federal Rules of Evidence.

Question # 41 - Constitutional Law
Answer: B

(A)   Incorrect. The commerce clause grants Congress plenary power to regulate the safety of air travel because airlines are instrumentalities of interstate commerce.

The due process clause of the Fifth Amendment provides the best ground for challenging the constitutionality of this statute. The U.S. Supreme Court held, in *Bolling v. Sharpe*, 347 U.S. 497 (1954), that the equal protection principles of the Fourteenth Amendment apply to actions of the federal government through the due process clause of the Fifth Amendment. The new security measures presumptively violate equal protection because they contain a racial classification: the new security measures apply only to individuals of one race. A court therefore would uphold the new security measures only if the government could prove that they are necessary to serve a compelling public interest, a standard that the government typically cannot meet.

(B)   Correct. The U.S. Supreme Court held, in *Bolling v. Sharpe*, 347 U.S. 497 (1954), that the equal protection principles of the Fourteenth Amendment apply to actions of the federal government through the due process clause of the Fifth Amendment. The new security measures presumptively violate equal protection because they contain a racial classification: the new security measures apply only to individuals of one race. A court therefore would uphold the new security measures only if the government could prove that they are necessary to serve a compelling public interest, a standard that the government typically cannot meet.

(C)   Incorrect. The privileges and immunities clause of Article IV prohibits actions by states that improperly discriminate against the citizens of other states. The clause does not apply to actions of the federal government.

The due process clause of the Fifth Amendment provides the best ground for challenging the constitutionality of this statute. The U.S. Supreme Court held, in *Bolling v. Sharpe*, 347 U.S. 497 (1954), that the equal protection principles of the Fourteenth Amendment apply to actions of the federal government through the due process clause of the Fifth Amendment. The new security measures presumptively violate equal protection because they contain a racial classification: the new security measures apply only to individuals of one race. A court therefore would uphold the new security measures only if the government could prove that they are necessary to serve a compelling public interest, a standard that the government typically cannot meet.

(D)   Incorrect. The privileges or immunities clause of the Fourteenth Amendment prohibits states from depriving individuals of the privileges or immunities of United States citizenship. The U.S. Supreme Court has never applied the clause to actions of the federal government.

The due process clause of the Fifth Amendment provides the best ground for challenging the constitutionality of this statute. The U.S. Supreme Court held, in *Bolling v. Sharpe*, 347 U.S. 497 (1954), that the equal protection principles of the Fourteenth Amendment apply to actions of the federal government through the due process clause of the Fifth Amendment. The new security measures presumptively violate equal protection because they contain a racial classification: the new security measures apply only to individuals of one race. A court therefore would uphold the new security measures only if the government could prove that they are necessary to serve a compelling public interest, a standard that the government typically cannot meet.

Question # 42 – Torts
Answer: D

(A)   Incorrect. A jury could conclude that the blender was defective at the time of sale because the accident is the sort of accident that ordinarily occurs as a result of a defect and no other cause was identified. *See* Restatement (Third) of Torts (Products Liability) § 3 illus. 1.

(B)   Incorrect. A jury could conclude that the blender was defective at the time of sale, and such a conclusion would support a claim based on strict product liability. *See* Restatement (Third) of Torts (Products Liability) § 3 illus. 1.

(C)   Incorrect. The jury may conclude that the blender was defective at the time of sale based on the circumstantial evidence presented, but it is not required to draw that conclusion. *See* Restatement (Third) of Torts (Products Liability) § 3 illus. 1.

(D)   Correct. A jury could conclude that the blender was defective at the time of sale because the accident is the sort of accident that ordinarily occurs as a result of a defect and no other cause was identified, but the jury is not required to draw that conclusion. *See* Restatement (Third) of Torts (Products Liability) § 3 illus. 1.

Question # 43 - Constitutional Law
Answer: A

(A)   Correct. Section 5 of the Fourteenth Amendment gives Congress the power to enforce the provisions of the Fourteenth Amendment by appropriate legislation. Congressional legislation is appropriate within the meaning of Section 5 if (1) it seeks to prevent or remedy actions by state or local governments that violate provisions of the Fourteenth Amendment, and (2) its requirements are congruent with and proportional to the Fourteenth Amendment violations it addresses. In this case, the legislation seeks to prevent actions by state agencies that violate the due process clause of the Fourteenth Amendment, and the requirements of the legislation appear to be proportional to and congruent with the Fourteenth Amendment violations Congress has sought to prevent.

(B)   Incorrect. Article I, Section 8 of the Constitution gives Congress the power to spend for the general welfare, but this power is inapplicable because the legislation at issue is not a spending measure.

The best source of authority for the statute at issue is Section 5 of the Fourteenth Amendment, which gives Congress the power to enforce the provisions of the Fourteenth Amendment by appropriate legislation. Congressional legislation is appropriate within the meaning of Section 5 if (1) it seeks to prevent or remedy actions by state or local governments that violate provisions of the Fourteenth Amendment, and (2) its requirements are congruent with and proportional to the Fourteenth Amendment violations it addresses. In this case, the legislation seeks to prevent actions by state agencies that violate the due process clause of the Fourteenth Amendment, and the requirements of the legislation appear to be proportional to and congruent with the Fourteenth Amendment violations Congress has sought to prevent.

(C)   Incorrect. The privileges and immunities clause of Article IV, Section 2 prohibits actions by states that improperly discriminate against the citizens of other states. The clause does not apply to actions of the federal government.

The best source of authority for the statute at issue is Section 5 of the Fourteenth Amendment, which gives Congress the power to enforce the provisions of the Fourteenth Amendment by appropriate legislation. Congressional legislation is appropriate within the meaning of Section 5 if (1) it seeks to prevent or remedy actions by state or local governments that violate provisions of the Fourteenth Amendment, and (2) its requirements are congruent with and proportional to the

Fourteenth Amendment violations it addresses. In this case, the legislation seeks to prevent actions by state agencies that violate the due process clause of the Fourteenth Amendment, and the requirements of the legislation appear to be proportional to and congruent with the Fourteenth Amendment violations Congress has sought to prevent.

(D)   Incorrect. The takings clause of the Fifth Amendment prohibits the federal government from taking property from an individual without paying fair compensation for the property taken. The takings clause does not apply because this legislation does not authorize the taking of anyone's property.

The best source of authority for the statute at issue is Section 5 of the Fourteenth Amendment, which gives Congress the power to enforce the provisions of the Fourteenth Amendment by appropriate legislation. Congressional legislation is appropriate within the meaning of Section 5 if (1) it seeks to prevent or remedy actions by state or local governments that violate provisions of the Fourteenth Amendment, and (2) its requirements are congruent with and proportional to the Fourteenth Amendment violations it addresses. In this case, the legislation seeks to prevent actions by state agencies that violate the due process clause of the Fourteenth Amendment, and the requirements of the legislation appear to be proportional to and congruent with the Fourteenth Amendment violations Congress has sought to prevent.

Question # 44 - Real Property
Answer: D

(A)   Incorrect. It is true that in the absence of a contrary express agreement there is an obligation to convey a marketable title. A mortgage is an interest held by a third party and does make title unmarketable. The time for title to be marketable, however, is at the closing, when the seller is to provide the warranty deed. The buyer has an obligation to make 290 more payments before the time for closing arises. A buyer may be able to object to title earlier only if it appears unlikely that the seller will be able to provide a marketable title at the time of closing. Under these facts, the seller has made all mortgage payments timely. The amount of the mortgage debt is 25 percent of the purchase price the buyer will pay and the land is four times more valuable than the debt owed. It is most likely that title will be marketable at the time when all payments have been made. If not, that is the time for the buyer to sue for damages.

(B)   Incorrect. An installment purchase contract is often treated as a mortgage, and on default there must be a foreclosure of the buyer's equity of redemption. In this case, the buyer may have stopped making payments, but the seller has not yet sought to enforce the installment purchase contract. Because it is the buyer who is seeking damages, the buyer's equity of redemption is not at issue.

(C)   Incorrect. This option correctly concludes that damages will not be awarded but for the wrong reason. An installment purchase contract is a seller's security device. Payments are made over time and, when all payments have been made, a deed will be given. Title does not have to be marketable until all payments have been made. An existing mortgage lien does make the title unmarketable, but it is likely that the lien will have disappeared when the deed is to be given. A buyer may be able to object earlier only if it appears unlikely that the seller will be able to provide a marketable title at that time. Under the facts given, the seller has made all mortgage payments timely. The amount of the mortgage debt is 25 percent of the purchase price the buyer will pay and the land is four times more valuable than the debt owed. It is most likely that title will be marketable at the time when all payments have been made under the agreement. If not, that is the time for the buyer to sue for damages.

(D) Correct. Title does not have to be marketable until the closing date when all payments have been received. The buyer still has 290 payments to make. A mortgage can render title unmarketable but it is most likely that title will be marketable when all payments have been made by the buyer under the agreement. The seller has made all mortgage payments timely. The amount of the mortgage debt is 25 percent of the purchase price the buyer will pay, and the land is four times more valuable than the debt owed, so it is likely that the mortgage debt will be paid off by the time the seller must provide the warranty deed, and thus the buyer is not entitled to damages at this time.

Question # 45 – Contracts
Answer: D

(A) Incorrect. The general rule is that a repudiating party may retract its repudiation. An attempted retraction is ineffective, however, if it occurs after the injured party has materially changed its position in reliance on the repudiation. The buyer's purchase of the second tract of land constituted such a change in position. Restatement (Second) of Contracts § 256.

(B) Incorrect. Ordinarily in a real estate transaction the tender of the purchase price and of the real property are to occur simultaneously. Here, however, the seller's repudiation and the buyer's subsequent action in reliance on the repudiation discharged the buyer's obligation to tender the purchase price on July 1. Restatement (Second) of Contracts §§ 234, 256.

(C) Incorrect. Repudiations may be retracted unless the injured party materially changes position or considers the repudiation final before the retraction. Restatement (Second) of Contracts § 256.

(D) Correct. The buyer's purchase of the second tract, which occurred before the seller's attempted retraction, constituted a material change in position and thus terminated the seller's ability to retract his repudiation. Restatement (Second) of Contracts § 256.

Question # 46 – Torts
Answer: B

(A) Incorrect. One who negligently injures another is liable to rescuers even when the rescuer voluntarily comes to the aid of the injured person.

(B) Correct. Even states that allow witnesses who are not in the zone of danger to recover for the emotional distress of observing an accident limit recovery to witnesses who are closely related to the injured person.

(C) Incorrect. One who negligently injures another is liable to rescuers who are physically injured in the course of the rescue, but pure emotional distress is not usually recoverable in a negligence action in the absence of physical harm or a close relationship with the injured person.

(D)   Incorrect. The bystander observed the accident from across the street. He was not in the path of the car so was not in the zone of danger.

Question # 47 - Constitutional Law
Answer: C

(A)   Incorrect. The usual rule prohibiting Congress from enacting a statute overruling a constitutional decision of the U.S. Supreme Court does not apply to enactments based on Congress's commerce power because the Constitution gives Congress plenary authority to regulate conduct that is within the commerce power. The congressional statute permitting any state to regulate the degree of light reflectiveness of the exteriors of commercial trucks using the state's highways is a valid enactment pursuant to the commerce power because commercial trucks are instrumentalities of interstate commerce.

(B)   Incorrect. The congressional statute permitting any state to regulate the degree of light reflectiveness of the exteriors of trucks using the state's highways did not overrule the U.S. Supreme Court's judgment. Thus, for example, if the Court had awarded damages or attorney's fees to the prevailing party, those awards would remain in effect after Congress enacted the statute. Congress's statute simply changed the law for future cases, which is an action that is within the legislative power of Congress and which does not encroach on the Court's judicial power to decide cases within its jurisdiction.

The usual rule prohibiting Congress from enacting a statute overruling a constitutional decision of the U.S. Supreme Court does not apply to enactments based on Congress's commerce power because the Constitution gives Congress plenary authority to regulate conduct that is within the commerce power. The congressional statute permitting states to regulate the degree of light reflectiveness of the exteriors of commercial trucks using the state's highways is a valid enactment of the commerce power because commercial trucks are instrumentalities of interstate commerce.

(C)   Correct. The usual rule prohibiting Congress from enacting a statute overruling a constitutional decision of the U.S. Supreme Court does not apply to enactments based on Congress's commerce power because the Constitution gives Congress plenary authority to regulate conduct that is within the commerce power. The congressional statute permitting any state to regulate the degree of light reflectiveness of the exteriors of commercial trucks using the state's highways is a valid enactment of the commerce power because commercial trucks are instrumentalities of interstate commerce.

(D)   Incorrect. While the Constitution gives Congress the power to appropriate money to promote the general welfare of the United States, it does not give Congress the power generally to enact statutes promoting the general welfare.

The proper constitutional source of congressional power for the statute at issue is the commerce clause of Article I, Section 8. The usual rule prohibiting Congress from enacting a statute overruling a constitutional decision of the U.S. Supreme Court does not apply to enactments based on Congress's commerce power because the Constitution gives Congress plenary authority to regulate conduct that is within the commerce power. The congressional statute permitting any state to regulate the degree of light reflectiveness of the exteriors of commercial trucks using the state's highways is a valid enactment of the commerce power because commercial trucks are instrumentalities of interstate commerce.

Question # 48 – Evidence
Answer: A

(A) Correct. This statement meets the requirements of Rule 803(5) of the Federal Rules of Evidence, the past recollection recorded exception to the hearsay rule. The witness once had knowledge but now has insufficient recollection to testify fully and accurately about her investigation. She made the recording when the matter was fresh in her memory, and she has testified that the recording was an accurate reflection of her memory.

(B) Incorrect. Although the officer's formal written report would qualify as a public record, the informal dictated comments she made to help her prepare the report would not. The tape recording would be admissible under the past recollection recorded exception to the hearsay rule.

(C) Incorrect. Although the tape recording is hearsay, it fits the hearsay exception of Rule 803(5) of the Federal Rules of Evidence as a past recollection recorded. It contains only informal comments so probably does not qualify as a "police report." Even if it were a police report, there is no prohibition against the admission of a police report in a civil case if it satisfies a hearsay exception.

(D) Incorrect. The tape recording was made prior to the written report and was used as a basis for the written report. It is not being offered to prove the content of the written report and hence its admission does not violate Rule 1002 of the Federal Rules of Evidence. Instead it is being offered to prove the factual details of the officer's investigation as she remembered them at the end of her shift when she made the tape recording.

Question # 49 – Contracts
Answer: A

(A) Correct. The law supports the settlement of debts and claims. However, consideration is required for a settlement to be enforceable. Under the pre-existing duty rule, the creditor's promise to forbear from suing to collect was not supported by consideration from the debtor since the amount due was liquidated and the debtor promised to do nothing more than he was already obligated to do. The creditor's promise here was not supported by consideration from the debtor since it allowed for payment of an undisputed amount, $1,000, after the time for payment of the debt had passed. Restatement (Second) of Contracts §§ 73, 74; E. Allen Farnsworth, Contracts § 4.23 (4th ed. 2004).

(B) Incorrect. The creditor's promise to forbear from filing suit would have been sufficient consideration to support the debtor's promise. There was, however, no consideration coming from the debtor to support the creditor's promise since the debtor promised nothing more than to pay an undisputed debt after it was due. Restatement (Second) of Contracts §§ 73, 74; E. Allen Farnsworth, Contracts § 4.23 (4th ed. 2004).

(C) Incorrect. This is an incorrect statement of the rule of *Foakes v. Beer* and the preexisting duty rule that requires consideration to enforce a promise to allow a debtor to delay payment on an undisputed debt. Restatement (Second) of Contracts §§ 73, 74; E. Allen Farnsworth, Contracts § 4.23 (4th ed. 2004).

(D) Incorrect. The debtor may have hoped that the creditor would forbear, but the debtor provided no consideration to support the creditor's forbearance. Restatement (Second) of Contracts § 73, 74; E. Allen Farnsworth, Contracts § 4.23 (4th ed. 2004).

Question # 50 - Criminal Law and Procedure
Answer: B

(A) Incorrect. The patron could not properly be convicted of robbing the sleeping man because robbery requires a larceny by violence or intimidation. The latter element cannot be satisfied here because the sleeping man was not aware of what was happening. *See* 3 Wayne R. LaFave, Substantive Criminal Law § 20.3(b).

(B) Correct. Larceny requires a trespassory taking and carrying away of the personal property of another with intent to steal it. All the elements were satisfied here. The asportation (carrying away) element requires movement of only a slight distance, so it was satisfied here even though the patron ultimately discarded the wallet. *See* 3 Wayne R. LaFave, Substantive Criminal Law § 19.3(b).

(C) Incorrect. The patron properly could be convicted of the more serious crime of larceny. *See* 3 Wayne R. LaFave, Substantive Criminal Law § 19.3(b). Thus, even assuming the patron could be convicted of attempted robbery, this offense is not the most serious possible crime of conviction, so the answer is wrong.

(D) Incorrect. The patron properly could be convicted of larceny, so attempted larceny is not the most serious crime of conviction and this answer is wrong. *See* 3 Wayne R. LaFave, Substantive Criminal Law § 19.3(b).

Question # 51 – Contracts
Answer: B

(A) Incorrect. Although contract law supports the principle of efficient breach, the principle does not discharge a breaching party's duty to perform or its responsibility to compensate the non-breaching party for damages arising from the breaching party's failure to perform. Restatement (Second) of Contracts § 346.

(B) Correct. The condition exception to the parol evidence rule permits the admission of extrinsic evidence to establish an oral condition to the parties' performance under the contract. Restatement (Second) of Contracts § 217.

(C) Incorrect. The builder made a definite commitment to perform even though it was conditioned on his other bid being rejected. The builder's promise to perform was not illusory since the possibility the condition might occur limited the builder's freedom of action by binding him to perform if the condition was satisfied. Restatement (Second) of Contracts § 76.

(D) Incorrect. The condition exception to the parol evidence rule allows for the admissibility of extrinsic evidence to establish that the parties' performance under a written contract was subject to an oral condition. As to the oral condition, the written agreement is not completely integrated. Restatement (Second) of Contracts § 217.

Question # 52 - Constitutional Law
Answer: D

(A)   Incorrect. The disparate impact of a law on women, without more, does not constitute sex discrimination, and thus is insufficient by itself to trigger heightened judicial scrutiny of the constitutionality of the law. In order for the ordinance to be considered discriminatory against women, a court must find that the city adopted the ordinance because it would have a disparate impact on women, and there are no facts upon which to base such a finding. Even if a court would find (incorrectly) that the ordinance discriminates against women, the appropriate standard of review would require the court to examine whether the ordinance is substantially related to an important government interest, and not whether the ordinance is necessary to advance a compelling government interest. The ordinance is constitutional because it is rationally related to a legitimate government objective.

(B)   Incorrect. Although the ordinance infringes on the freedom of babysitters to contract for their services, strict judicial scrutiny of the constitutionality of the ordinance is inappropriate because the freedom of contract is not a fundamental right. The ordinance is constitutional because it is rationally related to a legitimate government objective.

(C)   Incorrect. The appropriate standard of judicial review is not whether the burdens imposed by the ordinance outweigh the benefits of the ordinance. The ordinance is constitutional because it is rationally related to a legitimate government objective.

(D)   Correct. The disparate impact of a law on women, without more, does not constitute sex discrimination and thus is insufficient by itself to trigger heightened judicial scrutiny of the constitutionality of the law. In order for the ordinance to be considered discriminatory against women, a court must find that the city adopted the ordinance because it would have a disparate impact on women, and there are no facts upon which to base such a finding. The ordinance is constitutional because it is rationally related to a legitimate government objective.

Question # 53 - Real Property
Answer: C

(A)   Incorrect. If a contract of sale is silent as to quality of title, a court will imply a marketable title. An easement does affect the marketability of title. Although the seller has the duty to deliver a marketable title, the requirement of marketable title is for the benefit of the buyer. The buyer may waive the right to have a marketable title, which is what the buyer did in this fact situation.

(B)   Incorrect. The corporation does have an easement on the land and the easement does render title unmarketable. But while the seller has the duty to deliver a marketable title, the requirement of marketable title is for the benefit of the buyer, and the buyer may waive the right to receive a marketable title. The buyer may accept the land with the easement, as the buyer did in this fact situation.

(C) Correct. If a contract of sale is silent as to quality of title, the court will imply a marketable title, and an easement does affect the marketability of title. But while the seller has a duty to deliver a marketable title, the requirement of marketable title is for the benefit of the buyer. The buyer may waive the right to have a marketable title, which is what the buyer did in this fact situation.

(D) Incorrect. This option correctly concludes that the buyer will prevail but misstates the rationale. If a contract of sale is silent as to quality of title, the court will imply a marketable title, and an easement does affect the marketability of title. Title is to be marketable at the time of closing. If a buyer discovers a defect which makes title objectionable, the buyer must notify the seller with specificity and allow the seller a reasonable time to cure the defect. Under these facts, the buyer waived the right to have a marketable title and is not asking the seller to remove the defect, so the buyer can enforce the contract.

Question # 54 - Criminal Law and Procedure
Answer: B

(A) Incorrect. The common law does not require an overt act for conspiracy. *See* 2 Wayne R. LaFave, Substantive Criminal Law § 12.2(b). In any event, payment for the drugs likely would qualify as an overt act in jurisdictions imposing such a requirement. *Id.*

(B) Correct. The common law requires plurality of agreement and does not criminalize "unilateral" conspiracy where only one person actually agreed to commit the crime and the other only feigned agreement. 2 Wayne R. LaFave, Substantive Criminal Law § 12.2(c)(6).

(C) Incorrect. While the common law does not require an overt act, it does require plurality of agreement. Accordingly, the dealer could not properly be convicted for conspiring with an undercover officer. 2 Wayne R. LaFave, Substantive Criminal Law § 12.2(b) & (c)(6).

(D) Incorrect. The dealer cannot be convicted here because there was no plurality of agreement. 2 Wayne R. LaFave, Substantive Criminal Law § 12.2(c)(6). Accordingly, the dealer could not properly be convicted for conspiring with an undercover officer.

Question # 55 - Constitutional Law
Answer: B

(A) Incorrect. The city must prove that the ordinance is the least restrictive means of promoting a compelling government interest only if the court exercises strict scrutiny. The city's ordinance does not trigger strict scrutiny because it restricts signs regardless of their content. Because the ordinance is a content-neutral restriction of expression, it must satisfy only intermediate scrutiny, which requires the city to prove that the ordinance is narrowly tailored to an important government interest and that it leaves open alternative channels of communication.

(B) Correct. Because the ordinance is a content-neutral restriction of expression, it must satisfy intermediate scrutiny, which requires the city to prove that the ordinance is narrowly tailored to an important government interest and that it leaves open alternative channels of communication.

(C) Incorrect. The ordinance does not impose a prior restraint because it does not require the permission of a government official before signs may be posted. Because the ordinance is a content-neutral restriction of expression, it must satisfy only intermediate scrutiny, which requires the city to prove that the ordinance is narrowly tailored to an important government interest and that it leaves open alternative channels of communication.

(D)   Incorrect. The text of the city's ordinance restricts signs regardless of their content, and there are no facts to support a claim that the ordinance effectively operates as a content-based restriction on expression. Moreover, even if the ordinance effectively favors some categories of speech over others, this fact by itself would be insufficient to cause a court to invalidate the ordinance. Because the ordinance is a content-neutral restriction of expression, it must satisfy only intermediate scrutiny, which requires the city to prove that the ordinance is narrowly tailored to an important government interest and that it leaves open alternative channels of communication.

Question # 56 – Contracts
Answer: A

(A)   Correct. The manufacturer does not have an action for the price, which is available under three circumstances, none of which is present here—where the buyer has accepted the goods, the goods are lost or damaged within a commercially reasonable time after the risk of loss has passed to the buyer, or the seller is unable after reasonable efforts to resell the goods. UCC § 2-709.

(B)   Incorrect. UCC § 2-708(1) gives a seller the right to recover the difference between the contract price and the market price of goods when a buyer has wrongfully rejected the goods. Note, however, that since the manufacturer is a lost volume seller, it would be better off seeking damages under § 2-708(2), since it is unlikely that a market differential formula will result in the recovery of any direct damages by the manufacturer with respect to what appear to be standard goods.

(C)   Incorrect. Section 2-706 allows a seller to recover the difference between the contract price and resale price when a buyer has wrongfully rejected the goods. Note, however, that the manufacturer would be better off seeking damages under UCC § 2-708(2), since it is a lost volume seller and it is unlikely that a resale will result in the recovery of any direct damages by the manufacturer with respect to what appear to be standard goods.

(D)   Incorrect. UCC § 2-708(2) provides the lost volume seller (a seller not operating at full capacity) with an action to recover lost profit. A recovery under UCC § 2-708(2) would adequately compensate the manufacturer for its direct damages.

Question # 57 – Contracts
Answer: C

(A)   Incorrect. The statement accurately states that the insurance policy is not a divisible contract. The doctrine of divisibility is typically employed to permit a breaching party who is to receive money under the contract to recover a portion of the contract price for having completed a portion of the work. The doctrine of divisibility is not relevant here, however, since the focus of this question is the enforceability of a contract entered into in violation of a statute. Restatement (Second) of Contracts §§ 240, 179.

(B)   Incorrect. Generally, a contract that violates a regulatory statute may be unenforceable as against public policy if the policy against enforcement outweighs the interest of enforcement. This general rule is subject, however, to an exception when those intended to be protected by the statute would be harmed by a finding of unenforceability. Restatement (Second) of Contracts § 179 cmt. c, illus. 4.

(C)   Correct. A contract that violates a state statute may be declared unenforceable on grounds of public policy. Where, however, the contract violates a policy that was intended for the benefit of a contracting party seeking relief, the contract may be enforceable in order to avoid frustrating the policy behind the statute. Accordingly, public policy would not prevent the enforcement of the contract by those within the class of persons, including the homeowner, that the statute was intended to protect. Restatement (Second) of Contracts § 179 cmt. c, illus. 4; E. Allen Farnsworth, Contracts § 5.6 (4th ed. 2004).

(D)   Incorrect. While as a general rule an insurance policy is interpreted against the drafter, the insurance company, this rule is primarily applicable in disputes involving the interpretation of contract language, which is not at issue in this question. Restatement (Second) of Contracts §§ 206, 179 illus. 4.

Question # 58 - Criminal Law and Procedure
Answer: A

(A)   Correct. Model Penal Code section 5.03(1), by defining conspiracy as requiring agreement by the defendant but not by two or more persons, adopts a unilateral interpretation of conspiracy. In addition, many jurisdictions that require a bilateral conspiracy still allow conviction if one of the co-conspirators agreed to the crime but cannot be convicted based on lack of capacity or some other defense personal to the co-conspirator. 2 Wayne R. LaFave, Substantive Criminal Law § 12.4(c)(1).

(B)   Incorrect. The woman would not be entitled to dismissal, even if she knew of the diplomat's status, because the diplomat's capacity to be convicted of the crime would be irrelevant under a jurisdiction that adopted a unilateral view of conspiracy. *See* 2 Wayne R. LaFave, Substantive Criminal Law § 12.2(c)(1).

(C)   Incorrect. The Model Penal Code section 5.03(1) definition of conspiracy does not require that there be two guilty participants. In addition, even in many other jurisdictions that normally would require two guilty participants, an exception is made where two conspirators agreed to the crime but one cannot be convicted based on lack of capacity or some other defense personal to the co-conspirator. 2 Wayne R. LaFave, Substantive Criminal Law § 12.2(c)(1).

(D)   Incorrect. The woman properly can be convicted because, regardless of the diplomat's immunity, she agreed to commit a crime. *See* Model Penal Code section 5.03(1). The fact that the diplomat's conduct was a but-for cause of the conspiracy is irrelevant because the diplomat was not a government agent, and in any event there is no basis for finding that he entrapped her. 2 Wayne R. LaFave, Substantive Criminal Law § 12.2(c)(1).

Question # 59 – Torts
Answer: C

(A)   Incorrect. The interference with the homeowner's use and enjoyment of her property must be substantial and unreasonable. Restatement (Second) of Torts §§ 821F illus. 1, 822.

(B)   Incorrect. Priority in time may be a factor in determining the character of a neighborhood, but it is not determinative of whether an invasion is a nuisance. Dan B. Dobbs, The Law of Torts 1327–28 (2000).

(C)   Correct. Whether an invasion constitutes a nuisance turns on whether it causes significant harm of a kind that would be suffered by a normal member of the community. Restatement (Second) of Torts § 821F illus. 1.

(D)   Incorrect. Compliance with government requirements is not a defense to a claim of private nuisance. Dan B. Dobbs, The Law of Torts § 405 (2000).

Question # 60 - Criminal Law and Procedure
Answer: D

(A)   Incorrect. The friend and the man lacked the requisite criminal intent. Burglary requires unlawful entry with intent to commit a felony (in this case, larceny). 3 Wayne R. LaFave, Substantive Criminal Law § 21.1(e). Persons taking back their own property or taking property in the honest but mistaken belief that the property belongs to someone who has authorized them to take it lack the intent to steal required for larceny. 3 Wayne R. LaFave, Substantive Criminal Law § 19.5(a).

(B)   Incorrect. The friend lacked the requisite criminal intent. Burglary requires unlawful entry with intent to commit a felony (in this case, larceny). 3 Wayne R. LaFave, Substantive Criminal Law § 21.1(e). Persons taking property in the honest belief that the property belongs to them lack the intent to steal required for larceny. 3 Wayne R. LaFave, Substantive Criminal Law § 19.5(a).

(C)   Incorrect. The man lacked the requisite criminal intent. Burglary requires unlawful entry with intent to commit a felony (in this case, larceny). 3 Wayne R. LaFave, Substantive Criminal Law § 21.1(e). Persons taking property in the honest but mistaken belief that the property belongs to them or to someone who has authorized them to take it lack the intent to steal required for larceny. 3 Wayne R. LaFave, Substantive Criminal Law § 19.5(a).

(D)   Correct. Only the woman had the requisite criminal intent. Burglary requires unlawful entry with intent to commit a felony (in this case, larceny). 3 Wayne R. LaFave, Substantive Criminal Law § 21.1(e). Persons taking back their own property or taking property in the honest but mistaken belief that the property belongs to someone who has authorized them to take it lack the intent to steal required for larceny. 3 Wayne R. LaFave, Substantive Criminal Law § 19.5(a).

Question # 61 – Evidence
Answer: C

(A)   Incorrect. This report is admissible as a public record under Rule 803(8) of the Federal Rules of Evidence.

(B)   Incorrect. The fact that this is a civil case does not make the report inadmissible. Public records are admissible in both civil and criminal cases. In fact, they are more broadly admissible in civil cases than in criminal cases. The report is admissible as a public record under Rule 803(8) of the Federal Rules of Evidence.

(C)   Correct. The report is admissible as a public record under Rule 803(8) of the Federal Rules of Evidence. The facts of the problem indicate that the fire marshal had a legal duty to report. The fact that the fire marshal issued the citation indicates that he observed gasoline being stored in the banquet hall.

(D)   Incorrect. Although the exception for records of regularly conducted activity (Rule 803(6) of the Federal Rules of Evidence) might apply, this answer is incorrect because this exception does not require a showing of the unavailability of the fire marshal.

Question # 62 - Real Property
Answer: B

(A)   Incorrect. This option correctly notes that the brother will prevail, but misstates the reasoning. A tenant in common may bring an action to partition the property. Partition in kind, in which there is a physical division of the common property, is preferred; however, a partition by sale is allowed when a fair and equitable physical division of the property is impossible. The applicable zoning ordinance requires a frontage of 100 feet on a public street in order to build. It would not be fair or equitable to convey only 50 feet of frontage to the brother, who then could not build on his lot.

(B)   Correct. A tenant in common may bring an action to partition the property. Partition in kind, in which there is a physical division of the common property, is preferred; however, a partition by sale is allowed when a fair and equitable physical division of the property is impossible. The applicable zoning ordinance requires a frontage of 100 feet on a public street in order to build. It would not be fair or equitable to convey only 50 feet of frontage to the brother, who then could not build on his lot.

(C)   Incorrect. A tenant in common may bring an action to partition the property. Partition in kind, in which there is a physical division of the common property, is preferred; however, a partition by sale is allowed when a fair and equitable physical division of the property is impossible. Although the subject property can be physically divided, it would not be fair or equitable to give the brother only 50 feet of frontage on the public street when the applicable zoning ordinance requires 100 feet of frontage on a public street to build.

(D)   Incorrect. The interests in a tenancy in common need not be equal. Upon partition of the property, each co-tenant will receive either the ownership ratio in the land if the partition is in kind (in which the land is physically divided) or the ownership ratio in the proceeds if the partition is by sale. Partition in kind is preferred; however, a partition by sale is allowed when a fair and equitable physical division of the property is impossible. The applicable zoning ordinance will not allow the brother to build on his lot according to the proposal, and thus partition in kind would not be fair or equitable. The property can be sold, and one-third of the proceeds can be given to the brother and two-thirds of the proceeds given to the sister.

Question # 63 - Criminal Law and Procedure
Answer: B

(A)   Incorrect. The woman cannot be guilty of murder because the hit man did not in fact cause the neighbor's death. 1 Wayne R. LaFave, Substantive Criminal Law § 6.4(b) (discussing *People v. Dlugash*, 363 N.E.2d 1155 (N.Y. 1977)).

(B)   Correct. The woman cannot be guilty of murder, because the hit man did not in fact cause the neighbor's death, but she can be convicted of attempted murder. 1 Wayne R. LaFave, Substantive Criminal Law § 6.4(b) (discussing *People v. Dlugash*, 363 N.E.2d 1155 (N.Y. 1977)).

(C)   Incorrect. The woman properly could be convicted of attempted murder. 1 Wayne R. LaFave, Substantive Criminal Law § 6.4(b) (discussing *People v. Dlugash*, 363 N.E.2d 1155 (N.Y. 1977)). Accordingly, conspiracy is not the most serious crime of conviction.

(D)   Incorrect. The woman properly could be convicted of attempted murder. 1 Wayne R. LaFave, Substantive Criminal Law § 6.4(b) (discussing *People v. Dlugash*, 363 N.E.2d 1155 (N.Y. 1977)). Accordingly, solicitation is not the most serious crime of conviction.

Question # 64 – Contracts
Answer: B

(A)   Incorrect. The homeowner is not in breach; his duty to perform has not become due since the builder has not completed its performance. Where one party's performance requires a period of time, that party (the builder) must complete its performance before the other party is required to perform unless the language or circumstances indicate otherwise. Restatement (Second) of Contracts § 234.

(B)   Correct. Where one party's performance requires a period of time, that party must complete its performance before the other party is required to perform unless the language or circumstances indicate otherwise. Here the parties did not provide for progress payments. Therefore the builder was required to complete performance before the homeowner was obligated to pay for any of the work the builder had performed. The builder's abandonment of the job constituted a wrongful repudiation giving the homeowner an action for breach. Restatement (Second) of Contracts §§ 234, 235.

(C)   Incorrect. The homeowner is not liable because the builder's abandonment was unjustified since the homeowner was legally justified in refusing to make the $2,000 progress payment to the builder. Where one party's performance requires a period of time, that party (the builder) must complete its performance before the other party is required to perform unless the language or circumstances indicate otherwise. Restatement (Second) of Contracts §§ 234, 235.

(D)   Incorrect. The builder wrongfully repudiated by abandoning the project without justification. Where one party's performance requires a period of time, that party (the builder) must complete its performance before the other party is required to perform unless the language or circumstances indicate otherwise. Restatement (Second) of Contracts §§ 234, 235; E. Allen Farnsworth, Contracts § 8.11 (4th ed. 2004).

Question # 65 – Torts
Answer: B

(A)   Incorrect. The worker must prove that the press was either negligently made or defective in order to recover from its manufacturer. *See* Restatement (Second) of Torts § 281; Restatement (Third) (Products Liability) § 1.

(B)   Correct. A product is defective if it fails to include a feasible safety device that would prevent injuries foreseeably incurred in ordinary use.

(C)   Incorrect. The possibility that an employer would purchase the press without a safety device in order to save money is not only foreseeable but known to have occurred here, and it is precisely this possibility that should lead the manufacturer to install a safety device that cannot be removed.

(D)   Incorrect. Where it is feasible to install a safety device, a manufacturer does not fulfill its obligation to make a safe product by warning the purchaser that the product is unsafe.

Question # 66 - Constitutional Law
Answer: B

(A)   Incorrect. Even if the provision of medical services is traditionally a matter of legitimate local concern, states do not have unreviewable authority to regulate it. State regulation is always subject to constitutional limits. The appropriate constitutional standard of review is whether the law is rationally related to a legitimate government interest. The apparent legislative judgment that diagnostic centers not affiliated with hospitals would be less reliable than hospitals is rational, regardless of whether it is in fact correct.

(B)   Correct. The law does not trigger heightened judicial scrutiny because it neither classifies regulatory subjects on a constitutionally suspect basis nor unduly burdens the exercise of a fundamental right. The appropriate constitutional standard of review therefore is whether the law is rationally related to a legitimate government interest. The apparent legislative judgment that diagnostic centers not affiliated with hospitals would be less reliable than hospitals is rational, regardless of whether it is in fact correct.

(C)   Incorrect. The U.S. Supreme Court has not held access to medical services to be a fundamental right. Thus, even if the law unduly burdens such access, heightened judicial scrutiny would not be appropriate. The appropriate constitutional standard of review therefore is whether the law is rationally related to a legitimate government interest. The apparent legislative judgment that diagnostic centers not affiliated with hospitals would be less reliable than hospitals is rational, regardless of whether it is in fact correct.

(D)   Incorrect. The suit is ripe because the facts state that the physicians' group has immediate plans to open a diagnostic center in the state. The appropriate constitutional standard of review is whether the law is rationally related to a legitimate government interest. The apparent legislative judgment that diagnostic centers not affiliated with hospitals would be less reliable than hospitals is rational, regardless of whether it is in fact correct.

Question # 67 – Torts

Answer: C

(A) Incorrect. Punitive damages are available to victims of intentional torts. Dan B. Dobbs, The Law of Torts 80 (2000).

(B) Incorrect. Punitive damages are available to victims of intentional torts. Dan B. Dobbs, The Law of Torts 80 (2000).

(C) Correct. Punitive damages are not available in ordinary negligence cases. Restatement (Second) of Torts § 908(2).

(D) Incorrect. Punitive damages may be available to victims of reckless conduct. Restatement (Second) of Torts § 908(2).

Question # 68 – Evidence
Answer: D

(A) Incorrect. It is true that a report prepared in anticipation of litigation may qualify as work product. However, the work-product immunity is not absolute. Documents that are work product are still subject to discovery upon a showing of substantial need and the inability to obtain the substantial equivalent of the materials by other means. Moreover, a claim of work-product immunity must be asserted in front of and ruled on by the court. A party cannot simply destroy the material and claim work-product protection. Finally, here the plaintiff would not be asking the defendant to produce the report for the jury to see. The plaintiff would only ask whether such a report had been destroyed.

(B) Incorrect. It is proper for the jury to draw an adverse inference *in a civil case* from a party's assertion of the privilege against self-incrimination.

(C) Incorrect. The privilege against self-incrimination may be asserted in both civil and criminal cases.

(D) Correct. If a party destroys evidence, it is proper for the jury to draw an inference that the evidence was adverse to that party. It is also proper for the jury to draw an adverse inference *in a civil case* from a party's assertion of the privilege against self-incrimination. Thus, the court should allow the question to be asked, because it is proper regardless of how the defendant responds.

Question # 69 – Contracts
Answer: A

(A) Correct. The collector rightfully rejected the goods. However, the collector's exercise of ownership of the painting, after his original rejection, caused the gallery to otherwise dispose of the goods. Therefore, the collector's conduct in selling the painting was wrongful against the gallery and constituted conversion. The remedy for conversion is the fair market value of the goods at the time of the conversion. The collector's sale of the painting for $120,000 provides credible evidence of the painting's fair market value at the time of the conversion. UCC §§ 2-601 cmt. 2, 1-103.

(B)   Incorrect. The collector's exercise of ownership of the painting, after his original rejection, caused the gallery to otherwise dispose of the goods. Therefore, the collector's conduct in selling the painting was wrongful against the gallery and constituted conversion. The gallery should not be limited to the contract price for determining the value of the painting since the remedy for conversion is the fair market value of the goods at the time of the conversion, which occurred when the collector sold the painting for $120,000. UCC §§ 2-601 cmt. 2, 1-103.

(C)   Incorrect. The collector's exercise of ownership of the painting, after his original rejection, caused the gallery to otherwise dispose of the goods. Therefore, the collector's conduct in selling the painting was wrongful against the gallery and constituted conversion. The remedy for conversion is the fair market value of the goods at the time of the conversion. The collector's sale of the painting for $120,000 provides credible evidence of the painting's fair market value at the time of the conversion. UCC §§ 2-601 cmt. 2, 1-103.

(D)   Incorrect. The collector's exercise of ownership of the painting, after his original rejection, caused the gallery to otherwise dispose of the goods. Therefore, the collector's conduct in selling the painting was wrongful against the gallery and constituted conversion. The remedy for conversion is the fair market value of the goods at the time of the conversion. The collector's sale of the painting for $120,000 provides credible evidence of the painting's fair market value at the time of the conversion. In addition, the gallery is not a lost volume seller since the painting was a one-of-a-kind good, which means the gallery was operating at full capacity. UCC §§ 2-601 cmt. 2, 1-103.

Question # 70 - Real Property
Answer: B

(A)   Incorrect. The option correctly concludes that the landlord will prevail but misstates the reasoning. If the city had condemned all of the land, the lease would have terminated and the tenant might have been able to receive the sum by which the award exceeds the tenant's obligations under the lease. The city condemned only two-thirds of the land. Under these facts, the lease provision provided that the lease would terminate and that the landlord would receive the entire condemnation award.

(B)   Correct. The landlord and the tenant agreed in the lease that if any part of the land was condemned, the lease would terminate and the landlord would receive the entire condemnation award.

(C)   Incorrect. The taking of all or part of leased land under the power of eminent domain is not a breach of the landlord's warranty of quiet enjoyment. The condemnation occurred through no fault of the landlord. Under these facts, the lease provision provided that the lease would terminate and that the landlord would receive the entire condemnation award.

(D)   Incorrect. If all the leased premises had been condemned, the lease would have terminated by operation of law. Here, only a portion of the land was condemned. If the lease had not otherwise provided, the tenant's obligation under the lease to pay rent would have continued (though it might have been abated). Here the tenant and the landlord agreed that the lease would terminate upon condemnation of any portion of the land and that the landlord could retain all of the condemnation award. There was no unjust enrichment.

Question # 71 - Constitutional Law
Answer: A

(A)   Correct. The tax clause of Article I, Section 8 gives Congress plenary power to raise revenue through taxes. Application of the tax to the sale of newspapers does not violate the freedom of the press protected by the First Amendment because the tax is generally applicable and in no way targets press operations.

(B)   Incorrect. Application of the tax to the sale of newspapers does not trigger strict scrutiny because the tax is generally applicable and in no way targets press operations. Therefore, the government need not prove that the tax is necessary to serve a compelling interest. The tax clause of Article I, Section 8 gives Congress plenary power to raise revenue through taxes.

(C)   Incorrect. The Constitution does not reserve retail sales taxes for the states. The tax clause of Article I, Section 8 gives Congress plenary power to raise revenue through taxes.

(D)   Incorrect. Application of the tax to the sale of newspapers does not violate the freedom of the press protected by the First Amendment because the tax is generally applicable and in no way targets press operations. The tax clause of Article I, Section 8 gives Congress plenary power to raise revenue through taxes.

Question # 72 - Criminal Law and Procedure
Answer: B

(A)   Incorrect. Evidence seized pursuant to a search warrant would have to be suppressed if the warrant was obtained based on information discovered pursuant to an illegal search, if the search was in fact illegal. *See Murray v. United States*, 487 U.S. 533 (1988).

(B)   Correct. The marijuana plants were in plain view of the neighbors, and the woman has no standing to complain of any police trespass on the neighbors' property. *See Horton v. California*, 496 U.S. 128 (1990).

(C)   Incorrect. The marijuana plants were in plain view of the neighbors, and the woman has no standing to complain of any police trespass on the neighbors' property. *See Horton v. California*, 496 U.S. 128 (1990).

(D)   Incorrect. The woman has no standing to complain of any police trespass on the neighbors' property. *See Minnesota v. Carter*, 525 U.S. 83 (1998).

Question # 73 - Real Property
Answer: C

(A)   Incorrect. Lack of access to a public right-of-way may make the title unmarketable. The time to object regarding marketability of title, however, is prior to acceptance of the deed. The doctrine of merger provides that once a deed has been accepted it is too late to sue on title matters under the contract of sale. The colleague's remedy, if any, is under one of the title covenants, but in this case, no title covenants were breached.

(B)   Incorrect. The covenants of warranty and quiet enjoyment are breached when the grantee has been evicted from possession of the land by another with a superior title. The colleague has not been evicted by anyone with a superior title. The colleague merely does not have access to a public right-of-way. Lack of access may render a title unmarketable under a contract of sale; however, the time to challenge marketable title is prior to the acceptance of the deed.

(C)   Correct. Lack of access may render title unmarketable under the contract of sale; however, the time to challenge marketable title is prior to the acceptance of the deed. Under the doctrine of merger, the remedy, if any, is on the title covenant in the deed. Lack of access does not violate any of the title covenants. The colleague received the title the niece said she had. No one had a superior title and thus the covenants of seisin, right to convey, quiet enjoyment, and general warranty were not breached. The covenant against encumbrances provides protection for interests held by third parties such as easements for access. The land was not subject to an express easement nor may any easement be implied based on either prior use or necessity because the lands were never held in common ownership.

(D)   Incorrect. This option correctly concludes that the niece will prevail but misstates the reasoning. The Statute of Frauds does require that an agreement to sell land be in writing. Nonetheless, if the parties have both fully performed under an oral contract, the relationship is the same as if the statute had been fully complied with initially. It is too late for the colleague, having accepted the deed, to now complain that the Statute of Frauds was not complied with because the agreement was oral.

Question # 74 – Evidence
Answer: A

(A)   Correct. This evidence has some probative value because it links the knife in defendant's possession to the type of knife that could have caused the victim's wound. The evidence is not very strong, because other knives could also have caused the wound. But how much weight to give to the evidence is a decision for the jury. Rule 401 of the Federal Rules of Evidence requires only that evidence have "any tendency to make the existence of any fact that is of consequence to the determination of the action more probable or less probable than it would be without the evidence." Thus to be relevant, evidence need only have *some* probative value in establishing a fact. The Advisory Committee's Note to Rule 401 quotes the famous statement "A brick is not a wall," making the point that evidence is admissible even if it is only a single brick that is a part of a large wall of evidence establishing a party's case.

(B)   Incorrect. Evidence meets the relevancy requirement of Rule 401 of the Federal Rules of Evidence if it has "any tendency to make the existence of any fact that is of consequence to the determination of the action more probable or less probable than it would be without the evidence." The medical examiner's testimony, thus, would be admissible.

(C)   Incorrect. Rule 401 of the Federal Rules of Evidence does not require such a statement of probability. The medical examiner's testimony does not have to establish that defendant's knife caused the wound by any particular standard, such as beyond a reasonable doubt, by clear and convincing evidence, or by a preponderance of the evidence. It need only have probative value to be admissible.

(D)   Incorrect. Rule 401 of the Federal Rules of Evidence has a very broad and liberal standard of what is relevant: evidence that has "any tendency to make the existence of any fact that is of consequence to the determination of the action more probable or less probable than it would be without the evidence." Rule 403 allows evidence to be excluded under certain circumstances. But Rule 403 establishes what might be described as a presumption of admissibility, because evidence meeting Rule 401's definition of relevance is admissible unless its probative value is "substantially outweighed" by the danger of unfair prejudice. Here there does not appear to be any significant degree of unfair prejudice, let alone enough to "substantially outweigh" the value of the medical examiner's testimony.

Question # 75 – Torts
Answer: B

(A)   Incorrect. The defendant's belief that the force he used was necessary must be reasonable in order to support the privilege of self-defense. *See* Restatement (Second) of Torts § 63(1) & cmt. i.

(B)   Correct. The privilege of self-defense permits the use of force reasonably believed to be necessary given the threat posed by the plaintiff. *See* Restatement (Second) of Torts § 63(1).

(C)   Incorrect. Actual fear is insufficient to support the privilege of self-defense. The defendant is privileged to use only that force which is objectively reasonable given the threat. *See* Restatement (Second) of Torts § 63(1).

(D)   Incorrect. The privilege of self-defense does not permit retaliation or revenge, but only the use of force reasonably believed necessary to prevent further attacks. *See* Restatement (Second) of Torts § 63 & cmt. g.

Question # 76 – Evidence
Answer: B

(A)   Incorrect. The testimony is certainly admissible to impeach the defendant's testimony, but it can also be used substantively as an admission by a party-opponent under Rule 801(d)(2)(A) of the Federal Rules of Evidence.

(B)   Correct. This statement is admissible both to impeach the defendant's testimony as a prior inconsistent statement and as substantive evidence, because it is an admission of a party-opponent under Rule 801(d)(2)(A) of the Federal Rules of Evidence.

(C)   Incorrect. Under Rule 801(d)(2)(A) of the Federal Rules of Evidence, a statement of a party-opponent is "not hearsay."

(D)   Incorrect. The statement made to the witness does relate to the prior business fraud, but it is a statement by the defendant that in fact he *did* know about the fraud, when he testified in two trials that he *did not* know of it. Thus the statement is relevant to prove that the defendant's trial testimony was knowingly false and hence constituted perjury.

Question # 77 - Real Property
Answer: A

(A) Correct. The mortgage contains a valid due-on-sale clause. If the landowner conveys the land without the prior consent of the bank, the bank may accelerate the debt. A sale by use of an installment land contract is a transfer of the land which can trigger the due-on-sale clause.

(B) Incorrect. A due-on-sale clause in a mortgage granted to a nationally chartered bank is valid and is not an illegal restraint on alienation. The Garn-St. Germain Depository Institutions Act preempts any state law to the contrary.

(C) Incorrect. The landowner may sell the land by an installment land contract. Such a sale would be a transfer, however, which would allow the bank to accelerate the debt if the prior consent of the bank had not been received. It is irrelevant whether the mortgage payments are current at the time of the land contract execution.

(D) Incorrect. The proposed transfer will not make the neighbor personally liable on the debt. The neighbor would be personally liable on the mortgage debt only if the neighbor expressly assumed the mortgage debt. If the transfer is made without its consent, the bank may accelerate the debt. If the entire debt is not paid, the bank could bring a foreclosure proceeding.

Question # 78 – Contracts
Answer: D

(A) Incorrect. Expressions of doubt by a party as to its willingness or ability to perform do not amount to the affirmative manifestation of intent required to constitute an anticipatory repudiation. Expressions of doubt on one party's part may, however, give the other party the right to demand adequate assurance. Restatement (Second) of Contracts §§ 250 cmt. b, 251.

(B) Incorrect. A mere request by the excavator, who had reasonable grounds for making the request, is not a violation of the implied covenant of good faith and fair dealing. Restatement (Second) of Contracts §§ 250, 251.

(C) Incorrect. The contractor's cancellation of the contract would be wrongful and would entitle the excavator to monetary damages (anticipated profit), but not specific performance, which is available only where monetary damages are inadequate. Restatement (Second) of Contracts §§ 250, 359.

(D) Correct. An anticipatory repudiation occurs when a party unequivocally manifests an intention not to perform or an inability to perform. Expressions of doubt as to a party's ability to perform or a mere request by a party (excavator) that the other party (contractor) consider modifying their agreement would not constitute an anticipatory repudiation. Restatement (Second) of Contracts § 250 cmt. b.

Question # 79 - Constitutional Law
Answer: D

(A) Incorrect. The political question doctrine insulates from judicial review certain constitutional questions that the Constitution has committed either to the Legislative Branch or to the Executive Branch of the federal government. No such question is presented on these facts, which concern actions by a state government.

A more appropriate basis for a court dismissing the suit would be that the case is not ripe for adjudication. The agency's inspection does not itself pose any risk of harm to residents of the community. The residents face a risk of harm only if the agency selects their community as a site for a landfill, but on these facts it is unclear whether or when the community would be selected.

(B) Incorrect. There are no facts to suggest that strict judicial scrutiny of the state's site-selection decision is warranted. Therefore the state need not show that the selection of the community is necessary to serve a compelling interest.

A more appropriate basis for a court dismissing the suit would be that the case is not ripe for adjudication. The agency's inspection does not itself pose any risk of harm to residents of the community. The residents face a risk of harm only if the agency selects their community as a site for a landfill, but on these facts it is unclear whether or when the community would be selected.

(C) Incorrect. The Eleventh Amendment does not bar the suit because it was brought against state officers, and not the state itself, and because it seeks only prospective declaratory and injunctive relief, and not compensatory monetary relief.

A more appropriate basis for a court dismissing the suit would be that the case is not ripe for adjudication. The agency's inspection does not itself pose any risk of harm to residents of the community. The residents face a risk of harm only if the agency selects their community as a site for a landfill, but on these facts it is unclear whether or when the community would be selected.

(D) Correct. The case arguably is not ripe for adjudication because the agency's inspection does not itself pose any risk of harm to residents of the community. The residents face a risk of harm only if the agency selects their community as a site for a landfill, but on these facts it is unclear whether or when the community would be selected.

Question # 80 - Real Property
Answer: C

(A) Incorrect. The man's use of the neighbor's land for the past 15 years was without the permission of the neighbor and was thus adverse. It was open and notorious in that the neighbor could have seen him. His use was continuous and without interruption by the neighbor. His use was actual. These elements are needed to acquire a title by adverse possession. The man's use of the land, however, was not exclusive. The man shared the use of the path with the neighbor's tenants. Thus the man did not acquire a title by adverse possession. In addition, the man claims only a right to use the land, which would be an easement rather than ownership of the land itself.

(B) Incorrect. An easement by necessity may be implied only if the lands had been in common ownership and the strict necessity for the easement existed at the time of severance. The man's land and the neighbor's land have never been in common ownership.

(C)   Correct. The man is claiming a right to use the land of the neighbor, which is an easement. An easement by prescription requires that the use be without the neighbor's permission for the requisite period of time. The man has used the path for the past 15 years without the neighbor's permission. His use was open and notorious in that the neighbor could have seen him.

His use was continuous and without interruption by the neighbor. His use was actual. An easement acquired by prescription need not be exclusive. With an easement, the owner may make any use of the easement area that does not interfere with the use made by the easement holder unless the easement is expressly noted as exclusive. The use by the tenants of the neighbor did not interfere with the man's use, nor did his use interfere with theirs.

(D)   Incorrect. The man has acquired an easement by prescription. For the past 15 years, the man has used the path without the permission of the neighbor. His use was open and notorious because the neighbor could have seen him. His use was actual and without significant interruption by the neighbor, and thus he satisfied all of the requirements for an easement by prescription. An easement acquired by prescription need not be exclusive. With an easement, the owner may make any use of the easement area that does not interfere with the use made by the easement holder unless the easement is expressly noted as exclusive. The use by the tenants of the neighbor did not interfere with the man's use, nor did his use interfere with theirs.

Question # 81 – Evidence
Answer: A

(A)   Correct. This is a correct statement of the scope of cross-examination as set forth by Rule 611(b) of the Federal Rules of Evidence.

(B)   Incorrect. If a witness is declared hostile, the examining party may be allowed to examine the witness by leading questions. But a declaration that a witness is hostile does not mean that the cross-examination can go beyond the scope of direct. The rule governing the scope of cross-examination is the same for hostile and non-hostile witnesses.

(C)   Incorrect. Under Rule 611(b) of the Federal Rules of Evidence, cross-examination should be limited to the subject matter of the direct examination and matters affecting credibility. Although the court has discretion under this rule to permit inquiry into additional matters, defendant is not "entitled" to a wider scope of cross-examination.

(D)   Incorrect. There is no such rule permitting cross-examination of unlimited scope of an agent of a party. The scope of cross-examination for all witnesses is controlled by Rule 611(b) of the Federal Rules of Evidence.

Question # 82 – Torts
Answer: D

(A)   Incorrect. A reasonable jury could conclude that the supermarket was not negligent, and strict liability is not applicable where there is neither a sale of a product nor an abnormally dangerous activity. *See* Restatement (Second) of Torts §§ 402A, 519.

(B)   Incorrect. The plaintiff is not required to sue all possibly negligent persons. The defendant supermarket may join the building owner as a third-party defendant, if it chooses to do so. *See* Restatement (Second) of Torts § 882.

(C)   Incorrect. Under the theory of res ipsa loquitur, the jury can infer negligence where an accident would ordinarily not occur in the absence of negligence and the defendant is responsible for the instrumentality that inflicted the injury. Restatement (Second) of Torts § 328D.

(D)   Correct. Under the theory of res ipsa loquitur, the jury can infer negligence where an accident would ordinarily not occur in the absence of negligence and the defendant is responsible for the instrumentality that inflicted the injury. Restatement (Second) of Torts § 328D.

Question # 83 – Torts
Answer: B

(A)   Incorrect. The neighbor did not touch the man, so the neighbor is not liable for battery. *See* Dan B. Dobbs, The Law of Torts § 28 (2000).

(B)   Correct. The tort of intentional infliction of mental suffering or emotional distress allows recovery for personal injury despite the absence of physical injury or touching. On these facts, the neighbor was aware that his conduct would cause severe emotional distress, and he could be asked to compensate the man for the man's emotional suffering, as well as for the value of the cat. *See* Dan B. Dobbs, The Law of Torts § 303 (2000).

(C)   Incorrect. Trespass to chattels provides an action for intentional interference with the plaintiff's chattel in a way that causes recognizable harm to the chattel, which was the case here. In this action, though, the plaintiff could recover only $25, the value of the cat. *See* Dan B. Dobbs, The Law of Torts § 60 (2000).

(D)   Incorrect. Conversion provides a cause of action for interference with a chattel that is substantial enough to amount to the exercise of dominion or control, which was the case here. The standard remedy in conversion is a forced sale, however, so the plaintiff could recover no more than $25, the value of the cat. *See* Dan B. Dobbs, The Law of Torts § 67 (2000).

Question # 84 - Constitutional Law
Answer: A

(A)   Correct. The U.S. Supreme Court held, in *New York v. United States*, 505 U.S. 144 (1992), that the concept of federalism embedded in the Tenth Amendment disables Congress from requiring states to enact laws or to administer federal law.

(B)   Incorrect. The commerce clause of Article I empowers Congress to regulate economic or commercial activity that, in the aggregate, has a substantial effect on interstate commerce. The sale of controlled substances is a commercial activity. The facts disclose "a dramatic increase in the number of elementary and secondary school students bringing controlled substances to school for sale," suggesting that, in the aggregate, this activity has a sufficient effect on interstate commerce to bring the regulation within Congress's commerce power. In addition, the statutory limitation requiring that any controlled substance must have been previously transported in interstate commerce may provide a sufficient jurisdictional nexus with interstate commerce to bring Congress's statute within the commerce power.

Congress's statute is unconstitutional because the U.S. Supreme Court held, in *New York v. United States*, 505 U.S. 144 (1992), that the concept of federalism embedded in the Tenth Amendment disables Congress from requiring states to enact laws or to administer federal law.

(C) Incorrect. The statutory limitation requiring that any controlled substance must have been previously transported in interstate commerce may provide a sufficient jurisdictional nexus with interstate commerce to bring Congress's statute within the commerce power. Congress's statute nevertheless is unconstitutional because the U.S. Supreme Court held, in *New York v. United States*, 505 U.S. 144 (1992), that the concept of federalism embedded in the Tenth Amendment disables Congress from requiring states to enact laws or to administer federal law.

(D) Incorrect. Although the spending clause of Article I gives Congress power to appropriate money for the general welfare of the United States, there is no clause of the Constitution that gives Congress power generally to regulate for the general welfare. Nor does the commerce clause of Article I give Congress power to regulate any activity that, taken in the aggregate, has a substantial effect on interstate commerce. The regulated activity must be economic or commercial in nature to trigger Congress's commerce power. Although the activity here (the sale of controlled substances in or near a school) is commercial activity and the activity, in the aggregate, likely has a substantial effect on interstate commerce, Congress's statute is unconstitutional because the U.S. Supreme Court held, in *New York v. United States*, 505 U.S. 144 (1992), that the concept of federalism embedded in the Tenth Amendment disables Congress from requiring states to enact laws or to administer federal law.

Question # 85 – Evidence
Answer: B

(A) Incorrect. There is nothing in the fact pattern to suggest that the bank teller is an expert on handwriting, and merely working as a bank teller would not give a person such expertise.

(B) Correct. Rule 701 of the Federal Rules of Evidence allows lay opinion testimony when it is rationally based on the perception of the witness and is helpful to the jury. Here the teller knew the signature of the bank customer on whose account the check was drawn. This knowledge made it possible for her to recognize the signature on the check as a forgery. Her testimony that the signature was a forgery is testimony that the signature on the check presented was different from the signature of the owner of the account (a signature she knows). Obviously the owner of the account would be a stronger prosecution witness than the teller in establishing that the signature was forged, but this doesn't mean that the teller would not be allowed to testify.

(C) Incorrect. There is no rule in the law of evidence that would allow exclusion of the testimony on this basis. Moreover, there is no indication in the facts that there was fault on the part of the teller.

(D) Incorrect. Having an expert or even the jury members themselves compare an exemplar established as genuine with the disputed signature is one way to establish whether a signature is forged or authentic. This method of authentication is specifically recognized by Rule 901(b)(3) of the Federal Rules of Evidence. But it is not the only method authorized. Rule 901(b) also allows authentication by "[n]onexpert opinion as to the genuineness of handwriting, based upon familiarity not acquired for purposes of the litigation."

Question # 86 – Contracts
Answer: C

(A)   Incorrect. Generally, parties who make a contract for an intended beneficiary retain the right to modify the duty by a subsequent contract. The power to modify is terminated, however, when the intended beneficiary materially changes his position in reliance on the promise. The clerk materially changed his position in reliance on the promise when he purchased a retirement home. Restatement (Second) of Contracts §§ 302, 311.

(B)   Incorrect. The clerk was an intended beneficiary of the promise between the accountant and the bookkeeper since their promise clearly intended to benefit the clerk. The clerk's material reliance terminated the ability of the accountant and the bookkeeper to modify their duty. Restatement (Second) of Contracts §§ 302, 311.

(C)   Correct. The power of the bookkeeper and the accountant to modify their duty was terminated when the clerk, an intended beneficiary, materially relied on the promised performance by purchasing the retirement home. Restatement (Second) of Contracts §§ 302, 311.

(D)   Incorrect. Under the bargained-for-exchange test for consideration, acts performed in the past constitute past consideration, which does not amount to the consideration required to enforce a contract. The clerk's many years of employment constituted past consideration and would be insufficient to prevent the accountant and the bookkeeper from modifying their duty except for the clerk's reliance on their promise. Restatement (Second) of Contracts §§ 71, 302, 311.

Question # 87 - Real Property
Answer: B

(A)   Incorrect. The restrictive covenant created 25 years ago placed a burden on the 40-acre tract of land and gave the right to enforce the promise to the man who retained the ownership of the benefitted five-acre tract of land. The man may enforce the promise because he owns the benefitted tract of land. It may be that the owners in the subdivision also may enforce the promise; however, the man, as owner of the original benefitted five-acre tract of land, also may enforce it.

(B)   Correct. The restrictive covenant created 25 years ago placed a burden (that the land must be kept residential) on the 40-acre tract of land and gave the right to enforce the promise to the man who retained the ownership of the benefitted retained five-acre tract of land. The man may enforce the promise because he owns the benefitted land.

(C)   Incorrect. The restrictive covenant is not an interest which is affected by the Rule Against Perpetuities. The restrictive covenant is still valid, and no facts are stated which indicate that it has terminated.

(D)   Incorrect. The zoning ordinance does allow the doctor's proposed use. The zoning ordinance does not, however, preempt the valid restrictive covenant. The restrictive covenant, as the more restrictive of the two in terms of its limitations, prevails.

Question # 88 – Contracts
Answer: B

(A)   Incorrect. The mechanic contracted to complete the repairs by a specified time. His failure to execute the repairs within the time set forth in the contract constituted a breach entitling the textile company to damages. The recovery of consequential damages, however, requires more than a determination of breach. Additional requirements, such as foreseeability of the damages, must be satisfied. Restatement (Second) of Contracts §§ 346, 351; E. Allen Farnsworth, Contracts § 12.14 (4th ed. 2004).

(B)   Correct. Assuming other requirements are met, an aggrieved party is entitled to recover consequential damages only if they were reasonably foreseeable to the breaching party. The textile company did not inform the mechanic of its contract with the customer, and thus the mechanic had no reason to know what impact his failure timely to perform would have on the textile company's relationship with its customer. Restatement (Second) of Contracts § 351; E. Allen Farnsworth, Contracts § 12.14 (4th ed. 2004).

(C)   Incorrect. The facts are insufficient to support this conclusion since the textile company had contracted with the mechanic for repairs to be completed within a time frame that would have allowed the textile company to timely fulfill its contractual obligations to the customer. Restatement (Second) of Contracts § 351; E. Allen Farnsworth, Contracts § 12.14 (4th ed. 2004).

(D)   Incorrect. There are insufficient facts to support this conclusion. No information is provided concerning the actual damages sustained by the customer. Moreover, the facts assume the validity of the liquidated damages provision. Restatement (Second) §§ 351, 356; E. Allen Farnsworth, Contracts § 12.14 (4th ed. 2004).

Question # 89 - Real Property
Answer: D

(A)   Incorrect. The friend does not have an enforceable lien. The friend did have a lien on the lot when the investor granted the friend a mortgage. The friend, however, did not record the mortgage. The investor then sold the lot to the buyer. The buyer had no actual notice of the mortgage to the friend. The buyer had no notice based on possession because the lot was vacant. The buyer had no constructive notice of the mortgage because the mortgage to the friend had not been recorded when the buyer received title. The lot is located in a notice jurisdiction. Thus, the buyer took the lot free of any prior unrecorded documents. The fact that the friend later recorded the mortgage is irrelevant in a notice jurisdiction. The buyer took free of that mortgage. The bank's mortgage is an enforceable lien.

(B)   Incorrect. The friend does not have an enforceable lien. The friend did have a lien on the lot when the investor granted the friend a mortgage. The friend, however, did not record the mortgage. The investor then sold the lot to the buyer. The buyer had no actual notice of the mortgage to the friend. The buyer had no notice based on possession because the lot was vacant. The buyer had no constructive notice of the mortgage because the mortgage to the friend had not been recorded when the buyer received title. The lot is located in a notice jurisdiction. Thus, the buyer took the lot free of any prior unrecorded documents. The fact that the buyer was an innocent purchaser for value qualifies the buyer for protection in a notice jurisdiction. The bank does have an enforceable lien.

(C)   Incorrect. The friend does not have an enforceable lien. The friend did have a lien on the lot when the investor granted the friend a mortgage. The friend, however, did not record the mortgage. The investor then sold the lot to the buyer. The buyer had no actual notice of the mortgage to the friend. The buyer had no notice based on possession because the lot was vacant. The buyer had no constructive notice of the mortgage because the mortgage to the friend had not been recorded when the buyer received title. The lot is located in a notice jurisdiction. Thus, the buyer took the lot free of any prior unrecorded documents. The fact that the friend later recorded the mortgage and told the buyer is irrelevant. The buyer took free of the friend's mortgage. The buyer was an innocent purchaser for value when the buyer purchased the lot and took free of the friend's mortgage. The lot is not subject to the friend's mortgage and the fact that the buyer told the bank of the recorded mortgage is irrelevant. The notice given to the buyer was given too late. The bank's mortgage is an enforceable lien.

(D)   Correct. The friend does not have an enforceable lien. The friend did have a lien on the lot when the investor granted the friend a mortgage. The friend, however, did not record the mortgage. The investor then sold the lot to the buyer. The buyer had no actual notice of the mortgage to the friend. The buyer had no notice based on possession because the lot was vacant. The buyer had no constructive notice of the mortgage because the mortgage to the friend had not been recorded when the buyer received title. The lot is located in a notice jurisdiction. Thus, the buyer took the lot free of any prior unrecorded documents. The buyer was an innocent purchaser for value at the time the buyer received title. Later notice to the buyer and a later recording of the friend's mortgage are irrelevant.

Question # 90 - Criminal Law and Procedure
Answer: A

(A)   Correct. The friend is responsible for the unintended but reasonably foreseeable acts of her coconspirator in furtherance of the conspiracy. 2 Wayne R. LaFave, Substantive Criminal Law § 13.3(b) (discussing *Pinkerton v. United States*, 328 U.S. 640 (1946)). The store owner's sale of the gun, combined with his knowledge of the woman's plan to use it in a crime and his financial benefit from that knowledge, should suffice to impose accomplice liability. 2 Wayne R. LaFave, Substantive Criminal Law § 13.2(b).

(B)   Incorrect. The friend is responsible for the unintended but reasonably foreseeable acts of her coconspirator in furtherance of the conspiracy. 2 Wayne R. LaFave, Substantive Criminal Law § 13.3(b) (discussing *Pinkerton v. United States*, 328 U.S. 640 (1946)). The store owner's sale of the gun, combined with his knowledge of the woman's plan to use it in a crime and his financial benefit from that knowledge, should suffice to impose accomplice liability. 2 Wayne R. LaFave, Substantive Criminal Law § 13.2(b).

(C)   Incorrect. The store owner could also be convicted. The store owner's sale of the gun, combined with his knowledge of the woman's plan to use it in a crime and his financial benefit from that knowledge, should suffice to impose accomplice liability. 2 Wayne R. LaFave,

Substantive Criminal Law § 13.2(b).

(D)   Incorrect. The friend could also be convicted. The friend is responsible for the unintended but reasonably foreseeable acts of her coconspirator in furtherance of the conspiracy. 2 Wayne R. LaFave, Substantive Criminal Law § 13.3(b) (discussing *Pinkerton v. United States*, 328 U.S. 640 (1946)).

Question # 91 – Evidence
Answer: C

(A)   Incorrect. The statement is admissible as a present sense impression under Rule 803(1) of the Federal Rules of Evidence because it describes or explains an event or condition and was "made while the declarant was perceiving the event or condition, or immediately thereafter." But it is also admissible under Rule 803(5) of the Federal Rules of Evidence because it is a record "concerning a matter about which a witness once had knowledge but now has insufficient recollection to testify fully and accurately," and it was made by the witness "when the matter was fresh in the witness' memory" and "reflect[s] that knowledge correctly."

(B)   Incorrect. The tape recording is admissible under Rule 803(5) of the Federal Rules of Evidence because it is a record "concerning a matter about which a witness once had knowledge but now has insufficient recollection to testify fully and accurately," and it was made by the witness "when the matter was fresh in the witness' memory" and "reflect[s] that knowledge correctly." However, the statement is also admissible as a present sense impression under Rule 803(1) of the Federal Rules of Evidence because it describes or explains an event or condition and was "made while the declarant was perceiving the event or condition, or immediately thereafter."

(C)   Correct. The statement is admissible as a present sense impression under Rule 803(1) of the Federal Rules of Evidence because it describes or explains an event or condition and was "made while the declarant was perceiving the event or condition, or immediately thereafter." It is also admissible under Rule 803(5) of the Federal Rules of Evidence because it is a record "concerning a matter about which a witness once had knowledge but now has insufficient recollection to testify fully and accurately," and it was made by the witness "when the matter was fresh in the witness' memory" and "reflect[s] that knowledge correctly."

(D)   Incorrect. The statement on the recording is hearsay because it is an out-of-court statement offered for its truth. But it is admissible under Rule 803(1) of the Federal Rules of Evidence as a present sense impression and also under Rule 803(5) as a past recollection recorded.

Question # 92 - Criminal Law and Procedure
Answer: C

(A)   Incorrect. Intent to steal the car would not prove the man knowingly damaged the store. To have acted knowingly, a defendant must have been practically certain that his conduct would cause damage. 1 Wayne R. LaFave, Substantive Criminal Law § 5.2(b).

(B)   Incorrect. The fact that the man was in the process of committing another felony would not prove that the man knowingly damaged the store. To have acted knowingly, a defendant must have been practically certain that his conduct would cause damage. 1 Wayne R. LaFave, Substantive

Criminal Law § 5.2(b).

(C)   Correct. The instruction was wrong because to have acted knowingly, the man must have been practically certain that his conduct would damage the store. 1 Wayne R. LaFave, Substantive Criminal Law § 5.2(b).

(D)   Incorrect. Double jeopardy does not preclude conviction of two distinct crimes with separate legal elements. *Blockburger v. United States*, 284 U.S. 299 (1932).

Question # 93 – Contracts
Answer: C

(A)   Incorrect. UCC § 2-311(1) specifically rejects the notion that a contract that is otherwise sufficiently definite is invalid because the agreement failed to specify the assortment of goods to be delivered to the buyer.

(B)   Incorrect. The buyer's selection of candy bars was a constructive condition to the seller's performance obligation. UCC § 2-311.

(C)   Correct. UCC § 2-311 imposes a duty on a buyer to cooperate by specifying the assortment of goods where the contract fails to so provide. A seller can treat the buyer's failure to specify as a breach by failure to accept the contracted-for goods only if the buyer's failure to specify materially impacts the seller's performance. The seller had an available supply of candy bars and had entered into no new contracts. These facts support the conclusion that the buyer's failure to select did not materially impact the seller's performance. Therefore the seller unjustifiably refused to accept the buyer's selection of goods. UCC § 2-311.

(D)   Incorrect. The right of the seller to select is merely one of the options available to the seller when the buyer's failure to select has a material impact on the seller's performance. The buyer's failure to select did not have a material impact on the seller's performance, and the buyer still had the opportunity to select the assortment of candy bars. UCC § 2-311(3).

Question # 94 - Real Property
Answer: A

(A)   Correct. Fifteen years ago each of the parties granted a reciprocal right of first refusal (or a preemptive right) to the other. A right of first refusal is a conditional option. It provides that if the owner ever decides to sell the property, the one holding the right of first refusal has the right to purchase it. In this case, the price for the purchase was to be set by three qualified expert independent real estate appraisers and was thus fair. The right, however, violates the common law Rule Against Perpetuities. The right to purchase is triggered by the decision of one to sell his or her land. In this case, that decision might occur more than 21 years after a life in being at the time the right was granted. Thus, under the common law, the right of first refusal is struck ab initio. The question notes that the common law Rule Against Perpetuities is unmodified in this jurisdiction. Thus, there are no applicable statutory reforms to the rule, and because the question is written with the daughter winning, any statute which may exempt a commercial transaction is inapplicable.

(B)   Incorrect. Ten years ago, the grantee had the right to purchase the larger tract of land under the right of first refusal (or a preemptive right) given to the grantee. The grantee chose not to exercise that right. The fact that the grantee chose not to exercise the right of first refusal has no effect on whether the grantor can exercise the reciprocal right of first refusal regarding the grantee's land. In this case, however, the reciprocal rights of first refusal violated the common law Rule Against Perpetuities and would be struck at once, with neither party able to enforce the right. The right of first refusal is triggered by the decision to sell the land. That decision might occur more than 21 years after a life in being at the time the right was granted. Thus, under the common law, the right of first refusal is struck ab initio. The question notes that the common law Rule Against Perpetuities is unmodified in this jurisdiction. Thus, there would be no applicable statutory reforms to the rule.

(C) Incorrect. Fifteen years ago each of the parties granted a reciprocal right of first refusal (or a preemptive right) to the other. A right of first refusal is a conditional option. It provides that if the owner ever decides to sell the property, the one holding the right of first refusal has the right to purchase it. A right of first refusal may have been granted as to only one of the tracts of land. Here, the rights were reciprocal as to two tracts of land. It does not matter that the tracts were not adjacent. The reciprocal rights of first refusal, however, violate the common law Rule Against Perpetuities and would be struck at once, with neither party able to enforce the right. The right of first refusal is triggered by the decision to sell the land. That decision might occur more than 21 years after a life in being at the time the right was granted. Thus, under the common law, the right of first refusal is struck ab initio. The question notes that the common law Rule Against Perpetuities is unmodified in this jurisdiction. Thus, there would be no applicable statutory reforms to the rule.

(D) Incorrect. Fifteen years ago each of the parties granted a reciprocal right of first refusal (or a preemptive right) to the other. The reciprocal right of first refusal, however, violates the common law Rule Against Perpetuities and would be struck at once, with neither party able to enforce the right either for money damages or for specific performance. The right of first refusal is triggered by the decision to sell the land. That decision might occur more than 21 years after a life in being at the time the right was granted. Thus, under the common law, the right of first refusal is struck ab initio. The question notes that the common law Rule Against Perpetuities is unmodified. Thus, there would be no applicable statutory reforms to the rule.

Question # 95 - Constitutional Law
Answer: A

(A) Correct. Any permanent physical occupation by the government of private property is a taking for which just compensation to the property owner is required. It is irrelevant that in this case the portion of the owner's tract of land to be occupied by the government is unused and very small. Nor is it relevant that in this case the construction and operation of the facility will not affect any of the uses that the owner is currently making of the entire tract of land. The permanent physical occupation by the government of the owner's land would be sufficient by itself to constitute a taking.

(B) Incorrect. Constructing and operating the facility on the owner's land would not violate equal protection because the decision to do so was rationally related to the protection of national security, which is a legitimate government interest.

Any permanent physical occupation by the government of private property is a taking for which just compensation to the property owner is required. Because in this case construction and operation of the facility would constitute a permanent physical occupation by the government of the owner's land, the government would have to compensate the owner for having taken his property.

(C) Incorrect. Any permanent physical occupation by the government of private property is a taking for which just compensation to the property owner is required. It therefore is irrelevant in this case that the construction and operation of the facility will not affect any of the uses that the owner is currently making of the entire tract of land.

(D) Incorrect. Any permanent physical occupation by the government of private property is a taking for which just compensation to the property owner is required. The takings clause does not exempt takings that are necessary to protect a compelling government interest from the obligation to provide just compensation to the property owner. Therefore, in this case, the taking would be invalid without just compensation even if the government could show that construction and operation of the facility.

Question # 96 – Torts
Answer: C

(A) Incorrect. The possessor of a vicious dog may be strictly liable to those injured by the dog, but the landlord here is not in possession of the dog. Moreover, the liability, where it exists, is limited to cases in which the possessor has reason to know that the dog is unusually dangerous. Restatement (Second) of Torts §§ 343, 509.

(B) Incorrect. A landlord may have a nondelegable duty to protect persons who come upon the land from dangerous conditions of the property, such as cracked walks and broken stairs, but the presence of the dog is not such a condition. Also the duty is only a duty to act reasonably, and there is no evidence here that the landlord acted unreasonably. See Restatement (Second) of Torts § 422.

(C) Correct. Any duty that the landlord may have is at most a duty to act reasonably. If the landlord had no reason to know that the dog posed a risk to those on his property, his failure to take precautions against that risk was not negligent. Restatement (Second) of Torts §§ 343, 509.

(D) Incorrect. A landlord does owe a duty to those who are foreseeably on the land, including guests of his tenants. Because this is a business venture of the landlord, guests of his tenants would be the landlord's invitees. See Restatement (Second) of Torts §§ 332 cmt. k.

Question # 97 - Criminal Law and Procedure
Answer: B

(A) Incorrect. The Fifth Amendment also protects acts of production that would have testimonial significance by authenticating documents. See, e.g., United States v. Hubbell, 530 U.S. 27 (2000); Fisher v. United States, 425 U.S. 391 (1976).

(B)   Correct. Use and derivative use immunity sufficiently protects the constitutional privilege against self-incrimination in this situation. *Kastigar v. United States*, 406 U.S. 441 (1972).

(C)   Incorrect. The suspect did not have to be granted transactional immunity because use and derivative use immunity sufficiently protects the constitutional privilege against self-incrimination. *Kastigar v. United States*, 406 U.S. 441 (1972).

(D)   Incorrect. The suspect's privilege against self-incrimination may be overcome if the suspect is granted use and derivative use immunity. *Kastigar v. United States*, 406 U.S. 441 (1972).

Question # 98 – Evidence
Answer: A

(A)   Correct. The attorney-client privilege applies only to confidential communications made for the purpose of facilitating legal representation of the client, and the amount the defendant paid in legal fees does not qualify as such a communication. Fee arrangements and payments are generally outside the protection of the attorney-client privilege.

(B)   Incorrect. The attorney-client privilege can be invoked even where it conceals evidence of a past crime. However, the privilege applies only to confidential communications made for the purpose of facilitating legal representation of the client, and the amount the defendant paid in legal fees does not qualify as such a communication. Fee arrangements and payments are generally outside the protection of the attorney-client privilege.

(C)   Incorrect. The attorney-client privilege applies only to confidential communications made for the purpose of facilitating legal representation of the client. The amount the defendant paid in legal fees does not qualify as such a communication. Fee arrangements and payments are generally outside the protection of the attorney-client privilege.

(D)   Incorrect. The work-product doctrine provides a qualified immunity for materials prepared by an attorney or client in anticipation of litigation, such as witness statements, investigative reports, or trial memoranda. The amount a client paid to his attorney for legal representation is outside the protection of the work-product doctrine.

Question # 99 - Criminal Law and Procedure
Answer: A

(A)   Correct. The man could properly be convicted of murder, even though he lacked specific intent to kill, because his conduct created such a high risk of death and was so devoid of social utility that he could be found to have acted with a "depraved heart." *See* 2 Wayne R. LaFave, Substantive Criminal Law § 14.4(a), at 437–41 (2d ed. 2003).

(B)   Incorrect. The man could not properly be convicted of voluntary manslaughter because there was no adequate provocation for his conduct, and in any event this answer is incorrect because he could be convicted of the more serious offense of depraved heart murder. *See* 2 Wayne R. LaFave, Substantive Criminal Law § 14.4(a), at 437–41 (2d ed. 2003).

(C)   Incorrect. The man could properly be convicted of involuntary manslaughter but this answer is incorrect because he could also be convicted of the more serious offense of depraved heart murder. *See* 2 Wayne R. LaFave, Substantive Criminal Law § 14.4(a), at 437–41 (2d ed. 2003).

(D) Incorrect. The man could properly be convicted of assault in some jurisdictions but this answer is incorrect because he could also be convicted of the more serious offense of depraved heart murder. *See* 2 Wayne R. LaFave, Substantive Criminal Law § 14.4(a), at 437–41 (2d ed. 2003).

Question # 100 – Torts
Answer: A

(A)   Correct. The tort of interference with contract provides a cause of action against those who improperly interfere with the performance of a contract between another and a third person. In this case, the plaintiff and the defendant were parties to the contract, and any action between them would be based on the contract, rather than on tort. The proper defendant in the tort action would be the food company. *See* Restatement (Second) of Torts § 766.

(B)   Incorrect. The airline could sue the food company for tortious interference even though it was not in privity with the food company, but it did not do so. It sued the delivery service instead. *See* Restatement (Second) of Torts § 766.

(C)   Incorrect. Because the delivery service was a party to the contract with the airline company, any claim of breach is governed by contract law, rather than tort. *See* Restatement (Second) of Torts § 766.

(D)   Incorrect. There is no indication here that the delivery service encouraged or otherwise abetted the food company's decision to cancel its contract. In fact, the delivery service lost business because of that cancellation. *See* Restatement (Second) of Torts § 766.

MBE ANSWERS

Multistate Bar Examination - Answers to Questions – Section 2

MBE Practice Exam 2

Question 1 - Contracts
Answer: B

(A) Incorrect. The goal is to put the teacher in the position he or she would have occupied but for the breach. $4,000 is a wrong answer because it fails to provide for recovery of the $200 expense incurred in the reasonable, albeit unsuccessful, effort to mitigate damages by applying for the head counselor position at another nearby summer camp. The fact that the effort to mitigate was unsuccessful does not mean the expense is not recoverable. Accordingly, the teacher is entitled to recover the difference between the contract salary ($10,000) and the amount earned at the local summer school ($6,000), PLUS the reasonable expenses incurred in seeking to mitigate after the breach ($200 travel expenses).

(B) Correct. The teacher is entitled to be put in the position he or she would have been in if the contract had been performed. Application of this principle leads to recovery of the difference between the contract salary ($10,000) and the amount earned at the local summer school ($6,000), PLUS the reasonable expenses incurred in seeking to mitigate after the breach ($200 travel expenses). Mitigation expenses can be recovered, if reasonable, even if those particular expenses are not connected to a successful mitigation attempt.

(C) Incorrect. The goal is to put the teacher in the position he or she would have occupied but for the breach. An award of $10,000 would overcompensate the teacher, violating the principle of expectation damages. The teacher successfully sought other employment for the same time period as covered in the contract, and the amount earned on that job must be taken into account in calculating damages. There is no suggestion here that the teacher could have held both jobs simultaneously, earning both salaries. In addition, this answer fails to compensate the teacher for the travel expenses incurred in mitigating damages. The fact that the effort to mitigate was unsuccessful does not mean the expense is not recoverable. The proper recovery is the difference between the contract salary ($10,000) and the amount earned at the local summer school ($6,000), PLUS the reasonable expenses incurred in seeking to mitigate after the breach ($200 travel expenses).

(D) Incorrect. The goal is to put the teacher in the position he or she would have occupied but for the breach. An award of $10,200 would overcompensate the teacher, violating the principle of expectation damages. The teacher successfully sought other employment for the same time period as covered in the contract, and the amount earned on that job must be taken into account in calculating damages. There is no suggestion here that the teacher could have held both jobs simultaneously, earning both salaries. This answer does take into account the unsuccessful effort to mitigate damages, which is appropriate. Accordingly, the proper recovery is the difference between the contract salary ($10,000) and the amount earned at the local summer school ($6,000), PLUS the reasonable expenses incurred in seeking to mitigate after the breach ($200 travel expenses).

Question 2 - Constitutional Law
Answer: C

(A) Incorrect. Article I, Section 9, Clause 4 of the Constitution allows Congress to adopt direct taxes, provided they are in proportion to the national census. Courts defer to reasonable congressional taxing measures, such as the statute at issue in this case, as well as to expenditures that reasonably further the general welfare.

(B) Incorrect. It is true that the Fifth Amendment prohibits the taking of private property for public use without just compensation. But no such taking has occurred here. A tax on the sale of a computer takes no property from those who hold patents or copyrights on computer software. Likewise, the software distributed freely under the statute will first be purchased, rather than taken, by the government. Courts defer to reasonable congressional taxing measures, such as the statute at issue in this case, as well as to expenditures that reasonably further the general welfare.

(C) Correct. Article I, Section 8, Clause 1 of the Constitution gives Congress broad power to tax and to spend for the general welfare. Courts defer to reasonable congressional taxing measures, such as the statute at issue in this case, as well as to expenditures that reasonably further the general welfare.

(D) Incorrect. Although Article I, Section 8, Clause 8 of the Constitution gives Congress power to provide patent rights to inventors, this clause does not itself authorize federal taxes and appropriations. Courts defer to reasonable congressional taxing measures, such as the statute at issue in this case, as well as to expenditures that reasonably further the general welfare.

Question 3 - Criminal Law and Procedure
Answer: A

(A) Correct. The eight gang members are not guilty of murder, because they took no affirmative act and were merely present at what turned out to be a crime scene. *See generally* Wayne R. LaFave, Principles of Criminal Law § 10.4, at 442-49 (2003).

(B) Incorrect. This answer correctly states that the convictions should not be upheld, but it misstates the legal basis for this conclusion. Murder does not require specific intent to kill, but may be committed in other circumstances (e.g., intent-to-do-serious-bodily-harm murder, depraved-heart murder, and felony murder). *See* Wayne R. LaFave, Principles of Criminal Law §§ 13.3-13.5, at 569-91 (2003). In this case, the eight gang members are not guilty of murder because they took no affirmative act and were merely present at what turned out to be a crime scene. *See generally id.* § 10.4, at 442-49.

(C) Incorrect. The eight gang members did not have a legal duty, enforceable by the criminal laws, to save the informant. *See* Wayne R. LaFave, Principles of Criminal Law § 5.2, at 213-17 (2003). Moreover, they are not responsible for the murder because they took no affirmative act and were merely present at what turned out to be a crime scene. *See generally id.* § 10.4, at 442-49.

(D) Incorrect. The conclusion is wrong and the principle is inapposite. In this case, the eight gang members were not responsible for the murder regardless of whether they were sober or intoxicated. This is because they took no affirmative act and were merely present at what turned out to be a crime scene. *See generally* Wayne R. LaFave, Principles of Criminal Law § 10.4, at

442-49 (2003).

Question 4 - Real Property
Answer: A

(A) Correct. An assignment arises when a tenant transfers all or some of the leased premises to another for the remainder of the lease term, retaining no interest in the assigned premises. In this case, prior to the agreement with the friend, the tenant had privity of contract with the landlord because of the lease. The tenant also had privity of estate because the tenant was in possession of the apartment. Subsequently, an assignment arose when the tenant transferred the premises to the friend for the remainder of the lease term of nine months. The friend was then in privity of estate with the landlord as to all promises that run with the land, including the covenant to pay rent. The tenant was not released by the landlord, however, and thus remained liable on privity of contract.

(B) Incorrect. An assignment arises when a tenant transfers all or some of the leased premises to another for the remainder of the lease term, retaining no interest in the assigned premises. Here, the tenant transferred all the remaining time of the lease to the friend and retained no other interest. Accordingly, this was an assignment and the friend was in privity of estate with the landlord. The privity of estate remained with the friend until the end of the lease, because that was the friend's assigned interest. The friend made no assignment, and remained liable on privity of estate for the period after he vacated. Furthermore, because the landlord never released the tenant, the tenant remained liable for the full $3,500 on privity of contract.

(C) Incorrect. It is true that the friend is liable for $3,500 on privity of estate. However, because the landlord never released the tenant, the tenant remained liable on privity of contract based on the original lease. There was no express release, and a release would not be implied merely because the landlord accepted rent from the friend.

(D) Incorrect. This option assumes that the friend was a sublessee, which he was not. A sublease arises when a tenant transfers the right of possession to all or some of the leased premises to another for a time less than the remaining time of the lease, or when the tenant retains some other interest in the premises. Here, the tenant transferred all the remaining time of the lease to the friend and retained no other interest. Accordingly, this was an assignment and not a sublease. As an assignee, the friend was in privity of estate with the landlord as to all promises that run with the land, including the covenant to pay rent.

Question 5 - Evidence
Answer: A

(A) Correct. Federal Rule of Evidence 803(18), the learned treatise exception, provides that if the court finds a publication to be a reliable authority, then "statements" may be read into evidence, but that the publication may not be received as an exhibit. Thus, the jury is not allowed to bring learned treatises into the jury room. There is a concern that if juries were allowed unrestricted access to the whole publication, they may rely on parts of the publication that are not germane to the case. Moreover, the intent of the rule is that juries need to be guided through the pertinent parts of the publication by the testifying experts.

(B) Incorrect. Federal Rule of Evidence 803(18), the learned treatise exception, allows statements from a treatise to be read into evidence where the treatise is "called to the attention of an expert witness" and is found to be reliable by the court. The rule does not require that an expert *rely* on the treatise. In this case, the publication was called to the attention of the defendant's expert.

(C) Incorrect. Federal Rule of Evidence 803(18), the learned treatise exception, allows statements from a treatise to be read into evidence when the treatise is "established as a reliable authority by the testimony or admission of the witness or by other expert testimony or by judicial notice." In this case, one expert testified that the publication was reliable, but the other expert contests that assertion. The decision on reliability is for the court; it is not correct to say that the court should find the publication reliable simply because one expert has found it to be so. In addition, the rule allows "statements" from a learned treatise to be read into evidence, but does not allow the publication to be received as an exhibit.

(D) Incorrect. The statement is true so far as it goes, but it does not mean that the jury gets to consider any evidence that the parties wish to present. Federal Rule of Evidence 803(18), the learned treatise exception, requires the judge to determine that the publication is reliable before it can be considered by the jury. In addition, the rule allows "statements" from a learned treatise to be read into evidence, but does not allow the publication to be received as an exhibit.

Question 6 - Torts
Answer: B

(A) Incorrect. This answer correctly states that the driver's motion should be denied, but it misstates the legal basis for this conclusion. The firefighters' rule, although named with reference to firefighters, also covers police officers. They, too, are public servants at risk of injury by the perils that they have been employed to confront. Instead, the motion should be denied because being struck by a car in normal traffic is not one of the special risks inherent to dangerous police work.

(B) Correct. The driver could be held liable for his negligence because being struck by a car in normal traffic is not one of the special risks inherent to dangerous police work.

(C) Incorrect. But-for causation is not sufficient to support the firefighters' rule defense when the risk that materialized was not one of the unique risks inherent to the officer's dangerous work. The fact that the officer was returning from an emergency when she was struck is just a coincidence. The driver could still be held liable for his negligence because being struck by a car in normal traffic is not one of the special risks inherent in dangerous police work.

(D) Incorrect. The firefighters' rule only bars claims for injuries that result from risks that are unique or special to the plaintiff's inherently dangerous work. Workers' compensation, not the common law of torts, is the compensation system for on-the-job injuries. The driver could be held liable for his negligence because being struck by a car in normal traffic is not one of the special risks inherent to dangerous police work.

Question 7 - Contracts
Answer: C

(A) Incorrect. A quantity term expressed in terms of a manufacturer's requirements is enforceable. Uniform Commercial Code § 2-306 provides that "a term which measures the quantity by the . . . requirements of the buyer means such actual . . . requirements as may occur in good faith . . . ." Basically, the definiteness of quantity requirement is satisfied if there is an available objective method for determining the quantity, and the requirements of a manufacturer would generally satisfy that need. In this case, once the manufacturer provided the supplier with adequate assurance in the form of audited financial statements and a credit report, the supplier was bound to perform under the contract.

(B) Incorrect. Under Uniform Commercial Code § 2-609, a party to a contract who has reasonable grounds for insecurity is entitled to request assurances, and is also entitled to suspend performance pending receipt of that assurance. A failure to provide an adequate assurance within a reasonable time (not to exceed 30 days) can be treated as a repudiation, which may give rise to a right to terminate the contract. In this case, the supplier was entitled to seek assurance, but once the manufacturer provided the supplier with adequate assurance in the form of audited financial statements and a credit report, the supplier was bound to perform under the contract.

(C) Correct. A party to a contract with reasonable grounds to worry that the other party might not perform can request adequate assurances of performance, pursuant to Uniform Commercial Code § 2-609. The supplier in this case did so, but the information provided by the manufacturer would be regarded as satisfying the request for an assurance of performance. Therefore the supplier's refusal to continue performance constituted a breach of contract for which the manufacturer is entitled to compensation.

(D) Incorrect. This answer correctly concludes that the manufacturer will prevail, but it misstates the reason why this is so. Uniform Commercial Code § 2-609 provides that a party to a contract with reasonable grounds to worry that the other party might not perform can request adequate assurance of performance. In this case, the supplier heard rumors from a credible source that the manufacturer's financial condition was insecure. This would be enough to trigger the right to request assurance, and so it is incorrect to assert that the supplier was not entitled to request assurance. Nevertheless, the manufacturer will prevail because it in fact provided adequate assurance in the form of audited financial statements and a credit report. Therefore the supplier's refusal to continue performance constituted a breach of contract for which the manufacturer is entitled to compensation.

Question 8 - Constitutional Law
Answer: B

(A) Incorrect. It is true that the Green law is unconstitutional, but this answer misstates the basis for this conclusion. The contracts clause (Article I, Section 10, Clause 1 of the Constitution) does not forbid state laws affecting contractual relations between private parties so long as they are reasonably related to a legitimate state interest. Because the courts typically defer to state regulations of private contracts as reasonable, the statute at issue here is not likely to be found unconstitutional under the contracts clause. Rather, the law clearly violates the negative implications of the commerce clause (Article I, Section 8, Clause 3 of the Constitution), because it has a purely discriminatory effect against out-of-state toy manufacturers despite any number of less discriminatory alternatives available to the state to protect the legitimate interests cited in the law.

(B) Correct. The commerce clause (Article I, Section 8, Clause 3 of the Constitution) gives Congress the power to regulate commerce among the states and, by negative implication, restricts the regulatory power of the states with respect to interstate commerce. Any state law that has a substantial effect on interstate commerce must not be protectionist or otherwise impose an undue burden on interstate commerce. A protectionist law benefits in-state interests at the expense of out-of-state interests. A state law that discriminates against interstate commerce is protectionist unless it serves a legitimate local interest that cannot be served by nondiscriminatory legislation. By barring the sale in Green of the Martian toys manufactured in other states, the state law has a substantial effect on interstate commerce. Although the law does not explicitly discriminate against the out-of-state toy manufacturers, it has a purely discriminatory effect against them, and the state has less discriminatory alternatives available to protect the legitimate interests cited in the law. The state law therefore violates the negative implications of the commerce clause.

(C) Incorrect. State regulations of local matters are subject to the negative implications of the commerce clause (Article I, Section 8, Clause 3 of the Constitution) if they have a substantial effect on interstate commerce. By barring the sale in Green of the Martian toys manufactured in other states, the state law has such an effect. The law is unconstitutional under the commerce clause because it has a purely discriminatory effect against out-of-state toy manufacturers despite any number of less discriminatory alternatives available to the state to protect the legitimate interests cited in the law.

(D) Incorrect. The commerce clause (Article I, Section 8, Clause 3 of the Constitution) gives Congress the power to regulate commerce among the states and, by negative implication, restricts the regulatory power of the states with respect to interstate commerce. Any state law that has a substantial effect on interstate commerce must not be protectionist or otherwise impose an undue burden on interstate commerce. A protectionist law benefits in-state interests at the expense of out-of-state interests. A state law that discriminates against interstate commerce is protectionist unless it serves a legitimate local interest that cannot be served by nondiscriminatory legislation. By barring the sale in Green of the Martian toys manufactured in other states, the state law has a substantial effect on interstate commerce. Further, it has a purely discriminatory effect against out-of-state toy manufacturers. Although the state's interest in protecting children from faulty science is legitimate, it does not justify the law's discriminatory burden on interstate commerce because the state has less discriminatory alternatives available to protect the interest.

Question 9 - Real Property
Answer: C

(A) Incorrect. The deed to the friend was valid because it was in the proper form and was delivered to him. Delivery occurred at the time the landowner handed the deed to the friend. At that time the landowner was competent. The friend's subsequent recording of the deed had no effect on the deed's validity.

(B) Incorrect. The deed to the friend was valid because it was in the proper form and was delivered to him. Delivery occurred at the time the deed was handed to the friend with the words "this is yours." The subsequent misrepresentation that the friend made that he had destroyed the deed has no effect on the prior valid delivery.

(C) Correct. A deed must be delivered to be valid. Delivery is a question of intent. The words of the landowner included "this is yours," showing the necessary intent to strip himself of dominion and control over the deed and to immediately transfer the title. In addition, handing the deed to the grantee raises a rebuttable presumption of delivery. Recording the deed is not required and thus the request not to record the document until later is irrelevant so long as delivery was present.

(D) Incorrect. Recording a document has no effect on its validity. In this case, the deed to the friend was valid because it was in the proper form and was delivered to him. His subsequent recording of the deed had no effect on his claim of ownership, although recording will now provide constructive notice of his ownership.

Question   10 - Criminal Law and Procedure
Answer: A

(A) Correct. The common law of attempt required that the defendant commit some act (beyond mere "preparation") toward bringing about the intended crime. Wayne R. LaFave, Principles of Criminal Law § 10.4, at 442-49 (2003). Here, the drug dealer took no act, much less any act that would qualify at common law, toward obtaining the cocaine. *See, e.g., People v. Warren*, 489 N.E.2d 240 (N.Y. 1985) (finding no common law attempt on much stronger facts for prosecution than this fact pattern). Indeed, the drug dealer likely would not be guilty of attempt even under the Model Penal Code's broadened standards because there was no "substantial step" toward commission of the crime. *See* MPC § 5.01(1)(c).

(B) Incorrect. This answer correctly states that the drug dealer should not be convicted of attempted possession of the cocaine, but it misstates the legal basis of this conclusion. The legality or illegality of a defendant's arrest has nothing to do with whether the defendant was guilty of an attempt. The common law of attempt required that the defendant have committed some act (beyond mere "preparation") toward bringing about the intended crime. Wayne R. LaFave, Principles of Criminal Law § 10.4, at 442-49 (2003). Here, the drug dealer took no act, much less any act that would qualify at common law, toward obtaining the cocaine. *See, e.g., People v. Warren*, 489 N.E.2d 240 (N.Y. 1985) (finding no common law attempt on much stronger facts for prosecution than this fact pattern). Indeed, the drug dealer likely would not be guilty of attempt even under the Model Penal Code's broadened standards because there was no "substantial step" toward commission of the crime. *See* MPC § 5.01(1)(c).

(C) Incorrect. An agreement to commit a crime is neither necessary nor sufficient to constitute attempt. The common law of attempt required that the defendant have committed some act (beyond mere "preparation") toward bringing about the intended crime. Wayne R. LaFave, Principles of Criminal Law § 10.4, at 442-49 (2003). Here, the drug dealer took no act, much less any act that would qualify at common law, toward obtaining the cocaine. *See, e.g., People v. Warren*, 489 N.E.2d 240 (N.Y. 1985) (finding no common law attempt on much stronger facts for prosecution than this fact pattern). Indeed, the drug dealer likely would not be guilty of attempt even under the Model Penal Code's broadened standards because there was no "substantial step" toward commission of the crime. *See* MPC § 5.01(1)(c).

(D) Incorrect. Attempt under common law required more than an unequivocal expression of criminal intent; in addition, the defendant must also have committed some act toward bringing about the intended crime. Wayne R. LaFave, Principles of Criminal Law § 10.4, at 442-49 (2003); *see, e.g., People v. Rizzo*, 158 N.E. 888 (1927). Here, the drug dealer took no act, much less any act that would qualify at common law, toward obtaining the cocaine. *See, e.g., People v. Warren*, 489 N.E.2d 240 (N.Y. 1985) (finding no common law attempt on much stronger facts for prosecution than this fact pattern). Indeed, the drug dealer likely would not be guilty of attempt even under the Model Penal Code's broadened standards because there was no "substantial step" toward commission of the crime. *See* MPC § 5.01(1)(c).

Question 11 - Torts
Answer: B

(A) Incorrect. This answer correctly states that the father will not prevail, but it misstates the legal basis for this conclusion. The existence of a physical impact, or lack thereof, is irrelevant. If recovery for emotional distress were permissible in this situation, a showing of physical impact would not be required. Virtually all jurisdictions have rejected the impact rule in cases involving negligent infliction of emotional distress. Instead, the father will lose because, when a patient does not pose a threat to others, a medical professional's duty of care usually extends only to the patient.

(B) Correct. In most situations, a medical professional's duty of care extends only to his or her patient. Unlike *Tarasoff v. The Regents of California*, the patient here posed no threat to others. Considerations of privacy and confidentiality usually lead courts to deny a duty on the part of therapists to non-patients when only the patient himself is at risk.

(C) Incorrect. The fact that the father was a member of the patient's immediate family is irrelevant in this kind of emotional distress case. It might well be relevant in a different sort of case—for example, in a case brought by a bystander who suffers emotional distress upon witnessing negligently caused injury to a family member, or in a case where a psychiatrist might prevent harm to a family member who is threatened by the patient by warning the patient's family. In this case, however, the psychiatrist's duty of care extended only to the patient.

(D) Incorrect. Even if the father's emotional distress is foreseeable, it is not ordinarily sufficient to create a duty to the father, who is not a patient of the doctor. Foreseeability alone, even when the risk is high and the cost of precautions is relatively low, is not enough in negligent infliction of emotional distress cases; the duty is more limited than when physical injury is involved.

Question 12 - Evidence
Answer: A

(A) Correct. Under Federal Rule of Evidence 608(b), a witness can be impeached with prior bad acts that bear upon truthfulness. Failing to stop at a stop sign has no bearing on truthfulness. As a general matter, a witness also can be impeached with evidence that contradicts a part of his testimony that bears on an important issue in dispute. However, in this case, the prior bad acts do not contradict the witness's testimony that he stopped on this occasion. Essentially, the defendant is trying to show that the plaintiff is a careless driver. Carelessness is a character trait, and evidence of a person's character is not admissible in a civil case to prove how that person acted on the occasion in question.

(B) Incorrect. Under Federal Rule of Evidence 608(b), a witness can be impeached with bad acts that do not result in convictions. The reason that the prior acts are inadmissible is not because there were no convictions, but rather because the acts have no bearing on veracity or contradiction of prior testimony.

(C) Incorrect. Under Federal Rule of Evidence 608(b), a witness can be impeached with prior bad acts that bear upon truthfulness by demonstrating falsity, dishonesty, or the like. Otherwise, the probative value of the acts as to credibility are substantially outweighed by the risks of prejudice, confusion, and delay, and would be excluded under Federal Rule of Evidence 403. In this case, the plaintiff's prior acts may demonstrate carelessness, but they do not demonstrate dishonesty.

(D) Incorrect. A person can be acting carefully on one occasion and not another, so the prior acts are not contradictory of the plaintiff's testimony that he was careful in this instance. If the plaintiff testified that he had *never* run a stop sign, then the prior acts would contradict his testimony.

Question   13 - Constitutional Law
Answer: B

(A) Incorrect. The state fired the woman because of her speech (notifying federal officials that the state was not following federal rules). There thus is a viable argument that the woman's firing abridged her freedom of speech.

(B) Correct. The privileges and immunities clause of Article IV, Section 2, Clause 1 of the Constitution does not apply on these facts. The clause only reaches actions by a state that discriminate against citizens of other states. The woman is a citizen of the state that employed her because she was a resident of that state (Fourteenth Amendment, Section 1).

(C) Incorrect. The supremacy clause (Article VI, Section 1, Clause 2) invalidates any state action that is contrary to federal law. It is reasonable to argue that firing an employee for notifying federal officials that the state was not following federal rules was in furtherance of action in violation of federal law, and thus prohibited by the supremacy clause.

(D) Incorrect. The due process clause of the Fourteenth Amendment generally prohibits states from taking property from an individual without notice and opportunity for a hearing. In the context of a government job, where state law provides that state employees can be fired only for good cause, a person has a legitimate claim of entitlement to, and thus a property interest in, his or her job. Here, the state had such a law, and the woman was therefore entitled to notice and the opportunity for a hearing before she was fired.

Question 14 - Contracts
Answer: D

(A) Incorrect. This contract is governed by the common law of contracts, and not the Uniform Commercial Code. Unlike the UCC, the prevailing common law view is that a modification to a contract requires consideration to be valid. Here, there was no consideration for the elimination of the contractor's duty to pave the sidewalk. The contractor actually promised to do less than it was under a pre-existing duty to do, and so there was no enforceable modification of the contract.

(B) Incorrect. It is true that the contractor breached the contract, but there is no rule requiring the discharge of a contractual obligation to be in writing. There are many ways in which a discharge might arise, in addition to discharges by mutual agreement. But even in the case of discharge by mutual agreement, there is no general rule requiring a writing. The issue is whether the parties' oral exchange regarding the sidewalk resulted in an enforceable modification of the contract. Because this contract is governed by the common law of contracts, and not the Uniform Commercial Code, the modification required consideration to be valid. There was no consideration in this case for the elimination of the contractor's duty to pave the sidewalk. The contractor actually promised to do less than it was under a pre-existing duty to do, and so there was no enforceable modification of the contract.

(C) Incorrect. It is true that the contractor breached the contract, but the parol evidence rule is not applicable. The parol evidence rule applies to exclude some kinds of evidence with respect to discussions held, or correspondence exchanged, either prior to or contemporaneous with the making of a contract. In this case the crucial exchange occurred AFTER the contract was made, and so the issue is whether that exchange resulted in an enforceable modification of the contract. Because this contract is governed by the common law of contracts, and not the Uniform Commercial Code, the modification required consideration to be valid. There was no consideration in this case for the elimination of the contractor's duty to pave the sidewalk. The contractor actually promised to do less than it was under a pre-existing duty to do, and so there was no enforceable modification of the contract.

(D) Correct. This contract is governed by the common law of contracts, and not the Uniform Commercial Code. The prevailing common law view is that a modification to a contract requires consideration to be valid. Here, there was no consideration for the elimination of the contractor's duty to pave the sidewalk. The contractor actually promised to do less than it was under a pre-existing duty to do, and so there was no enforceable modification of the contract.

Question 15 - Real Property
Answer: D

(A) Incorrect. A joint tenancy is not devisable or inheritable, and cannot be severed by a will. In this case, therefore, the son's interest in the land terminated on his death. He had no separate interest in the land to convey by will to the cousin.

(B) Incorrect. Joint tenants traditionally received their interests at the same time and by the same document. The friend and the cousin received their purported interests by two different documents. Even if the formal requirements for a joint tenancy are not required to create the joint tenancy, there is no intent to create a joint tenancy between the friend and the cousin. In fact, because a joint tenancy is not devisable or inheritable, and cannot be severed by a will, the son's interest terminated on his death and he had no interest to convey to the cousin.

(C) Incorrect. It is true that a tenancy in common may be created by different documents. However, the son's interest in this case was a joint tenancy with the daughter. Because a joint tenancy is not devisable or inheritable, and cannot be severed by a will, the son's interest terminated on his death and he had no interest to convey to the cousin.

(D) Correct. A joint tenancy is not devisable or inheritable, and cannot be severed by a will. In this case, the son and the daughter received title as joint tenants with right of survivorship. On the death of the son, the interest of the daughter swelled and she then owned the land alone and in fee simple. She had the right to devise that interest by her will to the friend.

Question 16 - Evidence
Answer: D

(A) Incorrect. The prosecutor is trying to prove what the defendant said, not what the transcript says. Accordingly, Federal Rule of Evidence 1003, the Best Evidence Rule, is not relevant. Even assuming that the Best Evidence Rule applied here, this is not an accurate statement of the law. Under Rule 1003, a duplicate can be admissible without any showing that the original is unavailable. A showing of unavailability is required only if the party is seeking to introduce something other than a duplicate (e.g., oral testimony) to prove the contents of a document. *See* Federal Rule of Evidence 1004.

(B) Incorrect. Under Federal Rule of Evidence 612, the copy of the transcript is properly used to revive the officer's recollection. This is not a case of past recollection recorded, in which the prosecutor would have to show that the stenographer accurately recorded what the defendant said. In this case, the officer is testifying to his own recollection of what the defendant said, that recollection having been revived by looking at the transcript. A document used only to revive recollection does not have to be accurate or reliable, because the document is not being admitted into evidence. The officer's testimony is the evidence.

(C) Incorrect. Although Federal Rule of Evidence 1003 supports the admission of photocopies with some exceptions, this option assumes that the Best Evidence Rule applies here, which it doesn't. The prosecutor is trying to prove what the defendant said, not what the transcript says. The transcript here is being used to revive the officer's recollection under Federal Rule of Evidence 612, and Rule 1003 is not relevant.

(D) Correct. The prosecutor is trying to prove what the defendant said, not what the transcript says. Accordingly, Federal Rule of Evidence 1003, the Best Evidence Rule, is not relevant. It would be different, for example, if this were a contract and the parties differed over the wording of a clause in the contract. In this case, the copy of the transcript is properly used under Federal Rule of Evidence 612 to revive the officer's recollection.

Question 17 - Criminal Law and Procedure
Answer: B

(A) Incorrect. This answer correctly states that the conviction will be set aside, but it misstates the legal basis for this conclusion. The Constitution does not require 12-person juries. *Burch v. Louisiana*, 441 U.S. 130 (1979).

(B) Correct. The Constitution requires unanimity where only a 6-person jury is used. *Williams v. Florida*, 339

U.S. 78 (1970).

(C) Incorrect. This answer correctly states that the conviction will be set aside, but it misstates the legal basis for this conclusion. The Constitution does not require 12-person juries (*Burch v. Louisiana*, 441 U.S. 130 (1979)), although it does require unanimity where only a 6-person jury is used (*Williams v. Florida*, 339 U.S. 78 (1970)).

(D) Incorrect. The conviction will not be upheld because the Constitution requires unanimity where only a 6-person jury is used. *Williams v. Florida*, 339 U.S. 78 (1970).

Question 18 - Real Property
Answer: A

(A) Correct. The warranty deed conveyed a fee simple determinable title to the church and the grantor retained the future interest which is the possibility of reverter. The future interest becomes possessory immediately upon the occurrence of the limitation. A title is unmarketable when a reasonable person would not purchase it. This buyer plans to use the land as a site for business purposes, which would cause the limitation to occur and the title to be forfeited automatically to the grantor.

(B) Incorrect. This answer correctly states that the church is unlikely to prevail, but it misstates the legal basis for this conclusion. The quoted provision creates a fee simple determinable title in the church. If the stated limitation occurs, the fee simple estate terminates automatically and title is forfeited to the holder of the future interest (in this case, the grantor). A restrictive covenant involves a promise regarding the use of the land and is not the title itself. Because the title in this case will be forfeited to the grantor if the land is not used for church purposes, no reasonable third party is likely to buy the land, and the church's title is not marketable.

(C) Incorrect. When and if the limitation occurs, the interest of the present interest holder is automatically terminated and title goes to the grantor as the holder of the future interest. While it is true that the church may use the sale proceeds as it desires, it is unlikely to find a buyer because any change in use of the land would cause the title to be forfeited automatically to the grantor. Accordingly, the church's title is not marketable.

(D) Incorrect. The grantor conveyed a title, which was a fee simple determinable, to the church and retained the possibility of reverter in fee simple. The grantor did not breach any title warranty. If the property is not used for church purposes, the property automatically is forfeited to the holder of the future interest, who is the grantor. Accordingly, the church's title is not marketable.

Question 19 - Evidence
Answer: C

(A) Incorrect. Under Federal Rule of Evidence 607, "[t]he credibility of a witness may be attacked by any party, including the party calling the witness."

(B) Incorrect. The prior statement of the witness is inadmissible hearsay under Federal Rule of Evidence 802 only if offered to prove that the defendant was involved in the transaction. It is not hearsay if offered to impeach the witness whose trial testimony is inconsistent with it. This is because, whether true or not, the statement is probative to show that the witness is not credible— he said one thing at trial and said something else previously.

(C) Correct. Prior statements that are inconsistent with a witness's present testimony impeach the witness's credibility because they tend to show that the witness's trial testimony is not believable. The prior inconsistent statement was not made under oath, and so does not fit the exemption to the hearsay rule provided by Federal Rule of Evidence 801(d)(1)(A). There is no other hearsay exception that is satisfied under the facts. Therefore the statement is admissible only to impeach the witness and not for its truth.

(D) Incorrect. The first part of the statement is correct but the second part is incorrect. The prior inconsistent statement was not made under oath, and so does not fit the exemption to the hearsay rule provided by Federal Rule of Evidence 801(d)(1)(A). There is no other hearsay exception that is satisfied under the facts. Therefore the statement is admissible only to impeach the witness and not for its truth. Using the statement to prove the defendant's involvement would violate Federal Rule of Evidence 802, the hearsay rule.

Question 20 - Torts
Answer: C

(A) Incorrect. Negligence creating the risk of an icy surface cannot be inferred from the mere fact that the car owner allowed the water to accumulate; the cold snap was "sudden and unexpected." Because there is no reasonable inference of negligence and no evidence of negligence (the statute is irrelevant because it does not speak to the risk that materialized in this case), the car owner's motion should be granted.

(B) Incorrect. The statute was not enacted to reduce the risk of accumulating ice on the public walkways. In fact, complying with the statute by washing the car in a private driveway would not have reduced the risk of accumulating ice on pedestrian walkways and may even have increased that risk. Therefore, violation of the statute says nothing about whether the car owner was negligent. The statute is irrelevant to the cause of action, and because the pedestrian offered no evidence supporting the claim of negligence except the statute, the car owner's motion should be granted.

(C) Correct. The pedestrian offered no evidence supporting the claim of negligence except the statute, and the statute does not speak to the risk that materialized in this case. Accordingly, the car owner's motion should be granted.

(D) Incorrect. In this case, the statute was enacted solely to reduce a particular safety risk (congested traffic lanes) that neither materialized nor caused the pedestrian's injury. In fact, the car owner's motion should be granted, because the pedestrian offered no evidence supporting the claim of negligence except the statute, and the statute does not speak to the risk that materialized in this case.

Question   21 - Constitutional Law
Answer: A

(A) Correct. The provision is a bill of attainder in violation of Article I, Section 10, Clause 1 of the Constitution. A bill of attainder is a law that provides for the punishment of a particular person without trial. The challenged provision satisfies this definition because it deprives two named professors of their salaries, and thus, their employment.

(B) Incorrect. It is true that the court is likely to strike down the provision, but this answer misstates the basis for this conclusion. The fact that the professors' conduct preexisted the state law would be significant if the state law provided for a criminal penalty—it would then be unconstitutional as an ex post facto law in violation of Article I, Section 10, Clause 1 of the Constitution. The ex post facto clause, however, does not apply to laws attaching civil consequences to past conduct. In this case, the provision does not alter the criminal law, but provides for the punishment of particular people, without trial, by depriving the two named professors of their salaries. As such, it is an unconstitutional bill of attainder in violation of Article I, Section 10, Clause 1 of the Constitution, regardless of the timing of the professors' conduct.

(C) Incorrect. The Eleventh Amendment provides for state sovereign immunity from certain kinds of adjudications. It does not extend legislative authority of any kind to the states. The provision in this case deprives two named professors of their salaries without affording them a trial. As such, the court will strike it down as a bill of attainder in violation of Article I, Section 10, Clause 1 of the Constitution.

(D) Incorrect. The full faith and credit clause (Article IV, Section 1 of the Constitution) does not insulate state laws from constitutional challenge. It merely requires state courts to accord due authority to the laws of other states. The provision in this case deprives two named professors of their salaries without affording them a trial. As such, the court will strike it down as a bill of attainder in violation of Article I, Section 10, Clause 1 of the Constitution.

Question   22 - Criminal Law and Procedure
Answer: B

(A) Incorrect. This answer correctly states that the woman's motion to suppress the heroin should not be granted, but it misstates the legal basis for this conclusion. Even assuming there was probable cause to search the home, a warrant would have been required for entry had the woman not consented. *See, e.g., Payton v. New York*, 445 U.S. 573 (1980). The woman's consent justified the officers' entry, and the heroin was properly seized because it was in plain view. *See, e.g., Illinois v. Rodriguez*, 497 U.S. 177 (1990).

(B) Correct. The woman's consent justified the officers' entry, and the heroin was properly seized because it was in plain view. *See, e.g., Illinois v. Rodriguez*, 497 U.S. 177 (1990).

(C) Incorrect. The search of the man, even assuming it was improper, did not violate the woman's rights and therefore provides no basis for suppressing evidence found in her house. *Cf. Minnesota v. Carter*, 525 U.S. 83 (1998) (discussing what is commonly referred to as "standing" requirement). The woman's consent justified the officers' entry, and the heroin was properly seized because it was in plain view. *See, e.g., Illinois v. Rodriguez*, 497 U.S. 177 (1990).

(D) Incorrect. There is no requirement that officers inform individuals of their right to refuse consent. *See Schneckloth v. Bustamonte*, 412 U.S. 218 (1973). The woman's consent justified the officers' entry, and the heroin was properly seized because it was in plain view. *See, e.g., Illinois v. Rodriguez*, 497 U.S. 177 (1990).

Question 23 - Real Property
Answer: A

(A) Correct. The landowner's wife had a determinable life estate, evidenced by the words "for life" and "until remarriage" in the landowner's will. The daughter had a vested remainder and an executory interest. Both of the daughter's interests could be assigned to the friend. On the remarriage of the landowner's wife, the wife's life estate ended and it automatically went to the holder of the future interest, who was then the daughter's friend.

(B) Incorrect. The landowner's wife had a determinable life estate, evidenced by the words "for life" and "until remarriage." A fee simple estate has no such words of special limitation. On the remarriage of the landowner's wife, the wife's life estate ended and it automatically went to the holder of the future interest.

(C) Incorrect. The landowner's wife had a determinable life estate, evidenced by the words "for life" and "until remarriage." Had she not remarried, the wife's life estate would have been transferable; however, the words of limitation regarding remarriage terminated the wife's life estate immediately upon her remarriage, and her estate automatically went to the holder of the future interest.

(D) Incorrect. The landowner's wife had a determinable life estate, evidenced by the words "for life" and "until remarriage" in the landowner's will. On the remarriage of the landowner's wife, the wife's life estate ended and it automatically went to the holder of the future interest. The landowner's wife had no interest in the land to give to her new husband at the time she executed the deed.

Question 24 - Contracts
Answer: D

(A) Incorrect. When a seller induces a buyer's consent to a contract by means of a material misrepresentation, the resulting contract is voidable at the election of the buyer. Although there might be some instances in which a failure to independently inspect property might constitute a defense to a claim of misrepresentation, the facts of this case don't justify such a conclusion. The buyer asked a direct question about whether the car had ever been in an accident, and the seller gave an answer that a reasonable buyer would take as an assurance that the seller at least had no knowledge of the car's involvement in an accident. The buyer is entitled to rely on the truth of material representations made by the seller, and need not conduct independent tests to see whether the seller is lying, even if such an independent test would reveal the lie. In this case, the seller actively concealed the damage, and would not escape responsibility for misleading the buyer merely because the seller did not answer the question more directly—by saying, for example, "No, the car has never been in an accident."

(B) Incorrect. When a seller induces a buyer's consent to a contract by means of a material misrepresentation, the resulting contract is voidable at the election of the buyer. In this case, the buyer asked a direct question about whether the car had ever been in an accident, and the seller gave an answer that a reasonable buyer would take as an assurance that the seller at least had no knowledge of the car's involvement in an accident. The seller's statement, taken in context, and in light of the seller's active steps to conceal evidence of the damage and repair, would be the legal equivalent of a statement that the car had not been in an accident. The seller actively concealed the damage, and would not be permitted to escape being held responsible for misleading the buyer merely because the seller did not answer the question more directly—by saying, for example, "No, the car has never been in an accident."

(C) Incorrect. This answer correctly concludes that the buyer may rescind the contract, but it misstates the reason why this is so. When a seller induces a buyer's consent to a contract by means of a material misrepresentation, the resulting contract is voidable at the election of the buyer. Unconscionability arises when there are unfair terms, coupled with an unfair bargaining process. In some cases, unconscionability may be found where a seller has made misrepresentations, or concealed material facts, but not every case of misrepresentation presents a case of unconscionability. In this case, apart from the fact that the seller concealed the damage to the car, and gave a misleading answer to the buyer's question, there is insufficient evidence that the contract was unconscionable.

(D) Correct. When a seller induces a buyer's consent to a contract by means of a material misrepresentation, the resulting contract is voidable at the election of the buyer. In this case, the buyer asked a direct question about whether the car had ever been in an accident, and the seller gave an answer that a reasonable buyer would take as an assurance that the seller at least had no knowledge of the car's involvement in an accident. The accident history of the car would be material to the decision of a buyer. The seller's statement, taken in context, and in light of the seller's active steps to conceal evidence of the damage and repair, would be the legal equivalent of a statement that the car had not been in an accident. The seller actively concealed the damage, and would not escape responsibility for misleading the buyer merely because the seller did not answer the question more directly—by saying, for example, "No, the car has never been in an accident."

Question 25 - Constitutional Law
Answer: B

(A) Incorrect. The Supreme Court may review a judgment of the highest court of a state if the state court's decision turns on a question arising under federal law. The reason the Supreme Court will deny the petition for certiorari is that the state supreme court based its decision entirely on state law.

(B) Correct. The Supreme Court may not review a judgment by the highest court of a state if that judgment is supported entirely by state law and is wholly independent of the interpretation and application of federal law. In this case, although the defendant claimed a violation of the Sixth Amendment of the U.S. Constitution, the state supreme court based its decision entirely on the state constitution without addressing the federal constitutional issue.

(C) Incorrect. The Supreme Court would not reach the merits of the defendant's Sixth Amendment claim. The Supreme Court may not review a judgment by the highest court of a state if that judgment is supported entirely by state law and is wholly independent of the interpretation and application of federal law. In this case, although the defendant claimed a violation of the Sixth Amendment of the U.S. Constitution, the state supreme court based its decision entirely on the state constitution without addressing the federal constitutional issue.

(D) Incorrect. Although the Supreme Court may only review final judgments and decrees from the highest state courts, this judgment qualifies because it finally settled the confrontation issue. That issue would not arise again on re-trial, and thus, the present petition provided the U.S. Supreme Court its only opportunity to review the confrontation issue. The reason the Supreme Court will deny the petition for certiorari is that the state supreme court based its decision entirely on state law.

Question 26 - Criminal Law and Procedure
Answer: D

(A) Incorrect. The wife is not guilty of any crime because she did not have a legal duty, enforceable by the criminal laws, to warn the others about the bomb. *See* Wayne R. LaFave, Principles of Criminal Law § 5.2, at 213-17 (2003).

(B) Incorrect. The wife is not guilty of any crime because she did not have a legal duty, enforceable by the criminal laws, to warn the others about the bomb. *See* Wayne R. LaFave, Principles of Criminal Law § 5.2, at 213-17 (2003).

(C) Incorrect. The wife is not guilty of any crime because she did not have a legal duty, enforceable by the criminal laws, to warn the others about the bomb. *See* Wayne R. LaFave, Principles of Criminal Law § 5.2, at 213-17 (2003).

(D) Correct. The wife did not have a legal duty, enforceable by the criminal laws, to warn the others about the bomb. *See* Wayne R. LaFave, Principles of Criminal Law § 5.2, at 213-17 (2003).

Question 27 - Criminal Law and Procedure
Answer: A

(A) Correct. The woman is guilty of burglary because she unlawfully entered the neighbor's house at night with intent to commit a felony (larceny). The woman's actions constituted the requisite "entry" of the neighbor's house. *See* Wayne R. LaFave, Substantive Criminal Law § 21.1 (2d ed. 2003) (To constitute burglary it is "sufficient if any part of the actor's person intruded, even momentarily, into the structure. Thus it has been held that the intrusion of a part of a hand in opening a window, or the momentary intrusion of part of a foot in kicking out a window, constituted the requisite entry.").

(B) Incorrect. The woman's action proceeded beyond the point of attempted burglary. The woman is guilty of burglary because she unlawfully entered the neighbor's house at night with intent to commit a felony (larceny). The woman's actions constituted the requisite "entry" of the neighbor's house. *See* Wayne R. LaFave, Substantive Criminal Law § 21.1 (2d ed. 2003) (To constitute burglary it is "sufficient if any part of the actor's person intruded, even momentarily, into the structure. Thus it has been held that the intrusion of a part of a hand in opening a window, or the momentary intrusion of part of a foot in kicking out a window, constituted the requisite entry.").

(C) Incorrect. The woman may have been guilty of attempted larceny, but that crime arguably would merge into, and in any event was less serious than, the burglary crime. The woman is guilty of burglary because she unlawfully entered the neighbor's house at night with intent to commit a felony (larceny). The woman's actions constituted the requisite "entry" of the neighbor's house. *See* Wayne R. LaFave, Substantive Criminal Law § 21.1 (2d ed. 2003) (To constitute burglary it is "sufficient if any part of the actor's person intruded, even momentarily, into the structure. Thus it has been held that the intrusion of a part of a hand in opening a window, or the momentary intrusion of part of a foot in kicking out a window, constituted the requisite entry.").

(D) Incorrect. The woman is guilty of burglary because she unlawfully entered the neighbor's house at night with intent to commit a felony (larceny). The woman's actions constituted the requisite "entry" of the neighbor's house. *See* Wayne R. LaFave, Substantive Criminal Law § 21.1 (2d ed. 2003) (To constitute burglary it is "sufficient if any part of the actor's person intruded, even momentarily, into the structure. Thus it has been held that the intrusion of a part of a hand in opening a window, or the momentary intrusion of part of a foot in kicking out a window, constituted the requisite entry.").

Question 28 - Torts
Answer: B

(A) Incorrect. This answer correctly states that the guest will lose, but it misstates the legal basis for this conclusion. Even though the host did not intend to shoot her guest, she may well have intended to cause the guest to fear being shot. That apprehension, if it had been created, would have been adequate to support the intent of assault.

(B) Correct. The tort of assault requires that the plaintiff have an apprehension of an imminent bodily contact. That result did not occur here, because the guest knew that the revolver was not loaded and that the ammunition was in a locked basement closet.

(C) Incorrect. Assault requires that the bodily contact apprehended be imminent. It would take the host some time to retrieve the ammunition from a locked closet two floors below, so the guest had no reasonable fear of imminent contact.

(D) Incorrect. A threat is not enough to support a case for assault unless it actually results in an apprehension of immediate bodily contact. In this case, the guest knew that the revolver was not loaded and that the ammunition was in a locked basement closet, and so there was no reasonable fear of imminent contact.

Question 29 - Evidence
Answer: B

(A) Incorrect. Under federal common law, the spousal testimonial privilege is held by the witness, not by the defendant. If a spouse wants to testify, the defendant cannot prevent the spouse from doing so. The rationale is that the privilege is designed to preserve marital harmony, and if a witness wants to testify against his or her spouse, then there is no marital harmony left to preserve.

(B) Correct. This is a correct statement of federal common law, established by the Supreme Court in *Trammel v. United States*. If the witness and the defendant are married at the time of trial, the witness cannot be placed in contempt for refusing to testify against the defendant. The rationale for the rule is to preserve marital harmony, which would otherwise be damaged by one spouse testifying against the other.

(C) Incorrect. The rule is in fact the opposite. Under federal common law, the interspousal testimonial privilege applies only in criminal cases and not in civil cases.

(D) Incorrect. This statement confuses two different privileges under federal common law. The interspousal *communications* privilege protects confidential communications made between the spouses during the marriage. That privilege is not at stake in this fact situation as testimony about the defendant's appearance at the time of the crime would not disclose a confidential communication. But there is also a testimonial privilege allowing a spouse to refuse to testify against his or her spouse, regardless of whether the testimony would involve confidential communications. It is the *testimonial* privilege that is applicable in this fact situation.

Question 30 - Contracts
Answer: D

(A) Incorrect. This answer implies the existence of a rule which would make a contract modification ineffective where an assignee had no notice of it—but there is no such rule. The assignee bank in this case succeeded to the contract as it stood at the time of the assignment. The parties had modified the contract before the assignment, changing the term which specified the time payments were due. (Note that there was consideration for the promise to accept payments later; the consideration was the debtor's promise to make future payments by cashier's check.) Accordingly, the debtor can insist that the payments be due on the fifth of each month.

(B) Incorrect. It is true that if a party waives a condition, that party may reinstate the condition with respect to future acts of performance—but that rule is not applicable here. The assignee bank in this case succeeded to the contract as it stood at the time of the assignment. The parties had modified the contract by mutual agreement, changing the term which specified the time payments were due, and the opportunity to reinstate a condition was no longer available—that is, this case raises an issue of modification of terms, and not a mere waiver. (Note that there was consideration for the promise to accept payments later; the consideration was the debtor's promise to make future payments by cashier's check.) Accordingly, the debtor can insist that the payments be due on the fifth of each month.

(C) Incorrect. It is true that the debtor in this case can insist that the payments be due on the fifth of each month, but this answer misstates the reason why this is so. An assignee succeeds to a contract as the contract stands at the time of the assignment. In this case, the parties had modified the contract by mutual agreement prior to its assignment to the bank, changing the term which specified the time payments were due. (Note that there was consideration for the promise to accept payments later; the consideration was the debtor's promise to make future payments by cashier's check.) This is not a case where the creditor has waived prompt payment under the contract—the parties mutually agreed to modify the contract. Moreover, if there had been no modification, but simply a waiver of the due date by the creditor, then the assignee bank would have had the right to reinstate the condition that payments be made on the first of the month.

(D) Correct. An assignee succeeds to a contract as the contract stands at the time of the assignment. In this case, the parties had modified the contract as to the time payment was due. (Note that there was consideration for the promise to accept payments later; the consideration was the debtor's promise to make future payments by cashier's check.) Accordingly, the debtor can insist that the payments be due on the fifth of each month.

Question 31 - Contracts
Answer: C

(A) Incorrect. The Uniform Commercial Code controls. The seller is entitled to be put in the position it would have been in if the contract had been performed. Two dollars per set fails to accomplish that goal. This would have been a correct answer ONLY IF the seller had not yet begun manufacturing the ball bearings. The seller incurred those costs in preparing for performance, and is entitled to recover them in order to protect its expectation interest. The proper measure of damages here is set out in UCC § 2-708(2), which provides that a seller is entitled to the profit the seller would have made ($2 per set), plus an allowance for costs reasonably incurred ($8 per set), minus payments received for resale of the goods ($2 per set)—here, the salvage. Accordingly, the seller should recover $2 + $8 - $2 = $8 per set.

(B) Incorrect. The Uniform Commercial Code controls. The seller is entitled to be put in the position it would have been in if the contract had been performed. Six dollars per set fails to accomplish that goal. The difference between the cost of manufacture and the salvage price fails to take account of the lost profit the seller is entitled to recover. The proper measure of damages here is set out in UCC § 2-708(2), which provides that a seller is entitled to the profit the seller would have made ($2 per set), plus an allowance for costs reasonably incurred ($8 per set), minus payments received for resale of the goods ($2 per set)—here, the salvage. Accordingly, the seller should recover $2 + $8 - $2 = $8 per set.

(C) Correct. The Uniform Commercial Code controls. The seller is entitled to be put in the position it would have been in if the contract had been performed. The proper measure of damages here is set out in UCC § 2-708(2), which provides that a seller is entitled to the profit the seller would have made ($2 per set), plus an allowance for costs reasonably incurred ($8 per set), minus payments received for resale of the goods ($2 per set)—here, the salvage. Accordingly, the seller should recover $2 + $8 - $2 = $8 per set.

(D) Incorrect. The Uniform Commercial Code controls. The seller is entitled to be put in the position it would have been in if the contract had been performed. The statutory section which controls, UCC § 2-708 (2), contains no requirement that the goods be salvaged by sale at a public auction. The proper measure of damages here is the profit the seller would have made ($2 per set), plus an allowance for costs reasonably incurred ($8 per set), minus payments received for resale of the goods ($2 per set)—here, the salvage. Accordingly, the seller should recover $2 + $8 - $2 = $8 per set.

Question 32 - Torts
Answer: A

(A) Correct. A negligent tortfeasor is not generally liable for the criminal acts of third parties made possible by his negligence, but there is an exception when the tortfeasor should have realized the likelihood of the crime at the time of his negligence. The issue of foreseeability is generally a question for the jury. In this case, there had been many thefts from the construction area during the course of construction. Accordingly, there was enough evidence to support a jury verdict for the plaintiff, but it was not so overwhelming as to require the judge to take the rare step of granting summary judgment for the plaintiff.

(B) Incorrect. The issue of foreseeability is generally a question for the jury. In this case, there had been many thefts from the construction area during the course of construction. The jury should be asked to consider whether the failure to place warning lights could foreseeably create a situation in which a damaged vehicle would be left vulnerable to theft.

(C) Incorrect. It is true that a negligent tortfeasor is not generally liable for the criminal acts of third parties made possible by his negligence, but there is an exception when the tortfeasor should have realized the likelihood of the crime at the time of his negligence. The issue of foreseeability is generally a question for the jury. In this case, there had been many thefts from the construction area during the course of construction. Accordingly, there is enough evidence to support a jury finding that the theft was foreseeable, and the defendant's motion for summary judgment should be denied.

(D) Incorrect. Even a negligent tortfeasor is not liable for the criminal acts of third parties made possible by his negligence unless he should have realized the likelihood of such a crime at the time of his negligence. The issue of foreseeability is generally a question for the jury; a grant of summary judgment for a plaintiff on that basis is therefore rare. In this case, there remains a jury question as to whether the pattern of past thefts from the construction site made the theft of the goods from the delivery truck foreseeable.

Question 33 - Constitutional Law
Answer: A

(A) Correct. The Supreme Court has held that officially sponsored prayers as part of public high school commencement ceremonies, like the prayer at issue in this case, violate the establishment clause of the First Amendment.

(B) Incorrect. This question does not implicate the free exercise clause of the First Amendment because there is no state action here that restricts the religious beliefs or practices of those attending the commencement ceremony. Instead, the offering of the prayer as part of a public high school commencement ceremony constitutes the kind of official sponsorship of religious practice that violates the establishment clause of the First Amendment.

(C) Incorrect. The Supreme Court has held that officially sponsored prayers as part of public high school commencement ceremonies violate the establishment clause of the First Amendment even if the prayer at issue, like the one in this case, is voluntary in the sense that no one is compelled to pray.

(D) Incorrect. The Supreme Court has held that officially sponsored prayers at activities of public elementary and secondary schools, like the prayer at issue in this case, violate the establishment clause of the First Amendment even if the idea for the prayer originates with the students.

Question 34 - Evidence
Answer: C

(A) Incorrect. Under Federal Rule of Evidence 609(a)(2), misdemeanor convictions are not admissible to impeach a witness unless they involved dishonesty or false statement. Assault convictions do not involve dishonesty or false statement. If the misdemeanor convictions had been for, say, lying to a government official, then they would have been admissible to impeach the declarant.

(B) Incorrect. Expert testimony on credibility is usually found inadmissible because credibility issues are for the jury, not for the imprimatur of an expert. There have been a few cases in which expert testimony on credibility has been permitted, but the question asks for the most likely evidence to be admitted, and this is not the best answer.

(C) Correct. This is evidence of "bias." It shows that the declarant had a motive to implicate the defendant falsely, because by doing so he would remove the defendant from the position that he wanted to have. Evidence of bias is considered important and, generally speaking, it is liberally admitted. Note that the gang member can be impeached even though he is not at trial to testify. Federal Rule of Evidence 806 allows parties to impeach a hearsay declarant in the same ways that would be permitted if the declarant were to testify. This is because a hearsay declarant is essentially a witness in the case.

(D) Incorrect. This is "bad act" evidence and to be admissible to impeach a witness under Federal Rule of Evidence 608, it must tend to prove that the witness is an untruthful person. If its probative value is substantially outweighed by the risk of prejudice, confusion, and delay, then it must be excluded under Rule 403. Courts have ruled that evidence of drug activity is only minimally probative of truthfulness, and therefore is usually inadmissible to impeach the witness. While it is probably within the trial court's discretion to admit this evidence, at least in some cases, the question asks for the most likely evidence to be admitted, and this is not the best answer.

Question 35 - Criminal Law and Procedure
Answer: A

(A) Correct. Jeopardy does not attach at a preliminary hearing (*Collins v. Loisell*, 262 U.S. 426, 429 (1923)) or at a grand jury proceeding (*United States v. Williams*, 504 U.S. 36, 49 (1992)). *See generally Serfass v. United States*, 420 U.S. 377, 388 (1975) (jeopardy attaches in jury trial when the jury is sworn and in bench trial when the court begins to hear evidence).

(B) Incorrect. This answer correctly states that the motion should not be granted, but it misstates the legal basis for this conclusion. Jeopardy attaches prior to judgment (whether on conviction or acquittal): in a jury trial when the jury is sworn, and in a bench trial when the court begins to hear evidence. *See Crist v. Bretz*, 437 U.S. 28, 35-36 (1978); *Serfass v. United States*, 420 U.S. 377, 388 (1975).

(C) Incorrect. The double jeopardy clause does not attach to preliminary hearings. *Collins v. Loisell*, 262 U.S. 426, 429 (1923); *see generally Serfass v. United States*, 420 U.S. 377, 388 (1975) (jeopardy attaches in jury trial when the jury is sworn and in bench trial when the court begins to hear evidence).

(D) Incorrect. The double jeopardy clause does not bar a grand jury from returning an indictment when a prior grand jury refused to do so. *United States v. Williams*, 504 U.S. 36, 49 (1992).

Question 36 - Constitutional Law
Answer: B

(A) Incorrect. The executive branch does not have inherent rule-making authority over public lands. Article I, Section 8, Clause 17 gives Congress power to provide for the regulation of activity on such lands. The executive's rule-making authority over public lands is limited to that which is provided by Congress. In this case, it is Congress's proper delegation of rule-making authority to the Forest Service to issue campfire regulations and penalties that best supports the Service's rule.

(B) Correct. Congress may delegate rule-making authority to federal agencies through statutes that provide an intelligible principle governing the exercise of that authority. The Supreme Court has been very deferential in applying the intelligible principle requirement, and the statute's provision of authority to the Forest Service to issue regulations controlling campfires and establishing a penalty schedule likely satisfies the requirement.

(C) Incorrect. The compelling nature of the government's regulatory interest is neither necessary nor sufficient to justify the Forest Service's regulation. The constitutional requirement is that the regulation be pursuant to a valid act of Congress. In this case, it is Congress's proper delegation of rule-making authority to the Forest Service to issue campfire regulations and penalties that best supports the Service's rule.

(D) Incorrect. Although law enforcement is an executive function, the constitutional exercise of that function requires that the executive act pursuant to congressional authorization provided by law. In this case, it is Congress's proper delegation of rule-making authority to the Forest Service to issue campfire regulations and penalties that best supports the Service's rule.

Question 37 - Evidence
Answer: D

(A) Incorrect. The statement is hearsay, but it is admissible under Federal Rule of Evidence 803(2), the "excited utterance" exception to the general rule barring hearsay from evidence.

(B) Incorrect. The statement fits under the Federal Rule of Evidence 803(2) exception to the hearsay rule for excited utterances. Under the hearsay exceptions in Rule 803, there is no requirement that the declarant be made available to testify. In this case, the victim's statement would have been admissible even if she had not been available at trial. There is no requirement that she be asked about the hearsay statement.

(C) Incorrect. While the declarant does not have to die for a statement to be admissible as a dying declaration under Federal Rule of Evidence 804(b)(2), this statement fails to satisfy that exception for at least two reasons. First, the declarant has to be unavailable, as the dying declaration is one of the "unavailability-dependent" exceptions of Rule 804. Here, the victim testified and so obviously is not unavailable. Second, a dying declaration is admissible only in homicide prosecutions and civil cases. This is a criminal case for aggravated assault.

(D) Correct. Federal Rule of Evidence 803(2) admits a hearsay statement that would otherwise be barred under Rule 802 where the statement "relat[es] to a startling event or condition made while the declarant was under the stress of excitement caused by the event or condition." In this case, the assault was a startling event, and the victim made the statement immediately after the beating, trying to identify the perpetrator. Thus, all the admissibility requirements of Rule 803(2), the excited utterance exception, are met.

Question 38 - Contracts
Answer: A

(A) Correct. This is the correct answer, because the characterization of employment as "permanent" creates an employment-at-will relationship. In an employment-at-will relationship, either party can terminate the agreement at any time, without the termination being considered a breach (unless the termination was to violate an important public policy—which is not the case here). Accordingly, the chef is not liable for breach of contract.

(B) Incorrect. This answer correctly concludes that the bakery will not prevail in a breach of contract action against the chef, but it misstates the reason why this is so. The question of whether the job the baker took with the hotel was comparable to that she left at the bakery is not relevant here. The comparability issue DOES arise in cases in which an employee who has been terminated is offered another job; in such cases the employee's claim for breach would be reduced by wages which could have been earned on jobs which are not different and inferior. That is not the case in this problem. The issue here is the interpretation of the term "permanent employment" in the bakery-chef contract. It is well established that "permanent employment" means "employment-at-will" in this context. In an employment-at-will relationship, either party can terminate the agreement at any time, without the termination being considered a breach (unless the termination was to violate an important public policy—which is not the case here). Accordingly, the chef is not liable for breach of contract.

(C) Incorrect. This answer is grounded in an incorrect interpretation of the meaning of the word "permanent" in the context of employment agreements. It is well established that "permanent employment" means "employment-at-will." In an employment-at-will relationship, either party can terminate the agreement at any time, without the termination being considered a breach (unless the termination was to violate an important public policy—which is not the case here). Accordingly, the chef is not liable for breach of contract.

(D) Incorrect. This answer is incorrect because it presumes the existence of an "implied right of first refusal." While some contracts do create rights to first refusal, such rights must be created by express agreement, and not by implication. In the context of employment agreements, it is well established that "permanent employment" means "employment-at-will." In an employment-at-will relationship, either party can terminate the agreement at any time, without the termination being considered a breach (unless the termination was to violate an important public policy—which is not the case here). Accordingly, the chef is not liable for breach of contract.

Question 39 - Real Property
Answer: C

(A) Incorrect. A mortgage lien does not automatically have priority over a judgment lien. This is a race notice jurisdiction which protects a bona fide purchaser for value without notice who records first. The aunt had constructive notice of the judgment lien, which was filed before the aunt loaned money to the debtor and obtained the mortgage. Accordingly, the judgment lien has priority.

(B) Incorrect. The aunt is not a mortgagee under a purchase money mortgage, because the debtor already owned the property when he borrowed money from the aunt, signed the note, and signed the mortgage. Furthermore, a mortgage lien does not have automatic priority over a judgment lien. This is a race notice jurisdiction which protects a bona fide purchaser for value without notice who records first. The aunt had constructive notice of the judgment lien, which was filed before the aunt loaned money to the debtor and obtained the mortgage. Accordingly, the judgment lien has priority.

(C) Correct. This is a race notice jurisdiction which protects a bona fide purchaser for value without notice who records first. The creditor filed first, giving the aunt constructive notice of the judgment lien. Accordingly, the judgment lien has priority.

(D) Incorrect. Although this option correctly concludes that the creditor has priority, it misstates the reason why this is so. No one has a duty to make a title search. The creditor has priority because the judgment lien was filed first in a race notice jurisdiction.

Question 40 - Torts
Answer: A

(A) Correct. The situations in which a plaintiff can recover for purely emotional distress caused by negligence are limited, and this is not one of them. Recovery for negligent misrepresentation is usually limited to pecuniary loss unless it involves a risk of physical harm. In this case, the applicant found a comparable position promptly, so he suffered no harm from the personnel director's misrepresentation aside from his emotional distress.

(B) Incorrect. This answer correctly states that the applicant will not prevail, but it misstates the legal basis for this conclusion. It is not the case that the director's statement is purely speculative. Some of the information conveyed to the job applicant was factual; it was clearly intended to assure the applicant that the company was in fact at the time economically strong, and to induce reliance. The applicant will lose because the situations in which a plaintiff can recover for purely emotional distress caused by negligence are limited, and this is not one of them. Recovery for negligent misrepresentation is usually limited to pecuniary loss unless it involves a risk of physical harm.

(C) Incorrect. Reliance is essential for recovery in negligent misrepresentation, but it is not sufficient. Moreover, the situations in which a plaintiff can recover for purely emotional distress caused by negligence are limited, and this is not one of them. Recovery for negligent misrepresentation is usually limited to pecuniary loss unless it involves a risk of physical harm. In this case, the applicant found a comparable position promptly, so he suffered no harm from the personnel director's misrepresentation aside from his emotional distress.

(D) Incorrect. Recovery for negligent misrepresentation does not extend to all foreseeable damages. The applicant cannot prevail because recovery for negligent misrepresentation is usually limited to pecuniary loss unless it involves a risk of physical harm. In this case, the applicant found a comparable position promptly, so he suffered no harm from the personnel director's misrepresentation aside from his emotional distress.

Question 41 - Constitutional Law
Answer: D

(A) Incorrect. The Supreme Court has not held that housing is a fundamental right. Therefore, the zoning board's denial of the permit does not trigger strict scrutiny on that basis. The zoning board's denial of the permit discriminated against neither a suspect class nor a quasi-suspect class. Nor did it unduly burden the exercise of a fundamental right. The denial therefore triggers rational basis scrutiny.

(B) Incorrect. The Supreme Court has not held that convicts constitute a quasi-suspect class. Therefore, the zoning board's denial of the permit does not trigger intermediate scrutiny on that basis. The zoning board's denial of the permit discriminated against neither a suspect class nor a quasi-suspect class. Nor did it unduly burden the exercise of a fundamental right. The denial therefore triggers rational basis scrutiny.

(C) Incorrect. The Supreme Court has not held that convicts constitute a suspect class. Therefore, the zoning board's denial of the permit does not trigger strict scrutiny on that basis. The zoning board's denial of the permit discriminated against neither a suspect class nor a quasi-suspect class. Nor did it unduly burden the exercise of a fundamental right. The denial therefore triggers rational basis scrutiny.

(D) Correct. The zoning board's denial of the permit discriminated against neither a suspect class nor a quasi-suspect class. Nor did it unduly burden the exercise of a fundamental right. The denial therefore triggers rational basis scrutiny.

Question 42 - Criminal Law and Procedure
Answer: A

(A) Correct. Evidence generally will not be suppressed where police reasonably held a good faith belief that their actions leading to its discovery were authorized by a valid warrant. *See Arizona v. Evans*, 514 U.S. 1 (1995) (good faith exception to exclusionary rule applied where arrest and resulting incidental search were based on warrant that was quashed 17 days earlier but, due to court employees' clerical error, still showed up in computer database). In this case, the computer check on the license number of the driver's car revealed that there was an outstanding warrant for the driver's arrest based on unpaid parking tickets. The police had no reason to believe that the warrant was invalid, so the search of the car was proper.

(B) Incorrect. This answer correctly states that the motion to suppress should not be granted, but it misstates the legal basis for that conclusion. Absent a custodial arrest or probable cause, a traffic stop does not authorize a full-blown search of the passenger compartment. *See Knowles v. Iowa*, 525 U.S. 113 (1998). In this case, however, the troopers did arrest the driver of the car pursuant to an arrest warrant that they believed in good faith to be valid. Accordingly, the search was proper and the driver's motion to dismiss will be denied. *See Arizona v. Evans*, 514 U.S. 1 (1995) (applying good faith exception under similar circumstances).

(C) Incorrect. Evidence generally will not be suppressed where police reasonably held a good faith belief that their actions leading to its discovery were authorized by a valid warrant. Here, the arrest was made in the good faith belief that there was a valid outstanding warrant, so the court's clerical error would not require suppression. *See Arizona v. Evans*, 514 U.S. 1 (1995) (applying good faith exception under similar circumstances).

(D) Incorrect. Neither probable cause nor reasonable suspicion was required because the search was incident to an arrest. It is true that the arrest warrant turned out to be invalid, but evidence generally will not be suppressed where, as in this case, police reasonably held a good faith belief that their actions leading to its discovery were authorized by a valid warrant. *See Arizona v. Evans*, 514 U.S. 1 (1995) (applying good faith exception under similar circumstances).

Question 43 - Contracts
Answer: D

(A) Incorrect. This is not the best answer because it is not really responsive to the question. The debtor had a statute-of-limitations defense which was partially destroyed by the promise to pay $500. The debtor DID promise to pay $500, which implies that the payment would be made and that, at least as to that $500 there would be no reliance on the statute of limitations. A promise to pay a debt after the running of the statute of limitations, like the promise in this case, is enforceable without consideration. The enforcement of such a promise is a long-established exception to the requirement that there be consideration to support the enforcement of promises.

(B) Incorrect. A promise to pay a debt after the running of the statute of limitations is enforceable without consideration. The enforcement of such a promise is a long-established exception to the requirement that there be consideration to support the enforcement of promises. So while it is true that there was no consideration for the debtor's promise, none was required in this instance.

(C) Incorrect. This answer is incorrect because it is not really responsive to the question. Promises are not enforceable just because their performance would benefit the promisee. This is obvious if one remembers that a promise to make a gift is not enforceable even though the promise, if performed, would benefit the donee. Rather, the promise in this case is enforceable without consideration because it was a promise to pay a debt after the running of the statute of limitations. The enforcement of such a promise is a long-established exception to the requirement that there be consideration to support the enforcement of promises.

(D) Correct. A promise to pay a debt after the running of the statute of limitations, like the promise in this case, is enforceable without consideration. The enforcement of such a promise is a long-established exception to the requirement that there be consideration to support the enforcement of promises.

Question 44 - Evidence
Answer: D

(A) Incorrect. Federal Rule of Evidence 408 protects statements concerning a "claim" that is "disputed as to validity or amount." However, in this case there was no pending dispute at the time the statement was made. The homeowner was simply calling for help and had not complained about the plumber's work or in any other way indicated that there was a dispute between the parties. Accordingly, the statement does not qualify as an offer in compromise.

(B) Incorrect. Rule 801(d)(2)(A) exempts statements made by a party, used against the party, from the definition of hearsay. In this case, the plumber is a party and the statement is being offered against him. In this context, the statement is not hearsay.

(C) Incorrect. This option correctly states that the statement is admissible, but it misstates the reason why this is so. Federal Rule of Evidence 407 excludes evidence of measures taken that, had they been taken prior to the event that caused the injury, would have made the injury or harm less likely to occur. Here, no "measure" was taken at all. The plaintiff wants to introduce a statement, not any action that would have made the injury less likely to occur. Therefore Rule 407 is inapplicable.

(D) Correct. This is a party admission, admissible as a hearsay exemption under Rule 801(d)(2)(A). A statement made by a party cannot be excluded as hearsay when offered against him by the opponent. Moreover, the statement is probative. A person who makes a statement like this is likely to think he is at fault, and this is probative evidence that indeed he is at fault.

Question 45 - Real Property
Answer: A

(A) Correct. A grantee who does not assume the mortgage, but rather takes subject to the mortgage, is not personally liable for the debt. In this case, there was no express assumption. In fact, the parties agreed that the neighbor was not assuming the mortgage debt. The land is primarily liable and the grantor, the investor, is a surety for the debt.

(B) Incorrect. Although this option correctly concludes that the neighbor will prevail, it misstates the reason why she is not liable for the delinquent mortgage payments. Privity of estate arises when the parties share a relationship with the land (e.g., a landlord and a tenant), which is not present in these facts. The investor conveyed the land to the neighbor. The only possible privity might be instantaneous privity between the neighbor and the investor, which could provide horizontal privity in the area of the running of real covenants. However, real covenants are not at issue. The lack of privity between the neighbor and the partner has no effect on the mortgage debt. The neighbor is not liable on that debt because she did not assume it. The land is primarily liable and the grantor, the investor, is a surety for the debt.

(C) Incorrect. A due-on-sale clause is used to accelerate the debt in the event of a transfer of the property to a third party. Here, the partner is suing only for delinquent payments. Moreover, the neighbor is not liable on the mortgage debt because she did not assume it. The land is primarily liable and the grantor, the investor, is a surety for the debt.

(D) Incorrect. Privity of estate arises when the parties share a relationship with the land (e.g., a landlord and a tenant), which is not present in these facts. The investor conveyed the land to the neighbor. The only possible privity might be instantaneous privity between the neighbor and the investor, which could provide horizontal privity in the area of the running of real covenants. However, real covenants are not at issue, and in any event, the neighbor is not in privity with the partner. The neighbor is not liable on the mortgage debt because she did not assume it. The land is primarily liable and the grantor, the investor, is a surety for the debt.

Question 46 - Constitutional Law
Answer: D

(A) Incorrect. The government's acquisition of property is sufficient but is not necessary to establish a taking within the meaning of the Fifth Amendment, as applied to the county by the Fourteenth Amendment. A government regulation that eliminates the investment-backed expectation and economic value of an individual's property is a taking for which the government must pay just compensation. Because the county did not compensate the purchaser for the land, the county has violated the takings clause.

(B) Incorrect. Physical invasion or intrusion of property is sufficient but is not necessary to establish a taking within the meaning of the Fifth Amendment, as applied to the county by the Fourteenth Amendment. A government regulation that eliminates the investment-backed expectation and economic value of an individual's property is a taking for which the government must pay just compensation. Because the county did not compensate the purchaser for the land, the county has violated the takings clause.

(C) Incorrect. The Supreme Court does not use such a balancing test for determining whether a governmental action is a taking within the meaning of the Fifth Amendment, as applied to the county by the Fourteenth Amendment. A government regulation that eliminates the investment-backed expectation and economic value of an individual's property is a taking for which the government must pay just compensation, regardless of the reason for the regulation. Because the county did not compensate the purchaser for the land, the county has violated the takings clause.

(D) Correct. A government regulation that eliminates the investment-backed expectation and economic value of an individual's property is a taking within the meaning of the Fifth Amendment, as applied to the county by the Fourteenth Amendment. Because the regulation has this effect, it constitutes a taking of the purchaser's property, for which the county must pay just compensation. Because the county did not compensate the purchaser for the land, the county has violated the takings clause.

Question 47 - Criminal Law and Procedure
Answer: D

(A) Incorrect. The second set of photographs should be suppressed because the woman was acting as a government agent at the time she seized them. *See United States v. Jarrett*, 338 F.3d 339, 344-48 (4th Cir. 2003) (describing relevant considerations, and finding on facts less compelling than these that private hacker was not government agent).

(B) Incorrect. The woman's first entry of the computer and copying of the file constituted an entirely private search and did not trigger Fourth Amendment protections. *United States v. Steiger*, 318 F.3d 1039, 1045 (11th Cir. 2003); *see generally Walter v. United States*, 447 U.S. 649, 656 (1980). However, because authorities encouraged and offered to reward the second computer search, the woman was acting as a government agent with regard to that search, which did in fact violate the Fourth Amendment because it was conducted without a warrant. *See United States v. Jarrett*, 338 F.3d 339, 344-48 (4th Cir. 2003) (describing relevant considerations, and finding on facts less compelling than these that private hacker was not government agent). Accordingly, only the second set of photographs should be suppressed.

(C) Incorrect. Private violation of this statute does not itself require suppression of evidence. *United States v. Steiger*, 318 F.3d 1039, 1050-52 (11th Cir. 2003). However, because authorities encouraged and offered to reward the second computer search, the woman was acting as a government agent with regard to that search, which did in fact violate the Fourth Amendment because it was conducted without a warrant. *See United States v. Jarrett*, 338 F.3d 339, 344-48 (4th Cir. 2003) (describing relevant considerations, and finding on facts less compelling than these that private hacker was not government agent). Accordingly, only the second set of photographs should be suppressed.

(D) Correct. Because authorities encouraged and offered to reward the second computer search, the woman was acting as a government agent with regard to that search, which did in fact violate the Fourth Amendment because it was conducted without a warrant. *See United States v. Jarrett*, 338 F.3d 339, 344-48 (4th Cir. 2003) (describing relevant considerations, and finding on facts less compelling than these that private hacker was not government agent).

Question 48 - Contracts
Answer: C

(A) Incorrect. There is no requirement that a promise, like that made by the bank, be in writing. The parties could have made an enforceable oral agreement to reschedule the payments—so long as there was consideration for promises made by the parties. Because there was no consideration given by the dealer, the bank is not bound by its earlier waiver of the due date and may demand full payment at once.

(B) Incorrect. This answer mischaracterizes the transactions at issue, because the car dealer hasn't attempted to delegate its duty to pay under the contract. The dealer simply directed the car buyer to make payments to the bank rather than to it. Moreover, the bank may reinstate the due date despite its earlier waiver; because there was no consideration given by the dealer, the bank is not bound by the installment agreement and may demand full payment at once.

(C) Correct. The bank had a right to insist on payment of the note, and promised to allow the car dealer to pay the debt in installments. There was no consideration for the bank's promise. There WOULD have been consideration if the dealer had assigned its right to receive payment from the retail buyer; the benefit to the bank would have been the addition of another obligor from whom it could expect payment. There was no assignment here, but rather an instruction to the retail buyer to redirect his payments. Accordingly, the bank may reinstate the due date despite its earlier waiver; it is not bound by the installment agreement and may demand full payment at once.

(D) Incorrect. The transaction in this instance cannot properly be characterized as a novation. A novation is a three-party agreement in which one party is substituted for another, the other being released from obligation. So, for example, A owes B. A, B, and C all agree that C will undertake an obligation to B, and A will be released from any duties to B under the original agreement. That would be a novation. There was no attempted novation here. Moreover, the bank may reinstate the due date despite its earlier waiver; because there was no consideration given by the dealer, the bank is not bound by the installment agreement and may demand full payment at once.

Question 49 - Evidence
Answer: C

(A) Incorrect. Under Federal Rule of Evidence 201(g), a judge may not instruct a jury to find a fact in a criminal case, even if it is a fact that is subject to judicial notice. Such an instruction would violate the accused's Sixth Amendment right to a trial by jury on all elements of the crime. A judicially-noticed fact in a criminal case allows the court to instruct on a permissible inference, but nothing more.

(B) Incorrect. The government has the burden of proving all elements of a crime beyond a reasonable doubt. Under Federal Rule of Evidence 201(g), a judicially-noticed fact in a criminal case cannot shift that constitutionally mandated burden of proof. Here, the court may instruct on a permissible inference, but nothing more.

(C) Correct. This instruction complies with Federal Rule of Evidence 201(g), which states that in a criminal case, "the court shall instruct the jury that it may, but is not required to, accept as conclusive any fact judicially noticed." A judicially-noticed fact in a criminal case allows the court to instruct on a permissible inference, but nothing more.

(D) Incorrect. Under Federal Rule of Evidence 201(g), a judicially-noticed fact in a criminal case does not create a presumption. In civil cases, a judicially-noticed fact is conclusive; in a criminal case, because of the accused's constitutional right to trial by jury, the judicially-noticed fact can be brought to the attention of the jury, but the jury is free to reject it. Any instruction about a "presumption" is inappropriate in these circumstances. The court may instruct on a permissible inference, but nothing more.

Question 50 - Torts
Answer: A

(A) Correct. The professor can state a prima facie case of defamation, but he cannot prevail because the dean has a valid defense based on his reasonable belief that the professor invited him to speak. By authorizing his agents to investigate his case, the professor apparently consented to limited publication in response to their inquiries. Ill will, if it existed, would be irrelevant to this defense.

(B) Incorrect. This answer correctly states that the professor will lose, but it misstates the legal basis for this conclusion. Some jurisdictions may require evidence of pecuniary loss for oral statements that are not slander per se, but this is a written statement. At common law, damages to the professor's reputation would be presumed. The professor cannot prevail—despite stating a prima facie case of defamation—because the dean has a valid defense based on his reasonable belief that the professor invited him to speak. By authorizing his agents to investigate the case, the professor apparently consented to limited publication in response to their inquiries.

(C) Incorrect. The tort of defamation does not turn on whether an investigation, reasonable or not, has been conducted. Moreover, the professor cannot prevail—despite stating a prima facie case of defamation—because the dean has a valid defense based on his reasonable belief that the professor invited him to speak. By authorizing his agents to investigate the case, the professor apparently consented to limited publication in response to their inquiries.

(D) Incorrect. An oral statement of this sort would ordinarily support an action for defamation if there were no defense or privilege. In this case, despite stating a prima facie case of defamation, the professor cannot prevail because the dean has a valid defense based on his reasonable belief that the professor invited him to speak. By authorizing his agents to investigate the case, the professor apparently consented to limited publication in response to their inquiries.

Question 51 - Constitutional Law
Answer: C

(A) Incorrect. The full faith and credit clause of the Constitution (Article IV, Section 1) prevents the court in State A from hearing the man's suit. The fact that the woman drove the car to State A has no effect on the constitutional analysis of this problem.

(B) Incorrect. The full faith and credit clause of the Constitution (Article IV, Section 1) prevents the court in State A from hearing the man's suit. The location of the car has no effect on the constitutional analysis of this problem.

(C) Correct. The full faith and credit clause of the Constitution (Article IV, Section 1) prohibits state courts from re-litigating cases in which the courts of another state have rendered final judgment. Accordingly, the court in State A should dismiss the suit.

(D) Incorrect. The case arises under state law. The movement of the car across state lines does not create a federal question. Moreover, the full faith and credit clause of the Constitution (Article IV, Section 1) prevents the court in State A from hearing the man's suit.

Question 52 - Real Property
Answer: A

(A) Correct. This water is diffuse surface water. Although there are different views regarding the way an owner may expel such water, an owner such as the farmer may impound such water, especially in the absence of any malice.

(B) Incorrect. Although this option correctly concludes that the farmer will prevail, it misstates the reason why this is so. Especially in the absence of malice, either landowner may impound diffuse surface waters. Neither impoundment is illegal, and the doctrine of estoppel does not apply.

(C) Incorrect. Waters from melting snows and rain is diffuse surface water. Riparian waters are waters with defined beds and banks, such as streams, rivers, and lakes. A riparian owner is one whose land borders such waters. Here, the only water at issue is diffuse surface water. Although there are different views regarding the way an owner may expel such water, an owner such as the farmer clearly may impound such water, especially in the absence of any malice.

(D) Incorrect. Especially in the absence of malice, either landowner may impound diffuse surface water. Neither impoundment is illegal in itself, and the farmer's impoundment did not run counter to any past representation relied upon by the rancher. In these circumstances, the doctrine of estoppel does not apply, and the farmer will prevail.

Question 53 - Torts
Answer: A

(A) Correct. The strict products liability suit would fail because the dentist was not in the business of selling the product, and the malpractice suit would fail because the plaintiff could not establish that the defendant departed from the professional standard of care.

(B) Incorrect. There is no evidence (nor could there be on these facts) that the dentist departed from a professional standard of care. In fact, the patient cannot recover against the dentist based on either strict products liability or malpractice.

(C) Incorrect. The dentist is not in the business of selling needles. He is a service provider. Therefore, he would not be an appropriate defendant in a suit for strict products liability. In fact, the patient cannot recover against the dentist based on either strict products liability or malpractice.

(D) Incorrect. The patient cannot recover on the basis of products liability, because the dentist is not in the business of selling needles. He is a service provider. Therefore, he would not be an appropriate defendant in a suit for strict products liability. In addition, the patient cannot recover on the basis of malpractice, because there is no evidence (nor could there be on these facts) that the dentist departed from a professional standard of care. In fact, the patient cannot recover against the dentist on either basis.

Question 54 - Contracts
Answer: D

(A) Incorrect. This answer misstates the rule concerning consequential damages. Buyers generally ARE entitled to recover consequential damages, subject to certain specified limitations such as the requirement that damages, to be recoverable, must be foreseeable at the time the contract was made. The contract was created in this case when the wholesaler shipped the bottles. The terms consisted of the negotiated terms plus UCC gap-fillers. The subsequent acknowledgment form was not accepted by the bottling company, and never became part of the contract. There are no facts that would support an exception to the general rule that buyers are entitled to recover consequential damages, and the bottling company will prevail.

(B) Incorrect. The terms of a contract for the sale of goods are established upon acceptance of an offer. Under Uniform Commercial Code § 2-206, an offer to buy goods for prompt shipment is accepted when the seller ships the goods. Because the bottling company's acceptance (shipment of the bottles) occurred PRIOR to the receipt of the acknowledgment form, the acknowledgement form was an ineffective attempt to modify the parties' contract. The bottling company did not accept the proposed modification, and it will in fact recover consequential damages.

(C) Incorrect. This answer correctly concludes that the bottling company will recover consequential damages, but it misstates the reason why this is so. While disclaimers of consequential damages might sometimes be found unconscionable, the mere existence of such a disclaimer is not enough to establish unconscionability, and there is no evidence in this case that would otherwise suggest that the contract was unconscionable. The bottling company will recover consequential damages, however, because the acknowledgement form was an ineffective attempt to modify the terms of the parties' contract. Under Uniform Commercial Code § 2-206, an offer to buy goods for prompt shipment is accepted when the seller ships the goods. The contract was created in this case when the wholesaler shipped the bottles. The terms consisted of the negotiated terms plus UCC gap-fillers. The subsequent acknowledgment form was not accepted by the bottling company, and never became part of the contract.

(D) Correct. Under Uniform Commercial Code § 2-206, an offer to buy goods for prompt shipment is accepted when the seller ships the goods. The contract was created in this case when the wholesaler shipped the bottles. The terms consisted of the negotiated terms plus UCC gap-fillers. The subsequent acknowledgment form was an ineffective effort to modify the terms, and these proposed modifications were not accepted by the buyer.

Question 55 - Criminal Law and Procedure
Answer: D

(A) Incorrect. There was no reasonable explanation for the defendant becoming enraged. Although his intoxication prevented the kind of "cool reflection" required for first-degree murder, it did not preclude the mental state required for second-degree murder.

(B) Incorrect. Even assuming the correctness of this statement, *but cf.* Wayne R. LaFave, Substantive Criminal Law § 14.7(a) (2d ed. 2003) ("better view" requires more time for deliberation), the defendant's intoxicated anger prevented the kind of "cool reflection" required for deliberation. *See id.* (a "killer may, in a particular situation, be incapable of that cool reflection called for by the requirement of premeditation and deliberation, as where his capacity to premeditate and deliberate is prevented by emotional upset, [or] by intoxication . . . ."). Although his intoxication prevented the kind of "cool reflection" required for first-degree murder, it did not preclude the mental state required for second-degree murder.

(C) Incorrect. The defendant did not deliberate upon taking the life "of another person" (as required by the statute) prior to becoming intoxicated. Although his intoxication prevented the kind of "cool reflection" required for first-degree murder, it did not preclude the mental state required for second-degree murder.

(D) Correct. The defendant's intoxication did not preclude the mental state required for second-degree murder. *See* Wayne R. LaFave, Substantive Criminal Law § 9.5(b) (2d ed. 2003) (it is "generally held" that "intoxication cannot further reduce the homicide from second degree murder down to manslaughter").

Question 56 - Constitutional Law
Answer: B

(A) Incorrect. It is true that the statute at issue is unconstitutional, but this answer misstates the basis for this conclusion. The Supreme Court has held that a short waiting period does not constitute an undue burden on a woman's right to an abortion. On the other hand, the Court has held that parental notification requirements violate a minor's right to an abortion where, as in this case, there is not a satisfactory judicial bypass procedure.

(B) Correct. The Supreme Court has held that parental notification requirements violate a minor's right to an abortion unless there is a satisfactory judicial bypass procedure. Such a procedure must allow a court to approve an abortion for a minor without parental notification if the court finds: (1) the minor is sufficiently mature and informed to make an independent decision to obtain an abortion; or (2) the abortion would be in the minor's best interest. Because no such bypass procedure is included in the statute at issue, the court will hold the statute unconstitutional.

(C) Incorrect. The rights of parents to supervise the health care of their minor children do not always prevail over the individual rights of their children. The Supreme Court has held that parental notification requirements violate a minor's right to an abortion unless there is a satisfactory judicial bypass procedure, which is not included in the statute at issue. Accordingly, the court will hold the statute unconstitutional.

(D) Incorrect. The Supreme Court has held that parental notification requirements violate a minor's right to an abortion unless there is a satisfactory judicial bypass procedure. Such a procedure must allow a court to approve an abortion for a minor without parental notification if the court finds: (1) the minor is sufficiently mature and informed to make an independent decision to obtain an abortion; or (2) the abortion would be in the minor's best interest. Because no such bypass procedure is included in the statute at issue, the court will hold the statute unconstitutional.

Question 57 - Real Property
Answer: A

(A) Correct. The foreclosure sale of the bank's mortgage on the hotel was insufficient to pay the businessman's debt to the bank. The bank had received a judgment against the businessman for the entire amount of the defaulted loan. This lien was properly recorded and applied to all property owned by the businessman during the ten-year time period, including the parking garage. (The bank may have decided on this course of action because it deemed the businessman's equity in the garage was significant and the timing was bad for a hotel foreclosure.) After the financing company was paid in full from the funds generated by the foreclosure sale of its mortgage on the parking garage, the additional funds generated by that sale would be paid to the bank not as a deficiency judgment, but because of the unsatisfied amount of the prior money judgment.

(B) Incorrect. The judgment lien was properly filed against the businessman. Therefore, the garage was subject not only to the loan of the financing company, but also to the judgment lien as a second priority. The businessman would be entitled to surplus proceeds only if both liens had been fully paid.

(C) Incorrect. The foreclosure sale of the financing company's mortgage on the parking garage was sufficient to pay the businessman's debt to the financing company in full. The fact that the garage was sold for more money than was owed under the garage mortgage is irrelevant to the amount owed to the financing company. Because the bank's judgment lien was properly filed against the businessman, the lien had second priority once the financing company's loan was paid in full, and the surplus proceeds will be paid to the bank.

(D) Incorrect. The foreclosure sale of the financing company's mortgage on the parking garage was sufficient to pay the businessman's debt to the financing company in full. The fact that the garage was sold for more money than was owed under the garage mortgage is irrelevant to the amount owed to the financing company. Because the bank's judgment lien was properly filed against the businessman, the lien had second priority once the financing company's loan was paid in full, and the surplus proceeds will be paid to the bank.

Question 58 - Evidence
Answer: A

(A) Correct. Federal Rule of Evidence 408 excludes "[e]vidence of conduct or statements made in compromise negotiations." Here, there is a dispute, and the manager's statement was made in an effort to settle that dispute. As such the entire statement is protected under Rule 408.

(B) Incorrect. If not for Federal Rule of Evidence 408, which protects compromise negotiations, the statement about the slippery condition would be admissible even though the manager denied that it was the cause. Under Federal Rule of Evidence 801(d)(2)(A), party admissions are not considered hearsay when offered against the party who made the admission. Therefore, the plaintiff would be allowed to offer the part of the statement that favors the plaintiff's case, while the part that favors the defendant's case would be excluded as hearsay. The latter part would not be admissible under Rule 801(d)(2)(A), because it would be offered by the manager who made the statement.

(C) Incorrect. The statement is true as far as it goes. But that only means that the statement is not excluded as hearsay. There is another ground for exclusion, so the statement is inadmissible even though it satisfies the hearsay rule. Federal Rule of Evidence 408 excludes "[e]vidence of conduct or statements made in compromise negotiations." Here, there is a dispute and the manager's statement was made in an attempt to settle that dispute. Therefore, the statement would be excluded under Rule 408.

(D) Incorrect. Federal Rule of Evidence 408 protects not only offers of compromise, but also "conduct or statements made in the course of compromise negotiations." The rationale is to allow the parties and counsel to speak freely during settlement negotiations, without having to worry that their statements will be used against them at trial. Here, there is a dispute, and the manager's statement was made in an attempt to settle that dispute. Therefore, the statement would be excluded under Rule 408.

Question 59 - Torts
Answer: A

(A) Correct. The plaintiff's evidence that the decedent violated the statute and crossed over into her lane of traffic does establish a prima facie case of negligence. However, the decedent's estate successfully rebutted the plaintiff's evidence by providing an undisputed explanation of how the accident happened that is inconsistent with a finding of negligence (the decedent's unforeseeable heart attack made her unable to comply with the statute, or indeed with any standard of care).

(B) Incorrect. This answer correctly states that the decedent's estate will prevail, but it misstates the legal basis for this conclusion. The plaintiff's evidence that the decedent violated the statute and crossed over into her lane of traffic does establish a prima facie case of negligence. Nevertheless, the decedent's estate successfully rebutted the plaintiff's evidence by providing an uncontested explanation of how the accident happened that is inconsistent with a finding of negligence (the decedent's unforeseeable heart attack made her unable to comply with the statute, or indeed with any standard of care).

(C) Incorrect. It may or may not be true that accidents of this type do not ordinarily happen in the absence of negligence, but that is beside the point. In this case, the decedent's estate successfully rebutted the plaintiff's evidence by providing an undisputed explanation of how the accident happened that is inconsistent with a finding of negligence (the decedent's unforeseeable heart attack made her unable to comply with the statute, or indeed with any standard of care).

(D) Incorrect. The plaintiff's evidence that the decedent violated the statute and crossed over into her lane of traffic establishes only a prima facie case of negligence. The decedent's estate successfully rebutted the plaintiff's evidence by providing an undisputed explanation of how the accident happened that is inconsistent with a finding of negligence (the decedent's unforeseeable heart attack made her unable to comply with the statute, or indeed with any standard of care).

Question 60 - Constitutional Law
Answer: A

(A) Correct. The law school's denial of the meeting room to the student group violates the speech clause of the First Amendment. The meeting rooms are a limited public forum because the law school made the rooms generally available for extracurricular student use. Because the meeting rooms are a limited public forum, the law students had a First Amendment right to use a room for expressive activity consistent with their purpose (i.e., extracurricular student use). Because the law school's denial of the room was based on the content of the students' expression, the denial must be tested by strict scrutiny, which requires the law school to prove that its denial was necessary to serve a compelling governmental interest. It is unusual for the courts to uphold content-based speech restrictions at strict scrutiny, and the law school's concerns here are clearly insufficient to meet that test.

(B) Incorrect. This answer correctly states that the law school's action was unconstitutional, but it misstates the legal basis for that conclusion. Satisfying rational basis scrutiny is insufficient to justify the law school's denial of the meeting room to the student group. The meeting rooms are a limited public forum because the law school made the rooms generally available for extracurricular student use. Because the meeting rooms are a limited public forum, the law students had a First Amendment right to use a room for expressive activity consistent with their purpose (i.e., extracurricular student use). Because the law school's denial of the room was based on the content of the students' expression, the denial must be tested by strict scrutiny, which requires the law school to prove that its denial was necessary to serve a compelling governmental interest. It is unusual for the courts to uphold content-based speech restrictions at strict scrutiny, and the law school's concerns here are clearly insufficient to meet that test.

(C) Incorrect. The meeting rooms are a limited public forum because the law school made the rooms generally available for extracurricular student use. Because the meeting rooms are a limited public forum, the law students had a right under the speech clause of the First Amendment to use a room for expressive activity consistent with their purpose (i.e., extracurricular student use). The law school's concerns were based on feared effects stemming from the speech content of the debate (affirmative action). Because the law school's denial of the room was based on the content of the student group's expression, the denial is a presumptive violation of the speech clause of the First Amendment, and it must be tested by strict scrutiny. It is unusual for the courts to uphold content-based speech restrictions at strict scrutiny, and the law school's concerns here are clearly insufficient to meet that test.

(D) Incorrect. The meeting rooms are a limited public forum because the law school made the rooms generally available for extracurricular student use. Because the meeting rooms are a limited public forum, the law students had a right under the speech clause of the First Amendment to use the rooms for expressive activity consistent with their purpose (i.e., extracurricular student use). Because the law school's denial of the room was based on the content of the student group's expression, the denial is a presumptive violation of the speech clause of the First Amendment, and it must be tested by strict scrutiny. It is unusual for the courts to uphold content-based speech restrictions at strict scrutiny, and the law school's concerns here are clearly insufficient to meet that test.

Question 61 - Real Property
Answer: A

(A) Correct. To be binding, a restrictive covenant must be placed on property at the time it is conveyed. Here, neither the deed to the first buyer nor the deed to the doctor contains the restrictive covenant. The burden cannot be attached to Lot 1 at a later time by someone who has no interest in Lot 1. Therefore, the doctor may proceed with her plan to use part of the property as a medical office.

(B) Incorrect. This option correctly concludes that the doctor will prevail, but it misstates the reason why this is so. Zoning ordinances do not automatically override a private restrictive covenant. The stricter of either the zoning ordinance or the covenant will prevail. In this case, the doctor will prevail because the restrictive covenant was not in the deed to the first buyer of Lot 1, nor was it in the deed to the doctor.

(C) Incorrect. Public land use controls and private land use controls are separate issues. Zoning may be changed. In this case, the zoning was changed a year after the first buyer purchased Lot 1. The doctor's use of Lot 1 is governed by the zoning in existence during the time of the doctor's ownership, and the previous zoning of the property is irrelevant. The doctor may proceed with her plan to use part of the property as a medical office, because the restrictive covenant was not in the deed to the first buyer of Lot 1, nor was it in the deed to the doctor.

(D) Incorrect. To be binding, a restrictive covenant must be placed on property at the time when it is conveyed. Here, the burden was not placed on Lot 1 when the first buyer accepted the deed. The first buyer's actual knowledge of the covenant two years later is irrelevant, and does not incorporate Lot 1 into the common scheme of the subdivision. A common scheme argument may prevail as to subsequent purchasers of other lots in the subdivision. As to Lot 1, however, the doctor may proceed with her plan to use part of the property as a medical office, because the restrictive covenant was not in the deed to the first buyer, nor was it in the deed to the doctor.

Question 62 - Contracts
Answer: B

(A) Incorrect. The Uniform Commercial Code controls. UCC § 2-202, which is the UCC embodiment of the parol evidence rule, explicitly provides that, while a final written expression of agreement may not be contradicted by any prior agreement, it may be explained or supplemented "by course of dealing or usage of trade or by course of performance." A course of dealing, when inconsistent with a usage of trade, controls. This is true under both UCC § 1-205, the version of the UCC most widely in effect at this time, and UCC § 1-303, which is the proposed amended version, adopted in some states. The agreement in this case should be interpreted to embody the course of dealing of the parties, which provided for a 5% discount if payment was made within 15 days.

(B) Correct. The Uniform Commercial Code controls. UCC § 2-202, which is the UCC embodiment of the parol evidence rule, explicitly provides that, while a final written expression of agreement may not be contradicted by any prior agreement, it may be explained or supplemented "by course of dealing or usage of trade or by course of performance." A course of dealing, when inconsistent with a usage of trade, controls. Therefore, the agreement in this case should be interpreted to embody the course of dealing of the parties, which provided for a 5% discount if payment was made within 15 days.

(C) Incorrect. This question doesn't raise an issue of waiver or retraction of a waiver, because there is no indication that payment within 15 days at a 5% discount is inconsistent with the parties' agreement. In fact, the seller's invoice is silent on the matter. Instead, the question goes to the meaning of the agreement made by the parties. The Uniform Commercial Code governs. UCC § 2-202, which is the UCC embodiment of the parol evidence rule, explicitly provides that, while a final written expression of agreement may not be contradicted by any prior agreement, it may be explained or supplemented "by course of dealing or usage of trade or by course of performance." A course of dealing, when inconsistent with a usage of trade, controls. Therefore, the agreement in this case, which is silent on the discount matter, should be interpreted to embody the course of dealing of the parties, which provided for a 5% discount if payment was made within 15 days.

(D) Incorrect. The Uniform Commercial Code controls. UCC § 2-202, which is the UCC embodiment of the parol evidence rule, explicitly provides that, while a final written expression of agreement may not be contradicted by any prior agreement, it may be explained or supplemented "by course of dealing or usage of trade or by course of performance." In this case, the evidence as to the seller's previous discount for prompt payment is relevant, and the agreement should be interpreted to provide for a 5% discount if payment was made within 15 days.

Question 63 - Torts
Answer: A

(A) Correct. The woman gave no indication that she did not want to be subjected to the ordinary touches that are part of life in a crowded society. In the absence of such an indication from her, the passenger was entitled to believe that she implicitly consented to a light tap to get her attention. The passenger's touch was neither unreasonable nor inconsistent with ordinary social norms privileging such contacts.

(B) Incorrect. This answer correctly states that the woman cannot prevail, but it misstates the legal basis for this conclusion. It is true that the woman would have to prove that she thought that she was about to be touched in order to recover in an action for assault. But the elements of a negligence or a battery action could be established without any reference to whether she had an apprehension of this or any other sort. The reason she cannot recover, despite being seriously injured, is because she gave no indication that she did not want to be subjected to the ordinary touches that are part of life in a crowded society. The passenger's touch was neither unreasonable nor inconsistent with ordinary social norms privileging such contacts.

(C) Incorrect. People are presumed to have consented to the ordinary contacts of daily life. Although the passenger intended to touch the woman, he did not intend a harmful or offensive touching, and the woman gave no indication that she did not want to be subjected to the ordinary touches that are part of life in a crowded society. The touch was neither unreasonable nor inconsistent with ordinary social norms privileging such contacts.

(D) Incorrect. Serious injury is neither necessary nor sufficient to support either battery or negligence, although some damage would be required to recover in negligence. Here, although the woman was seriously injured, she will not prevail because she gave no indication that she did not want to be subjected to the ordinary touches that are part of life in a crowded society. The passenger's touch was neither unreasonable nor inconsistent with ordinary social norms privileging such contacts.

Question 64 - Constitutional Law
Answer: A

(A) Correct. Section 1 of the executive order is constitutional. The president, as the chief executive officer of the

U.S. government, has authority to direct the actions of federal executive agencies, so long as the president's directives are not inconsistent with an act of Congress. (The facts state that there is no applicable statute here.) Section 2 of the executive order is unconstitutional. At least as a general rule, the president does not have authority to direct the actions of persons outside the executive branch unless the president's direction is authorized by an act of Congress. There are no circumstances presented in the facts (such as a sudden attack on the U.S.) that might justify an exception to this general rule.

(B) Incorrect. Section 2 of the executive order is unconstitutional. At least as a general rule, the president does not have authority to direct the actions of persons outside the executive branch unless the president's direction is authorized by an act of Congress. There are no circumstances presented in the facts (such as a sudden attack on the U.S.) that might justify an exception to this general rule. Section 1 of the executive order is constitutional. The president, as the chief executive officer of the U.S. government, has authority to direct the actions of federal executive agencies, so long as the president's directives are not inconsistent with an act of Congress. (The facts state that there is no applicable statute here.)

(C) Incorrect. Section 1 of the executive order is constitutional. The president, as the chief executive officer of the U.S. government, has authority to direct the actions of federal executive agencies, so long as the president's directives are not inconsistent with an act of Congress. (The facts state that there is no applicable statute here.) Section 2 of the executive order, however, is unconstitutional. At least as a general rule, the president does not have authority to direct the actions of persons outside the executive branch unless the president's direction is authorized by an act of Congress. There are no circumstances presented in the facts (such as a sudden attack on the U.S.) that might justify an exception to this general rule.

(D) Incorrect. Section 2 of the executive order is unconstitutional. At least as a general rule, the president does not have authority to direct the actions of persons outside the executive branch unless the president's direction is authorized by an act of Congress. There are no circumstances presented in the facts (such as a sudden attack on the U.S.) that might justify an exception to this general rule. Section 1 of the executive order, however, is constitutional. The president, as the chief executive officer of the U.S. government, has authority to direct the actions of federal executive agencies, so long as the president's directives are not inconsistent with an act of Congress. (The facts state that there is no applicable statute here.)

Question 65 - Evidence
Answer: D

(A) Incorrect. The certification qualifies under Federal Rule of Evidence 803(10), the hearsay exception for a certification offered to prove the absence of a public record. To be admissible, the certification must be prepared by a public official and must on its face indicate that a diligent search of the records was conducted. This certification satisfies the requirements of the exception.

(B) Incorrect. No extrinsic evidence of authenticity is required to admit a domestic public document bearing a government seal under Federal Rule of Evidence 902(1). Here, the certification is from a public agency of the United States and bears the agency's seal. Therefore, it is self-authenticating under Rule 902(1), and is admissible under Federal Rule of Evidence 803(10), the hearsay exception for a certification offered to prove the absence of a public record.

(C) Incorrect. The certification qualifies under Federal Rule of Evidence 803(10), the hearsay exception for a certification offered to prove the absence of a public record. The certification can be offered for its truth, that there was no record of any issuance of a license to the defendant. Therefore its admissibility is not limited to impeachment; it can be used both for impeachment and as substantive proof of the disputed fact.

(D) Correct. The certification is hearsay, but it qualifies under Federal Rule of Evidence 803(10), the hearsay exception for a certification offered to prove the absence of a public record. The certification is offered for the proper inference that if a license had been issued, it would have been recorded in the public record. Thus, the fact that there was no record found is probative evidence that a license was never issued. To be admissible, the certification must be prepared by a public official and must on its face indicate that a diligent search of the records was conducted. This certification satisfies the requirements of the exception.

Question 66 - Real Property
Answer: C

(A) Incorrect. Although a covenant that title will be marketable is implied in a contract for the sale of land, the doctrine of merger provides that one can no longer sue on title matters contained in the contract of sale after the deed is delivered and accepted. In this case, if the investor has a remedy, it would be based on the deed he received, not on the contract of sale. The seller will prevail on the breach of contract claim.

(B) Incorrect. The doctrine of merger provides that one can no longer sue on title matters contained in the contract of sale after the deed is delivered and accepted. The investor's remedy, if there is one, would be based on the deed he received, not on the contract of sale. The facts do not justify any other claim for damages (e.g., misrepresentation). Accordingly, the seller will prevail on the breach of contract claim.

(C) Correct. Although a marketable title will be implied in a contract for the sale of land, the doctrine of merger provides that one can no longer sue on title matters contained in the contract of sale after the deed is delivered and accepted. The investor's remedy, if there is one, would be based on the deed he received and not on the contract of sale.

(D) Incorrect. This option correctly concludes that the seller will prevail, but misstates the reason why this is so. Even if the contract of sale is silent regarding title matters, the law will imply a requirement of a marketable title in a contract for the sale of land. Therefore, the language of the contract of sale in this case is not dispositive. Instead, the seller will prevail because the doctrine of merger provides that one can no longer sue on title matters contained in the contract of sale after the deed is delivered and accepted. In this case, if the investor has a remedy, it would be based on the deed he received, not on the contract of sale.

Question 67 - Torts
Answer: C

(A) Incorrect. The seller of a product with a manufacturing defect that is dangerous to the health of a consumer is strictly liable for the injuries it causes. In this case, there is nothing to indicate that the consumer actually saw the snail, and contributory negligence, if any, is no defense to a strict products liability action.

(B) Incorrect. The seller of a product with a manufacturing defect that is dangerous to the health of a consumer is strictly liable for the injuries it causes. Because the store sold the bottle in a defective condition to the consumer, it can be held strictly liable even though it did not bottle the soda.

(C) Correct. The seller of a product with a manufacturing defect that is dangerous to the health of a consumer is strictly liable for the injuries it causes.

(D) Incorrect. This answer correctly states that the consumer will prevail, but it misstates the legal basis for this conclusion. Liability is not based on exclusive control but on the sale to the consumer. In fact, the store did not have exclusive control over the bottle. Res ipsa loquitur is neither necessary nor appropriate here; if anyone was negligent, it was the bottler. Nevertheless, the store will be liable because the seller of a product with a manufacturing defect that is dangerous to the health of a consumer is strictly liable for the injuries it causes.

Question 68 - Evidence
Answer: B

(A) Incorrect. Under Federal Rule of Evidence 404(b), prior bad acts can be admitted to prove the defendant's conduct if offered for some purpose other than to show that the defendant is a bad person. In this case, the bad acts are very similar to the acts in dispute, and tend to show non-character purposes such as intent, knowledge, lack of accident, and modus operandi (i.e., that the defendant has a tendency to engage in particularized activity that sets her apart from others). Thus the bad acts can be offered as proof that the defendant committed the crime charged. In addition, Federal Rule of Evidence 609(a)(2) provides that evidence of a past conviction "shall be admitted" to impeach the credibility of a witness if the crime "involved dishonesty or false statement, regardless of the punishment." In this case, fraud convictions clearly involve dishonesty, and are therefore properly admitted to impeach the defendant. Accordingly, the convictions are admissible both to prove that the defendant committed the crime and to impeach the defendant.

(B) Correct. Under Federal Rule of Evidence 404(b), prior bad acts can be admitted to prove the defendant's conduct if offered for some purpose other than to show that the defendant is a bad person. In this case, the bad acts are very similar to the acts in dispute, and tend to show non-character purposes such as intent, knowledge, lack of accident, and modus operandi (i.e., that the defendant has a tendency to engage in particularized activity that sets her apart from others). Thus the bad acts can be offered as proof that the defendant committed the crime charged. Moreover, the convictions are automatically admissible to impeach the defendant's character for truthfulness; fraud convictions clearly involve dishonesty or false statement, and so the court "shall" admit the convictions under Rule 609(a)(2).

(C) Incorrect. It is true that the convictions are properly admitted to impeach the defendant under Federal Rule of Evidence 609(a)(2). However, the convictions are also properly admitted as substantive evidence to prove the defendant's guilt. Under Federal Rule of Evidence 404(b), prior bad acts can be admitted to prove the defendant's conduct if offered for some purpose other than to show that the defendant is a bad person. In this case, the bad acts are very similar to the acts in dispute, and tend to show non-character purposes such as intent, knowledge, lack of accident, and modus operandi (i.e., that the defendant has a tendency to engage in particularized activity that sets her apart from others). Thus the bad acts can be offered as proof that the defendant committed the crime charged.

(D) Incorrect. It is true that the convictions are properly admitted substantively under Federal Rule of Evidence 404(b). However, the convictions are also properly admitted to impeach the defendant. Federal Rule of Evidence 609(a)(2) provides that evidence of a past conviction "shall be admitted" to impeach the credibility of a witness if the crime "involved dishonesty or false statement, regardless of the punishment." In this case, fraud convictions clearly involve dishonesty, and are therefore properly admitted to impeach the defendant.

Question 69 - Criminal Law and Procedure
Answer: C

(A) Incorrect. Because the defendant killed the neighbor, the crime would not be attempted murder but would be either murder or manslaughter. Whether the defendant is guilty of murder, or guilty only of manslaughter, depends upon whether he fired the third shot in the heat of passion provoked by the neighbor's earlier attack. *See* Wayne R. LaFave, Principles of Criminal Law § 14.2, at 599 (2003).

(B) Incorrect. It is true that the defendant could properly be convicted of manslaughter. However, he could also be convicted of murder if he did not fire the third shot in the heat of passion. *See* Wayne R. LaFave, Principles of Criminal Law § 14.2(f), at 607 (2003).

(C) Correct. Whether the defendant is guilty of murder, or guilty only of manslaughter, depends upon whether he fired the third shot in the heat of passion provoked by the neighbor's earlier attack. *See* Wayne R. LaFave, Principles of Criminal Law § 14.2, at 599 (2003).

(D) Incorrect. The defendant was not in imminent fear of the neighbor, and therefore was not acting in self-defense, when he fired the third shot. *See* Wayne R. LaFave, Principles of Criminal Law § 9.4, at 407-10 (2003). Whether the defendant is guilty of murder, or guilty only of manslaughter, defends upon whether he fired the third shot in the heat of passion provoked by the neighbor's earlier attack *See* Wayne R. LaFave, Principles of Criminal Law § 14.2, at 599 (2003).

Question 70 - Real Property
Answer: A

(A) Correct. A gift may be made of real estate. A deed is required as are the elements for a gift. The homeowner had the requisite donative intent as shown by his words. Delivery occurred when the homeowner physically handed the deed to the nephew's friend as the agent of the nephew. Acceptance is presumed if the gift is beneficial. At this point, the homeowner could not recall the gift.

(B) Incorrect. Although the recording of a deed may raise the presumption of delivery, here the delivery occurred prior to the recordation of the deed. Delivery occurred when the homeowner physically handed the deed to the nephew's friend as the agent of the nephew, with the intent to pass the title.

(C) Incorrect. A gift causa mortis may only be made of personal property. In addition, the gift was not made in view of pending death from a stated peril. The facts only note that the homeowner was ill. This was a valid inter vivos gift of real property which was irrevocable on delivery of the deed to the nephew's friend.

(D) Incorrect. A testamentary document takes effect at the death of the testator and must have been executed with the requisite testamentary intent. The homeowner wanted the nephew to have title immediately and thus delivered the deed to the nephew's friend. The homeowner did not want to postpone delivery until his death. This was a valid inter vivos gift of real property which was irrevocable on delivery of the deed to the nephew's friend.

Question 71 - Criminal Law and Procedure
Answer: D

(A) Incorrect. The woman never had lawful possession of the money and so cannot be convicted of embezzlement. *See* Wayne R. LaFave, Substantive Criminal Law § 19.6(e) (2d ed. 2003). However, all the elements of larceny and robbery (which "may be thought of as aggravated larceny") were present. *See id.* § 20.3. The woman's threat of immediate harm to the clerk was sufficient to constitute the intimidation required for robbery. *See id.* § 20.3(d)(2). Note that because robbery and larceny are greater and lesser included offenses, she cannot be convicted of both for a single offense.

(B) Incorrect. The crime was not false pretenses because, among other things, the woman never obtained title to the cash. *See* Wayne R. LaFave, Substantive Criminal Law § 19.7(d) (2d ed. 2003). However, all the elements of larceny and robbery (which "may be thought of as aggravated larceny") were present. *See id.* § 20.3. The woman's threat of immediate harm to the clerk was sufficient to constitute the intimidation required for robbery. *See id.* § 20.3(d)(2). Note that because robbery and larceny are greater and lesser included offenses, she cannot be convicted of both for a single offense.

(C) Incorrect. It is true that all the elements of larceny and robbery (which "may be thought of as aggravated larceny") were present. *See* Wayne R. LaFave, Substantive Criminal Law § 20.3 (2d ed. 2003). The woman's threat of immediate harm to the clerk was sufficient to constitute the intimidation required for robbery. *See id.* § 20.3(d)(2). However, because robbery and larceny are greater and lesser included offenses, a defendant cannot be convicted of both for a single offense. *See* Wayne R. LaFave, Substantive Criminal Law § 20.3 & n.2; *cf. Carter v. United States*, 530 U.S. 255 (2000) (recognizing that robbery and larceny are greater and lesser included offenses under common law).

(D) Correct. All the elements of larceny and robbery (which "may be thought of as aggravated larceny") were present. *See* Wayne R. LaFave, Substantive Criminal Law § 20.3 (2d ed. 2003). The woman's threat of immediate harm to the clerk was sufficient to constitute the intimidation required for robbery. *See id.* § 20.3(d)(2).

Question 72 - Torts
Answer: C

(A) Incorrect. This might be correct under a pro rata allocation of damages, but it is not correct under comparative negligence with joint and several liability. Under joint and several liability, the entire amount can be collected from any one of the defendants. That defendant, in turn, can seek to recover a proportional (rather than a pro rata) share of the damages from the other defendants.

(B) Incorrect. This would be correct if liability were only several, rather than joint and several. Under joint and several liability, the entire amount can be collected from any one of the defendants. That defendant, in turn, can seek to recover a proportional share of the damages from the other defendants.

(C) Correct. Under joint and several liability, the entire amount can be collected from any one of the defendants. That defendant, in turn, can seek to recover a proportional share of the damages from the other defendants.

(D) Incorrect. This might be the rule under a traditional contributory negligence regime where the negligence of the parent is imputed to the child and bars all recovery, but it is not the approach under comparative negligence with joint and several liability. Under joint and several liability, the entire amount can be collected from any one of the defendants. That defendant, in turn, can seek to recover a proportional share of the damages from the other defendants.

Question 73 - Constitutional Law
Answer: A

(A) Correct. The incidence of the state sales tax on the collector's purchases of antiques is on the collector, who is independent of the National Park Service.

(B) Incorrect. This answer correctly states that the court should not issue the injunction, but it misstates the legal basis for that conclusion. State courts generally have concurrent jurisdiction with federal courts over cases arising under federal law, and no exception to that general rule is presented on these facts. However, the incidence of the state sales tax on the collector's purchases of antiques is on the collector, who is independent of the National Park Service. Accordingly, the court should not issue an injunction.

(C) Incorrect. The incidence of the state sales tax on the collector's purchases of antiques is on the collector, who is independent of the National Park Service. The fact that the collector passes the cost of the tax on to a federal agency when the collector sells an item to the agency does not change the incidence of the tax on the collector's purchase. Accordingly, the court should not issue an injunction.

(D) Incorrect. There is no indication in the facts that the sales tax on the collector's purchases conflicts with any federal law governing the Park Service's program. Moreover, the incidence of the state sales tax on the collector's purchases of antiques is on the collector, who is independent of the National Park Service. Accordingly, the court should not issue an injunction.

Question 74 - Evidence
Answer: D

(A) Incorrect. The question does not call for a statement that would be used for its truth. Therefore, it is not hearsay. Rather, the intent of the question is to test the witness's knowledge of the defendant's reputation on the one hand, and the quality of the community on the other. If the witness hasn't heard about the falsification, he might not be very plugged in to the community and so might be a poor reputation witness. On the other hand, if the witness answers "yes," then the jury might infer that the community in which the defendant has a reputation for complete honesty may be setting the honesty bar pretty low. In either case, the alleged falsification is probative impeachment whether or not it occurred.

(B) Incorrect. The alleged incident is not offered to prove income tax fraud. Rather, the intent of the question is to test the witness's knowledge of the defendant's reputation on the one hand, and the quality of the community on the other. If the witness hasn't heard about the falsification, he might not be very plugged in to the community and so might be a poor reputation witness. On the other hand, if the witness answers "yes," then the jury might infer that the community in which the defendant has a reputation for complete honesty may be setting the honesty bar pretty low. In either case, the alleged falsification is probative impeachment whether or not it occurred.

(C) Incorrect. Federal Rule of Evidence 405 prohibits evidence of specific acts indicative of a person's character when that character evidence is offered to prove that a person acted in accordance with the character trait on the occasion in question at trial. Thus, the prosecutor may not introduce the incident involving the medical school transcript for the inference that, because the defendant acted dishonestly on that occasion, she likely acted dishonestly with regard to her tax return.

(D) Correct. The incident can be offered on cross-examination of the character witness, the proper purpose being to show that the witness's assessment of the defendant's character for honesty is not credible. The intent of the question is to test the witness's knowledge of the defendant's reputation on the one hand, and the quality of the community on the other. If the witness hasn't heard about the falsification, he might not be very plugged in to the community and so might be a poor reputation witness. On the other hand, if the witness answers "yes," then the jury might infer that the community in which the defendant has a reputation for complete honesty may be setting the honesty bar pretty low. In either case, the alleged falsification is probative impeachment whether or not it occurred. Note that the courts require that the cross-examiner must have a good faith belief that the event actually occurred before inquiring into the act on cross-examination. In this case, that good faith standard is met by the evidence presented at the sidebar conference that the defendant was disciplined in medical school.

Question 75 - Torts

Answer: D

(A) Incorrect. Owners of dangerous animals are strictly liable even when the harm would not have occurred but for the operation of a force of nature.

(B) Incorrect. An owner of a wild animal or an abnormally dangerous animal is strictly liable for harm caused by that animal's dangerous nature. The contributory negligence of the worker would not be a defense to strict liability, and in any case there is nothing in the facts to indicate that the worker would have reason to foresee the risk of a poisonous snake.

(C) Incorrect. This answer correctly states that the worker will prevail, but it misstates the legal basis for this conclusion. There may not be enough evidence here to support a finding of negligence, and such a finding is not necessary to support liability. An owner of a wild animal or an abnormally dangerous animal is strictly liable for harm caused by that animal's dangerous nature. Even though the snake was defanged, the worker had no reason to know this; his injury falls within the risk run by the homeowner because it was caused by the worker's foreseeable reaction to seeing the escaped snake.

(D) Correct. An owner of a wild animal or an abnormally dangerous animal is strictly liable for harm caused by that animal's dangerous nature. Even though the snake was defanged, the worker had no reason to know this; his injury falls within the risk run by the homeowner because it was caused by the worker's foreseeable reaction to seeing the escaped snake.

Question   76 - Real Property
Answer: D

(A) Incorrect. When a contract for the sale of land contains no contingencies, both the seller and the buyer have an insurable interest once the contract is signed. In this case, at the time the building was destroyed, the seller had the legal interest and the buyer had the equitable interest under the doctrine of equitable conversion. Although jurisdictions differ on which party has the risk of loss, a finding for the seller in this case means the jurisdiction hearing the case places the risk of loss on the equitable owner of the property, the buyer, under the doctrine of equitable conversion.

(B) Incorrect. In a contract for the sale of land, absent a provision to the contrary, neither the seller nor the buyer has a duty to carry insurance. Accordingly, this option cannot accurately describe the basis for a court to find for the seller. Although jurisdictions differ on which party has the risk of loss, a finding for the seller in this case means the jurisdiction hearing the case places the risk of loss on the equitable owner of the property, the buyer, under the doctrine of equitable conversion.

(C) Incorrect. In a contract for the sale of land, absent a provision to the contrary, neither the seller nor the buyer has a duty to carry insurance. In this case, the seller's cancellation of the insurance would not transfer the risk of loss to the buyer and would not be a basis for a court to find for the seller. Although jurisdictions differ on which party has the risk of loss, a finding for the seller in this case means the jurisdiction hearing the case places the risk of loss on the equitable owner of the property, the buyer, under the doctrine of equitable conversion.

(D) Correct. Although jurisdictions differ on which party has the risk of loss, a finding for the seller in this case means the jurisdiction hearing the case places the risk of loss on the equitable owner of the property, the buyer, under the doctrine of equitable conversion.

Question 77 - Criminal Law and Procedure
Answer: B

(A) Incorrect. There was no robbery because the customer did not take the watch by force or threat of force. Instead, he committed larceny—a trespassory taking and carrying away of another's property with the intent to steal it. *See* Wayne R. LaFave, Principles of Criminal Law § 16.2, at 671 (2003). He obtained possession of, but not title to, the watch by lying about a present fact. *See id.* § 16.2(e), at 674.

(B) Correct. The customer committed a trespassory taking and carrying away of another's property with the intent to steal it. *See* Wayne R. LaFave, Principles of Criminal Law § 16.2, at 671 (2003). He obtained possession of, but not title to, the watch by lying about a present fact. *See id.* § 16.2(e), at 674.

(C) Incorrect. The crime was larceny, not false pretenses, because the customer obtained possession of, but not title to, the watch. *See* Wayne R. LaFave, Principles of Criminal Law § 16.2(e), at 674; § 16.7(d), at 697-99 (2003).

(D) Incorrect. The crime was larceny, not embezzlement, because there was a trespassory taking, so the customer never was in lawful possession of the watch. *See* Wayne R. LaFave, Principles of Criminal Law § 16.6(e), at 690 (2003).

Question 78 - Evidence
Answer: B

(A) Incorrect. The test for admissibility is whether the judge believes that the evidence is probative, not whether a reasonable jury could believe it to be so. This is established by Federal Rule of Evidence 104(a).

(B) Correct. This is the standard of relevance applied by the judge in determining admissibility under Federal Rule of Evidence 401. Under that rule, evidence is relevant if it has "any tendency to make the existence of any fact that is of consequence to the determination of the action more probable or less probable than it would be without the evidence."

(C) Incorrect. The judge determines admissibility and the jury determines sufficiency. It would be impossible for a party to build a case if every piece of evidence had to be sufficient to prove the point in dispute.

(D) Incorrect. The preponderance standard is applied by the jury to all of the evidence admitted. It is not applied by the court to determine whether a particular piece of evidence can be considered by the jury on the ultimate question. Thus, this answer confuses the standard of proof used by the jury with the standard of admissibility used by the judge.

Question 79 - Contracts
Answer: A

(A) Correct. The victim of a breach is entitled to recover only those damages which could not reasonably have been avoided. Failure to take reasonable steps to mitigate damages defeats only a claim for consequential damages. It does not deprive the victims of the breach of the opportunity to claim damages measured by the difference between contract and market price. Here, the mother and son could have paid just $1,000 more to hire a substitute teacher, and they are entitled to recover this amount—which is the amount necessary to put them in the position they would have been in had the contract been performed.

(B) Incorrect. Even though these damages might have been foreseeable, the losses were not CAUSED by the breach, since they could have been avoided had the plaintiff made reasonable efforts to mitigate damages. The victim of a breach is entitled to recover only those damages which could not reasonably have been avoided. Failure to take reasonable steps to mitigate damages defeats a claim for consequential damages. The victims of the breach may still claim damages measured by the difference between contract and market price, however. Here, the mother and son could have paid just $1,000 more to hire a substitute teacher, and they are entitled to recover this amount—which is the amount necessary to put them in the position they would have been in had the contract been performed.

(C) Incorrect. Where two parties contract for a service that both parties intend to directly benefit a designated third party, both the third party beneficiary and the promisee are entitled to sue upon the promissor's breach. Here, the woman and the tutor both intended that the tutor's services benefit the woman's son. Upon the tutor's breach, therefore, both the woman and her son—the intended beneficiary of the contract—may sue for damages. Their failure to take reasonable steps to mitigate damages defeats only the claim for consequential damages. It does not deprive them of the opportunity to claim damages measured by the difference between contract and market price. The victim of a breach is entitled to recover those damages which could not reasonably have been avoided. Here, the mother and son could have paid just $1,000 more to hire a substitute teacher, and they are entitled to recover this amount—which is the amount necessary to put them in the position they would have been in had the contract been performed.

(D) Incorrect. Failure to take reasonable steps to mitigate damages defeats only the claim for consequential damages, and does not deprive the mother and son of the opportunity to claim damages measured by the difference between contract and market price. The victim of a breach is entitled to recover those damages which could not reasonably have been avoided. Here, the mother and son could have paid just $1,000 more to hire a substitute teacher, and they are entitled to recover this amount—which is the amount necessary to put them in the position they would have been in had the contract been performed.

Question 80 - Constitutional Law
Answer: D

(A) Incorrect. The federal courts lack power to entertain a suit that is not ripe for adjudication, because such a suit does not present a "case" or "controversy" within the meaning of Article III, Section 2, Clause 1 of the Constitution. The court should dismiss the suit without deciding the merits of the brewery's claim because the Bureau has yet to announce the beer-quality standards, and therefore the case is not ripe.

(B) Incorrect. The federal courts lack power to entertain a suit that is not ripe for adjudication, because such a suit does not present a "case" or "controversy" within the meaning of Article III, Section 2, Clause 1 of the Constitution. The court should dismiss the suit without deciding the merits of the brewery's claim because the Bureau has yet to announce the beer-quality standards, and therefore the case is not ripe.

(C) Incorrect. The federal courts lack power to entertain a suit that is not ripe for adjudication, because such a suit does not present a "case" or "controversy" within the meaning of Article III, Section 2, Clause 1 of the Constitution. The court should dismiss the suit instead of issuing a stay because the Bureau has yet to announce the beer-quality standards, and therefore the case is not ripe. The court may not maintain jurisdiction over the suit by issuing a stay because it lacks the constitutional authority to retain control over the suit.

(D) Correct. The federal courts lack power to entertain a suit that is not ripe for adjudication, because such a suit does not present a "case" or "controversy" within the meaning of Article III, Section 2, Clause 1 of the Constitution. The court should dismiss the suit because the Bureau has yet to announce the beer-quality standards, and therefore the case is not ripe.

Question 81 - Contracts
Answer: D

(A) Incorrect. The substantial performance rule doesn't apply here, because the obligations were separable, and the builder DID substantially complete the first structure. The builder is likely to recover the agreed price of the first structure, less any recoverable damages caused to the landowner as a result of the builder's breach. Contract law acknowledges the fact that parties sometimes embody obligations which are in most respects separable into a single document or agreement. The rules for damages permit the separable components to be treated separately, which is appropriate here, since the structures were to be built on separate pieces of land, and there were prices related to each distinct property.

(B) Incorrect. Though willfulness might, in some cases, be a factor to be considered in a breach of contract case, it doesn't affect recovery in this case. The builder is likely to recover the agreed price of the first structure, less any recoverable damages caused to the landowner as a result of the builder's breach. The obligations of the builder were severable for purposes of calculating damages; the structures were to be built on separate pieces of land and there were distinct prices related to each distinct property.

(C) Incorrect. The first part of the statement is correct—the contract is divisible. But this does not mean that the victim of the breach is required to bring separate claims. Though the contract has separable components, for damages purposes, it is still a single contract. In addition, requiring separate claims would be inconsistent with the law's goal of providing for the disposition, in a single action, of closely related claims. The builder is likely to recover the agreed price of the first structure, less any recoverable damages caused to the landowner as a result of the builder's breach.

(D) Correct. Contract law acknowledges the fact that parties sometimes embody obligations which are in most respects separable into a single document or agreement. The rules for damages permit the separable components to be treated separately, which is appropriate here, since the structures were to be built on separate pieces of land, and there were prices related to each distinct property. Another rationale for the divisibility of obligations is to avoid a forfeiture.

Question 82 - Real Property
Answer: C

(A) Incorrect. The fact that the uncle was the owner of record on the date of transfer to the woman would be relevant in a dispute between the uncle and the woman, but is not relevant in a dispute between the nephew and the woman. In fact, the woman owns the land because the nephew will be estopped from claiming ownership of the land upon the death of his uncle.

(B) Incorrect. The woman does not have a duty to conduct a title search, although she would be charged with the notice that such a search would provide. In this case, a title search would have revealed that the uncle was the owner of record on the date of transfer, but the uncle's ownership is only relevant to a dispute between the woman and the uncle. It is not relevant in a dispute between the nephew and the woman. In fact, the woman owns the land because the nephew will be estopped from claiming ownership of the land upon the death of his uncle.

(C) Correct. Estoppel by deed applies to validate a deed, and in particular a warranty deed, that was executed and delivered by a grantor who had no title to the land at that time, but who represented that he or she had such title and who thereafter acquired such title. In this case, estoppel by deed would apply in the woman's favor to estop the nephew from claiming ownership of the land upon the death of his uncle.

(D) Incorrect. This option correctly states that the woman owns the land, but misstates the reason why this is so. The woman's recording of the deed provided notice of her interest from the time of recording, but had no bearing on the validity of her claim. In this situation, estoppel by deed would apply in the woman's favor to estop the nephew from claiming ownership of the land upon the death of his uncle.

Question 83 - Torts
Answer: B

(A) Incorrect. This answer correctly states that the judge should not let the case go to the jury, but it misstates the legal basis for this conclusion. In slip-and-fall cases, even if a customer was negligent, he could recover some of his damages under a system of pure comparative negligence if a jury determines that the grocer was also negligent. The case at issue, however, should not go to the jury, because there is no evidence to support a finding of negligence on the part of store staff. Unlike cases in which res ipsa loquitur is appropriate, the condition of the banana in the present case indicates that it had not been on the floor for a significant amount of time. Therefore, there is not enough evidence to support a jury verdict that the store staff was negligent in failing to remove it before the customer's fall.

(B) Correct. Unlike slip-and-fall cases in which res ipsa loquitur is appropriate, the condition of the banana peel does not indicate that it has been on the ground for any significant period of time. Therefore, there is not enough evidence to support a jury verdict that the store staff was negligent in failing to remove it before the customer's fall.

(C) Incorrect. Strict products liability is not applicable here because the banana was not defective. Moreover, the case at issue should not go to the jury, because there is no evidence to support a finding of negligence on the part of store staff. The fact that the peel came from a banana offered for sale by the grocer is not evidence of negligence. Unlike cases in which res ipsa loquitur is appropriate, the condition of the banana in the present case indicates that it had not been on the floor for a significant amount of time. Therefore, there is not enough evidence to support a jury verdict that the store staff was negligent in failing to remove it before the customer's fall.

(D) Incorrect. Foreseeability alone is not sufficient to establish that the grocer was negligent. The plaintiff must also offer evidence that the grocer fell below the standard of care, i.e., that he failed to adopt the precautions that a reasonably prudent person in his situation would adopt to avoid the foreseeable risk. There is no such evidence here. Moreover, unlike cases in which res ipsa loquitur is appropriate, the condition of the banana in the present case indicates that it had not been on the floor for a significant amount of time. Therefore, there is not enough evidence to support a jury verdict that the store staff was negligent in failing to remove it before the customer's fall.

Question 84 - Constitutional Law
Answer: B

(A) Incorrect. This balancing argument is appropriate only if: (1) Congress has not enacted a statute authorizing the state regulation at issue; and (2) the state law does not discriminate against interstate commerce. In this case, however, Congress has authorized state-of-origin labeling requirements on imported citrus fruit and the state law is discriminatory. The best argument in this case would rely on Congress's explicit authorization of state-of-origin labeling requirements on imported citrus fruit.

(B) Correct. Congress may use its commerce power (Article I, Section 8, Clause 3 of the Constitution) to permit states to discriminate against interstate commerce. The federal statute here explicitly authorizes states to enact state-of-origin labeling requirements on imported citrus fruit.

(C) Incorrect. The state law discriminates against out-of-state citrus growers because the law requires that all citrus fruit "imported" into the state be stamped with the state of origin, while the law imposes no such requirement on citrus fruit grown within the state. The best argument in this case would be that Congress has used its commerce power (Article I, Section 8, Clause 3 of the Constitution) to explicitly authorize the states to enact state-of-origin labeling requirements on imported citrus fruit.

(D) Incorrect. This argument paraphrases the burden on the state to justify a law that discriminates against interstate commerce. That burden is a heavy one, however, and states only rarely succeed in justifying discriminatory commercial regulations. The far better argument for the state is that the federal statute here explicitly authorizes states to enact state-of-origin labeling requirements on imported citrus fruit.

Question 85 - Contracts
Answer: B

(A) Incorrect. The amount of the loan is irrelevant here. The writing requirement arises under the suretyship provision of the statute of frauds. A person selecting this answer might be thinking of the $5,000 limit which may trigger a writing requirement in cases involving sales of goods under the UCC. The UCC does not apply here, since this is not a sale of goods. As to the enforceability of the mother's promise, the statute of frauds requires a writing in cases of promises to answer for the debt of another. But the memorandum sufficient to satisfy the statute needn't be written at the time of the making of the promise, nor need it be a writing addressed to the promisee. In this case, the letter written by the mother to her son, the nephew, is sufficient to satisfy the statute of frauds.

(B) Correct. There is a statute-of-frauds requirement in cases of promises to answer for the debt of another. But the memorandum sufficient to satisfy the statute needn't be written at the time of the making of the promise, nor need it be a writing addressed to the promisee. In this case, the mother's letter to her son, the nephew, satisfies the requirement of the statute of frauds.

(C) Incorrect. It is true that the statute of frauds requires a writing in cases of promises to answer for the debt of another. But the memorandum sufficient to satisfy the statute needn't be written at the time of the making of the promise, nor need it be a writing addressed to the promisee. In this case, the letter written by the mother to her son, the nephew, is sufficient to satisfy the statute of frauds.

(D) Incorrect. The issue in this case is not the enforceability of the nephew's promise, but the enforceability of the mother's promise. And even if the issue did involve the nephew's promise, there is no statute-of-frauds requirement that a promise to repay a debt be in writing. As to the enforceability of the mother's promise, the statute of frauds requires a writing in cases of promises to answer for the debt of another. But the memorandum sufficient to satisfy the statute needn't be written at the time of the making of the promise, nor need it be a writing addressed to the promisee. In this case, the letter written by the mother to her son, the nephew, is sufficient to satisfy the statute of frauds.

Question 86 - Criminal Law and Procedure
Answer: C

(A) Incorrect. A state may grant broader rights under its own constitution than are granted by the federal constitution. *See Michigan v. Long*, 463 U.S. 1032 (1983). Here, the state has a clear precedent that the recording violated the employee's state constitutional rights, and that it should be excluded as a remedy. The court should apply this precedent to grant the employee's motion.

(B) Incorrect. It is irrelevant what the police thought about the propriety of their actions under the federal Constitution where the state has granted broader rights under its own constitution as permitted by *Michigan v. Long*, 463 U.S. 1032 (1983). Here, the state has a clear precedent that the recording violated the employee's state constitutional rights, and that it should be excluded as a remedy. The court should apply this precedent to grant the employee's motion.

(C) Correct. A state may grant broader rights under its own constitution than are granted by the federal Constitution. *See Michigan v. Long*, 463 U.S. 1032 (1983). Here, the state has a clear precedent that the recording violated the employee's state constitutional rights, and that it should be excluded as a remedy. The court should apply this precedent to grant the employee's motion.

(D) Incorrect. The secret recording of a conversation with a defendant by a government informant, like the recording in this case, does not violate the Fourth Amendment. *See United States v. White*, 401 U.S. 745 (1971). However, the state in this case has a clear precedent that the recording violated the employee's state constitutional rights, and that it should be excluded as a remedy. Because states may grant broader rights under their own constitutions than are granted by the federal Constitution, the court should apply this precedent to grant the employee's motion.

Question 87 - Evidence
Answer: B

(A) Incorrect. In slander cases, where the defendant makes a statement that the plaintiff has an unsavory character, the plaintiff's character is considered "in issue" (i.e., an essential element of the claim or defense under the substantive law) in two respects: First, the plaintiff's actual character will determine whether the defendant was incorrect in his assessment, and thus liable for slander, because truth is a defense. Second, the plaintiff will allege that he is damaged by the statement, which is another way of saying that his true character has been besmirched; but if the plaintiff actually has a bad reputation anyway, then damages are limited. Thus, in slander cases like the one in this question, character evidence is relevant both to whether the plaintiff has a certain character and to the extent of damages. Under Federal Rule of Evidence 405, when character is "in issue" it can be proved by evidence of reputation, opinion, or specific acts.

(B) Correct. In slander cases, where the defendant makes a statement that the plaintiff has an unsavory character, the plaintiff's character is considered "in issue" (i.e., an essential element of the claim or defense under the substantive law) in two respects: First, the plaintiff's actual character will determine whether the defendant was incorrect in his assessment, and thus liable for slander, because truth is a defense. Second, the plaintiff will allege that he is damaged by the statement, which is another way of saying that his true character has been besmirched; but if the plaintiff actually has a bad reputation anyway, then damages are limited. Thus, in slander cases like the one in this question, character evidence is relevant both to whether the plaintiff has a certain character and to the extent of damages. Under Federal Rule of Evidence 405, when character is "in issue" it can be proved by evidence of reputation, opinion, or specific acts.

(C) Incorrect. In slander cases, where the defendant makes a statement that the plaintiff has an unsavory character, the plaintiff's character is considered "in issue" (i.e., an essential element of the claim or defense under the substantive law) in two respects: First, the plaintiff's actual character will determine whether the defendant was incorrect in his assessment, and thus liable for slander, because truth is a defense. Second, the plaintiff will allege that he is damaged by the statement, which is another way of saying that his true character has been besmirched; but if the plaintiff actually has a bad reputation anyway, then damages are limited. Thus, in slander cases like the one in this question, character evidence is relevant both to whether the plaintiff has a certain character and to the extent of damages. Under Federal Rule of Evidence 405, when character is "in issue" it can be proved by evidence of reputation, opinion, or specific acts.

(D) Incorrect. In slander cases, where the defendant makes a statement that the plaintiff has an unsavory character, the plaintiff's character is considered "in issue" (i.e., an essential element of the claim or defense under the substantive law) in two respects: First, the plaintiff's actual character will determine whether the defendant was incorrect in his assessment, and thus liable for slander, because truth is a defense. Second, the plaintiff will allege that he is damaged by the statement, which is another way of saying that his true character has been besmirched; but if the plaintiff actually has a bad reputation anyway, then damages are limited. Thus, in slander cases like the one in this question, character evidence is relevant both to whether the plaintiff has a certain character and to the extent of damages. Under Federal Rule of Evidence 405, when character is "in issue" it can be proved by evidence of reputation, opinion, or specific acts.

Question 88 - Torts
Answer: D

(A) Incorrect. The student is in legal possession of the apartment and thus has an interest that can be vindicated in a trespass action. There is evidence supporting compensatory damages (emotional distress, the removal of the faucets) and punitive damages (malicious intent, ill will). Because the lease is still in effect and the trespasses are repeated and ongoing, injunctive relief should also be available.

(B) Incorrect. Damage is not necessary to establish a cause of action in trespass, and, in any case, the removal of the faucets was damage to the property. There is evidence supporting compensatory damages (emotional distress, the removal of the faucets) and punitive damages (malicious intent, ill will). Because the lease is still in effect and the trespasses are repeated and ongoing, injunctive relief should also be available.

(C) Incorrect. Under these facts demonstrating a pattern of ongoing malicious behavior, the law student is unlikely to be limited to compensatory damages. In addition to compensatory damages for emotional distress and the removal of the faucets, the student is entitled to punitive damages (demonstrated by the landlord's malicious intent and ill will). Because the lease is still in effect and the trespasses are repeated and ongoing, injunctive relief should also be available.

(D) Correct. There is evidence supporting compensatory damages (emotional distress, the removal of the faucets) and punitive damages (malicious intent, ill will). Because the lease is still in effect and the trespasses are repeated and ongoing, injunctive relief should also be available.

Question 89 - Contracts
Answer: C

(A) Incorrect. There was no contract formed on May 3, because the uncle's original letter was not an offer. It was merely a statement indicating a possible interest in selling the truck, and a suggestion as to a price that might be acceptable. It would be regarded, if anything, as a statement soliciting an offer. The nephew's letter, mailed on May 3, constituted an offer to buy the pickup. The uncle's note, mailed on May 6, constituted an acceptance of the nephew's offer, and was effective when mailed. And so a contract arose on May 6.

(B) Incorrect. On May 5 the uncle received the offer from the nephew, but had not yet accepted it. As a result, there was no contract on May 5. The uncle's note, mailed on May 6, constituted an acceptance of the nephew's offer, and was effective when mailed. And so a contract arose on May 6.

(C) Correct. The uncle's original letter was not an offer. It was merely a statement indicating a possible interest in selling the truck, and a suggestion as to a price that might be acceptable. It would be regarded, if anything, as a statement soliciting an offer. The nephew's letter, mailed on May 3, constituted an offer to buy the pickup. The uncle's note, mailed on May 6, constituted an acceptance of the nephew's offer, and was effective when mailed. And so a contract arose on May 6.

(D) Incorrect. The nephew's letter, mailed on May 3, constituted an offer to buy the pickup. The uncle's note, mailed on May 6, constituted an acceptance of the nephew's offer, and was effective when mailed. And so a contract arose on May 6. The law would treat the nephew's May 3 letter as an offer, even though the nephew might have mistakenly believed it to be an acceptance of an offer. The nephew's May 7 phone call was too late to constitute a revocation of his May 3 offer, since it had already been accepted. The nephew's license revocation would not constitute a defense to the existence of the contract for sale.

Question 90 - Real Property
Answer: B

(A) Incorrect. A constructive eviction claim is raised in the context of a landlord and tenant relationship. It is inapplicable here, where the woman and the public school district own adjacent properties. However, the facts demonstrate a non-trespassory invasion of the woman's property rights that would support a damages award for private nuisance.

(B) Correct. Damages may be awarded if a private nuisance is proven. A private nuisance is a substantial and unreasonable interference with the use or enjoyment of one's land. The facts demonstrate a non-trespassory invasion of the woman's property rights.

(C) Incorrect. A public nuisance is a violation of a legal right that is common to the public as a group. The activities at the school, although a public school, are disturbing only one landowner. As such, the facts in this case demonstrate a non-trespassory invasion of the woman's property rights that would support a damages award for private nuisance.

(D) Incorrect. Damages for waste arise where ownership of a particular property is divided in time (e.g., a life estate) or is shared (e.g., a joint tenancy), and where one owner's use of the land impacts another owner's interest. In this case, the issue is between owners of adjacent properties, so waste is inapplicable. The facts here demonstrate a non-trespassory invasion of the woman's property rights that would support a damages award for private nuisance.

Question 91 - Criminal Law and Procedure
Answer: B

(A) Incorrect. Conspirators must agree on the essential objectives of the conspiracy. *See* Wayne R. LaFave, Principles of Criminal Law § 11.2(c)(2), at 478 (2003). In any event, the rationale offered here is inapposite, because the problem raised by the question is not failure to agree to the robberies, but not being present during the latter robberies. The defendant's motion for acquittal in this case should be denied, because a co-conspirator need not be present at the commission of each crime, nor does the arrest of one co-conspirator automatically terminate the conspiracy where other co-conspirators continue to carry out the goals of the conspiracy. *See, e.g., United States v. Williams*, 87 F.3d 249, 253 (8th Cir. 1996); *United States v. Mealy*, 851 F.2d 890, 901 (7th Cir. 1988); *United States v. Ammar*, 714 F.2d 238, 253 (3d Cir. 1983); *United States v. Killian*, 639 F.2d 206, 209 (5th Cir. 1981).

(B) Correct. A co-conspirator need not be present at the commission of each crime, nor does the arrest of one co-conspirator automatically terminate the conspiracy where other co-conspirators continue to carry out the goals of the conspiracy. *See, e.g., United States v. Williams*, 87 F.3d 249, 253 (8th Cir. 1996); *United States v. Mealy*, 851 F.2d 890, 901 (7th Cir. 1988); *United States v. Ammar*, 714 F.2d 238, 253 (3d Cir. 1983); *United States v. Killian*, 639 F.2d 206, 209 (5th Cir. 1981).

(C) Incorrect. The defendant is not entitled to acquittal of conspiracy, even if there was compliance with an alibi notice rule. A co-conspirator need not be present at the commission of each crime, nor does the arrest of one co-conspirator automatically terminate the conspiracy where other co-conspirators continue to carry out the goals of the conspiracy. *See, e.g., United States v. Williams*, 87 F.3d 249, 253 (8th Cir. 1996); *United States v. Mealy*, 851 F.2d 890, 901 (7th Cir. 1988); *United States v. Ammar*, 714 F.2d 238, 253 (3d Cir. 1983); *United States v. Killian*, 639 F.2d 206, 209 (5th Cir. 1981). In this case, even if the defendant showed that he was in prison during several of the robberies, he could be convicted of the conspiracy.

(D) Incorrect. The defendant is not entitled to acquittal of conspiracy, because a co-conspirator need not be present at the commission of each crime, nor does the arrest of one co-conspirator automatically terminate the conspiracy where other co-conspirators continue to carry out the goals of the conspiracy. *See, e.g., United States v. Williams*, 87 F.3d 249, 253 (8th Cir. 1996); *United States v. Mealy*, 851 F.2d 890, 901 (7th Cir. 1988); *United States v. Ammar*, 714 F.2d 238, 253 (3d Cir. 1983); *United States v. Killian*, 639 F.2d 206, 209 (5th Cir. 1981). In this case, even if the evidence showed that the defendant was in prison during several of the robberies, he could be convicted of the conspiracy. Furthermore, the reasoning stated in this answer, that "the government is bound by exculpatory evidence elicited during its case-in-chief," is incorrect.

Question 92 - Contracts
Answer: D

(A) Incorrect. This statement of the law is much too broad to be true. Courts look beyond the words of a condition, and if it is clear that the purpose of the condition was to benefit or protect one of the parties, the language of the condition will be interpreted as if that intention had been embodied in the contract terms. In this case it is clear that the language of the condition was intended for the benefit of the buyer, and so the seller's duty was not subject to the condition.

(B) Incorrect. The issue in this dispute does not concern the modification of the contract. The parties did nothing which could be interpreted as an attempt to modify the agreement. The issue is whether the seller's duty is conditional. Courts look beyond the words of a condition, and if it is clear that the purpose of the condition was to benefit or protect one of the parties, the language of the condition will be interpreted as if that intention had been embodied in the contract terms. In this case it is clear that the language of the condition was intended for the benefit of the buyer, and so the seller's duty was not subject to the condition.

(C) Incorrect. While it is true that the buyer changed position because of the seller's promise, that fact is not relevant to the question of whether the seller's duty to perform is subject to a condition. Courts look beyond the words of a condition, and if it is clear that the purpose of the condition was to benefit or protect one of the parties, the language of the condition will be interpreted as if that intention had been embodied in the contract terms. In this case it is clear that the language of the condition was intended for the benefit of the buyer, and so the seller's duty was not subject to the condition.

(D) Correct. Courts look beyond the words of a condition, and if it is clear that the purpose of the condition was to benefit or protect one of the parties, the language of the condition will be interpreted as if that intention had been embodied in the contract terms. In this case it is clear that the language of the condition was intended for the benefit of the buyer, and so the seller's duty was not subject to the condition.

Question 93 - Torts
Answer: C

(A) Incorrect. The duty of a landowner for dangerous artificial conditions exists only where the owner has reason to know that trespassers are in dangerous proximity to the condition and that they are unlikely to appreciate the risk. Even then, the duty is only to exercise reasonable care to warn trespassers of the danger, which was done here. The corporation will prevail because the obviousness of the risk, buttressed by a warning sign, would have been appreciated by a "bright nine-year-old child."

(B) Incorrect. For a condition on land to be considered an attractive nuisance, there must be evidence that the possessor has reason to know that children are likely to trespass, as well as evidence that the plaintiff did not appreciate the risk involved. No such evidence is mentioned in the facts; there is no suggestion that children often stray from the day care center. The corporation will prevail because the obviousness of the risk, buttressed by a warning sign, would have been appreciated by a "bright nine-year-old child."

(C) Correct. This is not a case in which the trespasser failed to appreciate the risk. The obviousness of the risk was buttressed by a warning sign written in words that a "bright nine-year-old child" should be able to read and understand.

(D) Incorrect. This answer correctly states that the corporation will prevail, but it misstates the legal basis for this conclusion. Even if the day care center had a duty to keep children from the ice, the corporation could also be liable if it was negligent. The reason the corporation will prevail is because the obviousness of the risk, buttressed by a warning sign, would have been appreciated by a "bright nine-year-old child."

Question 94 - Torts
Answer: C

(A) Incorrect. Day care centers are not strictly or absolutely liable for all injuries that occur to children under their care. The center's negligence must be established. Under the facts as described, there is no evidence of lack of reasonable care, and the day care center will prevail.

(B) Incorrect. The mere fact that the center is located near a pond is not in itself evidence of negligence. It might mean that reasonable care requires extra-vigilant supervision, but the facts specify that the center staff was in fact exercising "reasonable care." Accordingly, the day care center will prevail.

(C) Correct. Under the facts as described, there is no evidence of lack of reasonable care by the day care center.

(D) Incorrect. The child's status as a trespasser would only be relevant in litigation against an owner or possessor of land. Under the facts as described, there is no evidence of lack of reasonable care, and the day care center will prevail for that reason.

Question 95 - Constitutional Law
Answer: C

(A) Incorrect. The man communicated a threat with the intent to intimidate the recipient. The Supreme Court has held that such threats are not protected by the speech clause of the First Amendment. Because these threats are not constitutionally protected, states may outlaw them regardless of whether the speaker acts on the threat.

(B) Incorrect. This answer correctly states that the man may be convicted, but it misstates the legal basis for that conclusion. The state may not punish an individual for the content of his speech simply because he engages in unlawful conduct. The speech restriction itself must be consistent with the speech clause of the First Amendment. In this case, the man may be convicted because the Supreme Court has held that a threat communicated with the intent to intimidate the recipient, like the communication in this case, is not constitutionally protected speech.

(C) Correct. The Supreme Court has held that a threat communicated with the intent to intimidate the recipient, like the communication in this case, is not protected by the speech clause of the First

Amendment.

(D) Incorrect. The Supreme Court has not held racially motivated threats to violate the Thirteenth Amendment's prohibition of involuntary servitude. The reason the man may be convicted is that the Supreme Court has held that a threat communicated with the intent to intimidate the recipient, like the communication in this case, is not constitutionally protected speech.

Question 96 - Criminal Law and Procedure
Answer: A

(A) Correct. There is no obligation to retreat unless the defender intends to use deadly force. *See* Wayne R. LaFave, Principles of Criminal Law § 9.4(f), at 411 (2003).

(B) Incorrect. This answer correctly states that the defendant should not be convicted, but it misstates the legal basis for this conclusion. The reason the defendant was not required to retreat was because he used nondeadly force and not because he was in an occupied structure.

(C) Incorrect. Even where safe retreat is possible, it is not required before using nondeadly force in self-defense. *See* Wayne R. LaFave, Principles of Criminal Law § 9.4(f), at 411 (2003).

(D) Incorrect. A response of nondeadly force is justified where the defender reasonably believes the other is about to inflict unlawful bodily harm, which need not be deadly harm. *See* Wayne R. LaFave, Principles of Criminal Law § 9.4(b), at 407-08 (2003).

Question 97 - Contracts
Answer: A

(A) Correct. When parties attach significantly different meanings to the same material term, the meaning that controls is that "attached by one of them if at the time the agreement was made . . . that party did not know of any different meaning attached by the other, and the other knew the meaning attached by the first party." Restatement (Second) of Contracts § 201. In this case, the innkeeper did not know, at the time of contract formation, that the laundry company attached a different meaning to the term "daily service" than its apparent meaning of "every day." Conversely, the laundry company knew the innkeeper thought he was contracting for "every day" service. Accordingly, the innkeeper's understanding of the term will control.

(B) Incorrect. While it is sometimes the case that no agreement arises when parties attach significantly different meanings to the same material term, that principle is not applicable when, as here, one of the parties is aware of the meaning intended by the other. When parties attach significantly different meanings to the same material term, the meaning that controls is that "attached by one of them if at the time the agreement was made . . . that party did not know of any different meaning attached by the other, and the other knew the meaning attached by the first party." Restatement (Second) of Contracts § 201. In this case, the innkeeper did not know, at the time of contract formation, that the laundry company attached a different meaning to the term "daily service" than its apparent meaning of "every day." Conversely, the laundry company knew the innkeeper thought he was contracting for "every day" service. Accordingly, the innkeeper's understanding of the term will control.

(C) Incorrect. The parol evidence rule is not applicable here. The apparent meaning of "daily service" is "every day." This is the meaning asserted by the innkeeper, and so it is not the innkeeper that is seeking to alter the apparent meaning of the term, but rather the laundry company. That is, to the extent that there is extrinsic evidence here, it is not being offered by the innkeeper, but rather by the laundry company. When parties attach significantly different meanings to the same material term, the meaning that controls is that "attached by one of them if at the time the agreement was made . . . that party did not know of any different meaning attached by the other, and the other knew the meaning attached by the first party." Restatement (Second) of Contracts § 201. In this case, the innkeeper did not know, at the time of contract formation, that the laundry company attached a different meaning to the term "daily service" than its apparent meaning of "every day." Conversely, the laundry company knew the innkeeper thought he was contracting for "every day" service. Accordingly, the innkeeper's understanding of the term will control.

(D) Incorrect. While it is often the case that trade usages control the interpretation of terms in a contract, that is not true here. In this case, the laundry company knew that the innkeeper was not aware of the trade usage. When parties attach significantly different meanings to the same material term, the meaning that controls is that "attached by one of them if at the time the agreement was made . . . that party did not know of any different meaning attached by the other, and the other knew the meaning attached by the first party." Restatement (Second) of Contracts § 201. In this case, the innkeeper did not know, at the time of contract formation, that the laundry company attached a different meaning to the term "daily service" than its apparent meaning of "every day." Conversely, the laundry company knew the innkeeper thought he was contracting for "every day" service. Accordingly, the innkeeper's understanding of the term will control.

Question 98 - Real Property
Answer: B

(A) Incorrect. This option correctly states that the grantee will prevail, but it misstates the reason why this is so. A license is not subject to the statute of frauds; it may be oral, written, or implied. In this case, the neighbor had a valid license, but it was effectively revoked by the grantee.

(B) Correct. A license is permission to use the land of another. It is revocable, and is not subject to the statute of frauds. In this case, because the neighbor had the landowner's permission to use the road and did not expend any money, property, or labor pursuant to the agreement, the neighbor had a license that was effectively revoked by the grantee.

(C) Incorrect. For estoppel to apply, the neighbor must have expended money, property, or labor pursuant to the agreement. In this case, the landowner alone maintained the road. The neighbor's use of the land by permission, without expense, was a license that was effectively revoked by the grantee.

(D) Incorrect. An open and notorious use of the road suggests a claim for an easement by prescription. However, the use was with permission, which prevents a prescriptive claim, and the use was for a very short time, which negates any possible claim based on the discredited theory of lost grant. Instead, the neighbor's use of the land was a license that was effectively revoked by the grantee.

Question 99 - Contracts
Answer: A

(A) Correct. The carpenter is entitled to the contract price for the work done. The other items of damage are unrecoverable either because they were unforeseeable at the time the contract was made or because they were not caused by the breach. No unjust enrichment claim is viable on these facts, because an unjust enrichment claim cannot exceed the contract price when all of the work giving rise to the claim has been done and the only remaining obligation is the payment of the price. This limitation on unjust enrichment claims was recapitulated in the well known case of *Oliver v. Campbell*, 273 P.2d 15 (Cal. 1954), and represents the current rule in such cases.

(B) Incorrect. The carpenter is entitled only to the contract price for the work done. The medical expenses are unrecoverable because even if the heart attack was caused by the breach, which would be difficult to establish, the medical expenses were unforeseeable at the time the contract was made.

(C) Incorrect. The carpenter is entitled only to the contract price for the work done. The $2,000 for the loss of the bargain on the car was unforeseeable at the time the contract to do the work was made. That car contract was a special circumstance, of which the homeowner had no notice.

(D) Incorrect. The carpenter is entitled only to the contract price for the work done. No unjust enrichment claim is viable on these facts, because an unjust enrichment claim cannot exceed the contract price when all of the work giving rise to the claim has been done and the only remaining obligation of the homeowner is the payment of the price. The claim has been "liquidated" and the work substantially performed. This limitation on unjust enrichment claims was recapitulated in the well known case of *Oliver v. Campbell*, 273 P.2d 15 (Cal. 1954), and represents the current rule in such cases.

Question 100 - Evidence
Answer: A

(A) Correct. The doctor's letter is not a business record under Federal Rule of Evidence 803(6), because it was not prepared in the ordinary course of regularly conducted activity. In addition, it cannot be admitted simply because an expert relies upon it. Rule 703 does allow an expert to rely on hearsay in reaching a conclusion, so long as other experts in the field would reasonably rely on such information. But the rule distinguishes between expert *reliance* on the hearsay and *admitting* the hearsay at trial for the jury to consider. Generally speaking, hearsay will not be admissible when offered only because the expert relied upon it. The probative value of the hearsay in illustrating the basis of the expert's opinion must substantially outweigh the risks of prejudice and confusion that will occur when the jury is told about the hearsay. That strict balancing test is not met in this case. There is no other exception that appears even close to being applicable (and none listed in the possible answers), so the letter is inadmissible hearsay.

(B) Incorrect. This fact would only be relevant if the hearsay were offered under Federal Rule of Evidence 804 as one of the "unavailability-dependent" exceptions to the hearsay rule. None of those exceptions are pertinent here. Furthermore, if the hearsay qualified as a hearsay exception under Rule 803 (e.g., if it were a business record), then the doctor's availability would be completely irrelevant, because unavailability need not be shown for those exceptions. But the letter does not qualify under any of the Rule 803 exceptions. In particular, it is not a business record because it was not prepared in the ordinary course of regularly conducted activity.

(C) Incorrect. The letter is hearsay if offered to prove that the plaintiff's condition was as indicated in the letter. Federal Rule of Evidence 703 does allow an expert to rely on hearsay in reaching a conclusion, so long as other experts in the field would reasonably rely on such information. But Rule 703 distinguishes between expert *reliance* on the hearsay and *admitting* the hearsay at trial for the jury to consider. Generally speaking, hearsay will not be admissible when offered only because the expert relied upon it. The probative value of the hearsay in illustrating the basis of the expert's opinion must substantially outweigh the risks of prejudice and confusion that will occur when the jury is told about the hearsay. That strict balancing test is not met in this case.

(D) Incorrect. The doctor's letter clearly does not qualify under Federal Rule of Evidence 803(6) as a business record. It is not a medical record prepared in the ordinary course of regularly conducted activity. Rather, it is a letter written by the doctor on an ad hoc occasion. Thus, the letter lacks the earmarks of regularity that are critical for admissibility under the business records exception to the hearsay rule.

AMERIBAR BAR REVIEW

Multistate Bar Examination - Answers to Questions – Section 3

CONSTITUTIONAL LAW

Question 1
Answer: D

This question tests the concept of federal preemption.

The Preemption Doctrine provides that federal law overrides state law if the sate law conflicts with the federal law. This question presents a case of direct conflict between the federal statute—which allows interstate carriers to cancel unprofitable lines—with the state statute. The state statute prohibits the cancellation of routes where a community has no alternative form of transportation. The Supremacy Clause of the U.S. Constitution underlies the Preemption Doctrine, so in this question, the federal law is supreme to the state law. Foley is out of luck.

Choice (A) is wrong. Foley is, as a resident of the Shaley Mountains, directly affected by it, and threatened with imminent harm by the statute. He does have standing to sue.

Choice (B) is wrong. The case does not involve a substantial federal question.

Choice (C) is wrong. Because of the Preemption Doctrine, Foley cannot win. Further, a federal agency is not prohibited from ever interfering with essential state functions.

Question 2
Answer: B

This question tests the discretion of the Supreme Court in granting judicial review.

The highest state court is the final arbiter of the meaning of the state's constitution. Therefore, the Supreme Court will not involve itself in interpretation of a state law or constitution where there exists a valid and independent state ground that supports the decision made by the state's highest court. The Supreme Court is concerned only with the federal issues presented by the suit. In this question, the statute was held by the state court to violate the state constitution's equal protection clause. It was also held to have violated the Federal Equal Protection Clause. The Supreme Court can and will properly hear the question as to whether the Federal Clause was violated. As for the violation of the state constitution, there is no independent basis upon which that decision can stand (choice (C) is wrong) because the two equal protection clauses are interpreted the same way. This means that the Supreme Court will hear this appeal and, disagreeing, reverse and remand back to the state.

Question 3
Answer: B

This question tests the delegation powers of Congress.

The first half of the question is a correct description of acceptable delegation of legislative power. The delegate commission is given intelligible standards and guidelines on upon which to base the rules that it formulates and the licenses that it grants. However, once those decisions are made, Congress is permitted to essentially veto the decision by majority vote. This is not a permissible, constitutional method of disposing of an administrative decision. Even if the Congress delegated the power which was used to make that decision, a congressional majority vote does not have the unilateral power to set aside that decision once it is made. Presentment is required for that license to be denied once it has been granted.

Question 4
Answer: B

This question tests the doctrine of federal preemption.

Under the Preemption Doctrine, which is based on the Supremacy Clause, a federal law overrides a state law if the state law conflicts with the federal law. In this question, there is a direct conflict between the state and federal law. The state seemed to ignore the presence of the federal law in enacting the state statute.

Choice (A) is wrong. Timing is not of any importance. Otherwise, states would be free to circumvent any federal laws by simply enacting state laws after-the-fact.

Choice (C) is wrong. Even where a federal law does not explicitly state that it will occupy a certain field of the law, it may implicitly indicate the same. In this question, there is at least an implicit indication that the federal law is to govern all construction projects. It is occupying the field of construction standards.

Choice (D) is wrong. This is an off-the-wall option that should immediately be eliminated. Constitutionality is not measured by the safety risk posed to the construction workers.

Question 5
Answer: B

This question tests a state's police powers under the Tenth Amendment.

Police powers are those that a state employs to protect the public's health, safety, welfare, and morals. A state's exercise of police power is generally permissible as long as the U.S. Constitution is not otherwise violated. State and local legislatures are permitted to enact economic and social legislation subject to two constraints: (1) the legislation may not violate federal constitutional rights, and (2) the legislation must pass rational basis scrutiny. Where a matter is judged by rational basis scrutiny on the exam, it will rarely fail and be invalidated. Therefore, (C) and (D) are out. This legislation is likely to pass scrutiny. Choice (A) is wrong because it employs strict scrutiny—too rigorous a test for the kind of legislation proposed in the question.

Question 6
Answer: A

This question tests the Commerce Clause.

The Commerce Clause power to regulate applies to the instrumentalities of commerce, the channels of commerce, noncommercial activity that has a direct connection to interstate commerce, and to activities that produce a substantial effect on interstate commerce. This question presents a scenario in which all sales of consumable products must have a proper designation when a risk of cancer is present. This is a regulation which would produce a definite substantial effect on interstate commerce.

Choice (B) is wrong. The Fourteenth Amendment will come into play where a state statute is affecting a class of individuals regarding their due process rights or equal protection rights. This scenario is not present in the question.

Choice (C) is wrong. The general welfare justification tends to come into play where the question discusses a federal appropriations scheme or the like. While this question could very loosely be regarded as presenting a statute which does protect the general welfare of the people, the easier and more direct justification for the statute is the Commerce Clause.

Choice (D) is wrong. The promotion of science and the arts tends to encompass the making of federal grants to sponsor development in these areas. This statute does not promote science—rather, it seems to enforce science on the public.

Question 7
Answer: A

This question tests the sovereign immunity of states.

In *Hans v. Louisiana*, the Supreme Court expanded the Eleventh Amendment's prohibition of standing to lawsuits in a federal court by a state's citizens against that state. The Supreme Court decided in *Fitzpatrick v. Bitzer*, that Congress may establish exceptions to the Eleventh Amendment by enacting a statute that enforces the Fourteenth Amendment and authorizes lawsuits in federal court by a state's citizens against that state. The statute in question does just this. The equal protection implication is age discrimination perpetrated by the state.

Choice (B) is wrong. The power of Congress is not unlimited in authority to authorize private suits against a state for damages.

Choice (C) is wrong. Congress is limited in its ability to modify a state's sovereign immunity. For instance, Congress cannot compel a state to undo its immunity from suit within the state's own courts.

Choice (D) is wrong. The Eleventh Amendment has been expanded to cover suits by citizens against their own states.

Question 8
Answer: A

This question tests the concept of federal preemption.

In this question, there is a federal practice which mirrors an existing state practice regarding the same subject matter. They expressly conflict because one requires the use of an EPA licensed facility while the other requires the use of a state facility. Federal law supersedes any conflicting state laws. This federal statute implicitly indicates that it will occupy and govern the field of tire disposal in the country. Therefore, it will govern over the existing state practice. Because of preemption, it is apparent that choices (C) and (D) are incorrect.

Choice (B) is incorrect because it overlooks the concept of preemption. While it is true that some tires disposed of in the state facility will be purely intrastate tires, the federal statute will prevail because it covers the same subject matter as the state's laws or practice. The issue is not really a question of the Commerce Clause—it is a question as to whether federal interstate commerce laws will trump intrastate laws.

Question 9
Answer: A

This question tests conditional federal expenditures.

The spending power allows Congress to attach, as a condition of receiving federal funding, a requirement that a state voluntarily comply with a federal law. The Congress cannot impose compliance with the federal law using coercive means. The state must be free to opt out of the federal expenditures. In this question, Congress has required that, if federal funding is wanted for the restoration of courthouses, the facilities must be made handicap-accessible. This is a textbook example of conditional spending.

Choice (B) is wrong. While this answer sounds nice and politically correct, the rights of the disabled are judged like the rights of anyone else. The rights in question, though, are unclear. They may or may not be fundamental. The right to access the courthouse is a fundamental one, but the statement in this option is too broad. Not all of their rights are fundamental.

Choice (C) is wrong. The U.S. Constitution, through its spending power provisions, authorizes the federal government to affect the matters that might traditionally be left to state government.

Choice (D) is wrong. This is not a case of duress. This is merely a conditional federal expenditure. The state is free to accept or reject the restoration funding for its courthouse.

Question 10
Answer: B

This question tests the Commerce Clause.

The Commerce Clause is probably the most heavily tested congressional power on the bar exam. The Clause itself provides that Congress has the power to regulate commerce with foreign nations and among the several states. That power to regulate extends to the instrumentalities of interstate commerce, the channels of interstate commerce, and to those activities which produce a substantial effect on interstate commerce. In this question, Congress is passing regulations which will produce a substantial effect on interstate commerce, given the size of the over-the-counter drug industry. Further, it may be argued that these are regulations on the channels of interstate commerce because the regulation is of the chain of production and ultimate retail sale of the goods.

Choice (A) is wrong. Government spending is not the means by which the government seeks to combat look-alike drugs. The government is seeking to accomplish this through legislation.

Choice (C) is wrong. The General Welfare Clause is closely connected to the federal spending power. This question does not involve a federal appropriations scheme.

Choice (D) is wrong. The Congress is not addressing a Fourteenth Amendment "discrimination" issue such as due process or equal protection. The Fourteenth Amendment enforcement powers are generally used for these purposes.

Question 11
Answer: D

This question tests the Commerce Clause.

The state statute in question discriminates against businesses that use testing companies outside the state. This, because of its less favorable treatment of other states' companies, is a burden on interstate commerce. The state law would be constitutionally upheld if it advanced a **legitimate state interest** and **nondiscriminatory alternatives** were unavailable. However, it does appear that nondiscriminatory alternatives were available. There is nothing to suggest that the out-of-state testing is inferior to the in-state testing. The same goal of safety is achieved by either.

Choices (A) and (B) are wrong. While the law might be reasonably related to the issues of public safety and protecting the fabric industry in the state, there were alternative means available that were not as discriminatory. Choice (C) is wrong. Fabric Mill is being treated differently by a state other than its own. Equal protection issues usually arise where a state is treating its own citizens differently from one another.

Question 12
Answer: C

This question tests equal protection and fundamental rights.

This question concerns itself with the right of a child to a public education and discrimination by a state in the allocation of funding to public schools. The discrimination tends to be across wealth lines. Wealthy schools that, perhaps, need less of the state's funding, are being treated equally with poorer schools that have a greater need. A classification based on wealth is not a suspect classification. It is subject only to rational basis scrutiny and often will succeed if the state can show any legitimate reason for the statute. Choice (C) is the only option which applies the correct level of scrutiny. Choices (A) and (B) apply strict scrutiny, which is too high for this issue. Choice (D) applies intermediate scrutiny—also too high for this issue.

Question 13
Answer: A

This questions tests states' power to legislate.

The Federal Constitution and statutes are removed from consideration in this question where it states that no federal laws are applicable. The actions of the state reapportionment board, therefore, are governed only by the state's constitution. For the board's actions to be valid, it must comply with the state constitution. The best answer, therefore, to support the validity of the board's actions, would be an answer which proves constitutional compliance. Compliance with the state constitution is the only measuring stick by which the reapportionment's validity can be governed. Choice (B) is not based on comparing the reapportionment to the state constitution's standards.

Question 14
Answer: C

This question tests federal senatorial powers.

Choice (A) is a valid power of the Senate. The Senate can confer with the House through bicameralism and then presentment to make a proposed amendment into law. This is within Congressional powers.

Choice (B) is also a valid power of the Senate. The Senate can decide eligibility issues for its own members.

Choice (C) is incorrect. This option presents a situation in which the Senate has violated the doctrine of separation of powers. The kind of dispute at issue is one generally reserved to the Article III courts. The federal legislature does not have the power to adjudicate disputes. Therefore, in appointing a commission to do so, the Senate is unconstitutionally delegating judicial power that it does not itself possess.

Choice (D) is also a valid power of the Senate. The Senate can pass resolutions calling on various governmental figures to pursue certain policy.

Question 15
Answer: D

This question tests content-based restrictions on speech.

Content-based regulation means that the government is restricting some speech but not others, based on the content of the expression. Here, the content of the expression which is being banned is human sexual intercourse. The strict scrutiny standard applies to content-based restrictions and provides that the law will only be upheld if necessary to achieve a compelling purpose. This standard is rarely satisfied in the First Amendment context, so this is the strongest argument to be made against the constitutionality of the statute.

Choice (A) is wrong. This is not a prior restraint on the speech. It would be a prior restraint if the state, instead, taxed the production of these films because of their content.

Choice (B) is wrong. Arguably there is a legitimate national interest in having this act.

Choice (C) is wrong. Live theater versus movie theater is not a classification protected under the Fifth Amendment Equal Protection Clause. This kind of line drawing would actually be examined under rational basis scrutiny and would likely be upheld under such a test.

Question 16
Answer: A

This question tests speech in public employment and the Due Process Clause.

Immediately of importance in this question is the fact that the employee had a contract with a "for cause" firing provision. This loosely can be interpreted to mean that the employee was due some process upon termination, such as notice and a hearing. In this question, the reader must essentially infer that the comments constituted a "cause" for the firing because all other answers can be eliminated.

Choice (B) is wrong. A government employee is free to make comments that are inconsistent with current governmental policy, and he is protected in doing this when, for instance, his comments are on a topic of public concern.

Choice (C) is wrong. Though the statements may have been on a topic of public concern, this is not enough to make the statements permissible and immune from adverse employment action.

Choice (D) is wrong. A private person cannot claim the protections that are reserved to the publisher and the press once he has made comments.

Question 17
Answer: C

This question tests the concept of equal protection and private discrimination.

The first line of the question holds the answer. The companies perpetrating the discrimination in the state of Shoshone are private companies. There is no state action because the state does not regulate rates or policies. If a resident feels that he or she has been discriminated against by the insurance provider because he or she lives in a crime-ridden area, there is nothing to be done. A suit for violation of the Equal Protection Clause will be fruitless because private individuals are not held subject to it unless specifically authorized through federal statute. There is no federal statute present here which would subject the insurance companies to liability.

Choice (D) is a red herring. It does look like the discrimination is based on wealth. This categorization would receive rational basis scrutiny. The problem is that there is no state action, so the test need not be applied at all.

Question 18
Answer: D

This question concerns the original jurisdiction of the United States Supreme Court.

An immediate red flag should appear to the reader when he sees that Congress and the President have joined together to expand the original jurisdiction of the Supreme Court. The original jurisdiction of the Supreme Court is for cases that affect "Ambassadors, other public Ministers and Counsels, and those in which a State shall be a party." Under Article III, Congress may determine the Supreme Court's appellate jurisdiction, as well as the types of cases that the lower federal courts may adjudicate. Congress, however, cannot change the Supreme Court's original jurisdiction.

Question 19
Answer: A

This question tests congressional taxing power.

Congress has the power to impose and collect taxes for the national defense and public welfare. An Act of Congress that imposes a tax will be upheld as valid if the Act does in fact raise revenue. If the tax adversely impacts the taxed activity (air travel, for example), then it will be upheld: (1) if it is raising revenue; and (2) if it lacks provisions unrelated to the tax needs and purposes; and (3) if no language of the U.S. Constitution specifically prohibits it. In this question, the taxing power is being used to raise revenue for the construction of new major airports. The taxing scheme is completely related to its fundraising purpose and the Constitution allows for this kind of taxation for the general welfare. Nothing in the Constitution prohibits this taxing scheme. The tax monies are not required to be used for a purpose related to the item being taxed, though. A good example would be sin taxes that are levied on alcohol, tobacco, and lottery tickets. These tax monies are used to fund public education in many states.

Question 20
Answer: C

This question tests the constitutionality of state alienage statutes.

A state statute which discriminates on the basis of alienage will be subjected to strict scrutiny review. This rules out answer choices (B) and (D). They apply the wrong level or type of scrutiny.

Choice (A) is wrong because, although states do have plenary power over the spending of state funds, this power is still constrained by the Federal Constitution which prohibits, in some instances, discrimination based on the classification of alienage.

Choice (C) is correct because it uses the proper level of judicial scrutiny to examine the constitutionality of this state statute.

Question 21
Answer: C

This question tests the requirement of a case or controversy (standing).

Jones has no standing to bring suit in this case. He has not suffered an injury in fact. None of his rights have been violated. If an injury is recognized, though, Jones cannot prove that the existence of this statute is what caused his injury.

Choice (A) is wrong. This is not a substantial federal question arising under the Constitution, laws, or treaties of the United States.

Choice (B) is wrong. The political questions doctrine is not implicated here. This doctrine tends only to arise where a federal court is reviewing a federal law that implicates political issues.

Choice (D) is wrong. The Eleventh Amendment does not apply when a state citizen files an action against a local government that is a state's political subdivision. The local government lacks immunity from a lawsuit involving a federal question.

Question 22
Answer: A

This question tests the doctrine of preemption.

The Supremacy Clause of the U. S. Constitution underlies the Preemption Doctrine. The doctrine provides that federal law overrides state law if the sate law conflicts with the federal law. In this question, federal law is intended to "occupy the field" in the area of liability insurance and interstate carriers. The state tort law directly conflicts with this law because it does govern the relationship between the complaining parties on the basis of their contract. Therefore, because of the conflict, federal law will prevail.

Choice (B) is wrong. The Obligation of Contracts Clause is concerned with the passing of legislation that impairs or makes impossible contracts already in existence. There is no legislating going on in this question that impairs an already existing contract.

Choice (C) is wrong. This statement is contrary to the principles of federal supremacy.

Choice (D) is wrong. If this statement were true, all forms of insurance would be unconstitutional and non-existent.

Question 23
Answer: B

This question tests the Establishment Clause.

The Establishment Clause of the U.S. Constitution prevents Congress from legislatively establishing or directly assisting a religion or religions in general. Here, the city has passed a law that makes no preference of any religious group or sect. It is neutral. Therefore, the court will examine the purpose and effect of the law to determine if the Establishment Clause has been violated. The statute must have a secular purpose. Here, the purpose is the upkeep of a public cemetery. The law's primary effect must be a neutral one that neither advances nor inhibits religion. The effect of this law is the creation a uniform, respectful setting for the dead. There is no excessive entanglement with religions. In fact, quite the converse seems true. This statute allows for the full and free display of religious symbols on the grave markers themselves.

Choice (A) is wrong. The amount of funding is immaterial where the government has actually engaged in the establishment of any religion over another.

Choice (C) is wrong. Cities often maintain religious objects, especially during the holidays, and can do so without violating the Establishment Clause.

Choice (D) is wrong. The individuals are the ones with the fundamental right to the free exercise of religion and free expression.

Question 24
Answer: C

This question tests the Due Process Clause.

In this question, we have a denial of a boy's freedom of liberty after a short hearing that he violated the school's behavior code. State action that impairs, interferes with, denies, or deprives a person of life, liberty, or property requires substantial justification. Here, the right being deprived would probably be examined under heightened scrutiny, which requires that the least restrictive means be used in the deprivation. In this question, there were likely less burdensome means available to accomplish the school's purpose in enforcing discipline on its students. A 15-day punishment for a gum prank is actually the most restrictive option available to the school under its disciplinary program.

Choice (A) is wrong. This is not a privileges and immunities question. These tend to arise where citizens of one state are treated differently than non-citizens of that state.

Choice (B) is wrong. The rule itself may not be overbroad and therefore unconstitutional. The application of it, however, can be unconstitutional under the facts.

Choice (D) is wrong. Very rarely will there be a question on bills of attainder. A bill of attainder is a retrospective law that imposes punishment on named individuals or a readily identifiable group of individuals. It is an impermissible legislative penalty that precludes a person from receiving a minimum degree of procedural due process such as notice and a hearing. This question involves no bills of attainder. In fact, a hearing is guaranteed to the students under the school policy.

Question 25
Answer: C

This question tests the Due Process Clause.

Where a public employee has a property interest and entitlement in his or her job, the state must provide procedural due process safeguards for any potential termination of that job. The statute in question looks to be a pretty comprehensive provision for notice and hearings. However, one sentence in the statute should cause alarm. "...such an employee must, upon request, be granted a post-dismissal hearing before an administrative board..." Under the Due Process Clause, this hearing is not optional. It must take place, even if the terminated employee does not request it.

Choice (A) is wrong. Federal courts are authorized to determine the constitutionality of federal and state laws pursuant to controlling precedents of the federal courts.

Choice (B) is wrong. The standard of proof required by the statute is sufficient. The reasonable doubt standard is more appropriate for criminal proceedings.

Choice (D) is wrong. The Due Process Clause is not limited to only a statement of reasons and a hearing. Other procedural due process protections may be warranted in other situations. In any event, this option does not correspond well to the statute being tested because the statute does not guarantee a hearing to the employee—the employee must request one.

Question 26
Answer: D

This question tests a performer's "right of publicity."

The plaintiff in *Zacchini v. Scripps-Howard Broadcasting Co.* was a human cannonball performer whose paid public performance was, without his permission, broadcast over the television. The Supreme Court held that this violated his proprietary interest and that the broadcast was not protected under the First Amendment. The plaintiff in this case is just like *Zacchini*.

Choices (A) and (B) are statements that are not entirely true. The rights under the First Amendment are not absolute in many instances. These two choices overlook the fact that the performer has a proprietary interest in his commercially valuable name.

Choice (C) is a red herring answer. Yes, the performer is deprived of a property interest, but the examination of the issue is not undertaken using the Due Process Clause. It is a First Amendment question.

Question 27
Answer: C

This question tests the presidential pardon power.

Article II provides the President with "power to grant Reprieves and Pardons for Offenses against the United States, except in Cases of Impeachment." The Supreme Court construed the power as extending "to every offense known to the law." The President may pardon persons from convictions of federal offenses, subject to certain limitations that the Supreme Court has imposed. In this question, the Congress attempts to limit the pardon power to only those who have already served one-third of a sentence. The Supreme Court is the entity which may cast limitations on the power—not the Congress.

Choices (A) and (D) are red herring answers. The process for passing the law over a presidential veto was followed correctly, but the problem lies in the fact that this kind of law is itself unconstitutional—even if it is somehow passed by the Congress.

Choice (B) is wrong. The law is concerned with a power of the President—not a power held by Congress. The law does not allow the Congress to carry out any of its own powers. Rather, it limits the President in the ability to carry out his.

Question 28
Answer: B

This question tests the Commerce Clause.

The fact pattern in this question presents a scenario in which a state establishes a ceiling price level for manufacturers and wholesalers who sell goods to retailers within the state, in an effort to keep prices competitive with neighboring states. When a question talks about buying and selling, the Commerce Clause should immediately come to mind as a possible issue being raised in the question. This is a law created by the state but regulating interstate commerce. The law will only be upheld if it serves a legitimate state objective, the law is rationally related to that objective, and the state's interest in enforcing the law outweighs both its regulatory burden on commerce and its discrimination against interstate commerce. The strongest argument for the invalidation of the statute is that it does create an unreasonable burden on interstate commerce.

Choice (A) is wrong. There is no property interest or liberty interest to be protected. The only interest is the out-of-state companies' desire to sell to retailers in the state of Yellow. They do not have a protected right to do this at a certain price.

Choice (C) is wrong. The privileges of federal citizenship are the Fourteenth Amendment privileges and immunities. They include things such as the right to vote in federal elections, the right to petition the government, and the right to travel interstate. None of these rights is infringed upon by the Yellow state statute.

Choice (D) is wrong. While a weak argument could be made that similarly situated entities are being treated differently under the law, a state does have some right to treat foreign citizens and entities differently than its own. The only scrutiny applied, however, would be rational basis, which is rarely going to fail.

Question 29
Answer: C

This question tests the Supremacy Clause.

In certain respects, state government and laws are subordinated to the federal government and its laws. For instance, states are generally prohibited from enacting laws that interfere with the operations and activities of the federal government. The Supremacy Clause forbids a state from regulating the federal government unless the federal government has expressly consented to the regulation or the state law is consistent with existing federal law. In this question, there is no evidence that the state's pollution statute is consistent with an existing federal statute. Further, the federal government never consented to subjecting itself to the state pollution statutes. Therefore, the federal government is immune from the state pollution prosecution.

Choices (A) and (B) are wrong because they overlook the idea of federal supremacy. While it is true that pollution falls within a state's police power over the public health and welfare, the state law is not always the final word.

Choice (D) is wrong. There is no way to assess the truth or falsity of the statement in this option. Generally, if there is a violation of a state statute, the state law can reach that violation, even if it is a small one. However, state law cannot reach the violations in this question due to federal supremacy.

Question 30
Answer: C

This question tests the right to be a political candidate.

Every state passes some sort of regulation that impacts individuals' ability to run for elected office. These restrictions may be residency requirements, support requirements, and the like. In viewing the constitutionality of these restrictions, the appropriate test to apply is one that balances (1) the severity of the infringement on the rights protected under the First and Fourteenth Amendments with (2) the state interest for burdening that right to candidacy. Applied to this question, we have (1) complete denial of the ability to become a candidate once a person has lost in the primary weighed against (2) probably a state concern that losers in primaries ought not to run because of the potential for ballots full of frivolous candidates without sufficient voter support.

A state may pass regulations designed to keep primary losers from running on the general election ballot, but there must be alternative means for ballot qualification by which a candidate may still appear in the general election. In other words, the right to appear on that general election ballot cannot be completely denied or made too difficult. For example, a requirement that a primary loser in Ohio elections must collect signatures equaling 15 percent of the last election's votes cast was considered to be a suffocating restriction on the right to candidacy and struck down. A 5 percent requirement, though, was upheld for the State of Georgia. In this question, there are no alternative means by which the candidate might appear on the general election ballot. The correct answer applies strict scrutiny because the question presents a complete denial of the right to become a candidate once the primary is lost. The state should have to prove that the statute is the least restrictive means of achieving a compelling state interest.

Question 31
Answer: C

This question tests the laws of police power. One primary category of state authority under the general right of sovereign self-government is the police power. The police powers are those that a State employs to protect the public's health, safety, welfare, and morals. Generally, States may use their police power as long as (1) a conflicting federal law does not pre-empt the state law, (2) the state law does not exceed the limits of state power with respect to interstate commerce, and (3) the state law does not violate individual constitutional rights.

The problem at bar is an instance of proper police power. The Supreme Court has held in the past that States may regulate insurance rates. In this case, East Dakota regulates insurance rates without conflicting with a federal law, and only restricts insurance companies within its State, as not to offend interstate commerce., Finally, the statute does not infringe on any constitutional rights because the insurance companies are free to set their rates as market forces dictate.

(A) is incorrect. East Dakota's purpose is to protect its citizens from unfair insurance rates. Requiring insurance companies to charge citizens in the same county the same rates is rationally related to this purpose.

(B) is incorrect. The statute does not impose a burden on interstate commerce because the statute only regulates insurance companies within the State when dealing with the State's citizens.

(D) is incorrect. The case calls into question the U.S. Constitution. Thus, the case falls within the courts federal subject matter jurisdiction.

Question 32
Answer: C

This question tests the Tenth Amendment. The Tenth Amendment to the U.S. Constitution provides: "The powers not delegated to the United States by the Constitution, nor prohibited by it to the States, are reserved to the States respectively, or to the people." However, the Tenth Amendment does not give the states the power to act unconstitutional. Thus, if a state law violates the U.S. Constitution it is not protected under the Tenth Amendment. In the above case the Green tax statute will be void if it is found to violate the U.S. Constitution.

(A) is incorrect. This fact may be helpful if the state of Green is trying to show that the federal government lacks power to intervene under the Commerce Clause, because the tax does not affect interstate commerce.

(B) is incorrect. This fact may be helpful in showing that the tax affects in-state and out-of-state purchasers equally as to not violate the Privileges and Immunities Clause.

(D) is incorrect. This fact may be helpful in showing that the tax does not unduly burden interstate commerce as to not violate the interstate Commerce Clause.

Question 33
Answer: D

This problem tests the Fifteenth Amendment. The right to vote is a fundamental right protected under the Equal Protection Clause and the Fifteenth Amendment. A reviewing court will apply strict scrutiny to any challenged law that limits that right (except with regard to voter age, residency, and citizenship). The problem at bar deals directly with the citizens of Green City's right to vote; hence, the Fifteenth Amendment provides the basis for the claim.

(A) is incorrect. The Thirteenth Amendment to the U.S. Constitution provides in part that: "Neither slavery nor involuntary servitude, except as a punishment for crime whereof the party shall have been duly convicted, shall exist within the United States, or any place subject to their jurisdiction." This case does not present a slavery or involuntary servitude problem, only a voting issue.

(B) is incorrect. Though the state action may violate the Due Process Clause of the Fourteenth Amendment, the statute must first be challenged under the Fifteenth Amendment, because the state law is a direct violation of it.

(C) is incorrect. This provision prevents a state from depriving its citizens of the privileges and immunities of national or federal citizenship, which include the right to vote. However, the most basic and obvious ground for the above case would be the right to vote, which is protected under the Fifteenth Amendment.

Question 34
Answer: B

This question tests the federal government's taxing power. The congressional power of taxation arises under Article I of the U.S. Constitution, which states in part that "The Congress shall have Power to lay and collect Taxes." An Act of Congress that imposes a tax will be sustained as a valid use of its taxation power if, (1) *objectively*, the act in fact raises revenue, or (2) subjectively, the act is intended to raise revenue. Courts will uphold a tax that *adversely impacts* the taxed activity if the tax satisfies either prong of the above alternative test and if, (1) it lacks any provisions that are unrelated to the tax needs and purposes, and (2) no language of the U.S. Constitution prohibits it.

The case at bar represents a tax intended to raise revenue. The fact that the tax is intended to raise revenue mean it satisfies the first prong of the above test. Next, even if the tax adversely affects the events being taxed, it will still be upheld because the tax includes no provision unrelated to the objective of raising revenue and no language in the U.S. Constitution prohibits it.

(A) is incorrect. Reducing the federal budget is not a compelling end to reach the level of an emergency procedure.

(C) is incorrect. Though the tax may adversely impact the sporting events it will likely be upheld, because the Act does not include any provision unrelated to the tax and the Constitution does not expressly prohibit it.

(D) is incorrect. The equal protection standard in this case would be rational basis. Taxing tickets to championship sporting events is rationally related to the legitimate purpose of raising revenue.

Question 35
Answer: B

This question tests the Commerce Clause. The Commerce Clause grants Congress plenary power to regulate international and interstate activity of both a commercial and non-commercial nature. That authority extends to include, (1) instrumentalities of interstate commerce such as certain private or commercial trains, airplanes, and trucks, (2) channels or facilities of interstate commerce such as certain private or commercial railroads, roads, and airports, (3) noncommercial activity having a direct connection to interstate commerce, regardless of if it has any cumulative or aggregate effect, and (4) activities producing a substantial effect on interstate commerce in a cumulative manner or by inseverable aggregates.

Undeniably, computers can be linked to interstate comer in several ways. First, their components come from many different states, if not different countries. Second, they are usually shipped across state lines. Third, an overwhelming amount of international business is done over computers. For these reasons, the Commerce Clause allows Congress to regulate computers. The Commerce Clause has some exceptions, most notably that the activity being regulated must have affect interstate commerce either direct, indirect, or aggregately. Also, statutes attempting to regulate traditional state activities must be more closely tailored to ensure that some aspect of interstate commerce is involved.

(A) is incorrect. The Necessary and Proper Clause of the U.S. Constitution, provides additional congressional authority beyond the other specifically enumerated powers in the U.S. Constitution. The Clause is usually invoked when Congress makes laws necessary to implement powers enumerated to them in the Constitution.

(C) is incorrect. Congress may regulate interstate commerce. Since computers likely constitute interstate commerce, Congress may regulate them as they seem fit.

(D) is incorrect. Congress has the power to regulate interstate commerce. Though owning a computer may seem like a wholly local matter, Congress may regulate computers if they are interstate commerce, or affect interstate commerce. It is very likely that possessing computers and using them affects interstate commerce, thus Congress may regulate.

Question 36
Answer: C

This question tests the Supremacy Clause. Article II sets forth the Supremacy Clause, which makes the U.S. Constitution, federal law, and treaties the "supreme law of the land." The Supremacy Clause gives rise to the doctrine of intergovernmental immunity. That doctrine generally prevents the states from enacting laws that interfere with the operations and activities of the federal government. The Supremacy Clause prohibits a state from regulating the federal government unless (1) the state receives express consent from the federal government, or (2) the state law is consistent with federal law that is already in effect.

The United States Department of Energy is an extension of the federal government. Because of this, Centerville may not interfere with the Department's operations, as the city is effectively interfering with the operations of the federal government. As demonstrated above, since Centerville's regulations are inconsistent with the Department's operations, they are not valid unless Centerville has consent from Congress.

(A) is incorrect. When a state regulation is inconsistent with federal law, the Supremacy Clause dictates that the state regulation is invalid. No rational basis test is used in these situations.

(B) is incorrect. The Tenth Amendment does not change the Supremacy Clause, which prohibits states from interfering in the federal government's operations.

(D) is incorrect. The ordinance does not violate the Equal Protection Clause, because the regulation is rationally related to the health and safety of the public. However, this analysis is moot, because Centerville's regulation attempts to regulate a federal government activity, which is prohibited by the Supremacy Clause.

Question 37
Answer: D

This question tests the Equal Protection Clause of the Fourteenth Amendment. The Supreme Court construes the Fourteenth Amendment as requiring that all laws treat similarly situated people in the same manner. If such people do not receive equal treatment either under the laws or from a government, then a violation of their equal protection right might have occurred. Race, ethnicity, and national origin are the fully suspect classifications of individuals with respect to government laws or conduct. A court will ordinarily apply strict scrutiny to test the constitutionality of a statute's suspect classification.

In the problem above, the state's classification is based on national origin, because the statute classifies people based on their citizenship. Because the state uses a classification based on national origin, the Court will likely apply strict scrutiny. Under strict scrutiny analysis the classification must be necessary for a compelling purpose. Thus, Alien has the best chance of invalidating the statute through the Equal Protection Clause.

(A) is incorrect. The ex post facto law prohibition prevents the federal and state governments from punishing people for conduct that was lawful when it occurred and before a federal or state law subsequently rendered that conduct unlawful. In this case, not being an American citizen never became illegal. Non-citizens are not criminally punished in Chetopah; they are only excluded from employment as law enforcement officers.

(B) is incorrect. Under the Due Process Clause, the right to practice a trade or profession is not considered a fundamental right. Thus, the court would use a rational basis standard. Statutes are rarely invalidated under the rational basis standard.

(C) is incorrect. The Privileges and Immunities Clause of the Fourteenth Amendment only applies to certain particularly federal rights. Specifically, this provision prevents a state from depriving its citizens of the privileges and immunities of national or federal citizenship, which include: (1) the right to vote in federal elections, (2) the right to petition the federal government to address grievances, and (3) the right to travel interstate. Thus, the Privileges and Immunities Clause is inapplicable for purposes of this problem as it does not include the right to seek employment.

Question 38
Answer: A

This question tests the law of First Amendment rights. The First Amendment expressly refers to "freedom of speech," the Supreme Court construes that phrase to include freedom of expression by means other than speech, such as communicative conduct and graphic presentations. Freedom of association includes the right of one or more individuals or entities to communicate, meet, have relationships, and create organizations. When the statute in question is not content-based, the court will apply intermediate scrutiny, which involves three points of analysis: (1) Does the content neutral restriction reasonably serve a significant governmental interest? (2) Is the restriction narrowly tailored to exclude other content? (3) Does the restriction allow for alternative channels to communicate the information?

The case above concerns an ordinance that is content neutral in that the statute does not regulate or allow certain types of expression based on content. Instead, the statute seeks to control all forms of expression. As laid out above, the court will examine Rightville's ordinance using intermediate scrutiny, because it is a content-neutral statute. So, to satisfy the intermediate scrutiny standard the ordinance must be narrowly tailored to serve a substantial government interest, and must not unreasonably limit alternative avenues of expression.

(B) is incorrect. This choice describes rational basis scrutiny, because it states the ordinance must be rationally related to a legitimate government interest. In First Amendment cases when dealing with a content-neutral statute, intermediate scrutiny is applied.

(C) is incorrect. This choice uses rational basis review, because it states the ordinance must be rationally related to a legitimate government interest. In reality the court uses a more rigid standard, intermediate scrutiny, when examining content-neutral ordinances, as shown in the case above.

(D) is incorrect. This choice is not describing the intermediate standard, which the court uses in content-neutral First Amendment cases. The intermediate standard demands that a statute is narrowly tailored to serve a substantial government interest, and does not unreasonably limit alternative avenues of expression.

Question 39
Answer: C

This question tests the Fourteenth Amendment. The Fourteenth Amendment cannot be used to prohibit private conduct that infringes upon a private person's equal protection and due process rights under the Fourteenth Amendment. The Amendment does provide authority to regulate **private action** that occurs in conjunction with state officials and results in state action.

The Opossums is a private organization and its owners hired private contractors to build their stadium. Thus, the Opossums is a private entity and its owners act as private individuals who are not subject to the Fourteenth Amendment. Furthermore, the Opossums, through its owners, cannot be said to be acting in conjunction with the state, because a onetime grant does not establish a sufficient connection.

(A) is incorrect. The onetime grant is not sufficient to establish a substantial connection. To establish such a connection there must be more evidence of state involvement, such as a sustained plan to pay a portion of state money to the Opossums.

(B) is incorrect. The public's interest in a private activity has no bearing on whether the activity will be considered state action. To constitute state action, the private party must be acting in conjunction with state officials.

(D) is incorrect. No political questions problems exist here. The Fourteenth Amendment may only be invoked against state action. For a private party to be liable under the Fourteenth Amendment, the party must be working in conjunction with state officials.

Question 40
Answer: A

This problem tests the Commerce Clause. The Commerce Clause of Article I of the U.S. Constitution provides in part that Congress has the power: "To regulate Commerce with foreign Nations, and among the several States." In particular, Congress possesses exclusive power over foreign commerce. Generally, a state law may regulate interstate commerce only in a few instances, one being only when the law does not unduly burden interstate commerce.

Automobiles manufactured outside the U.S. are definitely foreign commerce, meaning that they fall under the Commerce Clause. So, Ames cannot regulate foreign cars if the ordinance unduly burdens foreign commerce. In this case, one can see that not allowing foreign cars to be parked in any parking lot or parking structure owned or operated by the state would burden that commerce.

(B) is incorrect. Using the Equal Protection Clause is not the strongest argument, because the court would only use a rational basis standard to evaluate this problem. Under rational basis the court would only look to see if banning foreign cars in public parking lots is rationally related to the legitimate state objective of fostering its domestic automobile companies. Invalidating the statute through application of the Commerce Clause is much more likely.

(C) is incorrect. The problem above does not concern a fundamental right. Therefore, the court would use a rational basis review. It is much more likely that the law would stand, because all the court would have to find is that banning foreign cars in state owned parking lots is rationally related to the legitimate state objective of fostering the domestic automobile companies.

(D) is incorrect. The Privileges and Immunities Clause of the Fourteenth Amendment only applies to certain particularly federal rights. Specifically, this provision prevents a state from depriving its citizens of the privileges and immunities of national or federal citizenship, which include: (1) the right to vote in federal elections, (2) the right to petition the federal government to address grievances, and (3) the right to travel interstate. The ordinance in the above problem does not violate any of these fundamental rights. Remember, banning a car from parking in state owned parking lots does not deny the owner of the foreign car from traveling interstate, as foreign cars are still allowed to park on the streets.

Question 41
Answer: A

This question tests the Property Clause of Section 3 of Article IV of the U.S. Constitution. Under the Property Clause, Congress may acquire, maintain, and eliminate the federal government's real and personal property. The Property Clause authorizes Congress to make any laws and regulations that are necessary to protect federal real and personal property, including wild animals.

The National Ecological Balance Act is simply a law that is necessary to protect federal property, specifically the wild animals. So, since the Act is constitutional, it supersedes Arkota's legislation because of the Supremacy Clause of the U.S. Constitution.

(B) is incorrect. The Necessary and Proper Clause would not apply here. The Necessary and Proper Clause applies to laws Congress must make to carry out enumerated powers in the U.S. Constitution.

(C) is incorrect. So long as a federal law is within constitutional bounds, the Supremacy Clause demands that it supersedes any state law in contravention of it. Hence, since it is established that it is within Congress' power to regulate federal property, including wild animals, the National Ecological Balance Act supersedes Arkota's Coyote Bounty Bill.

(D) is incorrect. The Full Faith and Credit Clause of the U.S. Constitution requires courts to recognize final decisions of courts of other states. The Full Faith and Credit Clause also requires that courts recognize official acts and records from other states. Hence, the Full Faith and Credit Clause does not apply in conflicts between the Federal and State governments.

Question 42
Answer: C

This question tests the Establishment Clause. The Establishment Clause of the U.S. Constitution prevents Congress from legislatively establishing or directly assisting a religion or religions in general. Under the Establishment Clause, the government may not promote or assist religion. Statutes that are neutral on their face will be examined by their purpose and effect. The purpose must be secular and the statute's effect cannot advance nor inhibit religion.

Revising a statute in order to make religious books exempt is effectively advancing religion. When the court examines Wonatol's statute, it will find that the purpose is raising revenue, which is secular and permissible. However, the court will find that the statute has the effect of assisting religion, making it invalid under the Establishment Clause.

(A) is incorrect. Magazine has standing because they can show a direct stake in the proceeding, as they are being taxed by this statute, while competitors may fall under the exception. Article III has merely been interpreted to say that a taxpayer usually does not have standing to challenge the government's expenditure of tax revenue.

(B) is incorrect. The Eleventh Amendment to the U.S. Constitution bars a plaintiff's standing in federal courts in a lawsuit seeking damages "against any one of the states by citizens of another state or by citizens or subjects of any foreign state." The Amendment has been extended to restrict a citizen of a state in terms of bringing a suit in a federal court against the citizen's state. However, this case has Magazine, an entity within Wonatol, suing in the proper state courts. So, the Eleventh Amendment is not applicable.

(D) is incorrect. Freedom of the press is not applicable here, as no conduct is being regulated or prohibited.

Question 43
Answer: D

This question tests the First and Fourteenth Amendment. Two of the freedoms protected by the First Amendment are freedom of speech and freedom of association. These freedoms are most commonly associated with political lobbying or demonstrations. Through the Fourteenth Amendment these freedoms have been extended to apply with respect to the states.

The clause in Kiowa's statute is basing acceptance of state money on waiving the First Amendment. Since fundamental rights are at issue in this case, the courts will examine the statute under strict scrutiny, making the possibility of the statute being declared invalid strongest.

(A) is incorrect. The fact that Kiowa is giving money to intrastate groups makes it difficult to constitute these groups as being or effecting interstate commerce, which is needed in order to be included under the Commerce Clause.

(B) is incorrect. The Contract Clause is used by the court to prohibit states from altering or modifying existing contracts. This case does not involve an existing contract that the state is attempting to alter.

(C) is incorrect. The Fifth Amendment provides that no person may be "deprived of life, liberty, or property, without due process of law." This provision applies to the conduct of the federal government. To extend this to the states, as is the case here, one would need to use the Fourteenth Amendment. Thus, the Fifth Amendment is inapplicable in this problem.

Question 44
Answer: A

This question tests structural limitations contained in U.S. Constitution. When the Supreme Court examines constitutional questions, they may use structural arguments. This means the Court examines if a statute violates the structure set up by the Constitution. Under Article III of the U.S. Constitution, Congress may determine the Supreme Court's appellate jurisdiction. The Supreme Court recognized that Article III allows Congress to expand or reduce appellate jurisdiction in *Ex Parte McCardle*. However, in *McCardle* Congress eliminated one particular avenue for appeal, habeas corpus. It is quite another matter when Congress attempts to eliminate all avenues for appellate review for a particular legal topic. This is because doing so seems to violate the structure of the Constitution, in that Congress is eliminating an entire area of constitutional law. The reason this argument is strong is because the Court's role is to interpret the Constitution. Therefore, the Court may determine that this statute interferes with the establishment of a supreme and uniform body of federal constitutional law and that violates the Constitution because Article III is not meant to be interpreted that broadly.

(B) is incorrect. Article III gives Congress the power to regulate the appellate jurisdiction of the Supreme Court. There is no limitation that specifies the cases may arise in federal courts.

(C) is incorrect. Article III gives Congress the power to alter the Supreme Court's appellate jurisdiction; a constitutional amendment is not needed.

(D) is incorrect. The Equal Protection Clause does not relate to the Supreme Court's appellate jurisdiction.

Question 45
Answer: A

This question tests the Supreme Court's appellate jurisdiction. Article III of the U.S. Constitution defines the Supreme Court's jurisdiction. Among the cases that the Court has appellate jurisdiction are cases involving a federal statute, treaty, or the U.S. Constitution.

In the above problem, the Blue Supreme Court interpreted a federal statute. Hence, the interpretation of the federal statute is at question in this case and the Supreme Court has appellate jurisdiction.

(B) is incorrect. The Blue Supreme Court clearly interpreted a federal statute, therefore the Supreme Court has jurisdiction.

(C) is incorrect. The Blue Supreme Court interpreted a federal statute to reach their decision. Therefore, the decision involves the interpretation of a federal statute and the Supreme Court has appellate jurisdiction.

(D) is incorrect. The Blue Supreme Court case is reviewable because the state court interpreted a federal statute to reach their decision. If a federal statute is in question, the Supreme Court has jurisdiction.

Question 46
Answer: B

This question tests the Thirteenth Amendment. The Thirteenth Amendment to the U.S. Constitution provides in part that: "Neither slavery nor involuntary servitude, except as a punishment for crime whereof the party shall have been duly convicted, shall exist within the United States, or any place subject to their jurisdiction." The Thirteenth Amendment further authorizes Congress to enact statutes that advance the purposes of the Thirteenth Amendment. Through case law, this Amendment has been expanded to uphold the Civil Rights Act of 1866, which includes private actors, and goes beyond the limited category of property rights.

The statute in this problem falls within the expansion of the Thirteenth Amendment. Since the Thirteenth Amendment has been interpreted to include private parties and multiple business transactions the statute would likely be upheld.

(A) is incorrect. The obligation to provide for the general welfare includes, at a minimum, federal entitlement programs. The General Welfare Clause is more often applied to federal expenditures and would not apply to such statutes.

(C) is incorrect. The transaction only has to be interstate commerce if the statute is being justified under the Commerce Clause. In this case the statute can be upheld through the Thirteenth Amendment and therefore does not need to regulate only interstate commerce.

(D) is incorrect. Preventing discrimination is not a traditional state power. Therefore, the statute does not violate state sovereignty as long as its purpose is to advance the Thirteenth Amendment.

Question 47

Answer: D

This question tests the First Amendment right to expression. The government is permitted to regulate expression in terms of time, manner, and place through content-neutral statutes, provided that the time, manner and place are reasonable. A court will apply the following version of the intermediate scrutiny test when reviewing such restrictions: (1) Does the content neutral restriction reasonably serve a significant governmental interest? (2) Is the restriction narrowly tailored to exclude other content? (3) Does the restriction allow for alternative channels to communicate the information?

The case at bar involves a prohibition by the National Park Service that advances a significant government interest, in that the government wants to protect and preserve the park. Second, the restriction prohibits every person from overnight camping and camp fires on Mt. Snow, not just the Friends of Lucifer. Third, the restriction is not prohibiting Friends of Lucifer from meeting on Mt. Snow, only from overnight camping and camp fires. Furthermore, the Friends of Lucifer would perhaps be permitted to perform their ritual in another area of the park. The foregoing analysis shows that the National Park Service restriction will likely be found to be valid.

(A) is incorrect. Under the Free Exercise Clause a rational basis level of scrutiny applies to determine the constitutionality of a broadly applicable law that incidentally affects religious conduct. Such a law will be valid if it applies to all persons and entities and does not target a particular religious group. The law in this case satisfies the rational basis standard.

(B) is incorrect. The facts do not show that the park purposely discriminated against Friends of Lucifer. The Park Service enforced a restriction that applies to everyone. Furthermore, the restriction enforced by the Park Service has been consistently enforced in the past on all park-goers.

(C) is incorrect. The Establishment Clause of the U.S. Constitution prevents Congress from legislatively establishing or directly assisting a religion or religions in general. Allowing religious ceremonies on federal land does not violate this Clause unless the government is only allowing certain religious groups to perform ceremonies and barring others from doing so.

Question 48
Answer: C

This question tests due process. In *Cleveland Board of Ed. v. Loudermill*, the Supreme Court held that terminating a tenured public employee requires that the employee receive a notice and an opportunity to be heard. Public employment constitutes a protected personal property right if an employee is only subject to termination "for cause" pursuant to a public employer's informal customs or policies, an employment manual and/or agreement, or a controlling statute.

Thus, in order to show that she was deprived of a personal property right without due process, Baker must show that she could only be terminated "for cause." To establish that she could only be fired "for cause," Baker must show that those terms are contained in a state statute or the employment procedures of her employer.

(A) is incorrect. The initial burden is on the plaintiff, in this case Baker, to show that she was deprived of a constitutionally protected right.

(B) is incorrect. The initial burden is on the plaintiff, in this case Baker, to show that she as deprived of a constitutionally protected right. The Green City Council only must demonstrate that Baker's termination was for good cause if Baker first shows that the city was indeed held to such a standard.

(D) is incorrect. To establish a protected personal property right, Baker must show that a state law or employment procedures created a standard that she could only be fired for cause. Baker's reasonable beliefs have nothing to do with whether she had a protected right under the U.S. Constitution.

Question 49
Answer: C

This question tests Executive powers. Article II of the U.S. Constitution defines the powers and responsibilities of the President of the United States. The President has broad authority to negotiate and sign executive agreements that are binding upon the United States when executed by a foreign nation's authorized leader and the President. An executive agreement is effective without ratification by Congress. An executive agreement cannot contravene or supersede federal law. Applying this power to the situation above, the President's action are constitutional because he has entered into an executive agreement with Ruritania and the agreement does not contravene or supersede a federal law.

(A) is incorrect. The power of the President to conduct foreign affairs does not authorize the president to do whatever action he or she deems necessary. There are certain limitations on this power, such as that an executive agreement cannot supersede or contravene a federal law.

(B) is incorrect. The President's power to appoint ambassadors is not the power that authorizes him to make the executive agreement illustrated in this problem. The power to make executive agreements is derived from the power of the President to negotiate with foreign nations.

(D) is incorrect. The duty of the President to execute faithfully the laws only means that the executive branch must execute federal laws. The duty does not give the President power to settle disputes between the federal and state governments and is inapplicable to this situation.

Question 50
Answer: C

This question tests Congress' spending power. Congress is constitutionally authorized to decide the amount and scope of federal fiscal appropriations and expenditures of tax revenues. The Spending Clause of Article I of the U.S. Constitution states in part that "The Congress shall have Power...to pay the Debts and provide for the common Defence and general Welfare of the United States." Courts apply a rational basis standard of review to congressional expenditures.

A court applying this standard of review to a federal spending statute inquires if: (1) A contested expenditure statute is reasonably related to the general welfare? (2) It states **concrete objectives**? and (3) It provides adequate **administrative criteria**?

Congress' spending in the above problem satisfies all of the rational basis criteria. First, basic research is rationally related to the general welfare of society because it helps develop new technology and discover a variety of things helpful to society. Second, the statute provides concrete objectives, in that it will distribute the research money to the top 10 best universities as voted on by all university presidents. Finally, the statute provides adequate administrative criteria by listing the accepted standards of academic quality upon which the presidents of each university are to base their vote.

(A) is incorrect. The statute provides a list of the administrative criteria and distributes the poll to university presidents who are presumed be in the best position to apply the criteria. Thus, the rational basis test is satisfied and the statute is likely valid.

(B) is incorrect. Congressional expenditures only must pass the rational basis test. Since this expenditure is certainly rationally related to the general welfare of society, it will be held constitutional.

(D) is incorrect. Congressional spending does not fall under the category of political questions, which the courts will not decide. Instead, the courts have applied a rational basis test to determine if congressional spending is constitutional.

Question 51
Answer: C

This question tests the Supremacy and Commerce Clause. Article II sets forth the Supremacy Clause, which makes the U.S. Constitution, federal law, and treaties the "supreme law of the land." The Commerce Clause grants Congress plenary power to regulate international and interstate activity, such as transportation and travel, of both a commercial and non-commercial nature. In the above case, the federal government is able to issue fishing permits, because fishing is likely interstate commerce. Moreover, if Fisher, Inc. is operating in multiple states, the company falls under the Commerce Clause. Thus, it is established that through the Commerce Clause the federal government may issue fishing and transportation licenses. Furthermore, because of the Supremacy Clause, Atlantica's law is superseded by federal law. Thus, Fisher, Inc. has a right to fish for oysters in Atlantica.

(A) is incorrect. First, all fishing in Atlantica may not fall under the Commerce Clause. Second, a reasonable fee for a fishing license will not likely cause an undue burden on interstate commerce.

(B) is incorrect. The courts examine a situation where out-of-state residents are barred completely from obtaining a license differently from a situation where a fee for a license is higher. In cases where an out-of-state entity is barred from obtaining a license a stricter standard is applied than if the out-of-state entity is charged a higher fee. If the out-of-state entity is charged a higher fee, as is the case here, the Privileges and Immunities Clause protects non-citizens of states from discrimination only with respect to essential activities and basic rights. Thus, charging a higher fee to obtain a license for fishing for oysters does not violate the Privileges and Immunities Clause.

(D) is incorrect. The expiration of Fisher, Inc's permit is not a taking of property, as the permit has a one-year expiration date. Thus, Fisher, Inc. was aware of the permit's expiration date, and no constitutional due process violation occurred.

Question 52
Answer: D

The problem tests the Supremacy Clause of Article VI of the U.S. Constitution. Under the Supremacy Clause, the federal government is immune from direct taxation by any state government. In *Van Brocklin v. Anderson*, the Supreme Court ruled that federal property is immune from local and state property taxes. However, in some cases the courts have found that states may tax lessees of federally owned buildings.

Regardless, Concessionaire can argue that the federal statute, which enables such concessions, states that they will be charged a nominal fee to rent the federally owned space. Thus, this statute supersedes the New Senora's tax statute.

(A) is incorrect. A state occupancy tax is unlikely to unduly burden interstate commerce. Furthermore, it is not certain that taxing Concessionaire would burden tourist trade at all.

(B) is incorrect. The occupancy tax is a tax on all owners of property that is not taxable. Thus, citizens and non-citizens can be equally impacted and the Privileges and Immunities Clause is not violated.

(C) is incorrect. The occupancy tax does not violate the Equal Protection Clause. The tax is rationally related to the government purpose of equalizing state tax burden, meaning it satisfies the rational basis standard of equal protection.

Question 53
Answer: A

This question tests the concept of "cases or controversies". The Supreme Court's construction of Article III of the U.S. Constitution provides for the adjudication of "cases or controversies" only. To ensure that there is a case or controversy, the parties must have proper standing. In order for a plaintiff to possess standing to bring a civil action, the party must possess a significant stake in the proceeding and its outcome. The elements include: (1) Injury in Fact: Evidence of a threat of imminent injury or evidence that a party suffered an actual injury in fact; (2) Causation: Evidence that the other part(ies) caused the injury; and (3) Redressability: A court is capable of affording relief to a party (through judicial relief).

The problem with the situation above is that the second element to determine standing is not satisfied. Candidate brought the action against the chairman of his political party. The chairman is not causing the injury to Candidate. The possible injury to Candidate is that he will not be able to run for mayor because of the five-year citizen rule. Thus, election officials, or possibly the legislators who enacted the residency ordinance, are causing Candidate's injury. Therefore, the chairman is not causing the injury, meaning that Candidate lacks standing.

(B) is incorrect. Candidate is challenging the ordinance on constitutional grounds. Therefore, the federal court has jurisdiction.

(C) is incorrect. The court cannot issue a judgment on this issue because Candidate lacks standing.

(D) is incorrect. The court cannot issue a judgment on this issue because Candidate lacks standing.

Question 54
Answer: D

This question tests the standards of review in equal protection cases. Gender is quasi-suspect type of classification. Laws containing gender classifications are usually subject to a heightened or intermediate scrutiny level of judicial review. Under that standard, a court will inquire if a contested law is substantially related to achieving an important government interest. The government possesses the burden of proving the law's validity under this test. Since a gender classification is being challenged in the case above, the school will have the burden of demonstrating that the admission policy is substantially related to an important governmental interest.

Choices (A) and (B) are incorrect. When reviewing gender classifications in equal protection cases the government, in this case the school, has the burden of proving the law's validity under the intermediate scrutiny test.

Choice (C) is incorrect. Gender classifications are reviewed under an intermediate standard. Thus, the policy must be substantially related to an important government interest.

Question 55
Answer: C

This question tests the right to abortion. For substantive due process purposes, a woman possesses a fundamental right to an abortion before fetal viability. A state cannot impose restrictions that are substantial obstacles to the exercise of that right. When a state statute does not unduly burden a woman's right to an abortion, a court will apply a rational basis analysis to adjudicate the statute's constitutionality. A state is not obligated to provide funding so that a woman may exercise the right to an abortion. The state has a legitimate interest in encouraging childbirth provided it does not go beyond encouragement and create an undue burden on a woman's right to an abortion. Here, we have a atate attempting to encourage childbirth by not allowing abortions to be performed in state owned and operated facilities, except under limited circumstances. Since the state of Wasminia is not obliged to fund a woman's abortion, generally the state may prohibit the procedure in state owned and operated facilities. Since this is the only action the state has taken in encouraging childbirth, the state has not unduly burdened Citizen's right to an abortion. Hence, the court would use rational basis review to analyze the statute and likely uphold it.

(A) is incorrect. States are not required to fund abortions. Therefore, state-owned or operated facilities may prohibit the procedure and it will not be considered an undue burden.

(B) is incorrect. States are not required to fund abortions. Therefore, they are legally permitted to prohibit the procedure in state owned or operated facilities. The absence of state funding has been found to not be an undue burden on the right to abortion.

(D) is incorrect. The use of state owned or operated facilities is not considered a privilege that can be conditioned on any basis. The reason that state owned or operated facilities may prohibit the performance of abortions is because they are not legally required to fund abortions.

Question 56
Answer: C

This question tests the Equal Protection Clause and the Supremacy Clause. First, if an alleged violation of the Equal Protection Clause does not involve a fundamental right, or a suspect or quasi-suspect classification, then the level of judicial review is rational basis analysis. Under the rational basis standard of review, a court will inquire if a contested law is rationally related to achieving a legitimate or conceivable government interest. Article II sets forth the Supremacy Clause, which makes the U.S. Constitution, federal law, and treaties the "supreme law of the land." This simply means that federal law trumps state law.

The instant problem deals with a non-fundamental right. The right to seek employment is treated with a higher standard only if the state law in question treats non-state citizens differently from state citizens. Since this problem does not have a law that makes such a classification, the right to seek employment is not fundamental, meaning the court would use a rational basis analysis. Thus, the stricter licensing requirements must be reasonably related to a legitimate public interest. The public interest in this case is the public's safety, which will likely be legitimate, while stricter licensing requirements are more than likely related to this interest. Finally, the state law is not inconsistent with the federal law because the federal government does not license radon testers; it only advises the nation on who they feel are accurate testers. Thus, the Magenta's statute does not violate the Supremacy Clause.

(A) is incorrect. The Full Faith and Credit Clause only applies between states, it does not relate to state and federal government. Therefore, the Full Faith and Credit Clause is inapplicable in this situation.

(B) is incorrect. The Supremacy Clause requires Magenta to follow federal law. However, Magenta's statute is not inconsistent with any federal law, because no federal law exists that licenses radon testers.

(D) is incorrect. This problem falls under the Equal Protection Clause, not the Commerce Clause, so there is not a requirement that radon testing must be interstate commerce.

Question 57
Answer: C

This question tests ripeness. Ripeness is a requirement that a party litigant must have experienced an actual harm, or been subject to an imminent threat of harm, in order for a civil legal proceeding to occur. This doctrine seeks to prevent the bringing of a civil action before it is appropriate for the action to be heard by a court. In the case at bar, Economy Electric has not suffered an actual harm nor is it subject to an imminent threat of harm. As of now, Economy Electric was approved for a rate increase and has no need to increase rates now or in the near future. Since Economy Electric is not demanding a rate increase now, and cannot pinpoint an exact date when it would need but be prohibited from increasing rates, the action is not ripe. Thus, the court would dismiss the complaint.

(A) is incorrect. The court would dismiss the case before examining the statute's constitutionality, because the action is not ripe for decision.

(B) is incorrect. The court would dismiss the case before examining the statute's constitutionality, because the action is not ripe for decision.

(D) is incorrect. Because the statute's constitutionality is being challenged, the federal courts have jurisdiction. However, this case would be dismissed, because the action is not ripe for decision.

Question 58
Answer: B

This question tests the First Amendment. The First Amendment generally preserves the freedom of expression and association. As a general rule, a person's exercise of expressive or association rights may not be a basis for denying the individual a job, a license (e.g., to practice law), or another public benefit such as employment.

In this case, Clerk was denied the right to public employment because he exercised his right to expression by making the comments about the Governor. To be able to fire Clerk for his comments, the state would have to show that the views he expressed negatively relate to his job performance. His job requirements do not involve him dealing with or advising the public, so his political views do not have a bearing on his job performance.

(A) is incorrect. Employment is not considered private real property. Thus, Clerk's termination does not constitute a taking.

(C) is incorrect. The state's interest in loyal and supportive employees is outweighed by an employee's right to free speech in most instances. The state cannot terminate an employee because of the employee's political views when the employee's job does not relate to his or her political opinions.

(D) is incorrect. Public employment is a privilege. However, a public employee cannot be denied employment solely because of their exercise of freedom of expression.

Question 59
Answer: B

This question tests the First Amendment. A government's legal restrictions on the time, place, and manner, of expression in any type of public forum must, at a minimum, be reasonable and content neutral. The Supreme Court in *City of Renton v. Playtime Theatres, Inc.,* concluded that: "'Content-neutral' time, place, and manner regulations are acceptable so long as they are designed to serve a substantial governmental interest and do not unreasonably limit alternative avenues of communication." The Supreme Court upheld a zoning ordinance that prohibited adult motion picture theaters from locating within 1,000 feet of certain non-commercially zoned property. The ordinance furthered the city's interest in preventing the adverse secondary effects of adult theaters on the surrounding community, rather than regulating the adult film's content. The Supreme Court did not use another standard of review because the ordinance neither banned freedom of expression nor outlawed adult entertainment.

In this problem we have an almost identical situation to the case mentioned above. Maple City has a substantial interest in preventing adverse secondary effects on the community, while the zoning restriction still allows for adult entertainment in other areas of Maple City. Thus, Maple City's ordinance satisfies the Supreme Court's test and is constitutional.

(A) is incorrect. First, the zoning restriction must be content-neutral meaning it cannot state a specific business it intends to prohibit. Second, the state's interest is preventing adverse secondary effects on the surrounding community. The businesses message should be of no concern to the state, only what effect the business's operations will have on the community. Finally, the city must not unreasonably limit alternative avenues of communication, meaning the city cannot completely ban a business.

(C) is incorrect. The state has a substantial interest in preventing adverse secondary effects of adult entertainment on the surrounding community. This interest outweighs the adult business owner's interests provided the state does not unreasonably limit other avenues of communication.

(D) is incorrect. The opposite is true. A city has a substantial interest in preventing the adverse effects of the adult entertainment industry on the community by zoning, rather than regulating the adult material's content.

Question 60

Answer: A

This problem tests the Equal Protection Clause. The Fourteenth Amendment includes the Equal Protection Clause, which provides in part that: "No State shall…deny to any person within its jurisdiction the equal protection of the laws." The Supreme Court construes the Fourteenth Amendment as requiring that all laws treat similarly situated people in the same manner. If such people do not receive equal treatment either under the laws or from a government, then a violation of their equal protection right might have occurred. In other words, a government's regulation or conduct might have interfered with or infringed upon those persons' right to equal protection. In the above case, Blue County's tax system does not provide equal treatment to similarly situated people. The fact that Owner must pay 200 to 300 percent higher taxes than other county residents with similar homes in similar neighborhoods violates the Equal Protection Clause. Furthermore, Blue County has no legitimate interest in this tax system, other than to raise revenue, which does not justify the current unequal property tax system.

(B) is incorrect. Blue County property tax is not based on a classification of non-county citizens and county citizens nor is there a federal property tax system. Therefore, the Privileges and Immunities Clause does not apply.

(C) is incorrect. A property tax is not considered a taking of private real property for public use.

(D) is incorrect. The ex post facto law prohibition prevents the federal and state governments from punishing people for conduct that was lawful when it occurred and before a federal or state law subsequently rendered that conduct unlawful. In this case we have no such situation as no one is being punished for past lawful conduct.

Question 61
Answer: A

This question tests burdens on interstate commerce.

When a statute in question treats out-of-state individuals or entities differently than those intrastate, one of two issues is likely being tested: the Commerce Clause or Privileges and Immunities Clause. A state statute places an undue burden on interstate commerce when it treats interstate commerce more adversely than intrastate commerce. This may be in the form of imposing increased regulations or obligations on out-of-state individuals or entities. In this question, there are no increased regulatory obligations on out-of-state barbers—there is a flat ban on them. This is a state law that discriminates against out-of-state individuals. Such laws are unconstitutional burdens on interstate commerce.

Choice (B) is incorrect. While this may very well be a question of privileges and immunities, it is not a question testing the Fourteenth Amendment Privileges and Immunities Clause, which concerns the right to vote, travel interstate, etc. Those privileges and immunities are different from the Article IV Privileges and Immunities that guarantee equal treatment of citizens and non-citizens in such areas as employment and access to state courts. This question presents an Article IV Privileges and Immunities Problem.

Choice (C) is incorrect. A statute that burdens interstate commerce can never be founded on the principle of economic protectionism.

Choice (D) is incorrect. Barbering is actually a non-fundamental right sometimes protected under Article IV privileges and immunities. It is the right to practice one's trade of choice.

Question 62
Answer: D

This question tests the law of equal protection under the laws.

The discriminatory scheme present in this question is a line drawn between those who are American citizens and those who are not. Whenever there is a line drawn which treats two groups of people differently, it is likely to be an equal protection question. Note that this question is not raising a privileges and immunities issue because it does not concern different treatment between in-state and out-of-state citizens. This concerns national citizenship.

Choice (A) is incorrect. This justification would not pass even rational basis scrutiny.

Choice (B) is incorrect. This question does not concern the state's police power because the statute is not aimed at safety, welfare, morals, etc.

Choice (C) is incorrect. This licensing requirement is not a bill of attainder.

Choice (D) is correct. There is a line drawn in this regulatory scheme on the basis of alienage. Alienage classifications are subjected to different levels of equal protection scrutiny depending on where the line-drawing originates. Federal alienage classifications are subject to rational basis review. State alienage classifications are subject to strict scrutiny. Since this is a state statute, there must be a compelling state interest behind the discrimination against aliens, and the employed scheme must be the least restrictive means available to achieve that interest. In this question, there is no compelling state interest in requiring that barbers be American citizens. Further, in *In re Griffiths*, the Supreme Court found that a state law banning aliens from the practice of law did not satisfy strict scrutiny. If aliens were entitled to be lawyers, then why not allow them to be barbers?

Question 63
Answer: D

This question tests federal court jurisdiction.

Federal courts have, via Article III, proper jurisdiction in cases where there is diversity of citizenship or in cases where a federal question is presented. This problem presents a federal question because it concerns the Federal Constitution and its provisions concerning the equal protection of the laws.

Choice (A) is wrong. It is true that there is no diversity of citizenship here, but that does not mean that the suit would be dismissed because it could still be a case presenting a federal question.

Choice (B) is wrong. The abstention doctrine is any one of several alternative doctrines that a federal court may invoke as its reason for refusing to hear a case otherwise properly before it. This is done when hearing the case would potentially intrude upon the powers of state courts. In this question, there is no indication that hearing this case would infringe the powers of the state of Aurora's courts.

Choice (C) is wrong. This is not a controversy between two states.

Question 64
Answer: C

This question tests the law of equal protection.

Generally, a residency requirement will be examined using the concept of privileges and immunities or the concept of equal protection. In this question, there is a line drawn which treats those longer-term residents differently than shorter-term residents.

Choice (A) is wrong. The Privileges and Immunities Clause that would be pertinent to this question is not in the Fourteenth Amendment. Rather, it is the Article IV Privileges and Immunities Clause.

Choice (B) is wrong. This is not a due process inquiry. Were the question addressing the revocation of a license, due process would come into play.

Choice (C) is correct. This is a case of governmental line-drawing which treats similarly situated groups differently.

Choice (D) is wrong. While there could theoretically be some ill effects to ongoing contracts in the state of Aurora, the Obligation of Contracts Clause is not the strongest argument presented.

Question 65
Answer: D

This question tests the Obligation of Contracts Clause.

No State shall pass any law impairing the obligation of contracts. This is generally how the Clause reads. This means that the U.S. Constitution limits the ability of local and state governments to alter or modify, for example, private contracts and public charters. This question presents a situation in which the legislation does precisely that—it renders the existing contract invalid. This is a violation of the Obligation of Contracts Clause.

Question 66

Answer: C

This question tests the area of government spending.

When the government is providing funds to certain groups or entities, it is entitled to attach conditions to the receipt of that funding. Congress holds the purse strings. The federal government may make any expenditure as long as doing so does not violate express constitutional prohibitions. A condition placed on the receipt of federal funding need only pass rational basis scrutiny in order to be upheld. The statute must be reasonable related to the general welfare. It must state concrete objectives, and it must provide adequate administrative criteria. This lessened scrutiny makes these general welfare provisions very hard to invalidate. Thus, the General Welfare Clause would be the strongest argument for the enactment of the statute in question.

Question 67
Answer: D

This question tests the concept of separation of powers.

The Congress in this question may, under the Necessary and Proper Clause, hold hearings and investigations into the conduct of government officials. But the federal statute in the question authorizes only the Attorney General to prosecute those persons when they are in contempt of Congress. The power to prosecute is exclusively a police power—a power delegated to the executive branch—and not the legislature. Therefore, the power to prosecute rests solely in the hands of the Attorney General, who cannot be compelled to prosecute by the legislative branch.

Question 68
Answer: A

This question tests the investigation powers of Congress.

Under the Necessary and Proper Clause, Congress is empowered to conduct investigations of other branches of government if the purpose and scope of the investigation is relevant to the legislative function of Congress. In this question, the conduct of the ambassador may or may not be related to any matter upon which Congress may legislate. If the matter is unrelated, then Congress has no power to investigate that matter, and Green does not have to answer those questions. This is a valid constitutional defense.

Question 69
Answer: D

This question tests the concept of state action.

In this question, the state of New Atlantic provides free secular textbooks to students in public and private schools. This is conferring a benefit on all schools. By doing so, however, the government is indirectly encouraging the admissions practices of Little White School—a school that obviously engages in racial discrimination. By providing books to the segregationist school, the government can be held legally accountable for that segregation. Thus, the best answer is (D).

Choice (A) is wrong. The distribution of textbooks does serve a legitimate educational function.

Choice (B) is wrong. The states are not forbidden to provide aid to public or private schools. The states simply cannot do so in a way that violates constitutional provisions, such as the Establishment Clause.

Choice (C) is wrong. The U.S. Constitution is a check on the powers and practices of the state and federal governments. It is not a limitation on the rights of private individuals or entities.

Question 70
Answer: C

This question tests the Establishment Clause.

Where a state law is passed that is sect-neutral or grants no preference to religion on its face, it must be examined using the test from *Agostini v. Felton*. The statute must, first, have a secular purpose. This statute does have a secular purpose. It is providing textbooks on secular subjects to all schools. The purpose is promotion of education. The statute must also have a primary effect which neither enhances nor inhibits religion. To determine if the statue does promote or inhibit religion, the test is to determine whether or not the statute fosters excessive entanglement between the state and the church.

In this question, the best way to argue for the constitutionality of the state law is to show that it passes the test in *Agostini*. The purpose and effect of the law is secular and does not entangle the state and religion. Choice (D) is incorrect because it is an argument founded on the Free Exercise Clause. This is an Establishment Clause question.

Question 71
Answer: B

This question tests the concept of due process.

Due process is essentially a guarantee that a person will not be deprived of his life, liberty, or property without due process of the law (e.g., notice and a hearing, etc.). As a general rule, tenured public employees are entitled to receive notice and an opportunity to be heard when they are faced with job termination. In this question, Barnes is not tenured. It may be argued that he has no entitlement or vested property interest that would entitle him to notice or a hearing. His employment contract does not create such an interest. Therefore, he must try to establish that he did have an interest based on the conduct of the employer. Choice (B) is the only option that presents conduct of another party that might establish a vested property right for Barnes. Choice (D), for example, is based on Barnes' own expectations.

Question 72
Answer: C

This question tests the concept of due process.

The tenure scheme established in the state in question requires that an employee work for five years before being eligible for tenure. Tenure is that classification which grants the public employee a vested property interest or entitlement in his job. Generally, only when tenured is the employee entitled to due process before termination of his property interest in employment. The best argument for the state college is that no due process was required for Barnes because of his short duration of employment with the school. There was no property interest, after three years, of which he could be deprived.

Question 73
Answer: B

This question tests the powers of Congress.

Under the Property Clause, Congress may acquire, maintain, and eliminate the federal government's real and personal property. The Property Clause also authorizes Congress to make any laws and regulations that are necessary to protect federal real and personal property. This includes wild animals.

Question 74
Answer: C

This question tests government regulation of business activity.

Choice (A) is wrong. There is no party alleging that life, liberty, or a property right is being deprived without due process of law. This is not a good challenge to the enacted statute.

Choice (B) is wrong. While a weak equal protection argument could be made in this instance, because discrimination between businesses is occurring on the basis of annual sales figures, the discrimination is not based on a category that receives any special scrutiny. It must only pass rational basis scrutiny. Therefore, this is not the strongest argument to be made.

Choice (C) is correct. The statute in this question creates a situation in which an entity is limited in its ability to engage in trade and commerce. Forcing businesses to spend in the state of Onondaga will likely create an undue burden on interstate commerce because it will impose different burdens on in-state and out-of-state entities. This kind of economic regulation, when imposed by a state, is impermissible.

Choice (D) is wrong. The Privileges and Immunities Clause of the Fourteenth Amendment only applies to certain particular federal rights. Specifically, the Clause prevents a state from depriving its citizens of the privileges and immunities of national or federal citizenship. The right of a business to spend its money in one state or another is not one of these federal rights.

Question 75
Answer: D

This question tests the concept of separation of powers and delegation of those powers.

Under the Appointment Clause in Article II of the U.S. Constitution, the President is given the power to appoint federal officials. Congress may authorize the federal judiciary, the President, and Cabinet members, to appoint other "inferior officers" for lower federal positions. Congress may not, however, provide the power of appointment to itself. Congress has *no* powers of appointment. Therefore, any congressional acts that purport to authorize or govern appointments by Congress are invalid.

Question 76
Answer: A

This question tests the concept of separation of powers.

Choice (B) is incorrect. Congress can constitutionally delegate away some of its rule-making powers. The Commission in the question was delegated some of that authority.

Choice (C) is incorrect. The makeup of the Commission is not reason enough to forbid that the Commission exercise those powers that were constitutionally and permissibly delegated to it. It may continue with its investigatory function with no problem.

Choice (D) is incorrect. The advice and consent of the Senate is needed for appointments of ambassadors, higher-level federal officials, and members of the federal judiciary. The members appointed here are not among those which require the Senate's advice and consent.

Choice (A) is correct. Investigation and recommendation are two powers and duties of the Commission that can continue without running into a power struggle between the branches of government.

Question 77
Answer: D

This question tests the difference between Article III judiciary members and Article I tribunal members.

An Article III judge is appointed by the President for a lifetime tenure with a guarantee of no decrease in salary. Article I authorizes Congress to create legislative courts that operate like those courts employed by administrative agencies. The purpose of the tribunals is oversight and recommendation. The Article I tribunal members do not enjoy a guarantee of lifetime tenure and freedom from salary cuts. In this question, Hobson was appointed to an Article I tribunal. He was not an appointed member of the judiciary pursuant to Article III.

Question 78
Answer: A

This question tests the concept of federalism and the Tenth Amendment.

Under the Tenth Amendment, a state has the power to regulate the activities of its own separate branches of government and to do so free of interference by the federal government. This is an element of state sovereignty retained under the Tenth Amendment. Because Kane is claiming that the wrongful acts were committed in the course of legislative business, this brings those wrongful acts under the state's jurisdiction and out of the jurisdiction of the federal regulations. The state, under Tenth Amendment sovereignty, must be allowed to govern its own legislators in the context of official duties.

Choice (B) is wrong. The wrongful acts in the question were likely not occurrences that would even fall under the speech and debate exception.

Choice (C) is wrong. A federal court does not have to follow state law respecting the scope of legislative immunity. The Supremacy Clause may step in to elevate federal law over the state law where the state law is in conflict with constitutional principles.

Choice (D) is wrong. There is no indication that application of the Federal Securities Act to state legislators would violate the Due Process Clause. The answer is too broad. Outside the scope of their official duties, the state legislators are subject to the Act just like every other individual.

Question 79
Answer: C

This question tests state sovereignty.

As mentioned in the previous question's explanation, a state has the power to regulate the activities of its own separate branches of government and to do so free of interference by the federal government. The best argument for the federal government, to uphold the prosecution, would be that it poses no interference to the state's power to govern and regulate its own branches of government.

Question 80
Answer: C

This question tests the doctrine of vagueness.

The doctrine of vagueness is implicated when a law that prohibits speech does not clearly define conduct so that a reasonable person could not ascertain what speech is allowed and what speech is banned. In this question, the statute is very vague in defining what speech is prohibited. Therefore, Smith cannot be punished under this statute, and choice (A) is wrong. This does not mean, however, that the state cannot punish the type of speech in which Smith had engaged. Therefore, choice (B) is wrong, and choice (C) is correct. Choice (D) is wrong. The average user of a public street may very well find that the words were not annoying. But the reason that the conviction will fail lies in the statute itself. It is too vague.

Question 81
Answer: D

This question tests the regulatory authority of Congress.

The right to marry is a fundamental right, but it is subject to some regulation by the states. Marriage regulations are left to the states and the states' police power. Regulation of marriage by the federal government will upset the balance between the state and federal governments. However, such a regulation would likely pass constitutional scrutiny if it were only applicable to the District of Columbia. Congress has the authority to regulate the territory of the United States, including the District of Columbia. This grants Congress sovereign authority in the District of Columbia. In that respect, Congress possesses the same police powers as a state legislature to regulate the District.

Question 82
Answer: B

This question tests the concept of standing.

In order for a party to bring suit, the party must possess a significant stake in the proceeding and its outcome. Generally, standing requires (1) that the party has suffered an injury in fact or is threatened with imminent injury, (2) the injury is caused by the other party, and (3) a court is able to give judicial relief to the injured party. In this question, the party with the most concrete injury or imminent injury is the party in answer (B).

Choice (A) is wrong. Taxpayer standing is a difficult type of standing to establish. Generally, an individual taxpayer lacks constitutional standing to challenge a federal expenditure. The taxpayer may only obtain standing to challenge a specific federal expenditure on the basis that the expenditure exceeds a certain limitation that the U.S. Constitution places on federal expenditures. There is no indication that this particular expenditure is one prohibited by the U.S. Constitution.

Choice (C) is wrong. The injury to the user of the highway is merely speculative at this point.

Choice (D) is wrong. Standing for an organization to challenge this expenditure would only exist if, individually, its members would have standing to bring such suit on their own. Again, the injury is still speculative to this point if a claim is made in any capacity outside being a taxpayer. And if standing of a taxpayer is sought, it will fail because the expenditure is not one in violation of constitutional provisions.

Question 83
Answer: C

This question tests the standard of review for federal expenditures.

Courts apply a rational basis standard of review to congressional expenditures. The courts determine if is it reasonable to conclude that the expenditure at issue will benefit or protect the public. (1) A contested expenditure statute must be reasonably related to the general welfare. (2) It must state concrete objectives, and (3) It must provide adequate administrative criteria. Therefore, the correct answer will be one that uses the language of the rational basis standard of review. This is choice (C). The Congress must have reasonably believed that the speed limit regulation would assure that the federal monies would result in benefits to the public.

Choice (A) is wrong. While accepting a federal grant to finance highways will subject the state to the authority of the federal government in some instances, it does not mean that all power over the highways has been ceded to the federal government.

Choice (B) is wrong. The federal government cannot regulate the use of state highways without limitation because that is contrary to the principles of federalism.

Choice (D) is wrong. Public opinion surveys are irrelevant. Congress is not bound by public opinion surveys, though the Congress is free to base its legislation on them.

Question 84
Answer: D

This question tests the justifications for federal expenditures.

Conditional expenditures are constitutional where the Congress makes such expenditures by means of its spending power. This does not mean that spending power is the only justification for such a statute. The Congress also has fairly broad power to regulate commerce. The Commerce Clause grants Congress plenary power to regulate interstate activity, such as transportation and travel. That authority extends to include channels or facilities of interstate commerce such as roads and highways.

Question 85
Answer: B

This question tests the constitutionality of restrictions on expressive conduct.

Choice (A) is wrong. A licensing requirement is a prior restraint on speech, but it is not always unconstitutional. As long as the criteria for licenses is content neutral and the licensing party is not granted any discretionary authority, the license requirement will not be an impermissible prior restraint.

Choice (B) is correct. Regulations on expressive conduct cannot be overbroad or unduly vague. They must be stated in terms clear enough that a reasonable person would be able to tell if his conduct was permitted or prohibited.

Choice (C) is wrong. While it is probably a good idea to make sure that the police force is not the final arbiter as to whether or not a gathering may be lawfully held, they are permitted to make a decision, provided that it is content neutral and not dependent on their discretion.

Choice (D) is wrong. While the First and Fourteenth Amendments do guarantee the right of association, like most other rights, it is not an absolute right. It is subject to regulation.

Question 86
Answer: D

This question tests the law of Fourth Amendment searches.

Because consent is a waiver of the Fourth Amendment right of privacy, only an individual who has that right of privacy may consent to the search. This right of privacy is not dependent on ownership, however. This means that the landlord, although the true owner of the apartment, does not have a privacy interest in that apartment. Thus, the landlord in this question had no right to consent to the search. This means that the search was not a waiver of the defendant's Fourth Amendment rights. The landlord's only authority of entry was for repair purposes. The landlord was not permitted, because of the privacy rights of the tenant, to allow the police to enter.

Question 87
Answer: B

This question tests the concept of standing.

In order for a defendant to challenge evidence as the fruit of an illegal search, the evidence must have been gathered in violation of the defendant's constitutional rights. As a general rule, though, the party making the challenge must also possess a significant stake in the proceeding and its outcome. Generally, standing requires (1) that the party has suffered an injury in fact or is threatened with imminent injury, (2) the injury is caused by the other party, and (3) a court is able to give judicial relief to the injured party. In this question, the defendant suffered an injury—an illegal search. The injury was caused by the state. And a court can grant him judicial relief by excluding the evidence obtained in that illegal search. The defendant has a property interest in his apartment even though he is now in custody.

Choice (A) is wrong. The fact that the items seized may be incriminating is not important. The crucial fact is the manner in which those items were seized. This is what may preclude them from being used as evidence against the defendant.

Choice (C) is wrong. The fact that the landlord consented to the search without being authorized to give such consent is actually a factor that helps grant the defendant standing.

Choice (D) is wrong. The defendant still has a property interest in his apartment when he is not present there.

Question 88
Answer: B

This question tests congressional spending powers.

Congress is constitutionally authorized to decide the amount and scope of federal appropriations and expenditures of revenues. Congress must enact legislation to authorize funding by means of appropriations. Congress may establish various funding levels of the appropriations that are different from those desired by the President. Although the President may decide to veto an appropriations bill, Congress may override that veto to effectuate different appropriations than those that the President had proposed.

Choice (A) is wrong. Passage of an appropriations bill over the President's veto does not necessarily mean that the spending will, in fact, occur.

Choice (C) is wrong. While the President's enumerated powers do tend to lend themselves towards the area of treaties and foreign relations, he does have implied powers, especially through his veto power, to affect congressional spending.

Choice (D) is wrong. Again, the President's veto power can cause the withholding of funds in areas other than foreign affairs if the veto is not subsequently overridden by the Congress.

Question 89
Answer: D

This question tests the concept of equal protection under the laws.

Exam issues involving fundamental rights, such as the right to vote, are often addressed in the context of equal protection, because they often involve laws classifying individuals. In this question, the law has classified potential voters into two groups—those who are literate and those who are not. The illiterate population is then denied this fundamental right to vote. A reviewing court will apply strict scrutiny to any challenged law that limits that right (except with regard to voter age, residency, and citizenship).

Choice (A) is wrong. The law in question still provides that the People of the states are those who will vote to elect Congress members. It simply provides that only those People who are literate may do so.

Choice (B) is wrong. Congress does have the power to make or alter state regulations concerning the time and manner of elections. This state law, however, does not violate that constitutional provision. The provision is the tool that Congress may use to change state laws that conflict with federal constitutional principles.

Choice (C) is wrong. The question is alleging unequal treatment of two groups of individuals. It does not present a situation in which the fundamental right to vote is being denied without any due process being given to the deprived group of people.

Question 90
Answer: C

This question tests the "one man, one vote" principle.

The one person, one vote principle may not apply in certain circumstances such as when a state elects certain functionaries whose duties are so far removed from normal governmental activities and so disproportionately affect different groups that the principle should not apply. The Supreme Court has specifically held that a water storage district, by reason of its special limited purpose and of the disproportionate effect of its activities on landowners as a group, is an exception to the rule. The same analysis will apply to this watershed improvement district election.

Question 91
Answer: B

This question tests the Supremacy Clause.

If a state law treats its citizens differently than non-citizens for the purposes of seeking employment or receiving contracts, the state must provide a substantial reason for the different treatment that the in-state and out-of-state workers receive. Otherwise, the statute cannot be upheld as constitutionally valid. In this question, however, the reader is told to examine the constitutionality of the statute under the Supremacy Clause. This means that the law is to be examined for direct conflict with constitutional provisions related to the subject matter of the particular law. The only answer choice which presents a constitutional provision is answer choice (B).

Question 92
Answer: A

This question tests the Commerce Clause.

A state law that regulates interstate commerce generally is subjected to rational basis review. The law will be upheld if it (1) serves a legitimate state objective, (2) is rationally related to that objective, and (3) the state's interest in enforcing the law outweighs both the regulatory burden on interstate commerce and the law's adverse effect upon interstate commerce.

In answer choice (A), the protection of local workers from competition by foreigners is a weak defense because it implicates the Privileges and Immunities Clause of Article IV. It must pass a higher degree of scrutiny upon review than the Commerce Clause rational basis standard. Further, it cannot be said that protecting local workers in the small area of government construction contracts is going to protect all workers of the state of Yuma from competition by foreigners.

Choices (B-D) are wrong. Each of these arguments presents or implies a legitimate state objective that could be served by the statute in question. The statute is rationally related to these objectives of employee dedication, a stable workforce, and qualifications.

Question 93
Answer: D

This question tests the Supreme Court's discretion to engage in judicial review.

The Supreme Court generally will not grant certiorari from a decision made by a state's highest court when that decision rests upon adequate and independent state grounds. A state court makes the ultimate determination of what that state's constitution means. The Supreme Court will not entertain any appeal from a state court decision where the state ground for invalidation of a statute is independent of the federal grounds for invalidation of the statute. Here, the Equal Protection Clause of the state's constitution has been violated. That is an adequate and independent reason for invalidation of the law and thus, the Supreme Court will not review that state court decision.

Question 94
Answer: B

This question tests the concept of taxpayer standing.

Generally, a taxpayer lacks constitutional standing to challenge a federal expenditure of tax revenue. However, the taxpayer may have standing to challenge a specific federal expenditure on the grounds that it violates an express constitutional provision. The statute in this question is a direct exercise of the Congress' powers to tax and spend. And the spending exceeds a specific constitutional limitation imposed on that spending by the U.S. Constitution—the Establishment Clause.

Choice (A) is wrong. Taxpayer standing is rarely sufficient to challenge federal spending. This is because the injury suffered is not an individual injury—it is a generalized grievance.

Choice (C) is wrong. There is a sufficient nexus between the taxpayer and the challenged expenditure because the congressional action being attacked as a violation of an express constitutional provision is a direct exercise of taxing and spending power under Article I of the U.S. Constitution.

Choice (D) is wrong. The action in this question is state action. The private party is merely the recipient, not the actor.

Question 95
Answer: D

This question tests the Establishment Clause.

If government takes action or passes a law that possesses no sect preference, then according to *Agostini v. Felton,* the court will examine the law's purpose and effect to determine if the action violates the Establishment Clause. (1) The statute must have a secular legislative purpose. If it does not, it is unconstitutional. (2) The law's primary effect must be one that neither advances nor inhibits religion. In determining whether the law satisfies this requirement, a court will examine whether the statute fosters an excessive government entanglement with religion.

The salary supplements, in this instance, will indirectly advance religion by adding to the salaries that private, religious schools are able to provide to their employees.

Choice (A) is wrong. While it is a true statement that the supplements will not be made to teachers who engage in religious instruction, this does not mean that the supplements will not otherwise contribute to or advance religion—the supplements will do so indirectly.

Choice (B) is wrong. To distinguish between public and private teachers is not religious discrimination. It is actually a way to comply with the Establishment Clause. The private teachers are not being prohibited from the practice of their own religious beliefs.

Choice (C) is wrong. There is no indication, though it probably is true, that some religions would benefit disproportionately. However, this is not the concern of the constitutional challenge. The challenge is based on an unconstitutional establishment of religion—not religious discrimination.

Question 96
Answer: B

This question tests the Establishment Clause.

If government takes action or passes a law that possesses no sect preference, then according to *Agostini v. Felton*, the court will examine the law's purpose and effect to determine if the action violates the Establishment Clause. (1) The statute must have a secular legislative purpose. If it does not, it is unconstitutional. (2) The law's primary effect must be one that neither advances nor inhibits religion. In determining whether the law satisfies this requirement, a court will examine whether the statute fosters an excessive government entanglement with religion.

In this question, the statute has a secular purpose—construction and promotion of education. The primary effect of the statute does not directly advance or inhibit religion. It is correct that bricks and mortar do not aid or advance religion in a way forbidden by the Establishment Clause.

Question 97
Answer: B

This question tests the concept of equal protection.

Where a question presents a scenario in which a private party is engaging in conduct or discrimination that would be prohibited if the party were the state, it is a good idea to look for links between the private party and the state such that the acts of the private party might be attributed to the state and considered state action. If this can be established, then the private party will be subjected to and bound by the Fourteenth Amendment. If anyone seeks to enjoin the discrimination, the best way to do so is to paint the school's actions as state actions.

Question 98
Answer: C

This question tests the Commerce Clause.

Generally, a state law may regulate interstate commerce when federal law expressly permits it, prior federal law does not preempt subsequent state law, there is no impermissible risk of inconsistent regulation by different state, there is no undue burden on interstate commerce, and the law does not discriminate against interstate commerce. In any of those situations, a law that would otherwise violate the Commerce Clause will be judicially upheld. The best way to challenge the statute would be to show one of the situations listed above—that the statute placed an unreasonable burden on interstate commerce.

Question 99
Answer: B

This question tests speech in public employment.

Where a loyalty oath is not overly broad or vague, it may be constitutional as a condition of public employment. It simply involves the affiant's giving affirmation to personally oppose the violent overthrow of the government and to support constitutional principles. Courts have pretty consistently upheld these oaths as valid. Choice (B) is correct because the oath really is a simple promise to abide by constitutional procedures while employed. Given that a public employee's acts are attributable to the state, the state has an interest in guaranteeing that those acts will not be contrary to constitutional processes and create liability for the state.

Choice (A) is wrong. Government employment may become a right if the employee gains a vested property interest in his or her job—such as being in a position where firing can occur for cause only.

Choice (C) is wrong. The First and Fourteenth Amendments may indirectly allow a state to set conditions for public employment, but the state does not have free reign. That power is curtailed by the U.S. Constitution. The First and Fourteenth Amendments actually serve to restrain the power of the states rather than to confer powers upon them.

Choice (D) is wrong. While a loyalty oath may appear to be a content based restriction on speech, and as such, be subject to strict scrutiny, this is not the prevailing test for loyalty oaths. They are generally examined for vagueness and for being overly broad.

Question 100
Answer: C

This question tests the concept of state action.

Where discrimination is practiced by a private party, little challenge may be made to such discrimination because it is not prohibited by the Federal Constitution. However, if the actions of the private party can be painted as the actions of the state, the discriminatory behavior will then be prohibited, most likely under the Fourteenth Amendment. The strongest challenge that a party can make to private discrimination is a state-action claim which shows that the discriminating party is an agent of the state. Therefore, answer (C) is the correct answer. The Bar Association can be called an agent of the state because the state itself has mandated membership in it for all lawyers and because state officials serve the Bar Association in a governing capacity.

Question 101
Answer: A

This question tests the court's screening process for alleged state-action cases.

Federal courts are authorized to determine the constitutionality of federal and state laws pursuant to controlling precedents of the federal courts. A basis for federal question jurisdiction exists where there is controversy arising under the U.S. Constitution, laws, or treaties of the United States. In this question, it is proper for a federal district court to hear this case because there is a controversy concerning state action and equal protection of the laws under the Fourteenth Amendment.

Question 102
Answer: D

This question tests the issue of ripeness.

The doctrine of ripeness seeks to prevent the bringing of a civil suit before it is appropriate to be heard by the court. A suit is ripe only if the litigant has actually experienced harm or is subject to imminent threat of harm. In this question, the litigant has not even applied for a marriage license. The couple is not even engaged. Therefore, there is no actual injury or threat of injury. The suit is not yet ripe.

Question 103
Answer: C

This question tests the fundamental right to marry.

When a challenge is brought to a statute which concerns a fundamental right, the burden will be on the state to defend the constitutionality of that statute. The right to marry, between a man and a woman, is recognized as a fundamental right, thus requiring elevated scrutiny. A substantial interference with that right will not be sustained on the grounds that the statute has a rational basis. The requirement of state-sponsored counseling prior to the issuance of a marriage license can present a substantial obstacle to some individuals who seek to get married. In this question, Pine is encountering that obstacle.

Note that this question could have a different answer if Pine (gender-ambiguous) were in fact a man. The right to marry a person of the same sex has not been recognized as a fundamental right under federal constitutional law as of this volume's preparation, but such law could be subject to change at any time without notice.

Question 104
Answer: D

This question tests multiple subjects pertaining to discriminatory behavior by the federal government.

Choice (A) is wrong. The right to retire at any specific age is not a privilege or immunity of national citizenship.

Choice (B) is wrong. Prentis lacks a private real property right in his occupation for which just compensation would be required.

Choice (C) is wrong. The requirement that people in, for instance, the Department of the Army, retire at a certain age arguably does fall under the enumerated power of Congress to make rules for the government and regulate the land and naval forces.

Choice (D) is correct. While age is not a category that receives strict scrutiny review when government conduct is questioned, this question presents an obvious case of age discrimination that would at least be reviewed under the Fifth Amendment because the discrimination is done by the federal government. This answer, though not necessarily a good one, is the best answer of the four choices.

Question 105
Answer: D

This question tests the Commerce Clause.

The Commerce Clause grants Congress plenary power to regulate interstate and international activity (like transportation or travel), of both a commercial and non-commercial nature. This power to regulate applies to instrumentalities of commerce, the channels of commerce, noncommercial activity that has a direct connection to interstate commerce, and to activities that produce a substantial effect on interstate commerce. Inseverable aggregates are a manner in which this substantial effect on interstate commerce is established. Common products that, as inseverable aggregates, have a substantial effect on interstate commerce are fuel sources. Therefore, the oil, natural gas, and electric power in this question are the kind of products produced in inseverable aggregates, and they have a substantial effect on interstate commerce. This is the strongest argument in favor of the statute's constitutionality.

Choice (A) is wrong. The General Welfare Clause tends to come into play where federal appropriations and expenditures of tax money are concerned.

Choice (B) is wrong. While the Commerce Clause does grant Congress the power to regulate the channels of interstate commerce, the channels are not what is being regulated by this statute. The price is being regulated.

Choice (C) is wrong. Congress may not regulate the price of every good and service in the United States because buying and selling goods and services does not necessarily constitute interstate commerce. Some buying and selling can take place purely intrastate—and out of the reach of the Commerce Clause—if there is no substantial impact on interstate commerce that results.

Question 106
Answer: B

This question tests the jurisdiction of the Supreme Court.

In Article III of the U.S. Constitution, the Supreme Court is listed to have original jurisdiction over cases affecting ambassadors, etc. It also states that the Court shall have appellate jurisdiction as to all other cases, under such regulations as the Congress shall make. This question is an example of a congressional regulation which confers appellate jurisdiction to the Supreme Court. Choice (A) is wrong. This question tests the jurisdiction of the Supreme Court. It is not a question about the power of Congress over the subject matter of energy. Choice (C) and (D) are wrong. As stated before, it is perfectly within congressional powers to establish rules and regulations governing the appellate jurisdiction of the Supreme Court.

Question 107
Answer: A

This question tests the Congressional power to regulate private conduct.

The Fifth and Fourteenth Amendments apply only to state action. Congress has the power to enact legislation based on these amendments for purposes such as their enforcement. Private conduct that can be linked to state conduct—for instance, interference with a state official's ability to give equal protection or due process to individuals—may be prohibited by Congress. However, when the discrimination is purely private, chances are slim that Congress will prohibit such private conduct.

Choice (A) is correct. This is conduct by a private citizen that prohibits a state actor from complying with the equal protection clause.

Choice (B) is wrong. This is private conduct amounting to racial discrimination. There is no state action.

Choice (C) is wrong. Since the school bus driver is operating under the sponsorship of a local church, his actions are considered private discrimination. There is no state action.

Choice (D) is wrong. This question is concerned with state action and the Fourteenth Amendment. Discrimination by a federal official would be examined under the Fifth Amendment.

Question 108
Answer: D

This question tests the presidential power of the executive order.

The President has general authority to issue executive orders that become the law of the land. Those orders are effective without congressional approval. An executive order, however, cannot contravene or supersede federal law. In this question, the Congress enacted a federal law, and the President may not deliberately disregard that law. This law states that all monies appropriated for the dental education program must be used for this purpose. Therefore, all $100 million must be used for that dental education program.

Choice (A) is wrong. Though it is true that the President could determine that this program is less worthy as a general welfare program, this does not mean that he can issue an executive order to unilaterally cut spending on that program. That kind of change has to come through Congress.

Choice (B) is wrong. An executive order may be issued where the executive order impacts the employees directly in the President's administration. However, the order cannot be used to contravene existing federal law.

Choice (C) is wrong. This is not an equal protection question. This question tests presidential powers. If this choice were a legitimate argument, then any federal appropriation or taxation would be an equal protection violation. Government programs and taxing schemes sometimes do treat different groups of individuals differently.

Question 109
Answer: B

This question tests the right to vote and the right to travel between states.

The right to vote is a fundamental right. Any law that infringes on this right will be subjected to strict scrutiny, except with regard to less severe interference with that right. These minor interferences include things such as age, residency, and citizenship requirements. Residency requirements have been upheld where the duration of residency required in order to vote was 50 days. But a residency requirement of more than 90 days will be strictly scrutinized. There must be a compelling government interest behind the statute, and the means chosen in the statute must be narrowly tailored, such that the least restrictive means were employed to fulfill that interest.

Choice (A) is wrong. A state may very well have an incentive that is compelling enough to justify excluding an entire class of persons from the election. For instance, a state may limit the body of voters in a water storage district to only landowners.

Choice (B) is correct. In challenging the constitutionality of this statute, it will be hard to argue that the state does not have a worthy interest in ensuring that its voters are not migratory college students. It will be a better argument that the means employed, which completely deny the voting right to college students, are too broad-sweeping.

Choice (C) is wrong. This is a weak argument. It is the same as choice (A), in effect. This argument simply states that it is unconstitutional to deny the right to vote to a certain group of individuals over the age of majority.

Choice (D) is wrong. This is a voting rights question about privileges and immunities. It is not a Commerce Clause question.

Question 110
Answer: C

This question tests the Thirteenth Amendment.

The Thirteenth Amendment states that: "Congress shall have power to enforce this article by appropriate legislation." This provision authorizes Congress to enact statutes that further the purposes of the Thirteenth Amendment. The Thirteenth Amendment's main purpose was to end the vestiges of slavery. It was further expanded to include an end to discrimination in the sale of real property, etc. This kind of expansion took place under the Civil Rights Act of 1866. Under the Act, Congress is empowered to make any laws necessary and proper to eliminate the remnants of slavery. The scope of the Act has further been expanded to cover racial discrimination by private parties even beyond property rights.

Choice (A) is wrong. The Obligation of Contracts Clause prohibits the states from enacting legislation that retroactively impairs existing contracts. This is not the scenario created in this question.

Choice (B) is wrong. The General Welfare Clause is usually tested in regards to federal appropriations legislation. This is not an appropriations question.

Choice (D) is wrong. While the Fourteenth Amendment does address the issue of racial discrimination, it focuses more on discrimination perpetrated by the state or its officials. The Thirteenth Amendment has been more effectively used to justify punishment of racial discrimination perpetrated by private citizens.

Question 111
Answer: A

This question tests the concept of separation of powers.

Choice (A) is correct because Congress, under its enumerated powers in Article I, holds the power to make all laws that are necessary and proper to carry into execution the powers vested in the federal government by the U.S. Constitution. Foreign affairs are generally left to the executive branch, but the Congress has power to maintain preserve the area of foreign affairs to that branch.

Choice (B) is wrong. The President must have statutory authorization to punish citizens who engage in the conduct described in this question. The President must have laws in order to enforce them. The President is an enforcer of the laws and cannot unilaterally legislate and then enforce his own legislation.

Choice (C) is wrong. Simply because a law deals with foreign relations does not mean that the First Amendment cannot be implicated by the enactment of enforcement of that law.

Choice (D) is wrong. The domestic versus international distinction is of no importance. Every law must be specific enough to avoid being declared void for vagueness. There is no reason to distinguish between international legislation and domestic legislation on the basis of their specificity.

Question 112
Answer: C

This question tests the Equal Protection Clause.

Where a state statute treats citizens of the United States differently from aliens, it is generally subjected to strict scrutiny review. The state must prove a compelling state interest and show that the least restrictive means available are being used to further that interest.

Choice (A) is wrong. Aliens do in fact receive some protection under the Equal Protection Clause of the Fourteenth Amendment.

Choice (B) is wrong. This option applies the wrong level of review to the alienage issue. It is not an intermediate standard of scrutiny to be applied. The correct standard is strict scrutiny.

Choice (C) is right. The justifications for the restriction are likely to fail under strict scrutiny review.

Choice (D) is wrong. The Privileges and Immunities Clause of Article IV provides that one state may not deprive the privileges and immunities of that state to an individual who is a non-citizen of that state.

Question 113
Answer: B

This question tests the power of Congress to regulate interstate commerce.

The Commerce Clause has been greatly expanded to allow Congress to legislate and regulate in areas that, on the surface, do not appear to be interstate commerce issues. This power to regulate applies to instrumentalities of commerce, the channels of commerce, noncommercial activity that has a direct connection to interstate commerce, and to activities that produce a substantial effect on interstate commerce. Inseverable aggregates are one manner in which this substantial effect on interstate commerce is established. Here, Congress could justify its regulation of the bicycle industry using the substantial effect that bicycles, as an aggregate, have on interstate commerce.

Choice (A) is wrong. The General Welfare Clause tends to come into play where federal appropriations and expenditures of tax money are concerned. It is not often linked to the regulation of property.

Choice (C) is wrong. This option attempts to make an intrastate versus interstate distinction. Note that the statute in question could constitutionally stand even if the bicycles mostly remain within one state. Purely intrastate activity can in fact be considered interstate commerce when it has a substantial effect on interstate commerce.

Choice (D) is wrong. If the matter at hand does fall within the legislative powers of Congress due to the Commerce Clause, then it will preempt state laws on vehicle registration and the Tenth Amendment is not an issue.

Question 114
Answer: B

This question tests the fundamental right to privacy.

Whenever a question is focused on sexual activity, whether it be the right to engage in sex acts, the right to an abortion, or the right to make decisions about one's own body, the topic probably being tested is the due process clause and a denial of a fundamental right. In *Griswold v. Connecticut*, the Supreme Court recognized the right of individuals to acquire and use contraceptives. A statute which bans the ability to acquire and use contraceptives to a group of individuals denies them this fundamental right.

Choice (A) is wrong. It is arguable that minors do not constitute large enough of the sexually active population to amount to this statute creating a significant burden on interstate commerce.

Choice (C) is wrong. The right to sell one's product within a state is not protected as a privilege and immunity of state citizenship.

Choice (D) is wrong. This may very well be a morals regulation, but not all morals regulations are premised on religious principles and subjected to scrutiny as violations of the U.S. Constitution.

Question 115
Answer: D

This question tests the Property Clause of Article IV.

Under the Property Clause of the U.S. Constitution, Congress has the power to dispose of and make any necessary rules and regulations concerning the territory or property of the United States. The land in this question is federally owned property subject to this Property Clause. Therefore, Congress may make a regulation that prohibits hunting or poaching on federal lands.

Question 116
Answer: D

This question tests the jurisdiction of federal courts.

For a federal court to exercise jurisdiction over a dispute, there must actually be a "case or controversy." In this question, there is no case or controversy to be settled, but rather a disagreement as to the distribution of federal funding. The federal court is authorized to render an opinion that is not even binding—as the head of the federal agency is under no obligation to execute the judgment if he feels that it is unfair or unlawful. The problem here is not with the subject matter of the disputes, but rather with the ability of the court to render a decision.

Choice (A) is wrong. It is true that federal grant-in-aid funding would likely present a federal question for purposes of federal jurisdiction in Article III courts, but there is an error with the statute that makes it unconstitutional.

Choice (B) is wrong. Much like choice (A), it does make a quasi-true statement concerning congressional ability to regulate the spending of federal monies, but this does not mean that the statute itself is constitutional.

Choice (C) is wrong. Again, since there is no true case or controversy created in the fact pattern, there is not really a suit from which a state would need to be immune under the Eleventh Amendment.

Choice (D) is correct. A federal court is prohibited from issuing advisory opinions about matters that do not arise from actual cases or controversies.

Question 117
Answer: C

This question tests the concepts of justiciability and political questions.

Under the doctrine of separation of powers, the federal courts will not take jurisdiction over cases that seek to resolve a political issue when that issue is either best addressed by another branch of the government or is inappropriate for judicial review. For instance, when a certain issue has a *textually demonstrable constitutional commitment* to another branch or political department, the judiciary will opt out of reviewing that case or controversy. The area of foreign relations and recognition of nations is delegated to the executive branch.

Choice (A) is wrong. Dunn actually would have standing, as a party to the contract with the federal government, to bring his suit.

Choice (B) is wrong. There is an adversarial relationship between Dunn and the defendants (however, immunity would likely come into play).

Choice (D) is wrong. The judiciary will likely refuse this case as being not justiciable because of the political question doctrine.

Question 118
Answer: A

This question tests a parent's interest in the upbringing of his or her child.

The rights of a parent to companionship, care, custody, and management of his or her children are fundamental rights, protected by state and federal constitutions. Great deference is accorded to these parental rights, based upon constitutionally protected rights to privacy and the goal of protecting the family unit. Where fundamental rights are concerned, strict scrutiny will usually be applied when that right or liberty interest is being denied. The state is responsible for presenting a compelling interest upon which the denial of liberty is warranted. In this question, the language of strict scrutiny review is not present in any of the offered choices. Therefore, the next best scrutiny will be the answer. The state will have to satisfy intermediate scrutiny.

Choices (B) and (D) are wrong because they apply a level of review that is too low for a fundamental right.

Choices (C) and (D) are wrong because the burden of proof is placed on the incorrect party.

Question 119
Answer: B

This question tests burdens placed on the electoral process. Political candidates may be subjected to legally permissible burdens imposed by state and local governments. The requirement of obtaining voter signatures is considered one of these reasonable and legally permissible burdens. It is subjected to a rational basis standard of review. There must be a legitimate state objective behind the law, and that law must be rationally related to achieving that state objective. A law subject to rational basis review will rarely be invalidated, but this does not mean that a challenge cannot be made.

Choice (A) is wrong. It is true that this requirement is burdensome. It is designed to be burdensome because the state has an interest in ensuring that those persons placed on the ballot are, in fact, legitimate candidates.

Choice (B) is correct. While it is recognized that the requirement is burdensome, the best argument made to challenge it is that there are less burdensome means that could be employed in order to ensure that the state's objective is satisfied.

Choice (C) is wrong.

Choice (D) is wrong. This is simply an expression of the legitimate state interest that is advanced by the law.

Question 120
Answer: A

This question tests the concept of separation of powers and the delegation doctrine.

Congress is the usual entity to conduct legislative actions. But Congress may also delegate a limited portion of its legislative authority to another coordinate branch—usually the executive branch. In this question, the Congress is delegating a limited bit of its legislative power to the President, to allow him to set a percentage of reduction for energy consumption. This kind of delegation is permissible as long as the delegate has been given intelligible standards and guidelines. Here, the President's authority is confined by this limited delegation of power. Pursuant to this administrative power to implement the statute, the President may only specify the percentage by which consumption of energy must be reduced.

Question 121
Answer: A

This question tests the Property Clause.

The Property Clause authorizes Congress to make any laws and regulations that are necessary to protect federal real and personal property, including wild animals. By virtue of the necessary and proper clause, the federal government may also legislate to protect wild animals in adjacent state property (if the law is necessary to protect the federal property including wild animals). In this question, the government has enacted a statute to protect the wildlife inhabiting the federal lands.

Choice (B) is wrong. It would be difficult to establish that hunting these particular deer would have a substantial effect on interstate commerce or that hunting has a direct connection to interstate commerce.

Choice (C) is wrong. While it could be argued that protecting wild animals falls under the police power of the federal government, the justification for this power is what is tested by this question. This power, as stated above, comes from the Property Clause, coupled with the Necessary and Proper Clause.

Choice (D) is wrong. While the statement made in this option is true, it is not a strong argument supporting the constitutionality of this statute.

Question 122
Answer: B

This question tests the concept of equal protection.

When a question presents itself as needing an equal protection analysis, the first determination which must be made is the level of scrutiny which must be applied to the statute in question. Is the governmental line drawing based on a protected or suspect category? In this question, the line is drawn differentiating between private individuals and common carriers. This is a differentiation that warrants only rational basis scrutiny. When the statute being challenged must pass only rational basis scrutiny, the contested law must be rationally related to achieving a legitimate state interest. A law subject to rational basis review will rarely be invalidated on the exam. This is why choice (B) is correct.

Choice (A) is wrong. The question presents itself as needing an equal protection argument. This option is not framed in terms of equal protection. It talks of property interests.

Choice (C) is wrong. As stated earlier, the governmental line drawing in this question is between private citizens and common carriers. Rational basis scrutiny is to be applied. This answer is incorrect because it applies strict scrutiny.

Choice (D) is wrong. Just like choice (A), this option is not stated in terms of the equal protection analysis.

Question 123
Answer: D

This question tests federal preemption.

When a state law directly conflicts with a federal law, the state law is invalid. When a state law impedes a specified federal objective, then that federal law also preempts the state law. In this question, there is a federal law regulating the design of snipe traps. There is also a state law that prohibits the possession of such traps. There is no direct conflict between these two laws because the safety requirements under the federal law are not impeded by the presence of the snipe trap ban in the state of Midland. The purposes of the laws are independent of each other. Therefore, the federal rule will not preempt the state rule. Both will stand. This means that choices (A) and (B) are out.

Choice (C) may also be excluded because it overlooks the Property Clause of the U.S. Constitution. Under that clause, the federal government does have power over and the ability to regulate wild animals that are located on federal lands. The power to regulate wild animals is not left exclusively to the states.

Question 124
Answer: A

This question is very similar to question 121 and tests the requirement of standing.

In order for a plaintiff to possess standing and proceed in a civil action, the party has to have a significant stake in the outcome of the action. There must be an injury in fact (either actual or imminent), causation by the accused party, and a court must be capable of affording relief to the complainant.

Choice (A) is correct. There is a definite injury to the business in the other state because under the Green state law, it will be losing about $10 million worth of revenues from the supplies it will no longer be able to sell the company that had $20 million in sales in the state of Green.

Choice (B) is wrong. The corporation in the question has not crossed the threshold figure for sales and will not even be affected by the statute. There is no injury in fact, nor does injury appear imminent.

Choice (C) is wrong. There is no standing in this option because there is no evidence of any injury. Further, if there is an injury, a suit brought on behalf of all residents of the neighbor state will probably be faced with the challenge that the injury is too generalized for standing to be upheld.

Choice (D) is wrong. While the corporation in the option might have standing, a bondholder will not. The injury is too speculative or attenuated for this standing to be upheld.

Question 125
Answer: D

This question tests the Free Exercise Clause.

The statute in question punishes those who engage in fraud for personal financial gain. Implied in this statute is a mens rea—a knowing or intentional defrauding. This means that the accused must have known that his representations were false. The accused in this question appears to have believed in the veracity of his religious claims, which would mean that the necessary mens rea could not be shown. Any challenge to his representations, however, would be a challenge to his religious beliefs. A court may not consider the reasonableness or truthfulness of any religious belief because a person's freedom to select a religion is absolute. Because the charge implied that the religious statements were false, the Free Exercise Clause has been violated. The prosecution, by its charge, placed it upon the court to determine the truth or falsity of Jones's religious beliefs.

Question 126
Answer: B

This question tests the Supremacy Clause and federal immunity from state taxation.

Under the Supremacy Clause, the federal government is immune from direct taxation by a state government. A state may impose, however, an indirect and nondiscriminatory tax upon the federal government. For instance, a state could impose a uniform tax upon all similarly situated taxpayers of a particular status, which happens to include federal government employees, but that does not adversely treat them differently. In this question, the state is imposing a uniform tax on all business conducted within that state. This is a broad application that does not adversely treat the federal contract partners when compared to any other business conducted in the state.

Choice (A) is wrong. A state does not have exclusive jurisdiction over all commercial transactions executed wholly within its borders. This is a lesson in the Commerce Clause. Even transactions wholly within one state may be governed federally because of the significant effect that they have, as an aggregate, on interstate commerce.

Choice (C) is wrong. There is no violation of the Supremacy Clause in this question because the tax imposed is nondiscriminatory.

Choice (D) is wrong. There is no evidence to suggest that this tax will create an undue burden on interstate commerce.

Question 127
Answer: C

This question tests the Due Process Clause.

A property interest may or may not be subject to due process protections. For example, a professor working at a public institution who is employed at will, possesses no entitlement to continued employment. An entitlement would exist if the professor had tenure, at which point he would fall under due process protections in the event of termination. In this question, the employee is a state employee who appears to be employed at will. There is no indication of any entitlement in his position which would make him deserving of due process protections if terminated.

Choice (A) is wrong. A bill of attainder is a retrospective law that imposes punishment on named individuals or a readily identifiable group of individuals. In this question, the rule or law in existence simply did not require hearings or notice in the event of employment termination. This is not a bill of attainder because it does not preclude individuals from receiving minimal due process. The rule simply said that hearings and notice were not required. Also, there was no property interest to protect because the professor was employed at will.

Choice (B) is wrong. Like choice (A), this argument will fail because any line drawing between employees will be subjected to rational basis scrutiny. A challenge to a distinction that receives rational basis scrutiny usually will fail.

Choice (D) is wrong. While it is true that authority over conditions of state employment is mostly reserved to the states, federal law will sometimes be involved. This question, though, is not concerned with preemption—it is concerned with due process.

Question 128
Answer: D

This question tests the Equal Protection Clause.

State law classifications based on alienage are generally subject to strict scrutiny review. Thus, a state law or action that classifies people by alienage violates the Equal Protection Clause of the Fourteenth Amendment if the state (1) cannot prove a compelling state interest in the law that discriminates against aliens or (2) cannot prove that the least restrictive means available were used to fulfill that interest.

Therefore, the state has the burden of proof and must satisfy the requirements of strict scrutiny. Choice (D) is the only option which pairs the state's burden with a strict scrutiny standard of review.

Question 129
Answer: B

This question concerns the federal property of the United States.

Under the Property Clause, Congress may act pursuant to that provision to "dispose of and make all needful rules and regulations respecting the territory or other property of the United States." This would include making commercial use of the federally owned property. The question asks for the easiest and most directly applicable clause of the U.S. Constitution to settle the issue. The first line of the question presents the answer. It speaks of real property that is owned by the United States. This is federal property subject to the Property Clause and fully at the disposal of the federal government.

Question 130
Answer: C

This question tests the constitutional scope of subject matter jurisdiction of federal courts.

Article III states that federal judicial power applies to all cases in law or equity that involve the following subject matter: federal questions, ambassadors and counsels, maritime law, controversies where the U.S. is a party, disputes between sister states, disputes between a state and the citizens of another, disputes over state lands, and disputes between a state and a foreign nation. A dispute between two private parties over a commercial matter does not fall within the aforementioned categories of cases or disputes. Therefore, a state court is the more appropriate forum for adjudication of this suit involving two adverse parties located in the same state arising under common-law contract theory, rather than any federal legal provision.

Choice (A) is wrong. Obligation of contracts is not a subject matter expressly subject to the subject matter jurisdiction of Article III courts. This subject matter, however, could possibly fall under the above referenced category of federal questions in the event of certain circumstances that do not exist here. Here, the facts do not indicate that a law impaired an existing obligation of contract—in violation of the U.S. Constitution's Obligation of Contracts Clause—that would give rise to a federal question subject to the subject matter jurisdiction of Article III courts.

Choice (B) is wrong. The transaction in question does not affect interstate commerce enough, on its own, to merit a federal court's attention as a federal question.

Choice (D) is wrong. There is an actual case or controversy. It simply is not one to be heard in the federal courts.

Question 131
Answer: B

The correct answer is (B). The Free Exercise Clause of the First Amendment applies to the states under the Due Process Clause of the Fourteenth Amendment. The Free Exercise Clause prevents governments from legislatively outlawing or controlling a religion or all religions. In *Employment Division v. Smith*, the Supreme Court stated that "the right of free exercise does not relieve an individual of the obligation to comply with a valid and neutral law of general applicability on the ground that the law proscribes...conduct that his religion prescribes..." If a law falls under *Smith*'s exception, it is subject to a rational basis standard of judicial review. A law that is rationally related to promoting a legitimate state interest is constitutional.

The parents are challenging the statute on the basis that it infringes upon their right of free exercise of religion by subjecting their deceased son to an autopsy. The parents are in effect seeking an exemption from the statute's application insofar as it interferes with their religious expression. The statute is a facially neutral regulation because it uniformly applies to all persons who die from other than obviously natural causes. The statute is a generally applicable law that has been consistently enforced for 50 years to discover and prosecute criminal activity. Consequently, it is subject to a rational basis analysis.

The correct answer is (B) because the statute is a generally applicable law that is rationally related to a legitimate state interest.

Answer (A) is incorrect. The fact that the parents' son is dead does not mean that he is not a person, such that he would be denied the protections of the Due Process Clause of the Fourteenth Amendment. The parents are the son's legal representatives and, as such, they have standing to assert his constitutional rights as a deceased person.

Answer (C) is incorrect. It uses the wrong standard of judicial review. The strict scrutiny test, which includes the compelling state interest element, does not apply under these facts because the law unintentionally interfered with religious expression.

Answer (D) is incorrect. It is an inaccurate conclusion based on the inapplicable intermediate standard of judicial review.

Question 132
Answer: D

The correct answer is (D). An act of Congress that imposes a tax will be sustained as a valid use of its plenary taxation power if

    (1) Objective test: the act in fact raises revenue; or
    (2) Subjective test: the act is intended to raise revenue.

Courts will uphold a tax that adversely impacts the taxed activity if the tax satisfies either prong of the above alternative test and if:

    (1) It lacks any provisions that are unrelated to the tax needs and purposes; and
    (2) No language of the U.S. Constitution prohibits it.

The correct answer is (D) because the tax statute is constitutional for three reasons: First, Congress exercised its plenary taxation power with the intention of raising revenue. Second, although the statute may adversely impact the alpha producers in Blue or the freshwater fishing industry, the tax lacks any provisions that are unrelated to the statute's needs and purposes. Third, no language in the U.S. Constitution prohibits the tax.

Answer (A) is incorrect because the tax statute's language is facially uniform among the states despite the fact that alpha is only mined in Blue.

Answer (B) is not correct because even if the tax statute adversely affects the freshwater commercial fishing industry, the Commerce Clause does not require Congress to protect, foster, or advance this industry.

Answer (C) is incorrect. The Necessary and Proper Clause of the U.S. Constitution is not the appropriate premise for the tax statute and does not provide federal authority over navigable waters.

Question 133
Answer: A

The correct answer is (A). A government may establish a race-conscious set-aside program to remedy documented past discrimination in a community. That purpose will fulfill the government's compelling remedial interest. Such a program will be unconstitutional if this remedy may be accomplished by race-neutral means. To determine the program's constitutionality, consider:

    (1) Does the evidence demonstrate a history of racial discrimination in a community?

(2) Is a race-based program required to remedy that past discrimination?

(3) Is a race-neutral means available to achieve that objective?

Water District, as a governmental entity, improperly issued its rules to establish a race-conscious set-aside program because it lacked a factual basis to justify remedying documented past discrimination within its community. The question states that the "community is racially, ethnically, and socioeconomically diverse, and the community has never engaged in any discrimination against members of minority groups." Based on this factual context, Water District lacks a compelling remedial interest to issue the challenged rules. This contested set-aside program that Water District created is unconstitutional because the remedy is not needed under these facts, even if it could have been accomplished by race-neutral means.

The correct answer is (A) because the rules would unconstitutionally deny other potential employees or contractors the equal protection of the laws under the Fourteenth Amendment.

Answer (B) is incorrect. The constitutional provision prohibiting the impairment of contracts does not apply because Water District's rule does not impact already existing contracts. It only would prospectively apply to future contracts.

Answer (C) is incorrect. The program is unconstitutional because the facts do not demonstrate a history of racial discrimination in the community. Thus, no race-based program is needed.

Answer (D) is incorrect. The program is unconstitutional and the proprietary function exception does not apply when Water District engages in the governmental function of supplying water.

Question 134
Answer: A

The correct answer is (A). The Tenth Amendment precludes Congress from directly mandating that a state regulatory agency take specific action. In *New York v. United States* and *Printz v. United States* the Supreme Court ruled that federal laws may not commandeer state legislatures by obligating states to pass and execute federal legislation. Such federal laws would impermissibly deprive a state of its sovereignty under the Tenth Amendment.

Congress exceeded its scope of authority by enacting this federal statute. The federal statute impinges upon the states' limited sovereignty that exists pursuant to the Tenth Amendment. The federal statute contradicts the states' right to regulate illegal drug related activities as a means of exercising its police power to protect the public health, safety, and welfare. The federal statute violates the Tenth Amendment because Congress directly mandated that the state legislatures to take specific action. Specifically the statute would operate to commandeer state legislatures contrary to the governing precedent. Congress exceeded the scope of its authority in enacting this law that obligates the states to pass and execute federal legislation.

Answer (B) is incorrect. This answer is premised upon the Commerce Clause of the U.S. Constitution, which may be a permissible basis for congressional legislation. Even if a sufficiently close nexus existed between the transportation of controlled substances in interstate commerce and the federal statute, the Tenth Amendment violation renders it invalid.

Answer (C) is incorrect. This answer is also premised upon the Commerce Clause. The federal statute's jurisdictional provision regarding any affect upon interstate commerce cannot overcome the Tenth Amendment violation.

Answer (D) is incorrect. This answer is premised upon the Commerce Clause and the Welfare Clause of the U.S. Constitution. Although Congress possesses the board authority that this answer describes, that fact does not trump the federal statute's invalid commandeering of the state legislatures.

Question 135
Answer: C

The correct answer is (C). The federal district court will not reach the merits of the lawsuit because the plaintiffs lack standing.

A professor's interest in increasing the clarity of criminal laws does not, without more, constitute a significant stake in the proceeding and its outcome under the following factors:

(a) *Threat*: A professor cannot present much evidence of a threat of imminent injury due to the statute's lack of clarity.

(b) *Injury*: A professor cannot show any evidence of suffering an actual injury in fact as a result of the statute's enactment.

(c) *Type*: A professor cannot show that a vague statute resulted in a violation of a constitutional or statutory right, an economic injury, or any other legally cognizable harm.

(d) *Causation*: A professor cannot show that the Attorney General produced any injury.

(e) *Redressability*: A federal court cannot afford relief to a professor who is not an investor when the Attorney General is not prosecuting him or her.

The association lacks standing to litigate on behalf of its members because, individually they would not possess standing to file a lawsuit unless they were present or future investors and/or being prosecuted by the Attorney General. This is the case, even though the association desires to invalidate the statute, which relates to its objective of clear criminal laws.

Again, the correct answer is (C) because the plaintiffs lack an interest in the statute's invalidation that is sufficient to provide an Article III "case or controversy."

Answer (A) is incorrect. The fact that the plaintiffs are raising a constitutional issue is not, of itself, enough for them to have standing to proceed against the Attorney General.

Answer (B) is incorrect. The fact that the plaintiffs are demanding real relief of a conclusive nature is not, of itself, enough for them to have standing to proceed against the Attorney General.

Answer (D) is incorrect. The plaintiffs' lack of standing does not result from the lack of the Attorney General's good faith effort to enforce the statute against them or a third party. They lack standing because they do not fulfill Article III's requirements.

Question 136
Answer: D

The correct answer is (D). General public forums include sidewalks. A government must make such forums available for the expression of speech if the speech satisfies applicable legal tests.

Commercial speech is speech that occurs in advertising and in business transactions. The First Amendment only protects truthful commercial speech that advances a lawful activity. A court reviews commercial speech under the intermediate scrutiny standard. Honest commercial speech is subject to state law to the degree that: (1) the regulation furthers a substantial government interest; and (2) it uses the least restrictive means available.

City's ordinance regulating the machines on its sidewalks is subject to the commercial speech rules. The First Amendment applies to the commercial advertisements in the publications that were dispensed by the machines on City's sidewalks. Under the intermediate scrutiny standard, a court would not find that the regulation directly advanced a substantial government interest. Rather, the government interest in protecting the aesthetics of its sidewalks and streets would only be considered legitimate. A court could also determine that the removal of 30 of the 300 machines did not constitute the least restrictive means possible to achieve the legitimate state objective of reducing the adverse affects of litter on the streets and sidewalks.

The correct answer is (D) because no reasonable fit existed between City's legitimate interest in preserving the aesthetics of its sidewalks and streets and the means that were used to advance this end. This is because City continued to allow machines dispensing other types of publications on the public sidewalks.

Answer (A) is incorrect. The rational basis standard of review generally does not apply to regulations of commercial speech that are protected by the First Amendment.

Answer (B) is incorrect. City only possesses a legitimate interest in protecting the aesthetics of its sidewalks and streets and its regulation was not a necessary means of vindicating the interest.

Answer (C) is incorrect because it is based on a less than optimal reason. The regulation may or may not be the least restrictive means available to satisfy City's aesthetic objective. However, even if it were, the fact that no reasonable fit existed between the legitimate interest in preserving the aesthetics and the means that were used to advance this end, would still result in the law's invalidation.

Question 137

Answer: C

The correct answer is (C). In *Cox Broadcasting Corp. v. Cohn*, the Supreme Court determined that a person's privacy interest about information that existed in the public record did not prevail over the strong interests of:

    (1) a free press in not having to censor itself; and
    (2) the public's need to know about activities of a government.

In *Cox*, the Court concluded that a state could not impose liability for:

    (1) public dissemination of true information (i.e., a crime victim's name);
    (2) contained in and obtained from official court records;
    (3) that were open to public inspection.

The correct answer is (C) because it is most closely based upon the controlling precedent cited in the rule.

Answer (A) is wrong. Although the statute equally treats the arrest and prosecution records of anyone who obtained an acquittal of a crime and those against whom criminal charges were dropped or dismissed, this fact does not balance the respective rights of public access to criminal records and protecting individual's right of privacy.

Answer (B) is incorrect because, although the rights of the press usually are no greater than those of citizens generally, on some occasions they are greater because the press acts as the citizens' representatives.

Answer (D) is wrong because a state's legislature cannot seal records on an irrational, unreasonable, arbitrary, or capricious basis.

Question 138
Answer: D

The correct answer is (D). Courts apply a rational basis standard of review to congressional expenditures. Thus, courts generally determine if is it reasonable to conclude that the expenditure at issue will benefit or protect the national public? A court applying this standard of review to a federal spending statute inquires if:

    (1) A contested expenditure statute is reasonably related to the general welfare;
    (2) It states concrete objectives;
    (3) It provides adequate administrative criteria.

A challenger of the law possesses the burden of proving its invalidity under this test.

It is reasonable to conclude that the appropriation of taxpayer funds for prize winning essay writers will benefit or protect the national public by combating drug abuse. The taxpayer will carry the burden of proving that the statute's creation of a nationwide essay contest is reasonably related to the general welfare that is harmed by drug abuse. The statute includes the concrete objectives of by obtaining "new, practical ideas for eliminating drug abuse." The statute includes administrative criteria for selecting winning essays, appointing contest judges, and the participant's eligibility.

The correct answer is (D) because the statute is constitutional, it is reasonably related to the general welfare, it states concrete objectives, and it provides adequate criteria for conducting the essay contest and awarding the prize money.

Answer (A) is wrong because the political question doctrine does not apply to these facts.

Answer (B) is incorrect because the statute provides sufficient guidelines for awarding prize money, such that it does not unconstitutionally delegate legislative power to the contest judges.

Answer (C) is wrong because the statute is rationally related to congressional spending power and thus the Necessary and Proper Clause of Article I does not apply.

Question 139
Answer: B

The correct answer is (B).

The term dormant Commerce Clause refers to certain negative or implicit implications of the Commerce Clause of the U.S. Constitution. The Commerce Clause grants the power to Congress to enact laws that may affect interstate commerce. This "Commerce" power implies a negative converse — that states are restricted from legislating in a manner that improperly burdens or discriminate against interstate commerce.

The types of laws that are subject to analysis under the dormant Commerce Clause are: (1) discriminatory laws (laws that expressly discriminate against out-of-state people or entities; and (2) laws that do not expressly discriminate, but unduly burden interstate commerce, which can be discriminatory against out-of-state people or entities.

A state statute may be unconstitutional if it unreasonably burdens interstate commerce. A state statute that impermissibly burdens interstate commerce treats that commerce more adversely than intrastate commerce by, for example, imposing increased regulatory obligations on out-of-state individuals or entities as compared to intrastate individuals or entities.

As a general rule, state or local laws that affect interstate commerce are unconstitutional unless the following elements are fulfilled:

(1) A legitimate governmental end is pursued by the law;

(2) A rational relation exists between the law and the end that is pursued;

(3) The law's benefits exceed its burden upon interstate commerce; and

(4) Nondiscriminatory alternatives are not available.

In this case, the law violates the dormant Commerce Clause. The Kelly County ordinance regulates interstate commerce although its terms concern taxicabs registered and operating in Kelly County and only its residents can register their taxicabs there. The ordinance will not be upheld despite the fact that it serves the legitimate objective of reducing traffic congestion and the law is reasonably related to the objective. The law's burden on interstate commerce exceeds any benefit. Additionally, nondiscriminatory options are available, but have not been pursued.

Answer (A) is incorrect because, even if the alleged fact it true, this does not render the ordinance an unreasonable means of reducing traffic congestion.

Answer (C) is incorrect because Kelly County is not entitled to a judgment if the ordinance does not discriminate against interstate commerce.

Answer (D) is incorrect because judgment should not be for Kelly County based on the improper standard of review for the question that implicates the Commerce Clause.

Question 140
Answer: D

The correct answer is (D). A government must utilize adequate and fair procedures when its action results in an intentional or reckless deprivation of a person's life, liberty, or property. Part of the test of procedural due process is inquiring if a deprivation of property occurred? A deprivation of a personal property interest occurs when a government takes an individual's occupational license.

In *Bishop v. Wood*, the Supreme Court allowed a state's local government to delineate, in an ordinance regarding public employment, the scope and nature of the interests that the ordinance created. Accordingly, a state or local government may describe a benefit by law or contract in a manner that does not confer any property or liberty interest. When a government does that, then an individual recipient of the benefit may not be entitled to judicial relief on claims of a deprivation of an interest.

The underlying premise of John's action is that procedural due process requires the city licensing officials to afford him a hearing because their issuance of a license to Sandy could adversely affect his interest in property (i.e., his taxicab operator's license). John could argue that granting licenses to others impairs those interests by increasing competition for customers.

The foregoing *Bishop v. Wood* exception applies here because the city's ordinance regarding public employment did not confer any property interest in an existing holder of a license in being free from competition. Thus, John is not entitled to the judicial relief of requiring the officials to conduct a hearing because no property interest is adversely affected by granting such a license to Sandy, even if it would impair the value of John's license.

The correct answer is (D) because the licensing ordinance did not provide John with any property interest in being free of competition from other licensees.

Answer (A) is wrong because its incorrect conclusion is premised on an inaccurate reason. The reason is an overbroad statement of the law that does not account for any exceptions.

Answer (B) is incorrect. Although the officials possess discretion as to whether to conduct a hearing, their exercise of that discretion may be subject to judicial review and correction.

Answer (C) is incorrect. John may challenge the law, regardless of whether it benefited him in the past.

Question 141
Answer: C

The correct answer is (C). The Equal Protection Clause of the Fourteenth Amendment requires that all laws treat similarly situated people in the same manner. If such people do not receive equal treatment either under the laws or from a government, then a violation of their equal protection right might have occurred.

The fundamental right to vote is protected under the Equal Protection Clause and the Fifteenth Amendment. A court considering cases involving fundamental rights apply the most rigorous standard of review—strict scrutiny. A court will inquire:

(1) Is a law necessary to achieve a compelling government purpose?
(2) Was the least restrictive alternative means used?
(3) Did no less burdensome means exist to accomplish the purpose? and
(4) Was the law sufficiently narrowly tailored to accomplish the purpose?

The government possesses the burden of proving the law's validity under the above test.

The Fourteenth Amendment will be most helpful to the new political party because the statute may violate the Equal Protection Clause. The party may contend that the statute does not treat the potential candidates of similarly situated political parties in the same manner, in violation of their equal protection rights.

A court considering the party's challenge to the statute would probably find that they are asserting the fundamental right to vote. As such, the strict scrutiny standard of review would apply. This level of review would provide the party with the greatest likelihood of prevailing in their lawsuit because State X possesses a difficult burden of proving the law's constitutionality.

Answer (A) is wrong because, although the First Amendment provides the freedom of association that allows for the formation of, and participation in, political parties, it does not directly concern voting rights.

Answer (B) is incorrect because the Thirteenth Amendment outlaws slavery and does not concern the issue of voting rights.

Answer (D) is wrong because, although the Fifteenth Amendment outlaws any infringement of a citizen's right to vote based on race or color, it does not apply to the equal protection issue.

Question 142
Answer: B

The correct answer is (B). Congress may exercise its plenary power under the Commerce Clause in the following ways:

(1) Delegate to the states certain power to regulate commerce;
(2) Share with the states its power to regulate commerce; or
(3) Prohibit the states from exercising the power to regulate commerce.

Congress is not required to outlaw all state laws that burden, or are discriminatory with respect to, interstate commerce. Congress may authorize a burdensome or discriminatory state law.

Congress properly invoked its authority under the Commerce Clause to enact the federal statute. The statute constitutionally delegates to Redville the power to regulate Airline Limousine Service (i.e., Service). The statute permissibly authorizes Redville to impose a burdensome or discriminatory rule with respect to Service and "without regard to the origin or destination of the passengers."

Service must comply with the rule because Redville regulates rates and service pursuant to the statute, even if the rule does not advance a legitimate state interest or imposes burdens upon Service. Service must comply with the rule even if nondiscriminatory alternative means of regulation exist.

Question 143
Answer: B

The correct answer is (B). Under Article II of the U.S. Constitution, the President's power to make certain appointments is subject to the Senate's "advice and consent." Congress may authorize the President to appoint other "inferior officers," for lower level federal positions. Congress may not, however, provide that power to itself. Congress lacks any power of appointment. Any congressional appointment is void. Any congressional regulations or rules that purport to authorize or govern appointments by Congress are invalid.

The court will declare the statute unconstitutional because it violates the above described Appointment Clause. Congress improperly exercised the appointment power by the term in the statute that appointed "the respective general counsel of the Senate and House of Representatives Committees on Government Operations." This provision renders the statute invalid, although the statute otherwise properly empowers the President to appoint three members of the Board subject to the Senate's advice and consent. Congress unconstitutionally usurped and exercised the power of appointment that it lacked. Its purported appointments are void.

Answer (A) is incorrect because Congress lacks any power of appointment.

Answer (C) is incorrect. Neither the Necessary and Proper Clause nor the Commerce Clause, separately or in combination, is a constitutional basis that trumps the Appointment Clause.

Answer (D) is incorrect. It improperly relies upon the power of Congress to make expenditures for the general welfare as a basis for Congress to improperly exercise the power of appointment.

Question 144
Answer: A

The correct answer is (A). The original jurisdiction of the Supreme Court (i.e., the Court) according to Article III of the U.S. Constitution is for cases that affect "Ambassadors, other public Ministers and Counsels, and those in which a State shall be a party." Congress may reduce or expand the appellate jurisdiction of the Court. Specifically, Article III provides that "In all other cases before mentioned [above], the Supreme Court shall have appellate Jurisdiction, both as to Law and Fact, with such Exceptions, and under such Regulations as the Congress shall make."

The original jurisdiction of the Court does not include the companies' lawsuit against the EPA because they are not the type of parties identified in Article III. Thus, the Court cannot grant certiorari as a tribunal of first resort. Congress exercised its Article III power to expand the appellate jurisdiction of the Court by enacting the statute. The Court, however, cannot exercise this appellate jurisdiction before a United States Court of Appeals exercises original jurisdiction over the lawsuit. Indeed, no lower court has made any decision with respect to the case.

Answer (B) is incorrect because the Court's appellate jurisdiction under Article III is not limited to cases arising under the Constitution. The Court's appellate jurisdiction also extends to cases arising under federal laws and treaties.

Answer (C) is a wrong because Article III's requirement of the existence of a "case or controversy" could be fulfilled by an action to enforce a federal agency rule and other actions, such a challenge to the procedural validity of the promulgation of the rule.

Answer (D) is an incorrect response because Article III does not expressly mandate that all cases not arising under the Court's original jurisdiction must be initiated in a federal district court.

Question 145
Answer: C

The correct answer is (C). A state law (e.g., a state statute or regulation, local ordinance or rule) that regulates interstate commerce generally is subject to a type of rational basis review when it is challenged in a lawsuit. The law will be upheld if:

(1) it serves a legitimate state objective;
(2) the law is rationally related to the objective;
(3) the state interest in enforcing the law outweighs both;
    (a) the law's regulatory burden on interstate commerce;
    (b) the law's adverse affect upon or discrimination against interstate commerce.

The statute regulating the acquisition of domestic corporations regulates interstate commerce only insofar as it affects out-of-state purchasers. The statute's legitimate state objectives are preserving jobs in State A and protecting its domestic corporations against their sudden acquisition.

The statute's requirement of takeover approval by a majority of shareholders is rationally related to the statute's objectives. The statute involves no undue burden on interstate commerce because it imposes the same burden on both in-state and out-of-state entities and shareholders seeking to acquire a domestic corporation. The statute does not discriminate against interstate commerce because it regulates only the acquisition of domestic corporations.

Answer (A) is incorrect. The statute applies to acquisitions by companies both within and outside of State A.

Answer (B) is incorrect. The statute regulates the acquisition of domestic corporations by other corporations whose shareholders reside in every state including State A.

Answer (D) is incorrect. The negative implications of the Commerce Clause may apply to states' corporation laws.

Question 146
Answer: C

The correct answer is (C). In *Roe v. Wade* the Supreme Court recognized a woman's privacy right to obtain an abortion on demand prior to the viability to a fetus at the beginning of the third trimester. During this period a state cannot impose any law that unduly burdens a woman's right to an abortion. After the point of fetal viability, no fundamental right to an abortion exists. Beyond this point states may outlaw abortion unless that procedure is required to save a mother's life.

For substantive due process purposes, a woman possesses a right to an abortion. A state cannot impose restrictions that unduly burden to the exercise of that right. When a state statute does not unduly burden a woman's right to an abortion, a court will apply a rational basis analysis to adjudicate the statute's constitutionality. If the state statute imposes an undue burden on a woman's right to an abortion, a court will apply strict scrutiny.

The challenged statute violates the rule of *Roe v. Wade* generally providing a right to abortion before the viability to a fetus in the third trimester. The statute unduly burden's a woman's right to an abortion by preventing her from obtaining an abortion on demand during the second trimester. The statute only complies with the rule of *Roe* by limiting her right to an abortion during the third trimester to when a physician determines that the abortion is needed for her life or health.

The statute imposes restrictions that are substantial obstacles to a woman's exercise of her right that is protected by substantive due process. The statute is subject to strict scrutiny upon judicial review because it imposes an undue burden on the right to an abortion.

Answer (A) is incorrect because it does not describe the applicable analytical approach.

Answer (B) is incorrect. This is an misstatement of the law.

Answer (D) is incorrect. The right to privacy that includes abortion is protected by the Due Process Clause, not the Equal Protection Clause, of the Fourteenth Amendment.

Question 147
Answer: B

The correct answer is (B). Article II of the U.S. Constitution provides in part that "The executive Power shall be vested in a President of the United States of America." The President is authorized to take any action that is allowed under the U.S. Constitution and not otherwise prohibited by law.

Pursuant to Article II, the President may exercise the executive power to appoint a Presidential Advisory Commission on Vaccination (i.e., Commission) for three reasons. First, Article II implicitly allows this presidential conduct. Second, the creation of this Commission is not prohibited by a federal statute. Third, Congress appropriated funds for the President to use in his discretion that could be used for the Commission's expenses.

Answer (A) is incorrect. It attributes to the President those police powers that the Tenth Amendment reserves to the states.

Answer (C) is incorrect because it is an over-generalized statement.

Answer (D) is incorrect. The Commission did not need to be congressionally created.

Question 148
Answer: D

The correct answer is (D). A state law (e.g., a state statute or regulation, local ordinance or rule) that regulates interstate commerce generally is subject to a type of rational basis review when it is challenged in a lawsuit. The law will be upheld if:

(1) it serves a legitimate state objective;

(2) the law is rationally related to the objective;

(3) the state interest in enforcing the law outweighs both;

        a)   the law's regulatory burden on interstate commerce;

        b)   the law's adverse affect upon or discrimination against interstate commerce.

Does the law protect or favor in-state businesses from out-of-state competition without adequate justification?

City's ordinance regulates interstate commerce by imposing a license tax with a "Green content" provision. The provision decreases license taxes based on the proportion of a computer's components that were produced in Green. The ordinance may serve a legitimate state objective of business taxation and could be rationally related to this objective. The state interest in enforcing the ordinance, however, is outweighed by its discriminatory effect upon interstate commerce. The ordinance favors in-state computer components over out-of-state computer components without adequate justification.

Answer (A) is incorrect because the tax upon Central City companies discriminates against interstate commerce by providing a tax reduction based on the favoring computer components made in Green over computer components made in other states.

Answer (B) is incorrect because here, improper legal means were used to foster and support businesses within the state.

Answer (C) is incorrect because it is an inaccurate statement of the law.

Question 149
Answer: D

The correct answer is (D). A permit or license requirement obligates an individual or entity to obtain governmental approval in order to engage in expressive conduct. The criteria for the issuance or revocation of a permit or license must generally be content neutral in terms of regulating the viewpoints of an individual or entity that seek its issuance. Refusal of a permit or license is only permissible if it will be used for expressive conduct that is not constitutionally protected.

City may not prevail in its action to revoke Driver's license because the ordinance unconstitutionally limits his expressive conduct. The ordinance's conditioning of the issuance of the license upon Driver's agreement not to display any political endorsements on his taxicab is not content neutral in regulating Driver's expression of view points. The ordinance's restrictive agreement requirement rests on an invalid justification because it does not regulate expressive conduct on the permissible basis that it is constitutionally unprotected.

Answer (A) is incorrect. It relies on a wrong premise because the acceptance of a license with notice of its condition does not affect one's standing to contest the licensing regulation.

Answer (B) is incorrect. It relies upon an incorrect premise because a license is a government issued personal property interest that is protected by the Due Process Clause of the Fourteenth Amendment.

Answer (C) is incorrect. It is based on an inaccurate statement of the law because the license is not a private real property interest that is protected by the Takings Clause and for which just compensation must be paid.

Question 150
Answer: C

The correct answer is (C). A state court makes the ultimate determination of what the state's constitution means. The Supreme Court will not entertain an appeal from a state court decision if an independent and adequate state ground supports that decision. When the Supreme Court reviews a state court decision, it usually only considers the federal law issues instead of the state law issues. In *Michigan v. Long,* the Supreme Court set forth the following rule for analyzing if a state court's decision rests on state or federal grounds: If a state court truly intended to rule based on state law, then the state court must make that intention apparent in its written decision.

The state supreme court's opinion in Agitator's case constituted an ultimate determination of the meaning of the state's constitution. Accordingly, the Supreme Court should not have granted certiorari to hear the state's appeal when the state supreme court's decision rested on an independent and adequate state ground. The Supreme Court did not need to review any federal law issues because the state supreme court did not render the opinion based on its discussion of federal law. The state supreme court's written opinion made clear its intention to decide the case based on state law.

Answer (A) is incorrect because the Supreme Court should not reach the merits of the case.

Answer (B) is wrong because the state supreme court's decision rests upon adequate state law grounds, so no federal constitutional law issues need to be resolved.

Answer (D) is incorrect because the state supreme court's decision concluded that Agitator engaged in speech that the state constitution protected.

Question 151
Answer: C

The correct answer is (C). The Supremacy Clause of the U.S. Constitution legally furthers the principle of federalism that, in certain respects, the state governments and laws are subordinate to the federal government and laws. The Supremacy Clause gives rise to the doctrine of intergovernmental immunity. That doctrine generally prevents the states from enacting laws that interfere with the operations and activities of the federal government.

Under the Supremacy Clause, the federal government is immune from direct taxation by any state government. A state may impose an indirect and nondiscriminatory tax upon the federal government. For instance, a state may impose a uniform tax upon all similarly situated taxpayers of a particular status, class, or category which happens to include federal government employees, but that does not adversely treat them differently.

The state income tax on the rental value of an automobile provided by a taxpayer's employer is not a direct tax on the federal government. The federal government supplies automobiles to its employees who, as taxpayers, are not immune from the state income tax for three reasons. First, the employees, not the federal government, are subject to the state's non-discriminatory tax on each automobile's rental value. Second, the tax does not discriminate against federal employees because it applies to all taxpayers who were employed by any employer. Third, the tax applies to the taxpayer's use of the automobile for both business and personal purposes.

Answer (A) is incorrect. The tax was not upon the United States directly.

Answer (B) is incorrect. Although the tax affected federal employees, it also equally affected all other taxpayers.

Answer (D) is incorrect because it is based on an accurate, but less than optimal, reason. In other words, it is not the "best" answer.

Question 152
Answer: A

The correct answer is (A). The Supreme Court in *City of Renton v. Playtime Theatres, Inc.* concluded that: "'Content-neutral' time, place, and manner regulations are acceptable so long as they are designed to serve a substantial governmental interest and do not unreasonably limit alternative avenues of communication." The Supreme Court upheld a zoning ordinance that prohibited adult motion picture theaters from locating within 1,000 feet of certain non-commercially zoned property. The ordinance furthered the city's interest in preventing the adverse secondary effects of adult theaters on the surrounding community, rather than regulating the adult film's content.

Here, the court should uphold the ordinance's adult entertainment provisions because they are not a blanket prohibition of that type of business within King City. The ordinance is a "content-neutral" time, place, and manner regulation because it does not control the content of adult entertainment. The ordinance serves King City's substantial governmental interest in protecting its commercial center from harmful uses. Sam can exercise other alternative avenues in which to conduct his proposed business.

Answer (B) is incorrect because certain non-obscene adult entertainment is expressive conduct protected by the free speech guarantee of the First Amendment as applied under the Fourteenth Amendment.

Answer (C) is incorrect because the ordinance does not prohibit adult entertainment on the basis of content, even if it is not "obscene" in nature.

Answer (D) is incorrect because it is based on an incomplete statement of the law.

Question 153
Answer: A

The correct answer is (A). A government must utilize adequate and fair procedures when its action results in an intentional or reckless deprivation of a person's life, liberty, or property. The two-part test of procedural due process is:

(1) Whether a deprivation of a personal property interest occurs when a government takes an individual's occupational license?

(2) What procedures are due under the circumstances?

In civil proceedings, evidentiary rules cannot infringe upon a litigant's fair trial right under the Due Process Clause of the Fourteenth Amendment.

John's optimal contention for setting aside the revocation is a denial of procedural due process resulting from his lack of opportunity to cross-examine the informants. John could assert that the procedural due process that the Board used to deprive him of his personal property interest in the license was inadequate under the circumstances.

John could assert that the Board's evidentiary rules violated his right to a fair hearing by admitting the hearsay evidence of the informant's affidavits without allowing him to cross-examine them. John may have lost his license based on inaccurate or fabricated out-of-court statements by informants whose credibility, bias, and motive went unchallenged.

Answer (B) is incorrect for two reasons. First, the Full Faith and Credit Clause requires a state to recognize and enforce a valid judgment that a court of another state granted. Second, the dismissal occurred prior to any criminal prosecution and is unrelated to the Board's hearing.

Answer (C) is incorrect because Article III applies to the federal government, not the Board in State A that derives its authority from the Tenth Amendment.

Answer (D) is incorrect because the facts do not indicate if federal laws preempt state action regarding drug trafficking. Even if they did, John's case concerns the status of his professional license and is not a criminal prosecution.

Question 154
Answer: A

The correct answer is (A). Article IV of the U.S. Constitution includes the Full Faith and Credit Clause. The Clause states in part that "Full Faith and Credit shall be given in each State to the public Acts, Records, and judicial Proceedings of every other State."

One effect of the Full Faith and Credit Clause is to require that a final judgment in a legal proceeding, which was rendered by a court of one state, must be recognized as valid by the courts in other states. The other states are required to deem the final judgment as res adjudicata. For example, the other states are obligated to allow a judgment creditor to maintain an action to enforce such a valid final judgment that is rendered for money damages.

The injured persons will obtain from the state of Red the entire balance of their Blue state court judgment pursuant to the Full Faith and Credit Clause. The Red state court must recognize the Blue state court judgment as valid and res adjudicata. The injured persons are judgment creditors who are entitled to prosecute their enforcement proceeding in Red state court and receive the amount awarded by the Blue state court from the state of Red.

Answer (B) is incorrect. The Full Faith and Credit Clause is controlling. An Equal Protection Clause violation may not exist because the Red state law is an economic regulation that only needs to be rationally related to a legitimate government interest.

Answer (C) is incorrect. It relies upon an inapplicable correct legal premise because, even if the state's public policy is otherwise enforceable, the Blue state court judgment is res adjudicata on the issue with respect to the parties.

Answer (D) is incorrect. The issue of the employees' liability for their conduct was already adjudicated in the Blue state court.

Question 155
Answer: C

The correct answer is (C). In *St. Pierre v. United States,* the Supreme Court defined a case as moot when "there is no subject matter on which the judgment of the court's order can operate." In other words, mootness occurs if a controversy ceases to exist at any point during litigation, such that it is too late for adjudication of an action because it is unlikely that the controversy will be revived.

Answer (C) is correct because the judge's motion should be granted when Alex's lawsuit became moot when the proceedings in Clark's case ended before Alex's lawsuit could be adjudicated. Thus, no subject matter existed upon which the court could render a judgment. Mootness occurred because when Alex's controversy ceased to exist it became too late for its adjudication. The resolution of Clark's case resulted in the judge's voluntary cessation of his prohibition against further televising of the trial, which probably will not reoccur in the future. Consequently, Alex's controversy became moot because it is unlikely that it will be revived.

It is important to note that one possible exception may apply. It can be argued that the controversy is capable of repetition but evading review. However, no answer choice relies upon this exception. Therefore, you must assume that the exception does not apply to this question.

Answer (A) is incorrect. The facts do not indicate that Clark will appeal and the facts show that is not likely that he would prevail on appeal.

Answer (B) is incorrect. It is a misstatement of the law.

Answer (D) is incorrect. The doctrine of mootness makes no exceptions based on the subject matter of a "case or controversy."

Question 156
Answer: D

The correct answer is (D). In *Dolan v. City of Tigard*, the Supreme Court followed the doctrine of unconstitutional conditions, which prohibits a government from requiring a landowner to relinquish a constitutional right in return for a discretionary benefit conferred by the government when the property that the government seeks has little or no relationship to the benefit. In considering a landowner's claim of unconstitutional conditions, a court needs to ascertain:

(1) Does an essential nexus exist between a legitimate state interest and the permit condition?

(2) If yes, a court must determine if the degree of the exactions of the landowner's property that a permit's conditions demand involves the required relationship of rough proportionality to the projected impact of the proposed development?

In deciding this second inquiry—if a government's findings are constitutionally sufficient to justify the conditions imposed on a landowner's permit—the necessary connection required by the Fifth Amendment is rough proportionality. The government must make some sort of individualized determination that the required dedication of the landowner's property is related both in nature and extent to the impact of the landowner's proposed development.

The doctrine of unconstitutional conditions applies because City's zoning requirement mandated that Company must surrender its right to property in exchange for the permit because its parking lot had a minimal relationship to the benefit of providing additional day care. Accordingly, a court may not find that an essential nexus exists between a legitimate state interest and the permit condition.

Even if such a nexus existed, the permit imposes an exaction upon Company's property that is equal to the amount of space that Company seeks to develop as a coffeehouse. The demand of the permit's condition is not roughly proportionate to the proposed development's projected impact because City failed to make an individualized determination that the mandatory use of Company's property is related to the impact of the proposed coffeehouse addition.

Answers (A), (B), and (C), are incorrect. They are based on incorrect standards of review.

Question 157
Answer: B

The correct answer is (B). In *Lynch v. Donnelly*, the Supreme Court ruled that public displays involving religious themes (e.g., Christmas or Easter) were lawful as long as primarily secular symbols surrounded the religious symbols. To analyze if a public display is constitutional, consider:

(1) Does the display include secular and religious symbols?

(2) Are many different faiths reflected by the religious symbols?

(3) Does the display, including religious symbols, depict and commemorate a religious event or season as a primarily secular holiday?

The state's display includes a religious symbol of Christmas for one month that is surrounded during the year by products that are manufactured in the state. The display lacks the symbols of any other religion with observances during this holiday season. In its context, the display's combined elements do not depict and commemorate a religious event or season as a primarily secular holiday.

Answer (A) is a correct conclusion based on a less than optimal reason, although state ownership is more unconstitutional than private ownership of the nativity scene.

Answer (C) is incorrect. Even if private citizens donated the nativity scene, it is state property.

Answer (D) is incorrect. Although the nativity scene is surrounded by the manufactured products, they neither depict nor commemorate the holiday season in a secular manner.

Question 158
Answer: B

The correct answer is (B). The Commerce Clause grants Congress plenary power to regulate international and interstate activity of both a commercial and noncommercial nature. That authority extends to include activities producing a substantial effect on interstate commerce in a cumulative or aggregate manner. Commercial activity, even if it occurs on an intrastate or local level and to a small degree, is subject to regulation if its aggregate impact has a substantial effect on interstate commerce.

The Commerce Clause provides Congress with sufficient authority to regulate the sale or rental of housing. Congress could use its plenary power to regulate this activity based on its commercial nature and substantial effect on interstate commerce in inseverable aggregates. Such commercial activity also transpires on an intrastate or local level and to a lesser degree. It may be federally regulated because its cumulative impact has a substantial effect on interstate commerce.

Answer (A) is incorrect because the General Welfare Clause limits the purposes of congressional taxing and spending.

Answer (C) is incorrect. The Enforcement Clause concerns prohibiting slavery, which is a racial issue as opposed to the gender issue of the proposed legislation.

Answer (D) is incorrect. The Fourteen Amendment applies to discriminatory conduct by governments through laws or state action. It does not authorize Congress to legislate with respect to private actors who engage in discrimination.

Question 159
Answer: D

The correct answer is (D). Private action includes many types of conduct that is undertaken by individuals or entities who are not serving in a public capacity. Not all private action needs to comply with the U.S. Constitution. Only the Thirteenth Amendment to the Constitution expressly applies to a private activity. The Fourteenth Amendment to the Constitution address issues regarding state action.

State action occurs when a government (federal, state, or local) engages in conduct that implicates the constitutional rights of a person without any involvement by a private individual or entity. State action may or may not involve private individuals or entities.

The organization is engaging in private action by holding its meeting in the city's auditorium. The organization is comprised of private individuals who do not serve in a public capacity. Their private meeting and officer selection process is not prohibited by statute or administrative rule and would only need to comply with the freedom of association provided by the First Amendment to the Constitution. The Thirteenth Amendment does not apply to the organization's private activity which does not involve involuntary servitude.

The city's leasing of the auditorium does not constitute state action because this conduct does not implicate the plaintiff's constitutional rights, either on its own or in conjunction with the organization. Thus, the Fourteenth Amendment does not apply to the organization's activities.

Answer (A) is incorrect. The Fourteenth Amendment does not apply to private organizations unless they engage in state action.

Answer (B) is incorrect. The organization's use of the city's auditorium does not make it a state actor.

Answer (C) is incorrect. The First Amendment protects the freedom of association and the city's lease does not interfere with the organization's private activity.

Question 160
Answer: A

The correct answer is (A). Gender is quasi-suspect type of classification. Laws containing gender classifications are usually subject to a heightened or intermediate scrutiny level of judicial review. Under this standard, a court will inquire:

    (1) Is a contested law substantially related to

(2) achieving an important government interest?

The government possesses the burden of proving the law's validity under the above test.

Under the intermediate review standard, the state court may conclude that the panel selection process involved a gender-based denial of equal protection of the laws. The gender classification that the state's attorney applied does not fulfill the intermediate scrutiny requirements because it was not substantially related to achieving an important government interest. The state could not carry its burden of proving that women, as a group, would necessarily be biased in favor of another woman who was claiming sexual harassment.

Note that you were not required to make any close judgment of law in order to answer this question. If you knew that gender based discrimination requires intermediate scrutiny, then you could immediately eliminate the other choices.

Answer (B) is a incorrect. A jury of one's peers is not necessarily comprised of only people of the same gender or race.

Answer (C) is incorrect. The strict scrutiny standard of review does not apply to gender classifications.

Answer (D) is incorrect. The rational basis standard of review does not apply to gender classifications.

Question 161
Answer: B

The correct answer is (B). The Speech and Debate Clause of Article I of the U.S. Constitution states that "for any Speech or Debate in either House [all Congress members] shall not be questioned in any other Place." That provision applies to the official activities of the members of Congress while they participate in the legislative function. It generally protects them by making their communications in that capacity privileged from civil or criminal suit, including grand jury proceedings. The staff of members of Congress may also assert the privilege for their conduct that occurs in the scope of their work on behalf of their member of Congress.

The court should grant the motions of both defendants because the Speech and Debate Clause affords them immunity from William's defamation action. Although Senator's speech misidentified William, it occurred while performing official activities during his participation in the legislative function. On the same basis William may also assert the privilege because he researched and wrote the speech when working for Senator.

Answer (A) is incorrect. The First Amendment's freedom of speech guarantee does not apply to defamation by Frank regardless of his carelessness. Senator possesses the ordinary freedom of speech rights of a constituent part of the government, as well as her privilege under the Speech and Debate Clause.

Answer (C) is incorrect because Senator's legislative immunity is not contingent upon the relevancy of her speech to pending legislative business. Frank is entitled to equal immunity with Senator.

Answer (D) is incorrect because he is protected by the Speech and Debate Clause as Senator's employee.

Question 162
Answer: B

The correct answer is (B). Article IV of the U.S. Constitution states that: "The Citizens of each State shall be entitled to all Privileges and Immunities in the several States." According to this Privileges and Immunities Clause, a first state may not deprive a citizen of any other state the fundamental privileges and immunities that the citizens of the first state enjoy. Fundamental rights of state citizenship may include seeking employment and access to licenses.

The Redville Hospital rule is a form of Red state action depriving Doctor, a resident (i.e., citizen) of Green, the fundamental privilege and immunity (i.e., right) to use her license to practice medicine, which the citizens of Red enjoy. Doctor's use of her medical license in Red is an exercise of her fundamental right of state citizenship regarding employment and licensing. The Redville Hospital rule unconstitutionally interferes with this right.

Answer (A) is incorrect because the Bill of Attainder Clause retrospectively criminalizes the conduct of certain individuals.

Answer (C) is incorrect because, although the Redville Hospital rule interferes with Doctor's property interest in her Red license to practice medicine, the Privileges and Immunities Clause of Article IV is more relevant than the Due Process Clause because the interference is based on her citizenship in the state of Green.

Answer (D) is incorrect because the Red Hospital rule is not an ex post facto law when it does not punish Doctor for previously legal conduct.

Question 163
Answer: A

The correct answer is (A). Overbreadth exists when a law restricts or prohibits a wider scope of expression than it is necessary to prohibit. A court may rule that an overly broad law is unconstitutional if it does not satisfy the strict scrutiny test.

Vagueness exists when a law that prohibits expression fails to clearly define conduct so that reasonable person could not ascertain what expression is allowed and what expression is prohibited. A court may rule that a vague law is unconstitutional if it fails the strict scrutiny test.

Overbreadth would be an effective argument for Store. The law criminalizes significantly more conduct than is necessary in order to reach its objective. Thus, the law may not survive strict scrutiny because it is overbroad.

Vagueness would also be an effective argument for Store. The language of the law is vague and does not specifically identify what type of conduct is criminalized. The law criminalizes the display of "any material that may be harmful to minors because of the violent or sexually explicit nature of its pictorial content." What is it that may be harmful to minors, and who determines what conduct satisfies the standard? A reasonable person would not be put on notice of what is prohibited because of the subjective nature of the law's harmful material standard.

Answer (B) is an incorrect conclusion because, although it refers to the controlling constitutional provisions, it does not accurately state the controlling law.

Answers (C) and (D) are incorrect because the Equal Protection Clause is less controlling than the First Amendment with respect to matters of freedom of speech.

Question 164
Answer: D

This question tests the delegation powers of Congress.

The first half of the question is a correct description of acceptable delegation of legislative power. The delegate agency is given intelligible standards and guidelines on upon which to base the rules that it formulates. However, once those rules are made, a small committee of congressmen is permitted to essentially veto the rule by majority vote. This is not a permissible, constitutional method of disposing of an unwanted rule. Even if the Congress delegated the power which was used to make that rule, a congressional committee does not have the unilateral power to set aside that rule once it is made. The same procedures used to enact a rule are also needed to retire the rule.

Choice (A) is wrong. The way to ensure that the rules issued by the agency will be consistent with the will of Congress is by providing intelligible standards and guidelines to that agency.

Choice (B) is wrong. While the grants may be discretionary under the statute, this does not give Congress free reign over their administration. Congress must still abide by traditional methods of legislation.

Choice (C) is wrong. This is not an equal protection inquiry. If this argument were legitimate, it would spell the end for all committees in Congress because appointment of one committee would violate the rights of those not appointed to that committee.

Question 165
Answer: C

This question concerns the Supremacy Clause.

The U.S. Constitution provides that "this Constitution, and the Laws of the United States which shall be made in Pursuance thereof..." shall be the supreme law of the land. In this question, the building was constructed pursuant to a federal contract premised on federal statutory requirements. These federal requirements are superior, under the Supremacy Clause, to state requirements for construction.

Choice (A) is wrong. No interest of the company is being denied by requiring a sprinkler system.

Choice (B) is wrong. There is no denial of equal protection of the laws. All companies and all buildings constructed are subject to the same requirements.

Choice (D) is wrong. The Obligation of Contracts Clause is applicable where a state law is passed which retroactively impairs contractual duties and rights. There is no retroactive concern presented in this question.

MBE ANSWERS

AMERIBAR BAR REVIEW

Multistate Bar Examination – Answers to Questions – Section 4

CONTRACTS

Question 1
Answer: C

This question tests the law of consideration. Generally, courts presume that any degree of detriment is adequate to sustain a promise. In other words, a court is reluctant to invalidate a contract because one person receives a seemingly beneficial bargain because he gave up too little.

In this question Geriatrics and Ohlster had a valid express contract in which Geriatrics would supply lifetime care in exchange for Ohlster's $20,000. Geriatrics incurred the legal detriment of having to supply lifetime care to Ohlster in exchange for Ohlster's $20,000. Therefore consideration was exchanged and the contract will be enforced despite Geriatrics getting a beneficial bargain.

Answer choice (A) is incorrect because Geriatrics and Ohlster had a valid express contract, unjust enrichment does not apply in this situation.

Answer choice (B) is incorrect because frustration of purpose occurs when events that occur before the contract's performance result in destroying a party's purpose of entering into the contract. In this case the contract's performance began on October 1, prior to Ohlster's death.

Answer choice (D) is incorrect. This question does not test Geriatrics detrimental reliance.

Question 2
Answer: D

This question tests the law of breach of contract damages. A court seeks to afford a non-breaching party with the benefit of the bargain from a breaching party. With that relief, the non-breaching party will be placed into the position he or she expected to have been if the parties' contract had been performed. This includes any profits that would have been received. New businesses are able to recover lost profits if they can establish such profits with reasonable certainty.

Answer choice (A) is incorrect because the court incorrectly stated the law by limiting recovery to reasonably foreseeable damages.

Answer choice (B) is incorrect because the issue of damages is not solely a jury question.

Answer choice (C) is incorrect. Swatter is entitled to benefit of the bargain damages which include reasonably expected profits.

Question 3
Answer: C

This question tests the law of exclusive dealing and implied promises. Because this transaction involves the sale of goods the UCC applies. Section 2-306(2) of the UCC states that: "A lawful agreement by either the seller or the buyer for exclusive dealing in the kind of goods concerned imposes unless otherwise agreed an obligation by the seller to use best efforts to supply the goods and by the buyer to use best efforts to promote their sale." Despite the decline in demand for the buns, Bonnie's Buns still had an obligation to use their "best efforts" to sell the buns.

Answer choices (A) and (B) are incorrect. Section 2-306 of the UCC concerns requirement contracts, which are supported by sufficient legal detriment to be enforceable. Under such a contract the promisor undertakes to supply all of the output that a promisee needs. Such a contract implies that both of those parties will make a good faith determination of the requisite quantities. Therefore the contract will not fail for indefiniteness.

Answer choice (D) is incorrect because this question addresses the implied promise of Bonnie's Buns to use their best efforts to market the buns.

Question 4
Answer: C

This question tests the law of summary judgment proof. Summary judgment is appropriate only when there are no triable issues of fact. In this question whether Superpastries gave adequate notice of termination and whether their cessation of production was justified are both triable issues of fact. Therefore both issues are inappropriate for a summary judgment determination given the suggested facts.

Answer choice (A) is incorrect because Superpastries could terminate the contract upon reasonable notice. A triable issue of fact exists as to whether Superpastries gave reasonable notice therefore summary judgment is inappropriate.

Answer choice (B) is incorrect. This choice seeks to impute notice on Bonnie's Buns and imputed notice is clearly not provided for in the contract.

Answer choice (D) is incorrect. Given the termination clause in the contract Superpastries is not required to share its profits from the dog biscuits with Bonnie's Buns.

Question 5
Answer: A

This question tests the law of mutuality of obligation. The doctrine of mutuality of obligation provides that unless both parties to a contract are bound, neither is bound. If performance of a contractual obligation, which is the consideration for the contract, is elective, rather than mandatory, and the other party is required to perform some other duty, then there is no mutuality of obligation and therefore, no valid enforceable contract. In this case Acme's performance of the contract was elective prior to September 1 therefore no contract was formed as of July 22.

Answer choice (B) is incorrect. Acme's attempted offer failed because it was illusory. It was completely elective as to Acme as of July 22.

Answer choices (C) and (D) are incorrect because no contract was formed on July 22.

Question 6
Answer: A

This question tests the law of formation of a contract. A contract is a legally enforceable promise. Snowco's delivery of the shovels on September 15 was an acceptance of Acme's promise to pay for the shovels. After September 1, Acme's promise to purchase the shovels was legally enforceable assuming Snowco's acceptance was valid.

Because this transaction involved the sale of goods, the UCC governed it and Snowco had to comply with the perfect tender rule. Under section 2-601 of the UCC (the perfect tender rule): "[I]f the goods or the tender of delivery faii in any respect to conform to the contract, the buyer may: (a) reject the whole, (b) accept the whole, or (c) accept any commercial unit or units and reject the rest." Because Snowco's shipment conformed in all respects to Acme's order, the perfect tender rule was satisfied and Acme was required to accept and pay for the shovels.

Answer choice (B) is incorrect because this transaction did not involve an option contract. An option contract results when an offeror receives consideration from an offeree in order to keep an offer open for a certain period. There was no such consideration exchanged between Snowco and Acme.

Answer choice (C) is incorrect because this transaction did not involve a condition subsequent. A condition subsequent is an event that the parties agree will discharge a duty of performance after it has become absolute. Acme's right to cancel the order was not a condition subsequent.

Answer choice (D) is incorrect because Snowco complied with the terms of Acme's offer after September 1.

Question 7
Answer: C

This question tests the law of contract damages. Because this transaction involves the sale of goods the UCC applies. Under the UCC, usually either a non-breaching seller or a non-breaching buyer may recover expectation damages from a breaching party in a contract action. Section 1-106(a) of the UCC provides that the UCC's remedies, "shall be liberally administered to the end that the aggrieved party may be put in as good position as if the other party had fully performed." Thus, a seller may receive any profit that the seller could have made if full performance had occurred.

Answer choice (A) is incorrect because Zuma is entitled to the portion of his advance that does not represent an actual or expected loss suffered by Hydro-King.

Answer choice (B) is incorrect. Zuma is entitled to a portion of his advance payment that does not represent an actual or expected loss suffered by Hydro-King. Furthermore the lost volume sale rationale may apply if the standard measure of damages is inadequate to put the seller in as good of a position as would have performance of the contract.

Answer choice (D) is incorrect. The UCC does not provide for that award of damages.

Question 8
Answer: B

This question tests the law of acceptance by conduct. Generally, if beginning performance is a reasonable mode of acceptance, then it will constitute acceptance in a bilateral contract. In this case Waterman's beginning of drilling the well was a reasonable mode of acceptance. Therefore upon Waterman's drilling of the well a valid contract existed between he and Dewar.

Some contracts do not precisely spell out the obligations of each party. However, an examination of the facts may indicate that an obligation is presumed. In this case the facts indicate that Waterman had the obligation to drill the well to completion. This constituted an implied promise by Waterman to complete the well.

Answer choice (A) is incorrect because a contract was not formed when Dewar signed Waterman's proposal. Waterman's performance obligated him on the contract.

Answer choices (C) and (D) are incorrect because Waterman's performance by beginning drilling the well obligated him to finish the well.

Question 9
Answer: B

This question tests the law of the Parol Evidence Rule. The Parol Evidence Rule (Rule) is an exclusionary rule that requires the parties to incorporate into a contract, all of the terms and conditions to which they have agreed. The Rule provides that if the parties intend that a writing represent their agreement's final terms and conditions, the writing cannot subsequently be contradicted with extrinsic evidence of previous or contemporaneous agreements that supplement or contradict their contract's terms. However there are exceptions to the Rule that allow extrinsic evidence relating to conditions precedent to the written agreement or evidence that the contract was voidable. In this question the approval of Ohner's spouse was required as a condition precedent. Therefore the oral agreement is admissible in a breach of contract action brought by Planner.

Answer choice (A) is incorrect because approval by a third party by itself is not an exception to the Parol Evidence Rule.

Answer choice (C) is incorrect. The evidence at issue satisfies an exception to the Rule.

Answer choice (D) is incorrect. Typically the Rule bars contradictory extrinsic evidence, but in this case the extrinsic evidence satisfies an exception to the general exclusionary function of the Rule.

Question 10
Answer: C

This question tests the law of waiver of a condition. A condition is an event that must occur to obligate a party to perform under a contractual term or condition. If conditions are not fulfilled by a breaching party, they relieve a non-breaching party of any legal obligation under a contract. However, a party to a contract is entitled to waive a condition or conditions of the contract. By waiving a condition, the party relinquishes any right to that condition being satisfied. The waiver must occur before a duty to perform that condition becomes absolute.

Ohner arguably waived the condition of his law partner's approval of the landscaping design before his law partner's duty of approval became absolute and thereby relinquished any right to that condition being satisfied. Even if Ohner waived his law partner's approval of the landscaping design after his law partner's duty to approve the design became absolute, Ohner still ordered Planner to proceed with the work. This order, combined with Planner's 40 percent performance of the work pursuant to the design, makes Ohner's waiver irrevocable.

Answers (A), (B), and (C) are incorrect because the question asks which concept "best supports Planner's claim". In this question Ohner's waiver of his law partner's approval obligated him on the contract with Planner. Therefore waiver best supports Planner's breach of contract claim.

Question 11
Answer: A

This question tests the law of delegable duties. Contractual duties are generally delegable by a party to a contract. However, a duty is not delegable when a delegate's performance would materially vary from a promisor's performance. Contractual duties involving the exercise of special or unique talents are non-delegable. The exculpatory clause in the contract between Gyro and Tower was evidence that Tower hired Gyro based on its expertise in lifting and placing equipment atop tall buildings. It can be assumed that Tower would not have granted such a clause to a company that did not have Gyro's unique skills. Therefore the exculpatory clause limits Gyro's potential liability best supports Tower's contention that Gyro's duties under the contract were non-delegable.

Answer choice (B) is incorrect. Generally construction contracts or subcontracts involving objectively measurable performance are delegable. These per diem damages are clearly objectively measurable and therefore were delegable.

Answer choice (C) is incorrect because the "time is of the essence" clause does not overcome the presumption that contractual duties are generally delegable.

Answer choice (D) is incorrect because the extra-work clause does not make the contract non-delegable.

Question 12

Answer: A

This question tests the law of assignment of rights. Most contract rights are assignable. However, the promisor may bring an action against the assignor to obtain damages for violating a covenant in the contract. Therefore the promisor, Tower, may bring an action against the assignor, Gyro, to obtain damages resulting from Copter's negligent performance of the contract. Copter's negligent installation of the wrong equipment was therefore a breach of the contract for which Tower was liable.

Answer choice (B) is incorrect. No consideration is needed to make an assignment valid. While Tower is able to recover against Gyro in this breach of contract action, it is not because of a lack of consideration.

Answer choice (C) is incorrect. A novation is a type of substitute agreement that replaces at least one of the parties to a prior agreement into a subsequent agreement with a new party. The new party becomes a successor promisor to the original promisee under the subsequent agreement, which releases the predecessor promisor from the prior agreement. In this case there was no substitute agreement which released Tower from the initial contract. Gyro merely allowed Copter to perform the remainder of Tower's contract with Gyro; it did not substitute Copter with Tower.

Answer choice (D) is incorrect because the liquidated damages clause does not excuse negligent performance of the contract.

Question 13
Answer: B

This question tests the law third-party beneficiary contracts. An intended beneficiary is entitled to enforce the contract although the beneficiary did not assent to or know about it when it was made. The beneficiary's action may seek either damages or specific performance. Therefore, Elda, as the intended beneficiary, can succeed in an action on the contract between Alice and Barry.

Answer choice (A) is incorrect because Alice and Barry made an express contract which Elda as the third-party beneficiary can enforce.

Answer choice (C) is incorrect. Parents and children are free to contract, and upon breach pursue normal breach of contract remedies.

Answer choice (D) is incorrect. Alice and Barry entered into a contract enforceable by either of them as parties to the contract or by Elda as a third-party beneficiary.

Question 14
Answer: A

This question tests the law of enforcement of a third-party beneficiary contract. Under a third-party beneficiary contract, a promisor and a promisee agree that a third party, instead of the promisee, will receive the promisor's performance. Either party to the contract can seek of enforcement of the contract. Alice, as a party to the contract, is entitled to Barry's specific performance of the contract, an equitable remedy generally available in the absence of adequate remedy at law.

Answer choice (B) is incorrect because, absent the contract, Barry probably would not be legally required to support his mother, despite the burden this may place on Alice.

Answer choice (C) is incorrect because the fact that a contract requires the payment of money does not preclude specific performance of the contract.

Answer choice (D) is incorrect. Alice will be able to require that Barry continue to make the payments pursuant to their contract regardless of whether she was directly financially harmed. By definition, a breach of a contract intended to benefit a third-party beneficiary may result in harm to the third-party's interest alone.

Question 15
Answer: B

This question tests the law of impossibility of performance and mutual mistake. Mutual mistake can occur when neither party is aware of facts that existed before a contract's formation that make the contract impossible to perform. In this question, the enactment of the federal statute made it impossible for Barrel and Slidebolt to perform their contemplated contract because the statute rendered its subject matter illegal.

Because this transaction involves the sale of goods, the UCC firm offer rule applies. Under section 2-205 of the UCC, a merchant's (one who deals in such goods) offer contained in a signed writing is usually irrevocable for up to three months (90 days) without consideration. Such an offer by a merchant is called a firm offer. Therefore, Barrel had up to 90 days to accept Slidebolt's offer (assuming that the statute had not been enacted in the interim—consequently making this offer's subject matter illegal).

Answer choice (C) was flagged as a possible correct answer, indicating that a large number of test takers who did well on this question answered it with choice (C). The reason answer choice (B) is the correct answer, as opposed to choice (C), is because after the enactment of the federal statute performance became impossible, not impracticable.

Section 2-615(a) of the UCC provides in part that a seller's non-delivery, or a delay in delivery, is excused if "performance as agreed has been made impracticable by the occurrence of a contingency the non-occurrence of which was a basic assumption on which the contract was made." Impracticability occurs in situations where, for example, a significant shortage of required materials has prevented delivery of a particular good. In this case, it became illegal to make the sale. Therefore, impossibility of performance based on mutual mistake, not impracticability, was the correct answer.

Answer choice (A) is incorrect. The June 10 sale would have been a revocation if Barrel had known of the sale. In the absence of such knowledge, the offer to Barrel was not revoked due to the firm offer rule.

Answer choice (D) is incorrect. This choice incorrectly states the mailbox rule. The mailbox rule provides that an offeree's written communication of an acceptance (not rejection) occurs when it is placed into the mail in an authorized manner.

Question 16
Answer: A

This question tests the law of consideration. A contract must possess consideration for the contract to be formed. Consideration is required to enforce a promise. Generally consideration consists of a bargained for exchange of legal value in return for a legal benefit between two contracting parties. A bargained-for promise to relinquish a valid legal claim is adequate consideration to support a reciprocal promise.

In this question, Midas relinquished his valid claim to sue to collect the note until after December 31 in exchange for Spender's promise to pay interest until December 31. Therefore, the agreement is a valid defense for Spender to the suit filed by Midas on May 1.

Answer choice (B) is incorrect because reliance is not applicable in this case because consideration was exchanged.

Answer choice (C) is incorrect because consideration was exchanged to support Midas's promise not to pursue his claim against Spender until after December 31.

Answer choice (D) is incorrect. A reciprocal promise requires consideration to be enforceable.

Question 17
Answer: D

This question tests the law of promise. A party cannot gain relief on a promise in which they were the breaching party. As of April 1, Midas and Spender had a valid agreement in which Midas would not sue on the overdue note within a certain interval in exchange for Spender's promise to pay by December 31. When Midas filed suit in the small claims court on May 1, he breached his promise to Spender. Therefore, their April 1 agreement is not a claim upon which Midas can gain relief.

Answer choice (A) is incorrect because Midas breached this promise before Spender's performance was due.
Answer choice (B) is incorrect because generally a promise cannot be enforced based solely upon a moral obligation to perform the promise. Moreover, a majority of jurisdictions rule that a debtor's promise to pay a creditor for a pre-existing debt that otherwise a statute of limitations would preclude may be enforced, (1) although no new consideration supports it; and (2) if the

debtor made the new promise in a signed writing. However, this rule is not applicable to this question because new consideration was exchanged between Midas and Spender.

Answer choice (C) is incorrect. This question does not test the policy justifications for statutes of limitation.

Question 18
Answer: C

This question tests the law of suretyship and the Statute of Frauds. An agreement to answer for another's legally enforceable debt or duty must be in a writing. A surety has a collateral obligation relative to a separate arrangement between a creditor and the third-party debtor. The Statute of Frauds requires that the collateral obligation be reflected in a written agreement in order to be enforceable. The written agreement must be signed by the party to be charged.

One exception to the Statute of Frauds, the Main Purpose Rule, provides that when a promisor's primary reason for making the suretyship promise is to further some interest of the promisor, that promise does not fall under the Statute of Frauds. Therefore, Pater's best defense is that the primary purpose for making the promise was not to benefit him, but that it was made for another reason. If Pater can prove this, he will not be held liable for the debt because his agreement with Tertius was not in writing.

Answer choice (A) is incorrect because this question deals with Pater's role as a surety.

Answer choice (B) is incorrect because the Statute of Frauds requires that a suretyship agreement be in writing.

Answer choice (D) is incorrect. The agreement between Tertius and Carmen is enforceable despite the lack of a stated interest rate.

Question 19
Answer: B

This question tests the law of partial breach of contract. A partial or immaterial breach of a contract is one that does not fully impair its value and usually does not justify a non-breaching party in ceasing to perform under the contract. The non-breaching party may bring an action against a breaching party to recover damages that resulted from the immaterial breach.

The ordinary purpose of receiving damages for a breach of contract is to place a non-breaching party the position that the party would have been in had no breach occurred. Therefore, because three months of non-payment does not fully impair the value of the loan between Bower and Geetus, Geetus will only be able to recover $300 plus accrued interest for the partial breach.

Answer choice (A) is incorrect. Geetus can recover for a partial breach when it occurs.

Answer choice (C) is incorrect because failing to make three payments is a partial, not material, breach.

Answer choice (D) is incorrect. No facts in the question lead to the conclusion that Bower is insolvent.

Question 20
Answer: D

This question tests the law of formation. A legally enforceable contract requires an offer, acceptance, and consideration. Death of an offeror operates as a rejection of his offer.

Choice I is incorrect because Cash was serving as a surety for Bower therefore the consideration was Geetus's consent to loan Bower the $1000 based on Cash securing the loan. Choices II and III are incorrect because Geetus accepted Cash's offer to serve as a surety when he agreed to loan Bower the $1000 on September 15, one day prior to Cash's death. Because Geetus accepted Cash's offer on September 15, prior to the death of Cash, Geetus accepted prior to revocation of the offer by virtue of Cash's death.

Therefore, I, II, and III are incorrect choices.

Question 21
Answer: D

This question tests the law of contract interpretation. Because this transaction involved the sale of goods the UCC governs. Under section 2-208(1) of the UCC, evidence of an agreement's terms or meaning can be another party's approval and acquiescence thereof without making an objection. In this case there is evidence that Tune allowed Bill's to return undefective radios in the past. This is evidence of course of performance and will be admissible.

Answer choice (A) is incorrect. The Parol Evidence Rule will not bar this course of performance evidence.

Answer choice (B) is incorrect. There were no express terms in the contract prohibiting Bill's return on undefective radios.

Answer choice (C) is incorrect. The agreement does fall within the Statute of Frauds because the value of subject matter of the agreement for the sale of goods exceeds $500.

Question 22
Answer: B

This question tests the law of accord and satisfaction. Because this transaction involves the sale of goods the UCC governs. A majority of the states have enacted laws based on section 3-311 of the UCC. It provides that by depositing or cashing a qualifying check, a creditor fully discharges a debt. A creditor may, however, preserve its right to obtain a full payment of the debt by returning the debtor's payment within 90 days from receiving it. Therefore, by cashing Bills' check that stated "payment in full," Tune discharged any remaining duty Bill's had to purchase the 25 returned radios.

Answer choice (A) is incorrect. This question asks for Bill's best defense, which is accord and satisfaction, not estoppel.

Answer choice (C) is incorrect. A novation is a type of substitute agreement that replaces at least one of the parties to a prior agreement into a subsequent agreement with a new party. Clearly, novation does not apply to these facts.

Answer choice (D) is incorrect. The good faith dispute over the 25 radios did not suspend Bill's duty to pay other undisputed debts to Tune.

Question 23
Answer: A

Under the pre-existing duty rule, a contract modification will not be enforceable where no new consideration was provided in support of the modification. In this case, Paul was already obligated to paint Alice's office for $1,000, and she received no new consideration for the extra $200.

(B) is incorrect because Alice knew that additional amount would be $200 so the amount was not uncertain.

(C) is incorrect because Alice was not unjustly enriched as she was already entitled to getting her office painted for $1,000.

(D) is incorrect because performance was not impossible as evidenced by the fact that the job was completed. Performance is not impossible merely because it is time-consuming or costly.

Question 24
Answer: B

This question tests quasi-contracts. A quasi-contract is a legal fiction used by courts to prevent injustice. In this case, Paul invested time and money into completing half of the job and it would be unjust if he did not receive some compensation for the work which he completed.

(A) is incorrect because it would be unjust to bar Paul from recovery.

(C) and (D) are incorrect because Alice's contractual duty is also discharged because her purpose for entering the contract has been destroyed (frustration of purpose).

Question 25
Answer: A

This question tests the applicability of reformation. Reformation is a judicial modification of a written contract's original provisions in order to conform it to the parties' agreement. A party seeking reformation must show that: (1) the parties reached an agreement; (2) the parties decided to reduce their agreement to writing: (3) a variance exists between their agreement and the writing: and (4) the variance is a mutual mistake. Choices (B), (C), and (D) are incorrect because those mistakes were not mutual. Choice (A) is correct because there was a mutual mistake.

Question 26
Answer: D

This question tests orders or offers seeking a prompt shipment of goods. Under the UCC, a seller may accept an offer that seeks a prompt shipment of goods by promptly shipping them. Generally, when a seller sends the wrong goods its actions constitute an acceptance and a breach, not a counter-offer. A buyer may reject the goods within a reasonable time after their delivery. Thus, Fruitko does not have to accept the wrong goods. In this case, Orchard's shipment of the wrong type of peaches was an acceptance of Fruitko's offer. Fruitko is not required to accept No. 2 Royal Fuzz peaches because it ordered No. 1 Royal Fuzz peaches.

(A) and (B) are incorrect because Orchard's shipment was an acceptance, not a counter-offer.

(C) is incorrect because Fruitko may reject the wrongfully sent goods within a reasonable period of time after delivery.

Question 27
Answer: C

This question tests gratuitous assignments. If there is no consideration for an assignment, the assignment is gratuitously made and is not enforceable against an assignor. In this case, Aunt did not receive any consideration from Niece in exchange for Aunt's gift promise. Thus, the assignment of Debtor's $1,000 debt from Aunt to Niece was gratuitous. Moreover, Aunt's acceptance of the $1,000 from Debtor without objection revoked the assignment. Therefore, Niece cannot enforce the assignment.

(A) is incorrect because the assignment was gratuitous.

(B) is incorrect. A novation is a type of substitute agreement that replaces at least one of the parties to a prior agreement into a subsequent agreement with a new party. Clearly, novation does not apply to these facts.

(D) is incorrect because Aunt was free to assign her interest in the debt and Debtor was obligated to repay it.

Question 28
Answer: D

This question tests the method of acceptance. An offeror may dictate the method of acceptance. In this case, Koolair's offer explicitly stated that the acceptance had to be received on or before March 20. Hotz's letter arrived on March 21 and thus the attempted acceptance was ineffective.

(A) and (B) are incorrect because, if the written offer was signed, pursuant to the firm offer rule it had to be left open until March 20 because Koolair is a merchant selling goods under the Uniform Commercial Code.

(C) is incorrect because there is no rule that a revocation must be mailed, and Koolair's offer did not specify that mail was the only authorized means of revocation.

Question 29
Answer: B

This question tests the Parol Evidence Rule. The Parol Evidence Rule provides that if the parties intend that a writing represent their agreement's final terms and conditions, the writing may not be contradicted with extrinsic evidence of previous or contemporaneous agreements that supplement or contradict their contract's terms. In this case, the signed writing clearly indicated that Equinox could choose a gray horse. Equinox's claim that Stirrup orally agreed to let Equinox choose a gray or brown horse contradicts the written terms of their written contract. Thus, evidence of this claim is barred by the Parol Evidence Rule. Evidence of an oral agreement regarding the saddle, however, would be admissible because it does not contradict the language of the contract.

Question 30
Answer: C

This question tests compromise and settlement of claims. A settlement agreement is enforceable if (1) the parties had a good faith dispute when (2) they entered into a valid contract that resolved the dispute. In this case, Bypast did not bring the suit in good faith because he knew that Testator was competent but claimed otherwise. Thus, Bypast is not entitled to recover.

Question 31
Answer: B

This question tests the rules of land-sale contracts and specific performance. Ordinarily, time is not of the essence in land-sale contracts unless the parties expressly stipulate that it is. An exception to this rule occurs when the property in question is subject to great fluctuations in value. In this case, the value of the property actually increased by $10,000. The fair monthly rental value was $5,000 and Farmer lost half of one month's use of the property valued at $2,500. There was no express stipulation that time was of the essence and the value of the land did not decrease so the general rule applies.

(A) is incorrect because Green could have tendered the deed on January 15.

(C) is incorrect because time is generally not of the essence in land-sale contracts.

(D) is incorrect because a specific parcel of land is a unique item and money damages would not provide an adequate remedy. Thus, Green will probably succeed in an action against Farmer for specific performance.

Question 32
Answer: C

This question tests limitations on damages. A plaintiff can recover damages by showing that the damages were caused by the breach of the contract to a reasonable certainty, and that the breaching party could have foreseen the damages. In this case, the loss of the fair rental value was foreseeable and recoverable for the 15 day period. But the cost of grazing damages was not foreseeable because Green did not know that Farmer had purchased the cattle. Thus, Farmer may not recover this cost.

(A) is incorrect because Farmer specifically reserved the right to damages.

(B) is incorrect because the market value of the property still would have increased if Farmer had taken possession on January 15. And, therefore, he is still entitled to the fair rental value of Greenacre for 15 days.

(D) is incorrect because the damages for the cost of grazing were not foreseeable.

Question 33
Answer: A

This question tests the rule of incidental beneficiaries. When performance under a contract will not run directly to the third party to the contract, that individual or entity is an incidental beneficiary and may not sue to enforce rights under a contract. In this case, Collecta was an incidental beneficiary to the Broker-Hoarder contract and thus may not sue for the breach of that contract.

(B) is incorrect because Hoarder did sustain $2,000 in damages.

(C) is incorrect because Collecta was not an intended beneficiary of the Broker-Hoarder contract.

(D) is incorrect because Collecta did not take an assignment of Hoarder's claim against Broker.

Question 34
Answer: C

This question tests the difference between mutual mistake and uncertainty. A mutual mistake occurs when two parties make an assumption about a key fact on which their contract was premised and that assumption is incorrect. In this case, neither party hired an expert to test for granite. Also, there is no evidence that Venture assumed that there was no granite under the plot of land. Since neither party knew whether or not there was granite under the land, uncertainty existed and Bildko assumed the risk.

(A) is incorrect because severe impracticability does not fall under the doctrine of supervening impossibility.

(B) is incorrect because neither party knew whether or not there was a granite layer because neither party hired an expert and thus there was no mutual mistake.

(D) is incorrect because uncertainty existed and Bildko assumed the risk.

Question 35
Answer: D

This question tests the doctrine of promissory estoppel. Promissory estoppel can apply when a party relies on a promise and alters its position accordingly. However, the promise will only be enforced to the extent required to avoid injustice. In this case, there may not be any injustice.

(A) is incorrect because a gift promise may be enforceable under the doctrine of promissory estoppel.

(B) is incorrect because there is no rule that the gift need be equivalent to the reliance loss.

(C) is incorrect because the promisor need not receive an economic benefit.

Question 36
Answer: B

This question tests option contracts between contractors and subcontractors. When a contractor relies on a subcontractor's bid, an option contract is created and a contractor may recover the reliance loss from the subcontractor if the subcontractor pulls out.

Pursuant to the correct choice (B), Gennybelle would have a reliance loss because of the bid bond that the owner had required Gennybelle to submit. (A), (C), and (D) are incorrect because if Gennybelle could have amended or withdrawn its bid without forfeiting that bond, Gennybelle would not be not entitled to damages from Mural.

Question 37
Answer: D

This question tests unilateral mistake. If one party makes a unilateral mistake about a basic fact the contract will usually be upheld. However, it will not be upheld if the non-mistaken party (1) had knowledge of the mistake, (2) should have been aware of the mistake, (3) caused the mistake, or (4) took advantage of the mistake. In this case, Gennybelle had reason to suspect that Mural had made an error when calculating the sub-bid because his was $4,000 less than the other sub-bid amounts. If Mural could prove that, it would best support his defense.

(A) is incorrect because the subcontractor should have reasonably anticipated that the contractor's reliance on the bid would have created an option contract.

(B) is incorrect because Gennybelle's alleged unilateral mistake supports Mural's defense better than that provision of his sub-bid.

(C) is incorrect because Gennybelle's net profit is irrelevant.

Question 38
Answer: A

Section 2-204(a) of the UCC states that "a contract for the sale of goods may be made in any manner sufficient to show agreement." In this case, the parties made identical offers which may be sufficient to show agreement. Moreover, they made and received their respective offers on the same dates.

(B) is incorrect, although an accurate statement of law, because no traditional offer and acceptance occurred between Mater and Nirvana.

(C) is incorrect because identical cross-offers are not the same as an offer and acceptance because circumstances may change within the time between the sending of the cross-offers.

(D) is incorrect because Nirvana's status as a merchant affects its ability to revoke an offer, but does not estop Nirvana from denying that the counter-offers in this case created a binding contract.

Question 39
Answer: B

This question tests third-party beneficiary contracts. Courts will enforce an express contract for a third party's benefit if the third party is an intended beneficiary. In this case, Dilbert was expressly mentioned as a beneficiary in the contract so Dilbert is an intended beneficiary. Dilbert's rights became vested when he relied on the contract and sold his Cheetah and Nirvana was aware of this reliance.

(A) is incorrect because Mater made no assignment to Dilbert.

(C) is incorrect because Dilbert was an intended beneficiary, according to the express language of the contract.

(D) is incorrect because Nirvana had been informed that Dilbert sold his Cheetah, and Nirvana's sale to another party was unreasonable in light of its knowledge of Dilbert's reliance.

Question 40
Answer: C

Under section 2-209 of the UCC, no consideration is required to modify a contract subject to the UCC. However, the modification must be in writing if the UCC's Statute of Frauds applies to the contract. In this case, the contract falls under that Statute of Frauds because it involved goods worth at least $500. Here, the modification was in writing. Thus, under the UCC, no consideration was required to modify the contract.

(A) and (B) are incorrect because of the pre-existing duty rule.

(D) is incorrect because under section 2-302 of the UCC, unconscionability is based on the circumstances that existed when the contract was formed and not unexpected expenses encountered after contract formation.

Question 41
Answer: C

This question tests modifications. Under the modern rule, a modification may occur if (1) unanticipated or unforeseen problems occur that would cause an impracticable situation for one party and (2) the modification is considered to be fair. In this case, both elements are satisfied so Structo is entitled to $520,000.

(A) is incorrect because consideration is not required for modifications under the modern rule.

(B) is incorrect because there is no evidence of a threat or a wrongful act by Structo and the modification was motivated by unanticipated difficulties.

(D) is incorrect because the reasonable value of Structo's performance is not relevant to the modification.

Question 42
Answer: D

This question tests material breach. If a breaching party performs in bad faith or willfully fails to perform contractual duties, the non-breaching party may (1) suspend performance, (2) refuse performance by the breaching party, and (3) commence a lawsuit to recover damages. The amount of damages available to the non-breaching party is the amount required to put that party in the position it would have been in if the contract had been fully performed. In this case, Structo breached the contract by building a ramp that trucks and cars could not use safely. If Structo had fully performed its contractual duties, Bailey would have the ramp it wanted for $500,000. Bailey will have to spend $30,000 to achieve this position so Structo is only entitled to the $470,000 already paid by Bailey.

(A), (B), and (C) are incorrect because Bailey is entitled to damages to be in the position it would have been in had Structo not breached the contract.

Question 43

Answer: A

This question tests the Parol Evidence Rule. The Parol Evidence Rule excludes extrinsic evidence of previous or contemporaneous agreements that supplement or contradict a contract's terms. However, the Rule does not apply to evidence about the meaning of ambiguous contractual terms. In this case, the phrase "all tires required by this agreement" is much different than if the contractual language had been "all the tires required by County." The latter would constitute a requirement contract, but the former is not very clear. Thus, the advertisement concerning the possibility of multiple awards should be admitted by the Court because it relates to the ambiguous term.

(B) is incorrect because the advertisement did not need to be in writing.

(C) is incorrect because the Parol Evidence Rule does not apply to evidence which helps to define ambiguous contractual terms.

(D) is incorrect because the court would likely find an implied promise by County in the contract.

Question 44
Answer: B

This question tests requirement contracts. Under section 2-306(2) of the UCC, "a lawful agreement by either the seller or the buyer for exclusive dealing in the kind of goods concerned imposes (unless otherwise agreed) an obligation by the seller to use the best efforts to supply the goods and by the buyer to use the best efforts to promote their sale." In this case, if the court finds a requirements contract, Tyres will be able to recover under the UCC because County is in violation by not dealing exclusively with Tyres.

(A) is incorrect because there is no mention of requirement contracts in the Obligation of Contracts Clause of the U.S. Constitution.

(C) and (D) are incorrect because under section 2-306(2) of the UCC, there is mutuality of obligation, the buyer and seller must use their best efforts to supply and use the goods, and the quantity need not be exact.

Question 45
Answer: A

This question tests adequacy of consideration. Generally, courts presume that any degree of detriment is adequate to sustain a promise even if one party receives a seemingly beneficial bargain because he or she gave up too little. In this case, Betsy agreed to pay $3,000, which is a clear detriment. The Court is likely to find Betsy's payment adequate to sustain the contract.

(B) is incorrect because generally moral obligation is insufficient consideration to render a promise enforceable.

(C) is incorrect because the consideration is adequate even though Betsy appears to have received a beneficial bargain.

(D) is incorrect because Rollem is responsible for the actions of its employees.

Question 46
Answer: D

This question tests legal detriments. Under the majority rule, a promisee must incur a legal detriment. A legal detriment is an obligation to do something one would otherwise not be able to do or to refrain from doing something which one has a legal right to do. In this case, Graceful was not legally obligated to run a six minute mile before Loomis made his promise, despite the fact that Graceful had run six minute miles in the past. Graceful's motives for running in this case are irrelevant because Graceful incurred a legal detriment and performed the specified mile as requested.

(A) is incorrect because inducement is not required under the majority rule.

(B) is incorrect because Graceful still incurred a legal detriment.

(C) is incorrect because a task does not need to be significantly demanding to constitute a legal detriment.

Question 47
Answer: B

In this case, no mention was made of progress payments so Karp was not entitled to progress payments. Manor is thus not in breach of the contract. Karp, however, has failed to perform by abandoning the job. Therefore, Karp has breached the contract.

(A) and (C) are incorrect because Manor has not breached the contract. (C) and (D) are incorrect because Karp has breached the contract.

Question 48
Answer: C

This question tests assignment of rights. Contract rights are generally assignable. However, if the assignor materially breaches the contract, the assignee's rights are worthless. In this case, Karp materially breached the contract with Manor. Banquo (Karp's assignee) cannot recover from Manor.

(A) and (B) are incorrect because Karp materially breached the contract and the rights Karp assigned to Banquo are worthless.

(D) is incorrect because priority of claims is not determined by which claim arose first.

Question 49
Answer: D

This question tests the "Battle of the Forms." Under section 2-207 of the UCC, the mirror-image rule no longer applies. Rather, a written confirmation acts as an acceptance even if it adds terms or is in a different form, unless acceptance is expressly made conditional on assent to the different or additional terms. In this case, acceptance was not made expressly conditional on assent to the liability-limitation clause. Thus, there is an enforceable contract but the liability-limitation clause is not a part of the contract.

(A) is incorrect because a material alteration is excluded from, but does not negate, a contract.

(B) is incorrect because there is still a contract under section 2-207 of the UCC.

(C) is incorrect because liquidation of damages must be reasonable and limiting liability to $100 on a $10,000 contract is unreasonable.

Question 50
Answer: B

This question tests promissory estoppel. Promissory estoppel applies if (1) an offeror makes a promise to an offeree (2) under circumstances that the offeree would reasonably anticipate the promise to be fulfilled and (3) the offeror would reasonably anticipate that the offeree would alter positions based on that promise. In this case, all three elements are satisfied, so Dominique does have a cause of action against Hardcash under promissory estoppel.

(A) is incorrect because demolishing the building was not an acceptance.

(C) is incorrect because bargained-for exchange is not a requirement of promissory estoppel.

(D) is incorrect because the project did not need to be financially sound for Dominique to rely on Hardcash's promise.

Question 51
Answer: C

This question tests relief under the doctrine of promissory estoppel. Under promissory estoppel, a promise is only enforced to the extent required to avoid injustice. This means that only reliance damages can be recovered. In this case, Dominique relied on Hardcash's promise when she had the building demolished.

(A) and (B) are incorrect because relief under promissory estoppel is for reliance damages, not expectancy damages.

(D) is incorrect because Dominique's reliance loss can be calculated.

Question 52
Answer: B

This question tests conditions precedent. A condition precedent is an event that must happen before a duty to perform under a contract becomes due. In this case, there was a condition precedent that Kranc notify Schaff in writing no later than January 2 that Kranc had arranged to resell the engine to a third person or "there is no deal." Kranc did not notify Schaff in writing by January 2, so the condition precedent failed.

(A) is incorrect because the secretary's clerical error is not a mutual mistake because the parties did not make an incorrect assumption about a key fact on which their contract was premised.

(C) is incorrect because the principal purpose of the contract has not been frustrated. Also, there is no evidence suggesting that the parties assumed that the engine's value would not fluctuate.

(D) is incorrect because evidence of a condition precedent is not excluded by the Parol Evidence Rule. Thus, the oral agreement is admissible.

Question 53
Answer: C

Waiver is a voluntary relinquishment of a known right. In this case, Schaff waived the right to require Kranc to provide written notice by January 2. The waiver of this condition precedent supports Kranc's claim.

(A) is incorrect because Kranc has not paid anything yet. Thus, Kranc has not substantially performed.

(B) is incorrect because there was no condition subsequent.

(D) is incorrect because Kranc (not Trimota) is still the buyer. So, there is no novation.

Question 54
Answer: B

This question tests rescission for a unilateral mistake. Judicial relief from a unilateral mistake may occur when a mistaken party establishes the following elements:

     (1) a mistake in a basic assumption upon which the contract is premised; and
     (2) the mistake materially affects or imbalances the parties' performances; and
     (3) the plaintiff does not bear the risk of mistake; and
     (4) either the non-mistaken party knew of or had reason to know of the mistake; or
     (5) the mistake makes enforcing the contract unconscionable.

Answer choice (B) is the only choice in which element (4) is satisfied.

(A) and (C) are incorrect because they focus on Walker's knowledge which is not relevant to element (4).

(D) is incorrect because there is no suggestion that Sherwood knew or should have known about the mistake.

Question 55
Answer: A

This question tests rescission for a mutual mistake. Judicial relief from a mutual mistake may occur when a mistaken party establishes the following elements:

(1) a mistake in a basic assumption upon which the contract is premised; and

(2) the mistake materially affects or imbalances the parties' performances; and

(3) the plaintiff does not bear the risk of mistake.

Answer choice (A) best supports a rescission action by Sherwood because the three elements are more likely to be satisfied in (A) than in the other answer choices.

(B) is incorrect because rescission seeks to return each party to their respective positions that existed before the contract's execution, and Sherwood has profited since the sale.

(C) is incorrect because the contract was not premised on which horse sired Aberlone.

(D) is incorrect because animals sometimes go berserk. Also, Sherwood is more likely to have assumed that risk than to have assumed the risk that Aberlone suffered from a rare heart defect.

Question 56
Answer: C

This question tests constructive conditions. All contracts contain a constructive condition that if a first party expects reciprocal performance from a second party, then the first party must perform its contractual duties. In this case, Kabb breached the contract by buying from another supplier. Consequently, Petrol is not obligated to reciprocally perform.

(A) and (B) are incorrect because Petrol is not obligated to perform due to Kabb's breach.

(D) is incorrect because a third party beneficiary to a contract is not required to provide consideration.

Question 57
Answer: A

This question tests contract modification when a third party beneficiary is involved. The parties to a contract may mutually alter or eliminate third party rights under a contract before those rights vest. Third party rights vest when a third party (1) discovers a third-party contract and assents to it, (2) materially alters his or her position based upon a promise, or (3) commences a suit to enforce a promise. In this case, Artiste declined to accept another contract due to her reliance on the Petrol-Kabb contract before Kabb told Petrol that Petrol no longer had to advertise with Artiste. Thus, the third-party rights vested before the original parties attempted to eliminate them. Therefore, Artiste will likely succeed in a breach of contract action against Petrol.

(B) is incorrect because Petrol would be in breach of the contract even if Kabb had acted in good faith.

(C) and (D) are incorrect because the third-party rights vested before the original parties attempted to eliminate them.

Question 58
Answer: A

This question tests liquidated damages provisions. A court will enforce a contract's liquidated damages provision only when actual damages are (1) difficult to ascertain or uncertain in amount and (2) reasonably estimated either at a contract's formation or when the contract was breached. In this case, Mermaid had to stay out two hours beyond the customary return time and made $100 less for the day. It would be difficult for Mermaid to establish her actual damages but the sum of $200 appears reasonable. Thus, the Court will enforce the liquidated damages provision. Mermaid is entitled to retain the $200 deposit.

(B) is incorrect because the $50 Mermaid would be allowed to keep is less than her $100 loss in money for the day and does not even take into account her lost time.

(C) is incorrect because Mermaid has not been unjustly enriched since her time is also worth money damages.

(D) is incorrect because the damages are not unreasonably large. Thus, they do not act as a penalty.

Question 59
Answer: A

This question tests impossibility. A party's contractual duty may be discharged by impossibility when an unforeseen event occurs or unexpected circumstances arise which render the duty impossible to perform. In this case, all vessels of Mermaid's size were banned from leaving the harbor. So, the contract was discharged due to impossibility.

(B) is incorrect because mistake relates to misunderstandings about existing facts at the time of contract formation. The "heavy weather" warnings, however, came after contract formation.

(C) is incorrect because all small vessels were banned from leaving the harbor. So, even if Mermaid's boat would have been seaworthy, taking it out of the harbor would have been impossible.

(D) is incorrect because the liquidated-damages clause was only applicable if Phinney canceled or failed to appear. It did not cover impossibility. Also, liquidated damages provisions are disfavored by courts.

Question 60
Answer: C

This question tests impossibility. A party's contractual duty may be discharged for impossibility when an unforeseen event occurs, or unexpected circumstances arise, which render the duty permanently impossible to perform. In this case, Megahawg's illness was likely to last until after the fair was over, so performance was impossible. Thus, all remaining duties under the contract were discharged.

(A) is incorrect because written assurances are asked for after an expression of doubt (not after performance becomes impossible). Additionally, any repudiation would not be actionable because the duties of both parties were discharged for impossibility.

(B) is incorrect because there was no breach of contract because the duties of both parties were discharged for impossibility.

(D) is incorrect because there is no substitute for a world champion animal since there is only one world champion.

Question 61
Answer: A

This question tests a seller's right to cure. Under section 2-508(1) of the UCC, when a non-conforming tender of goods is rejected before the time of performance expires, the seller may notify the buyer of his intention to cure. Further, the seller may make a conforming delivery within the contract time. In this case, the time for performance expired on June 1. Thus, Trailco had a right to cure the defect by then.

(B) is incorrect because section 2-508(1) of the UCC mitigates the perfect tender rule.

(C) and (D) are incorrect because Nimrod is not required to accept a defective product.

Question 62
Answer: B

This question tests orders or offers seeking a prompt shipment of goods. Under the UCC, a seller may accept an offer that seeks a prompt shipment of goods by promptly shipping them. A shipment of non-conforming goods is an acceptance and breach. However, a shipment of nonconforming goods with a reasonable notice of accommodation constitutes a counter-offer, instead of an acceptance and breach. The buyer may reject or accept the counter-offer.

In this case, Zeller shipped non-conforming goods to Buyem by sending red widgets instead of blue widgets. Zeller also included the price and quantity of widgets in its reasonable notice of accommocation. In under these facts, Zeller's conduct constitutes a counter-offer, rather than an acceptance and breach. Buyem is free to accept the terms of the counter-offer or to reject them.

(A) and (C) are incorrect because Zeller never accepted the contract for blue widgets so there was no breach.

(C) and (D) are incorrect because if Buyem accepts Zeller's counter-offer, Buyem must pay the list price.

(D) is incorrect because Buyem is not required to buy conforming widgets from another seller in order to reject Zeller's offer.

Question 63
Answer: D

(I) is incorrect because the only types of duties that are generally non-delegable are those involving a confidential relationship, those involving unique talents, and those requiring personal skill, knowledge, or judgment.

(II) is incorrect because a delegate is not required to make an express promise to perform because the delegate is obligated to perform after being assigned all of the delegator's contracts.

(III) is incorrect because "assignment" refers to both the assignment of rights and the delegation of duties.

Question 64
Answer: D

(I) is incorrect because Eclaire could only deny accepting the delegation if Miller's performance would materially vary from that of Staff.

(II) and (III) are incorrect because, though Staff remained obligated to Eclaire, Staff assigned the contract right to receive payments to Miller.

Question 65
Answer: B

This question tests accord and satisfaction. A creditor who deposits or cashes a check with "payment in full" written on it in good faith is subject to a valid accord and satisfaction if the debt (1) is subject to an honest dispute and (2) is not definite in amount. In this case, Lawyer deposited Client's check that stated "Payment in full" without objection. Also, they honestly disputed the amount of the debt. Thus, an accord and satisfaction occurred.

(A) is incorrect because the risk of unexpected title problems is not allocated to a seller's attorney.

(C) and (D) are incorrect because there was an accord and satisfaction.

Question 66
Answer: B

This question tests modifications. Under section 2-209(1) of the UCC, no consideration is necessary to modify an agreement for the sale of goods. In this case, Barrister was not required to provide any consideration in exchange for the stacks.

(A) is incorrect because Barrister provided no consideration.

(C) is incorrect because the original contract was modified, not rescinded.

(D) is incorrect because no consideration is necessary to modify a contract under the UCC.

Question 67
Answer: B

This question tests revocations. An offeror may revoke an offer at any time before an offeree accepts it, in the absence of (1) consideration exchanged to keep the offer open, (2) detrimental reliance (reasonably suffered) by the offeree, or (3) the offeror being a merchant selling goods under the UCC. In this case, all three elements are absent. Thus, the communication operated as a legally effective revocation.

(A) is incorrect because contracts can be modified without consideration under the UCC. Thus, Barrister's pre-existing duty is not relevant.

(C) is incorrect because there was no consideration to keep the offer open, no reasonably suffered detrimental reliance, and Debbit is not a merchant.

(D) is incorrect because Barrister's reliance was not reasonable because Barrister is a lawyer.

Question 68
Answer: B

This question tests specific performance. Specific performance is usually not enforced on personal service contracts because: (1) the Thirteenth Amendment to the U.S. Constitution bars involuntary servitude; and (2) it is difficult to force adverse parties to collaborate on a project.

(A) is incorrect because one year might not constitute an unreasonable delay in filing suit especially since Galley spent time searching for another party to remodel.

(C) is incorrect because there is no bar to equitable relief in cases of anticipatory repudiation.

(D) is incorrect because specific performance is an available remedy where money damages would not provide adequate relief even if nominal damages could have been recovered.

Question 69
Answer: B

Under the common law, a court seeks to afford a non-breaching party with the benefit of the bargain from a breaching party. The non-breaching party is placed in the position it expected to be in if the contract had been performed. In this case, Joiner expected to make a $3,000 profit and is thus entitled to $3,000 in expectation damages.

(A) is incorrect because Joiner is still entitled to expectation damages despite failing to mitigate.

(C) and (D) are incorrect because Joiner should not have relied on the contract after Galley repudiated it.

Question 70
Answer: C

This question tests implied-in-fact contracts.   An implied-in-fact contract arises from an agreement manifested by the parties' conduct. A contract will be implied-in-fact when an intention is not manifested by words between the parties, but may be gathered by deduction from their conduct, language, or other circumstances.   In (C), an implied-in-fact contract exists because Nabor's silence while watching Asphalt pave his driveway acted as an acceptance.

(A) is incorrect because there is a contract, which may be rescinded on the basis of mutual mistake.

(B) is incorrect because Ryder did not act in a way to suggest that a contract existed.

(D) is incorrect because there is a traditional offer and acceptance occurred.

Question 71
Answer: D

This question tests trade usage. According to the UCC, trade usage is "any practice or method of dealing having such regularity of observance in a place, vocation or trade as to justify an expectation that it will be observed with respect to the transaction in question." In this case, trade usage evidence may be used to define the contract term "promote in good faith the sale of Fizzy Cola." If it is customary practice for distributors to handle only one brand of cola, it is unlikely that a distributor promoting more than one brand is acting in good faith.

(A) is incorrect because if Happy-Time is free to distribute more than one brand of cola, the disparaging remarks are irrelevant.

(B) is incorrect because the decrease in sales could have been caused by many different factors.

(C) is incorrect because what a Happy-Time representative said before the deal is not a part of the contract as signed. Also, it is likely barred by the Parol Evidence Rule.

Question 72
Answer: D

This question tests election. An election is a choice to waive a condition by a non-breaching party after a breaching party's failure to fulfill the condition. In this case, Bitz failed to fulfill a condition for three years and Presskey elected to waive the condition. Bitz relied on Presskey's conduct of not complaining about the lack of fulfillment of the condition when Bitz purchased new equipment.

(A), (B), and (C) are incorrect because waiver of a condition does not require a contract modification.

Question 73
Answer: D

This question tests suretyship contracts. A suretyship is an agreement to answer for another party's legally enforceable debt or duty. Contracts of suretyship require broad disclosures to the surety (i.e., guarantor). In this case, Freund had to be given notice of the sale to Wrench for the suretyship agreement to be enforceable by Tuff.

(A) is incorrect because the Statute of Frauds does apply to suretyship contracts.

(B) is incorrect because acting upon an offer is the proper way to accept a unilateral contract.

(C) is incorrect because Freund induced Tuff to give credit to Wrench, so Freund's promise is enforceable.

Question 74
Answer: A

This question tests expressions of doubt. A mere expression of doubt about a party's willingness or ability to perform a contract will not serve as an anticipatory breach. In this case, Broker can argue that writing that requiring his performance would be unfair is not a repudiation of the contract. That would allow Broker to have until the end of the contract period to perform.

(B) is incorrect because specific performance is reserved for cases in which money damages would not provide an adequate remedy. In this case the value of the coin can be ascertained. Also, Broker no longer has the coin so specific performance would be impossible.

(C) is incorrect because impossibility does not include impracticability.

(D) is incorrect because Hoarda is not required to ask Broker to retract his repudiation before filing suit.

Question 75
Answer: C

This question tests repudiation. When a party repudiates a contract, the other party may file a lawsuit for breach of contract before the end of the contract term. In this case, Broker repudiated the contract. Thus Hoarda had the right to file suit before the end of the contract term.

(A) is incorrect because Hoarda was not required to sue immediately and could have waited until after the contract period expired.

(B) is incorrect because the repudiatee does not need to owe a duty to the repudiator.

(D) is incorrect because anticipatory repudiation may support a breach of contract claim, not a tort claim.

Question 76
Answer: B

This question tests the UCC's provision for a merchant's confirmatory memo, a type of exception to the Statute of Frauds. When the parties to a purported contract are merchants who have not executed a formal written agreement, a written memorandum may satisfy the Statute of Frauds if it (1) confirms the contract, (2) the sending merchant signs it, (3) the receiving merchant who gets the memorandum has reason to know of its contents, and (4) does not object to it in writing within 10 days after receiving it. In this case, all four elements were satisfied. Thus, the faxed confirmatory memo was sufficient to make the contract enforceable.

(A) is incorrect because identifying and tendering alone would not satisfy the Statute of Frauds.

(C) is incorrect because a signed writing is not required because the memo is sufficient.

(D) is incorrect because Slalome did not need to pay for the goods or accept them in order to be bound by the contract.

Question 77
Answer: D

This question tests the pre-existing duty rule. The pre-existing duty rule usually precludes enforcement of a contract modification if no new consideration is provided in support of the modification. An exception applies, however, when the promisee's duty is owed to a different party than the party to which this pre-existing duty is owed. In this case, Snoop's pre-existing duty was owed to Artistic and his new duty was owed to Collecta. Therefore, the pre-existing duty rule does not apply and Snoop wins.

(A) and (B) are incorrect because (1) Snoops pre-existing duty was owed to Artistic, and (2) Snoop's duty under the subsequent agreement was owed to Collecta.

(C) is incorrect because it does not matter under which scenario Collecta would be better off.

Question 78
Answer: C

This question tests capacity to contract for minors. Minors have the capacity to enter into contracts that are voidable. A minor may disaffirm or ratify a contract after reaching the age of majority. If a minor expressly ratifies a contract after reaching the age of majority, the minor will be liable only to the extent acknowledged in the ratification. In this case, Starr acknowledged a debt of $75 so that is what she is liable for.

(A) is incorrect because the original contract was voidable, not void.

(B) is incorrect because no new consideration was required.

(D) is incorrect because Starr only acknowledged owing $75 after reaching the age of majority.

Question 79
Answer: D

This question tests implied promises. Sometimes, courts will imply a duty to use reasonable efforts when a promise would otherwise be illusory. In this case, Starr's promise to pay as soon as she is able appears to be illusory because she may never be able. However, courts tend to err on the side of enforcing contracts. In this case, courts are likely to imply a duty for Starr to raise enough money to pay for the telescope.

(A) is incorrect because (D) is correct.

(B) is incorrect because (1) courts presume that all contracts contain a requirement of good faith performance and (2) courts tend to err on the side of enforcing contracts.

(C) is incorrect because the party seeking enforcement must prove his or her claim.

Question 80
Answer: D

This question tests assignments. Assignments normally do not need to be made in writing. However, one exception is that an assignment made in consideration of marriage must be in writing. In this case, Dr. Pulmonary's oral assignment to Bridey was not effective because it was made as a wedding gift. Pulmonary's assignment to Margin was in writing and is legally binding.

(A) and (B) are incorrect because a promisor is only required to render performance to an assignee if the promisor possesses knowledge of the assignment.

(C) is incorrect because the assignment to Bridey did not satisfy the Statute of Frauds.

Question 81
Answer: C

This question tests the law of breach of contract. A total or material breach of contract occurs when a breaching party fails to substantially perform the contract and a non-breaching party has no means to cure that breach. To determine if the breach is material one must consider: (1) Did a party fail to abide by the contract's terms? (2) To what degree is a non-breaching party deprived of a reasonably expected benefit? (3) To what degree will damages sufficiently compensate a non-breaching party? (4) To what degree has a breaching party partially performed? (5) How probable is it that a breaching party will cure the breach? (6) How willful is the breach under the circumstances? (7) To what extent is a there a delay in performance? (8) To what degree will a breaching party suffer forfeiture?

In this case, Bell would be liable for total breach of contract if Ames properly or substantially painted the porch because (1) Ames completed his obligations under the contract, and (2) Bell has refused to fulfill his obligation of paying Ames $2,000. When Bell's breach is analyzed to determine if it was material, one finds that Bell failed to follow the express term of paying $2,000. Ames, the non-breaching party, is completely deprived of receiving $2,000, which will be sufficiently compensated by damages. Bell made no attempt to pay any of the money owed to Ames, hence he has not partially performed. One can gather from the facts that Bell has no intention of paying Ames. Bell willfully refused to pay after performance was completed. So, Bell would receive the complete benefit from the contract without fulfilling his duty. As the above analysis shows, Bell's breach was material.

(A) is not correct because Bell materially breached the contract.

(B) and (D) are not correct because had Ames not properly or substantially painted the porch Bell would not likely be found to have breached the contract.

Question 82
Answer: C

This question tests the law of compromise and settlement of claims. A promise to relinquish a valid claim is a detriment and, when bargained for, is consideration. A promise to relinquish an invalid claim is a detriment if a claimant makes it in good faith and a reasonable man could believe that the claim was well founded. The *Restatement* provides that either good faith or objective uncertainty as to a claim's validity is sufficient. A settlement agreement is enforceable if the parties to it (1) had a good faith dispute when (2) they entered into a valid contract that resolved the dispute.

In this case, Bell and Ames were having a dispute over the $2,000 Bell owed Ames. Bell's check for $1,800 that stated, "In full on the Ames-Bell painting contract as per letter dated June 18" was consideration for the contract described in the letter of June 18 (Bell would pay Ames $1,800 if Ames repainted Bell's porch). Hence, when Ames cashed the check he accepted the terms of the contract and promised to relinquish his claim, thus ending the dispute.

Ames' claim for $2,000 is most likely valid. And if the claim were invalid, the facts indicate that a reasonable man would believe the claim is well founded, and that Ames' made it in good faith. The facts also indicate Bell is refusing to pay based on his good faith belief that Ames did not do an adequate job. So, both parties are acting in good faith and have entered into a valid contract that has resolved the dispute.

(A), (B), and (D) are incorrect because when Ames cashed Bell's check he agreed to a new contract, which ended the dispute over the $2,000.

Question 83
Answer: A

This question tests the law of acceptance. Acceptance by conduct occurs when a party's actions could be found by a reasonable person to imply assent to the contract. It is important to remember that acceptance by conduct is an objective standard, and a party's subjective intent does not matter.

In this case, Bell offered Ames a new contract on June 18 via the letter, which acted as an offer, proposing that Ames repaint the porch in exchange for $1,800. Ames never responded to this offer. From an objective point of view, Ames has neither accepted nor rejected the offer at this point. When Ames receives Bell's check on June 30, the check clearly states that this is the $1,800 promised in the June 18 contract. Ames says nothing and cashes the check. Using the objective standard, a reasonable man could find that Ames' actions show intent to assent to Bell's contract. Objectively, Ames has said nothing concerning the newly proposed contract. Ames cashed Bell's check, which was clearly intended by Bell to fulfill his promise in the new contract of paying Ames $1,800. When one studies these objective circumstances, one can conclude that Ames intended to assent to Bell's contract.

(B) is incorrect because mere silence generally is not acceptance. Usually, there must be some manifest action on Ames' part to give rise to the inference of acceptance.

(C) is incorrect because Ames did accept the offer by cashing Bell's check.

(D) is incorrect because there was consideration to support Ames' promise. Ames' promise was to repaint the porch in exchange for $1,800. There is detriment to Ames, because he is bound to repaint Bell's porch, something he was not legally bound to do. Furthermore, Ames has impliedly promised to relinquish his claim of $2,000, another detriment.

Question 84
Answer: D

This question tests your understanding of immaterial breach. An immaterial breach occurs when the breaching party is guilty of a minor breach. To determine if a breach is minor the breaching party must show that he or she acted in good faith or that a non-breaching party did not suffer great hardship due to the alleged breach. If the breaching party can establish either of the above defenses, the breach will be considered immaterial. In the case of an immaterial breach, the non-breaching party's only remedy is damages. Thus, the non-breaching party could not suspend performance or terminate the contract.

In this case, Bertha's breached the contract when she was unable to perform for a week. Bertha can show that she acted in good-faith because she did not intend, in bad-faith, to breach the contract, she simply became ill and could not perform. Furthermore, Bertha's failure to perform for one week most likely did not result in Albert suffering great hardship, as Bertha was out for a relatively short period of time. Thus, Bertha has established the defenses necessary to show that her breach was immaterial, meaning Albert is not allowed to terminate her contract.

(A) is incorrect. In order to be severable, a contract must either contain a "severability clause" or contain multiple promises to do multiple things based upon distinct considerations. In this contract, Bertha's only promise is to perform her role for six months. Bertha being compensated every two weeks is likely not enough to show severability, because she has no separate promises to fulfill.

(B) is incorrect because the terms of the contract were subjectively impossible. In other words, the terms were only impossible for Bertha to perform, but a third party could have performed the terms. Subjective impossibility is not a valid basis for nonperformance of a contractual duty.

(C) is incorrect because detrimental reliance usually applies to the offeror's ability to revoke an offer. In this case, the offer has already been accepted. Albert is attempting to terminate the contract. Detrimental reliance can be used after performance begins, but only in cases of a unilateral contract. In this case, we clearly have a bilateral contract. Thus, detrimental reliance does not apply.

Question 85
Answer: C

The correct answer is (C). This question tests compromise and settlement of claims. A settlement agreement is only enforceable if (1) the parties had a good faith dispute when (2) they entered into a valid contract that resolved the dispute. In this case, Bypast did not bring the suit in good faith because he knew that Testator was competent but claimed otherwise. Thus, Bypast is not entitled to recover.

Question 86
Answer: D

This question tests your knowledge of the Statute of Frauds. The Statute of Frauds requires certain contracts to be in writing. Two of these contracts are suretyship and land contracts. Suretyship is when a contract is made for the purpose of paying another's legally enforceable debt. Suretyship does have an exception known as the Main Purpose Rule. The Main Purpose Rule provides that when a promisor's primary reason for making the suretyship promise is to further some interest of the promisor, that promise does not fall under the Statute of Frauds. A land contract applies to the sale of parcels, leases, and mortgages.

In this problem, the suretyship entered into between Byer and Zeller for the benefit of Quincy falls under the Main Purpose Rule because Byer's purpose of making the suretyship was to further his interest of buying Zeller's home. In other words, the main purpose for the Byer-Zeller contract was for Byer to purchase the house, not to pay Zeller's debt, thus this contract is not required to be in writing and is still enforceable.

The second part of the problem deals with the contract for Zeller's land. This contract is required by the Statute of Frauds to be in writing because it deals with a parcel of land. As per the Statute of Frauds, this transaction was put into writing by Byer's secretary, meaning the contract for Zeller's land is valid. However, this would only result in two agreements. One written agreement for the sale of Zeller's land, and a second, oral agreement for Byer to pay $25,000 to Quincy.

Question 87
Answer: A

This question tests your knowledge of the Parol Evidence Rule. The Parol Evidence Rule (Rule) is an exclusionary rule that requires the parties to incorporate into a contract, all of the terms and conditions to which they have agreed. The Rule provides that if the parties intend that a writing represent their agreement's final terms and conditions, the writing cannot subsequently be contradicted with extrinsic evidence of previous or contemporaneous agreements that supplement or contradict their contract's terms. The Rule is applied through the four corners test, which allows the written document to be examined. If the document appears to be complete and unambiguous, the contract is declared totally integrated. This means that no extrinsic evidence can be introduced regarding the contract.

Today, many jurisdictions also apply the Collateral Contract Rule, which allows a court to look outside of the written contract. It provides that the existence of a total integration does not preclude the introduction into evidence of "collateral agreements" that do not contradict the main agreement.

In this case, if the contract is found to be totally integrated, no extrinsic evidence showing a separate agreement would be permitted. Such evidence would be excluded because paying $25,000 of the purchase price to Quincy specifically contradicts the written contract. It states that the entire purchase price is to be paid to Zeller. Under the four corners rule, once a contract has been found to be totally integrated, a court cannot go beyond the contract to discover more evidence. Under the Collateral Contract Rule, the court would be able to go outside of the totally integrated contract. However, that Rule still only allows separate agreements that do not contradict the written contract. As stated above, paying $25,000 of the purchase price to Quincy likely contradicts the written terms of the contract.

(B), (C), and (D) are incorrect because the admissibility of each element's evidence hinges on whether the contract is found to be completely integrated or not. Evidence of the separate agreement, involving Quincy, would only be considered if the contract was found not to be totally integrated. Thus, oral agreements between Byer and Zeller, which show their negligence in not including the separate agreement in the written document or agreements making Quincy a third party beneficiary to the contract, would not be admissible unless the contract was found to not be completely integrated.

Question 88
Answer: B

This question tests the law of third party beneficiaries. Original parties to a contract may mutually rescind the rights of a third party in the contract, and this rescission may be verbal. Generally, the original parties may alter or eliminate a third party's rights before those rights vest. Under the *Restatement,* one of the ways a third party's rights can vest is if the third party discovers the contract and assents to it.

In this case, Byer and Zeller mutually agree to rescind Quincy's rights on March 5, before Quincy discovers the contract. Thus, Quincy's rights never vest, and Byer and Zeller are able to mutually eliminate them.

(A) is incorrect because a lack of consideration to support Zeller's prior promise to pay Quincy would afford Byer a less effective defense than rescission of the oral agreement of Zeller and Byer.

(C) is incorrect because if a statute of limitations barred an action by Quincy prior to March 1, then the action Quincy had accrued before and does not deal with this contract. A statute of limitations only bars action after a certain amount of time from when the cause of action accrued. Thus, if a statute of limitations barred Quincy from taking action against Byer before March 1 (the date the contract was formed), then the action does not deal with the contract.

(D) is incorrect because an intended third-party beneficiary of a contract is entitled to enforce the contract although the beneficiary did not assent to or know about it when it was made. Thus, Quincy does not have to assent to the contract in order to enforce his rights under the contract.

Question 89
Answer: C

This question tests the law of mistakes in contracts. Under the *Restatement,* a mutual mistake occurs when two parties make an assumption about a key fact on which their contract was premised and that assumption is incorrect. In that event, the contract may be avoided if, because of the mistake, a different transaction would have occurred than the one that they contemplated. In the case of a mutual mistake, the contract is avoidable. In the case of a unilateral mistake, the contract will usually be upheld unless the party can show that the unmistaken party had knowledge of the mistake, should have been aware of the mistake, caused the mistake, or took advantage of the mistake.

In this problem, if Zeller can show that there was a mistake in integration the contract would be voidable. In that event, Zeller could avoid the contract entirely. Both Zeller and Byer were under the assumption that the land was being sold for $46,000. Since the contract states $45,000, a different transaction would have occurred because of this mistake in integration, making the contract avoidable. Furthermore, the contract would also be voidable if Zeller can show a unilateral mistake. Zeller can show that Byer had previously agreed to $46,000. Zeller can also show that Byer's secretary mistakenly typed $45,000. This means that Byer has, in effect, caused the mistake.

(A) is incorrect because the courts generally will rely on the objective theory of contracts. Simply put, the court would only analyze Zeller's outward conduct to determine his intent. Here, Zeller's conduct never suggests that he intends the contract to be a sham.

(B) is incorrect. When a contract is not fully integrated, parol evidence may be permitted to complete the agreement. However, it is only admitted to the extent that the terms do no contradict the written terms of the agreement. Accordingly, Zeller would not be allowed to introduce evidence of an orally agreed upon price different from the price in the written contract because it is clearly contradictory.

(D) is incorrect. There was no misunderstanding between the parties in this case over the price of the land. To be a misunderstanding there must be an ambiguous term, which both parties construe a different way. There is no ambiguous term in this case, only a selling price, which is unambiguous.

Question 90
Answer: A

This question tests the law of consideration. Consideration is required to enforce a promise. Generally consideration consists of a bargained for exchange of legal value in return for legal benefit between two contracting parties. A bargained for exchange exists when there is a promise to perform by a promisor that causes a promisee to perform pursuant to that promise. The majority rule requires the promisee to incur a legal detriment, while the minority rule will accept the promisor receiving a legal benefit in the absence of legal detriment.

In this case, Charles promises to pay for any of Betty's losses as a result of the accident. To be legally enforceable, this promise by Charles would have to cause Betty to perform pursuant to Charles' promise, thus constituting a bargained for exchange. Furthermore, Betty incurs no detriment, as she does not have to do anything in exchange for the promise; hence there is no legal detriment. Legal benefit does not exist either, as Charles receives no benefit by paying

Betty's losses. In the absence of a bargained for exchange and no legal benefit or detriment, there is no consideration to enforce this promise.

(B) is incorrect. In this case there is no valid contract. One can only use the defense of mistake when there is a valid contract in dispute. In this case, we only have a promise by Charles.

(C) is incorrect. Charles' promise looks like a suretyship agreement or an executor or administrator contract. The Statute of Frauds can only be raised when there is a valid contract. In this case, however, we only have a promise by Charles.

(D) is incorrect. It would be difficult to argue that Charles' promise was indefinite. An indefinite promise does result in insufficient consideration. However, in this case, since Betty made no effort to make a counter promise, it would be best for Charles to use the lack of consideration defense.

Question 91
Answer: C

This question tests the law of bargained-for consideration. Bargained-for consideration exists when there is (1) a promise to perform by a promisor (2) that causes a promisee to perform pursuant to that promise.

Looking first at the situation where Physician has not begun treating Betty, one will note that Charles' promise to Physician will result in Physician performing medical treatment on Betty pursuant to Charles' promise. It is important that Physician has no yet begun treating Betty before Charles calls him, because there is no question now that Charles' promise is compelling Physician to perform. So, statement I is significant in determining whether there was bargained-for consideration to support Charles' promise to Physician.

Next, we look at statement II. Charles having a contract with Betty is also important, because this fulfills the first requirement of bargained-for consideration. That first requirement is a promise to perform by the promisor. The existence of a legally binding promise to Betty to pay for all of her expenses solidifies the fact that Charles made a clear, definite promise, which is necessary for bargained-for consideration. If Charles' promise was found to be indefinite, it would not constitute bargained-for consideration. Thus, Charles' promise would be unenforceable for indefiniteness, and Physician's promise would be unenforceable for lack of consideration.

Question 92
Answer: D

This question tests the law of third-party beneficiaries. Intended beneficiaries are those third parties that the first and the second parties to a contract designate to receive the primary benefit of the contract. A third party beneficiary is created when there is a valid contract between two parties who agree that the benefit of the contract will go to a third party. This means that when determining if a contract is valid, one only must look for all the elements of a valid contract between the original two parties, not the third party beneficiary. A third-party beneficiary is also entitled to enforce his or her rights under a contract.

Argument I would not be an effective defense because Betty, as a third-party beneficiary, does not have to furnish any consideration. There only must be consideration between Charles and Physician, the original parties to the contract.

Argument II is also irrelevant because Betty is the third-party beneficiary of the contract between Physician and Charles. As a third-party beneficiary, Betty may enforce her rights under the contract.

Argument III is ineffective because Physician's obligation to Betty arose out of his contract with Charles. To have a novation there has to be a prior agreement between two parties. Then a third party must enter and become a substitute to one of the original contractual parties. The substitute party assumes all duties of the original party, and the original party is discharged. In this case, we only have one agreement between Charles and Physician. This agreement includes Betty as a third party beneficiary. A new agreement, involving one party substituting for another, is never made. Therefore, there is no novation.

Question 93
Answer: B

This question tests the law of consideration. A bargained-for promise to relinquish a valid legal claim is adequate consideration to support a reciprocal promise.

In this case, Dodge promised to relinquish his valid legal claim against Arthur's estate. This is a detriment to Dodge, and it is adequate consideration to support Charles' reciprocal promise to pay $200.

(A) is incorrect. Detrimental reliance can only be used if there is not a valid contract. In this case, we have bargained-for consideration. Thus, detrimental reliance cannot be used.

(C) is incorrect. Agreeing to relinquish an invalid legal claim can also act as adequate consideration when in good faith, a promisor thinks, (1) the claim is valid, and (2) that a legal detriment may only arise in that matter. No facts in this problem contradict either of those two factors.

(D) is incorrect. We have shown that there is adequate consideration; thus, Charles promise is more than a moral obligation.

Question 94
Answer: C

This question tests the law of accord and satisfaction. An accord is an agreement to accept substituted performance (e.g., less money). A satisfaction occurs when the substituted performance occurs. A debtor is not discharged from an existing duty until the debtor has performed pursuant to the accord's terms. When a debtor makes an offer for an amount less than what the creditor wants, and the creditor accepts the amount, the creditor is subject to a valid accord and satisfaction if the debt is, (1) subject to an honest dispute, or (2) is unliquidated (not a definite amount).

In this situation, Dodge, the creditor, requests $200 from Charles, the debtor. Charles offers $150 to settle the dispute and Dodge accepts. The fact that both men honestly believed the amount was in controversy shows there was an honest dispute, meaning Dodge is subject to a valid accord and satisfaction. Because Dodge is bound by a valid accord and satisfaction, he is unable to bring a suit for the remaining $50.

(A) is incorrect. First, there is nothing in the facts that supports the notion that Arthur's $200 debt was a liquidated amount. Second and most importantly, the facts show that both men honestly believed different amounts were owed, resulting in an honest dispute.

(B) is incorrect. Dodge does honestly believe that he is owed $200. However, once he agreed to $150, he was bound by the accord and satisfaction.

(D) is incorrect. Regardless of whether Charles was legally obligated to pay $200 in the first place, both men have agreed to a valid accord and satisfaction. Once a valid accord and satisfaction occurs, both men are subject to it.

Question 95
Answer: B

This problem tests the law of parol evidence. The Parol Evidence Rule (Rule) is an exclusionary rule that requires the parties to incorporate into a contract, all of the terms and conditions to which they have agreed. The Rule provides that if the parties intend that a writing represent their agreement's final terms and conditions, the writing cannot subsequently be contradicted with extrinsic evidence of previous or contemporaneous agreements that supplement or contradict their contract's terms.

The Rule allows for evidence that shows the writing was not intended to be final. The Rule also allows for evidence that shows the existence of additional consistent terms that supplement the parties' written agreement, if the agreement is final but incomplete.

If HDS can show that the memorandum was not completely integrated, they can introduce the evidence at issue. They can do so because that evidence would show an additional consistent term that supplements the parties' written, incomplete agreement.

(A) is incorrect. The Rule is applied through the four corners test. Under this test, the court may not look beyond a written document that appears to be complete and unambiguous. Here, the court would likely conclude that the written memorandum is complete and unambiguous and not allow the evidence to be introduced.

(C) is incorrect. Detrimental reliance is only used when there is not a valid contract. In this case, there is no question whether HDS and CP have a valid contract. The only question is whether HDS can introduce evidence to show an additional oral agreement connected with the written contract. For these reasons, detrimental reliance is inapplicable.

(D) is incorrect. Showing that the memorandum was not a partially integrated document could mean that the document was fully integrated. Under the four corners rule, extrinsic evidence would not be allowed when the written document is fully integrated. In this case, HDS would have to hope the court uses the Collateral Contracts Rule. This Rule allows for extrinsic evidence, even though the contract is fully integrated, so long as the extrinsic evidence does not contradict the written document. This uncertainty makes (D) an inferior choice to (B).

Question 96
Answer: D

This question tests the law of express conditions. An express condition is a condition that is explicitly stated in a written or verbal agreement. A promisee must strictly comply with an express condition in order for a promisor's duty of conditional performance to apply.

In this problem, one must look at the written agreement and factual circumstances of the transaction to interpret that phrase "within one month of completion." The writing contains no mention of paying CP after one-half of the job is complete. Furthermore, the written agreement conditions the payment to CP on the final product meeting certain standards. HDS has no way of knowing if their standards will be complied with half-way through the performance. Thus, the condition is construed to mean within one month after completion. There must be strict compliance with this condition.

(A) is incorrect. The writing does not support this interpretation of the phrase "within one month of completion."

(B) is incorrect. The writing makes no mention of completing the job half way. When interpreting a condition you must look at what the written agreement suggests.

(C) is incorrect. Express conditions must be strictly complied with. In the problem, the condition lists standards that CP must specifically meet. Substantial performance would only apply if the condition was implied; the condition is express in this case.

Question 97
Answer: A

This question tests the law of modification. The common law has two requirements for a modification, (1) mutual consent, and (2) consideration. Usually an oral modification is valid if there is not restriction in the contract against it and the Statute of Frauds does not require the contract to be in writing. However, if the oral modification would be invalid as to either of those standards, it may still be enforceable if one of the parties to the contract materially alters his or her position based on that modification.

In this problem, the escrow agreement is an oral modification. The modification satisfies the common law's requirements in that both parties agreed to the modification, and CP agreed to relinquish their legal claim. The *Restatement* provides that either good faith or objective uncertainty to a claim's validity is sufficient to constitute consideration. In this case, CP honestly believed it had a valid claim. Also, there is a certain amount of uncertainty, which resulted in CP agreeing to relinquish their claim as valid consideration. The next issue is that the written contract between HDS and CP forbids an oral modification. However, CP, by agreeing to continue working and not seeking $10,000, materially altered its position based on the escrow agreement; thus, the oral modification is valid.

(B) is incorrect. The Statute of Frauds applies to subsequent oral modifications of a contract when the Statute requires the original contract to be in writing.

(C) is incorrect. Because CP materially altered its position as a result of the oral modification, the modification is valid even though the contract required written modifications.

(D) is incorrect. CP suffered a detriment by agreeing to relinquish a legal claim, which constituted adequate consideration to support the oral modification.

Question 98
Answer: C

This question tests the law of waiver. A waiver is one party giving up a known and existing right in a contract. A waiver may be implied from the factual circumstances or expressly made.

In this problem, it appears that HDS waived the condition that CP must complete the project by July 1. This waiver is implied by two surrounding factual circumstances. First, HDS failed to take any action when CP went over the July 1 deadline. Second, HDS made no mention of the deadline as a reason for their dissatisfaction with CP's performance.

(A) is incorrect. The July 1 condition was impliedly waived by HDS.

(B) is incorrect. Substantial performance applies to all constructive conditions, including commercial contracts. Regardless, the July 1 deadline is an express condition.

(D) is incorrect. A liquidated damages clause is used to provide an agreed upon sum that is to be paid in case a breach occurs. The absence of a liquidated damages clause does not affect a party's ability to renounce the contract.

Question 99
Answer: D

This question tests the law of satisfaction of conditions. When dealing with contracts for mechanical fitness or suitability for purpose a contract may include a term requiring that a payment to a promisee by a promisor be made subject to that party's satisfaction. That is a question of mechanical fitness or suitability for a particular purpose. In these types of contracts, a court will use an objective standard and determine whether the work would be satisfactory to a reasonable person.

This case involves a contract for mechanical fitness or suitability for purpose. The terms of the contract require that the computers must cut HDS's processing time for financial transactions in half. CP failed to satisfy this condition by only cutting processing time by 47 percent. Using the objective standard, this work would not be satisfactory for two reasons. First, HDS expressly stated in the contract that processing time must be cut by 50 percent. Second, express conditions must be strictly complied with.

(A) is incorrect. Express conditions must be strictly complied with.

(B) is incorrect. The express condition stated that HDS wanted their processing time cut in half. Express conditions must be strictly complied with, and saving HDS money was not what the conditions specified.

(C) is incorrect. Shortening the processing time by one-half was not a condition subsequent. A condition subsequent is an event that the parties agree will discharge a duty of performance after it has become absolute. The processing time condition was an express condition precedent because it was an event that must have occurred before HDS's duty to pay CP became due.

Question 100
Answer: B

This question tests the law of restitution. If a party justifiably refuses to perform on the ground that his remaining duties of performance have been discharged by the other party's breach, the party in breach is entitled to restitution for any benefit that he has conferred by way of part performance or reliance in excess of the loss that he has caused by his own breach.

Although CP breached the contract, they still conveyed a benefit to HDS because HDS has continued using their programs. According to the law of restitution, CP is entitled to any benefit that CP has conferred on HDS.

(A) is incorrect. HDS's continued use is speculative in this answer. The important factor in this case is the actual benefit CP has provided to HDS.

(C) is incorrect. According to the law of restitution, CP is entitled to restitution for any benefit it has provided to HDS.

(D) is incorrect. A claim by HDS for breach of contract in this case would not yield an inconsistent result. HDS would be entitled to damages resulting from the breach; however, those damages would likely be outweighed by the benefit CP provided. Thus, HDS would likely not recover damages in a breach of contract claim against CP.

Question 101

Answer: C

This question tests the law of acceptance. In this case, we have a unilateral contract. The only way to accept a unilateral contract is by performance of the specified terms in the contract. Public offers are offers that are made to everyone, and everyone may perform the specified act. Determining the terms of a public offer requires interpreting the offer.

In this problem, we have a public offer. Since the offer was made to the public, it is proper to assume that the performance requested is for information leading to the arrest and conviction of the arsonist. This is true because an offer to the public would likely not request some specialized service to be performed (i.e. an arrest).

(A) is incorrect. A unilateral offer cannot be accepted by a return promise, but only by performance.

(B) is incorrect. To make an arrest and assist in the arsonist's conviction would require specialized skills. Such an offer would not be made to the public at large.

(D) is incorrect. A unilateral offer may only be accepted by full performance. Assent is not necessary.

Question 102
Answer: D

This question tests the law of terminating an offer. All offers can be terminated by a lapse of time, whether or not the offer has a specified duration of time. When the duration of the offer's acceptance period is not specified, it is open for a reasonable time. Whether the time is reasonable depends on the subject matter, the medium of the offer, business custom, and price fluctuation. Moreover, a public offer can only be revoked by direct communication. In that event, if an offer was communicated to the public, then a revocation of that announcement must be made in a similar manner to that by which it was initially communicated. Reasonable means, such as by newspaper or broadcast media, must be used. Reasonable means does not require that every member of the public must in fact receive notice of the revocation.

In this situation, the city made a public offer. Thus, the offer can be terminated by a reasonable lapse of time. Alternatively, the city can revoke the offer through direct communication using similar means as were used to announce the offer.

(A) is incorrect. There is no precise time that an offer with no specified termination date expires. Instead, the offer is open for a reasonable time. The "reasonable" amount of time depends on the subject matter, the medium of the offer, business custom, and price fluctuation.

(B) is incorrect. Offers may be terminated by a lapse of time.

(C) is incorrect. Offers may be revoked, provided that the offer has not been accepted or performance has not begun. In regard to a public offer, as here, the offeror must revoke the offer through direct communication using reasonable means.

Question 103
Answer: C

This question tests the law of revoking a public offer. When dealing with a public offer, revocation must be made by direct communication using reasonable means. A revocation of a public offer must be made in a similar manner to that by which it was initially communicated. Reasonable means, such as by newspaper or broadcast media, must be used. Reasonable means does not require that every member of the public must in fact receive notice of the revocation.

The key to this problem is understanding that revocation only has to be similar, not exact. The communication to revoke the offer must reasonably have the capability of reaching the same depth of people who received the offer. As long as the offeror uses reasonable means to revoke the offer as compared to how the original offer was conveyed, the revocation will be valid. Thus, using a comparable medium and frequency of communication will satisfy the reasonableness test.

(A) is incorrect. The newspaper would likely not be a similar medium as the TV station. The TV station likely reached more people, who would not be aware of the revocation. Revoking an offer communicated over the television by placing the revocation in print would not be reasonable, as these are two different mediums that reach a different depth of people.

(B) is incorrect. The revocation only must be similar using reasonable means, not identical.

(D) is incorrect. Reasonable means does not require that every member of the public must in fact receive notice of the revocation.

Question 104
Answer: D

This question tests the law of unilateral contracts. A unilateral contract is created by an exchange of one party's promise for another party's performance of certain conduct. In other words, a promise is exchanged for an act (which is not promised). A unilateral contract cannot be formed when an offeree makes a promise in return for an offeror's promise.

In this case, the contract formed between Humongous and Gimlet reads that Humongous promises to pay Gimlet $200 "for each day's work you actually perform in investigating our fire." In other words, Humongous is making a promise to pay Gimlet $200 every day he performs the act of investigating the fire. Thus, the offer breaks down into a series of unilateral contracts where Gimlet has a task to perform everyday in exchange for the promised $200.

(A) is incorrect. The offer is a series of daily unilateral contracts. Humongous has promised to pay Gimlet $200 every day he performs the act of investigating the fire. Thus, Gimlet completes his performance and is entitled to receive $200 at the end of each day.

(B) is incorrect. The offer never creates a condition that Gimlet must succeed in his investigation.

(C) is incorrect. A bilateral contract is the exchange of promises. In this problem, Humongous promises to pay Gimlet provided Gimlet performs the act of investigating the fire. In order for Humongous to be bound to pay Gimlet, Gimlet must perform. Therefore, the contract is unilateral.

Question 105
Answer: B

This problem tests the law of public offers. A reward offer made by the government is considered to be like a bounty. Anyone doing the act specified by the reward offer is entitled to the reward. This is the case regardless of whether the person was aware of the reward. Also, an offeree who knows that an offer has been made but does not know the terms of the offer may still assent to the offer.

In this case, Gimlet did not know about the offer of reward. But he may still be entitled to the reward because the offer was a government offer, and Gimlet performed the requested act. If the government's offer is seen as a bounty, Gimlet is entitled to the reward—even though he has no knowledge of it—because he performed the specified act.

(A) is incorrect. (A) indicates an argument for detrimental reliance. Detrimental reliance would be difficult to show here because Gimlet was being compensated in another contract for his services.

(C) is incorrect. There is no good-faith requirement for revocation. Generally, an offeror may revoke his or her offer any time before acceptance.

(D) is incorrect. Moral obligation would be difficult to prove, as the city did not make any specific promise directly to Gimlet. Also, Gimlet is already being compensated for his services, which lessens the appearance of a moral obligation on the city's part.

Question 106
Answer: D

This question tests the law of equitable conversion. Under the doctrine of equitable conversion, when a contract for the sale of land is entered into, the buyer becomes the equitable owner of the land. During that time period until the closing, the seller holds legal title to the property. The equitable conversion occurs at the time of execution of the contract. This is the rule even regardless of whether the buyer does not take immediate possession or pay the contract price.

Under the doctrine of equitable conversion, once VanMeer entered into an enforceable agreement with Landover for Highacre, VanMeer became the owner in equity of the land. Therefore, VanMeer owned the land and became liable for it. Thus, VanMeer must close the deal regardless of the condition of the apartment because Landover merely holds legal title to ensure VanMeer pays the full purchase price.

(A) is incorrect. VanMeer was under no duty to insure Highacre. Still, it was in his best interest to inquire about Highacre's insurance coverage before entering into an enforceable contract.

(B) is incorrect. Although some disputes over real estate may be remedied by specific performance, this does not answer the question. The question is why would Landover prevail in his dispute, not what type of remedy is available.

(C) is incorrect. A court sitting in equity looks at all of the surrounding circumstances to determine what is fair and just, when there is not an adequate legal remedy.

Question 107
Answer: B

This question tests the law of interpreting contracts. In many jurisdictions, contracts for personal services contain an implied promise that the work is to be completed in a workmanlike manner. This means that the work is to be completed to general requirements and specifications determined by custom or law. If this implied or expressed term is not met, it results in a breach and the breaching party is subject to applicable remedies. This is to ensure that these type of contracts accomplish intent of the parties.

In the current problem, if Mechanic did not complete the work in a workmanlike manner, he will likely be found to have breached the contract, even though the contract does not mention the term. This is to ensure that the Ohner-Mechanic contract is suitable to accomplish the purpose of fixing Ohner's machine, which is what both parties sought to achieve upon entering the contract.

(A) is incorrect. Jones does not need to be capable of performing Mechanic's work because Mechanic is only making Jones a third party beneficiary. Mechanic is not delegating his duty to Jones.

(C) is incorrect. Most all non-assignment covenants are unenforceable, meaning that almost all of one's rights in a contract are able to be assigned. Assigning the benefit of a contract to third party is almost universally accepted, and covenants against it are unenforceable.

(D) is incorrect. Jones does not need to be an intended beneficiary in order to receive the benefit of the contract. In this case, Jones is not an intended beneficiary. Mechanic has merely assigned his right to receive Ohner's performance to Jones. An intended beneficiary is found in the original contract itself. Whereas, an assignment is made by one party to a third party after the contract is created.

Question 108

Answer: D

This question tests the law of express conditions. An express condition is a condition that is explicitly stated in a written or verbal agreement. A promisee must strictly comply with an express condition in order for a promisor's duty of conditional performance to apply.

In the problem above, BCD's promise to pay 5 percent is conditioned on Bobb's billing being actually rendered. When Bobb was billed, John was no longer an employee, therefore the condition to receive the commission was never fulfilled during John's employment. Specifically, the commission is subject to a condition precedent, which must be completed before BCD has an obligation to pay John. The condition was never completed before John was terminated.

(A) is incorrect. The condition precedent to John receiving commission was Bobb being actually billed for the machine. Thus, his procuring the sale does not satisfy the condition.

(B) is incorrect. John's promise to Bobb is irrelevant when determining if the condition precedent was satisfied.

(C) is incorrect. Quantum meruit is used with respect to quasi-contracts. Quasi-contracts are created by the court when no contract exists to prevent unjust enrichment. Quantum meruit basically means giving a party "as much as he deserves," or a reasonable value for the benefit conveyed by the plaintiff. In this case, quantum meruit would not apply because Franklin conveyed no benefit to BCD.

Question 109
Answer: C

This question tests the law of condition precedent. A condition precedent is an event that must happen before a duty to perform under a contract becomes due. Because the condition is express, it must be strictly complied with.

Here, the condition precedent to receiving a 5 percent commission is the actual billing of the customer. John was fired before this billing of Bobb took place. Thus, the condition precedent was never completed, and BCD was under no duty to pay John's commission.

(A) is incorrect. The court looks at the benefit the plaintiff provided to the defendant when it is sitting in equity (i.e. quasi-contract or promissory estoppel). If a valid contract exists, as it does here, the court generally will not sit in equity.

(B) is incorrect. BCD's contract included an express provision regarding the payment of commissions. A promise cannot be implied-in-fact when it contradicts an express provision in the contract.

(D) is incorrect. John's promise to assist the customer is irrelevant when determining the benefit he conveyed to the company.

Question 110
Answer: C

This problem tests the law of mutual mistake and employment at will. An adversely affected party may seek judicial rescission of a contract on the basis that both of the parties to the contract were mistaken regarding a basic assumption on which the contract was formed. To show a mutual mistake, the plaintiff must show: (1) a mistake in a basic assumption upon which the contract is premised; (2) the mistake materially affects or imbalances the parties' performances; and (3) the plaintiff does not bear the risk of the mistake. Furthermore, a terminated employee may show an exception to at will employment if he or she can show that the employer violated public policy by terminating the employee.

If both parties were mistaken about John's sales quotas, John can have the contract rescinded. John can satisfy the requirements to show mutual mistake because: 1) John's sales quotas were the basic assumption of his termination; 2) the mistake certainly affected the parties' performances because it resulted in John's termination; and 3) John did not bear the risk of the mistake, as it was both parties' responsibility to keep track of sales quotas. Also, if John was fired because the company's president wanted to have his son have the commission instead, then bad faith would be easy to show. Firing an employee only to profit one's son is probably against public policy.

The number of years John has worked for BDS would not matter if John were to have broken a set standard used to measure employees' performance (i.e. sales quotas).

Question 111
Answer: C

This question tests the law of assignments. Contractual provisions against assignment are usually unenforceable. Most contract rights are assignable. Even if the assignor violates a covenant with a promisor, the assignment may still be validly made, such that the promisor must continue to perform its contractual duties for the assignee. However, the promisor may bring an action against the assignor to obtain damages for violating the covenant.

In this situation, Stretch's assignment did breach the contract, and Stretch is liable to Sartorial for damages. However, the assignment is still effective, and Sartorial must continue to perform its promise for Finance Company, the assignee.

(A) is incorrect. Most provisions against assignment are unenforceable. Thus, even when a provision against assignment exists, the promisor still must perform for the assignee.

(B) is incorrect. Although covenants against assignment are not usually enforceable, they still have legal force. By violating the covenant, Stretch is liable to Sartorial for damages.

(D) is incorrect. A covenant against assignment can apply to either the buyer or the seller.

Question 112

Answer: B

The question tests the law of assignment. A promisor is only required to render performance to an assignee if the promisor possesses knowledge of the assignment. Until the promisor receives that notice, the promisor may continue to render performance to the assignor (i.e., the promisee).

In the above problem, Sartorial was not aware of the assignment and therefore had no duty to pay Finance Company. Stretch is liable to Finance Company for the $5,000 because Stretch is in debt to Finance Company and made an agreement with Finance Company regarding the debt. Thus, Stretch has privity of contract with Finance Company and is liable.

(A) is incorrect. Without knowledge of the assignment, Sartorial is not required to render performance to Finance Company.

(C) is incorrect. Sartorial did not have knowledge of the assignment, meaning Sartorial was not required to render performance to Finance Company. Thus, Sartorial is not liable to Finance Company.

(D) is incorrect. Stretch has entered into a contract with Finance Company, meaning that Stretch is liable to Finance Company for money that is rightly Finance Company's under the agreement.

Question 113
Answer: D

This question tests the law of third-party beneficiaries. When determining if there is an intended beneficiary who is able to enforce its rights in a contract, the most important factor is the intent of the contracting parties. The contracting parties can rescind a third party's rights by mutual rescission before the third-party's rights vest. The mutual rescission does not need to be in writing. A third party's rights vest when the third party (1) becomes aware of the rights, (2) materially alters his or her position based on the supposed rights, or (3) commences a suit to enforce the promise. An incidental beneficiary is not a party to the contract, but the promises in the contract indirectly affect the incidental beneficiary.

First, Virginia Wear and Son, Inc. is not an incidental beneficiary of the Stretch-Sartorial contract. The contract, on its own, in no way affects Virginia Wear and Son, Inc. Virginia Wear and Son, Inc. is only affected if it is an intended beneficiary of the contract.

Second, Virginia Wear and Son, Inc. only possesses a prior right to $5,000 if it is an intended beneficiary. There is little question that the parties intended to make Virginia Wear and Son, Inc. an intended beneficiary when the contract was formed, as it specifically states so. However, the parties mutually rescinded the rights of Virginia Wear and Son, Inc. before those rights vested. These rights would have vested in the contract when Virginia Wear and Son, Inc. became aware of them. By Sartorial paying $5,000 to Stretch, and Stretch accepting the payment, these parties impliedly rescinded Virginia Wear and Son, Inc.'s rights before those rights had vested. Accordingly, it was a valid mutual rescission of Virginia Wear and Son, Inc.'s third-party beneficiary rights.

Question 114
Answer: D

This question tests the law of impracticability. Section 2-615 of the UCC states that the non-performance of a contractual obligation in a contract for sale is not a breach if the performance has been made impracticable "by the occurrence of a contingency the nonoccurrence of which was a basic assumption on which the contract was made."

Simply stated, section 2-615 of the UCC says that if something occurred to Sartorial, that was not foreseeable when the contract was made, and the occurrence has made the contract impractical, Sartorial is not in breach of contract. In this case, Sartorial went out of business, making their promise to purchase elasticized fabric impracticable. It is important that Sartorial's clothing business ceased in good faith, because the occurrence is usually judged by foreseeableness and reasonableness.

(A) is incorrect. Generally, most all rights in a contract are assignable, including personal rights, so long as they do not materially alter a promisor's duty.

(B) is incorrect. The duties in this problem's contract are delegable. Duties for the delivery of goods are generally always delegable. To be non-delegable, the duties must require unique talents, skill, knowledge, or judgment.

(C) is incorrect. The contract is supported by sufficient consideration because both parties made promises that cause the other party to act pursuant to the promise. Thus, the parties created a bargained for exchange. Sartorial promised to buy all the elasticized fabric it required from Stretch for three years. In return, Stretch must deliver the requisite amount of fabric to Sartorial.

Question 115
Answer: C

This question tests the law of express conditions. If an express condition is not a material part of a contract and its occurrence becomes impossible due to neither party's fault, then the condition is legally excused. In that event, the intended beneficiary of the condition must still otherwise perform under the contract. A promisee must strictly comply with an express condition in order for a promisor's duty of conditional performance to apply. An express condition is clearly communicated, either verbally or in a written agreement, by terms like "on condition that" or similar verbiage.

The above dispute would hinge on whether the express condition Seth breached was a material part of the contract. Assuming that the delays in construction were neither parties' fault, unforeseeable, and made it impossible for Seth to complete his performance by the specified time, we must determine if the condition of time is material. If the condition of time is material to the contract, Seth will not be excused. To be material, the condition must threaten the value of the contract. Thus, if the wording of the contract makes time of the essence, it is inferred that the duration affects the value of the contract and Bob would be able to terminate it.

(A) is incorrect. If time is a material condition, Seth's failure to meet the requirement cannot be excused; it must be strictly complied with.

(B) is incorrect. Undue hardship does not necessarily make a condition material. Bob cannot show undue hardship because Seth breached an immaterial condition. Bob would not be able to cease performance, but only recover damages.

(D) is incorrect. Regardless of good faith, Bob still must show that Seth's breach was material in order to be able to cease performance under the contract.

Question 116
Answer: C

The question tests the law of assignment. An assignor, as a promisee in a valid contract, may transfer contractual rights to a third party assignee. An assignment of contractual rights occurs when the assignor manifests an intent to presently transfer those rights to an assignee. However, a contract right may not be assigned if doing so would materially alter a promisor's duty.

In this problem, the assignment, assuming it was made properly, does not material alter Boone's duty. Boone's duty remains the same and the assignee has similar experience and reputation. Boone still expects the same quality performance. Since most rights are assignable, and Boone's position is not changed as a result of the assignment, Boone will be required to accept performance by Coot.

(A) is incorrect. Addle is not in breach of contract because there was no term expressed or implied in the document that prohibited assignment.

(B) is incorrect. Boone may not refuse to accept performance by Coot because most rights are assignable. The fact that Coot has similar expertise as Addle also shows that the assignment does not materially alter Boone's position. Thus, Boone must accept performance.

(D) is incorrect. There is no novation in this situation. In a novation, Addle would be replaced by Coot. This is not the case. Addle may still be liable in certain cases. Also, a novation requires consideration, which is lacking in this case.

Question 117
Answer: A

Generally, for an assignee to take on the assignor's liability, this liability must be specifically stated. Otherwise, it is presumed that liability is not transferred.

Although Coot was assigned the entire contract, Addle remains liable on the contract because the Addle-Coot assignment agreement never specifically stated that Coot takes on Addle's liability.

(B) is incorrect. Coot did not take on Addle's liability because such a term was not specifically stated in his agreement with Addle.

(C) is incorrect. Coot does not incur any liability as a result of his breach because he did not take on Addle's liability in the assignment. Thus, Addle is the only party liable to Boone.

(D) is incorrect. Boone waived no rights by permitting Coot to perform. First, under the rules of assignment, Boone had no choice but to allow Coot to perform. Second, an assignment does not transfer liability to the assignee unless specifically stated. Thus, Addle remains liable to Boone.

Question 118
Answer: C

This question tests the law of the UCC, specifically a buyer's right to inspection. The UCC recognizes that all buyers have a right to inspection, even if it the right is not stated in the contract. A buyer who pays for goods before inspecting them also has the right to inspect the goods after delivery, but before acceptance. Thus, the buyer still has the right to inspect the goods and is able to invoke any applicable remedies if the good are not satisfactory.

(A) is incorrect. The buyer always has the right to inspect good before accepting them.

(B) is incorrect. The buyer always has the right to inspection, and does not waive any remedies by agreeing to pay before inspection.

(D) is incorrect. The buyer is still required to pay before inspection. So the provision is still valid, even though the provision does not cause the buyer to sacrifice any rights.

Question 119
Answer: C

This question tests the remedies available to immaterial breach. A partial or immaterial breach of a contract is one that does not fully impair its value and usually does not justify a non-breaching party in ceasing to perform under the contract. The non-breaching party may bring an action against a breaching party to recover damages that resulted from the immaterial breach. The ordinary purpose of receiving damages for a breach of contract is to place a non-breaching party the position that he would have been had no breach occurred.

The difference between no. 1 and no. 2 quality wool likely does not destroy the value of the contract. Therefore, the remedy for McHugh's breach would be damages. In this case, to put Johnston back in the position that he would have been in if the breach had not occurred, McHugh would be liable for the difference of the contract price and substitute goods purchased, plus the price Johnston already paid.

(A) is incorrect. Because the breach may be remedied by damages, specific performance is not necessary.

(B) is incorrect. These damages would not sufficiently compensate Johnston for the money he was forced to pay for substitute goods.

(D) is incorrect. Johnston waived no remedies by agreeing to pay before inspection.

Question 120
Answer: B

This question tests the buyer's right of rejection under the UCC. Section 2-711(3) of the UCC provides that a buyer who reject a seller's goods may sell them at a public or private sale if the buyer already paid for the goods. The buyer must only provide a seller with notice of his or her intent to resell the goods in a private sale. Thus, if Johnston is to resell the wool in a private sale he must give notice to McHugh.

(A) is incorrect. Johnston must give McHugh notice before reselling the goods in a private sale.

(C) is incorrect. Johnston may resell the goods in a public or private sale.

(D) is incorrect. Johnston may resell the goods in a public or private sale.

Question 121
Answer: D

This question tests the law of revocation. An offeror may revoke an offer at any time before an offeree accepts it, in the absence of, (1) consideration exchanged to keep the offer open, (2) detrimental reliance by the offeree, or (3) the offeror is a merchant selling goods under the UCC. In a unilateral contract, the offeror may revoke the offer anytime before performance begins.

The language in the contract in question does not affect the right to revocation, only meeting one of the three factors stated above would abolish the offeror's power of revocation.

(A) is incorrect. To force an offeror to keep his or her offer open for a specified amount of time there must be consideration exchanged. There was no consideration to force Duffer to keep his offer open.

(B) is incorrect. Slicker was able to accept the offer any time before noon, November 12.

(C) is incorrect. Options must be supported with valid consideration. There was no consideration to force Duffer to keep his offer open.

Question 122
Answer: B

This question tests the law of acceptance in regards to a unilateral contract. To accept a unilateral contract, the offeree must perform the specified act. The offeror may revoke the offer anytime before the offeree begins performance of the contract.

Duffer extended a unilateral offer to Slicker. Duffer promised to pay Slicker for his bike in return for Slicker performing the act of bringing his bike to Duffer's house before noon on November 12. Duffer's power to revoke can only be prevented if Slicker performs the contract or begins performance. Thus, Slicker's letter has no effect on Duffer's power to revoke, because it does not involve Slicker performing or beginning to perform the contract.

(A) is incorrect. A unilateral offer can only be accepted by actual performance, not a promise to perform.

(C) is incorrect. Duffer made a unilateral offer, meaning Slicker must perform the specified action to accept.

(D) is incorrect. A unilateral offer can only be accepted by actual performance of the contract. The letter would only constitute acceptance for a bilateral offer.

Question 123
Answer: B

This question tests termination of an offeree's power to accept. One way an offeree's power to accept can be terminated is if the offeror takes action contradictory to continuing the offer, and this action is communicated to the offeree. The offeree must reasonably believe the communication, but the communication does not need to be directly from the offeror. Koolcat's conversation with Slicker terminates Slicker's power of accepting because it acts as a communication to Slicker of action contradictory to continuing the offer.

(A) is incorrect. Duffer's offer was not irrevocable because there was no consideration to support holding the offer open until November 12.

(C) is incorrect. The fact of whether a prospective buyer or seller made the offer is irrelevant.

(D) is incorrect. This option describes a counter-offer. A counter-offer can only be made if Duffer had first made an offer to Koolcat. In this case, however, Koolcat's communication only terminates Slicker's power to accept.

Question 124
Answer: D

This question tests the law of revocation. Revocation is the manifestation of intent not to enter into a proposed contract made by one party, after that party has already made an offer. A revocation may occur before an offeree accepts an offer. The majority rule is that a revocation is effective when received.

Ohner telephoning Byer on May 5 and telling him that lots 102 through 150 were sold to someone else is a direct revocation of the previous May 1 offer that stated "Will sell you any or all of the lots …" After an effective revocation, Byer had no power to accept.

(A) is incorrect. In order for an offeror to be bound to keep an offer open for a certain amount of time, there must be consideration. There was no consideration to keep the offer open until June 1 in this problem.

(B) is incorrect. A revocation may be direct or indirect. In the case of direct revocation, the offeror only has to communicate the revocation directly to the offeree over whichever means of conveyance he or she chooses.

(C) is incorrect. Ohner's sale of the lots to another party only constituted revocation because it was directly communicated to Byer. In order for the sale of the lots to act as effectively terminating Byer's power to accept, the sales would have to be either directly or indirectly communicated to Byer.

Question 125
Answer: C

This question tests the power of acceptance. A contract consists of an offer and an acceptance. Once an offeree accepts an offer and the agreement is supported by consideration, the offeree's power to accept is extinguished.

The problem above involves Ohner making an offer to Byer that stated, "Will sell you any or all of the lots in Grover subdivision at $5,000 each…" Ohner accepted this offer by accepting to buy lot 101. Thus, Ohner and Byer had an enforceable agreement in place, and Byer's May 6 telegram is unenforceable because, in reality, there was nothing for Byer to accept as Ohner had not made another offer.

(A) is incorrect. A party's contractual duty may be discharged by impossibility when an unforeseen event occurs, or unexpected circumstances arise, which render the duty permanently impossible to perform. Usually impossibility of performance occurs from natural disasters, unexpected conditions, or other uncontrollable forces. Furthermore, this case would only be an instance of subjective impossibility, meaning only Ohner could not perform the contract, and impossibility is usually only a defense when there is objective impossibility, meaning no one can perform the contract.

(B) is incorrect. If a first party makes a unilateral mistake about a fact that involved a basic assumption upon which the contract was formed, the contract will be upheld unless the non-mistaken party, (1) had knowledge of the mistake, (2) should have been aware of the mistake, (3) caused the mistake, or (4) took advantage of the mistake. Since the above problem does not satisfy any of the exceptions, Ohner could not use unilateral mistake as a defense.

(D) is incorrect. A condition precedent is an event that must happen before a duty to perform under a contract becomes due. A condition precedent is usually found in unilateral contracts and not bilateral contracts like the contract involved in this problem. First, a condition precedent is usually a condition that must be satisfied by the offeree in order to force the offeror to perform his side of the contract. Second, the basic assumption of the above contract was the land; thus, it cannot be a condition precedent.

Question 126
Answer: D

A contract will be implied-in-fact when an intention is not manifested by words between the parties, but may be gathered by deduction from their conduct, language, or other circumstances. In this case, Doctor can show an implied-in-fact contract, because Victim sent him a copy of the contract, stating the promise to pay. The intention of Victim to give his settlement money to Doctor is then reinforced when he sends a copy of his contract with Second to the Doctor. This conduct by Victim shows he intended the Doctor to be paid by his settlement money.

(A) is incorrect. To qualify as a creditor beneficiary, one must enter into a contract with the intent to pay one's debt. A creditor beneficiary's rights do not vest until the third party alters its position by relying on the contract. Doctor did not know about the contract when he performed services for victim, so he never materially altered his position relying on the contract.

(B) is incorrect. A donee beneficiary is a third-party who, under a contract, is an intended recipient of a gift from a promisee and may bring an action against a promisor to recover. In this case, there is no gift only a possible settlement for an unnamed physician.

(C) is incorrect. In contract law, there is no rule where creditors whose services were essential to the preservation of Victim's health would receive assets first.

Question 127
Answer: D

This question tests the law of third party beneficiaries. A third party is considered a creditor beneficiary when a promisor enters into a contract to pay a debt that a promisee owes to the third party. The creditor beneficiary receives an assignment of the promisee's right of performance from a promisor. A creditor beneficiary's rights vest as a result of altering its position by relying on the contract.

Doctor did not know about the contract before he treated Victim. Thus, Doctor never altered his position in reliance on the contract. This means that Doctor's rights never vested, and First can show his rights as a third party beneficiary were extinguished by the parties before they vested.

(A) is incorrect. First, most anti-assignment clauses are unenforceable and the promisor must continue their contractual duties with the assignee. However, the anti-assignment clause is not void because the promisor may still collect damages as a result of the assignor's violation.

(B) is incorrect. First's relyiance on Victim's letter of release to his detriment would go to show an equitable relief such as promissory estoppel. However, this type of relief is only used when there is no valid contract. In this case, the court would be interpreting a valid contract.

(C) is incorrect. There is no attorney-client contract exception regarding third party beneficiaries.

Question 128
Answer: A

This question tests the law of novation. A novation is a type of substitute agreement that replaces at least one of the parties to a prior agreement into a subsequent agreement with a new party. The new party becomes a successor promisor to the original promisee under the subsequent agreement, which releases the predecessor promisor from the prior agreement. To be a valid novation, all of the original promisor's debt must be completely discharged.

In the case at bar, if Doctor can show that he impliedly assented to the Victim-First contract then the novation is not valid. If Doctor had assented to the Victim-First contract, First's obligations were not completely discharged as he still had an obligation to pay settlement money to Doctor.

(B) is incorrect. Victim was not unjustly enriched in this case because all of his settlement money went to his creditors leaving him with nothing.

(C) is incorrect. Releasing a party from a contract does not need to be supported by consideration.

(D) is incorrect. Though First's contract duties were personal and likely not delegable, this would only mean that Victim had the right to refuse the delegation. Since Victim did not refuse and entered into a substitute agreement with Second, this defense would not be helpful.

Question 129
Answer: C

This question tests the law of third party beneficiaries. The key to any intended beneficiary category is the third party must be intended. The court will look at the contract itself to determine whether the parties intended to benefit a third party. The court looks at the following factors, (1) whether the contract expressly identifies the third party, (2) whether the performance runs from the promisor to the third party, (3) whether the contract reflects an "intent to benefit" the third party, and (4) whether the third party reasonably relies on the contract as conferring an intended benefit.

The above case lacks almost all of these factors. The contract does not expressly identify Doctor. The contract was not made with the intent to benefit Doctor. Instead the writing's main purpose is to represent Victim and Doctor, who never relied on the contract because he performed his services before he knew of the agreement. Considering all of the surrounding circumstances it would be difficult to show Doctor as a third party beneficiary.

(A) is incorrect. Second entered into a written substitute agreement with victim, which released First of his obligations. This act is known as a novation and not a mere promise.

(B) is incorrect. At the time Second entered into agreement with Victim, Doctor had already performed his services and was informed of the existing contract when Victim mailed him the document. Thus, Doctor's rights likely had already vested when Second entered. Furthermore, if a contract does not name or identify a third party beneficiary when it is signed, the third party who will benefit under the contract only needs to be identified when that party's performance is due, rather than when the contract is formed.

(D) is incorrect. To determine if Doctor's rights vested, one would examine whether he altered his position by relying on the original contract, not Second's promise to take over the contract.

Question 130
Answer: D

This question tests the Statute of Frauds. The Statute of Frauds identifies certain types of contracts that must be in writing to be valid. Two of the more common types of contracts that the Statute of Frauds requires to be in writing are contracts for the sale of land and any contract that takes over one year to perform. In the above case, the subject matter of the contract deals with building on and altering certain parcels of land. However, neither of the contracts involves the sale of land, nor does performance take over a year to complete, hence they are not covered by the Statute of Frauds and do not have to be in writing to be valid.

Question 131
Answer: B

The correct answer is (B). This question tests the law of repudiation. When a repudiation occurs the non-breaching party may suspend performance, refuse performance from the breaching party, or sue for damages. When determining damages the court will consider a variety of factors such as a contracts valueand the actual damages that were sustained. The court will subtract those costs that were avoided and add any consequential and incidental damages.

In the problem above, Brown certainly has the option of suspending his performance of digging the channel without being liable for breach because Green repudiated the contract. Brown will likely not recover $2,500, however, because the court will consider all of the factors stated above while accessing the cost of damages. The $2,500 figure in the contract to be paid for completing the boathouse is not a liquidated figure, thus it is only a starting point for the court to determine damages.

Question 132
Answer: A

This question tests the law of contract remedies. Upon a material breach the non-breaching party has the right to suspend performance or sue for damages. If the breach is immaterial, however, the non-breaching party may only sue for damages. The key to determining whether a breach is material or immaterial is substantial performance. The contract has not been substantially performed if the breaching party fails to perform a term of the contract willfully or in bad faith. A material breach will normally ruin the value of the contract.

The above situation illustrates what would likely be construed as an immaterial breach. Assuming that the time of the contract was not essential, finishing the project late will not ruin the value of the contract.

Brown has still built a boat house and a canal, thus substantially performing the performance of which the contract was based on. Green will be allowed to sue for damages caused by the month delay, but he is still bound to perform his duty of paying $5,000 under the contract.

Question 133
Answer: C

This question tests the principle of equitable conversion. Under the doctrine of equitable conversion, the purchaser becomes the equitable owner of the land once the contract for the land is executed.

Under the doctrine, the seller continues to hold legal title, only to ensure that the full purchase price is paid. Conceptually, once the agreement is made, the seller of the land holds only money (the agreed on price) while the Buyer is the owner of the land.

Applying equitable conversion to this problem would mean that when Seller died his land had been converted to money, personal property, even though he had not closed the sale. Since Perry inherited his personal property, he is entitled to the proceeds of the sale when it closes.

(A) is incorrect. Death terminates an offeree's power to accept. In this case Buyer had already accepted Seller's offer before death.

(B) is incorrect. Equitable conversion applies to all contracts for the sale of land, if the jurisdiction recognizes the principle.

(D) is incorrect. Death does not render a title unmarketable.

Question 134
Answer: A

This question tests the law of terminating a contract. Death of an essential party to a contract before acceptance usually terminates a contract. However, once a contract is formed, depending on the subject matter of the contract, the agreement may be enforceable. For example, the death of a party in a personal services contract, where the service is unique or requires special talents, would terminated the contract. But the same does not hold true when another party may fulfill the duties of the deceased party.

In this situation, a contract is already in place because Buyer accepted Seller's offer before death. The closing simply involves Buyer fulfilling his contractual duty by paying Seller the agreed on price of the contract. Paying money is a duty that can be performed by another party, thus Buyer's heir may enforce the agreement because the contract is not terminated.

(B) is incorrect. Seller has no such right, because his position is not altered by the death. He is still entitled to receive the agreed on price from Buyer's heirs, and must accept performance from him or her.

(C) is incorrect. Death only terminates an agreement when the promisee's duties cannot be performed by another party. In this case, the duty of paying can be performed by a substitute party.

(D) is incorrect. Death does not render a title unmarketable.

Question 135
Answer: B

This question tests the law of damages. When a material breach occurs, the damages available to a non-breaching party are in an amount that will place the non-breaching party in the position that he would have been if the contract had been fully performed. Applying this rule to the problem above, the court would basically order Sawtooth pay the difference between what it would have cost if he finished the house and what it actually costs for another party to finish the house. By ordering this, the court ensures that Farquart will pay the same amount of money he would have paid if Sawtooth had fully performed the contract.

(A) is incorrect. Restitution is used when a contract has not been properly formed. In this case, we have a valid contract.

(C) is incorrect. The difference in market values of the partly completed house and fully completed house may not fully cover the loss incurred by Farquart, therefore not placing him in a position that he would have been in if no breach occurred.

(D) is incorrect. Damages for emotional distress are generally not allowed in contract cases, only tort cases.

Question 136
Answer: C

This question tests consequential damages. Consequential damages are those resulting from a breach of contract, even if they are not part of the contract. Consequential damages arise in the ordinary course of events that flow from the breach. A breaching party is not required to have in fact foreseen those damages. The question is: Could a breaching party have reasonably foreseen the damages based on what they knew at the contract's formation?

Consequential damages would be appropriate in this case because Sawtooth knew of the surrounding circumstances, such as the house was for Farquart's son and fiancé to live in after marriage. Being that Sawtooth knew that Farquart was furnishing the house for his son and daughter-in-law, he could have reasonably foreseen that Farquart would be forced to secure substitute housing as a result of his breach. Thus, consequential damages for the additional expense Farquart incurred in providing a house for Junior and his bride are appropriate.

(A) is incorrect. Consequential damages deal with additional, foreseeable damages incurred by the non-breaching party as a result of the breach. Hence, expenses that Junior and his bride incur would not be covered under consequential damages.

(B) is incorrect. First, Junior's incurred expenses would not be covered under consequential damages. Second, Junior's bride leaving him for another man who has a new house is not a reasonably foreseeable consequence of Sawtooth's breach.

(D) is incorrect. Farquart's own negligence after Sawtooth's breach is not a reasonably foreseeable consequence of the breach. Sawtooth cannot be held responsible for Farquart's actions after his breach. To the contrary, consequential damages require that Sawtooth only be liable for the ordinary course of events that flow from the breach.

Question 137
Answer: D

The correct answer is (D). This question tests what happens when the seller sends the wrong goods under the UCC. When a seller sends the wrong goods, its actions constitute an acceptance and a breach. The buyer may reject the goods within a reasonable time after delivery or tender according to section 2-602(1) of the UCC. "The buyer has no further obligation with regard to goods rightfully rejected." UCC § 2-602(2)(c). In this case, Orchard accepted Fruitko's offer by sending the wrong goods. However, Fruitko is under no obligation to accept the shipment.

(A) and (B) are incorrect because Orchard's shipment was an acceptance according to the UCC.

(C) is incorrect because Fruitko is not required to accept the peaches even though a contract was formed.

Question 138
Answer: C

This problem tests the contract law of conditions. A condition subsequent is an event that the parties agree will discharge a duty of performance after it has become absolute. Beta tendering good title to the farm is not a condition subsequent because its performance will not discharge a duty of performance. If anything, Beta tendering good title will likely bind Alpha to tender good title to the apartment house.

(A) is incorrect. Depending on a court's interpretation of the written contract, it could be determined that Alpha must first tender good title to the apartment house to make Beta's duty to convey good title come due.

(B) is incorrect. Depending on a court's interpretation of the written contract, it could be determined that Beta must first tender good title to the farm to make Alpha's duty to convey good title come due.

(D) is incorrect. Depending on a court's interpretation of the written contract, it could be determined that Beta and Alpha must both perform their duty of conveying good title concurrently.

Question 139
Answer: A

A condition subsequent is an event that the parties agree will discharge a duty of performance after it has become absolute. A condition precedent is an event that must happen before a duty to perform under a contract becomes due.

Alpha's removal of the shed within three months of the exchange of good title is condition subsequent in form, because the duty to remove the shed comes after both parties have exchanged good title to their respective properties. Thus, failing to remove the shed will result in discharging the parties' duties after they have performed. However, Beta also has a duty to pay $1,000 within six months of the exchange, thus Alpha's duty to remove the shed must occur before Beta is bound to pay the $1,000, making the condition precedent in substance.

(B) is incorrect. The form of the contract is not a condition precedent, as both the parties have performed their duties of exchanging good title before the condition must be met. Furthermore, the substance of the shed removal condition is that it must occur before Beta pays $1,000, making it a condition precedent in substance.

(C) is incorrect. The condition must be performed before Beta pays $1,000, which would make it a condition precedent.

(D) is incorrect. The removal of the shed is a condition to Beta's duty to pay the $1,000, because if the shed is not removed Beta is under no obligation to pay $1,000.

Question 140
Answer: A

This question tests the law of implied contracts. Contract law is governed by the objective theory of contracts. This means that the court only looks at surrounding outwardly manifested circumstances to determine the intent of the parties. Contracts may be implied, depending on the parties' conduct and relevant history.

James is attempting to show that he and Digits entered into a contract based on their interaction. Thus, he must show that Digits made a promise to him in return for his promise to bring his manuscripts to X-L. So, if James can show that "When" and "Wouldn't that be nice" implied a promise to type the manuscript based on what a reasonable person would objectively think and given their past history of doing business together, he can successfully show this was an implied contract.

(B) is incorrect. James relying on Mary Digit's statement may be helpful to show how he interpreted her comments, but does little to determine whether Digit's actually made a promise.

(C) is incorrect. X-L doing good work for James in the past is a fact helpful to determine what a reasonable person would interpret from the James-Digit conversation. But it is of little value to ultimately decide whether Digits made a promise.

(D) is incorrect. James forgoing the service of another service provides good insight to how James interpreted his conversation with Digits. But this fact does not help determine whether Digits made a return promise to James.

Question 141
Answer: B

Universal contracts are created when there is an offer to the public. When a universal contract is created it is usually unilateral. In the case at bar, the law school made a clear offer to all of its students. Thus, the law school at made a public offer, which allowed any student to accept.

(A) is incorrect. The law school's offer is not analogous to advertisements for the sale of goods, because the terms of acceptance were specific and definite, while the potential offerees were clearly defined as law school students.

(C) is incorrect. The offer was a universal offer and named all students at the law school as the offerees.

(D) is incorrect. The law school's offer was not a gift, because it is supported by consideration. Consideration would certainly be found by the detriment suffered by students who choose to accept the offer by preparing papers by the May 1 deadline. The school also receives a benefit in that they satisfy their need for more legal research.

Question 142
Answer: C

This question tests the law of unilateral contracts. The only way to accept a unilateral contract is by performance. An offeror may revoke an offer for a unilateral contract at any time before an offeree begins performance. Once that occurs, then the parties' performance obligations become absolute.

The key to the problem above is that Student stepped up his efforts to create a winning paper when he became aware of the law school's offer, meaning he began performance to accept the offer. Once Student began performance the law school could not revoke their offer.

(A) is incorrect. Student had already relied on the offer and began performance, meaning the offer was irrevocable when the second notice was posted.

(B) is incorrect. Unilateral contracts may be revoked anytime before performance begins, there is no reasonable time standard.

(D) is incorrect. A unilateral contract may be revoked anytime before performance. To constitute a valid revocation the law school only needs to post the revocation in comparable ways it used to post the offer.

Question 143
Answer: A

This problem tests the law of universal contracts. When a public offer is made, provided that the offerees are clearly defined and the terms of acceptance are specific and definite, the offer is a unilateral one. This means that the only way to accept the offer is by performance.

The law school posted a public offer to all students. The offer indicated specific terms of accepting the offer and made it clear that the offer was for all of the students at the law school. Thus, the offer proposed a unilateral contract.

(B) is incorrect. Public offers that clearly indicate the offerees and make terms of acceptance specific and definite propose unilateral contracts only.

(C) is incorrect. The offeree never has the option of what to make a contract. The offeror defines the contract through the terms of his or her offer.

(D) is incorrect. Unilateral contracts do not ripen into bilateral contracts. The only way to accept a unilateral contract is through performance. A return promise will never constitute acceptance in regards to a unilateral contract.

Question 144
Answer: B

This question tests the law of acceptance of a universal contract. Contrary to non-universal contracts, even if an offeree performs in response to an offer for a universal contract, the offeree's death will not extinguish that offer.

Thus, once Student performed on April 15 in response to the faculty's offer, his death would not extinguish the offer because he was acting under a universal contract.

(A) is incorrect. Promissory estoppel is used when there is no valid contract. In this case the faculty made an offer and Student accepted the offer by performing the specified terms of acceptance.

(C) is incorrect. There is no stated policy that prohibits the forming of a noncommercial agreement between Student and his teachers.

(D) is incorrect. Student was under no known contractual agreement with the National Competition. It is clear from the facts that Student increased his efforts to perform the terms of the faculty's offer.

Question 145
Answer: B

This question tests the law of satisfaction in personal service contracts. A services contract may include a term requiring that a payment to a promisee by a promisor be made subject to that party's satisfaction, which is a question of quality. A court will uphold and enforce such a term provided that the determination of satisfaction was made in good faith (subjective standard). Thus, the promisor's obligation to pay a promisee is not absolute.

The contract between Daniel and Paul states that the cards are guaranteed to be "fully satisfactory." The satisfactory clause in the agreement can be used by Daniel as a defense to not paying Paul. The court will judge this by a good faith standard.

(A) is incorrect. The rest of Daniel's family liked the cards, thus objectively they were satisfactory. The cards were not satisfactory only to Daniel, which is a subjective standard.

(C) is incorrect. The cards were not delivered on time due to Daniel. Daniel cannot penalize Paul for breaches caused by Daniel's fault.

(D) is incorrect. Daniel's illness did not render the contract impossible to perform. The contract could still be substantially completed, with only a two-day delay in delivery of the cards.

Question 146
Answer: D

This question tests the law of conditions precedent. A condition precedent is an event that must happen before a duty to perform under a contract becomes due. In this case, Paul must perform his duty of creating and delivering 200 acceptable cards to Daniel before Daniel's performance of paying $100 comes due.

(A) is incorrect. Paul's cards must first be created, delivered, and to Daniel's satisfaction before Daniel must pay Paul. Therefore, Daniel's payment of $100 comes due after Paul performs, hence Daniel's duty is not a condition precedent.

(B) is incorrect. Daniel does not have to pay Paul until Paul performs his duty to Daniel's satisfaction, therefore the duties are not concurrent.

(C) is incorrect. A condition subsequent is an event that the parties agree will discharge a duty of performance after it has become absolute. Daniel's payment of $100 completes the contract.

The payment does not discharge any party of a duty of performance, because both parties will have completed the contract by this time.

Question 147
Answer: C

This question tests the law of impossibility. A party to a contract can be justified in non-performance of a condition if performance of such condition is objectively impossible, meaning no one can perform the contract.

It was impossible for Paul to complete his duty on time because of Daniel's illness. Daniel was essential to Paul's duty being performed because Paul needed a picture of Daniel and his family. Therefore, Daniel's illness justified the breach of the December 15 condition.

(A) is incorrect. This statement is true and is governed by a reasonableness standard. Paul completed his performance in a reasonable time considering Daniel's illness and related developments.

(B) is incorrect. It is an implied condition that Daniel was responsible for promptly telling Paul when he had recovered from his illness, as it was essential for Paul to know that information in order to complete his duty.

(D) is incorrect. Daniel's conduct, of not promptly telling Paul that he had recovered from his illness, shows that performance by December 15 was not essential and that Paul would not be bound by the date; thus, waiving the condition.

Question 148
Answer: B

This question tests the law of implied promises. Some contracts do not precisely spell out the obligations of each party. However, an examination of the facts may indicate that an obligation is presumed. Above, Chase and Scott are entering into a written, detailed contract for the sale of land. A basic assumption in a contract for the sale of land is that Chase possesses and will convey good title. "... it is implied in a contract to convey land, unless differently agreed, that the vendor will give a marketable title." *Townsend v. Stick*, 158 F.2d 142 (C.C.A. 4th Cir. 1946).

(A) is incorrect. In cases like above, where the contracting parties have entered into a detailed agreement, courts will be reluctant to pronounce the agreement unenforceable only because a basic assumption to the contract is not included in the writing.

(C) is incorrect. It is a basic assumption that Chase own marketable title to the land his is selling. Chase must convey the land described in the contract.

(D) is incorrect. Chase must convey marketable title. The contract describes, in detail, the land Scott is purchasing. Therefore, a basic assumption or implied promise is that Chase will convey a marketable title for the land.

Question 149
Answer: C

This question tests moral obligation. The general rule is that a moral obligation constitutes insufficient consideration to render a promise enforceable. In this case, Brill saved Mary's life before Ace made a promise to Bill. Therefore, the promise was based on a moral obligation and saving Mary's life cannot be regarded as sufficient consideration.

(A) is incorrect because a moral obligation does not constitute sufficient consideration.

(B) is incorrect because Ace was materially benefited before he made his promise to Brill, so there is no adequate consideration.

(D) is incorrect because a bargain is not required to be equal in order to be enforceable.

Question 150
Answer: B

This question tests relinquishment of claims. A bargained-for-promise to relinquish a valid legal claim is adequate consideration to support a reciprocal promise. A promise to relinquish an invalid claim constitutes adequate consideration if the promisor believes (1) that the claim is valid and (2) that a legal detriment may only arise in that manner. In this case, if Brill reasonably believed that he had a valid claim, his case is strengthened.

(A) is incorrect because the promise not to file a claim did not have to be made in writing.

(C) is incorrect because moral obligation does not constitute adequate consideration regardless of how much Mary contributed.

(D) is incorrect because $1 is nominal consideration, and the relinquishment of an invalid legal claim is only adequate consideration only if the promisor believes the claim is valid as in (B).

Question 151
Answer: A

This question tests settlement of claims. A promise to relinquish an invalid claim is a detriment if a claimant makes it in good faith, and a reasonable man could believe that the claim was well founded. Brill is most likely to recover under the theory that he and Ace made a compromise by agreeing to settle Brill's potential claim against Ace's estate, even though that claim was likely invalid.

(B) is incorrect because when Brill saved Mary's life, he had no reasonable expectation of receiving compensation for it. Thus, Ace was not unjustly enriched.

(C) is incorrect because there is no evidence of Brill's reliance on the promise.

(D) is incorrect because a unilateral contract is accepted by performance, and Brill made no acceptance by performance.

Question 152
Answer: A

This question tests impossibility. A party's contractual duty may be discharged by impossibility when an unforeseen event occurs, or unexpected circumstances arise, which render the duty permanently impossible to perform. In this case, if Carpenter could only work during the month of March, the flood which prevented him from working during that month made the duty impossible to perform.

(B) is incorrect because if Householder's use is not be affected by delays, the impossibility caused by the flooding was only temporary and Carpenter's duty was suspended but not discharged.

(C) is incorrect because if the rate of increase of costs was foreseeable, then Carpenter may not claim impracticability.

(D) is incorrect because if Carpenter was aware that flooding was likely, he assumed the risk of delays caused by flooding and could have done more of the work in February.

Question 153
Answer: D

This question tests revocation. Under the majority rule, a revocation can occur before an offeree accepts an offer. In this case, the offer was revoked on March 12, two days before Dawes attempted to accept the offer.

(A) is incorrect because Dawes provided no consideration in exchange for keeping the offer open, Dawes did not detrimentally rely on the offer, and Adams is not a merchant selling goods under the UCC.

(B) is incorrect because the offeree should have reasonably concluded that the offer was no longer open.

(C) is incorrect because Adams repudiated the contract if the offer did have to be held open through March 14.

Question 154
Answer: C

This question tests misrepresentation. A misrepresentation is an untrue statement that one party makes to another party. The elements of a misrepresentation are (1) falsity, (2) scienter, (3) deception, and (4) injury. In this case, Page can only prevail if Carver made an untrue statement.

If Carter told Page that the stock was not worth more than $6 a share, all four elements of misrepresentation would be satisfied. In the absence of an untrue statement, Page cannot prevail on a misrepresentation claim.

(A) and (B) are incorrect because misrepresentation requires an untrue statement.
(D) is incorrect because the availability of the financial statement would not matter if Carver had made an untrue statement to Page.

Question 155
Answer: A

This question tests shipment contracts. A shipment contract occurs when the parties' agreement provides that a seller is to ship goods F.O.B. and lists the place where the risk of loss is transferred. A seller bears the risk of loss until the goods reach the F.O.B. location at which point the risk is transferred to the buyer. In this case, the contract specified that the risk of loss was transferred from the seller to the buyer when the goods were delivered to the carrier at Singer's place of business. Thus, the risk of loss is on Byer who is liable for the $10,000 contract price. Provisions prohibiting assignment are usually unenforceable.

(B) is incorrect because Byer is liable for the full contract price because the risk of loss was on Byer after the chairs reached the carrier.

(C) is incorrect because the goods only had to reach the carrier, not the final destination.

(D) is incorrect because provisions prohibiting assignment are usually unenforceable.

Question 156
Answer: D

This question tests shipment contracts. A shipment contract occurs when the parties' agreement provides that a seller is to ship goods F.O.B. and lists the place where the risk of loss is transferred. A seller bears the risk of loss until the goods reach the F.O.B. location at which point they are transferred to the buyer. In this case, the contract specified that the risk of loss was transferred from the seller to the buyer when the goods were delivered to the carrier at Singer's place of business.

(A) is incorrect because the contract allocated the risk to Byer after the chairs reached the carrier.

(B) is incorrect because the risk of loss was on Byer.

(C) is incorrect because Singer has already performed under the contract's terms.

Question 157
Answer: D

This question tests counter-offers. A counter-offer serves as a rejection of the initial offer and terminates the power of acceptance. In this case, when Plummer replied "will not do it for less than $3,500," that counter-offer served as a rejection of Ohner's initial offer.

(A) and (B) are incorrect because Plummer's March 15 counter-offer was a rejection of Ohner's initial offer. Plummer may not accept Ohner's offer after rejecting it.
(C) is incorrect because silence does not constitute acceptance unless there was a duty to respond or an expectation of a response was warranted by the relationship of the parties.

Question 158
Answer: A

This question tests the Parol Evidence Rule. The Parol Evidence Rule excludes extrinsic evidence of previous or contemporaneous agreements that supplement or contradict a contract's terms if the parties intended that a writing represent their agreement's final terms and conditions. However, the Parol Evidence Rule does not operate to exclude evidence regarding a condition precedent to a contract. In this case, there was a condition precedent that Ohner was able to obtain a $5,000 loan. Evidence of this oral agreement is admissible and Ohmer has a sound defense.

(B) is incorrect because it is less optimal than (A), although the oral modification did not violate the Statute of Frauds.

(C) is incorrect because evidence regarding a condition precedent is admissible.

(D) is incorrect because Ohner is free to deny the validity of the written agreement.

Question 159
Answer: D

This question tests the extinguishment of the rights of third-party beneficiaries. The parties to a contract may mutually alter or eliminate third party rights under the contract before those rights vest. Under the *Restatement*, a third party's contractual rights vest when a third party (1) discovers a third-party contract and assents to it, (2) materially alters his or her position based upon a promise, or (3) commences a suit to enforce a promise. In this case, Neese's rights under the contract did not vest prior to the contract modification because none of the scenarios above occurred.

(A) is incorrect because the parties were free to eliminate Neese's rights before the rights vested.

(B) is incorrect because including a third-party beneficiary in a contract is different from assigning rights.

(C) is incorrect because third-party beneficiaries are not required to provide consideration.

Question 160

Answer: C

This question tests the Statute of Frauds. The Statute of Frauds requires that some types of contracts are only enforceable if they are in writing. One of the types is suretyship contracts in which a person agrees to answer for another's legally enforceable debt or duty. In this case, Miller promised to be responsible for Gray's obligation and thus became a surety. However, Miller did not make the promise in writing so the Statute of Frauds is not satisfied.

Question 161
Answer: B

This question tests bargained for exchange. A bargained for exchange of promises occurs if (1) a promisor makes a promise to convince a promisee to perform, and (2) a promisee is convinced to perform based on the promise that the promisor made. In this case, Esther will probably successfully argue that Gray's promise was made to convince her to study hard and that she studied hard based on Gray's promise.

(A) is incorrect because the remedy under promissory estoppel is for reliance damages, not expectation damages.

(C) is incorrect because Gray's promise was intended to induce Esther to get "A's".

(D) is incorrect because Esther was under no such legal obligation.

Question 162
Answer: C

This question tests the perfect tender rule. Under the UCC's perfect tender rule, "if the goods or the tender of delivery fail in any respect to conform to the contract, the buyer may reject the whole". In this case, Zeller's tender of only 95 bushels failed to conform to the contract. Thus, Baker was allowed to refuse to accept or pay for the wheat, and Zeller has breached the contract.

(A) is incorrect because of the UCC's perfect tender rule.

(B) is incorrect because Zeller's duty would only be discharged if it was permanently impossible to perform and there is no evidence that it was even temporarily impossible to perform.

(D) is incorrect because Zeller's time to cure under section 2-508 of the UCC expired on August 1.

Question 163
Answer: C

This question tests expressions of doubt. A mere expression of doubt about a first party's willingness or ability to perform a contract will not serve as an anticipatory breach. If such an expression occurs, the first party who anticipates a breach may request written assurance of performance. If no written assurance is given, the party that requested it may file a lawsuit for breach of contract. In this case, Selco expressed doubt that it could perform on May 10. After this expression of doubt, Byco can suspend its performance and demand assurances that Selco will perform but cannot win a breach of contract claim.

(A) and (B) are incorrect because an expression of doubt is not an anticipatory repudiation.

(D) is incorrect because Byco is not required to make the May 15 payment after Selco's expression of doubt.

Question 164
Answer: D

This question tests anticipatory repudiation. Under the UCC, when a party repudiates a contract, the aggrieved party may suspend its own performance and (1) resort to any remedy for breach or (2) await performance by the repudiating party for a commercially reasonable time. In this case, Selco has repudiated the contract, so Byco can sue for breach of contract or await performance by Selco. However, Byco is not required to give Selco a commercially reasonable time to perform. Therefore, (D) is an incorrect statement and consequently is the correct answer.

(A) is a correct statement because Byco could not bring a successful breach of contract claim if Selco retracts its repudiation.

(B) is a correct statement because Byco can rescind the contract while awaiting Selco's performance.

(C) is a correct statement because Byco may only wait for a commercially reasonable time because damages after that point could have been mitigated.

Question 165
Answer: D

This question tests the Parol Evidence Rule. The Parol Evidence Rule bars extrinsic evidence of previous or contemporaneous agreements that supplement or contradict a written contract's terms. In this case, Gritz's oral commitment to repay the loan by July 1 contradicts the written contract's repayment date of September 1. Therefore, evidence of the oral commitment is barred by the Parol Evidence Rule.

(A) is incorrect because evidence of the oral agreement is barred regardless of whether or not there was independent consideration.

(B) is incorrect because such evidence is barred by the Parol Evidence Rule.

(C) is incorrect because the pre-existing duty rule does not serve to bar evidence.

Question 166

Answer: D

This question tests the Statute of Frauds. The Statute of Frauds requires that contracts be in writing when they relate to certain topics. One type of contract that must be in writing is the suretyship contract. A suretyship contract is an agreement to answer for another's legally enforceable debt or duty. In this case, Gritz's oral promise to guarantee the loan does not satisfy the Statute of Frauds.

(A) is incorrect because the memorandum does not include a promise to guarantee the loan.

(B) is incorrect because the evidence is barred by the Statute of Frauds regardless of whether Gritz is a third-party beneficiary or not.

(C) is incorrect because the guarantee promise was part of the consideration exchanged for the loan.

Question 167
Answer: C

When Perez signed the contract, Perez agreed to take title "subject to easements, covenants, and restrictions of record" at the time of contract formation. However, the easement to Electric Company was not of record at the time the contract was signed, so Perez did not agree to take title subject to it.

(A) and (B) are incorrect because O'Neal is not entitled to specific performance because Perez agreed to take title subject only to easements in place at the time of signing the contract.

(D) is incorrect because high-voltage power lines are not a nuisance under all circumstances.

Question 168
Answer: B

This question tests option contracts. After Cutter exercised the option he held, he was obligated to pay Bard $325,000 for Broadacres. Bard relied on Cutter's exercise of his option when Bard exercised his own option. A court may order specific performance when money damages would not provide an adequate remedy. The likelihood that a court will order specific performance increases the more unique an item is. Courts enforce agreements for real estate conveyances because they involve unique property. Thus, Bard is entitled to specific performance.

(A) is incorrect because specific performance, not money damages, is the appropriate remedy for real estate conveyances because land is unique property.

(C) is incorrect because Bard is entitled to specific performance as well.

(D) is incorrect because Bard is entitled to keep the money paid by Cutter in exchange for the option.

Question 169
Answer: D

This question tests third-party beneficiaries. Intended beneficiaries have actionable rights whereas incidental beneficiaries do not. Intended beneficiaries are third parties that the first and second parties to a contract designate to receive the primary benefit of the contract. In this case, the right to distribute "Premium Vintage-Bouqet" wine is not the primary benefit of the Bouquet-Vintage contract. Thus, the court will conclude that the parties did not intend to benefit Claret and made the contract to protect or serve their own interests. The "if feasible" language also suggests that the parties' motive was not to benefit Claret.

(A) is incorrect because Claret was an incidental beneficiary.

(B) is incorrect because Claret was unreasonable in relying on the contract because of the "if feasible" language.

(C) is incorrect because the parties did not have to expressly agree that Claret would have enforceable rights for rights to vest with Claret.

Question 170
Answer: C

This question tests assignments. An assignment is not valid if it would materially affect the non-assigning party's duty. In this case, Vintage can argue that forcing it to account for profits materially alters its duty.

(A) is incorrect because express authorization is not necessary to make an assignment.

(B) is incorrect because a partner may assign his or her interest in a contract.

(D) is incorrect because Amicusbank did not need to be a third-party beneficiary to have contract rights assigned to it.

Question 171
Answer: A

This question tests non-delegable duties. Those duties requiring special skill, knowledge, or judgment are non-delegable. In this case, the delegatee's employees had no experience or reputation in the wine industry, whereas the delegator was well known. Therefore, the delegation created a significant risk of diminishing profits for Bouquet. So, Bouquet is likely to prevail.

(B) is incorrect because no provision expressly authorizing delegation is required.

(C) and (D) are incorrect because growing grapes for wine requires special knowledge and judgment.

Question 172
Answer: A

This question tests the perfect tender rule. Under section 2-601 of the UCC, "unless otherwise agreed..., if the goods or the tender of delivery fail in any respect to conform to the contract, the buyer may (a) reject the whole; or (b) accept the whole; or (c) accept any commercial unit or units and reject the rest." In this case, Clothier was entitled to reject the non-conforming delivery on June 3 because Kravat tendered two-inch ties instead of three-inch ties as Clothier requested.

(B) is incorrect because Clothier could have still properly rejected the nonconforming goods even if Kravat had notified Clothier that they were shipped as an accommodation.

(C) is incorrect because even if the shipment of nonconforming goods acted as an acceptance, Clothier properly rejected the delivery under section 2-601 of the UCC.

(D) is incorrect because Clothier had no obligation to return the nonconforming goods because they were rejected.

Question 173
Answer: C

This question tests the seller's right to cure. Under section 2-508(2) of the UCC, "when any tender or delivery by the seller is rejected because non-conforming and the time for performance has not yet expired, the seller may seasonably notify the buyer of his intention to cure and may then within the contract time make a conforming delivery." In this case, Kravat had the right to cure the defective delivery through June 30 and did so. Clothier did not properly reject the ties on June 30.

(A) and (B) are incorrect because Kravat had until the end of the contract time to cure the defective delivery.

(D) is incorrect because there was no modification to the contract in this case.

Question 174
Answer: D

This question tests marketable title. A title is usually unmarketable if the purchaser would be subject to a real risk of litigation by acquiring the property. In this case, there is a strong likelihood for litigation because a portion of the Santos' house is in violation of a zoning ordinance.

(A) and (B) are incorrect because the title to the house is unmarketable.

(C) is incorrect because an immaterial breach usually does not justify a non-breaching party to cease performance.

Question 175
Answer: D

This question tests the rights of third-party beneficiaries. The parties to a contract may eliminate the rights of third party beneficiaries before those rights vest. A third party's contractual rights vest when the third party (1) discovers a third-party contract and assents to it, (2) materially alters his or her position based upon a promise, or (3) commences a suit to enforce a promise. In this case, none of those three scenarios occurred so the third party rights had not vested and the original parties were free to revoke them.

(A) and (B) are incorrect because third party rights may be revoked before they vest.

(C) is incorrect because Prodigal did not have to acquire physical possession of the passbook for the third party rights to vest.

Question 176
Answer: C

This question tests revocation of gratuitous assignments. Gratuitous assignments are terminable by a notice of termination from the assignor to the assignee, by the death of the assignor, or by a subsequent assignment of the same right. The assignment must be terminated before the gift is completed, however. A gift is completed when it is delivered to the assignee. In this case, the assignment was gratuitous but cannot be revoked because the gift was delivered.

(A) and (B) are incorrect because delivery was completed so the gift was not revocable.

(D) is incorrect because Prodigal would have to show reliance on the promise in order to prevail under promissory estoppel.

Question 177
Answer: D

This question tests anticipatory repudiation. When a first party tells a second party of an unequivocal and anticipated lack of ability or willingness to perform contractual obligations, the communication may be considered to be a repudiation and the second party can suspend its performance and bring a breach of contract claim. In this case, Fido repudiated the contract on October 15, so Toy Store's motion should not be dismissed because the complaint alleges an actionable breach.

(A) is incorrect because Fido breached the contract by repudiating it.

(B) is incorrect because the lawsuit is not premature since Fido repudiated the contract.

(C) is incorrect because repudiation of the contract allows a potential breach of contract claim, not a tort claim.

Question 178
Answer: A

This question tests assignments. In this case, Fido assigned its interest in the Fido-Toy Store contract to High Finance in exchange for a loan. However, Fido did not delegate to High Finance any of its duties under the contract, so High Finance is not liable to Toy Store for Fido's breach.

(B) is incorrect because assignments are not required to be public to be effective.

(C) and (D) are incorrect because Fido's contractual duties were not delegated to High Finance, so High Finance is not responsible for Fido's breach.

Question 179
Answer: C

This question tests capacity to contract for minors. Minors have the capacity to enter into contracts which are voidable, not void. A minor has no obligation under a contract unless he ratifies it after turning the age of majority. Even if a minor ratifies a contract after turning the majority age, he is still only liable to the extent acknowledged in the ratification. In this case, Ohm acknowledged being liable for $300 in ratifying the contract so that is his liability.

(A) is incorrect because Ohm ratified the contract.

(B) and (D) are incorrect because Ohm is liable for the amount acknowledged ($300).

Question 180
Answer: D

This question tests the duration of offers. When the duration of the offer's acceptance period is not specified, it is open for a reasonable time. In this case, no period was specified. So, Gourmet could accept the offer if Gourmet mailed the check and memo within a reasonable time after receipt of Eureka's letter.

(A) is incorrect because both parties do not have to be merchants for an offer to be open for a reasonable time.

(B) is incorrect because Eureka did not have to have 24 LBVC's in stock for Gourmet to accept Eureka's offer.

(C) is incorrect because Gourmet had a reasonable time which may have been three months, more than three months, or less than three months.

Question 181
Answer: C

This question tests offer and acceptance. When an offer is accepted, the offeror cannot force new terms upon the offeree at shipping. In this case, if Eureka's written reply quoting the $39.99 price per LBVC was an offer accepted by Gourmet, then the invoice restriction was not a part of the contract, and Eureka has no cause of action against Gourmet.

(A) is incorrect because Eureka didn't need to be a non-merchant to have a cause of action against Gourmet for violating the invoice restriction.

(B) is incorrect because if the invoice restriction materially altered pre-existing terms, the restriction did not become a part of the contract.

(D) is incorrect because the statement was not part of Eureka's written reply and thus is not a part of the contract.

Question 182
Answer: C

This question tests limitations on specific performance. A court usually will not enforce specific performance on a personal services contract because the Thirteenth Amendment of the U.S. Constitution prohibits involuntary servitude, and it is difficult to force two adverse parties to collaborate on a project. In this case, the Plannah-Threedee contract is a personal services contract, so Threedee is not entitled to specific performance.

(A) and (B) are incorrect because specific performance is not an appropriate remedy for personal services contracts.

(D) is incorrect because Plannah was not allowed to delegate the duties because the duties under a personal services contract are generally non-delegable.

Question 183
Answer: A

(I) is a correct statement because a delegator's duty is discharged only after a delegatee performs.

(II) is a correct statement because a delegatee's duty is discharged only if the delegatee performs.

(III) is incorrect because the fee was to be paid upon completion and Drafty abandoned the project prior to completion.

Question 184
Answer: A

This question tests expectation damages. Courts seek to afford a non-breaching party with the benefit of the bargain from a breaching party. The non-breaching party is placed into the position he or she expected to be in if both sides had performed the contract fully. In this case, Hardsell is entitled to recover the profit it would have made by selling a Doppelpferd to Shift. The profit is calculated by subtracting the manufacturer's price from the $9,000 sale price.

(B) is incorrect because expectation damages are not calculated from the local wholesale price because Hardsell ordered directly from the manufacturer.

(C) is incorrect because Hardsell already had a contract to sell one Doppelpferd to Karbuff, so Hardsell would have sold two if Shift had not repudiated.

(D) is incorrect because there is no evidence that Shift lacked the ability to negotiate any of the terms.

Question 185
Answer: A

This question tests retraction of repudiation. A party repudiates a contract when he or she communicates to the other party an unequivocal lack of ability or willingness to perform contractual obligations. Such a repudiation constitutes a breach of contract and the non-breaching party may suspend its own performance and bring a breach of contract claim. A repudiation may be retracted only if the promisee has not materially altered his or her position. In this case, Awl repudiated the contract on February 1 and Howser materially changed positions by hiring Gutter to do the work. Awl's repudiation could not be retracted after this change, so Awl committed a total breach of contract.

(B) is incorrect because Howser could not prevail if Awl was permitted to retract his repudiation because the original contract price was less than $75,000.

(C) is incorrect because Howser was not required to inform Awl of the hiring of Gutter.

(D) is incorrect because Awl could not retract his repudiation after Howser hired Gutter.

Question 186
Answer: D

This question tests expectation damages. Courts seek to give non-breaching parties the benefit of the bargain from breaching parties. This means placing non-breaching parties in the positions they expected to be in if the contracts had been performed by both sides. To fulfill a non-breaching party's expectations, the amount awarded may be measured by the sum that was required to obtain reasonable substitute performance. In this case, the $75,000 Howser-Gutter contract was a reasonable substitute because $75,000 was the fair market cost of the work to be done. Thus, Howser will recover $15,000.

(A) is incorrect because the fair market value of the completed house may be more or less than the cost of the construction of the house.

(B) is incorrect because the amount Awl demanded is irrelevant to the calculation of expectation damages.

(C) is incorrect because Howser was not required to pay Gutter $10,000 more than the contract price.

Question 187
Answer: C

This question tests novation. A novation is a substituted agreement that replaces at least one of the parties to a prior agreement with a new party. The new party becomes a successor promissory to the original promissee under the subsequent agreement, which releases the predecessor promissory from the prior agreement. A novation discharges the original party that is not a part of the substitute agreement. In this case, Ann would lose if there was a novation substituting Carolyn for Brenda because such a novation would discharge Brenda's duties under the original contract.

(A) is incorrect because there is no evidence that Ann failed to assert her right in a timely manner after Carolyn ceased making payments.

(B) is incorrect because an accord and satisfaction involves substituted performance, not substituted parties.

(D) is incorrect because an attornment is the acceptance by a tenant of a new landlord, not the acceptance by a landlord of a new tenant.

Question 188
Answer: B

This question tests liquidated damages. Courts disfavor liquidated damages provisions and enforce them only when actual damages are (1) difficult to ascertain or uncertain in amount and (2) reasonably estimated at the contract's formation or when the contract was breached. In this case, actual damages are not reasonably estimated at $500 per day because Homey could not have occupied the house during the period of delay anyway. The liquidated damages provision is not enforceable and Homey is entitled to actual damages, if any.

(A) is incorrect because the liquidated damages provision is not enforceable.

(C) is incorrect because Homey was aware of the delay and did not waive it.

(D) is incorrect because Homey did not consent to a modification of the completion date.

Question 189
Answer: A

If payment is contingent upon the approval of an expert, that expert must grant or deny approval in good faith. In this case, Bilevel explicitly stated that Structo "did a great job" and that Bilevel found "no defects worth mentioning." Therefore, Bilevel's refusal to issue the certificate was done in bad-faith, and consequently the nonoccurrence of the condition was excused.

(B) is incorrect because the nonoccurrence of one of the conditions was the result of bad faith by the architect.

(C) and (D) are incorrect because Structo is entitled to the final payment if the architect withheld the certificate in bad faith even if Homey overpaid Structo or Structo can still make a net profit without the payment.

Question 190
Answer: C

This question tests the assumption of risk. A mistake does not include an erroneous belief by one or more parties regarding what might occur in the future. When there is uncertainty about when or if an event will occur at the time of contract formation, the parties involved have assumed the risk that it will take place. In this case, the length of Ohlster's life was a risk assumed by both parties.

(A) is incorrect because the parties assumed the risk, so there was no unjust enrichment.

(B) is incorrect because frustration of purpose occurs when events that take place before the contract's performance result in destroying a party's purpose. In this case, the contract was fully performed by Geriatrics because Ohlster was given lifetime care despite the short time period.

(D) is incorrect because Geriatrics is not required to show reliance because this is not an estoppel case.

Question 191
Answer: B

This question tests nondisclosure. Generally, there is no duty to disclose information unless (1) disclosure is required by a statute or regulation or (2) a party makes affirmative efforts to hide the truth. In this case, there is no suggestion that disclosure was required or that Bill or Sally took affirmative efforts to hide the truth. In fact, Paul was free to ask questions, but there is no suggestion that he did so even after the "as is" language was included in the contract. If the "as is" language is controlling, Paul cannot win unless disclosure was required by statute, or Bill or Sally took steps to actively conceal the truth.

(A) is incorrect because the disclosure had to be made to Paul, and Sally is responsible for the actions of her agent, Bill.

(C) is incorrect because knowledge of an agent does not constitute knowledge of a principal.

(D) is incorrect because the seller must make disclosures if required by statutes or regulations and may not take steps to hide the truth.

Question 192
Answer: C

This question tests restitution. Restitution damages may be available where the plaintiff is the party that materially breached an enforceable contract and cannot recover for breach of contract. The non-breaching party, however, is entitled to his or her reliance loss. In this case, Hydro-King would have sold two power boats if Zuma had not breached the contract so it is entitled to retain the lost profit from the sale of one of the boats. Therefore, Zuma's claim should be upheld for the advance payment minus the lost profit from the contract with Hydro-King.

(A) is incorrect because a breaching party can still obtain restitution.

(B) is incorrect because $4,000 is more than the profit lost by Zuma's breach.

(D) is incorrect because Hydro-King is entitled to its reliance loss, not statutory damages under the UCC.

Question 193
Answer: B

If the parties intended that a writing represent their agreement's final terms and conditions, the Parol Evidence Rule bars extrinsic evidence that supplements or contradicts the written contract's terms. However, evidence is admissible to show that the writing was not intended to be final. In this case, evidence that the writing was not to be binding unless Ohner's spouse approved is admissible because it suggests that the writing was not meant to be final.

(A) is incorrect because an oral agreement that the written document was not meant to represent the final terms and conditions is admissible even if third-party approval was required.

(C) and (D) are incorrect because the Parol Evidence Rule does not bar evidence suggesting that a written agreement was not meant to be final.

Question 194
Answer: C

The correct answer is (C). This question tests waiver of condition. A party to a contract is entitled to waive a condition of the contract but in doing so relinquishes the right to that condition being satisfied. In this case, Ohner waived the condition requiring the law partner's approval, and Planner relied on that waiver by starting performance. The waiver cannot be revoked.

(A) is incorrect because 40 percent completion may not constitute substantial performance.
(B) is incorrect because the remedy for promissory estoppel is the reliance loss, and Ohmer can receive a higher damages award by pursuing the expectation loss.

(D) is incorrect because Planner should not pursue an unjust enrichment claim under quasi-contract theory because there was a contract in this case.

Question 195
Answer: D

This question tests what happens when the seller sends the wrong goods under the UCC. When a seller sends the wrong goods, its actions constitute an acceptance and a breach. The buyer may reject the goods within a reasonable time after delivery or tender according to section 2-602(1) of the UCC. "The buyer has no further obligation with regard to goods rightfully rejected." UCC § 2-602(2)(c). In this case, Orchard accepted Fruitko's offer by sending the wrong goods. However, Fruitko is under no obligation to accept the shipment.

(A) and (B) are incorrect because Orchard's shipment was an acceptance according to the UCC.

(C) is incorrect because Fruitko is not required to accept the peaches even though a contract was formed.

Question 196
Answer: C

This question tests the Statute of Frauds and suretyship contracts. Suretyship contracts must be in writing to satisfy the Statute of Frauds except when a promisor's primary reason for making the promise is to further his or her own interest. In this case, Pater's promise was not made in writing, so the Statute of Frauds is not satisfied. However, the promise does not fall under the Statute of Frauds if Pater's primary purpose in making the promise was self-benefit.

(A) is incorrect because a suretyship promise does not require consideration from the guarantor.

(B) is incorrect because the agreement could be performed within one year.

(D) is incorrect because a court may supplement the agreement with reasonable gap fillers and enforce the supplemented contract.

Question 197
Answer: B

This question tests the right of lateral support. A plaintiff can invoke the right of lateral support if a defendant acted negligently or if subsidence would have occurred to land in its natural condition. *Noone v. Price.* In this case, Pam must prove negligence in order to recover from Dora.

(A) is incorrect because the cause of action requires negligence.

(C) is incorrect because a landowner may still invoke the right of lateral support if the support was needed in the absence of the building to support the land in its natural state.

(D) is incorrect because Dora was also under the obligation not to act negligently.

Question 198
Answer: D

This question tests private nuisance. The is no legal right to free light or air flow, so disrupting such a flow does not constitute a private nuisance. *Fontainebleau Hotel v. Fort-Five Twenty-Five.* In this case, Pam has no cause of action because there is no legal right to the free flow of light.

(A), (B), and (C) are incorrect because disruption of light does not constitute a private nuisance because there is no legal right to free light or air flow.

Question 199
Answer: D

This question tests the rules of admissibility. Course-of-performance evidence is admissible because post contract formation behavior which is accepted without objection is assumed to have evidentiary value about what was intended at the time of contract formation. In this case, Tune had previously accepted return of undefective radios for credit which suggests that the parties intended the return of undefective radios to be allowed.

(A) is incorrect because the Parol Evidence Rule only applies where the extrinsic evidence contradicts the terms and conditions of the writing.

(B) is incorrect because the course of performance is not inconsistent with the express terms of the agreement.

(C) is incorrect because the time period covered by the agreement was longer than one year, so the agreement fell within the Statute of Frauds.

Question 200
Answer: B

A substituted agreement discharges a prior agreement between the parties and replaces it with a new agreement. In this case, a substituted agreement was formed when Tune, with knowledge of the wording on the check, deposited it without protest.

(A) is incorrect because there is no evidence that Bill's relied on the acceptance of the check by Tune's credit manager.

(C) is incorrect because novation requires replacement of one of the parties.

(D) is incorrect because a successful good-faith conduct defense makes a breach minor but would not remove liability from Bill's.

Question 201
Answer: C

This question tests compromise and settlement of claims. A settlement agreement is only enforceable if (1) the parties had a good faith dispute when (2) they entered into a valid contract that resolved the dispute. In this case, Bypast did not bring the suit in good faith because he knew that Testator was competent but claimed otherwise. Thus, Bypast is not entitled to recover.

Question 202
Answer: B

The correct answer is (B). This question tests the law of contract modification. UCC Article II, which applies to sales of goods, contains the UCC's Statute of Frauds. A contract for a sale of goods with a value of $500 or more must be in writing, contain essential terms, and be signed by the party to be charged. An exception, section 2-209(1) of the UCC, allows for an oral agreement to modify such a written contract if the contract as modified is not subject to the Statute of Frauds. If, however, the contract that the parties attempt to modify is subject to the Statute of Frauds and they attempt to orally modify it, section 2-209(4) of the UCC applies. It provides that an attempted modification may result in a waiver (1) if the oral modification is not retracted or (2) if a party materially changed his position in reliance on the waiver.

Fixtures, Inc. ("Fixtures") and Druggist are merchants under the UCC because they engage in the sale of goods. The subject matter of their written contract is the storage cabinets, to which the UCC's Statute of Frauds applies. Ordinarily, the parties' changes to their contract would need to be in writing to be effective under section 2-209(1) of the UCC because the sale is for more than $500. However, section 2-209(4) of the UCC applies because the parties' failed to make a valid modification of their written contract. Section 2-209(4) allows this failed modification to operate as a waiver of the written contract's delivery date of August 15. Because neither party revoked the change, Fixtures materially changed its position in reliance, the oral modification would constitute a waiver, and Druggist would be in breach for failing to accept the goods.

Answer (A) is incorrect because the UCC's Statute of Frauds required the initial contract and the modification to be in writing, but the exception operated to allow the oral modification.

Answer (C) is incorrect because UCC §2-209(1) does not require consideration for a modification to be valid.

Answer (D) is incorrect because the Parol Evidence Rule operates to exclude evidence of previous or contemporaneous agreements. The agreement here was a modification after the contract was signed and an acceptable modification.

Question 203
Answer: C

The correct answer is (C). This question tests the law of anticipatory repudiation. When a first party communicates to a second party an unequivocal anticipated lack of ability or willingness to perform contractual obligations, it may be considered an anticipatory repudiation of the contract. The second party is entitled to suspend its own performance of the contract. The second party may also bring an immediate breach of contract suit against the repudiator.

A seller's remedy of lost-volume profits is one type of actual damages recovery from a buyer in the event of incomplete performance of a contract for the sale of goods. A seller may receive any profit that the seller could have made if full performance of the contract had occurred. Further, the seller may recover its actual incidental damages and costs. Incidental damages may be awarded for miscellaneous costs or expenses resulting from responding to a breach of contract. A non-breaching party sustains incidental damages in attempting to mitigate damages or obtaining a contract's value.

Materboard repudiated the agreement on the day of performance and failed to fulfill its written promise to pay Ram for and take the computer on the agreed upon date. Materboard lacked any justification for its failure to perform. Thus, Materboard breached the parties' contract by means of anticipatory repudiation. Ram subsequently sold the computer to Byte in a private sale for the same amount as provided by the parties' contract. Had Materboard performed, Ram would have received the profits from two sales rather than one. Thus, Ram is entitled to actual damages for the lost sale to Materboard in the amount of anticipated profit, plus any incidental damages attributable to the private sale to Byte.

Question 204
Answer: A

The correct answer is (A). This question tests the law of unilateral contracts. A unilateral contract is created by an exchange of one party's promise for another party's performance of certain conduct. The parties to a contract may modify their contractual duties at any time after have entered into the contract. For a modification to be valid, the traditional common law required that mutual assent and consideration support it. The law's modern trend allows a modification in the absence of consideration if unanticipated problems arise that could make it impractical to perform a contract without altering the expected performance. In that event, the question one would ask is whether the modification is fair under the circumstances?

Painter and Farmer entered into a written unilateral contract because of Farmer's promise to pay Painter for painting three barns. Painter's request for payment after painting only two barns, when the contract provided for payment after all three barns were painted, is an attempted oral modification of the contract. No evidence of mutual assent and consideration exists to warrant such a modification under the common law. In terms of the law's modern trend, no evidence shows that unanticipated problems made it impractical for Painter to perform the contract without changing the expected performance with respect to the third barn.

Answer (B) is incorrect. Painter did not waive a right to payment on a per barn basis because no such contractual right existed.

Answer (C) is incorrect. Farmer lacks a payment obligation under the contract for the painting of only two barns. This obligation is not divisible but entire because it conditions payment on Painter's completion of painting all three barns.

Answer (D) is incorrect. Farmer lacks a payment obligation under the contract for the painting of only two barns. The substantial performance doctrine does not apply because the facts do not indicate a breach of contract. Specifically, Painter did not indicate a refusal to paint the third barn.

Question 205
Answer: C

The correct answer is (C). This question tests the law of restitution. When a party has materially breached a contract, he or she is not entitled to recover expectation damages for performance of the contract. The materially breaching party may be able to recover restitution damages. At common law, the breaching party (plaintiff) must prove the following elements to recover under a restitution theory: (1) the plaintiff conferred a benefit on the defendant, (2) under a reasonable expectation of receiving compensation for it, and (3) the defendant expressly or implicitly requested the benefit or the plaintiff did not voluntarily confer it, (4) the defendant would be unjustly enriched if the defendant was not obligated to compensate the plaintiff, and (5) it would be inequitable for the defendant not to pay for the benefit.

In this case, Painter has painted two barns at a value to Farmer of $4,000. However, Farmer will have to hire someone else to paint the third barn, and the cost of that person's work is unknown. Because Painter did confer a benefit on Farmer, requested by Farmer, for which he expected compensation, and Farmer would be unjustly enriched by retaining that benefit without paying for it, Painter would be entitled to recover for the reasonable value of his work. But anything over the $2000 that Farmer expected to pay for the third barn would be deducted from that amount.

Answer (A) is incorrect. Although the contract did make Farmer's payment conditional upon full performance, Painter may still recover for painting two barns on the basis of restitution.

Answer (B) is incorrect. Although Painter may recover an amount up to $4,000 from Farmer, his recovery would be tempered by any damages incurred by Farmer.

Answer (D) is incorrect. Painter's recovery would be measured based on the contract, not upon a measure of an increase in the two barns' value.

Question 206
Answer: A

The correct answer is (A). This question tests the Firm Offer Rule. Under section 2-205 of the UCC, a merchant's offer contained in a signed writing is usually irrevocable for up to three months without consideration. In order for a firm offer to remain valid beyond three months, the offer must expressly state its total duration. If a merchant provides a signed writing that offers to sell or buy goods and provides assurances that the offer shall remain open for a certain period, then the offer is irrevocable for the period that is stated in the offer; and no consideration is required.

Section 2-205 of the UCC applies because Stationer is a merchant. Stationer's offer is comprised of both the catalog and a signed letter, which constitutes a signed writing for the purposes of section 2-205. Stationer's signed letter, which offered to sell goods and provided assurances that this offer would remain open, is irrevocable for one year even in the absence of consideration from Lawyer.

Lawyer effectively accepted Stationer's firm offer by faxing in the order. Stationer is bound by Lawyer's acceptance because, Lawyer was aware of the offer, intended to accept the offer, and took steps to accept the offer by drafting the order faxing it. Because Stationer did not revoke its firm offer before Lawyer placed an order that accepted the offer, the acceptance was effective.

Answer (B) is incorrect because Stationer did not receive consideration to keep the option open, and therefore did not create an option contract.

Answer (C) is incorrect. Although section 2-205 of the UCC provides for a three-month limitation by default, Stationer's firm offer provided a 12 month duration for acceptance. Therefore, the firm offer met the statutory requirement to extend it beyond the three months.

Answer (D) is incorrect. Lawyer's acceptance did not need to occur within a reasonable time because Stationer's offer allowed for the acceptance to occur within a calendar year.

Question 207
Answer: B

The correct answer is (B). This question tests the Firm Offer Rule. Under section 2-205 of the UCC, a merchant's offer contained in a signed writing is usually irrevocable for up to three months without consideration. In order for a firm offer to remain valid beyond three months, the offer must expressly state its total duration. If a merchant provides a signed writing that offers to sell or buy goods and provides assurances that the offer shall remain open for a certain period, then the offer is irrevocable for (1) either a reasonable time not exceeding 90 days (if the offer states no period); or (2) for the period that is stated in the offer; and (3) no consideration is required. An offer that meets these requirements is irrevocable for the duration.

Section 2-205 of the UCC applies because Stationer is a merchant. Stationer's offer is comprised of both the catalog and a signed letter, which constitutes a signed writing under section 2-205. Although under section 2-205 the offer could have expired as of April due to a lack of any additional consideration to hold it open longer, the offer's letter provided assurances that this offer would remain open for a year. Even though Lawyer did not reply to Stationer's offer,

Stationer's January 15 notification to Lawyer that the price of certain items would be increased as of February 1 is not effective to change the original offer. The January 15 notification is null and void because Stationer's firm offer, including both the letter and catalog, is irrevocable.

Answer (A) is incorrect because the original offer and its price term was irrevocable under section 2-205 of the UCC, not under the promissory estoppel doctrine.

Answer (C) is incorrect. Section 2-205 of the UCC does not require consideration to make an offer irrevocable.

Answer (D) is incorrect. The price increases are not effective because Stationer's offer effectively assured Lawyer that the prices would remain the same for one year.

Question 208
Answer: A

The correct answer is (A). This question tests the law of consideration. Formation of a bilateral contract occurs when two parties exchange mutual promises. Consideration is required to enforce a promise. Generally consideration consists of a bargained for exchange of legal value in return for legal benefit(s) between two contracting parties. A bargained for exchange exists when there is (1) a promise to perform by a promisor (2) that causes a promise to perform pursuant to that promise. Parties may condition their performance upon express conditions, even if those conditions may never be fulfilled, without affecting consideration.

The facts indicate the formation of a written bilateral contract as a result of an exchange of mutual promises between Buyer and Shareholder. Buyer promised to purchase all of Shareholder's stock in order to convince Shareholder to relinquish ownership and control of the stock. Shareholder agreed to sell all of her stock in XYZ corporation based on the Buyer's promise. These bargained for exchanges constitute consideration.

Answer (B) is incorrect because Shareholder received Buyer's promise as consideration for her promise to sell.

Answer (C) is incorrect because (1) both parties were bound when they entered the contract, which satisfies the doctrine of mutuality of obligation, and (2) if Buyer were to not perform due to failure of the condition, then Shareholder would likewise no longer be bound.

Answer (D) is incorrect because parties are allowed to orally modify a contract if (1) no contractual provision prevents that type of modification and (2) the contract is not subject to the Statute of Frauds. The contract in question does not prohibit the modification here, and because the contract is not subject to the Statute of Frauds, there is no bar to the modification.

Question 209
Answer: A

The correct answer is (A). This question tests the law of conditions. A condition is an event that must occur to obligate a party to perform under a contractual term or condition. If conditions are not fulfilled by a breaching party, they relieve a non-breaching party of any legal obligation under a contract. A party to a contract is entitled to waive a condition or conditions of the contract. By waiving a condition, the party relinquishes any right to that condition being satisfied. The waiver must occur before duty to perform that condition becomes absolute.

Shareholder assented to Buyer's statement of an express condition that it needed Conglomerate's approval of the parties' contract. Thus, the approval constituted a prerequisite to consummation of the contract. Shareholder contends that Buyer's failure to obtain Conglomerate's approval resulted in breaching their contract, which relieves Shareholder of its legal obligation to convey the stock.

Buyer, however, may contend that it exercised the right to waive this condition prior to the duty to perform that condition. Buyer may waive it because the condition directly affects Buyer and Conglomerate. Buyer voluntarily imposed this condition upon itself after the parties entered into their written contract. Although Shareholder assented to the condition, Seller cannot prevent Buyer from waiving it. Buyer effectively relinquished the right to satisfy the condition before the obligation to perform it became absolute.

Answer (B) is incorrect. Although Buyer should prevail in its action, it will not be on the basis of detrimental reliance upon Shareholder's obligation to perform. Buyer will prevail based on its waiver of the condition precedent of Conglomerate's approval.

Answers (C) and (D) are incorrect. Buyer will prevail in its action because the express condition had been waived, and waiving a condition before the time for absolute performance is not a material breach.

Question 210
Answer: B

The correct answer is (B). This question tests the Parol Evidence Rule. The Parol Evidence Rule (Rule) requires that if the parties intend that a writing represent their agreement's final terms and conditions, the writing cannot subsequently be contradicted with extrinsic evidence of previous or contemporaneous agreements that supplement or contradict a contract's terms. Evidence, however, is admissible to show the existence of additional consistent terms that supplement the parties' written agreement if the agreement is final but incomplete. The Rule does not operate to exclude evidence regarding a condition precedent to the parties' integrated written contract.

The parties executed their written contract before Buyer verbally communicated the express condition that Conglomerate needed to approve the contract. Shareholder verbally assented to this condition. The Rule applies because this situation involves an oral agreement that supplements the contract's terms. Thus, this extrinsic evidence would be inadmissible under the Rule except that it seeks to show that the condition provides an additional consistent term that supplements the contract. Additionally, Conglomerate's approval was a condition precedent to the parties' integrated written contract, and therefore the extrinsic evidence would be admissible.

Answer (A) is incorrect. Although the oral condition is admissible, it is not evidence of a collateral agreement because the condition is not an agreement independent of the integrated agreement.

Answer (C) is incorrect because even if the agreement is integrated, the Rule would not operate to exclude evidence of the condition.

Answer (D) is incorrect. The oral condition is admissible because it does not contradict the written contract, but rather supplements it.

Question 211
Answer: A

The correct answer is (A). This question test the law of quasi-contracts. A quasi-contract is not an express agreement, but an obligation that the law imposes to do justice even when the parties neither made nor intended any promise. It is a non-contractual obligation that is treated like a contract and serves to prevent unjust enrichment to one party from another party. In the absence of an express contract, a promisee's claim for recovery will be based on a promisor's unjust enrichment through the promisee's conduct.

Although Glazier and Landlord had no express agreement for the completed repair work, a contract between them could be implied in law from the facts in order to prevent Landlord's unjust enrichment from Glazier's window replacement. Landlord would have paid to replace the window had this replacement happened outside of Tenant's lease. But because Tenant arranged to replace it and then breached the lease, Landlord would receive the benefits of both a new window and the $2,000 deposit. Because Landlord would be unjustly enriched at Glazier's expense by retaining the deposit, the courts will likely imply a quasi-contract and require that Landlord pay Glazier.

Answer (B) is incorrect because the promissory estoppel doctrine does not apply when the parties did not exchange any promises that needed consideration to be enforceable.

Answer (C) is incorrect because no implied-in-fact contract existed between the parties. Their conduct did not give rise to facts that would support an agreement between them. The only contract existed between Glazier and Tenant.

Answer (D) is wrong because Glazier is not an intended beneficiary of the lease.

Question 212
Answer: B

The correct answer is (B). This question tests the law of accord and satisfaction. An accord is an agreement to accept substituted performance (e.g., less money). A satisfaction occurs when the substituted performance occurs. An accord and satisfaction occurs when a debtor tries to obligate a creditor to take less than a debt's entire amount in full satisfaction of the debt by writing on a check or in an accompanying letter, "payment in full." A creditor who deposits or cashes such a check is subject to a valid accord and satisfaction if the debt: (1) is subject to an honest dispute; or (2) is unliquidated (not definite in amount).

Tenant failed to create an accord agreement—whereby Glazier would accept substituted performance—by making the notation on the check. No satisfaction occurred when Tenant provided the substituted performance of mailing a check to Glazier for half of the total amount due under the parties' contract. Although Glazier cashed the check, Glazier is not subject to a valid accord and satisfaction because the debt did not involve either an honest dispute or an indefinite amount of debt. The correct answer is (B) because the amount that Tenant owed to Glazier was liquidated and undisputed.

Answer (A) is incorrect because Tenant's debt was liquidated, and therefore Glazier is not bound by the notation.

Answer (C) is incorrect. Tenant will not prevail because Glazier did not implicitly agree to accept the check as full payment by cashing it without awareness of the notation.

Answer (D) is incorrect because Glazier's failure to write a reservation of rights notation on the check will not allow Tenant to prevail because the claim was liquidated and undisputed.

NOTE: The common law governs this question, although only a minority of states follow it, because the question does not provide for the application of a statute that controls this subject. Such a statute is the majority rule based on section 3-311 of the UCC. Only UCC Articles 1-2, and 9 regarding fixtures automatically apply to Multistate Bar Exam questions.

Question 213
Answer: D

The correct answer is (D). This question tests the law of anticipatory repudiation. When a first party communicates to a second party an unequivocal anticipated lack of ability or willingness to perform contractual obligations (i.e., "I will not perform"), it may be considered an anticipatory repudiation of the contract. Under the UCC, when either party repudiates the contract, an aggrieved party may suspend its own performance and: for a commercially reasonable time await performance by the repudiating party; or resort to any remedy for breach.

Bye Bye's letter of June 9 communicated to Vendor an unequivocal lack of willingness to perform any contractual obligations. Thus, the letter constitutes an anticipatory repudiation of the contract that the parties' correspondence had created. The UCC applies because the contract involves a sale of goods by Vendor, a merchant that deals in those goods. Because Bye Bye repudiated the contract, Vendor was entitled to suspend its own performance and choose one of two courses of action. In light of Bye Bye's letter of repudiation, Vendor reasonably exercised its option to sell the 100 QTs to another buyer, rather than wait a commercially reasonable time for Bye Bye to perform.

Answer (A) is incorrect. Vendor's telegram of June 2 regarding prices and availability can, under the circumstances, be construed as an offer rather than a quote.

Answer (B) is incorrect. Section 2-207 of the UCC applies when an offeror presents an offer for the purchase or sale of goods and an offeree responds by "accepting" the offer using a document containing different or additional terms.

Answer (C) is incorrect because Bye Bye's use of the mails was an effective means of acceptance in response to Vendor's telegram.

Question 214
Answer: C

The correct answer is (C). This question tests the law of delegable duties. Contractual duties are generally delegable by a party to a contract. A duty is not delegable when a delegate's performance would materially vary from a promisor's performance. The following types of contractual duties are not delegable by a party to a third party: (1) those between a professional and a client that involve a personal and confidential relationship; (2) those involving the exercise of special or unique talents; and (2) those requiring personal skill, knowledge, or judgment.

The duties under a personal services contract are ordinarily not delegable, especially when a promisee's interest in a promisor's taste, reputation, or personality is intended to achieve a certain outcome. The fact that a contract contains a provision preventing delegation indicates that the contract was for personal services.

Deligor's duty of designing the interior of Gourmet's new restaurant is not delegable because the performance of Newman, a delegate, could materially vary from Deligor's performance in style, if not in quality. Deligor's contractual duties to Gourmet are not delegable to Newman because they involve a personal relationship, special talent, and require his personal skill, knowledge, or judgment. These duties arise under Deligor's personal services contract with Gourmet, who is significantly interested in Deligor's taste, reputation, or personality in order to achieve a certain outcome. His duties may not be delegated because Newman's performance could materially breach the contract.

Answer (A) is incorrect because the lack of such a prohibition does not necessarily validate any assignment or delegation.

Answer (B) is incorrect because the adequate assurances of Newman's ability are insufficient to overcome the improper delegation of duties involving personal services.

Answer (D) is incorrect because Gourmet would have to accept the delegation to create a novation.

Question 215
Answer: D

The correct answer is (D). This question tests the law of delegation and third party beneficiaries. A promisor in a personal services contract cannot be discharged from contractual duties on the basis of its delegation of duties to a delegate because a promisee entered into the contract based on a significant interest in the promisor's talents and the results that they would achieve.

Intended beneficiaries are those third parties that the first and the second parties to a contract designate to receive the primary benefit of the contract. A presumption applies that the first and the second parties have entered into a contract for their own benefit and not for the third party's benefit. A court, however, will enforce the parties' express contract for a third party if that contract confers actionable rights upon that individual or entity as a beneficiary.

Deligor, a promisor in a personal services agreement with Gourmet, is not discharged from his contractual duties on the basis of the delegation of duties to Newman, a delegate, because Gourmet, a promisee, entered into their agreement based on a significant interest in the promisor's special talents and the results that they would achieve. In the alternative, Gourmet is an intended beneficiary of the assignment agreement between Deligor and Newman because Gourmet will receive its primary benefit. This agreement may be deemed to confer enforceable rights upon Gourmet. Because Gourmet has rights under either theory, he may recover from either individual.

Answer (A) is wrong because, although the assignment agreement did not discharge Deligor's duty to Gourmet, Gourmet is an intended beneficiary of this agreement and may therefore bring an action against Newman.

Answer (B) is incorrect because the assignment agreement did not discharge Deligor's duty to Gourmet.

Answer (C) is wrong because, although Gourmet is an intended beneficiary of the assignment agreement, this agreement did not discharge Deligor's duty to Gourmet.

Question 216
Answer: C

The correct answer is (C). This question tests the law of unconscionability. The test is of unconscionability from section 2-302 of the UCC is if, under the commercial background and needs of a specific case or trade, the contractual provisions at issue are sufficiently one-sided so as to be unconscionable under the circumstances that existed when the contract was formed. The UCC enables courts to strike down unconscionable provisions.

Under section 2-107 of the UCC, the sale of timber apart from the land is a sale of goods to which the UCC applies. A court could determine that, based on the "regionally prevailing price for comparable time rights" and Landholder's lack of knowledge about the timber values, the contract's price term was sufficiently one-sided so as to be unconscionable. A court could cancel the contract on this basis.

Answer (A) is incorrect. Although Logger probably made its offer in bad faith, his duty of good faith and fair dealing arises in contract performance or enforcement. UCC § 1-203. Bad faith conduct may cause a breach of contract, which has not occurred here in the absence of performance.

Answer (B) is wrong because equitable estoppel only applies when a first party objects to or rejects a second party's contractual performance. Neither Landholder nor Logger has performed their contract.

Answer (D) is incorrect because Landholder voluntarily accepted Logger's offer. Duress does not occur here because Logger neither made a threat nor engaged in a wrongful act that prevailed over Landholder's free will.

Question 217
Answer: A

The correct answer is (A). This question tests the law of third-party beneficiary contracts. When the performance under a contract will not run directly to the third party to the contract, that individual or entity is an incidental beneficiary. An incidental beneficiary may not sue to enforce rights under a contract because a promisee did not intend that it the contract benefit the third party, and a promisor's performance of the contract did not run to the third party

The neighbor is an incidental beneficiary who cannot seek a judicial remedy to Logger's anticipatory repudiation when Landholder did not intend that the contract benefit the neighbor, and Logger's performance did not run to the neighbor. The contract did not identify neighbor. Neighbor cannot reasonably rely on the contract as deliberately affording it the benefit of a clearer view of the lake.

Answer (B) is incorrect because the neighbor brought a breach of contract action, not a tort action for nuisance.

Answer (C) is incorrect because the neighbor is not an intended beneficiary of the contract. An intended beneficiary is a third party that the first and the second parties to a contract designate to receive the primary benefit of the contract.

Answer (D) is an incorrect conclusion because Landholder did not assign his rights under the contract to the neighbor.

Question 218
Answer: A

The correct answer is (A). This question tests the law of the Parol Evidence Rule. The Parol Evidence Rule (Rule) is an exclusionary rule that requires the parties to incorporate into a contract all of the terms and conditions to which they have agreed. The Rule provides that if the parties intend that a writing represent their agreement's final terms and conditions, the writing cannot subsequently be contradicted with extrinsic evidence of previous or contemporaneous agreements that supplement or contradict a contract's terms. The Rue does not operate to exclude what the parties understood to be the meaning of an ambiguous contractual term.

Boss's evidence is admissible to show the parties' understanding of a contractual term to determine if only Builder, instead of Boss individually, was to be legally responsible for performing the contract. Neither the signature nor the contract language is clear as to whether Boss is individually liable, so the introduction of the negotiation information would not contradict those terms.

Answer (B) is incorrect because the evidence would not be admissible if it contradicted the signature or the writing.

Answer (C) is a wrong conclusion resting upon an incorrect basis when admissible parol evidence may be used to explain the legal effect of Boss's signature.

Answer (D) is wrong because its correct conclusion is based on an inaccurate statement when the "four corners" rule is superseded by legal developments.

Question 219
Answer: B

Answer (B) is correct. This question tests the law of indefiniteness in contract law. Under the UCC, a contract does not fail for indefiniteness if the parties intended to make a contract and there is a reasonably certain basis for giving an appropriate remedy. Certain open terms are permitted to be read into sales and lease contracts. Under the UCC, open terms can include price, payment, delivery, time, and assortment of goods. UCC § 2-204(3).

In the absence of a written agreement's provision that a seller extended credit to a buyer, the buyer must pay for goods when and where the buyer will receive them (e.g., either party's place of business). In the absence of a written agreement's provision regarding the location of delivery, a buyer must obtain the goods wherever they might be. UCC § 2-309.

The correct answer is (B) because Apartments is responsible for obtaining the sets at Fixture's place of business where they are located. Apartments must pay Fixtures for them at that time.

Answer (A) is incorrect because the contract does not require Fixtures to deliver either installment of sets to Apartment. Apartments must pay for them upon tender.

Answer (C) is wrong because, although March 1 is the date when Fixtures must tender the first installment, Apartments must make payment for it upon tender.

Answer (D) is incorrect because, although March 1 is the date when Fixtures must tender the first installment, Apartments is required to make separate payments for each installment when they are tendered.

Question 220

Answer: D

Answer (D) is the correct answer. This question tests exceptions to the UCC's Perfect Tender Rule. Under section 2-612(1) of the UCC, an installment sales contract "requires or authorizes the delivery of goods in separate lots to be separately accepted," even if the contract "contains a clause [stating that] 'each delivery is a separate contract' or its equivalent." Section 2-612(2) of the UCC provides that under an installment contract for a sale of goods, "the buyer may reject any installment which is non-conforming if the non-conformity substantially impairs the value of that installment and cannot be cured."

When a seller makes an offer to a buyer that the seller will cure a nonconforming installment, and provides the buyer with adequate assurances about that cure, the buyer has to accept the installment unless the nonconformity substantially impaired the entire contract's value. Under section 2-612(3) of the UCC, if a "nonconformity or default with respect to one or more installments substantially impairs the value of the whole contract," then the buyer may reject the seller's other installments and cancel the contract.

The parties' installment sales contract provided for two separate shipments of the fixtures pursuant to section 2-612(1) of the UCC. Fixture performed the contract by sending the first shipment. Section 2-612(2) of the UCC does not permit Apartments to reject the first non-conforming installment because the non-conformity did not substantially impair the installment's value and will be promptly cured by Fixtures. Fixtures provided Apartments with an adequate assurance that it would cure the one set that suffered damage in transit. Thus, Apartments must accept the first installment that did not result in a breach of the contract. Accordingly, Apartments may not cancel the contract under section 2-612(3) of the UCC because the non-conformity did not substantially impair the value of the whole contract. Apartments must accept Fixture's cure and a conforming second installment.

Answers (A) and (B) are incorrect because Apartments must accept all of the conforming sets and cannot cancel the contract based on the nonconforming set that will be cured or with respect to the second installment.

Answer (C) is an incorrect because Apartments must accept the 24 sets and may not cancel the second installment because the value of the contract has not been substantially impaired.

Question 221
Answer: B

Answer (B) is the correct answer. This question tests the law of damages. Consequential damages are those resulting from a breach of contract, even if they are not part of the contract. Consequential damages arise in the ordinary course of events that flow from the breach. A breaching party is not required to have in fact foreseen those damages. The question is: Could a breaching party have reasonably foreseen the damages based on what they knew at the contract's formation?

The correct answer is (B) because Mechanic lacked any basis to foresee that Knitwear would incur consequential damages from its delayed performance. The contract did not specify that Mechanic must repair the machine by a particular time, and Knitwear subsequently entered into the contract with Textiles and did not notify Mechanic of it.

Answer (A) is incorrect. Mechanic might have been liable for consequential damages even absent a clause stipulating that time is of the essence if it could have foreseen that its delay would lead to the sustained damages.

Answer (C) is incorrect because under Textiles' contract with Mechanic there should not have been a delay that caused the damages.

Answer (D) is incorrect because even if the liquidated damages do exceed the actual damages, Mechanic might still have been liable for the consequential damages if they could have been foreseen.

Question 222
Answer: D

Answer (D) is the correct response to this contracts law question because none of the principles of contract law would support Owner's defense. Thus, answers (A)-(C) are wrong.

I. The Parol Evidence Rule (Rule) is not helpful because no previous or contemporaneous agreements exist to supplement or contradict the construction contract. The Rule provides that if the parties intend that a writing represent their agreement's final terms and conditions, the writing cannot subsequently be contradicted with extrinsic evidence of previous or contemporaneous agreements that supplement or contradict a contract's terms. It does not apply to modifications after formation.

II. The pre-existing duty rule is not helpful to Owner's defense because Contractor materially altered his position because of the modification. The pre-existing duty rule generally operates to invalidate oral modification of contracts when there is a contractual provision preventing that type of modification, but an exception exists when there has been detrimental reliance by one party on the modification. In such situations, the provision against modification is waived.

III. The contract's requirement that any modification be in writing was an express condition to Contractor's adding of the "extras." The parties' failure to comply with this express condition and mutual oral agreements regarding the "extras" resulted in a waiver of it. Waiver may be implied from the factual circumstances.

IV. Although the parties agreed that all modifications should be in writing, the Statute of Frauds does not require that the subject matter of their oral modifications be in writing. Verbal agreements are valid and enforceable if they do not cover topics that are subject to the Statute of Frauds.

Question 223

Answer: A

Answer (A) is the correct response. This question tests the law of revocation. An offeror may terminate an offeree's power of acceptance through revocation. A revocation may be implied or indirect if (1) an offeror takes steps that are inconsistent with (2) an ongoing intent to enter into a contract, and (3) an offeree gains knowledge of the offeror's steps.

In this case, Owner offered an option contract to Buyer, and in order to accept the offer Buyer had to pay $100. Owner attempted to revoke the offer by selling the property to Citizen, which was a step inconsistent with the intent to enter into the option contract. Buyer, though, lacked notice of Owner's actions. Because Buyer acted within a reasonable period of time to accept, as the offer was to remain open for 30 days, the acceptance was valid, and Owner is likely liable for breach of contract.

Answer (B) would not support Buyer's lawsuit because his application for financing does not constitute sufficient part performance of the parties' oral agreement to create an option contract to avoid the Statute of Frauds.

Answer (C) would not support Buyer's action because Owner made an inaccurate statement of law that could not operate as a waiver of the option contract rule that the offeror must receive consideration to keep the option open.

Answer (D) would not support Buyer's action because their professional status does not exempt them from the option contract rule.

Question 224
Answer: D

Answer (D) is the correct response. This question tests the remedies for breach of contract. Generally, the damages for a breach of an option contract are measured by the same standard used for a breach of a sell and buy contract. If a seller intentionally breaches a sell and buy contract, a buyer may recover the difference between the real property's market value on the date that the closing is to occur and the contract price.

Because the court determined that Owner breached the parties' contract, Buyer is entitled receive the difference between $100,000 and Greenacre's market value when Owner sold it to Citizen.

Answer (A) is incorrect because Buyer is not limited to nominal damages. Buyer is not entitled to specific performance of the contract because, as aforementioned, damages at law are adequate.

Answer (B) is wrong because Buyer is entitled to recover the difference between market value and contract price for Greenacre, not to recover for the value of his contract.

Answer (C) is incorrect because the law of damages does not take into consideration the difference in amount between Citizen's purchase price and the contract's purchase price.

Question 225
Answer: D

Answer (D) is the correct response. This question tests the law of anticipatory repudiation. When a first party communicates to a second party an unequivocal anticipated lack of ability or willingness to perform contractual obligations (e.g., "I will not perform"), it may be considered an anticipatory repudiation of the contract, entitling the second party to suspend its own performance of the contract and bring an immediate breach of contract suit against the repudiator. A mere expression of doubt about a first party's ability to perform a contract will not serve as an anticipatory breach (e.g., "I doubt that I will be able to perform."). The second party should the request a written assurance of performance, and if none is received, he may then sue for breach prior to the date for performance.

Buyer's statement to Seller on October 1 did not reflect an unambiguous lack of ability or willingness to perform the parties' contract of June 1. Buyer's statement simply communicated doubt about her willingness, not ability, to perform the contract in two months. Thus, Buyer did not commit a breach of contract by anticipatory repudiation. Seller failed to properly respond by requesting a written assurance of performance from Buyer. Thus, Seller prematurely filed his action without allowing Buyer to provide any assurances before the closing date.

Answer (A) is an incorrect conclusion under the foregoing analysis.

Answer (B) is incorrect because even if Seller had reasonable grounds for insecurity, he did not seek assurances from Buyer.

Answer (C) is incorrect because Seller could request written assurances and, if none were provided, bring suit for breach prior to the closing date.

Question 226
Answer: C

Answer (C) is the correct response. This question tests the law of retraction of repudiation. A repudiation can be retracted by the promising party so long as there has been no material change in the position of the other party in the interim. A retraction of the repudiation restores the other party's obligation to perform on the contract. The other party's request for a retraction of the repudiation does not operate as a waiver of the repudiation if it is not retracted.

At no time prior to the date of closing did Buyer respond to Seller's request that she retract her repudiation of their contract. Buyer's attempted tendering of the purchase price to Seller on the closing date could not operate as an implied retraction of her repudiation. Seller lawfully rejected Buyer's attempted performance of the contract because Seller had materially changed his position in response to the unretracted repudiation. Seller could no longer perform due to his material change by selling the ranch to Rancher.

Answer (A) is an incorrect because Seller lacked a legal duty to notify Buyer of a pending sale to Rancher after her repudiation was not retracted.

Answer (B) is incorrect because Seller's request that Buyer retract the repudiation did not operate as a waiver of the repudiation.

Answer (D) is incorrect because Buyer's repudiation removed any obligation for Seller's performance.

Question 227
Answer: C

Answer (C) is the correct response. This question tests the law of expectation damages. A court seeks to afford a non-breaching party with the benefit of the bargain from a breaching party. With that relief, the non-breaching party will be placed into the position when he or she expected to have been if the parties' contract had been performed. To fulfill the non-breaching party's expectations, the amount awarded may be measured by the sum that was required to obtain substitute performance. Reasonable substitute performance must be provided to the extent that the circumstances warrant.

Kontractor, a non-breaching party, is entitled to the benefit of the bargain from Subbo, a breaching party. Subbo breached their $200,000 contract after receiving $100,000 from Kontractor. Kontractor obtained substitute performance from a subcontractor for the cost of $120,000. Thus, Kontractor paid a $20,000 more than the contract price to have the work completed. To place Kontractor in the position that it expected to be upon completion of the contract, Subbo must pay the $20,000 in damages for Kontractor to cover its loss arising from Subbo's breach of contract.

Answer (A) is an incorrect conclusion because, as the breaching party, Subbo is not entitled to the unpaid amount of the benefit that it conferred upon Kontractor.

Answer (B) is an incorrect conclusion because, as the breaching party, Subbo is not entitled to the unpaid amount of the benefit that it conferred upon Kontractor, minus $20,000.

Answer (D) is an incorrect conclusion because Kontractor is entitled to its expectation damages after Subbo breached the contract.

Question 228
Answer: D

Answer (D) is the correct response. This question tests the UCC's Perfect Tender Rule. Under the UCC, if the delivery fails to conform in any way with the contract, the buyer has the right to reject or accept the whole, or accept a part. UCC § 2-601. Section 1-205 of the UCC provides that "any usage of trade…in which [the parties] are engaged…[shall] give particular meaning to and supplement or qualify terms of an agreement." The express terms of the agreement will be construed as consistent with trade usage unless such a construction is unreasonable, in which case the express terms control. UCC § 2-208.

Because the contract is for the sale of goods, the UCC applies. In this case, the 30-day leeway would be used to give particular meaning to the time for delivery. It does not appear to be unreasonable to construe the 30-day leeway and the delivery date as consistent because the date was not strictly specified. Unless the usage was expressly negated, the leeway would likely support Computers' recovery.

Answer (A) is incorrect. While there may not have been material harm, under the UCC's Perfect Tender Rule, Bank was entitled to reject the computer for Computers' failure to comply with the contract terms.

Answer (B) is an incorrect conclusion resting on an invalid assumption lacking a factual or legal basis.

Answer (C) is incorrect. In order for the delay in performance to be excused under section 2-615 of the UCC, Computers would have needed to notify Bank of the delay, which it failed to do.

Question 229
Answer: D

Answer (D) is the correct response. This question tests impossibility in the performance of a contract and the assumption of risk. Impossibility, when objective, may provide a valid basis for nonperformance of a contractual duty. Impossibility will not excuse nonperformance, however, when the breaching party assumed the risk that performance would become impossible. The UCC exemptions for failure to deliver goods "do not apply when the contingency in question is sufficiently foreshadowed at the time of contracting to be included among the business risks." UCC § 2-615, Comment 8.

Answer (D) is correct because Computers assumed the risk that its intended development of the novel magnetic memory would not work. If Computers had not assumed the risk, an objective impossibility would exist as a valid basis for its nonperformance of the contractual duty to build a mainframe. Here, though, the circumstances indicate that Computers knew that it was possible that its new technology would not work properly because the technology was still under development, and no other manufacturer had yet perfected it either. By agreeing to sell a product that was still in testing, Computers assumed the risk that the product would not work reliably.

Answer (A) is an incorrect conclusion based on an inaccurate statement because the objective impossibility of Computer's performance would not excuse it from liability for breach of contract because it assumed the risk.

Answer (B) is incorrect. Even if Computers exercised best efforts in performing the contract, doing that could not excuse Computers' material breach of failing to build the mainframe.

Answer (C) is incorrect because section 2-615(a) of the UCC, which incorporates impossibility of performance, applies to the parties' contract involving goods, and Computers is a merchant.

Question 230

Answer: B

Answer (B) is the correct response. This question tests the law of promissory estoppel. In the absence of a bargained for exchange, a promise is subject to enforcement if grounds exist for a court to find the existence of a substitute for consideration, such as promissory estoppel. Promissory estoppel applies if: (1) an offeror makes a promise to an offeree; (2) under circumstances that the offeree would reasonably anticipate the promise to be fulfilled; and (3) the offeror would reasonably anticipate that the offeree would alter positions based on that promise.

Loyal is entitled to recover damages from Mutate on the basis of promissory estoppel because the parties did not mutually bargain for an exchange of promises regarding a lifetime pension. Mutate's written resolution promised Loyal a lifetime pension. Loyal could reasonably anticipate that Mutate would fulfill the promise based on the resolution. Mutate could reasonably anticipate Loyal altering his position by resigning and buying a recreational vehicle in light of his stated retirement goals. Most importantly, Loyal did that in reasonable reliance on the resolution.

Answer (A) is incorrect because Loyal's retirement did not constitute bargained for consideration that created a contract with Board.

Answer (C) is incorrect because Mutate acted on its promise by making pension payments, and Loyal's conduct in response to the resolution created his enforceable reliance interest.

Answer (D) is an incorrect conclusion because Loyal's contractual status as an employee is irrelevant to the parties' course of dealings with respect to post-employment lifetime pension.

Question 231
Answer: B

Answer (B) is the correct response. This question tests the law of intended beneficiaries. When a third party asserts a right to enforce a contract as its beneficiary, the courts may consider evidence using the following factors to ascertain if a third party is an intended beneficiary: (1) Does the contract expressly identify the third party? (2) Does the performance run from the promisor to the third party? (3) Does the contract reflect an "intent to benefit" the third party? And, (4) May the third party reasonably rely on the contract as conferring an intended benefit? An intended beneficiary is entitled to enforce the contract although he did not assent to or know about it when it was made.

Minivanity Fair may enforce Goodbar's promise to Walker as an intended third-party beneficiary. This promise constitutes an enforceable oral agreement because valid and sufficient consideration supported it, and Walker performed his obligation for it. Minivanity Fair is the contract's intended beneficiary, although the contract does not expressly identify it as such. Goodbar agreed that his performance would to run to "anyone" such as Minivanity Fair. Goodbar's promise of payment shows his intent to benefit Minivanity Fair as a third party. Fair may reasonably rely on the contract as conferring an intended benefit to it. Minivanity Fair may enforce the contract although it did not assent to it or know about it when it was made.

Answer (A) is incorrect because the promissory estoppel doctrine applies in the absence of consideration to create an enforceable agreement, and Minivanity Fair did not rely on the promise when selling the van.

Answer (C) is incorrect because Goodbar's promise is not subject to the suretyship clause of the Statute of Frauds when the promise did not apply to an existing debt.

Answer (D) is incorrect because Goodbar's promise did not need to identify Minivanity Fair explicitly, and Minivanity Fair did not need to be aware of the promise when selling the minivan in order to enforce it.

Question 232
Answer: C

Answer (C) is the correct response. This question tests the law of assumption of risk. The lawful obligations of a voidable contract may be avoided by either party who disaffirms it. A contract may be avoidable on the basis of a mutual mistake if both parties were mistaken regarding a basic assumption on which the contract was formed. In such a situation, the parties would be returned to their respective positions prior to the contract. Two defenses to mistake are assumption of the risk and ratification of a contract with knowledge of the risk.

Pigstyle should succeed because Breeder assumed the risk that the boar might be sterile. Although both parties were mistaken as to the boar's fertility, Breeder knew, as admitted in the action, that it was impossible to determine the boar's fertility before it was 12 months old. Yet Breeder chose to purchase the boar at the higher price at 2 months old. Because Breeder assumed the risk that in 10 months he might discover that the Boar was infertile, Breeder cannot rescind the contract and recover based on mistake.

Answer (A) is incorrect because although the parties were mistaken about the boar's fertility, Breeder assumed the risk that it might be infertile.

Answer (B) is incorrect because Pigstyle and Breeder both knew that fertility could not be determined until later, and selling the boar sooner at the higher price did not imply a warranty that the boar would indeed be fertile.

Answer (D) is incorrect because the mistake would have been mutual, but it was excused through assumption of risk.

Question 233
Answer: C

Answer (C) is the correct response. This question tests the law of breach of contract. A total, absolute, or material breach of a contract threatens its value and warrants a non-breaching party in taking responsive action. A total breach of contract occurs when a breaching party fails to substantially perform the contract and a non-breaching party has no means to cure that breach. If a breaching party willfully fails to perform contractual duties, then the non-breaching party may commence a lawsuit to recover damages.

A quitclaim deed includes no promises or covenants from a grantor to a grantee. Consequently, a grantee takes title "as is" under a quitclaim deed.

Gourmet committed a material breach of his contract with Hope by failing to make his second annual payment to her. His breach threatened the contract's value of five other installments, which warranted Hope in seeking to recover the contract's unpaid value. Gourmet failed to substantially perform the contract and Hope lacked any means to cure his breach. Hope properly commenced her lawsuit to recover the missing payments because Gourmet willfully failed to perform his duty of payment. Gourmet accepted a quitclaim deed that provided no promise or covenant from Hope that she possessed a valid claim of title to the land. Thus, the probate court ruling against Hope did not provide Gourmet with an excuse for the breach.

Answer (A) is incorrect. Hope's awareness of the questionable nature of her claim of title to the land cannot affect the contract's enforceability because the quit claim deed did not guarantee the title's validity.

Answer (B) is incorrect because Hope suffered legal detriment by executing the quitclaim deed. Specifically, she then possessed a claim to title that could have been adjudicated in her favor.

Answer (D) is incorrect because Hope has nothing to convey to Gourmet, and therefore his performance is excused.

Question 234
Answer: B

Answer (B) is the correct response. This question tests the law of the Statute of Frauds. Under section 2-201(1) of the UCC, a writing regarding a sale of goods for a sum greater than $500 is required. In order for a writing to satisfy that Statute, at a minimum it must include the essential terms. The writing would be sufficient if it identifies the parties, quantity of goods, and is signed. A court will only enforce the contract to the extent of the stated quantity amount. Conversely, the courts will not enforce the contract if it fails to state a quantity.

A form of writing that will satisfy the Statute is a confirmatory memo between two merchants that the first merchant signs and to which the second merchant makes no objection. The merchant that received the memorandum of confirmation will be bound by it if the first merchant: (1) had reason to know of the memorandum's contents; and (2) failed to object to it within 10 days after receiving it.

Retailer and Manufacturer are merchants whose contract for a sale of goods exceeded a $500 value. Thus, it is subject to the UCC's Statute of Frauds, and their oral agreement would not normally be enforceable. Manufacturer's confirmatory memo, though, contained the essential terms by identifying the parties, stating a 500 towel quantity, and including Manufacturer's signature. Retailer is bound by the letter because it because it had reason to know of the letter's contents and did not object to the letter within 10 days of receiving it. The court would therefore enforce the contract for 500 towels.

Answer (A) is an incorrect conclusion because the letter's quantity term of 500 towels is controlling notwithstanding Manufacturer's contrary tender of 1,000 towels and the oral agreement that mentioned 1,000.

Answer (C) is incorrect because the parties had an enforceable contract under the UCC despite Retailer's lack of signature on the memo.

Answer (D) is an incorrect conclusion because the letter stated the essential terms and price is not an essential term.

Question 235
Answer: D

Answer (D) is the correct response. This question tests the law of acceptance. Under the UCC, if the acceptance of an offer occurs by any medium reasonable in the circumstances, the acceptance is effective when it is dispatched out of an offeree's possession. If an offeree uses an unauthorized means of acceptance, then the acceptance is effective when it is received instead of when it is sent.

The UCC applies because Seller is a merchant whose letter of January 7 operated as an acceptance of Buyer's order that constituted an offer. Seller's letter served as a reasonable medium of communication under the circumstances because Buyer used the mail to deliver his offer. Seller's acceptance was effective upon dispatch the day it received Buyer's order, and the offer cannot be rejected after it is accepted.

Answer (A) is incorrect because Seller accepted the offer by sending its letter before Buyer attempted its verbal revocation.

Answer (B) is incorrect because Seller accepted the offer by sending the letter, and Buyer did not need to expressly agree to the price.

Answer (C) is incorrect because even though it may have been irrevocable, the acceptance was valid before revocation was attempted.

AMERIBAR BAR REVIEW

Multistate Bar Examination - Answers to Questions – Section 5

CRIMINAL LAW & PROCEDURE

Question 1
Answer: A

This question tests the law of self-defense and deadly force.

For Harold to assert the self-defense argument, he must prove three elements: (1) The aggressor presented an immediate threat to him; (2) He possessed an objectively reasonable belief that the aggressor was about to use force against him; and (3) compared to the aggressor's threatened harm, he did not use excessive force. The use of deadly force to defend oneself is warranted only if the accused reasonably believes that deadly force is necessary to avoid the aggressor's immediate and unlawful use of deadly force. Harold, based on Jones's threat, could (and did) reasonably believe that deadly force was necessary to avoid being killed himself. Thus, his use of deadly force was justified, and the claim of self-defense should be upheld.

Question 2
Answer: A

This question tests the law of felony murder and arson.

In order for Shore to be liable for felony murder, the prosecution must establish an underlying inherently dangerous felony. Such felony must be inherently dangerous to life, the death must naturally and probably result from such felony, and the felony must be independent of the death itself. Arson is considered an inherently dangerous felony. Under common law, arson is the malicious burning of another's dwelling, though this definition has been expanded by state statutes. Today, an individual can be guilty of arson in burning his own building, and that building need not be a residence or dwelling. The malice element is established by showing intent that the structure burn or reckless disregard for the known risk that the structure would be damaged.

Choice (A) is correct because arson is the inherently dangerous felony that naturally resulted in the death of the vagrant. Shore intended to burn the structure, and the felony of arson was itself independent of the death.

Choices (B-D) are incorrect. Although Shore may have engaged in or been complicit to each of these crimes, none of them is the natural and probable cause of the vagrant's death.

Question 3
Answer: C

This question tests the law of accomplice (or accessory) liability and solicitation.

Accomplices are individuals who aid a principal actor in committing an offense by conduct such as planning, participation, or evasion of capture. For the accomplice to be liable, he must (1) have intent to encourage or assist the principal in committing the offense, (2) actually encourage or assist in committing the offense, and (3) the principal must actually commit the offense charged to the accomplice.

Choice (C) is correct. The principal in Case C is the council member. The defendant who bribed the principal did not intend to encourage or assist the principal in committing the offense of accepting a bribe. The crime intended was the bribery itself. The first element for accomplice liability cannot be met, and thus, the defendant is not guilty as an accomplice. Lipsky, in this case, also did not intend to assist or encourage the officer in the commission of the offense of selling narcotics. The crime intended was the purchase or possession of narcotics. The officer himself, as the principal selling the narcotics, could not even be guilty of the offense charged to Lipsky. Thus, Lipsky cannot be guilty as an accomplice to the sale of narcotics.

Question 4
Answer: B

This question tests accomplice liability and solicitation.

In case B, defendant is convicted as an accomplice to the offense he solicited despite the innocence of the principal actor. Similarly, in choice (B), there is an innocent actor solicited for an offense by the defendant. Following case B, George is an innocent actor under the statutory rape law—since the jurisdiction does not define it in terms of strict liability. But Howard is guilty as an accomplice to statutory rape because of his solicitation of the crime.

Question 5
Answer: A

This question tests accomplice liability.

Accomplices are individuals who aid a principal actor in committing an offense by conduct such as planning, participation in, or evasion of capture. For the accomplice to be liable, he must (1) have intent to encourage or assist the principal in committing the offense, (2) actually encourage or assist in committing the offense, and (3) the principal must actually commit the offense charged to the accomplice.

In case A, defendant/accomplice knowingly enabled principal actors to avoid detection by the police. The facts in this question are parallel to the fact pattern of case A. The defendant/accomplice knowingly enabled the principal actor to avoid detection by the police. Thus, choice (A) is correct.

In case D, though the facts are somewhat similar to the facts in question, there was no conviction of the prostitutes upon which the third element of accomplice liability could be premised. Thus, this fact pattern is different from the question, in which there is a conviction upon which accomplice liability can be based.

Question 6
Answer: C

This question tests the doctrine of merger.

The doctrine of merger requires that lesser included charges be merged into the more serious offense. The two offenses present are attempted robbery and assault. Robbery is the trespassory taking and carrying away of another's personal property with the intent to steal such property. Robbery requires the use of force, and the victim must feel subjectively threatened. These last two elements are, themselves, the elements of assault. Thus, assault is a lesser included charge within robbery. The only offense of which Max might be convicted is attempted robbery.

Question 7
Answer: D

This question tests the law of Fourth Amendment searches of vehicles the scope of such searches.

An officer may lawfully search a vehicle without a warrant if probable cause exists that the vehicle contains an item subject to seizure. If such probable cause arises, then any part of the vehicle which might contain the item is subject to being searched. Probable cause arose in this instance when the officers identified the vehicle and one potential suspect, based on the information provided by the undercover officer. There is no problem with the search of the tool box and glove compartment. They are places in which drugs like marijuana could be hidden.

Question 8
Answer: A

This question tests the law of vehicle searches and the scope of such searches.

Under *Wyoming v. Houghton*, the Supreme Court held that the personal belongings of a passenger may also be searched incident to the lawful search of a vehicle, if they may hold the items sought. In this question, the woman was no longer a passenger of the vehicle at the time of the search, so *Houghton* is inapplicable. Independent of the vehicle search, a search of the woman or her belongings would only be justified by probable cause. Under *Ybarra v. Illinois*, it is explained that a person's mere presence near others independently suspected of criminal activity does not, without more, give rise to probable cause to search that person. No probable cause had arisen as to her because she did not fit the description of two male suspects as given by the undercover police officer.

Question 9
Answer: C

This question tests the law of murder and the defenses of duress and necessity.

In the jurisdiction's definition of first-degree murder, intent and premeditation are required. Generally, premeditation exists when the accused has taken time to reflect on the thought of the killing. In this question, there is evidence that Smith reflected on the killing, first by refusing it and then reconsidering. An entire day passed during which he made the decision to kill. He satisfied the requirements for first-degree murder.

A duress defense *cannot* be presented in response to a charge of murder. Choice (A) is wrong.

A necessity defense will be successful only where the accused (1) faced a clear and present danger, (2) reasonably believed the action taken would prevent harm, (3) lacked lawful means of avoiding the harm, (4) caused a less serious harm than the harm he sought to avoid, and (5) did not place himself where he participated in the criminal conduct. In this case, Smith cannot claim necessity because he did have lawful means of avoiding the harm caused to Hardy. Further, the harm caused was just as serious as the harm Smith himself faced.

Question 10
Answer: D

This question tests the law of arson—and interpretation of a given statute.

Generally, arson is defined under common law as the intentional burning of the dwelling of another. Though most states have enacted statutes that do not limit arson to the property of others, the jurisdiction in this question has not. Arson is limited by the jurisdiction to include only those structures belonging to someone other than the accused. Thus, Arnold could not even attempt arson if the target was his own building. His mistaken belief is of no import.

Question 11
Answer: C

This question tests a specific exception to the Exclusionary Rule.

Under *United States v. Calandra*, the Supreme Court concluded that the exclusionary rule does not apply during the course of grand jury proceedings. A party seeking to suppress the illegally obtained evidence at this stage will not prevail.

Question 12
Answer: B

This question tests the law of receipt of stolen property.

The elements for receipt of stolen goods are as follows: (1) the accused received personal property, (2) a thief had stolen that property from its true owner, (3) the accused knew the property was stolen, and (4) the accused intended to permanently deprive the true owner of the property. Property that was once stolen but has since been restored to its true owner or to the police has lost its characterization as stolen property. Thus, if a thief works undercover with police to sell once-stolen goods, the receiving party cannot be guilty of receiving stolen goods.

Choice (A) is incorrect. The used car lot is being operated in connection with the police. It appears that the stolen car has been restored to the police. It can no longer be considered stolen goods.

Choice (C) is incorrect. The stolen car had been caught by the police, thus losing its characterization as stolen property.

Choice (D) is incorrect. A thief never stole the car from its true owner. The owner merely reported it as stolen.

Choice (B) is correct. Morrow received the car, knowing it was stolen, and he intended to permanently deprive the true owner of the car. Here, unlike in the other choices, there is outstanding stolen property. Despite the participation of an undercover agent along with thief Ball, the car was never restored to the police prior to its sale to Morrow.

Question 13
Answer: A

This question tests the law of the admissibility of a confession.

As a general rule, consider the totality of circumstances in determining whether a confession was made voluntarily, including the person's situation and the conduct of the officer. Considerations include the defendant's age, race, gender, education, physical condition, and mental state. The defendant's mental condition is only one factor to be considered in determining the voluntariness and admissibility of the confession. Similarly, the defendant's mental condition is only one factor to be considered in determining the voluntariness of his waiver of the right against self-incrimination. Finally, the conduct of the officer will be examined for the presence of coercion.

Choice (A) is correct. Though mentally ill, there is no evidence of coercion by the police.

Choice (B) is incorrect. Dan was in custody at the time of the confession.

Choices (C-D) are incorrect. As noted above, mental illness is just one factor to consider among the totality of circumstances in determining the voluntariness and admissibility both of a confession and a waiver of Miranda rights.

Question 14
Answer: A

This question tests the defenses of mistake of law and mistake of fact.

As a general rule, ignorance of the law is not a valid defense to a crime. Mistake of fact, however, can be a defense where, if the facts were as the accused believed them to be at the time of the offense, the accused could not have committed the offense for lack of mens rea. Choice (A) is an instance of ignorance of the law. It is not a defense to the crime of bigamy. Choices (B-D) are instances of mistake of fact in which the mens rea for the charged crime is absent due to that mistake of fact.

Question 15

Answer: A

This question tests the common law of murder.

Under the common law, murder is the unlawful killing of another with malice aforethought. The concept of malice requires a finding of an intent to kill or inflict serious bodily harm, depraved heart (reckless regard for human life), or death that occurs in commission of an inherently dangerous felony. A defendant is not guilty of common law murder unless such malice can be proven.

Choice (A) is correct. If there was no intent to kill or harm the child, the necessary malice element for common law murder is absent, and there can be no conviction of murder.

Choice (B) is incorrect. A defense based on the exercise of religion will fall to the state's higher interest in the preservation of human life.

Choice (C) is incorrect. A jury would likely find that the actions of Jim and Joan were, indeed, the proximate cause of Kathy's death.

Choice (D) is incorrect. Premeditation and deliberation are of importance only where a state employs statutory degrees of murder. Here, the jurisdiction operates under the common law definition.

Question 16
Answer: C

This question tests the elements of common-law murder.

Under the common law, murder is the unlawful killing of another with malice aforethought. The concept of malice requires a finding of an intent to kill, intent to inflict serious bodily harm (causing death), depraved heart (reckless regard for human life), or death that occurs in commission of an inherently dangerous felony. A defendant is not guilty of common-law murder unless such malice can be proven.

Choice (A) is incorrect. True, defendant may be found guilty of murder if intent to kill is proven. But this is not a complete answer. Intent to inflict serious bodily injury, which then results in death, will also suffice to convict. Thus, (C) is correct.

Choice (B) is incorrect. The provocation defense will not work if a reasonable person would have "cooled off" during the period between the provocation and the subsequent homicide. A reasonable cooling off period had expired in this question.

Choice (D) is incorrect. While felony murder is included under common law murder, the felony committed must be independent of the subsequent death. A felony of aggravated assault that results in a death is not independent of that death.

Question 17
Answer: C

This question tests the law of burglary and larceny.

First, apply the definition of burglary as it is written in the question. The elements presented are (1) an unlawful entering of a building with (2) intent to commit a crime. Here, David possessed the intent to commit a crime. However, his entrance to the museum was lawful. Thus, there can be no burglary, and choices (A) and (B) are incorrect.

Apart from burglary, David may still be guilty of larceny. Larceny is the taking and carrying away of the personal property of another with the intent to steal such property. Here, David took and carried away a photocopy of an etching. This was personal property of the museum. It was taken with the intent to steal it. Thus, he is guilty of larceny and (C) is correct. It does not matter that he failed to "steal" his intended target. The elements of larceny are still satisfied.

Question 18
Answer: A

This question tests the law of murder and transferred intent.

A question that charges a defendant with murder, without any reference to a statute or to degrees of murder, is most likely testing the common law definition of murder—the killing of another human with malice aforethought. This malice requirement is satisfied if there is proof of depraved heart—extreme recklessness or willful disregard of the risk to human life. Thus, Jack should be found guilty of murder because of his extremely reckless conduct in sending Chip (an enraged, jealous husband) to confront his wife's alleged paramour after suggesting the use of a weapon.

Choice (B) is incorrect. The doctrine of transferred intent is applicable where the victim of a crime is someone other than the intended target. Here, the victim was the intended target.

Choice (C) is incorrect. It does not matter that Jack did not intend for Chip to take a bullet.

Choice (D) is incorrect. Jack can be guilty of murder even though he did not himself pull the trigger.

Question 19
Answer: A

This question tests the law of murder.

There is evidence in the question that Jack did intend the killing of Morgan. It does not matter that Jack himself did not act using the gun. It is enough that he intended to kill Morgan and then set the events into motion that could lead to such killing. Jack's culpability is the same as if Jack had "hired" Chip to kill Morgan. The result is attempted murder.

Choice (B) is incorrect. Jack was intentional—not extremely reckless—as to Morgan. The extreme recklessness was present with regards to Chip.

Choice (C) is incorrect. Arguably, Morgan was in imminent danger. The intervening killing of Chip is what saved Morgan.

Choice (D) is incorrect. Chip would likely be guilty of voluntary manslaughter—or mitigated murder—due to his acting in the heat of passion. The heat of passion defense serves only to mitigate the actor's culpability. Here, Jack was not the actor. He cannot rely on Chip's heat of passion to reduce his own culpability.

Question 20
Answer: C

This question tests the law regarding guilty pleas.

A guilty plea results in a person's waiver of his Fifth Amendment right against self-incrimination and his Sixth Amendment rights of a jury trial and confrontation of witnesses. Because the guilty plea is a waiver, it must satisfy the due process requirements for waiver. It must be made intelligently, voluntarily, and knowingly. To satisfy these requirements, the court must determine that the accused does understand the consequences of making the guilty plea. The court must inform him of those consequences if he has not already been advised of them.

Thus, the court must make sure that the accused comprehends both the potential maximum and minimum sentences faced as well as the loss of a right to jury trial. Here, the accused was never informed that his plea would result in a loss of the right to a trial by jury.

Question 21
Answer: D

This question tests the law of rape and statutory rape.

Generally, statutory rape is a strict liability offense with no available defenses. Specific intent is not an essential element of rape or statutory rape. Where a rape is not completed, however, specific intent to commit the rape is a required element for attempted rape. If Michael was attempting to violate the statute as defined in the question, then he necessarily intended to have sexual intercourse with a girl under age 16. Here, his intent was sexual intercourse with a girl he though to be about 18 years old.

Question 22
Answer: B

This question tests the law of misdemeanor-manslaughter.

An accused who causes the unintentional death of another while committing a misdemeanor offense will be criminally liable for that death if three elements are satisfied: (1) the misdemeanor was inherently dangerous to life; (2) the death naturally and probably resulted from the misdemeanor; and (3) the misdemeanor was independent of the death.

Elements (1) and (3) are satisfied by the Parnell fact pattern. Thus, to be acquitted, he must show that element (2) is not satisfied. Choice (B) will show just this. If the collision would have occurred when Parnell was sober, then it cannot be said that the death of the other driver was naturally or probably caused by the misdemeanor of driving while intoxicated.

Question 23
Answer: D

This question tests the law of kidnapping.

To establish a kidnapping, the accused must confine and detain the victim for a duration as well as transport the victim for some distance. In this question, there is no evidence that Doris was in fact detained at the apartment, nor was she transported to the apartment by John. She was voluntarily present. Further, there was no attempt to transport her. Thus, John cannot be guilty of attempted kidnapping or kidnapping.

Question 24
Answer: A

This question tests Fifth Amendment procedural safeguards.

Under the Supreme Court's decision in *Miranda v. Arizona*, a statement made by a person during custodial interrogation, if the police have not provided legally sufficient safeguards, would be considered a compelled statement in violation of the person's Fifth Amendment right against self incrimination.

Here, despite the lack of Miranda warnings, Alice's statements are admissible because they are not the product of custodial interrogation. She may have been in custody, but she was not being interrogated or even generally questioned.

Question 25
Answer: B

This question tests the law of Fourth Amendment searches and the exclusionary rule.

An individual may possess a right to privacy even when in a public place. Where the person has a reasonable expectation of privacy within a closed public area, a search requires probable cause. A fitting room in a public store is a good example of such a closed public area. Here, Davis was surreptitiously viewed in a fitting room where she had an expectation of privacy. This surveillance was done without probable cause specific to Davis. Thus, the dress removed from her purse is the product of an illegal search and should be suppressed as evidence.

Question 26
Answer: B

This question tests the requirement of proof beyond a reasonable doubt.

The due process right to a fair trial requires that the prosecution show that the defendant is guilty beyond a reasonable doubt of all elements of a charged offense. In this question, the elements of the offense are (1) sexual intercourse, (2) with a female who is not the accused's wife, and (3) without the consent of that female.

In this question, the jury was instructed using the standard of "beyond a reasonable doubt"—but only as to the issue of sexual intercourse and lack of consent. This same standard was not employed as to the issue of Sally's status as wife. In fact, the instructions did not place the burden on the prosecution at all to show that she was not his wife, as the elements required.

Question 27
Answer: B

This question tests culpability and strict liability.

Where an offense is a strict liability offense, the intent of the accused is irrelevant. An accused may be found guilty of a criminal offense simply by having engaged in the prohibited activity. Here, the statute creates strict liability for the full-time employment of children under age 17. Crouse hired/employed children aged 15 and 16. Thus, he is guilty of the offense.

Question 28
Answer: D

This question tests vicarious liability for criminal acts.

An employer is not generally required to answer for the criminal acts perpetrated by his employee. However, where the violation took place because of delegation or opportunity afforded to the employee, the employer may be held liable. Here, Morton delegated his hiring power to Crouse, who misused it. Morton will also be strictly liable for the child labor violation because he exercised control over the hiring process.

This question may be equated with a hypothetical involving the sale of intoxicating liquors to minors in a state where it is a strict liability offense. The agent or employee of the store does not check identification and sells beer to a child of 15 years. The employee's own liability does not negate the liability of the liquor store. The store is also liable.

Question 29
Answer: B

This question tests the law of transferred intent and statutory degrees of murder.

Choice (A) is incorrect. Duncan did not knowingly kill the burglar across the street, nor was there a period of cool reflection or deliberation due to the siege of the liquor store.

Choice (B) is correct. Using the doctrine of transferred intent, the prosecution can convict Duncan of reckless homicide—which under the statutory scheme in the question is within "all other murder at common law except felony murder." Reckless murder is included in the common law definition.

Choice (C-D) are incorrect. While Duncan did indeed commit felony murder and voluntary manslaughter, he can be charged with a greater degree of murder as explained above.

Question 30
Answer: A (key)   B (popular response)

The correct answer is (A)—according to MBE examiners. However, choice (B) was selected by a large number of high-scoring applicants.

This question tests the false pretense offenses.

To establish a violation of a false pretense offense, the following elements are required: (1) the accused makes a false representation of fact that the victim believes to be true: (2) the victim transfers property or other consideration to the accused: (3) the accused knows his representation is false; and (4) the accused intended to defraud the victim.

Here, choice (A) is correct because there was no intent by Smith to defraud the store owner of his furniture. He did intend to pay for the items. Thus, there was no obtaining of property by false pretenses.

Question 31
Answer: A

This question tests the admissibility of a confession and the ability to consent to a search.

A confession made voluntarily is generally admissible when the person made the confession outside custodial interrogation. To determine whether or not the statement was made voluntarily, the totality of the circumstances are to be considered, such as the person's situation, the conduct of the police, and the presence of deception or coercion. In this question, there is no evidence of coercion or deception by the police. Further, the statement was made voluntarily in the defendant's diary. He was not compelled to confess in the diary.

Apart from the voluntary confession made outside custodial interrogation, the confession can still be excluded as evidence if it was illegally obtained. The search of the home was done without a warrant, but consent was given by Larson. There is no evidence that his lack of short-term memory prohibits him from allowing or disallowing the presence of police officers in his home.

Question 32
Answer: B

This question tests your knowledge of the felony-murder rule and the death penalty.

First, one must establish that Dawson can be convicted of felony murder. An accused is criminally liable for an unintended death of a human being while attempting to commit a felony if the felony was inherently dangerous to life, and if the death naturally and probably resulted from the felony.

In this case, the felony of robbery is inherently dangerous, and the death was the natural and probable result of the robbery. There is no question that Dawson was involved because the facts indicate that Dawson agreed to drive to the bank and to wait outside while Smith went in to rob it. As such, Dawson is criminally liable on a charge of felony murder.

The second step is to determine whether the death penalty may be sought. There is no flat prohibition the imposition of the death penalty for felony murder. The Supreme Court has held that the death penalty generally may not be imposed on a person who did not kill, attempt to kill, or intend that a killing take place. However, the death penalty may be imposed on someone who was a major participant in the underlying felony and acted with reckless indifference to human life.

In this case, Dawson did not kill, attempt to kill, or intend that the killing take place. Additionally, Dawson did not act with a reckless indifference to human life because he was merely waiting in the getaway car.

Therefore, although Dawson may be convicted of felony murder, the death penalty will not be imposed.

(A) is incorrect because the death penalty may not be imposed under the circumstances.

(C) and (D) are incorrect because Dawson is guilty of felony murder.

Question 33
Answer: A

This question tests the law of attempt. As a general rule, proof of a specific intent and an act in furtherance is required to establish an attempt to commit a crime. On an attempted murder charge, for a person to be guilty, he must possess the specific intent to kill. The facts indicate that Jones wanted to kill Adams. Therefore, the intent requirement is satisfied.

In addition to intent, a person guilty of attempt to commit a crime must commit an act in furtherance of the crime more than just preparation. In this case, the facts indicate that Jones fired five shots at Adams. So long as Jones was unaware of the limitation, the act of shooting the gun was made in furtherance of the intent to kill Adams. Therefore, the intent and act requirements are both met.

This question also raises the issue of factual impossibility, as the facts indicate that Adams was out of the range of the gun. The law provides, however, that factual impossibility is not a valid defense to the offense of attempt.

(B) is incorrect because it is the actual subjective intent that is relevant to a charge of attempt, not the objective standard of whether a reasonable person would have been aware of the limitation.

(C) is incorrect because factual impossibility is not a defense to the charge of attempt.

(D) is incorrect because the elements of attempt have been satisfied and no defense exists.

Question 34
Answer: A, B, D

The correct answers to this question are choices (A), (B), and (D). For this question, the examiners gave credit for three answer choices. This occurs on many exams. It is possible that the vague fact pattern permitted an argument to be made for all three of these selections.

The question tests the doctrine of imperfect self-defense.

Under this doctrine, an accused's unreasonable but honest belief that his life was in danger from another person would provide a basis for an imperfect self-defense to the charge of murdering that person. The defense cannot fully excuse the accused's criminal liability for the homicide, but it may be used to mitigate a murder charge to manslaughter.

Choice (A) was given credit because, under the facts, it is possible that Ralph may have reasonably feared for his life.

Choice (B) was given credit because the court could find that the belief was unreasonable, but honest, which could result in an instruction on manslaughter.

Choice (D) was given credit because, without additional facts, a court could find that the use of the knife was unreasonable under the circumstances, which could only result in a charge for murder.

Choice (C) is incorrect because the duty to retreat is irrelevant because there was no threat of deadly force by Sam.

Question 35
Answer: C

This question tests the intent standard of malice. Many examinees mistakenly believe that the question tests defense of property or some other issue of defense. However, it does not. As with many questions, the resolution is dependent upon the correct interpretation of the quoted words. The facts indicate that second-degree assault is defined in the jurisdiction as "maliciously causing serious physical injury to another."

The malice intent standard is a standard slightly above general intent, but not quite specific intent. Malice exists if a person *knowingly disregards a substantial risk* that the prohibited consequences would come about. Knowingly disregarding a substantial risk is also known as recklessness. The only answer which correctly addresses the malice standard is choice (C). The facts indicate that Armando fired a shotgun filled with non-lethal buckshot into bushes along his back fence where he believed the intruders might be hiding. This indicates that he was taking a substantial risk that someone may be hit by the buckshot, and such a shot could cause injury short of death. Therefore, Dawson is guilty because he was reckless (satisfying the malice requirement of the statute).

It is important to note that the examiners did not include an answer choice that Dawson was not guilty because he was not being reckless. This is an argument that can be made and may even succeed, if Dawson can show that he was not aware of the substantial risk of injury. The omission of such an answer choice is what makes choice (C), although not a perfect choice, the best available answer. Focusing on an answer with a correct legal standard, and eliminating other selections, is a strategy that can help you gain points on the exam.

Choice (A) is incorrect because protecting real property from trespass does not authorize the use of force under the circumstances.

Choice (B) is incorrect because the intent to kill or cause serious physical injury is not relevant to a crime with a malice intent requirement.

Choice (D) is incorrect because the age of the person is not relevant to the issue of privilege.

Question 36
Answer: A

Because the question does not indicate that a statute or degree of murder is involved, it is fair to assume that the question tests the common law of murder.

Under the common law, a murder is the unlawful killing of another human being with malice aforethought.

The malice may either be express or implied from the factual situation surrounding the offense. The concept of malice in the context of murder requires finding the existence of one or more of the following:

(1) Intent to kill a living human being;

(2) Intent to inflict serious bodily injury on a human being (causing death),

(3) Depraved heart as an extremely reckless or willful and wanton disregard of a risk to human life; or

(4) Death that occurs in the commission of an inherently dangerous felony (felony murder rule).

In order for the conviction to stand, one of these four circumstances must exist. Phillips possessed no intent to kill or to inflict serious bodily harm. The death did not occur in the commission of an inherently dangerous felony. The facts only raise the issue of whether this was a depraved heart murder.

Finding a depraved heart murder requires that an accused possess a reckless disregard for human life. Your task, according to the call of the question, is to determine whether sufficient evidence exists to support the verdict, not to substitute your judgment.

In this case, there are several factors that support the finding that a depraved heart murder occurred.

For example, the facts indicate that, Phillips "noticed that the area beyond a clearing contained several newly constructed houses that had not been there before." The facts also establish that, between the houses there was a small playground where several children were playing at the time (presumably in sight). Phillips nailed a paper target to a tree and went to a point where the tree was between himself and the playground. Thus, he clearly positioned himself in a place where the children were in the direct line of sight of his weapon. Accordingly, it could reasonably be inferred by the jury that Dawson was acting with a callous disregard for human life, even though he did not specifically intend to kill any of the children.

Choices (B), (C), and (D) are incorrect because the facts are sufficient to uphold a finding of depraved heart murder.

Question 37
Answer: D

Because the question does not indicate that a statute or degree of murder is involved, it is fair to assume that the question tests the common law of murder.

Under the common law, a murder is the unlawful killing of another human being with malice aforethought.

The malice may either be express or implied from the factual situation surrounding the offense. The concept of malice in the context of murder requires finding the existence of one or more of the following:

(1) Intent to kill a living human being;

(2) Intent to inflict serious bodily injury on a human being (causing death),

(3) Depraved heart as an extremely reckless or willful and wanton disregard of a risk to human life; or

(4) Death that occurs in the commission of an inherently dangerous felony (felony murder rule).

This is a clear cut case that tries to appeal to your emotions in order to convince you to select the wrong answer choice. In this case, the facts demonstrate that, although Harold wished his wife did not want to die, he intended to kill her when he pulled the trigger. Emotion or motive is irrelevant. If the intent to kill exists, the malice required for murder exists. There is no defense involving this situation. Therefore, Harold is guilty of murder.

Question 38
Answer: D

This question tests your knowledge of the "knowingly" intent standard. The statute makes it a crime to "knowingly violat[e] a regulation of the State Alcoholic Beverage Control Board." The regulation prohibits selling alcohol to a person under the age of 18 or failing to obtain identification from a person between the age of 18 to 22 years old. Knowingly criminal conduct exists when an accused is aware that his conduct is of a specific nature. In this case, the prosecution must demonstrate that Dart knew he sold alcohol to a 17 year old. If Dart mistakenly believed the purchaser was 24, he would not have knowingly sold the alcohol to a 17 year old, or knowingly failed to ask for identification. This would be the strongest defense to this crime requiring the knowingly intent standard.

Choice (A) is incorrect because the existence of a false identification demonstrating that the person is 21 is irrelevant, especially since it was not shown to Dart.

Choices (B) and (C) are incorrect because mistake or ignorance of law is no defense. So long as the prosecution can demonstrate that Dart knowingly sold prohibited liquid to a 17 year old, knowledge of the legal prohibition is irrelevant.

Question 39
Answer: A

This question tests the admissibility of a co-defendant's statements.

The admission at a joint trial of a non-testifying co-defendant's confession, which incriminates the other co-defendant being tried with the declarant, violates the other co-defendant's Sixth Amendment right to confront the witnesses against him. Using a non-testifying co-defendant's confession at a joint criminal trial violates the other co-defendant's confrontation rights even if the accused's allegedly interlocking incriminating statements, corroborating the co-defendant's confession, are also introduced at the trial. If Penn testified at trial, then Smith would have had the opportunity to confront one of the witnesses against her, and there would have been no problem with the admission of the confession.

Question 40
Answer: D

This question tests the law of accomplice liability.

Accomplices may be held liable for the crime committed by a principal. However, an accessory-after-the-fact is only criminally liable for the crime of being an accessory-after-the-fact to the crime. An accessory before the fact encourages, supports, assists, abets, aids, or facilitates the commission of a felony offense. An accessory after the fact knowingly aids a principal who perpetrated a felony to prevent or hinder the principal's capture, prosecution, or conviction by the lawful authorities. In this case, if her purpose in moving was to prevent Lester's conviction, Sylvia would be guilty of knowingly aiding Lester to evade prosecution for the crime, and hence, being an accessory–after-the-fact.

Choice (A) is incorrect because conviction of the principal is not required.

Choice (B) is incorrect because aiding after the crime is what an accessory after the fact does.

Choice (C) is incorrect because knowledge of the indictment is not necessary. All that is required is the intent to knowingly aid the principal to prevent or hinder prosecution, capture, or conviction.

Question 41
Answer: B

This question tests the law of robbery and attempt. Robbery is (1) the trespassory taking and carrying away (2) of the personal property of another (3) with the intent to steal the property, (4) without any consent and using violence, intimidation, or force. Under the fourth element, the victim must subjectively feel threatened. In this case, the first three elements have been established. However, the facts indicate that attendant knew Robert and "did not believe that he was violent or had a gun." He felt sorry for Robert, which is why he handed over the cash. Therefore, Robert cannot be guilty of robbery. Thus, (A) is incorrect. However, although the attendant did not feel threatened, Robert nonetheless attempted to commit robbery.

In order to be guilty of attempted robbery, a person must intend to commit robbery and commit an act in furtherance of the intended robbery. In this case, Robert intended to commit robbery when he became agitated and made the threat. The act of placing his hand in his pocket was also sufficient as an act in furtherance of the robbery. Therefore, Robert is most likely guilty of attempted robbery.

Choice (C) is incorrect because the elements of false pretenses are not met. Proof of the following elements is required to establish the false pretense offense: (1) An accused makes a false representation of a fact; (2) To a victim who transfers his property's title, or other valuable consideration, to the accused; (3) The accused knew that his representation was false; and (4) The accused intended to defraud the victim; and (5) The victim must actually believe the false representation to be true. In this case, two of the elements are clearly not present. First, Robert did not intend to defraud the victim because he gave the victim the check. Second, to the extent that the threat is considered the false representation, Attendant did not believe it.

Choice (D) is incorrect because larceny requires taking possession of property, not title. In this case, Robert took title to the money.

Question 42
Answer: B

This question tests the concepts of mistake of law and statutory interpretation.

Once again, the information in quotes is critical to resolving the question. The kidnapping statute in State A makes it a crime to "take a child from the custody of his custodial parent, knowing he has no privilege to do so." Accordingly, one element of the crime is that the person takes the child "knowing he has no privilege to do so." In this case, the facts indicate that Dave did not know that he had no privilege to take Maria. He took Maria believing that he was entitled to take her back to State B. Therefore, Dave should be acquitted because he lacked a necessary element of the crime.

Choice (A) is incorrect because mistake of law is not a valid defense, even if it is based on the advice of an attorney.

Choices (C) and (D) are incorrect because Dave could not be convicted because an element of the crime is lacking.

Question 43
Answer: A

This question tests the law of felony murder and double jeopardy.

In this question, there is an acquittal as to the felony of attempted rape but a conviction for assault. The assault results in death long after the conviction for assault, leading to a trial for felony murder. For a charge of felony murder, the underlying felony must be sufficiently independent of the victim's death. Thus, an assault that results in death is not independent of the death. The only crime which could be the underlying felony for the charge against Donald would be rape. But, Donald has not been convicted of rape. To charge him with felony murder would mean also charging him with the underlying felony of rape. That rape charge would amount to double jeopardy because of his prior acquittal.

Question 44
Answer: C

This question tests a defendant's legitimate expectation of privacy.

An individual has no legitimate expectation of privacy in those matters, such as appearance, which are knowingly exposed to the public. An in-court identification is inadmissible unless the government can show by clear and convincing evidence that the in-court identification was based upon observations of the suspect other than at the lineup identification. In determining whether there is an independent source for the in-court identification, the court will consider factors including the witness' opportunity to observe the criminal act. In this question, the identifications of Devlin were based on the witnesses' observations at the time the crime was committed and not on a subsequent lineup. Therefore, the request for the in-court identification is permissible. Choice (D) is incorrect because it is not a true statement that a defendant in a criminal trial never has a legitimate expectation of privacy.

Question 45
Answer: D

This question tests the law regarding larceny by trick and false pretenses.

Larceny by trick applies when an accused (1) acquires possession of a victim's property through lies, (2) intends to fraudulently convert the property, and (3) does fraudulently convert the property. In this case, Smith acquired title, not possession, of the money. Additionally, even if title was not given, the facts do not indicate that Smith intended to convert the money at the time he acquired it. Therefore, Smith did not commit larceny by trick.

Proof of the following elements is required to establish the false pretense offense: (1) Misrepresentation: An accused makes a false representation of a fact which the victim actually believes to be true; (2) Obtain Title to Property: To a victim who transfers his property's title, or other valuable consideration, to the accused; (3) Scienter: The accused knew that his representation was false; (4) Intent to Defraud: The accused intended to defraud the victim. An accused does not intend to defraud if he (a) believes the property is his own, (b) intends to return the property within a reasonable time, or (c) obtains the property in satisfaction of a debt he honestly believes the victim owes him.

In this case, Smith promised Jones that he would repay the money in two weeks. Nothing in the fact pattern indicates that Smith believed the representation to be untrue. Presumably, Smith did not intend to lose money gambling. Therefore, the misrepresentation may not have been false when made. Additionally, the intent to defraud element may not be satisfied because the facts indicate that Smith intended to return the money in two weeks. Therefore, Smith did not commit false pretenses.

Question 46
Answer: D

This question tests the law regarding larceny, burglary, and trespass.

First, let's examine Horace's potential crime. An accused commits a trespass upon a victim's real property by (1) loitering, prowling, or wandering, (2) on the property of another, (3) without permission. In this case, by giving Horace the key, Horace obtained Sam's permission to enter onto the property. Therefore, Horace did not commit trespass.

Horace is not guilty of burglary because he did not intend to commit a felony when he entered the property. Having a party, although morally repugnant under the circumstances, is not a felony. Therefore, Horace did not commit burglary. Horace is guilty of no crime.

Because Horace committed no crime, the only possible remaining correct answer is choice (D). Lewis is guilty of larceny because, by pocketing Sam's rings, he committed a trespassory taking of Sam's personal property.

Question 47
Answer: D

This question test aerial surveillance of curtilage.

Aerial surveillance of curtilage is generally permissible where the overflight takes place within public navigable airspace and the observed items are readily discernable or identifiable to the naked eye. This question is based on the case *California v. Ciraolo*, in which the officer observed marijuana plants from an airplane. The observation was found not to constitute a search because, for one, any member of the public could have been flying overhead and observed the same things that were seen by the police. Therefore, there was no reasonable expectation of privacy as to those things that can be seen from the vantage of public airspace.

Question 48
Answer: D

This question tests an exception to the fruit of the poisonous tree doctrine.

Unconstitutionally obtained evidence is admissible if obtained by warrant, even if that warrant turns out to be defective, if (1) the officer obtaining the warrant did not lie to the magistrate, and (2) the officers executing the warrant acted in good faith. In this question, the evidence from the search will be upheld as long as Officer Jones was truthful in his application for the warrant. If he knew of the falsity of Susie's statements, then the marijuana evidence should be excluded.

Choice (A) is wrong. A warrant application may contain a false statement. This does not mean that the subsequent search is tainted, however, if the officer applying for the warrant acted in good faith.

Choice (B) is wrong. Apart from the false statement, which, as indicated above, is not always grounds for excluding evidence, the fact that marijuana was found is not important. The marijuana could have been found in plain sight within the home or in any places that would reasonably be searched for the presence of cocaine.

Choice (C) is wrong. The exclusionary rule is intended to prevent police misconduct. It cannot be argued that evidence should be excluded because someone other than the police is the one who engaged in the misconduct. It can be argued that Officer Jones acted in good faith because he did not know that the statement was false.

Question 49
Answer: D

This is an excellent question to illustrate the principle that, on the exam, the best answer is not necessarily a good answer. This question tests the felony murder rule. In order to get to the best answer, for this question, it is imperative to eliminate the absolutely incorrect choices, which leaves you with the best answer.

Choice (A) is incorrect because intent to kill is not relevant to a felony murder rule inquiry. A person can be guilty of felony murder regardless of possessing an intent to kill.

Choice (B) is incorrect because the crime of robbery does not need to be completed in order for a dangerous felony to occur. Attempted robbery resulting in a death is sufficient.

Choice (C) is incorrect because possessing an intent to create a risk of intent to kill is not relevant to a felony murder rule inquiry. A person can be guilty of felony murder regardless of possessing an intent to kill.

This leaves choice (D) as the correct choice. Of all four answer choices, the only one that could even be made in good faith is the argument in choice (D). Steve could argue that he is not responsible for the acts of the customer because the acts of the customer are not a natural and probable result of the crime. In all likelihood, this argument would not succeed. However, the question merely asks for the best argument, not a winning argument. Of the four selections, this is the only one that could be made in good faith. The other answer choices are irrelevant to the issue, and therefore, incorrect.

Question 50
Answer: A

This question tests your knowledge of how burdens of proof work with relation to directed verdicts. It is masquerading as a question testing the Model Penal Code (MPC) standard for insanity. However, if you understand burdens of proof, then knowledge of the MPC standard is unnecessary.

The question indicates that the state employs the MPC test for insanity, and requires the state to prove sanity, when it is in issue, beyond a reasonable doubt. Therefore, the state, not the defendant, bears the burden of proof.

As such, the court could only grant a directed verdict if (1) no reasonable jury could conclude that the prosecution met the burden or (2) no reasonable jury could conclude that the prosecution has not met the burden. Because the prosecution bears the burden, those are the only two circumstances under which the directed verdict may be granted.

Choice (A) is correct because it correctly sets for the standard for the motion under the circumstances. If the judge believes that the jury could not find the prosecution to have proved sanity beyond a reasonable doubt, then granting the directed verdict in favor of the defense is appropriate. Alternatively, if the judge believes that the jury could only find that the prosecution proved sanity beyond a reasonable doubt, it would be appropriate to grant to motion in favor of the prosecution. However, this second alternative is not an option in this question.

Choice (B) is incorrect because, even if the judge believes that Askew's witnesses are not believable, the prosecution must still meet the burden of proof beyond a reasonable doubt.

Choice (C) is incorrect because the use of lay or expert witnesses is not relevant to the directed verdict issue. The only thing that is relevant is the extent to which the burden of proof was or was not met.

Choice (D) is incorrect because it does not accurately set for the standard for a directed verdict motion. The standard is whether a reasonable jury could not find that the burden was or was not met, not whether the judge is convinced by the evidence. If there is evidence that can support a finding either way, then the fact that the judge is convinced one way or the other is irrelevant. The judge cannot substitute her judgment for that of the jury.

Question 51
Answer: B

This question tests the common law of murder. Because no statute or degree of murder is involved, it can be assumed that the common law standard for murder is being tested. Common law murder is the unlawful killing of another human with malice aforethought. The malice mental state requirement is satisfied under the following four circumstances: (1) intent to kill, (2) intent to commit serious bodily injury, (3) death during commission of inherently dangerous felony; and (4) demonstrating a reckless disregard for human life.

In this case, Trelawney certainly possessed no intent to kill or inflict serious harm on the child. Additionally, he did not commit an inherently dangerous felony, such as robbery. He also did not act with a reckless disregard for human life. Although not reporting the bruises may not have been wise, it was not a reckless disregard for human life. Actions constituting a reckless disregard for human life include shooting a gun into a crowd of people, playing Russian roulette with a gun, or driving a vehicle into a crowd of people, among other things.

Choice (A) is incorrect because mistake of law is no defense. Additionally, the mistake of law set forth in choice (A) is a mistake regarding an uncharged law.

Choice (C) is incorrect. However, it is a commonly selected incorrect answer. Understanding why it is not as good of a choice as choice (B) is an integral for getting a good grasp of how this exam works. Choice (C) is incorrect because lack of proximate causation is a second best defense. It can be argued that the child's death was a foreseeable result of failing to report the conduct. Presumably, that is the reason for the statute in the first place. Although the existence of proximate cause may be argued, no argument can be made regarding mental state. Clearly, none of the four required mental states exist. Therefore, choice (B) is the better selection.

Choice (D) is incorrect both factually and legally. Trelawney is still guilty of violating the requirements of the statute, even if he was directed not to do so. Nonetheless, even if his omission is excused, guilt (or the lack thereof), under the statute, does not equate to guilt for the charge of murder.

Question 52
Answer: D

This question tests the defenses of intoxication and self-defense. First, the defense of voluntary intoxication is not available for non specific-intent crimes. Manslaughter is not a specific intent crime. Therefore, voluntary intoxication is not a valid defense and choice (B) is incorrect.

Self-defense, however, may be available if an accused fears for his own safety. If the accused possesses an objectively reasonable belief that an aggressor is about to use force against the accused, then the accused may be justified in using force in his own defense. The rule, however, requires that the belief must be reasonable. Therefore, even if the belief of the threat is honestly held, it must be reasonable under the circumstances in order to take advantage of the defense.

Choice (A) is incorrect because a reasonable belief, not honest belief of the threat, is required.

Choice (C) is incorrect because, although he acted recklessly, the fact that he was in no danger is of no consequence in this question. Remember, the standard for self-defense is reasonableness.

Choice (D) is correct because he acted recklessly (satisfying the standard for involuntary manslaughter), and his apprehension was not reasonable. Choice (D) is certainly not a perfect answer because it is not clear that self-defense would be available even if the apprehension was reasonableness. However, because reasonableness of the apprehension is the relevant standard for self-defense, not an honest belief, this answer is better than choice (C), and therefore, correct.

Question 53

Answer: D

This question tests the requirements for a valid search.

Generally, a Fourth Amendment search requires a warrant based on probable cause. In this question, the search of the student's backpack was done without a warrant. However, a warrant may be excused where there is spontaneously arising probable cause and exigent circumstances that require the officers to forego the application for a warrant. In this question, there is no indication that circumstances were so exigent as to make the search without a warrant necessary. The officers could have gotten a warrant and then proceeded with the search.

Question 54
Answer: D

This question tests the admissibility of a defendant's confession.

Where a defendant has confessed voluntarily and is not under custodial interrogation, that confession is generally admissible. In this question, however, the defendant was in custody. To determine if his confession was voluntary, a court will look at the totality of the circumstances surrounding the confession. The court will look at the person's situation (age, race, mental and physical states, education, etc.). The court will also look at the conduct of the officers. A scheme of deception or coercion may render the statement involuntary and invalid. In this question, a showing of such a scheme would be a good argument for excluding the statement.

Choice (A) is wrong. Merely being in custody does not automatically render an incriminating statement inadmissible.

Choice (B) is wrong. There is no evidence to suggest that the police did not comply with the request for a lawyer. The police merely let the parents see their child before a lawyer was present.

Choice (C) is wrong. Where a right to counsel is invoked, the police cannot ask questions or interrogate the defendant outside the presence of that defendant's lawyer. This does not mean that the police are categorically banned from listening to the statements and questioning conducted by someone else.

Question 55
Answer: A

This question tests your knowledge of the crime of arson. The common law definition of arson is the malicious burning of another's dwelling. The property burned in this question is the accused's own store, not a dwelling. However, no answer choice is dependent upon the lack of the dwelling or other's property elements. Therefore, it can be assumed that the jurisdiction at issue, like most jurisdictions, has adopted a modern modification of arson making it applicable to any building, even the accused's own building. Consequently, for this question, arson can be defined as the malicious burning of property for an improper purpose.

In this case, the property was clearly burned and the burning was for the improper purpose of collecting insurance proceeds. Therefore, the only element that is uncertain is the malice intent requirement.

The malicious element is satisfied if an accused (1) intended that the dwelling would burn; or (2) possessed a reckless disregard for a known risk that the structure would be damaged. In this case, there was no concurrent intent to burn the building with the reflexive action of dropping the match. However, once the match fell, defendant made a conscious decision not to put the fire out. In that moment, Defendant possessed a reckless disregard for the known risk that the building would burn. Accordingly, the malice requirement was satisfied and the elements for arson were satisfied.

Choice (B) is incorrect because whether Defendant was negligent is not the dispositive issue. Some jurisdictions have enacted an alternative negligence standard for arson, such as when discarding a lit cigarette in a forest. However, these jurisdictions have retained the intentional and reckless standards. The reckless standard is the standard that is satisfied in this question.

Choices (C) and (D) are incorrect because, as detailed earlier, the act of starting the fire by dropping the match is not the relevant act for the arson crime under these circumstances. Because the recklessness standard was met, instead of the intentional standard, the relevant act or omission is that, despite causing the fire and disregarding a known risk that the building would be damaged, Defendant did nothing to stop the fire.

Question 56
Answer: B, D

This question tests the crimes of battery and conspiracy. In order to resolve the question, you must analyze whether the elements of either, or both crimes, are present.

The elements of battery include the act, intent, and the result. Specifically, an accused must engage in an intentional act or failure to act if a duty exists, that results in a victim suffering an offensive touching or a bodily injury. The accused must also intend to injure a human being or engage in criminal negligence (which is essentially recklessness) with regard to the result. In this case, the parties' act caused a harmful result. Therefore, the act and result prongs are clearly met. The intent element is not as clear. Slick and Hope clearly did not intend the contact. However, intent is not the only mens rea that satisfies the battery crime. The intent element will also be satisfied if the accused engaged in criminal negligence. Criminal negligence is equated to recklessness – substantially disregarding a known risk of the contact. In this case, it can be argued that Hope and Slick were criminally negligent, but a good argument can be made against the proposition as well. Therefore, the Examiners accepted answer choices finding Hope and Slick guilty and not guilty of battery.

A conspiracy exists when more than one person agree to, and intend the commission of, an illegal act or a legal act by illegal means. The elements of agreement and intent must be established to prove the existence of a conspiracy. In this case, there is no intent to commit a battery. Hope and Slick agreed to set off the alarm, but not to commit battery. If a battery occurred, as set forth earlier, it is only as a result of the criminal negligence standard. Therefore, Hope and Slick are not guilty of entering into a conspiracy to commit battery.

Question 57
Answer: B

Choice (B) is correct because the defendant would likely be guilty of murder. The four mens rea alternatives that will satisfy a charge for murder are (1) intent to kill, (2) intent to inflict serious bodily harm, (3) reckless disregard for human life, and (4) death resulting from commission of an inherently dangerous felony. Choice (B) specifically states that Defendant intended to inflict a serious injury. Therefore, Defendant has the required mens rea for common law murder and will be guilty, even though he did not intend to kill Victim.

Choice (A) is incorrect because attempt is a specific intent crime. Defendant did not specifically intend to introduce adulterated drugs into interstate commerce.

Choice (C) is incorrect because the mens rea requirement for arson was not met. The accused must either intend to burn or act with a reckless disregard to a known risk of the building being damaged. Defendant did not intend to burn the building. Additionally, Defendant could not have known of the risk posed by smoldering wires that were unknown to him.

Choice (D) is incorrect because the mens rea for involuntary manslaughter was not met. Criminal-negligence manslaughter occurs when an accused kills a human being in the course of a lawful act because of the accused's failure to use due caution and circumspection. The relevant inquiry is whether the accused actions involved a high degree of risk of death or serious bodily harm. In this case, the use of the plastic rattlesnake cannot be said to have involved a high degree of risk of death or serious bodily harm. Therefore, Defendant would be not guilty of manslaughter.

Question 58
Answer: A

This question tests the crimes of larceny and embezzlement.

Proof of the following elements is required to establish an embezzlement offense: (1) Intent: An accused must specifically intend to take possession; (2) Lawful Possession: The accused is entrusted with an owner's property; (3) Fiduciary Relationship: Exists between the accused and the owner; (4) Conversion: The accused fraudulently converts the property; and (5) Interference: The accused interfered with the owner's rights. In this case, the lawful possession requirement is not met. In order to be guilty of embezzling property, an accused must be entrusted with possession of the property. Merely leaving a safe open in a room with the accused does not constitute entrusting him with possession of the property. Therefore, Eddie is not guilty of embezzlement.

Larceny is the trespassory taking and carrying away of the personal property of another with an intent to steal. In this case, Eddie took the money, which was not his property, and left. The facts do not suggest that he intended to return the property. Therefore, Eddie is clearly guilty of larceny.

Question 59
Answer: B

This question tests the Sixth Amendment right to counsel.

The first line in this question holds key information to the proper answer—an indictment is brought against Daniels. This means that he has been formally charged. Once this charging takes place, the defendant now has the Sixth Amendment right to counsel, which, unlike the Fifth Amendment right to counsel, does not have to be affirmatively invoked. Rather, it attaches until it is waived. No more questioning of the defendant can be conducted without the presence of his counsel. In this question, Daniels is questioned by the undercover informant outside the presence of his counsel. While this would not necessarily be prohibited prior to the charging of a defendant, it is prohibited after the charge.

Choice (A) is wrong. The privilege against self-incrimination comes into play where there is custodial interrogation of the defendant. There was no interrogation of the defendant in this situation.

Choice (C) is wrong. While it is true that Daniels did receive his Miranda warnings, simply receiving Miranda warnings may not be enough to render a confession valid, voluntary, and admissible. There are often instances in which the accused must receive the Miranda warnings again, even after the initial warnings given at the time of arrest.

Choice (D) is wrong. It is correct that Daniels was not interrogated by Innis, but this does not mean that there were no other problems with the conduct of the police.

Question 60
Answer: D

This question tests the defense of entrapment and the constitutionality of burdens of proof.

A state may place the burden for an affirmative defense upon the defendant. Therefore, placing the burden of persuasion for the entrapment defense on the defendant is not a valid ground for reversal. Consequently, choices (B) and (C) are incorrect.

A valid entrapment defense possesses two elements: (1) state inducement of the crime, and (2) the defendant's lack of predisposition to engage in the criminal conduct. In this case, the prosecution introduced evidence of prior convictions as substantive evidence regarding the predisposition element of the entrapment defense, not as substantive evidence that the defendant committed the crime in question. Therefore, the introduction of the convictions was proper and not a valid ground for reversal. Thus, choice (A) is incorrect and choice (D) is correct.

Question 61
Answer: B

This question tests the law of murder and transferred intent.

The doctrine of transferred intent provides that a person engaging in illegal conduct with any criminal state of mind will be liable for the results of that crime, even when it is perpetrated against someone other than the intended victim. Here, the intended victim was Adams. The attempted murder, however, was perpetrated against Brooks. Thus, the intent transferred to Brooks.

Question 62
Answer: D

This question tests the requirement of mens rea.

The statute in question makes it a misdemeanor to knowingly fail to file the required report. The accused has testified that he did not realize the amount of his prescription drug sales. If true, this negates the mens rea required for a violation of the statute. He could not knowingly violate the statute unless he knew the amount of his sales was greater than the threshold.

Question 63
Answer: B

This question tests the law of involuntary manslaughter.

There is no evidence in the question of John intending to cause the death of his child. However, this does not rule out homicide. Involuntary manslaughter is the unintended killing of another human being. It involves recklessness or criminal negligence. Where parent and child are concerned, an omission may constitute recklessness or negligence. To commit involuntary manslaughter, the accused must (1) have a legal duty to act and (2) the failure to act was the but-for cause of the death. Here, the parent-child relationship poses the duty to act, and but for John's refusal to accept "charity," the child would have survived.

Question 64
Answer: B

This question tests the law of murder and its statutory degrees.

Applying the degrees of murder as defined in the question, first-degree murder is either (1) premeditated or (2) felony murder. All other murder is second-degree murder.

Choice (A) is incorrect. The killing took place without premeditation or deliberation.

Choice (B) is correct. Defendant deliberated and premeditated the killing, actually going to buy the poison and then inserting it into the victim's coffee.

Choice (C) is incorrect. Though the attack itself was premeditated, the killing was not. There was no intent to kill.

Choice (D) is incorrect. The presence of alcohol negates the possibility of premeditation or deliberation.

Question 65

Answer: C

This question tests the requirement of general intent.

The offense charged to Rose does not present an express requirement of intent. However, all laws require at least a general intent (unless the offense is a strict liability offense). Thus, she is not guilty if the jury finds that she honestly believed the signs had been abandoned. In that event, Rose lacks even a general intent.

Question 66
Answer: B

This question tests the law of self-defense. Self-defense serves to mitigate the severity of an accused's offense. To satisfy or successfully claim self-defense, (1) the aggressor must have presented an immediate threat to the accused; (2) the accused possessed an objectively reasonable belief that the aggressor was about to use force against him; and (3) the accused cannot use excessive force compared to the force used by the aggressor. Here, Ted was attacked with a deadly weapon, which entitled Ted to respond using deadly force as well.

Question 67
Answer: D

This question tests the law of robbery.

Robbery is the trespassory taking and carrying away of another's personal property by use of force. There must be some element of violence, intimidation, or force used against the victim. In this question, there is no element of force in choice (D). The victim in choice (D) was too drunk to feel subjectively threatened, nor was there any violence. At most, choice (D) presents a case of larceny. It is not robbery.

Question 68
Answer: D

This question tests the law of burglary and specific intent.

Burglary is the breaking and entering of the dwelling of another (at night in common law) with the intent to commit a felony inside. Burglary is a specific intent crime. If the accused does not possess the specific intent when committing a criminal act, then the accused cannot be guilty of the act. Here, Harry did not have the specific intent to commit a felony.

Choice (A) is incorrect. There was a "breaking" into the neighbor's house even though no force was used.

Choice (B) is incorrect. Harry could not consent to the entry at the neighbor's house. He only consented to the entry at his own.

Choice (C) is incorrect. Harry could potentially be liable for burglary even though he was not the principal actor. An accessory before the fact can be charged with and convicted of the same offense as the principal actor.

Question 69
Answer: C

This question tests the viability of the defense of mistake of fact.

A mistake of fact occurs when, if the facts were as the accused believed them to be at the time of the offense, the accused could not have committed the offense. Here, if the house had been Harry's house, as Bill believed it was, then Bill would not be guilty of burglary because he had the consent to enter Harry's house.

Choice (B) is wrong. Bill did not have the consent of the owner of the house into which he entered. He had the consent of Harry. This defense would work only if Bill had actually entered Harry's house.

Question 70
Answer: B

This question tests the law of conspiracy.

In order for conspiracy to exist, more than on person must agree to and intend the commission of an illegal act. A person cannot be guilty of conspiring with a party who does not intend to commit the crime. Here, there was no intent by either Harry or Bill to commit the offense of burglary, as everything was done with permission or consent of the would-be victim. Rather, any conspiracy that existed would probably be in the area of fraud.

Question 71
Answer: B

This question tests the defense of involuntary conduct.

For an assault to take place, the accused must intend to place another person in a reasonable apprehension of imminent physical harm. For a battery, there is also a requirement that the accused intend to injure the other person. In the instance of involuntary conduct, the action taken is not under the volition of the accused, and therefore the accused will not be subjected to criminal liability. Such involuntary conduct may result from a seizure. Here, the involuntary conduct defense is the strongest.

Question 72
Answer: A

This question tests the law of Fourth Amendment searches.

The key to this question is that the state law empowered the officer to arrest Dexter for the offense of speeding. Thus, there is a valid custodial arrest, followed by the search of Dexter's person. The requirements for this type of warrantless search are that: (1) it occurs concurrently with the arrest; and (2) the arrest is of a custodial nature. Here, both requirements are satisfied.

Question 73
Answer: C

This question tests the Fifth Amendment right against self-incrimination.

The Fifth Amendment right against self-incrimination is founded upon the general principle that confessions or incriminating statements must be made voluntarily. If such a statement is made while the person is in custody and under interrogation, there lies the potential for disregarding such statement under the exclusionary rule, acknowledging that custodial interrogation could coerce or involuntarily force a confession. If a confession is voluntarily made when a person is not under custodial interrogation, as in the question at hand, then the confession is admissible.

Question 74
Answer: C

This question tests the elements of robbery.

Robbery is the trespassory taking and carrying away of another's personal property—with the requirement that such property be taken by force. The victim must feel subjectively threatened. Here, the victim was dead. Thus, there was no need to use force to take the identification papers. Without the use of force, there is no robbery.

Question 75
Answer: D

This question tests the law of self-defense.

In order for an accused to assert a claim for self-defense, the accused must possess an objectively reasonable belief that the aggressor is about to use force against him. While this defense does depend on the objective belief of the accused—that belief must also be a reasonable one. Thus, merely believing one is threatened with harm is not enough if the belief is unreasonable. Here, David may honestly believe that Bill was going to attack him, as suggested by choice (C). But that belief is judged by the reasonable person standard. The correct answer is (D).

Question 76
Answer: C

This question tests the reasonableness of Fourth Amendment searches.

In *Katz v. United States*, the Supreme Court held that a person's protection against unreasonable searches under the Fourth Amendment applies whenever the person possesses a reasonable expectation of privacy in the area that is being searched. The person must have both a subjective expectation of privacy and that expectation must be one that society will accept as an objectively reasonable one. Here, a person's private dorm room is a place in which there is a recognized expectation of privacy. To search this place, there must be a warrant or an exception to the warrant requirement. Here, there was no warrant, and further, there was no consent to the search. The president of the college cannot give consent for the search of the dorm room because he is not the person with the reasonable expectation of privacy in that room. Consent could only come from the student. Other justifications for a warrantless search do not exist, either—such as spontaneously arising probable cause or exigent circumstances.

Question 77
Answer: A

This question tests the law of homicide and causation.

For criminal liability to arise, an act must be both the proximate and actual cause of the illegal act, and no intervening act may exist. Here, the death was the natural and probable consequence of the poisoning of an already weakened victim. Further, the death would not have occurred but for the act of poisoning.

Question 78
Answer: C

This question tests the issue of a mistake of law.

An accused who mistakenly believes that the law does not prohibit the accused's actions nonetheless commits a crime—even if the accused held a mistaken belief about the law. The converse also holds true. An accused who mistakenly believes himself to be engaging in criminally prohibited conduct cannot commit a crime if the conduct engaged in is, under the law, not criminalized. Thus, despite the criminal intent, the actus reus itself is not criminal.

Choice (A) is incorrect. When the goods were recovered by police, they were no longer stolen goods. This means that Defendant will not be guilty of actually receiving stolen property, but he will still be guilty of attempt because he specifically intended to commit the crime of receiving stolen property, and he committed an act in furtherance of the crime by making the purchase.

Choice (B) is incorrect. Defendant knew the representation made to the banker was false, and he intended to defraud the banker of a loan. While the banker was not fooled, and thus the crime of obtaining property by false pretenses was not completed, Defendant is still guilty of attempt. He intended to commit the crime and took an affirmative step towards the commission of that crime by visiting the bank and making the false representation.

Choice (D) is incorrect. Defendant possessed the intent to kill and acted in furtherance of the killing by shooting at the intended victim. It matters not that the victim was already dead and that the killing became a physical impossibility. The elements for attempt are still satisfied.

Question 79
Answer: D

This question tests a witness's privilege against self-incrimination.

The court must determine the viability of a witness's invocation of the Fifth Amendment right against compelled self-incrimination. The court will ask whether any direct answer to a proposed question has a tendency to incriminate the witness. For the privilege to be invoked, the court must find that the witness's fear of self-incrimination is reasonable and well-founded. There is no requirement of a heightened burden of proof.

Question 80
Answer: A

This question tests common law murder.

Common law murder requires that the killing take place with malice aforethought—which can be established four ways. One of these ways is depraved heart murder. Depraved heart murder involves an extremely reckless disregard of the risk to human life. Shooting a gun into a crowd of people which causes the death of someone is a textbook example of depraved heart murder.

Choice (B) is incorrect. This option more resembles voluntary manslaughter, in which the accused is provoked to the killing during a heat of passion.

Choice (C) is incorrect. This is involuntary manslaughter.

Choice (D) is incorrect. This would also be involuntary manslaughter. There was merely an intent to injure—not to kill.

Question 81
Answer: A

This question tests interpretation of the statutorily defined defense of intoxication.

The statute in question provides that intoxication is not a defense to a crime unless it negates an element of the offense. Therefore, to invoke the defense against a claim of murder, the intoxication must cancel out one of the statutory elements of murder in that jurisdiction. In this question, there are two kinds of murder: (1) premeditation with intent to kill, and (2) killing during the commission of rape, robbery, burglary, or arson. Intoxication, in this question, can cancel out one of the required elements of burglary as defined by the jurisdiction. It requires an intent to commit a crime once inside the building. When intoxicated, there it is possible that the defendant did not intend to commit a crime when inside. Thus, the jury should be instructed that intoxication can be a defense to the second kind of murder by eliminating the underlying offense of burglary. However, there may still be murder if there had been premeditation and intent to kill. Thus, choice (A) is the correct jury instruction.

Question 82
Answer: A

This question tests interpretation of a statutory definition of manslaughter.

In the jurisdiction in this question, manslaughter is the killing of a human being in a criminally reckless manner. Criminal recklessness requires conscious disregard of a substantial and unjustifiable risk. Where a person is tried for manslaughter, the defense may try to negate the element of recklessness by showing there was no conscious disregard for the risk posed by the conduct. This would be defendant's best argument.

Question 83
Answer: C

This question tests the viability of a defense of intoxication.

If the defense in the question attempts to claim that the intoxication rendered the accused unable to consciously disregard the risk he posed to others, the response of the state would be to trace back occurrences in the chain of causation. The voluntary manner in which the alcohol was consumed, with knowledge it may cause drunkenness, was the conscious disregard for the risk associated with drunk-driving.

Question 84
Answer: C

This question tests specific intent.

Assault is a specific intent crime. The accused must both intend to commit the criminal act and desire the act's consequences. Therefore, for Edward to be guilty, he must have intended to attempt to commit the offensive touching or battery. The intent was not present.

Question 85
Answer: D

This question tests the concept of self-defense.

While Margaret may very well have caused an offensive touching to Edward, she was justified in doing so because of her subjective and reasonable fear of being struck by Edward. She was presented with the immediate threat of being hit and responded without use of excessive force. While it may be argued that this is a question testing the concept of justification, the pushing was not done to escape an unavoidable result, nor would the result (being hit in the face) have been irreparable. Self-defense is the better explanation.

Question 86
Answer: C

This question tests the law of Fourth Amendment searches and privacy.

While a dog sniff and permitted entry into the home were, in and of themselves, legal searches, the whole chain of events must be considered. The entry into the backyard (private property) of the defendant, without authorization or permission, was an invasion of a space about which the defendant both subjectively and objectively would expect privacy. A person's backyard and back porch would also be considered by society as a place where there is a justified expectation of privacy. Thus, the entry into the backyard violated that reasonable expectation of privacy—rendering any subsequently discovered evidence inadmissible.

Question 87
Answer: B

This question tests the mens rea requirement for accessories to crimes.

In order for a person to be an accessory to a crime, that person must have the intent to encourage or assist the other person in perpetrating an offense. In the present question, Carl could not have the intent to encourage the commission of bigamy because he was unaware of Alan's existing marriage. Thus, he did not have the mental state required to aid and abet Alan in the crime.

Question 88
Answer: C

This question tests the Fifth Amendment privilege against self-incrimination.

In *Griffin v. California*, the Supreme Court decided that the prosecution's referencing of an accused's failure to testify in her own behalf violated her right to due process under the Fourteenth Amendment. The references were considered a penalty for the exercise of a constitutional right against self-incrimination.

Question 89
Answer: C

This question tests the elements of larceny.

Choice (A) is wrong. Larceny requires that the accused intend to steal the other's property. Defendant has the defense of no intent, because he was going to return the television the next day.

Choice (B) is wrong. The intent requirement behind larceny can also be negated if the accused is attempting to satisfy a debt owed to him.

Choice (C) is correct. Mistake of law is no defense in this instance.

Choice (D) is wrong. Intent to commit larceny is also negated by the defendant's belief of his own right to the property. Here, Defendant believed that the car was actually his.

Question 90
Answer: B

This question tests application of statutorily defined elements of a crime.

Here, the charge of burglary requires (1) breaking and entering, (2) into a building or structure, (3) with intent to commit a felony or steal therein. In this question, there was no breaking and entering into the convenience store. Jim walked in through a door open to the public. Thus, there can be no burglary.

Question 91
Answer: C

This question tests the law of conspiracy.

Choices (A) and (B) are incorrect. For a conspiracy to exist, two or more people must agree to complete an unlawful act or lawful act by illegal means. Here, the only agreement was the sale/purchase of stolen food stamps. There was no agreement between Crowley and the other two defendants to actually steal the stamps.

Choice (C) is correct. Again, Crowley never agreed to participate in or commit the act of theft. His only agreement was to the purchase of stolen goods.

Choice (D) is incorrect. The fact that the two other defendants were not convicted of or even charged with conspiracy has no bearing on Crowley's guilt or innocence of that crime. If they had actually been acquitted of the charge of conspiracy, then it would be true that Crowley could not be guilty of conspiracy as the lone remaining defendant.

Question 92
Answer: D

This question tests the law of robbery.

Robbery is the trespassory taking and carrying away of another's personal property with the intent to steal it. Robbery requires that the taking be done by force, subjectively placing the victim at fear. Paul will likely be charged with robbery because he was an accessory. If charged, he needs to negate the elements of robbery. Here, the teller was not placed in fear, nor was any force used in taking the dollar bill. Thus, there can be no robbery.

Question 93
Answer: C

This question tests the law of Fourth Amendment searches.

Though the search was conducted without a warrant, there is an exception to the warrant requirement where the person gives consent to the search. Under the circumstances, Paul had Jack's permission to be in and use the car. The stop was for a legitimate traffic offense. Paul had the authority to consent to a search of the car.

Question 94
Answer: B

This question tests the law of conspiracy.

A conspirator may be held liable for criminal offenses committed by his co-conspirator when those offenses are (1) in furtherance of the conspiracy and (2) reasonably foreseeable as a necessary or natural consequence of the conspiracy. In this question, the brothers conspired to sell illegal liquor. They kept weapons nearby for defensive reasons. When Adam shot the officer, committing battery, Bailey could be held liable because (1) the shooting was in furtherance of their conspiracy to sell the illegal liquor, and (2) it was a reasonably foreseeable offense, given that the brothers kept weapons with the intent to use them if necessary.

Question 95
Answer: C

This question tests the law of misdemeanor-manslaughter.

An accused that causes the unintended death of another while committing a misdemeanor is criminally liable for that death if (1) the misdemeanor was inherently dangerous to life, (2) the death was a natural and probable result of the misdemeanor, and (3) the misdemeanor was independent of the death. Here, misdemeanor-manslaughter fails on both of the first two elements. Choice (C) presents the argument that there is no misdemeanor-manslaughter because the offense of driving with an expired license was not the proximate, nor even the natural and probable, cause of the death.

Question 96
Answer: B

This question tests the defense of intoxication.

The intoxication defense generally arises where the defendant seeks to negate the culpable mental state required for the charged offense. Intoxication may give rise to other defenses such as diminished capacity or mistake of fact.

Choice (A) is wrong. Manslaughter does not require a showing of intent to kill in this instance, so the claim of intoxication will be immaterial.

Choice (B) is correct. If defendant is charged with assault with intent to kill, the intoxication will serve to negate the requirement of intent in the charge.

Choice (C) is wrong. The argument is that the drunkenness made defendant unaware of whether the gun was loaded. This argument will merit nothing. A better argument would be that the intoxication negated his specific intent to commit the robbery.

Choice (D) is wrong. Statutory rape is generally a strict liability crime. Voluntary intoxication may not be used as a defense to strict liability crimes.

Question 97
Answer: C

This question tests the law of larceny and robbery.

For a conviction of either offense named above, the jury must find beyond a reasonable doubt that all elements of the crimes are satisfied. Given the testimony, it is possible that the jury would find beyond a reasonable doubt that Defendant engaged in the trespassory taking and carrying away of victim's property by force (robbery). It is also possible that the jury would not find that any force was used, thus reducing the offense to larceny.

Choice (D) is incorrect because of the merger doctrine. Larceny is a lesser included offense within the elements of robbery. Defendant could not be convicted of both crimes where the elements of one are necessarily included in the other.

Question 98
Answer: B

This question tests the application of a statutorily defined crime.

Larceny, given its lack of definition in the question, is simply common law larceny. Larceny is the trespassory taking and carrying away of another's personal property with the intent to steal it. Burglary, in this question, requires that Defendant have committed a breaking and entering offense. Here, the door to the room was left open. There was no breaking and entering into the room. Thus, Defendant can only be convicted of larceny.

Question 99
Answer: C

This question tests the law of accomplice liability.

An accomplice may be criminally liable for the offense committed by the principal actor where three elements are satisfied: (1) the accessory had the intent to encourage or assist the principal in committing the offense; (2) the accessory actually did encourage or assist; and (3) the principal did commit the offense charged. In this question, Sam had the intent to encourage the murder of Vic. He shouted such encouragement to Bill. Bill then committed the offense of murder.

Question 100

Answer: A

This question tests the law of accomplice liability.

An accomplice may be criminally liable for the offense committed by the principal actor where three elements are satisfied: (1) the accessory had the intent to encourage or assist the principal in committing the offense; (2) the accessory actually did encourage or assist; and (3) the principal did commit the offense charged. Here, Tom may have had the intent to encourage the killing and even approved of it, but he did nothing to further that intent. The charge of murder fails on the second element. Tom did not actually encourage or assist in the perpetration of the murder.

Question 101
Answer: C

This question tests the law of murder.

Though it may appear that this was an unintentional killing that should be classified as involuntary manslaughter, the question asks for the most serious crime with which Defendant could possibly be charged. There is enough given in the fact pattern to convict Defendant of common law murder. The common law elements of murder are (1) unlawfully killing another human with (2) malice aforethought. Obviously the first element is satisfied. The second element is also satisfied because, under common law, malice can be established by the defendant's possession of an intent to inflict serious bodily injury (which then results in the death). Defendant in this question possessed such intent.

Question 102
Answer: A

This question tests the law of manslaughter.

Involuntary manslaughter is an unintended killing of a human being. In this question, there is no evidence of intent to kill. It does appear that Defendant acted in self-defense. However, a claim of self-defense is weak in this instance because the aggressor did not present an immediate threat to the accused, who could have escaped from the shop. If the jury does not buy into the self-defense argument, then the most serious crime of which Defendant could be convicted is involuntary manslaughter.

Question 103
Answer: B

This question tests the elements of larceny, embezzlement, and false pretenses.

Choices (A) and (C) are incorrect. Larceny is the trespassory taking and carrying away, with the intent to steal, another's property. Here, the property was entrusted to the pawn shop owner. There was no trespassory taking of property.

Choice (D) is incorrect. False pretense offenses require a misrepresentation to the victim, upon which the victim relies in transferring property to the accused. The accused must know he makes a false representation and intend to defraud the victim. Here, at the time of the representation to the victim, there was not an intent to defraud.

Choice (B) is correct. Embezzlement requires that the accused intend to and lawfully take possession of the property in a fiduciary relationship. Then, the accused must fraudulently convert the property, thereby interfering with the owner's rights. The fact pattern presents all five elements of embezzlement.

Question 104
Answer: B

This question tests the law of embezzlement.

Regardless of the shop owner's attempt to ameliorate the situation with the victim, all elements of embezzlement are still satisfied. A potential common law defense to embezzlement would be if the accused intended to provide an equivalent of the property to the victim, thereby eliminating the conversion of the property. Here, however, at the time the shop owner took lawful possession, there was intent only to return the ring—not an equivalent of the ring—if the debt was paid back timely.

Question 105
Answer: B

This question tests the defense of insanity.

Under the M'Naghten test, an accused is not guilty by reason of insanity if, as a result of his mental disease, he either (1) did not know the quality and nature of his actions or (2) did not know his action was morally wrong. In this instance, Brown would be spared if the elements of both answer choices (A) and (C) were satisfied, but the options of quality and nature are not presented together. Therefore, the best answer is (B)—that he did not know his action was morally wrong. Rather, it is apparent that he felt the act was morally justified, given his mental defect.

Question 106
Answer: B

This question tests the law of testimonial privilege.

A witness may claim the privilege against self-incrimination even during cross-examination. The defense attorney cannot invade a state witness' protection against self-incrimination during cross-examination. If that witness invokes the privilege in response to questions concerning the details of the direct examination, though, the witness either must answer on cross-examination or the court must strike the witness's direct examination testimony. Here, Waite had testified on direct examination for the state and then refused to answer questions concerning details that had arisen during that direct examination. Thus, Waite had to answer or the direct examination testimony would be stricken. If Waite refused to answer, then defense counsel could not properly cross-examine him.

Question 107
Answer: C

This question tests accomplice liability.

Choice (A) is wrong. A principal and an accessory can be tried together.

Choice (B) is wrong. While Monroe may be a victim, this does not preclude him from also being an accessory.

Choice (C) is correct. Professors are the only persons who may violate the law in question. A student cannot violate this law, as it is intended to punish professors for taking bribes from students. Thus, a student cannot aid and abet the violation of the statute. Any potential liability on the student's part would be based on his own actions which may have constituted an offense.

Choice (D) is wrong. Arguably, Monroe was a necessary component in the violation of the law. This is a weak argument.

Question 108
Answer: B

This question tests the laws of larceny, embezzlement, and false pretense offenses.

Choice (A) is wrong. A necessary element of larceny is that there be a trespassory taking and carrying away of another's property. Here, the property was voluntarily relinquished to Defendant.

Choice (B) is correct. Larceny by trick requires that the accused acquire possession of the property by using lies. The accused must intend to and actually convert that property. Here, Defendant lied in order to gain possession and intended to convert—seriously interfere with owner's rights in—the car. Then in possessing the car for a day, there was such interference. It does not matter that the car was returned because Defendant changed his mind. He had already completed all necessary elements for larceny by trick.

Choice (C) is wrong. In order for property to be obtained under false pretenses, the accused must intend to defraud the victim. The accused does not intend to defraud the victim where it can be shown that the accused intended to return the property within a reasonable time. Here, Defendant merely sought to borrow the car for the evening and return it within a reasonable time.

Choice (D) is wrong. While defendant did take lawful possession of the car and convert it for a period of time, the element of a fiduciary relationship is absent, thus eliminating the possibility of a charge of embezzlement.

Question 109
Answer: D

This question tests the requirement of criminal intent.

The jurisdiction in question imposes a knowing mental state for the crime of perjury. If the jury believes that Walters testified about his prior convictions on the basis of what his attorney told him, then he necessarily did not know that he really had been convicted of a crime. Thus, he did not possess the requisite mental state for perjury.

Question 110
Answer: A

This question tests the law of vehicle stops and searches.

An officer is not authorized under the Fourth Amendment to randomly stop cars simply to inspect identification, registration, etc. The officer must possess a reasonable belief that the driver/occupants are engaged in criminal activity to justify stopping the car. In this question, the officer possessed no reasonable belief or suspicion as to this particular car. Therefore, the stop itself was not justified, and the marijuana was the fruit of an illegal search of the vehicle.

Question 111
Answer: B

This question tests the law of common-law murder.

Common-law murder is the killing of another human being with malice aforethought. The element of malice can be established several ways: (1) intent to kill, (2) intent to inflict serious bodily injury that later causes death, (3) willful and wanton disregard of the risk to human life, or (4) death occurring in the commission of an inherently dangerous felony.

Choice (A) is wrong. Defendant can make an argument for self-defense to mitigate his murder charges or completely absolve himself. Deadly force was used in response to what Defendant perceived to be deadly force.

Choice (B) is correct. Defendant caused the death of the customer during the commission of an inherently dangerous felony, robbery. Thus, there was a death and malice aforethought.

Choice (C) is wrong. This is involuntary manslaughter.

Choice (D) is wrong. The death is obviously not intentional in this situation, but the determination as to whether there existed a willful and wanton disregard for the risk to human life is open for argument. It is possible that this would establish malice aforethought, but choice (B) is the clearer example.

Question 112
Answer: B

This question tests the common-law definition of murder.

The jurisdiction's definition of murder is the equivalent of common-law murder. To be convicted, the state must prove (1) an act or failure to act if a duty exists, (2) malice aforethought, (3) causation, and (4) sometimes, that the death occurred within a year and one day after the injury. In this question, all elements are present except for causation. The actual cause of death was cancer and not malnutrition, according to the doctors. Therefore, the father's conduct was not the cause of the death, and he should be acquitted.

Question 113
Answer: C

This question tests the law of attempt.

As a general rule, proof of intent and an act are required to establish an attempt to commit a crime. In this question, entry onto another's property with the intent to commit a violent crime is the defined offense. Dodd had the intent to shoot Vance. Thus, he had the required intent to commit a crime. Further, he acted by moving towards entering Vance's property. Thus, there is intent and an act. He is guilty of attempting to violate the statute.

Question 114
Answer: C

This question tests the law of merger and double jeopardy.

The doctrine of merger mandates that lesser included charges merge into more serious offenses. In this case, robbery is not a lesser included offense within premeditated murder because of the differing element concerning property. Therefore, it is permissible to convict Dillon, the defendant, on both murder and robbery charges arising from the same incident.

Choice (A) is wrong. As long as there are violations of two distinct statutory provisions, it is no matter that the charges stemmed from the same incident.

Choice (B) is wrong. Again, robbery is not a lesser included offense within murder.

Choice (D) is wrong. Estoppel may sometimes apply when the defendant is charged with violating two statutes. This may happen when the two statutory provisions do not require any different additional facts from one another.

Question 115

Answer: D

This question tests the law of larceny and conspiracy.

For a conspiracy to exist, there must exist: (1) an agreement between two or more persons; and (2) intent to commit an illegal act. In this question, Adams claims no intent to commit the crime of larceny. He acted upon belief that the property actually belonged to Curtis. Thus, there was no intent to steal and no intent to commit larceny.

Question 116
Answer: C

This question tests the law of larceny and conspiracy.

As in the question above, the accused must possess the requisite intent to commit a crime if there is to be a conspiracy or the underlying crime itself. If the jury believes Bennett, it should find him not guilty because he did not possess the intent to commit a crime.

Question 117
Answer: D

This question tests the law of conspiracy.

Under the common law approach, which is the governing law in the question, if all of the alleged co-conspirators have been acquitted, then a remaining lone defendant cannot be convicted of conspiracy. If Adams and Bennett did not possess the intent necessary for a conviction, then Curtis must also be found not guilty.

Question 118
Answer: D

This question tests the common law definition of murder.

Choice (A) and (C) are wrong. There are several ways to establish the malice required for a conviction under the common law definition of murder. One is a showing of intent to kill, but that is not present in the fact pattern. The intent was merely to scare. Another example, not present in the fact pattern, is the intent to cause serious bodily injury which then results in death. There was no intent to injure on the part of the defendant.

Choice (B) is wrong. Under the felony murder doctrine, it is required that the death be independent of the underlying felony. The felony of aggravated assault that results in death is not a felony independent of the death.

Choice (D) is correct. One way to establish malice under common law murder is to show a depraved heart on the part of the defendant. This means that the defendant acts in willful and wanton disregard of the risk to human life, even if there is no intent to kill. Dobbs acted in this manner.

Question 119
Answer: D

This question tests strict liability principles.

A strict liability offense does not require proof of any criminal mens rea. The controlling consideration in determining criminal liability is whether or not the prohibited act occurred. Choice (A) is incorrect because shoplifting requires some sort of criminal mental state. The same is true for possession of heroin and failure to register a firearm, so choices (B) and (C) are also incorrect. Choice (D) is the only choice which presents a strict liability offense. It is a crime to simply sell the milk if it is adulterated. The circumstances surrounding the sale are irrelevant.

Question 120
Answer: B

This question tests the law of burglary.

Common law burglary is defined as the breaking and entering into another's building/dwelling/etc. with the intent to commit a felony once inside. Most questions, if not specifically declaring the common law definition of burglary, tend to omit the nighttime requirement and dwelling requirement. In this instance, these elements are immaterial because they are not possible answers. The tested element in this question is the intent to commit a felony/crime. In the question, Donaldson intended to look at exam answers, which, despite his belief, is not a crime in the jurisdiction. Therefore, it cannot be said he entered with the intent to commit a crime. He entered with the intent to engage in an activity that was not in reality criminalized.

Question 121
Answer: B

This question tests the law of voluntary manslaughter.

Voluntary manslaughter is homicide, but its severity is mitigated due to the provocation of the accused. To mitigate the offense, the following elements must be satisfied: (1) the victim provoked the accused; (2) the accused intentionally killed the victim; (3) the accused acted in heat of passion; (4) the heat of passion would have overcome a reasonable person; and (5) no time had elapsed during which the accused would have "cooled off." Here, it is possible that a jury would find the umbrella attack to be sufficient provocation causing the immediate, heat of passion killing of the victim.

Question 122
Answer: B

This question tests the defenses to a charge of obtaining property by false pretenses.

Whenever there is a false-pretenses offense, the only valid defenses are those that negate the required elements of the crime. For instance, the accused may actually believe his representation to be true. Or, the accused may not have the requisite intent to defraud the victim. One defense that will not prevail, however, is the behavior of the victim. If the victim acted in a particularly gullible or foolish manner, it is no defense to a false-pretense offense.

Question 123
Answer: D

This question tests potential defenses to homicide charges.

Choice (A) is incorrect. Intoxication may allow the defendant to negate the premeditation element required for a charge of first-degree murder, but it generally will not reduce a charge of second-degree murder.

Choice (B) is incorrect. Lack of malice aforethought is applicable to a charge of common-law murder. This question is not testing the requirements of common-law murder.

Choice (C) is incorrect. A claim of self-defense will only prevail where the accused is acting only with a reasonable amount of force. In this question, it appears that excessive defensive force was used against the elderly woman.

Choice (D) is correct. By process of elimination, choice (D) remains. However, it is the most plausible defense to the murder charge because of the described presence of a mental defect.

Question 124
Answer: A

This question tests the law of robbery.

Robbery is the taking and carrying away of another's property by use of force. In this question, the assailant had the intent to steal and used force to carry out that intent. The victim of the robbery was James, who, in all likelihood, subjectively felt threatened and intimidated by the gun held to Mary's head. The gun need not be held to James's own head in order for him to be intimidated or forced into giving up his property.

Question 125
Answer: D

This question tests the law of felony murder.

If the prosecution cannot prove the requisite elements of an inherently dangerous felony underlying the killing, then the accused cannot be held liable for that underlying felony or the killing itself. In this instance, the underlying crime was not an inherently dangerous felony. It was larceny. There is no evidence that force was used in taking the cash from the register. If there was no intent to commit an inherently dangerous felony, then the prosecution cannot convict Dunbar of the underlying felony or the murder. Dunbar, believing she was collecting on a debt owed to her and her own right to the money, had no intent to steal as is required for larceny or robbery.

Question 126
Answer: C

This question tests accomplice liability.

A conspirator may be held liable for the criminal acts of his co-conspirators if those criminal acts are (1) in furtherance of the conspiracy and (2) reasonably foreseeable as necessary or natural consequences of the conspiracy. In this question, Dunbar can negate the second element above by showing that it was unforeseeable that Balcom would be armed and would shoot Stone because there was no agreement, and thus no conspiracy, to use force in collecting on the debt owed by Stone.

Question 127
Answer: A

This question tests the law of burglary and larceny.

Larceny is the trespassory taking and carrying away of another's property with the intent to steal it. All elements of larceny are present in this question. It matters not that the intent element disappeared after the crime had been completed. At the time of the commission of the offense, the required intent was present. Burglary is the breaking and entering into another's dwelling with the intent to commit a felony inside. The common law definition included the element that the breaking and entering take place at night. In this question, the intent to commit a felony existed at the time of the breaking and entering into the home. Again, it does not matter that the intent element disappeared after the crime had already been completed.

Question 128
Answer: B

This question tests the law of felony murder.

Felony murder is a killing that occurs during the commission of or as a natural result of the commission of an inherently dangerous felony. In establishing a felony murder, however, the underlying felony itself must be sufficiently independent of the death. Arson is independent of the death. Attempted rape is independent of the death. Burglary is independent of the death. However, the crime of manslaughter is death itself. It cannot be said that this offense is independent of the death. Choice (B) is correct.

Question 129

Answer: C

This question tests the admissibility of incriminating statements.

Barber was not given any Miranda warnings when he visited the police station. He was not in the custody of the police, nor was he under any interrogation. The Fifth Amendment privilege against self-incrimination is designed to protect the accused against an invasive inquisition by telling the accused that he retains the right to stay silent. In this instance, no Miranda warnings were necessary. Barber gave his statement freely and voluntarily. He was not entitled to Miranda warnings because he was not in custody or being interrogated. Indeed, he was not even a suspect.

Question 130
Answer: D

This question tests an accused's reasonable expectation of privacy.

In *Katz v. United States*, the Supreme Court held that a person's protection against unreasonable searches under the Fourth Amendment applies whenever the person possesses a reasonable expectation of privacy in the area that is being searched. The person must have both a subjective expectation of privacy and that expectation must be one that society will accept as an objectively reasonable one. Though an individual may believe that his checking account balance is worthy of Fourth Amendment privacy protection, he must realize that the bank's records are the property of the bank—and as such, the individual has no right of privacy in them.

Question 131
Answer: D

This question tests strict liability offenses and the law of attempt.

Strict liability offenses are generally without any requirement of mens rea or intent. Accordingly, a defendant may not be held criminally liable for attempt to commit such an offense because those offenses do not require a showing of intent. Attempt requires that the defendant intend to commit the crime.

Question 132
Answer: D

This question tests the law of complicity.

In order to be criminally liable as an accomplice, three elements must be satisfied: (1) the accessory must have the intent to encourage or assist a principal in perpetrating an offense; (2) the accessory must actually encourage or assist the principal in committing the offense; and (3) the principal must perpetrate the charged offense. In this instance, Jordan possessed no intent to assist Hammond in killing his wife. Therefore, Jordan cannot be an accomplice to any form of criminal homicide.

Question 133
Answer: A

This question tests the laws of murder and conspiracy.

Choices (C) and (D) are immediately incorrect because the murder was fully completed, not just attempted. The question, then, is whether a conspiracy conviction will be plausible along with the murder conviction. Hammond is guilty of murder. He intended to kill his wife and did so. The mistaken belief that he was using poison and not antibiotics is of no import. A conspiracy conviction, however, will require that two guilty people conspire together to commit an illegal act. In this question, there was not an agreement between Jordan and Hammond to commit an illegal act. A person will not be guilty of conspiring with an individual who does not intend to the commit the crime. Jordan did not intend to commit murder. Therefore, there could be no conspiracy between the two.

Question 134
Answer: D

This question tests the common-law definitions of burglary and arson.

Burglary is the breaking and entering into another's dwelling, at night, with the intent to commit a felony inside. This is the common law definition. In this question, Murphy broke into a house at night with the intent to commit larceny. Thus, she is guilty of burglary. It does not matter that she did not actually take any property. Arson is the malicious burning of another's dwelling. In this question, Murphy set a couch on fire within the dwelling. This is enough to satisfy the requirement of malice. Malice exists where the accused possessed a reckless disregard for a known risk that the structure would be damaged. Along with the malice, part of the structure's ceiling actually did burn. The elements of arson are also satisfied.

Question 135
Answer: B

This question tests the validity of a waiver of Miranda rights.

If an accused chooses to make a statement after receiving Miranda warnings, then the waiver is only proper if it is voluntary, knowing, and intelligent. The waiver is voluntary if it did not occur as a result of coercion. A confession that resulted from deliberate deception would not be considered voluntary. In this question, the statement by Dirk appears voluntary and absent of any deliberate deception or coercion by the police. A waiver must also be made knowingly and intelligently. This does not mean that the accused must be fully aware of all potential charges against him. This merely means that the person must understand the nature of his rights and the consequences of relinquishing those rights. In this question, Dirk understood his rights and the potential results of waiver. The waiver was valid.

Question 136

Answer: C

This question tests the defenses to homicide liability.

Choices (A) and (B) are incorrect. Every crime requires both an actus reus and mens rea. Here, there is an obvious mental element—Smythe readily admits to intending the death of his wife. There is also an obvious actus reus—he pushed her down the stairs.

Choice (D) is also incorrect. The defense of justification is similar to that of necessity. The accused must prove that his criminal conduct served to escape unavoidable and irreparable results. In this case, his subjective belief is not proof that his conduct was actually necessary.

Choice (C) is correct. Given the facts presented in the question, it does appear that Smythe suffered from some sort of mental defect. His best defense would be that he was not responsible for the death due to insanity. It is possible that he could prove that, at the time of the killing, he suffered from a mental disease that rendered him incapable of controlling his conduct, even if he knew that conduct to be wrong. Or, he may be able to prove that, due to the mental disease, he did not know that his actions were morally wrong. Either way, insanity looks like the best defense among those offered.

Question 137
Answer: A

This question tests the law of murder.

Murder is generally defined as an intentional killing of another human being. Under the common law definition, however, all that is required is a killing with malice aforethought. Malice can be established even without intent. Depraved heart murder takes place where the accused acts with an extremely reckless or a willful and wanton disregard for the risk posed to human life. In this question, it can be argued that Rimm acted with such disregard, causing the death of Hill. Rimm could be convicted of murder.

Question 138
Answer: D

The correct answer is (D).

Attempt is an inchoate (i.e., incomplete) offense involving both the requisite intent (i.e., mens rea) and necessary act (i.e., actus reus). Attempted selling of cocaine involves both the intent to complete the offense of selling cocaine as well as the taking of a substantial step towards completing this offense. A "substantial step" involves the engaging in conduct in preparation for, or in the furtherance of, or towards the completion of, the ultimate offense.

Beth purchased the white powder from Albert after requesting that he sell her cocaine. She reasonably believed that he sold cocaine to her based on his reputation for selling cocaine and his provision of a white powder. No legal obligation required her to test the substance to verify its chemical composition. Beth then divided and packaged the white powder for the purpose of selling it to a third party. Beth intended to sell cocaine to Carol when she exchanged some of the white powder for money from Carol. This combined intent and conduct of Beth would constitute the offense of selling cocaine if the white powder had, in fact, been cocaine. Because the white powder was not cocaine, however, the prosecution charged Beth with attempting to sell cocaine. The above facts indicate that Beth both possessed the intent to sell cocaine and took substantial steps to do that. Beth's intent is clearly evident based on her dealings with, and representations to, Albert and Carol. Beth's substantial steps towards selling cocaine include her purchase of the white powder from Albert, her packing of it, and her provision of it to Carol in exchange for payment.

Although Beth could not have been convicted of selling cocaine to Carol because the white powder was not cocaine, she would be convicted of attempting to sell cocaine.

Answer (A) is wrong because it is not completely correct. Although it accurately states that Beth is guilty of attempting to sell cocaine, it inaccurately states that Albert is guilty of attempting to sell cocaine. Albert is not guilty of this offense because, while he led Beth to believe that he was selling cocaine to her, the facts do not indicate that he in fact intended to sell her cocaine. He intended to sell her fake cocaine—white powder. Thus, the requisite element of intent to commit an attempt does not exist. Without that element, the fact that he took the substantial step of supplying the white powder is insufficient to find him guilty of attempting to sell cocaine.

Question 139
Answer: B

The correct answer is (B).

The common law elements of robbery include:

(1) Intent: An accused must specifically intend to permanently deprive a victim of personal property;
(2) Caption: Taking and carrying away a victim's personal property;
(3) Asportation: Permanently depriving a victim of that property; and
(4) Force: Without any consent and using violence, intimidation, or force.

The defense of voluntary intoxication applies if an accused knowingly ingested a substance (e.g., alcohol or drugs) that caused the intoxication prior to the accused's commission of a criminal offense. The defense of mistake of fact is available when, if the facts were as an accused considered them to be when an offense occurred, the accused could not have committed the offense.

Caption occurred because Mel took the briefcase from the passenger's possession. Asportation occurred because Mel started to walk away from the passenger before being arrested. Force occurred in the physical struggle between Mel and the passenger.

Mel voluntarily induced his own intoxication that caused him to incorrectly believe that the passenger was carrying his briefcase. This intoxication occurred before the alleged robbery and prevented Mel from forming the specific intent required for robbery. Mel's altered perception led him to mistakenly believe that the passenger was holding Mel's briefcase. Thus, Mel's mistake of fact precluded his formation of the specific intent required for robbery.

The correct answer is (B) because although Mel's behavior fulfilled the other elements of robbery, he lacked the requisite mental state to commit the offense.

Answer (A) is incorrect, although it accurately indicates that Mel should be acquitted and also recognizes that intoxication would be a reason for that result. The absence of any threats is irrelevant to the offense and the defenses.

Answer (C) is incorrect for two reasons. First, Mel should not be convicted. Second, this answer incorrectly applies the law to conclude that voluntary intoxication should result in Mel's conviction.

Answer (D) is incorrect for two reasons. First, Mel should not be convicted. Second, this answer incorrectly applies the law to conclude that mistake of fact is not a defense to robbery.

Question 140
Answer: A

The correct answer is (A) because Joe completed the offense of larceny.

Answer (B) is incorrect because Joe did not commit attempted larceny.

Answer (D) is wrong because Joe committed larceny. Joe possessed both the criminal intent and committed the criminal act. Joe's intent to permanently deprive Marty of the watch existed when he decided take the watch after Marty left it on the blanket. Caption and asportation occurred when Joe took Marty's watch by lifting it from the blanket.

Answer (C) is not correct because Joe did not commit embezzlement. Although Joe intended to obtain possession of Marty's watch, when he picked it up Joe was not in lawful possession of the watch. Marty only sought to entrust Joe with the watch after it was in Joe's possession due to a completed larceny. Although Marty subjectively intended to give the watch to Joe, Joe did not receive any objective notice of that intent until after Joe took possession of the watch. Moreover, no fiduciary relationship existed between Joe and Marty. The facts do not indicate that Joe fraudulently converted the property, although he interfered with Marty's right of watch ownership.

Joe is not guilty of an attempted larceny because he completed the offense of larceny. Joe is not guilty of an attempted embezzlement because the facts only show Joe's intent, but he did not take substantial steps to fulfill all elements of that offense.

Question 141
Answer: A

The correct answer is (A).

A confession is a person's self-incriminating statement that typically is made prior to judicial proceedings. Generally, if it is voluntarily made when the person is neither in custody nor under interrogation, then the confession will not need to be suppressed under the exclusionary rule. Conversely, if a confession is involuntarily made when the person is in custody and under interrogation, then the confession may need to be suppressed under the exclusionary rule.

Under the Supreme Court's decision in *Miranda v. Arizona*, a statement by a person during custodial interrogation will be considered to be compelled in violation of the person's Fifth Amendment right against self-incrimination, absent evidence that the police provided legally sufficient procedural safeguards of that right.

Miller's admission that he killed Jones in a fight is a confession because of its self-incriminating nature and occurrence before judicial proceedings. Miller involuntarily made the confession for two reasons. First, the deputy who pinned Miller down had him in custody. Second, the deputy who asked the threatening question engaged in interrogation. Thus, the confession should be suppressed under the exclusionary rule.

Miller's statement during custodial interrogation was compelled in violation of his Fifth Amendment right against self-incrimination because the deputies failed to give Miller any Miranda warning about his right to remain silent.

Answer (B) is incorrect because the deputies' conduct violated Miller's constitutional right against self-incrimination.

Answer (C) is incorrect because, although a valid search and seizure of Miller occurred, a violation of his constitutional right against self-incrimination occurred.

Answer (D) is incorrect because even if the questioning occurred during a police emergency search, the questioning violated Miller's constitutional right against self-incrimination.

Question 142
Answer: C

The correct answer is (C).

In *Hester v. United States*, the Supreme Court stated that: "the special protection accorded by the Fourth Amendment…is not extended to the open fields." Thus, a person lacks a reasonable expectation of privacy in certain yard areas of the person's dwelling. The Court defined open fields in *Oliver v. U.S.* as an undeveloped or unoccupied area that is located beyond the curtilage of a dwelling, regardless of it is a field or if it is open. In that case, the Court reasoned that "an individual may not legitimately demand privacy for activities conducted out of doors in fields, except in the area immediately surrounding the home."

The exclusionary rule affords a person with a remedy that prevents the prosecution's admission at trial of evidence that an officer gathered in violation of the person's constitutional rights.

The clothing that deputies seized during their warrantless search of Miller's fields is admissible because he lacked a reasonable expectation of privacy there. The exclusionary rule does not apply to prevent the prosecution's admission at trial of the clothing because it was not obtained in violation of the Fourth Amendment. Thus, Miller's motion will be denied.

Answer (A) is incorrect because the deputies did not need a warrant to search the fields when no expectation of privacy existed there.

Answer (B) incorrect because no violation of substantive or procedural due process occurred.

Answer (D) is incorrect because the identity of the clothing's owner is irrelevant.

Question 143
Answer: A

The correct answer is (A).

Involuntary manslaughter is an unintended killing of a living human being. It is a lesser degree of homicide because it does not require that an accused possess a specific level of intent to kill another human being. It instead involves a reckless or careless type of criminal negligence.

Answer (A) is correct because the issue of causation is more dispositive regarding Martha's criminal liability for the teacher's death than the other defenses' issues. If the causal connection between Martha's false accusation and the teacher's death is weak or non-existent, then she will not be found guilty of involuntary manslaughter beyond a reasonable doubt.

Answer (B) is incorrect because the offense of involuntary manslaughter does not require the prosecution to prove that Martha intended to kill the teacher when making her false accusation.

Answer (C) is incorrect because the offense of involuntary manslaughter does not require the prosecution to prove that Martha maliciously made her false accusation.

Answer (D) is incorrect because extreme emotional distress, a torts law concept, is not a legally recognized defense to a criminal charge.

Question 144
Answer: B

The correct answer is (B), but (C) may be correct under current law.

An officer is permitted to stop a person if the officer possesses a reasonable suspicion that the person committed, or is in the process of committing, a crime. By running away upon seeing an officer, a person may increase the officer's reasonable suspicion of criminal activity to the level of probable cause if the person's conduct is not otherwise ambiguous to the officer. However, at the time this question was written, that fact alone would not be a basis for reasonable suspicion. Neither would the fact that the person was in a high crime area.

Thus, under then existing law, Sandra's conduct did not justify the officers in chasing and seizing Sandra without probable cause or a warrant to arrest her. Although the officers were in a neighborhood known to be frequented by drug dealers, the officers lacked a basis for reasonable suspicion that Sandra was involved in criminal activity. Thus, the fact that she turned and walked away, alone could not provide them with reasonable suspicion to chase Sandra because her conduct was ambiguous. Consequently, they lacked probable cause to arrest her when she discarded the bag. Thus, the bag's contents could not provide probable cause to arrest her.

However, since this question was administered, the Supreme Court has affirmed a police stop of a person on the street in a high crime area, who fled upon seeing the police. Thus, under current law, choice (C) would most likely be correct.

Question 145
Answer: D

The correct answer is (D).

"[T]he Double Jeopardy Clause protects against…a second prosecution for the same offense after conviction" *U.S. v. Halper*, 490 U.S. 435, 440 (1989). The protection of the Double Jeopardy Clause of the U.S. Constitution is usually limited to when:

      (1) the same "sovereign" (i.e., government) seeks to prosecute
      (2) the same person more than once for
      (3) the same offenses arising from a person's unlawful conduct.

A statute of limitations restricts the prosecution from conducting a criminal proceeding against an accused after a certain time from the date that an alleged offense occurred.

The Double Jeopardy Clause does not protect Debra against the grand jury's indictment for manslaughter of Peggy because it is not a second prosecution of her by the state because manslaughter is a different offense than reckless driving that arose from the same unlawful conduct.

The statute of limitations does not restrict the grand jury from indicting Debra for manslaughter or the prosecution from conducting a criminal proceeding against her because its three year period runs from the date of Peggy's death. The grand jury indicted Debra within this interval when measured from when Peggy died.

Question 146
Answer: D

The correct answer is (D).

This question is, to some extent, a trick question. Whether the arrests of Joan and Steven were proper is not the main issue presented by this question. Instead, this question is testing whether dismissal of an indictment is the proper remedy for an unlawful arrest (the facts state that "[b]oth moved to *dismiss the indictment* on the ground that their arrests violated the Fourth

Amendment"). The answer is a definitive no. A dismissal would serve no purpose because the officers could obtain a warrant and arrest the suspects immediately. The appropriate remedy for an unlawful arrest is the suppression of evidence discovered at the time of the arrest.

Question 147
Answer: C

The correct answer is (C).

A solicitation consists of an accused's demanding, encouraging, or advising that someone else perform an illegal act on behalf of the accused. The accused must have been actively involved in facilitating a crime. The following elements must be established in order to prove the offense of solicitation:

> (1) Intent: An accused possesses the intent that another person commit a crime; and
> (2) Act: The accused asks or directs the other person to commit the crime.

Smart should be convicted of solicitation because he requested and directed that Johnson perpetrate a double murder on his behalf. Smart actively participated in planning the killing of his girlfriend's parents and arranging to pay Johnson. The prosecution will establish the following elements to prove the offense of solicitation:

> (1) Intent: Smart intended that Johnson commit the murders; and
> (2) Act: Smart asked or directed Johnson to do that.

The fact that Smart called off the plan before paying Johnson does not eliminate his criminal liability for the offense of solicitation.

Answer (A) is incorrect because Smart's ineffective attempt to withdraw occurred after he completed the offense.

Answer (B) is incorrect because Smart committed the requisite acts for a solicitation.

Answer (D) is incorrect. Agreement by the person solicited is not an element of solicitation, and is not required. The crime occurs once the act of solicitation is complete, regardless of the response by the person solicited.

Question 148
Answer: D

The correct answer is (D).

The common law requires proof of these elements to establish that a murder occurred:

> (1) An accused's act or failure to act when a duty to act exists;
> (2) The accused's malicious state of mind; and
> (3) The accused's conduct must "legally cause" a living human being's death.

The common law requires proof of these elements to establish that a voluntary manslaughter occurred:

(1) A victim provoked an accused;
(2) The accused intentionally killed the victim;
(3) During the accused's heat of passion;
(4) The heat of passion would have overcome a reasonable person; and
(5) No time transpired in which the accused could have reduced the passion.

Proof of the element of intent does not exist to establish that a murder occurred if Defendant used Victim's gun based on an honest belief that it was a stage prop. Even if all of the other elements were established, the absence of this one element, malice, precludes the jury from finding Defendant guilty of this offense.

Proof of the element of intent does not exist to establish that a voluntary manslaughter occurred if Defendant used Victim's gun based on an honest belief that it was a stage prop. Even if all of the other elements were established, the absence of this one element precludes the jury from finding Defendant guilty of this offense. Additionally, Defendant was not provoked.

Question 149
Answer: B

(B) is the correct response to this criminal law question.

Self-defense is a possible defense to a criminal charge such as battery. Proof of the following elements is needed to establish self-defense:

(1) An aggressor presents an immediate threat to an accused;
(2) The accused possesses an objectively reasonable belief that the aggressor is about to use force against the accused; and
(3) Compared to the aggressor's threatened harm, the accused cannot use excessive force.

A mistake of fact occurs when, if the facts were as an accused considered them to be when an offense occurred, the accused could not have committed the offense. The accused may be exculpated from criminal liability based on such a mistake when the accused did not know of the actual state of facts or lacked the requisite mens rea to commit the offense.

An accused who believes that the law does not prohibit his or her conduct is guilty of a mistake of law. An accused, however, cannot prevail with a mistake of law defense by relying on one's own interpretation of the law or on that of one's legal counsel.

The correct answer is (B) because it illustrates an instance when Defendant properly used force. The undercover police officer did not announce his title to Defendant or place him under arrest. Thus, Defendant reasonably believed that the officer presented an immediate threat. In response, Defendant was entitled to use non-lethal force to avoid further harm. Although the officer might have reasonably made a mistake of fact regarding Defendant's identity, his failure to inform Defendant of his identity or the nature of his conduct prevents him from invoking a privilege to use force to apprehend a criminal suspect.

Answer (A) is incorrect because the local ordinance makes selling alcoholic beverages to minors a strict liability offense. Consequently, the fact that Defendant relied upon a false identification as a mistake of fact is not a valid defense.

Answer (C) is wrong because the statute makes sexual relations with a child under 16 years of age a strict liability offense. Thus, Defendant's reliance upon the prostitute's misrepresentation of age as a mistake of fact is not a valid defense.

Answer (D) is not correct because ignorance of the law is no excuse. Further, defendant will not be protected from criminal liability on the basis of a mistake of law because his reasonable reliance upon his attorney's advice is not a viable defense to violating the law against bigamy.

Question 150
Answer: C

The correct answer is (C).

Warrants are usually required under the Fourth Amendment in order for state officers to conduct legally valid searches and seizures. In *New York v. Burger*, the Supreme Court sustained the constitutionality of an administrative inspection of a vehicle junkyard that occurred without a warrant pursuant to a state statute regulating vehicle dismantlers. The statute permissibly eliminated the warrant requirement for several reasons.

The purpose of State X's statute is similar to that of New York's statute in *New York v. Burger*. The facts show that police officers enforced this statute by making periodic junkyard inspections to monitor for illegal activity involving stolen vehicles. The officers correctly informed Janet that she had no choice in whether they would inspect the premises of her business. The officers provided an accurate answer because they did not need her consent to conduct the inspection when the statute empowered them to conduct it. Indeed, if Janet had refused to cooperate with, or obstructed, the officers, she would have been criminally liable for a felony offense under State X's statute.

The correct answer is (C) because Janet's motion should not be granted when State X's statute reasonably addresses a highly regulated industry. Because State X's statute expressly authorized the inspection of Janet's premises that the officer's properly conducted, the exclusionary rule would not apply to warrant sustaining her motion to suppress.

Answer (A) is incorrect. The conclusion rests on an incorrect premise that the statute is invalid. The language of the statute cannot be reasonably construed as providing unbridled discretion to the officers and limits the time and place of an administrative inspection.

Answer (B) is incorrect because the conclusion rests on a faulty premise that the statute is invalid.

Answer (D) is incorrect because it misconstrues the Court's holding in *New York v. Burger*.

Question 151
Answer: C

The correct answer is (C).

Proof of these elements is required to establish a forgery offense:

(1) Intent: An accused intends to defraud a victim, even if no victim is defrauded;
(2) Writing: An accused creates a writing or alters (i.e., a materially changes) an apparently valid writing; and
(3) Apparent legal significance: The writing, if authentic, could have legal effect by establishing a legal right, duty, or liability.

Proof of the following elements is required to establish the false pretense offense:

(1) Misrepresentation: An accused makes a false representation of a fact;
(2) Causation: To a victim who transfers his property's title or valuable consideration to the accused;
(3) Scienter: The accused knew that his representation was false; and
(4) Intent: The accused intended to defraud the victim.

Rachel intended to, and did defraud, the collector who purchased the letter. Rachel created on very old paper what purported to be a hand-written letter. Rachel used her calligraphy skills to make the handwriting and signature resemble that of Thomas Jefferson. Even if the letter was authentic, it lacked any legal effect because it did not establish a legal right, duty, or liability. Thus, Rachel could not be guilty of forgery.

Rachel made a false representation of fact about the letter's origin to the purchasing collector. The purchasing collector gave money to Rachel in exchange for ownership of the letter. Rachel knew of the falsity of her representation about the letter's origin. Rachel intended to defraud the purchasing collector based on her creation of, and selling of, the letter.

The correct answer is (C) because, although Rachel did not commit forgery due to the letter's lack of apparent legal significance, she committed false pretenses by misrepresenting its source.

Answer (A) is incorrect because although Rachel committed false pretenses, she did not commit forgery.

Answer (B) is incorrect because it involves two wrong conclusions. First, Rachel did not commit forgery because the false document that she created with the intent to defraud lacked apparent legal significance. Second, Rachel did commit false pretenses because she fulfilled all elements of that offense.

Answer (D) is incorrect because, although it correctly states that Rachel committed forgery, it incorrectly states that did not commit false pretenses. Whether or not Rachel made a misrepresentation about the letter's authenticity is irrelevant because she fulfilled the elements of forgery.

Question 152
Answer: C

The correct answer is (C).

Jurors may be challenged and excused based on a party's discretion. However, the prosecution's exclusion of jurors on the basis of race may violate the Equal Protection Clause of the Fourteen Amendment. In *Batson v. Kentucky* the Supreme Court required a person to present the following evidence to make a prima facie case of unconstitutional racial discrimination in the exercise of peremptory challenges:

(1) A person is a member of a specific racial group;
(2) The prosecution has eliminated other members of that group by peremptory challenges;
(3) Such peremptory challenges could be for discriminatory purposes; and
(4) The circumstances raise an inference of intentional racial discrimination by the prosecution.

Nora could present a prima facie case of unconstitutional racial discrimination based on the prosecution's conduct. Although Nora is a white defendant and the excluded jurors were nonwhite, she represented their interests and in that respect shared their racial status. Nora could show that the prosecution used its peremptory challenges to exclude all non-white jurors on the basis of race. Nora could establish that such challenges were made for discriminatory purposes because she trespassed on the company's premises to draw attention to its racially discriminatory practices against nonwhites. The facts of the case and of the prosecution's exercise of challenges raise an inference of the prosecution's intentional racial discrimination.

The correct answer is (C) because the prosecution exercised racially-motivated peremptory challenges contrary to the Equal Protection Clause.

Answer (A) is incorrect. The conviction should not be affirmed because Nora represented the interests of nonwhites.

Answer (B) is incorrect. The conviction should not be affirmed because the peremptory challenges of nonwhites could deprive Nora of an impartial jury of her peers in terms of interests.

Answer (D) is incorrect. Although this reason could be true, the facts and the law do not directly support it.

Question 153
Answer: B

The correct answer is (B).

The selective incorporation doctrine applies the protections of certain constitutional amendments to the states under the Due Process Clause of the Fourteenth Amendment. No federal constitutional right to raise an insanity defense is incorporated to the states under the Due Process Clause. The states may establish their own standards for the burden of proof for the prosecution in presenting its case or a defendant in raising an affirmative defense.

Proposal A's elimination of the insanity defense is valid because no constitutional right exists to raise this defense.

Proposal B's placing of the burden of proving insanity upon a defendant is a constitutional allocation of the responsibility for proving a defense. Under the U.S. Constitution, the state must prove the elements of a crime beyond a reasonable doubt. The defense of insanity is not an element of a crime.

Question 154
Answer: A

The correct answer is (A).

Common law murder requires proof of these elements:

(1) An accused's act or failure to act when a duty to act exists;

(2) The accused's malicious state of mind; and

(3) The accused's conduct must "legally cause" a living human being's death.

Depraved heart murder requires that an accused possess, and intentionally act with, an extremely reckless disregard for human life. Thus, to establish the offense of reckless or negligent killing, an accused should have been aware that the accused's conduct posed an unjustifiable or substantial risk to human life.

The common law defines arson as an accused's malicious burning of a victim's dwelling. The malicious element is satisfied if an accused:

(1) intended that the dwelling would burn;

(2) inew that the dwelling would burn; or

(3) possessed a reckless disregard for the results of his conduct.

Augie committed murder because his conduct fulfilled the elements. His driving of the car into the pump resulted in Homer's death. Augie possessed the requisite malicious intent to kill because his conduct occurred while being enraged at Homer. Augie's conduct of severing the pump from its base was the legal cause of Homer's death from the resulting fire. Augie committed depraved heart murder because his conduct indicates an extremely reckless disregard for human life. He should have been aware that driving the car into the pump posed an unjustifiable or substantial risk to Homer's life.

Augie committed arson by maliciously burning Homer's dwelling. Homer lived in the building. Even if Augie neither intended nor knew that the store would burn as a result of his conduct, this conduct reflects a reckless disregard for its results.

The correct answer is (A) because Augie committed both murder and arson.

Question 155
Answer: B

The correct answer is (B).

The question contains the controlling statute in the jurisdiction. Under the statute, first-degree murder is an intentional and premeditated killing or one occurring during the commission of a common-law felony. The homicide in this example is not first-degree murder because it was not intentional or premeditated. There are no facts that indicate that Diane intended to kill Victor and arranged for the bullet to discharge when the gun was pointing at Victor. Essentially, Victor and Diane played a game of chance.

Under the statute, second-degree murder is all other murder at common law. Proof of these elements is required to establish common law murder:

(1) An accused's act or failure to act when a duty to act exists;

(2) The accused's malicious state of mind; and

(3) The accused's conduct must "legally cause" a living human being's death.

The concept of malice involves three situations of culpability that relate to this question:

(1) intent to kill a living human being;

(2) intent to inflict serious bodily injury on a human being (causing death), or

(3) depraved heart as an extremely reckless or willful and wanton disregard of a risk to human life.

If the prosecution can establish malice under one of these three alternatives, then Diane will be guilty of second-degree murder. The facts indicate that Diane did not intend to kill or seriously injure Victor. Therefore, the only malice ground that may exist is the depraved heart murder. Playing "Russian Roulette" or "Spin the Barrel" with a pistol is a classic example of depraved heart murder. It demonstrates a reckless indifference to human life because there is a significant likelihood that death will result. Thus, Diane committed a depraved heart murder and is guilty of second-degree murder.

Answer (C) is incorrect because Diane's actions demonstrated a reckless disregard for human life, not criminal gross negligence.

Answer (D) is wrong because the assumption of risk defense usually applies to tortious conduct, not criminal conduct.

Question 156
Answer: C

The correct answer is (C).

Even in the absence of probable cause, a warrantless search for weapons or evidence that occurred incident to lawful arrest is constitutionally permissible. The prerequisites for this type of search are:

> (1) The search must occur concurrently with an arrest; and

> (2) The arrest must be of a custodial nature.

An officer may search for weapons and contraband in the person's possession. That search may include the clothing that a person is wearing when arrested, as well as in the person's pockets or any containers within those pockets.

The exclusionary rule affords a person with a remedy that prevents the prosecution's admission at trial of evidence that an officer gathered in violation of the person's constitutional rights.

Although the police possessed and executed a warrant to search Jason's home, they lacked a warrant for his arrest. They found him in possession of the suitcase full of cocaine for which they conducted the search. Consequently, they had probable cause to lawfully arrest him then by putting him in handcuffs. The warrantless search of his person that they conducted was constitutionally permissible for two reasons. First, the search occurred simultaneously with the arrest. Second, the arrest was custodial.

The police reasonably searched Jason for contraband and seized the knife and pistol that were in his possession. Jason is not entitled to exclusion of the knife and pistol from evidence at trial because the police did not violate his rights under the Fourth Amendment. Accordingly, Jason's motion to suppress should be denied and knife and pistol are admissible evidence.

Answer (A) is wrong because this search and seizure resulted from a lawful execution of the search warrant.

Answer (B) is incorrect. Placing Jason in handcuffs indicated that he was under arrest and the failure to provide Miranda rights could not affect the validity of the search incident to the arrest.

Answer (D) is an incorrect conclusion because it is not pertinent to the search incident to the arrest.

Question 157
Answer: C

The correct answer is (C).

A confession is a person's self-incriminating statement. Generally, if it is voluntarily made when the person is neither in custody nor under interrogation, then the confession will not need to be suppressed under the exclusionary rule. Conversely, if a confession is involuntarily made when the person is in custody and under interrogation, then the confession may need to be suppressed under the exclusionary rule.

Under the Supreme Court's decision in *Miranda v. Arizona*, a statement by a person during custodial interrogation will be considered to be compelled in violation of the person's Fifth Amendment right against self-incrimination, absent evidence that the police provided legally sufficient procedural safeguards of that right.

The Miranda rule requires that a person actually be in an officer's physical custody when an interrogation occurs. Custody exists when a reasonable person would believe that the person's freedom of action is restricted to the extent of an arrest. Custody may involve a period of detention or confinement, such as while a person is in shackles, in an officer's vehicle, or in some building that is under the officer's control.

Jason made a self-incriminating statement to the police out of court. It was voluntarily made while he was in legal custody because he was handcuffed, but not during an interrogation by the police. Although the police had Jason in their physical custody and failed to utilize Miranda's procedural safeguards, no interrogation occurred because the police did not question him. Thus, no violation of his constitutional right against self-incrimination occurred. Accordingly, Jason would not prevail in his motion to suppress the statement because the exclusionary rule would not prevent the prosecution's admission at trial of Jason's statement.

Answer (A) is wrong because the police reasonably executed the search warrant by forcing open the door when nobody opened it for them after they knocked on it and announced their presence.

Answer (B) is an incorrect conclusion because the police's failure to read Jason his Miranda rights is not dispositive when he volunteered his statement while in custody and in the absence of police interrogation.

Answer (D) is an incorrect conclusion because Jason made the statement following the police's execution of a valid search warrant.

Question 158

Answer: A

The correct answer is (A).

In *Maryland v. Buie*, the Supreme Court concluded that a when a person is subject to a lawful arrest in a home, an officer may conduct a protective "sweep" search of the home if the officer reasonably believes that it contains another person who would present a risk of danger to the officer. The scope of the search must be reasonable in terms of what the officer is looking for and where the officer looks within a home.

Jason experienced a lawful arrest in his home. Afterwards, the police conducted a protective "sweep" search of the home to determine if it contained other people who could present a risk of harm to them. The scope of the protective search should have been limited to any area from which another person could have attacked the police. The police improperly expanded the scope of their search and obtained the Uzi by opening a box inside a closet. Accordingly, Jason's motion should be granted because the exclusionary rule precludes the admission of the Uzi as evidence because the police obtained it in violation of his constitutional rights.

Answer (B) is wrong because the protective sweep search was permissible even after the police secured the object of the warrant.

Answer (C) is incorrect because in order to find the Uzi the police opened a closet and a box therein on its top shelf.

Answer (D) is an incorrect conclusion because, although the police were lawfully in the house, probable cause did not exist to believe that it contained weapons.

Question 159
Answer: B

The correct answer is (B).

Accessories (also referred to as accomplices) are people who aid a principal in perpetrating an offense by conduct such as planning, participation, or evasion of apprehension. The test of an accessory's criminal liability is:

(1) Did an accessory have the intent to encourage or assist a principal in perpetrating an offense?

(2) Did the accessory encourage or assist the principal in perpetrating the offense?

(3) Did the accessory have the intent that the principal perpetrate the offense charged?

(4) Did the principal perpetrate the offense charged?

An accessory before the fact encourages, supports, assists, abets, aids, or facilitates the commission of a felony offense. An accessory after the fact knowingly aids a principal who perpetrated a felony to prevent or hinder the principal's capture, prosecution, or conviction by the lawful authorities.

An accessory may be held vicariously criminally liable for a principal's completed crime. Such derivative liability only applies when an accessory could be culpable if a principal was convicted of an offense. To be convicted of the crime, the prosecution must establish that the accessory's conduct coincided with intent to commit the crime.

In this case, no facts show that Sam's companions intended to, or actually did, encourage or assist him, as a principal, with manslaughter. No facts show the companions intended that Sam perpetrate the manslaughter. The companions could not be accessories before the fact because they observed the beating, rather than watching out for police or witnesses. The companions could only be accessories or accomplices after the fact. The companions cannot be held vicariously criminally liable for Sam's completed crime because the jury did not convict him of manslaughter.

Answer (A) is incorrect because its correct conclusion is premised on a less than optimal basis. Sam's companions would not be convicted because they did not act as accomplices, not because Sam was not convicted.

Answer (C) is incorrect. They are not being charged with being accessories after the fact.

Answer (D) is incorrect. The accessories' lack of intervention does not render them criminally liable.

Question 160
Answer: A

The correct answer is (A).

The common law defense of voluntary intoxication applies if an accused knowingly ingested a substance (e.g., alcohol or drugs) that caused the intoxication prior to the accused commission of a criminal offense. "Knowingly" may be construed to mean conduct that occurs with knowledge of the existence of specific circumstances or facts. An accused must prove an absence of specific intent that resulted from voluntary intoxication. Both attempted murder and assault are specific intent crimes.

The evidence of Martin's drinking of alcohol prior to the party is admissible because it supports his defense of voluntary intoxication. The proffered evidence tends to show that his intoxicated state existed before he perpetrated the alleged crimes. The evidence should be admitted because it goes to proving his lack of specific intent to commit attempted murder and assault.

Answer (B) is also an officially correct alternative answer because some jurisdictions consider assault a general intent offense.

Answers (C) and (D) are incorrect because both charges are for specific intent offenses.

Question 161
Answer: D

The correct answer is (D).

Common-law murder requires proof of these elements:

(1) An accused's act or failure to act when a duty to act exists;

(2) The accused's malicious state of mind; and

(3) The accused's conduct must "legally cause" a living human being's death.

Malice can be demonstrated in one of three ways: (1) intent to kill, (2) intent to inflict serious bodily harm, and (3) depraved heart (reckless disregard for human life). Depraved heart murder requires that an accused possess, and intentionally act with, an extremely reckless disregard for human life. Thus, to establish the offense of murder through a depraved or malignant heart, an accused should have been aware that the accused's conduct posed an unjustifiable or substantial risk to human life.

In this case, there is no doubt that the act and causation requirements have been satisfied. Thus, the only question involves whether Sally acted with malice. Sally fired an automatic weapon into the air in a room full of people. This act creates a substantial risk to the lives of the people in the room. As a result, she satisfies the requirements for depraved heart murder, and is guilty of common-law murder.

A conspirator may be held liable for criminal offenses committed by a co-conspirator if those offenses are (1) in furtherance of the conspiracy, and (2) reasonably foreseeable as a necessary or natural consequence of the conspiracy

In this case, Sally's act was clearly done to further the objectives of the conspiracy. Additionally, Sally and Ralph were both armed with automatic weapons. Therefore, the use of the weapons was foreseeable as a necessary or natural consequence of the conspiracy. Consequently, Ralph would also be guilty of common-law murder.

Question 162
Answer: D

The correct answer is (D).

In order to establish the offense of larceny, an accused must specifically intend to permanently deprive a person of personal property by taking and carrying away another person's property, with the intent to permanently deprive that person of the property.

Alice committed the offense of larceny because she fulfilled its elements. Alice possessed specific intent to permanently deprive the store of the purse when she decided to take it without paying for it. Alice manifested caption by placing the purse under her coat and carrying it a few steps. Alice also intended to permanently deprived the store of the purse. Alice basically committed the crime, and returned the purse afterwards.

Answer (A) is incorrect because the elements of larceny do not require removal of the purse from the store.

Answer (B) is incorrect. Withdrawing from a criminal enterprise is only an exculpatory basis with respect to the offense of conspiracy.

Answer (C) is incorrect. Alice committed larceny by possessing both the intent to, and engaging in the conduct of, taking the purse.

Question 163
Answer: A

The correct answer is (A).

The facts fulfill the elements requisite to establish the offense of burglary.

> (1) Intent: Dirk intend at the time of:
> (2) Entry: to break and enter into the;
> (3) Dwelling: of John and Marsha's apartment;
> (4) Nighttime: at 11:00 p.m.; and
> (5) Felony: with intent to commit the felony of robbery in the apartment.

The facts fulfill the elements requisite to establish the offense of robbery:

> (1) Intent: Dirk specifically intended to permanently deprive John and Marsha of the diamond necklace;
> (2) Caption: Dirk took and carried away the necklace;
> (3) Asportation: Dirk permanently deprived John and Marsha of the property; and
> (4) Force: Without their consent and using intimidation to accost them and force to bind and gag John and tie up Marsha. John and Marsha subjectively felt threatened.

Because Dirk caused an unintended death of John as a result of committing the felony of robbery, Dirk is criminally liable for the death. Although John's fatal heart attack was not immediately foreseeable to Dirk, the felonies of Robbery and Burglary are inherently dangerous to life. John's death naturally and probably resulted from the felonies and the felonies were independent of the death. Thus, Dirk is guilty of murder under the felony-murder rule.

Question 164
Answer: D

The correct answer is (D).

Grace's conduct established the following elements of attempt:

> (1) Intent: She possessed the intent to engage in conduct that would constitute the offense of larceny based on her desire to obtain Sam's portable TV; and
> (2) Act: Grace, by instructing Roy to find and remove the TV from Sam's house, took a substantial step in preparing to commit the offense.

The evidence satisfies the following elements of the completed offense of larceny. Specifically, Grace possessed the specific intent to permanently deprive a Sam of his TV. Pursuant to Grace's instruction about their game, Roy acted as her innocent agent in taking and carrying away Sam's TV. But for Sam's return to his house, Grace would have permanently deprived him of the TV.

Grace cannot avoid being completely responsible for the larceny on the basis that Roy performed its acts.   The innocent instrumentality doctrine protects Roy from criminal liability as an accessory because he was a child and was tricked into aiding Grace.

Answer (A) is incorrect because, although Roy is a minor who unwittingly served as Grace's innocent agent, she is guilty because he acted entirely at her will.

Answer (B) is incorrect because the completed offense of larceny occurred before Sam regained possession of the TV.

Answer (C) is incorrect because Roy lacked accomplice liability because he did not aid or encourage Grace in committing a crime.

Question 165
Answer: D

The correct answer is (D).

The common law requires proof of these elements to establish that a murder occurred:

> (1) An accused's act or failure to act when a duty to act exists;
> (2) The accused's malicious state of mind; and
> (3) The accused's conduct must "legally cause" a living human being's death.

A use of force that results in death, regardless of whether death is intended, is deadly force. An accused is warranted in using deadly force to protect himself or herself only if the accused reasonably believes that deadly force is necessary to avoid the aggressor's immediate and unlawful use of deadly force. In a majority of jurisdictions, an accused has no duty to retreat if an aggressor attacks the accused in his or her home.

Matt was warranted in using deadly force to defend himself because he reasonably believed that it was necessary to warn Fred and prevent his immediate and unlawful use of a knife. Matt lacked a duty to retreat because Fred attacked Matt in his house.

Answer (A) is incorrect because Matt's use of deadly force was not an unreasonable response to Fred's brandishing of the knife.

Answer (B) is incorrect because, even if Matt had a clear opportunity to retreat, in a majority of jurisdictions, no legal duty requires him to retreat if attacked in his home.

Answer (C) is incorrect. Acting in self-defense, John did not intend to kill Fred. Even if John intended this killing, however, it arguably is excused because of the doctrine of self-defense.

Question 166
Answer: D

The correct answer is (D).

Proof of the following elements is required to establish the offense of burglary:

> (1) Intent: An accused must specifically intend at the time of;
> (2) Entry: to break and enter into a (forceful entry is not required);
> (3) Dwelling: another person's dwelling;
> (4) Nighttime: during the night; and
> (5) Felony: with intent to commit a felony in that dwelling.

The jurisdiction defines aggravated assault as assault with intent to cause serious bodily injury. Proof of the following elements is required to establish a criminal assault.

> (1) Intent: An accused must specifically intend to commit a battery; and
> (2) Attempt: The accused tries to commit a battery.
> (3) Causation: An accused intentionally and physically causes a victim;
> (4) Apprehension: to reasonably apprehend an imminent bodily harm.

An accused commits a trespass upon a victim's real property by intentionally physically entering upon the property with the accused's body.

The correct answer is (D) because of Hannah's trespass by intentionally physically entering into the hotel and sleeping there.

Answer (A) is incorrect because (1) Hannah did not commit an assault (per Answer (C) discussion below); and (2) she did not intend to cause serious bodily injury. Hannah's intent in using the fire extinguisher was not to hurt the security guard, but to defend herself from him.

Answer (B) is a wrong conclusion because Hannah did not commit burglary. She lacked the specific intent to break and enter into another person's dwelling to commit a felony there. Instead, she intended to obtain shelter in the hotel.

Answer (C) is an incorrect conclusion because Hannah did not commit an assault. She lacked the specific intent to commit a battery. Her response to being beaten on the head with a flashlight constituted an intentional act of self-defense. In other words, if she committed an assault, she was excused from liability for the assault because of the doctrine of self-defense.

Question 167
Answer: D

The correct answer is (D).

Consent is a general exception to the warrant requirement. To be valid, a person's consent to an arrest, a search, or a seizure must be voluntarily given without any use of fraud, duress, or coercion by an officer.

A person must have standing in order to make an in-court challenge to a violation of constitutional rights. To obtain standing, a person must have a reasonable expectation of privacy in an item that was seized or a place that was searched. A person who lacks a possessory interest in a place searched lacks standing to challenge the search.

The exclusionary rule affords a person with a remedy that prevents the prosecution's admission at trial of evidence that an officer gathered in violation of the person's constitutional rights.

By calling the police and leaving his front door open, Henry invited them into his house and consented to their search for Scott without either probable cause or a warrant. Scott lacks standing to file the motion contesting the warrantless entry of the house as a violation of his constitutional rights. As Henry's guest, Scott had no reasonable expectation of privacy in Henry's house based on his status as a guest who lacked a possessory interest. Scott's motion to suppress evidence will be denied because his Fourth Amendment rights were not violated in an unlawful search and seizure.

Answer (A) is incorrect. Scott lacked standing to challenge the police's entry because of Henry consent to the entry, even if they possessed a warrant.

Answer (B) is incorrect. Scott lacked standing to challenge the police's entry because of Henry's invitation that they enter, even if they had probable cause.

Answer (C) is incorrect. Henry's ownership of the premises authorized him to consent to the police's entry when Scott lacked an ownership or possessory interest in them.

Question 168
Answer: B

The correct answer is (B).

In order to prove the existence of a conspiracy, the prosecution must show: (1) an agreement by and between two or more accused people; (2) a common intent of the people to be bound by the agreement; (3) a common goal of the people to complete an unlawful act or a lawful act by unlawful means; and (4) most state's statutes require proof that the people took substantial steps towards accomplishing the goal of their agreement.

However, no conspiracy liability exists when only one of the two parties could be liable for the completed offense of statutory rape. Under these facts, Emma is a victim, not a perpetrator, of the crime. Therefore, she cannot not be guilty of conspiracy to commit the crime, and as a result, neither can Kenneth alone.

Answer (A) is incorrect because, although they agreed to have sexual intercourse, Emma could not commit statutory rape.

Answer (C) is incorrect because statutory rape may be committed without an agreement so Wharton's Rule does not apply.

Answer (D) is incorrect because one could conspire with a person too young to consent, but the consent would be invalid. The key in this problem is that Emma is the victim, not a perpetrator.

Question 169
Answer: A

The correct answer is (A).

The common law requires proof of these elements to establish that a murder occurred:

    (1) An accused's act or failure to act when a duty to act exists;
    (2) The accused's malicious state of mind; and
    (3) The accused's conduct must "legally cause" a living human being's death.

Answer (A) is correct because Sam's conduct fulfilled the common law elements of murder.

    (1) Sam's installed a bomb in the company car;
    (2) Sam possessed a malicious (intent to kill) state of mind when he installed the bomb; and
    (3) Sam's conduct constituted the "legal cause" of Lois's death.

Sam committed murder in the first degree because of his premeditation and deliberation based on his planning of the explosion and installation of the bomb.

Answer (B) is incorrect because Sam's conduct constituted first-degree murder. The transferred intent doctrine applies to transfer Sam's malicious intent against Anna towards Lois.

Answer (C) is wrong because Sam installed the bomb with deliberation and the premeditated intent to kill Anna. His subsequent efforts to prevent the explosion cannot negate his prior intent and act because its planned result occurred.

Answer (D) is incorrect because Sam's intent and act, not the security officer's negligence, caused Lois's death when the security officer did what Sam asked him to do.

MBE ANSWERS

AMERIBAR BAR REVIEW

Multistate Bar Examination – Answers to Questions – Section 6

EVIDENCE

Question 1
Answer: B

The question tests the determination of the admissibility of hearsay evidence. Federal Rule of Evidence (FRE) 104(a) allows judges to determine preliminary questions of fact that determine the admissibility of evidence that is objectionable under an exclusionary rule. Furthermore, with respect to determining the admissibility of hearsay evidence, the judge is not limited by the rules of evidence. In this case, the affidavit is being considered by the judge to determine whether the victim's note properly falls within the dying declaration exception to hearsay.

Question 2
Answer: A

The question tests the admissibility of character evidence and impeachment evidence. Evidence of a witness's prior bad acts, which are specific instances of misconduct, is only admissible on cross-examination, and extrinsic evidence is not permitted. In this case, the testimony of Wesley's former employer regarding prior bad acts is not a cross-examination of Wesley and is extrinsic evidence. Therefore it is inadmissible.

Choice (B) is incorrect because evidence of a criminal defendant's reputation is admissible under FRE 404(a)(1) and 405(a) if it is used to rebut evidence presented by the defendant that he possesses a pertinent character trait that is inconsistent with the charged offense. In this case, the testimony described in choice (B) is used to rebut the evidence presented in Wesley's testimony that Dirk is a peaceful and nonviolent person.

Choice (C) is incorrect because FRE 608(a) allows a witness's credibility to be attacked by opinion or reputation evidence of that witness's character for truthfulness or untruthfulness. In this case, testimony by a neighbor of Wesley is being used as reputation evidence of Wesley's untruthful character.

Choice (D) is incorrect because extrinsic and direct evidence of a witness's bias or interest in the outcome of a case is admissible. In this case testimony by Dirk's former cellmate is being used as evidence that Wesley has an interest in the outcome of the case.

Question 3
Answer: B

The question tests the admissibility of highly prejudicial evidence. Under FRE 403, evidence is inadmissible if its prejudicial effect outweighs its probative value. In this case, Wallace's testimony that she passed a lie detector test was unfairly prejudicial because the results may be deemed unreliable in light of the jurisdiction's ban on evidence of lie detector test results.

Question 4
Answer: D

The question tests of the application of hearsay rules to three types of evidence. Under FRE 801(c), in order to be hearsay, a statement must be made by someone other by the defendant while at the trial or hearing and be offered to prove the truth of the matter asserted. In this case, none of the three items of evidence offered by the defendant relating to the description Dinet heard over the radio are being offered to prove the truth of the matter asserted–that a man fitting a specific description committed armed robbery. Rather, the evidence is being offered to show that Dinet reasonably believed that Park was an armed robber.

Question 5
Answer: A

This question tests the admissibility of evidence of a prior conviction. Under FRE 609(b), evidence of a prior conviction is not admissible as impeachment evidence if it is offered more than 10 years after the date of the conviction or the release of the witness from confinement, whichever is later. In this case, Dalton was released from prison more than 10 years prior to the offering of evidence of his conviction.

Question 6
Answer: B

The correct answer is choice (B). Dawson's statement to the police is a prior inconsistent statement. Testimony of a second witness may be used to establish that a first witness made statements prior to testifying that were inconsistent with the first witness's trial testimony. The testimony about the prior inconsistent verbal statement may be used to impeach the first witness, but not as substantive evidence in the case.

Choice (A) is incorrect because Wallington's testimony is not admissible as a present sense impression. A declarant's sudden and extemporaneous statement that describes an event when it occurs, or soon afterwards, is admissible. In this case, while Minter's statement to Wallingford may have taken place soon after the accident occurred, it was not sudden and extemporaneous. Rather it was made in response to Wallingford's investigation. Furthermore, choice (C) is incorrect because, while a party was not allowed to impeach his or her own witness under the old common law, modern law and the Federal Rules allow such impeachment.

Question 7
Answer: B

This question tests the application of the Fifth Amendment privilege against self-incrimination to cross-examination. A defendant's choice to testify acts as a waiver of the privilege with regards to questions on cross-examination that concern matters touched upon in direct examination. In this case, the testimony of Watts is admissible hearsay because it is a statement made by a party-opponent. In addition, it does not violate Deetz's Fifth Amendment privilege against self-incrimination because the evidence is offered to impeach him as the defendant and to rebut his claim that the killing was done in self-defense.

Question 8

Answer: A

This question tests the application of hearsay rules to employees of party-opponents. Admissions made by party-opponents are not hearsay, and statements made by employees of party-opponents within the existence and scope of an employment relationship are admissible as if they were made by the party-opponent. In the present case, the statement made by Dunlevy's executive assistant was made within the existence and scope of an employment relationship with Dunlevy. Therefore, the statement is admissible as though it were made by Dunlevy himself, a party-opponent.

Question 9
Answer: D

This question tests the admissibility of evidence of prior bad acts and of character evidence. Evidence of a criminal defendant's prior bad acts is generally inadmissible unless it is being used to prove an element of the charged criminal defense, is being used to rebut an affirmative defense, or is being used to prove motive, intent, absence of mistake, identity, common plan or scheme, knowledge, opportunity, or preparation if the probative value of such evidence is not substantially outweighed by the danger of unfair prejudice. In addition, character evidence may only be used by the prosecution to rebut the defendant's evidence of good character and innocence; or to rebut the defendant's evidence of a victim's bad character.

In this case, evidence that Decker committed two robberies in the past year may be admissible as evidence of a common plan or scheme; however, the probative value of such evidence is substantially outweighed by its highly prejudicial character. Furthermore, presenting the evidence of two prior robberies by Decker for the purposes of proving a personal trait and Decker's action in conformity therewith would be inadmissible. Therefore, choice (A) is incorrect. Additionally, because evidence that Decker robbed two other stores in the past year does not prove intent in the instant case, choice (B) is incorrect. In addition, the prosecution is not presenting evidence of the two prior robberies committed by Decker to either rebut his evidence of good character and innocence or to rebut his evidence of the victim's bad character.

Question 10
Answer: C

This question tests the application of the Best Evidence Rule. FRE 1002, commonly known as the Best Evidence Rule, requires that an original writing, recording, or photograph be produced in order to prove the contents therein. In this case, the Paulsen Corporation must produce the records in question in order for Wicks to testify as to their contents because his testimony is offered to prove contents of those records—that the fuel deliveries were actually made.

Question 11
Answer: B

This question tests the application of the presumptions in civil actions. If a party establishes a foundation for a presumption and no contrary evidence is introduced, a trial judge will instruct a jury on the presumption.   However, if the opposing party produces credible evidence in opposition to the presumption, then the judge will not instruct the jury about the presumption and jury may determine a contested proposition based on the jury's evaluation of both parties' evidence.   In this case, Defendant's testimony that she never received the notice is credible evidence in contradiction of the presumption that a notice properly addressed and stamped has been delivered.   Therefore, the jury must weigh the evidence and it may determine whether the notice was received.

Question 12
Answer: A

The correct answer is choice (A).   Business records are admissible hearsay if they were made contemporaneously or around the time when an act, condition, or event that the records concern occurred; they were made by, or from information transmitted by, a person possessing personal knowledge of that occurrence; and they were made and maintained in the normal course of regularly conducted business activity.   In this case, Payne's hospital chart was a record of regularly conducted business activity excepted from the general rule against the admissibility of hearsay because it (1) was made at or around the time of Payne's surgery, (2) was drafted from information obtained from an operating physician who had personal knowledge of Payne's operation, and (3) was made and maintained in the regular course of business.

Question 13
Answer: D

In cases where a federal court possesses federal question jurisdiction, the federal common law of privilege applies.   In addition, when a patient brings about a judicial proceeding that places her physical or mental condition in issue, the physician-patient privilege is waived.   In this case, the claim at issue arose in federal court under federal question jurisdiction because it stems from a violation of the federal civil rights law.   In addition, the court would reject the claim of privilege, because Parr voluntarily brought an action against Davis regarding his injuries.   Therefore, he has waived his physician-patient privilege with regard to those injuries.

Question 14
Answer: C

This question tests the admissibility of hearsay testimony.   Under FRE 803(1), a statement made by a declarant that describes an event as it occurs or immediately afterwards is admissible.   In this case, rather than focusing on the witness' relationship to the declarant, the proximity of the statement to the event is the key factor.   In choice (C), the declarant (Valerian) made the statement to the Witness (Wharton) describing the assault immediately after it occurred. Therefore, the statement is admissible as a present sense impression.

Question 15
Answer: D

This question tests the admissibility of character evidence presented by the prosecution in a criminal case. If a criminal defendant produces evidence of his good character, that evidence may only be rebutted by the prosecution in two ways: by cross-examining the defendant's witness as to the witness's knowledge of certain instances of the defendant's prior conduct; or by calling a prosecution witness to testify about his or her opinion of a defendant's character or about the witness's knowledge of the defendant's reputation in the community. In this case, the evidence at issue involves certain instances of Darrow's prior conduct; therefore it may only be admissible if it inquired into during the cross-examination of Goode.

Question 16
Answer: B

The correct answer is choice (B). This question tests the use of hypothetical questions in the examination of expert witnesses. Hypothetical questions must contain all material facts in evidence that are essential to the a rational opinion by the expert. In this case, Pitt's childhood horseback riding accident is a material fact to the case; therefore, the hypothetical question is objectionable because it did not include the childhood horseback riding accident.

Question 17
Answer: B

This question tests the admissibility of hearsay evidence. Under FRE 803(2), a statement that is made in reaction to an unexpected event or condition that relates to the unexpected event or condition and that was made when the declarant experienced stress that the event or condition caused is an excited utterance that is admissible hearsay. In this case, the statement made by Dagget's wife was made in reaction to a murder, related to the murder, and was made under the significant stress of witnessing such a crime. Therefore, the statement is admissible as a report of an excited utteramce.

Question 18
Answer: A

This question tests the admissibility of impeachment evidence. A party-opponent may try to impeach the credibility of a witness on cross-examination by inquiring about partiality, bias, interest, or motivation. In this case, the question is designed to show that Wendy had an improper motivation to accuse Darby falsely. Therefore, it may be asked on cross-examination.

Question 19
Answer: C

This question tests the admissibility of evidence of offering to pay medical bills. Under FRE 409, evidence that one party agreed to pay the medical bills of the adverse party is inadmissible if it is offered to prove the one party's liability. In this case, the testimonial evidence that Dyer offered to pay Paul's hospital bills is being used to prove that Dyer was responsible for Paul's injuries. Therefore, the testimony is inadmissible.

Question 20
Answer: B

This question tests the admissibility of hearsay evidence. When a witness' statement involves multiple levels of hearsay, each hearsay statement must be analyzed for admissibility, and the statement as a whole is only admissible if each hearsay statement is admissible. In this case, Wixon's testimony involves multiple levels of hearsay because her statement includes two hearsay statements: (1) Dooley's statement to Melville that Melville owed him money; and (2) Melville's statement to Wixon.

An out-of-court statement made by a person other than the witness that is being offered to prove the truth of the matter asserted is hearsay. In this case, Dooley's statement to Melville is not hearsay because it is not being offered to prove that Melville owed him money. Rather, it is being offered to show that Dooley is guilty of conspiracy to dispose of stolen property. Therefore, that portion of Wixons's statement is admissible.

When a declarant is unavailable at trial, statements made by that declarant that are contrary to her pecuniary, penal, or proprietary interests at the time when the statements were made are admissible. In this case, Melville's statement to Wixon exposed him to criminal liability, and Melville was unavailable at trial. Therefore, his statement to Wixon is admissible hearsay.

Question 21
Answer: B

This question tests the admissibility of hearsay evidence. Statements that are made regarding the cause of, or who is at fault for, an injury may be admitted only if they are pertinent to the declarant's diagnosis or treatment. In this case, the notation indicating that Payne said he was attacked by Dabney is inadmissible because it was not made for the purposes of medical diagnosis or treatment. Rather, it was an accusation having little to do with Payne's actual injuries.

Question 22
Answer: A

This question tests the admissibility of prior wrongful acts. Evidence of specific prior wrongful acts is admissible if it is not being used to prove character, and it has independent significance, such as by proving motive, intent, absence of mistake, identity, knowledge, opportunity, preparation, or a common plan or scheme. In this case, the evidence presented through Wilma's testimony is admissible because it is not being used to prove Dexter's character, and tends to show he is the killer by establishing a common plan or scheme. In addition, the evidence is not inadmissible as unfairly prejudicial because the two acts are so similar that the probative value of the evidence is high enough to not be substantially outweighed by the prejudice of the evidence.

Question 23
Answer: B

This question tests the admissibility of prior inconsistent statements. Evidence of a witness' prior inconsistent statements does not violate the prohibition against hearsay if it is presented to impeach the witness and the statement was not made under oath and subject to the penalty of perjury. If the statement was made under oath and subject to the penalty of perjury, then it may be presented as substantive evidence of the truth of the matter asserted. Furthermore, under FRE 613(b), extrinsic evidence of a prior inconsistent statement of a witness may be admissible if the witness is given an opportunity to explain or deny the inconsistency.

In this case, Smythe's statement to Walton is admissible as a prior inconsistent statement for the limited purpose of impeachment, because the statement was made between two cellmates rather than under oath and subject to the penalty of perjury. In addition, the statement is admissible as extrinsic impeachment evidence because Smythe was still subject to recall as a witness and could be cross-examined. Note that because Smythe's statement to Walton was not made under oath, the jury may only consider the statement as evidence that tends to impeach Smythe's credibility and not as substantive evidence of Davidson's guilt or innocence.

Finally, choice (A) is incorrect because this case does not fit within the statements against penal interest exception to hearsay. Statements against penal interest made by a declarant are excepted from the prohibition against hearsay only when the declarant is unavailable to testify at trial. In this case, Smythe's statement was against his own penal interest; however, Smythe was available to testify at trial. Therefore, the evidence of Smythe's statement does not fall within the statements against penal interest exception to hearsay.

Question 24
Answer: C

This question tests the proof requirements for authentication. Under FRE 901, documents can be authenticated in several ways: (1) a party-opponent admits or stipulates that it is genuine; (2) a jury makes a comparison between two pieces of evidence; (3) through circumstantial evidence that shows the document's authenticity; and (4) through a witness' testimony that the document is genuine. Furthermore, the following types of witnesses may testify as to authenticity: (1) a person who executed a document; (2) a witness who saw the person execute the document; (3) an expert witness who compared samples of the person's handwriting and signature with the handwriting and signature on the documents; or (4) a lay witness who is familiar with the person's handwriting. However, under FRE 901(b)(2), that familiarity may not have been acquired for the purposes of litigation.

In this case, choice (C) does not provide a sufficient basis for admitting the letter into evidence because it is testimony by a nonexpert lay witness who acquired familiarity with the document in order to be a witness at trial. Rather, that familiarity has to be acquired by a lay witness naturally, other than for the purposes of litigation, to authenticate a document.

In contrast, choice (A) would be a sufficient basis to admit the letter, because Parker has familiarity with Dix's handwriting that was acquired independently of trial preparation. In addition, choice (B) is sufficient because allowing the jury to compare the letter with an admitted signature of Dix is explicitly contemplated by FRE 901, allowing the jury to compare two pieces of evidence. Finally, choice (D) would be a sufficient basis for admitting the letter because evidence that Dix wrote the letter as a response to a prior letter addressed to him and written by Parker is valid circumstantial evidence that shows the letter's authenticity.

Question 25
Answer: A

This question tests the admissibility of hearsay evidence. Under FRE 803(3), a declarant's spontaneous and impromptu statement regarding a then existing mental, emotional, or physical condition is admissible. In this case, Walter's testimony is admissible because Vera's statement to him shows her mental state at the time she made the statement. In addition, the statement is relevant because it tends to disprove Dale's contention that the killing occurred in self-defense, because it diminishes the likelihood that Vera had any intention to hurt Dale.

Question 26
Answer: D

This question tests the applicability of the attorney-client privilege. A communication made by a person or entity to obtain legal representation or advice is a privileged communication and the contents may not be disclosed to a third party or testified about at trial. However, the privilege is not available when an attorney's services were requested to assist in planning or committing a crime or a fraud. In this case, Defendant sought Attorney's legal advice for the purpose of transferring records to a Mexican safe-deposit box in contravention of a subpoena. Therefore, Defendant was seeking legal counsel for the purpose of committing a crime or fraud. As a result, regardless of whether Attorney knew or did not know about the Defendant's illegal purpose in seeking the legal advice, the privilege does not apply.

Question 27
Answer: C

This answer tests the prejudice of evidence weighted against its probative value. Evidence is inadmissible if its probative value is substantially outweighed by its prejudicial effect. In this case, both the evidence of the duplicate insurance and Denn's threats against his ex wife are highly probative of his guilt. Though they are prejudicial, this does not substantially outweigh the probative value of the evidence.

Question 28
Answer: A

This question tests the applicability of hearsay rules to a statement. Under the FRE, "Hearsay is a statement, other than one made by the declarant while testifying at the trial or hearing, offered in evidence to prove the truth of the matter asserted." In this case, the statement at issue—that Roberta Monk planned to write her next novel under the pen name of Roberta Rector—is not hearsay because it is not being offered to prove the truth of the matter asserted. While Peter is testifying as to a statement that was not his own, the statement was not being offered into evidence as proof that Roberta Monk actually did write a book under the name Roberta Rector.

Rather, the statement is being offered as circumstantial evidence that Roberta Monk was on the plane.

Choice (B) is the incorrect answer because it concerns an exception to the prohibition against hearsay evidence. In this case, because the statement at issue was not hearsay, the hearsay exceptions are irrelevant.

Choice (C) is incorrect because the length of time a declarant has been missing does not affect the hearsay analysis of his or her statements.

Finally, choice (D) is incorrect because it incorrectly assumes that the statement at issue was hearsay.

Question 29
Answer: C

This question tests the authentication requirements for various documents. Under FRE 902, certain kinds of writings are self-authenticating and do not require any extrinsic evidence of authenticity such as that provided by a supporting witness. These writings include: newspapers and periodicals; labels and marks that indicate the source of a product, ownership, and control; and all books, pamphlets, and publications that issue from a public authority. In this case, choice (A) is incorrect because newspapers and periodicals do not require a supporting witness to establish the authenticity of the writing. Choice (B) is incorrect because the label on the can identifies the source of the product and thus does not require a supporting witness to establish the authenticity. Choice (D) is incorrect because the pamphlet at issue is published by an official authority, the State Highway Department. Therefore, no supporting witness is required. Finally, choice (C) is correct because corporate memorandums are not included in the list of self-authenticating documents. Therefore, a memorandum purporting to be from the Defendant Company must be authenticated with extrinsic evidence such as that provided by a supporting witness.

Question 30
Answer: C

This question tests the application of the rule excluding relevant evidence. Under FRE 403, relevant evidence may be excluded if its probative value is substantially outweighed by either its prejudicial effect on the jury; the danger that it will confuse the issues or mislead the jury; or the risk that it will waste the time of the court, cause undue delay, or be merely cumulative of evidence already presented. In this case, the risk that the opposing party will be surprised by evidence and unprepared to meet it is not an appropriate consideration in determining whether relevant evidence should be excluded. Therefore, choice (C) is correct. In addition, choices (A), (B), and (D) are incorrect because the risks of jury confusion, unfair prejudice, and the extension of the trial by trivial evidence should all be considered in determining whether relevant evidence should be excluded.

Question 31
Answer: A

This question tests judicial notice of facts. Under FRE 201, a judge may take judicial notice of a fact that is common knowledge from sources which guarantee accuracy or are a matter of official record, without the need for the introduction of evidence establishing the fact. This determination may be made without request on a discretionary basis by the judge, or by request if the party seeking judicial notice offers sufficient information for the judge to take notice of the fact. Furthermore, FRE 201(g) requires judges to instruct juries that judicially noticed facts should be accepted as conclusive.

In this case, the fact that Capitan is the state's capital is common knowledge that could be garnered from accurate or official sources. As a result, the judge may take judicial notice of the fact on a discretionary basis without a request by Pixley. Therefore, choice (A) is correct.

Choice (B) is incorrect because if Pixley had requested the judge to take judicial notice of the fact, an authenticated copy of the statute that designates Capitan as the capital would not be required. Pixley would only need to provide information sufficient for the judge to make that determination, which could be an unauthenticated official publication, map, or other accurate or official sources. Choices (C) and (D) are incorrect because once the judge takes judicial notice of a fact, the jury must be instructed to accept that fact as conclusive.

Question 32
Answer: B

Under FRE 608(b), an attorney may impeach a witness on cross-examination through questions about the witness' prior bad acts that are probative of the witness' truthfulness. In this case, the question at issue is probative of Watts' truthfulness or credibility because filing a false affidavit is a highly dishonest activity. Therefore, it is admissible under FRE 608(b) and choice (B) is correct.

Question 33
Answer: D

This question tests the applicability of the Best Evidence Rule. The Best Evidence Rule generally requires an original version of a writing, recording, or photograph to be entered into evidence in order to establish the contents of such evidence. However, the terms writing and recording, are narrowly defined in FRE 1001 as "letters, words, or numbers . . . set down by handwriting, typewriting, printing, photostating, photographing, magnetic impulse, mechanical or electrical recording, or from other data or compilation. Furthermore, photographs are defined as including "still photographs, X-ray films, video tapes, and motion pictures." In this case, Poole wishes to testify about the appearance of a model animal robot. That robot model does not fit within the definitions of writing, recording, or photograph. Therefore, the Best Evidence Rule does not apply.

Question 34
Answer: B

Under FRE 104(a), the trial judge determines preliminary questions of fact that that bear on witness competency, testimonial privilege, and the admissibility of evidence, and the judge is only limited by the FREs with regard to testimonial privileges. In this case, it must be determined whether the West is qualified to be an expert witness. Because this is a preliminary question of fact, the decision should be made by the judge. In addition, because the judge is only limited by the FREs with regard to testimonial privilege, the hearsay does not apply.

Question 35
Answer: C

This question tests governing law on decisions over presumptions. Federal common law regarding presumptions governs in many federal actions. However, in civil actions grounded in diversity jurisdiction, the federal court should apply the presumption law of the state whose substantive law is applied. In this case, because the action is brought in diversity jurisdiction, the law of the state whose substantive law is applied should be used to determine the presumption.

Question 36
Answer: A

This question tests the application of hearsay rules to an animal's reactions. Under the FRE, "Hearsay is a statement, other than one made by the declarant while testifying at the trial or hearing, offered in evidence to prove the truth of the matter asserted." Under this definition, noises or reactions of a nonhuman may not be considered hearsay. In this case, Walker's testimony regarding the dog's reaction to Dahle's suitcase contains no hearsay because the declarant was a dog rather than a human being. Therefore, choices (B) and (C) are incorrect. In addition, choice (D) is incorrect because the issue of how reliable the dog's reaction was goes to credibility, and that is an issue for the jury to decide. Therefore, the evidence is not hearsay and is admissible.

Question 37
Answer: A

This questions tests the admissibility of evidence of specific instances of conduct. FRE 608(b) prohibits the use of extrinsic evidence of a witness' prior bad acts to prove a witness' character for truthfulness or untruthfulness. In this case, the evidence of Peterson's prior theft is not being offered to impeach his credibility by proving his character for truthfulness or untruthfulness. Rather, the evidence is being offered as substantive evidence that Peterson is a thief, to show that Dylan's letter to Peterson's employer was true and therefore not libelous.

Choices (B) and (C) are incorrect because they are both built on the incorrect conclusion that the evidence of Peterson's theft is being offered to impeach Peterson's credibility or prove his character for untruthfulness. Furthermore, choice (D) is incorrect because the evidence of

Peterson's prior theft is highly probative to the ultimate issue of whether Dylan's statement was, in fact, libelous. Generally, truth provides a defense to a defamation claim such as libel.

Question 38
Answer: A

This question tests the authentication of real evidence. All real evidence admitted at trial must be authenticated and identified pursuant to FRE 901 by showing that the evidence is relevant to a fact of consequence in the case and by producing sufficient evidence to show that the item is in fact what the proponent claims it to be. Part of this requirement is to prove a chain of custody establishing that the evidence was not tampered with or altered in any substantial way. However, courts interpreting FRE 901 often hold a complete chain of custody is not always necessary. In this case, there is sufficient evidence to identify the bag of white powder as being that which belonged to Dickinson. The police identified Dickinson with the bag and witnessed him drop it. Then, after taking Dickinson into custody and only five minutes later, the police returned to the scene where Dickinson dropped the bag and recovered it. Likely, from that point on, an easy chain of custody could established, assuming that the bag of white powder was properly stored as evidence. While neither the police nor Dickinson were in possession of the bag of white powder during pursuit, that was not likely enough time to break the chain of custody.

Furthermore, choice (B) is incorrect because establishing a chain of custody is merely one aspect of the identification of real evidence.

Question 39
Answer: C

The correct answer is choice (C). This question tests the determination of preliminary questions of fact that bear on the admissibility of evidence. Preliminary questions of fact that bear on the admissibility of evidence are decided by the court on a more likely than not evidentiary standard. In this case, each answer choice provides evidence that shows Defendant's call to be admissible as an admission by a party-opponent. However, while each answer choice tends to prove that Defendant made the phone call, only choice (C) does so with extrinsic evidence that is subject to verification.

Question 40
Answer: C

This question tests the admissibility of hearsay evidence to impeach hearsay declarants. Under FRE 806, a declarant of an admissible hearsay statement is subject to impeachment in the same manner as if the declarant were a witness testifying at that trial. In this case, the evidence, introduced by Poe, that Ellis made a statement that Davies ran the red light is admissible hearsay under the excited utterance exception to the general prohibition against hearsay evidence. Therefore, Ellis may be impeached in the same manner as any other witness that was testifying at the trial.

Hearsay evidence that is offered to impeach a witness is being used to show discord between the witness' original testimony and the hearsay evidence, rather than for the purposes of proving the truth of the underlying hearsay statement. In this case, Witt's testimony contains a statement by Ellis. Therefore, to the extent that this statement is being used to prove the truth of the matter asserted—that Davies actually went through a yellow rather than red light—the statement is hearsay and must fall within a hearsay exemption or exception. However, if the statement is not being offered to prove that the light was yellow, but to impeach Ellis by showing that his statement that the light was red was not credible, then the statement is not hearsay and is admissible.

Question 41
Answer: A

This question tests the admissibility of learned treatises. The Federal Rules of Evidence recognize an exception to the hearsay rule for scholarly or learned materials that are relied upon by an expert witness in direct examination or are called to the attention of the expert witness upon cross-examination. However, such statements, contained in published treatises, periodicals, or pamphlets on a subject of history, medicine, or other science or art, must be made by a reliable authority as established by the testimony or admission of the witness or by other expert testimony or by judicial notice. If deemed reliable, the statements may be read into evidence but may not be received as exhibits. The evidence will be considered as both substantive evidence (i.e., for proof of its content in the action) and for impeachment purposes.

In this case, Dr. Will established the reliability of the text through his own testimony. In addition, he has explained how the text has informed his own opinion on the proper standard of care. Moreover, the text is being offered as substantive evidence of the proper standard of care. Therefore, because Dr. Will has testified as to the reliability of the text and has read it into evidence, it is admissible as both a basis for his opinion and as substantive evidence of the proper standard of care.

Question 42
Answer: A

This case tests the applicability of attorney-client privilege. A communication made by a person or an entity to an attorney for the purpose of obtaining legal representation or advice, is confidential, and client or prospective client who holds the privilege may prevent the attorney from disclosing the contents of the confidential communication to any third party. While this privilege continues even after the client or prospective client has died, it ceases to exist if the client waives the privilege by disclosing the contents of the confidential communication to a third party, or if the client or the attorney breaches a duty that one owes to the other.

In this case, the audiotape would no longer be privileged and would be subject to subpoena if Denby had played the audiotape for his father to get his reactions. Such action would constitute a waiver of the privilege because Denby's father, though close family, is a third party to the confidential communication. Therefore, choice (A) is correct.

Furthermore, choice (B) is incorrect because a client or prospective client's criminal behavior does not generally affect the attorney-client privilege. However, one exception does exist. If a party seeks the legal advice of an attorney for the purpose of planning or committing a crime or fraud, then the privilege is inapplicable.

Choice (C) is incorrect because giving a deposition neither waives any privilege nor breaches a duty between attorney and client.

Finally, choice (D) is incorrect because the death of a client or prospective does not end the privilege with regard to confidential communications between attorney and client.

Question 43
Answer: D

This question tests the admissibility of hearsay evidence and specifically, the problem of multiple levels of hearsay.

If an out–of-court statement that a party proffers as evidence includes an additional out-of-court statement, and both of the statements are admitted to prove their truth, a trial judge must separately analyze both levels of potential hearsay to determine their admissibility under the hearsay rule. If either of the statements constitutes hearsay and does not qualify under a hearsay rule exception, that combination of statements is inadmissible. A double hearsay situation arises if one party offers another party's oral out-of-court declaration into evidence.

In this case, the two separate statements include (1) the statement from Young to Dalton and (2) the statement from Young to Witt.

The statement that Young told Witt, that Young "told the manager he had better fix that torn carpet," asserts two things–(1) that the carpet was torn and therefore defective, and (2) that the manager had been told of the defect and therefore had notice of the defect. For the purposes set forth in choices (A) and (C), Young's statement is hearsay because it is being offered to prove its truth (that the carpet was defective).

That leaves choices (B) and (D). Young's statement to Dalton may be admissible to show notice of the defect, as set forth in choice (B). However, evidence of the statement may not be recounted by Witt. This is because the separate statement, from Young to Witt, is also hearsay not within any exception. As such, Witt's testimony about Young's statement is inadmissible. Note that Young may be permitted to testify directly as to the statement for the purpose of demonstrating notice of the defect.

Question 44
Answer: A

This question tests the admissibility of hearsay evidence. Former testimony of a presently unavailable declarant is admissible if it was made under oath in a former trial, hearing, proceeding, or deposition that concerned the same topic as the present trial, hearing, proceeding, or deposition and in which the party-opponent against whom the evidence was presented had an opportunity and similar motive to develop the former testimony by direct, redirect, or cross-examination.

In this case, Defendant's wife's former testimony at a bankruptcy proceeding was assumedly made under oath because it was part of a court proceeding. In addition, the bankruptcy proceeding involved similar issues as the present fraud trial. Furthermore, even though the wife was not seriously impeached on cross-examination, the opportunity to do so, or at least develop her testimony in some way, was there. Finally, the wife is deceased and is therefore unavailable at the present trial. As a result, the testimony given by Defendant's wife at the bankruptcy proceeding is admissible under the hearsay exception for former testimony.

As a final note, despite the existence of a spousal immunity, choice (D) is incorrect. Spousal immunity, sometimes referred to as spousal incompetency, allows one spouse to refuse to testify against the other spouse in a criminal case. However, it is the witness, not the spouse who is the party to the case, that holds the privilege. In this case, spousal immunity would only be relevant if the wife had refused to testify against her husband at trial.

Question 45
Answer: B

This question tests the admissibility of official documents. Under FRE 803(15), a statement is admissible hearsay if it is contained in a document that purports, establishes, or affects an interest in property if the statement made was relevant to the purpose of the document. In this case, the state motor vehicle registration listing Defendant as the owner clearly establishes or purports to establish Defendant's property interest in the car. In addition, as the evidence is used in choice (B), to show the Defendant's close connection with the car, it is admissible under this exception. Showing a close connection with a car is more than relevant to the purpose of motor vehicle registration, it is the purpose of motor vehicle registration. Therefore, choice (B) is correct.

Choice (A) is incorrect because the motor vehicle registration cannot be used as a statement against self-interest in this case. For a statement to admissible as a statement against self-interest, the declarant must be unavailable to testify. In this case, Defendant is the declarant. Therefore, because he is not unavailable, the registration may not be admitted as a statement against self-interest.

Question 46
Answer: A

This question tests the personal knowledge requirement. A witness must have personal knowledge of the subject matter to which he or she is testifying. In this case, Dint may testify as to the larger amounts of money he had given Post because he was personally aware of the amounts of money he was giving to Post. Furthermore, choice (C) is incorrect because the Best Evidence Rule only applies to testimony regarding the contents of a writing, recording, or photograph. In this case, Dint's testimony does not concern the contents of the ledger. Rather, Dint's testimony specifically describes his recollections and disputes the contents of the ledger.

Question 47
Answer: A

This question tests the role of the judge and the role of the jury in determining preliminary questions of fact. Under FRE 104, preliminary questions of fact are to be determined by the court rather than the jury. In addition, hearings on such preliminary matters are to be conducted outside the jury's presence when required by the interests of justice. In this case, Vetter's statement is only admissible as a dying declaration if Vetter believed his death was imminent at the time he implicated Dix. Therefore, the determination should be made by the judge. Furthermore, Vetter's statement would be so probative of Dix's guilt that the jury should not hear the evidence at all until the judge decides whether Vetter believed his death was imminent. Therefore, the hearing regarding the Vetter's belief that his death was imminent should be made with the jury not present. Finally, because nothing in the Federal Rules of Evidence limit the participation in hearings on preliminary questions of fact to only one party, the correct answer is choice (A).

Question 48
Answer: D

This question tests the applicability of exclusionary rules for evidence that causes undue prejudice. When the prejudicial effect of evidence outweighs its probative value, the evidence is inadmissible. In this case, a judgment for another plaintiff against Davis Co. in another case involving substantially similar facts is not admissible because the prejudice caused by the evidence substantially outweighs the probative value of the evidence.

In contrast, the fact that the defective part bears Davis Co.'s insignia or trademark, testimony that the part was purchased from a parts house to which Davis Co. regularly sold parts, and comparison between the part itself and a concededly genuine part manufactured by Davis Co. are highly probative forms of evidence in determining whether the Davis Co. actually manufactured the part. In addition, none of those pieces of evidence are highly prejudicial to the Davis Co. Therefore, choices (A), (B), and (C) are incorrect.

Question 49
Answer: C

This question tests the applicability of testimonial privileges. Limited privileges exist between married spouses, attorney and client, patients and physicians, and patients and psychotherapists that allow some testimony to be excluded at trial. However, the privilege applicable to communications between patients and physicians and patients and psychotherapists does not extend to nurses and other medical personnel. In addition, some jurisdictions further restrict the privilege by making it inapplicable in criminal trials. In this case, the communication at issue was between Dean and a nurse, rather than a physician or psychotherapist. Therefore, that privilege does not apply. Furthermore, Dean and the nurse were neither spouses nor in an attorney-client relationship. Therefore, no privilege applies in this case and the nurse may testify.

Question 50
Answer: A

This question tests the use of impeachment evidence. Evidence of bias or interest is allowed for the purposes of impeachment, and evidence that a witness in a criminal case has been granted leniency, immunity, is awaiting sentence, or is under indictment all show a witness' self-interest in testifying. In this case, Wagner has been promised that the charges against him will be dropped if he testifies against Damson. That evidence shows that Wagner had bias or self-interest in testifying at Damson's trial. Therefore, the evidence about the prosecutor's comment is admissible as a proper impeachment of Wagner.

Question 51
Answer: D

This question tests the admissibility of evidence presented by jurors as witnesses. The Federal Rules of Evidence and the common law generally prohibit jurors from testifying, either by affidavit or direct testimony, about statements or matters they considered in their deliberations, unless the testimony involves an improper outside influence or exposure to extraneous prejudicial information. In this case, the testimony that Wall learned from a court clerk that Doxie had been accused of fraud in several recent lawsuits is certainly extraneous prejudicial information. The information would be inadmissible at trial on the grounds that its prejudicial effect substantially outweighs is probative value, and because the information is coming from an outside source, the court clerk, rather than evidence presented at trial. Therefore, the motion would likely only be granted upon that testimony by Wall, because that is the only admissible testimony included among the answer choices.

Question 52
Answer: B

This question tests the admissibility of evidence of prior wrongful conduct in criminal proceedings. While evidence of prior wrongful conduct may not be presented in a criminal proceeding as evidence of character or that the defendant had a propensity or predisposition to commit a charged offense, the evidence may be admissible if it possesses independent relevance, such as by proving motive, intent, absence of mistake, identity, common plan or scheme, knowledge, opportunity, or preparation. In this case, Wallman's and Witler's testimony concerns prior wrongful conduct because it identifies Deben as having fraudulently purchased prescription drugs on the same day and in a similar manner as the purchase at Smith's Drugstore, for which Deben is on trial. This testimony would therefore be inadmissible to prove Deben's character or propensity or predisposition to fraudulently purchase prescription drugs. However, it is admissible to identify Deben as the man who presented the prescription at Smith's Drugstore.

Question 53

Answer: A

This question tests the admissibility of hearsay evidence. Under FRE 803(1), a declarant's sudden and extemporaneous statement that describes an event when it occurs, or soon afterwards, is admissible as an exception to the general prohibition against hearsay. In this case, May Wong's statement containing her recital of the license plate number described a crime and the subsequent getaway as it occurred. Thus, the statement fits squarely within the present sense impression hearsay exception and is therefore admissible.

Question 54
Answer: C

Evidence of bias or interest is allowed for the purposes of impeachment, and shared membership in an organization is allowed to show bias in favor of a party. In this case, the question is being asked for the purpose of showing that Winters' testimony is biased in favor of Day City Community Church because she is a member of that organization. Therefore it is admissible for the purposes of impeaching her.

Choices (A), (B), and (D) are each incorrect because those answers misconstrue the purpose for which the question is being asked. The question, though necessarily touching upon Winters' religion, is not being asked for the purpose of prying into her religious beliefs in order that the jury may draw an inference as to her credibility based on those beliefs.

Question 55
Answer: C

This question tests the applicability of spousal immunity. Spousal immunity, sometimes referred to as spousal incompetency, allows one spouse to refuse to testify against the other spouse in a criminal case. However, in federal courts, it is the witness, not the spouse who is the party to the case, that holds the privilege. In this case, Mrs. Denby holds the spousal immunity privilege because she is being called as the witness. Therefore, she has the privilege of refusing to testifying against her husband if she so desires.

In addition, the spousal immunity privilege does not prevent a spouse from being called as a witness, it merely allows them to refuse to testify once they raise the privilege. Therefore, choice (A) is incorrect. In addition, choice (A) is also incorrect because the spousal immunity privilege only applies to the spouse who is testifying, not to the spouse who is a party to the proceeding. Thus, Mr. Denby may not object to his wife's testimony on the grounds of spousal immunity. Therefore, choice (B) is also an incorrect answer because it incorrectly assumes that Mr. Denby may object to his wife's testimony on the grounds of spousal immunity.

Question 56
Answer: B

This question tests the admissibility of hearsay evidence. Under FRE 801(d)(2), a party-opponent's out-of-court statement is not considered to be hearsay and may be admitted as evidence if the statement is offered by another party against the party-opponent and the party-opponent's position is inconsistent with the out-of-court statement. In this case, Daniel's letter does not constitute an explicit admission that he has evaded taxes; however, the admission is implicit in the letter. Therefore, the letter is admissible non-hearsay because it is an admission of a party-opponent.

Furthermore, choice (A) is an incorrect answer because there is no statement of present intention or plan exception to the hearsay rule.

In addition, choice (C) is an incorrect answer. While communications made in an effort to reach a compromise or settle a claim are inadmissible under FRE 408, that rule only extends to civil actions, not criminal matters such as Daniel's trial for tax evasion. Furthermore, while some statements made during the course of plea discussions are inadmissible in civil and criminal cases under FRE 410, Daniel's letter to the IRS does not constitute a bona fide plea negotiation because it was anonymous and because it was a blind letter not addressed to any official who could negotiate a plea arrangement on the government's behalf.

Finally, choice (D) is an incorrect answer because, while the letter is somewhat prejudicial, its probative value is incredibly great.

Question 57
Answer: C

The correct answer is choice (C). This question tests the admissibility of evidence of prior wrongful conduct in criminal proceedings. Evidence of prior wrongful conduct may not be presented in a criminal proceeding as evidence of character used to prove that the defendant acted in conformity with that character trait or as evidence that the defendant had a propensity or predisposition to commit a charged offense. In this case, Willy's testimony is being used to show that Doppler has a propensity to shoot people without provocation and then claim self-defense, and that, therefore, he shot Vezy without provocation and is now dishonestly claiming self-defense. Therefore, Willy's testimony is impermissible character evidence. Choice (D) is incorrect because Willy's testimony may be factually relevant, but not legally relevant.

Question 58
Answer: A

This question tests the admissibility of hearsay evidence. A presently unavailable declarant's statement is admissible if it was made contrary to a declarant's pecuniary, penal, or proprietary interests at the time when made by the declarant. In this case, Ronald's statement to his doctor that the injuries he sustained in the automobile collision were his own fault was against his own pecuniary interest at the time it was made, because it was an admission that he could both not likely recover against Driver, and could possibly be sued by Driver for causing the collision.

Choice (B) is an incorrect answer because a statement is only admissible as a dying declaration if the declarant made the statement under a belief that his or her death was imminent. In this case, though Ronald did die one day after making the statement, there is nothing to suggest that he believed he was going to die very shortly after the statement was made. Choice (C) is an incorrect answer because Ronald's statement is not a reflection of his state of mind, it is merely a statement of his responsibility for the collision. Finally, choice (D) is an incorrect answer because the statement is only admissible as an excited utterance if it was a spontaneous and unprompted statement, which is made under the stress of an exciting or startling event and relates to that event. In this case, Ronald's statement regarding his responsibility for the collision was not made under the stress of the collision itself. Rather, it was made later, while he was receiving medical treatment following the collision.

Question 59
Answer: A

This question tests the admissibility of hearsay evidence. A declarant's spontaneous and impromptu statement regarding a then existing (present but not past) mental, emotional, or physical condition is admissible as a statement of mental, physical, or emotional condition. This includes a declarant's statement of a current state of mind or intent to do something in the near future. In this case, Dover's letter to his sister stating that he would see her in Utah on March 5 states his intent to travel to Utah. In addition, it was made only one week in advance of the intended trip. Therefore, the statement is admissible because it falls within the state of mind exception to the hearsay rule.

Question 60
Answer: B

This questions tests the application of hearsay exceptions to multiple hearsay evidence. Statements made by anyone other than the declarant while testifying at trial that are offered into evidence to prove the truth of the matter asserted are hearsay. In this case, Plaintiff Plaza Hotel is attempting to offer memoranda into evidence to prove that telephone callers, cab drivers, customers, and others regularly confused the two hotel names. The memoranda constitute hearsay because the declarants are the hotel employees who created each memorandum. However, the employees are not testifying at trial as to their observations, rather the memoranda themselves are being entered into evidence. Therefore, the memoranda must fit within one of the exemptions or exceptions to the hearsay rule.

Records of regularly conducted business activity are admissible as an exception to the hearsay rule when the business records were made and maintained in the normal course of regularly conducted business activity by a person possessing personal knowledge of that occurrence, and made contemporaneously or around the time when an act, condition, or event that the records concern occurred. In this case, each memorandum was created by a hotel employee at the end of his or her work day. Therefore, it is likely that the memoranda would be found to have been made, if not contemporaneously with the employee's observation of another's confusion, at least around the time of the confusion. In addition, because the memoranda were made by each employee in reaction to witnessing the confusion of another, the personal knowledge requirement is likely satisfied.

However, the memoranda are nonetheless inadmissible. Because the memoranda were made in preparation of litigation, they would not likely be held to have been made in the course of regularly conducted business. Furthermore, this conclusion is bolstered by the requirement that regularly kept records of business exhibit a requisite level of trustworthiness to be admissible under the hearsay exception. Memoranda made in the course of litigation preparation are made for self-serving purposes and therefore do not possess the requisite trustworthiness that regularly kept records of business possess.

In addition, it should be noted that this memoranda evidence constitutes hearsay within hearsay. First, there are the statements of the telephone callers, cab drivers, customers, and others that express confusion over the hotel names. These statements are hearsay that do not fall within any exceptions. In addition, the statements of the hotel employees recording those interactions in each memorandum constitute hearsay as well. Therefore, for this statement to be admissible, each hearsay statement must be admissible either as non-hearsay or through an exception to the general prohibition against hearsay.

Question 61
Answer: B

This question tests the scope of examination and the standard of relevancy applied to it. Determinations regarding the admissibility of evidence are within the discretion of the trial judge and will not be reversed unless the decision contributes to a unfair trial. In this case, while evidence relating to the frequency of quarreling in Don's marriage may not be relevant, the trial judge may nonetheless allow Don to rebut Peter's testimony because allowing Don to rebut evidence that has already been admitted is not likely to contribute to a unfair trial.

Question 62
Answer: D

This question tests the assertion of the physician/psychotherapist-patient privilege. A patient holds the privilege over confidential communications regarding medical treatment that occur between a patient and a physician or psychotherapist and may assert that privilege to prevent a physician or psychotherapist from divulging confidential information that is obtained in the course of providing medical treatment to the patient. In addition, the physician or psychotherapist also may assert the privilege on behalf of the patient.

In this case, Michael Zadock holds the privilege with regards to communication at issue. Therefore, Zadock, or an attorney representing him, would be the best person to assert that privilege. Therefore, the correct answer is choice (D).

In contrast, choice (A) is an incorrect answer. Dr. Webb may assert the privilege on behalf of Zadock; therefore, the first several words of choice (A) are technically correct. However, that choice goes on to describe the doctor-patient privilege as belonging to Dr. Webb. This is incorrect. Rather than the doctor holding a privilege that prevents a patient from disclosing information, the doctor-patient privilege is held by the patient and prevents the doctor from disclosing confidential information.

Question 63
Answer: C

This question tests the use of leading questions. Courts generally allow leading questions to be asked during cross-examination but not direct examination. However, leading questions are allowed during direct examination when (1) the witness is having difficulty answering questions either because they are a young child, an individual with a severe speech impediment, mentally disabled, or a hostile witness; or (2) for the purposes of obtaining preliminary information such as the person's name and address. Here, choice (C) is the correct answer because leading questions are not generally allowed during a direct examination and a disinterested witness does not fall within one of the exceptions discussed above.

In contrast, choice (A) is an incorrect answer because leading questions are allowed on cross-examination regardless of whether the witness is an expert or a lay witness. Furthermore, choice (B) is incorrect because young children may often be asked leading questions on direct examination because they have difficulty answering other forms of questions. Furthermore, choice (D) is incorrect because leading questions may be asked on direct examination if they are only related to preliminary matters such as the name or occupation of the witness.

Question 64
Answer: C

This question tests the role of the jury in determining issues of fact. Questions of fact, such as whether a party breached a duty owed to another party, are generally determined by the jury. In this case, it is the role of the jury to determine whether Abel and Baker breached the standard of care owed to Client. While evidence presented through the testimony of either local or in-state legal experts regarding whether a breach did in fact occur may be informative to the jury in its fact-finding role, it is not necessary. Therefore, choices (A) and (B) are incorrect answers. Furthermore, choice (D) is an incorrect answer because, aside from preliminary questions of fact regarding the admissibility of evidence, the judge may only determine questions of law. The issue of whether Abel and Baker breached the standard of care owed to Client is a questions of fact outside of that scope.

Question 65
Answer: C

This question tests the admissibility of lay opinion testimony. A lay witness may present opinion testimony that will assist in obtaining a clear understanding of the witness's testimony and that is rationally based on the witness' perception. Accordingly, a lay witness may generally testify regarding his or her opinion about intoxication, sanity, weight, speed, and height. In this case, Wood's testimony is lay opinion testimony of his belief, based on his perception on the night of the accident, that Chase was intoxicated. Therefore, this is permissible lay opinion testimony.

In addition, the statement is admissible even though it is hearsay because it falls under the present sense impression exception to hearsay. A sudden and extemporaneous statement that describes an event when it occurs, or soon afterwards, is admissible. In this case, Wood's statement regarding Chase's intoxication described his observation of Chase as he observed him. Therefore, choice (C) is the correct answer.

In contrast, choice (D) is an incorrect answer because witnesses need not establish their expertise to testify in regards to a subject's intoxication.

Furthermore, choice (A) is an incorrect answer, because an excited utterance must relate to and be made in reaction to an unexpected event or condition and be made under the stress of that event. In this case, witnessing a bar patron's intoxication is not an unexpected event and is not an event that puts most people under a great deal of stress. Therefore, Wood's statement was not an excited utterance.

Finally, choice (B) is incorrect because prior consistent statements may only be admissible if brought in to rebut an allegation by a party-opponent that the witness' statement was a recent fabrication or that there was some improper motive or influence over the testimony. In this case, Wood was not alleged by Duke's Bar to have made up his story or to have been influenced or motivated improperly.

Question 66
Answer: B

This question tests the admissibility of prior inconsistent statements. A witness's own prior inconsistent statements may be admissible at trial. If the statement was not made under oath, it may only be used for impeachment purposes. However, if the statement was made under oath in a hearing, trial, or deposition and the witness was subject to cross-examination, then it is also admissible as substantive evidence of the truth of the matter it asserted. In this case, Chase's prior statement was made under oath during a deposition during which he was assumedly subject to cross-examination. Therefore, the statement is admissible both as substantive evidence that Chase was sober and as impeachment evidence against the credibility of Chase's testimony at trial.

Furthermore, under the historical common law, the statement would have been inadmissible because a party could not impeach its own witness. Under this rubric, choice (C) would have been a correct answer. However, under modern law, a party may impeach its own witness. Therefore, choice (C) is incorrect in the present day.

Question 67
Answer: D

This question tests the admissibility of evidence of subsequent remedial measures. Under FRE 407, evidence of subsequent remedial measures is inadmissible to prove the fault or negligence of a defendant. However, such evidence may be used (1) to prove that a defendant owned or controlled something that harmed a plaintiff, (2) to prove the feasibility of precautionary measures if a defendant controverts them, or (3) to impeach the defendant.

In this case, choice (A) is an incorrect answer because using the evidence to show that Duke's Bar was negligent is facially inadmissible.

In addition, choice (B) is incorrect because using the evidence to show the need for taking precautionary measures implies that until taking those precautionary measures, Duke's Bar was negligent.

Furthermore, choice (C) is incorrect because the actions of a manager at Duke's Bar, acting within the scope and purview of his employment, may be attributed to the employer, Duke's Bar, under an agency theory.

Finally, choice (D) is the correct answer because it reflects the policy choices at play in restricting the use of evidence of subsequent remedial measures. If parties are aware that evidence of remedial measures, taken to ensure the safety of others, may be used against them in litigation to prove fault or negligence, then people will be less likely to take subsequent remedial measures during the pendency of litigation.

Question 68
Answer: A

This question tests the admissibility of hearsay evidence. A statement made by a party-opponent that is inconsistent with that party's position at trial and offered against that party is admissible as non-hearsay evidence. In this case, the statement of the owner of Duke's Bar that Chase was drunk the night of the accident is admissible because it was a statement attributable to a party-opponent. Here, the owner had the authority to act for Duke's Bar. In addition, the statement was inconsistent with Duke's Bar's position that it did not negligently over-serve Chase. And, finally, it is being offered by Penn against Duke's Bar.

Choice (B) is an incorrect answer for two reasons. Under FRE 408, any admissions of fact that a first party makes to a second party during their settlement negotiations are not admissible evidence at a trial. In this case, the owner's offer to pay Penn's medical bills was not made as part of a bona-fide settlement negotiations. Rather, the statement does not qualify as an offer of compromise because it was made with no strings attached. Therefore, even if Penn allows the Duke's Bar owner to pay his medical bills, he may still sue Duke's Bar. Furthermore, if the conversation were part of a settlement negotiation and the rule on offers to compromise applied, then the evidence would be inadmissible under that rule.

Choice (D) is also an incorrect answer. An offer to pay another's medical expenses may not be used as evidence to prove the fault or negligence of the offeror. However, other statements made while offering to pay another's medical expenses are admissible. In this case, while the owner's statement that he would pay Penn's hospital bills is inadmissible, the other statements, including the statement that Chase was drunk when he left the bar, would be admissible.

Question 69
Answer: A

This question deals with the proper methods of voice identification. Under FRE 901(b)(5), a person's voice, regardless of the media on which it is conveyed, may be identified by the opinion of a lay person that is "based upon hearing the voice at any time under circumstances connecting it with the alleged speaker." In addition, all witnesses must have personal knowledge of the subject matter to which they are testifying. In this case, only one answer choice is given in which the lay witness has had no opportunity to hear Daly's voice, choice (A). In that choice, the witness has based her lay opinion on the word of Daly's brother. As a result, she has does not have personal knowledge of Daly's voice and may not give opinion testimony on whether the voice on the tape belongs to Daly. Therefore, choice (A) is the correct answer.

Choices (B), (C), and (D) are each incorrect answers because in each of those fact situations the lay witness has personal knowledge of Daly's voice and uses that knowledge to form an opinion as to whether the voice on the tape recording belongs to Daly. Note that the time and circumstances of becoming acquainted with a person's voice, whether through years of friendship or for trial preparation, are irrelevant to the sufficiency of testimony to authenticate a voice.

Question 70
Answer: B

This question tests the proper use of impeachment evidence. Evidence of a witness' bias or interest may be presented on cross-examination to impeach the credibility of a witness' direct testimony. In this case, the question in choice (A) asks if Louis is a close friend of the plaintiff. This question is proper because it seeks to reveal that Louis' direct testimony is not credible because he is biased in favor of Potts. Therefore, choice (A) is an incorrect answer.

Under FRE 608(a), the credibility of a witness may be attacked by evidence in the form of both opinion and reputation referring to that witness's character for truthfulness or untruthfulness. In this case, the question in choice (B) is made in regards to reputation evidence of Louis' character. However, Louis' reputation as an alcoholic does not reflect on his character for truthfulness or untruthfulness. Specifically, rather than being used to discredit Louis' direct testimony by showing that Louis is dishonest, the question merely seeks to injure Louis' reputation independently of his character for truthfulness or untruthfulness. Therefore, the question in choice (B) is improper. Thus, that is the correct answer.

Under FRE 608(b), a witness may be questioned on cross-examination regarding the prior bad acts of a witness, so long as those prior bad acts are probative of truthfulness only. In this case, failing to report all income on a tax return is probative of truthfulness. Therefore, the question listed in choice (C) is improper. Thus, that choice is an incorrect answer.

Under FRE 609(a)(2), any witness is subject to impeachment by evidence that the witness was convicted of a misdemeanor or felony offense that involved an element of "dishonesty or false statement." In this case, Louis' conviction for obtaining money under false pretenses involves dishonesty or a false statement. Therefore, the question listed in choice (D) is improper. Thus, that choice is an incorrect answer.

Question 71
Answer: D

This question tests the applicability of the Fifth Amendment privilege against self-incrimination. A trial judge should allow a witness to exercise his or her Fifth Amendment privilege to remain silent on the stand if there is a reasonable possibility that the risk of self-incrimination exists. A witness is not required to show that the witness' testimony will incriminate himself or herself. Therefore, choice (D) is the correct answer because the judge only needs to find that some reasonable possibility exists that Bystander will incriminate herself.

Question 72
Answer: C

This question tests the admissibility of character evidence. Under FRE 404(b), evidence of character is inadmissible to show that because a defendant is has a criminal character that he is more likely to commit crimes. However, evidence of character may be presented to prove motive, opportunity, intent, preparation, plan, knowledge, identity, or absence of mistake or accident, if the probative value of such evidence is not substantially outweighed by the danger of unfair prejudice.

In this case, the evidence that Miller had heroin and a hypodermic needle, implying that he is a drug addict, is of very low probative value in determining whether he had the motive, opportunity, intent, preparation, plan, knowledge, identity, or absence of mistake or accident in the robbery of the First Bank of City. Conversely, the evidence has a highly prejudicial effect on Miller. Therefore, the evidence should be excluded, and as a result, choice (C) is the correct answer.

Choice (A) is incorrect. Courts have consistently held that while evidence of possession of narcotics may be presented as evidence of the direct result of a crime, it may not be presented to show that the crime was motivated by the need for funds to purchase narcotics. Therefore, this evidence may not be admitted to show motive. Thus, choice (A) is an incorrect answer.

Furthermore, choice (B) is a incorrect answer because character evidence may not be presented to prove a defendant's propensity to commit crimes.

Finally, choice (D) is incorrect because character evidence may be offered to prove motive, opportunity, intent, preparation, plan, knowledge, identity, or absence of mistake or accident, rather than simply to rebut evidence of good character presented by a defendant.

Question 73
Answer: D

This question tests the applicability of hearsay exceptions. A statement made by a party-opponent that is inconsistent with that party's position at trial and offered against that party is admissible as non-hearsay evidence. In addition, a party's failure to respond to a statement or an act (in the nature of a provocative accusation or event) may constitute an admission if: (1) the party-opponent against whom such evidence is proffered heard, comprehended, and had the ability to respond to the statement; and (2) a reasonable person in a party-opponent's position would have responded by refuting that statement or act.

In this case, Miller's silence does not constitute an admission. While it appears that Miller heard, comprehended, and had the ability to respond to the bartender's statement, there is no reason why he, or any reasonable person, would have responded to it. The bartender's statement is best interpreted as a light-hearted joke aimed at establishing a rapport with a would-be patron. Not only would most reasonable people decide not to refute the "allegation," an immediate response refuting the statement would have been awkward, out of place, and not in-keeping with the spirit of the remark. Therefore, the statement is inadmissible because Miller had no reason to respond to the bartender's statement.

Question 74
Answer: C

This question tests the admissibility of hearsay evidence. Statements made by someone other than the witness while testifying at trial that are used to prove the truth of the matter asserted are not admissible unless they fall within one of the non-hearsay exemptions or one the exceptions to the hearsay rule. In this case, the sketch of a person resembling Miller constitutes hearsay because (1) the sketch is a statement of what the teller believed the robber looked like and (2) it is being used at trial to prove that the robber looked like Miller. Therefore, the sketch is inadmissible unless it falls within an exemption or an exception to the hearsay rule. Furthermore, because none of the hearsay exceptions or other choices listed in this question apply, choice (C) is the correct answer.

Choice (A) is an incorrect answer because a declarant's prior identification of a party, such as through the sketch in this case, is only admissible when the declarant is presently testifying. Because the teller died prior to the trial, he cannot testify. Therefore, the sketch is not admissible as a prior identification.

Choice (B) is an incorrect answer because past recollections recorded may only be admissible when the witness who recorded the recollection is testifying at trial, does not recollect the information, and is not refreshed by presentation of the document. Once again, because the teller died and will not testify at trial, the sketch is not admissible under this hearsay exception.

Choice (D) is incorrect because there is no opinion exception to hearsay.

Question 75
Answer: C

This case tests the admissibility of hearsay evidence. Statements made by someone other than the witness while testifying at trial that are used to prove the truth of the matter asserted are not admissible unless they fall within one of the non-hearsay exemptions or one the exceptions to the hearsay rule. In this case, Miller's statement to the police was not made while testifying at trial. Furthermore, the statement is being used to show that he had not been to the bank he is accused of robbing. Therefore, the statement is being offered to prove the truth of the matter asserted. As a result, the statement is inadmissible unless it falls within a hearsay exception. Furthermore, because none of the hearsay exceptions or choices listed in this question apply, choice (C) is the correct answer.

Of the four possible answers, only one, choice (B), deals with an exception to hearsay. Therefore, unless that exception is applicable, choice (C) must be the correct answer. Prior consistent statements are only admissible when they are offered to rebut an allegation of a "recent fabrication or improper influence or motive" in present testimony. In this case, there has been no such allegation. Therefore, this hearsay exception is inapplicable. As a result, Miller's statement to police is inadmissible because it is hearsay not within any exception.

Question 76
Answer: A

This question tests the admissibility of evidence of a prior conviction. Evidence of a prior conviction may be used to impeach the credibility of a witness' direct testimony if it was a crime involving dishonesty or a false statement. In this case, Miller's prior conviction of tax fraud involved dishonesty and false statements. Therefore, the prosecutor may question Miller about it on cross-examination to show that Miller is inclined to lie because that impeaches the credibility of his direct testimony. Choice (B) is an incorrect answer because evidence of prior crimes may not be presented to prove a defendant's propensity to commit crimes.

Question 77
Answer: B

This question tests the authentication of documents. Under FRE 901, the authenticity of a document may be established through circumstantial evidence such as testimony that a letter being offered into evidence appears to be a reply letter coming from the addressee of a prior letter. In this case, the testimony of Investigator is being sought for the purpose of establishing that the letter, allegedly written by Denucci, was a reply letter to a prior letter Investigator had written to Denucci.

Furthermore, Investigator may testify as to contents of the letter despite the Best Evidence Rule's requirement of the original. Under FRE 1004, an original document is not required in order to establish its contents when the party against whom it would have been proffered has possession of the document and failed to produce it despite receiving adequate notice that it was needed at the hearing. In this case, the defendant, Denucci, apparently has possession of a prior letter written by Investigator, and Peri's attorney arguably seeks Investigator's testimony against Denucci to establish that Denucci wrote the libelous reply letter. Therefore, Investigator's testimony is admissible regardless whether the prior letter is produced or a showing of its unavailability is made.

Question 78
Answer: D

This question tests the authentication of documents. FRE 1002 requires that an original version of a writing, recording, or photograph be produced in order to establish the contents of such evidence through testimony. However, under FRE 1004, if such evidence is either destroyed or lost and its proponent did not lose or destroy the item due to bad faith misconduct, then the original does not need to be produced. In this case, Investigator may only testify to the contents of Denucci's letter if the judge finds that the original letter is unavailable and it was not lost or destroyed due to bad faith misconduct.

Question 79
Answer: B

Choice (B) is correct. While FRE 404 states that evidence of a person's character is generally inadmissible to show that the person "acted in conformity therewith on a particular occasion," a criminal defendant may present evidence of his good character to prove his or her good character and innocence. In this case, Wilma's testimony is admissible because it is being presented by Drew, a criminal defendant, to prove his good character and innocence.

Furthermore, character evidence, when allowed, may be presented in the form of opinion or reputation evidence. In this case, Wilma is testifying as to Drew's reputation in his community. Therefore, the testimony is a proper mode of proving character in a situation in which character evidence may be admitted.

Question 80
Answer: A

This question tests the admissibility of hearsay evidence. A declarant's statement of a current state of mind or intent to do something in the near future is admissible as an exception to the general prohibition against hearsay evidence. In this case, William is testifying that Drew said he was going to leave that day to visit relatives in a different state. That statement by the declarant, Drew, evinces an intent to travel out of state in the very near future (that day). Therefore, the statement is admissible under the present mental state exception to the hearsay rule.

Furthermore, the statement is relevant because if Drew was traveling out of state on July 20, it is less likely that he committed the murder at issue on July 21.

Question 81
Answer: A

This question tests the admissibility of impeachment evidence. Evidence regarding a witness' bias or interest in a case is admissible to impeach the credibility of a witness' testimony. In this case, the prosecution is seeking to impeach the credibility of Wilson's alibi testimony by showing that the Wilson and Drew are cousins. This tends to show that Wilson is biased in favor of Drew and that, therefore, his testimony may not be as reliable as that of a disinterested witness. Therefore, the question is proper because it goes to bias.

Question 82
Answer: B

This question tests the admissibility of impeachment evidence. Evidence that is otherwise admissible may be excluded if its probative value is substantially outweighed by the risk of unfair prejudice. In this case, any answer to the prosecution's question would be of little probative value. The mere membership of a witness on a particular jury gives little or no insight into the credibility of that juror's testimony at a subsequent and unrelated trial. However, an affirmative response to the prosecutor's question would certainly have the potential of greatly and unfairly prejudicing the jury against Warren, because it may lead the jury to believe that Warren is biased in favor of Drew.

Furthermore, choice (A) is an incorrect answer. Impeachment evidence is within the scope of allowable cross-examination. While any answer to the prosecution's question would be of very little, if any, probative value, the question is being asked to impeach the credibility of Warren's testimony on direct examination. Therefore, the question is within the scope of cross-examination.

Choice (C) is incorrect because leading questions are proper on cross-examination.

Finally, choice (D) is incorrect because there is a presumption of witness competency and prior jury service has no bearing on that presumption.

Question 83
Answer: B

This question tests the scope and order of questioning. The scope of questioning on redirect examination is limited to questions regarding a witness's testimony on cross-examination that raised significant new issues, such as by impeachment evidence.

Question 84
Answer: A

This question tests the authentication of physical evidence. Evidence of distinctive characteristics in the evidence such as "[a]ppearance, contents, substance, [or] internal patterns" may be used to establish an identifying circumstance of a crime or action. FRE 901. In this case, Winthrop's testimony regarding the red paint on the barrel of Dennis' gun is admissible because the paint is a distinctive characteristic of the firearm. Because most guns do not have red paint on the barrel, the testimony of two parties that they were robbed by Dennis who wielded a gun with red paint on the barrel is admissible to establish an identifying characteristic of Alice's robbery.

Question 85
Answer: D

This question tests the admissibility of hearsay evidence. Statements made by someone other than the witness while testifying at trial that are used to prove the truth of the matter asserted are not admissible unless they fall within one of the non-hearsay exemptions or one the exceptions to the hearsay rule. In this case, Rider's counsel seeks to introduce an affidavit containing statements made by Dr. Bond other than while testifying at the trial. Therefore, the affidavit is only admissible if it falls within one of the hearsay exceptions. Because no hearsay exception applies to Dr. Bond's affidavit, the judge should rule the affidavit inadmissible, because it is hearsay, not within any exception. As a result, choice (D) is the correct answer.

A declarant's statements regarding past or present mental, emotional, or physical condition is admissible if it was made for the purpose of treatment or diagnosis by a physician. In this case, Rider's statements to Dr. Bond may be admissible as falling within a hearsay exception if Dr. Bond were testifying about the statements, but the affidavit must be admissible as well, which it is not. Therefore, choice (A) is an incorrect answer because it deals only with the admissibility of Rider's statements to Dr. Bond and not Dr. Bond's affidavit.

Furthermore, choice (B) is an incorrect answer. If a presently unavailable declarant testified under oath in a former trial, hearing, proceeding, or deposition, that testimony is admissible in a subsequent proceeding if it concerned the same topic as does the present trial, hearing, proceeding, or deposition; and the adverse party had an opportunity and similar motive to develop the former testimony by direct, redirect, or cross-examination. In this case, the evidence at issue is an affidavit by Dr. Bond obtained in preparation for trial. It does not fall within this hearsay exception because Transit Company had no opportunity to develop Dr. Bond's testimony through cross-examination.

Finally, choice (C) is an incorrect answer because Dr. Bond's affidavit regarding Rider's injuries is relevant to the issue of whether Rider did, in fact, sustain injuries during the accident.

Question 86
Answer: A

This question tests the admissibility of hearsay evidence. A party-opponent's out-of-court statement may be admitted as non-hearsay if the statement is offered by another party against the party-opponent, and the party-opponent's position is inconsistent with the out-of-court statement. In this case, Rider's statement, contained in Observer's testimony, is being offered against Rider. In addition, the statement—that Rider had recently suffered a recurrence of an old back injury—is inconsistent with Rider's position that Transit Company's negligence caused his injury. Therefore, Observer's testimony is admissible as an admission of a party-opponent.

Furthermore, choice (B) is incorrect because the hearsay contained in Observer's testimony does not qualify as a spontaneous declaration, usually referred to as an excited utterance. A declarant's spontaneous and unprompted statement, made under the stress of an exciting or startling event and relating to that event, is admissible as an exception to hearsay. In this case, Rider's statement to Observer was spontaneous and unprompted and likely made under the stress of the accident, which was a startling event. However, the statement does not relate to the accident. Rather, it is a statement regarding Rider's own health before, and independent of, the accident.

Finally, choice (C) is an incorrect answer because Dr. Bond's affidavit regarding Rider's injuries is relevant to the issue of whether Rider did, in fact, sustain injuries during the accident.

Question 87
Answer: B

This question tests the applicability of the attorney-client privilege. A communication that is made by a person or an entity to an attorney to obtain legal representation or advice, or in preparation for litigation, is confidential and therefore legally privileged from disclosure. In this case, Def Company's general manager, acting for Def Company, prepared a report of the accident for Def Company's attorney to prepare for trial. Therefore, the report is a privileged communication taking place between a client and its attorney for the purpose of litigation.

Choice (A) is an incorrect answer because, though the report could possibly also be considered a business report, it is first and foremost a privileged communication between attorney and client.

Furthermore, choice (C) is an incorrect answer, because the fact that a document may contain hearsay does not affect whether it should or should not be produced during discovery. In this case, while the report may be inadmissible hearsay at trial (though there are not enough facts to make such a determination), this question only asks whether the report must be produced to Pace. Therefore, hearsay is not an issue that warrants consideration at this stage.

Finally, choice (D) is an incorrect answer because the self-serving nature of a report does not affect its discoverability.

Question 88
Answer: D

This question tests the admissibility of character evidence. Under FRE 404(a), evidence of a person's character or character trait is generally inadmissible to show that the person "acted in conformity therewith on a particular occasion." In this case, White's testimony that Dan had a reputation in the community as being a reckless driver and was known as "dare-devil Dan" is evidence of Dan's character. Furthermore, using such evidence to show that that Dan was negligent is an improper use of character evidence because it seeks to show that Dan acted in conformity with his reputation as a reckless driver on a specific occasion, the time of his accident with Park.

However, evidence of character is admissible in several contexts. In criminal trials, evidence of a pertinent character of a criminal defendant may be presented by the defendant to prove his or her good character and innocence. Also, the prosecutor may present such evidence to rebut the defendant's evidence of good character and innocence or to rebut the defendant's evidence of a victim's bad character. In addition, a criminal defendant may present opinion or reputation evidence regarding an alleged victim's "pertinent trait of character" if that evidence is relevant to his or her defense, and the prosecution may offer evidence to rebut the same. Finally, in both civil and criminal cases, character evidence may be sued to impeach a witness in conformity with FREs 607-609. Therefore, choice (A) is an incorrect answer because character evidence may not be admitted as habit evidence.

Furthermore, choice (B) is incorrect because using White's testimony to prove that Dan was negligent at the time of this collision is inadmissible, as discussed above.

Finally, choice (C) is an incorrect answer. That choice correctly implies that had Dan presented evidence of his good character, the rules as to what character evidence Park may seek to enter would certainly change. However, White's testimony would nonetheless be inadmissible in this case because evidence of a defendant's good character is only admissible in the criminal context, and this is a civil case. Furthermore, opinion and reputation evidence of the character of a witness may be presented to impeach the credibility of a witness' testimony insofar as it refers to the witness' character for truthfulness or untruthfulness. In this case, White's testimony constitutes reputation evidence. However, it does not refer to Dan's reputation for truthfulness or untruthfulness. Therefore, regardless of whether Dan had testified or not, White's testimony is inadmissible.

Question 89
Answer: C

This question tests the admissibility of silence as a statement by a party-opponent. A party's failure to respond to a statement or an act (in the nature of a provocative accusation or event) may constitute an admission. However, an adoptive admission will not result if the party possesses a constitutional right to remain silent. In this case, Sam possessed a constitutional right to remain silent under the Fifth Amendment. Regardless of whether the police had finished reading Sam and Alex the Miranda warning, they each had the right to remain silent. Therefore, Sam had no duty to respond to Alex's accusation and an adoptive admission did not result from Sam's silence. Moreover, Sam's failure to object to Alex's statement may not be used against him.

Choice (B) would be a technically correct statement if the facts offered in the question had been different. Alex's statement, as given at the time of his interrogation, would be inadmissible hearsay at Sam's trial. However, Alex would be allowed to testify at trial that Sam planned the robbery and executed it with his help. Here, however, Alex's statement is being used for another purpose, as evidence that Sam is guilty because he did not rebut Alex's statement at the time it was made during interrogation. Therefore, under the circumstances, choice (B) is an incorrect answer.

Question 90
Answer: B

This question tests the admissibility of hearsay evidence. Hearsay evidence is generally inadmissible unless it falls within an exception to the hearsay rule. Harry's affidavit is hearsay because it is a statement made by Harry other than while he was testifying at trial.

Public records and reports, or official documents as stated in choice (C), that were created by public agencies and officials within the scope of their duties are admissible despite being hearsay. In this case, Harry's affidavit does not fall within the public record and report exception because Harry is not (assumedly) a public official, and his observations regarding his brother's competence were not made as part of the scope of his public duties. Therefore, choice (C) is an incorrect answer.

In addition, ancient documents, which are properly authenticated documents that are at least 20-years old, are admissible despite being hearsay. In this case, while Harry's affidavit has been properly authenticated, it is not 20-years old because it was created shortly after the deed was executed, which took place only 15 years prior. Therefore, choice (D) is an incorrect answer.

Finally, while opinion evidence is generally admissible, it may not be presented as evidence if it is being offered in the form of hearsay. While the affidavit is inadmissible, choice (A) is an incorrect answer because it is the wrong grounds to exclude the evidence. Therefore, choice (B) is the correct answer.

There are only several instances when an affidavit can be introduced as evidence without running afoul of the hearsay rule. Such evidence could be presented as either a prior inconsistent statement used to impeach Harry had he testified inconsistently or as a past recollection recorded had Harry testified and been unable to remember the information he provided in the affidavit even after perusing it to refresh his memory.

Question 91
Answer: B

This question tests the admissibility of incriminating statements made by criminal suspects to the police. Confessions are generally admissible unless there is no corroborating evidence of the corpus delicti, the confession is coerced, or it is made during a custodial interrogation without Miranda rights having been read.

In this case, Sam's statement to the police constitutes a confession to the murder of his wife because that is really the only clear meaning of his statement. Furthermore, Sam made the statement at the scene when the police arrived. He had not been placed under arrest, or handcuffed, or restrained in any way that would constitute custody. Furthermore, the police officer's question does not constitute an interrogation because it was not a question that could be reasonably construed as being designed to elicit an incriminating response. Rather, it was merely an appropriate question by an officer on the scene who was seeking to determine the purpose of his investigation. Therefore, the confession is admissible because it was neither coerced nor the product of custodial interrogation.

Furthermore, choice (A) is an incorrect answer because res gestae is a disfavored ground for admitting evidence.

Question 92
Answer: D

This question tests the admissibility of evidence that a document is authentic. The authenticity of a document may be shown by the testimony of a lay witness who is familiar with the handwriting of the person who, it is argued, wrote the document. However, the witness's familiarity may not have been acquired for the purposes of the litigation. In this case, Alice may testify as to the authenticity of the document because she is familiar with John Smith's handwriting, and she became familiar with his handwriting as a result of being his teacher, rather than by preparing for litigation. Furthermore, Alice is testifying as a lay witness rather than an expert because she does not appear to have any special training or formal education as a handwriting expert. Therefore, Alice must be testifying as a layman. Thus, choice (D) is the correct answer.

Question 93
Answer: D

This question tests the limits of relevant evidence. Only relevant evidence is admissible, and evidence is relevant if it relates to, and possesses probative value regarding, an event, people, or time, at issue in litigation. In this case, evidence that people other than the Paula did not fall down in the week prior to her fall is irrelevant to show that Lee had exercised due of care on that specific occasion. Marks' testimony neither relates to, nor presents probative value regarding, Lee's exercise of due care at the time Paula fell. Nor does Marks' testimony relate to, or present probative value regarding, Lee's exercise of due care at all.

Furthermore, choice (A) is incorrect because Marks' testimony is irrelevant, once again, to the condition of the hallway at the specific time of Paula's fall. In addition, the safety of prior patrons possesses no relevance to the care exercised by Paula herself.

In addition, choice (B) is an incorrect answer because evidence of a general condition of safety is irrelevant in determining whether conditions were safe at the specific moment when an individual was injured.

Finally, choice (C) is incorrect because there is no evidentiary prohibition against self-serving evidence.

Question 94
Answer: A

This question tests the admissibility of evidence of subsequent remedial measures. Evidence of subsequent remedial measures is inadmissible to prove the fault or negligence of a defendant. However, such evidence is admissible (1) to prove that a defendant owned or controlled something that harmed a plaintiff, (2) to prove the feasibility of precautionary measures if a defendant controverts them, or (3) to impeach the defendant. In this case, while evidence that Horne replaced the flooring after Paula's fall would be inadmissible to prove that he was negligent, it is admissible for the purpose of showing that Horne, rather than Lee, controlled the hallway, despite Horne's position to the contrary.

It should be noted that choice (D) is incorrect because it fails to take into account the situations in which evidence of subsequent remedial measures is admissible. However, it nonetheless provides an accurate statement of one of the policies behind the prohibition of such evidence to prove the fault or negligence of a defendant.

Question 95
Answer: D

This question tests the admissibility of impeachment by contradiction evidence.

Generally, a party may not impeach a witness by contradiction on a collateral matter with extrinsic evidence. In this case, the color of the sweater that Derrick was wearing at the time of accident is a collateral matter because it has no bearing on a material fact, such as who was at fault. Rather, the evidence is only being offered to undercut the credibility of Bystander by showing that he thought the sweater was green rather than blue and, therefore, must have remembered other facts wrong as well. Furthermore, Wilson's testimony constitutes extrinsic evidence because it is not being offered by Bystander, the witness who is being impeached. Therefore, the evidence is inadmissible. Additionally, choice (C) is incorrect because it goes too far. Making a mistake regarding the color of the sweater has some, albeit little, bearing on the capacity of Bystander to observe.

Question 96
Answer: B

This question tests the admissibility of hearsay evidence. A party-opponent's out-of-court statement may be admitted in the lawsuit if the statement is offered by another party against the party-opponent and the party-opponent's position is inconsistent with the out-of-court statement. In this case, Derrick's statement to Officer is an out-of-court statement. In addition, it is being offered by Price against Derrick. Finally, Derrick's statement to Officer that he was traveling at 40 m.p.h. at the time of the accident is inconsistent with Derrick's position at trial that he was only traveling at 30 m.p.h. Therefore, the statement is admissible under the admission by a party-opponent exception to the hearsay rule.

While Derrick's statement to Officer is inconsistent with his direct testimony at trial, it nonetheless does not fall within the prior inconsistent statement exception to the hearsay rule. That exception applies only to a witness's own prior inconsistent statements in sworn testimony at another trial, hearing, proceeding, or deposition. In this case, Derrick's statement to Officer took place at the scene, not while under oath in sworn testimony. Therefore, choice (A) is an incorrect answer.

Question 97
Answer: C

This question tests the admissibility of hearsay evidence. Hearsay evidence is generally inadmissible unless it falls within an exception to the hearsay rule. In this case, Bystander's testimony constitutes hearsay because it includes statements made by Passenger other than by Passenger while testifying at trial.

Choice (A) is an incorrect answer because Passenger's statement does not qualify as an admission of a party-opponent. A party-opponent's out-of-court statement may be admitted in the lawsuit if the statement is offered by another party against the party-opponent and the party-opponent's position is inconsistent with the out-of-court statement. In this case, Peters, not Passenger, is the party-opponent of Davis. Therefore, only an out-of-court statement by Peters could possibly fall within the admission of a party-opponent exception.

In addition, choice (B) is an incorrect answer because Passenger's statement does not qualify as a declaration against interest. A presently unavailable declarant's statement is admissible if it was made contrary to a declarant's pecuniary, penal, or proprietary interests at the time when made by the declarant. In this case, Passenger's statement was not made contrary his pecuniary, penal, or proprietary interest, because the statement would not give rise to liability on the part of Passenger. Because he was not the driver of the automobile, his statement was really only contrary to Peters' pecuniary, penal, or proprietary interest.

Finally, choice (D) is an incorrect answer because the mere fact that a statement constitutes an opinion is not proper grounds to exclude it. Therefore, because none of the hearsay exceptions listed or unlisted among the answer choices are proper grounds to admit Bystander's testimony, and because the hearsay statement being an opinion is not proper grounds to exclude the testimony, choice (C) is the correct answer.

Question 98
Answer: A

This question tests the admissibility of hearsay evidence. A declarant's sudden and extemporaneous statement that describes an event when it occurs, or soon afterwards, is admissible as an exception to the general prohibition against hearsay.

In this case, Witness' statement, captured in Bystander's testimony, was a sudden exclamation that described the condition of Peters' car immediately after the accident occurred. Because it was a sudden statement describing the accident, and because it occurred so shortly after the accident, it is admissible as a present sense impression. Thus, choice (A) is the correct answer and (C) is an incorrect answer.

Furthermore, when a statement qualifies as a present sense impression, the availability of the declarant, in this case Witness, is immaterial. Therefore, choice (B) is an incorrect answer.

Finally, choice (D) is an incorrect answer because Dead Man's Statutes only apply to situations in which a survivor offers evidence of a transaction with a deceased person against the deceased person's estate. The facts contained in this question do not give rise to such a statute being applicable.

Question 99
Answer: C

This question tests the application of the attorney-client privilege. A communication that is made by a person or an entity to an attorney to obtain legal representation or advice is confidential and therefore legally privileged from disclosure. Furthermore, an attorney may include third party agents in confidential communications with clients without losing the attorney-client privilege. Defendants with a common interest may hold joint discussions with all respective lawyers representing them without waiving their privilege. This privilege is held by the client. In situations involving multiple defendants with a common interest, each individual defendant holds the privilege with respect to any information dealing with themselves, and the privilege continues regardless of any falling out between the defendants. In this case, the communications between Owner and Driver and Attorney are privileged communications because they were made for the purpose of obtaining legal advice.

Because Irving was acting as an agent of Attorney when he sat in on the consultation, his presence does not constitute a waiver of the privilege. Therefore, choice (A) is incorrect.

In addition, regardless of the cross-claim by Owner against Driver, Owner's statements to Attorney in Driver's presence are nonetheless privileged. Therefore, Owner may still prevent Driver from testifying as to the statements made by Owner during the consultation. Therefore, choice (B) is an incorrect answer. Once again, because the communications between Owner and Attorney are privileged, Driver's testimony regarding that communication is inadmissible because of the attorney-client privilege.

In addition, it should be noted that choice (D) is an incorrect answer but nonetheless presents an interesting issue. While Irving's notes of the conference would be hearsay and would therefore have to fall within an exception to hearsay to be admissible, they would not likely be inadmissible on the grounds of privilege. Because notes of a conversation are not a communication, they are not subject to attorney-client privilege unless they are read back to the lawyer, or the client examines and initials the documents.

Question 100
Answer: A

This question tests the applicability of the attorney-client privilege. Defendants with a common interest may hold joint discussions with all respective lawyers present without waiving their privilege. However, the privilege only exists between lawyers, clients, and the outside world, not between the defendants with a common interest. In this case, the communications made between the defendants, Owner and Driver, and Attorney are privileged communications because Owner and Driver are defendants with a common interest. However, the privilege only exists between Attorney, Owner, Driver, and the outside world, not between Owner and Driver. Therefore, in a suit between Owner, Driver, and Litigant, the privileged communications they made to Attorney are inadmissible as privileged. However, in the suit between Owner and Driver, the evidence is admissible.

Question 101
Answer: C

This question tests the admissibility of evidence of subsequent remedial measures. Evidence of subsequent remedial measures taken by a defendant is inadmissible to prove the fault or negligence of a defendant. In this case, the evidence that Mammoth put speed governors on its trucks subsequent to the accident cannot be offered into evidence to show fault or negligence on the part of Mammoth. This prohibition is rooted in the strong public policy favoring subsequent remedial measures by defendants. One public policy reason for the prohibition against such evidence is that admitting evidence of subsequent remedial measures to prove fault or negligence on the part of a defendant will discourage defendants from taking precautionary measures to prevent future accidents.

Question 102
Answer: A

This question tests the admissibility of hearsay evidence. A party-opponent's out-of-court statement may be admitted in the lawsuit if the statement is offered by another party against the party-opponent and the party-opponent's position is inconsistent with the out-of-court statement. Furthermore, if an employee of a party-opponent made the statement within the existence and scope of an employment relationship, then the statement is admissible as if the party-opponent had made that statement. In this case, Edwards' statement, presented through Helper's testimony, is being offered by Pemberton against Mammoth. Also, the statement—that Edwards was not wearing glasses at the time of the accident—is inconsistent with Mammoth's position that Pemberton caused the accident. Finally, because the statement was made by Edwards, an employee of Mammoth, within the scope of his employment when driving a truck, it falls within the statements attributable to a party-opponent exception to the hearsay rule.

Question 103
Answer: A

This question tests the admissibility of hearsay evidence. A party-opponent's out-of-court statement may be admitted in the lawsuit if the statement is offered by another party against the party-opponent and the party-opponent's position is inconsistent with the out-of-court statement. In this case, the statement was made by Pemberton and is being offered by Mammoth, through Sheriff's testimony, against Pemberton. Also, the statement is inconsistent with Pemberton's position at trial that Mammoth's driver caused the accident. Therefore, the statement is admissible as an admission of a party-opponent.

Question 104
Answer: D

This question tests the requirement of original writings referred to in testimony. Under the collateral document exception to the Best Evidence Rule, when a witness' testimony describes writings that have only a peripheral relationship to any disputed issues of a trial, the original writing does not need to be produced. In this case, the newspaper story to which Ward refers to while testifying has only a peripheral relationship to the issues addressed at trial. Rather than being determinative of any major issue in the contract dispute, the article simply serves as evidence of how Ward remembered the date of a specific conversation. Therefore, because the newspaper was a collateral document, Ward may refer to it without the original having to be produced. Therefore, the motion should be denied for the reason stated in correct answer (D).

It should be noted that choice (B) is an incorrect answer because Ward's testimony does not constitute hearsay for the purposes for which it is offered. Hearsay occurs when an out-of-court statement is offered to prove the truth of the matter asserted. In this case, the hearsay statement, an article announcing the engagement of Ward's daughter, is not being offered to prove that she is, in fact engaged. Rather it is being offered to prove that Ward correctly remembered the date of a meeting.

Choice (C) is incorrect because a court may only take judicial notice of a local newspaper's existence, not its contents.

Question 105
Answer: B

This question tests the admissibility of hearsay evidence. Hearsay evidence that is offered to impeach a witness is being used to show discord between the witness' original testimony and the hearsay evidence. As a result, such evidence is not being offered to prove the truth of the underlying hearsay statement and does not, therefore, qualify as hearsay.

As a result, such evidence is admissible to the extent that it is being used to impeach a witness, rather than as substantive evidence. In this case, Wall's testimony contains an out-of-court statement made by Pitt. However, Pitt's statement to Wall does not qualify as hearsay because it is not being used to prove that Pitt was murdered by Jack. Instead, the statement is being used to impeach the credibility of Pitt's statement to a priest during last rites, recounted by the police officer. Therefore, Pitt's statement to Wall is admissible to the extent it is being used to impeach Pitt, the dead declarant, rather than to prov that Jack committed the murder.

Question 106
Answer: A

This question tests the law of character evidence.

According to FRE 404(b), evidence of other crimes, wrongs, or acts is not admissible to prove the character of a person in order to show action in conformity therewith. It may, however, be admissible for other purposes, such as proof of motive, opportunity, intent, preparation, plan, knowledge, identity, or absence of mistake or accident. The evidence may also be used to establish the elements of a crime. It must be presented in the form of specific acts, rather than as reputation or opinion evidence. A trial judge must determine if the risk of undue prejudice from the evidence of the prior wrongful acts and past crimes substantially outweighs its probative value.

In this case, the act is so similar in method to the crime charged that it would be extremely unlikely that two different criminals were involved. Both the prior act being offered into evidence and the crime alleged by the state involved a female victim, the taping of each victim's hands, and strangulation of each victim in the same location. Because of the similarity of these two separate acts, the evidence would admissible as tending to show that Dexter is the killer.

Question 107
Answer: A

This question tests the identification of an individual during a telephone conversation. Under FRE 901(b)(6), a party to a telephone conversation may be identified by evidence that a call was made to a specified number assigned to a person if that person self-identifies over the phone. In this case, evidence was offered, through Jones' testimony, that Jones looked up Smith's phone number in the directory and used the phone to call the specific number assigned to Smith. In addition, when Smith answered the telephone, he identified himself as Smith. Therefore, the combination of Jones' testimony that he called Smith's assigned telephone number and that Smith identified himself as Smith is sufficient evidence to identify Smith. Thus, the conversation is admissible. Finally, note that the conversation is admissible as an exception to the hearsay rule because Smith's answer to Jones' question constitutes an admission by a party-opponent.

Question 108
Answer: A

This question tests the authentication of pictorial evidence. Pictorial evidence is admissible, without the need for any supporting testimony, if a witness who observed the person or event that was photographed testifies to the accuracy of the photograph. In this case, the photograph of the cornfield may be admitted if it is authenticated by a person who observed the damage to the cornfield. Because Jones observed the damage to his crops, he may authenticate the photograph by testifying that it fairly and accurately portrays the condition of the cornfield after the damage was done.

Question 109
Answer: C

This question tests the admissibility of hearsay evidence. Statements, other than those made by the declarant while testifying at trial, are hearsay and must fall within an exception to the hearsay rule in order to be admissible. In this case, the accident report completed by Handy is hearsay because the report is essentially a statement that Handy made out of court.

Choice (A) is an incorrect answer because res gestae is a disfavored ground for admitting hearsay evidence because a great deal of what was once considered res gestae is now specifically admissible under the present sense impressions, excited utterances, and statements of present bodily conditions exceptions to the hearsay rule. In this case, Handy's report does not fall within any of those exceptions because it was not made as the accident occurred or very shortly afterward, and it was a required statement rather than an impromptu or unsolicited exclamation. Further, the statement did not discuss any of Handy's bodily conditions.

In addition, choice (B) is incorrect because accident reports, though made in order to collect information on which management may act, do not constitute regularly kept business records because they are not made systematically or as a routine business matter. Additionally, the report at issue in these facts is self-serving because it was drafted by Handy, an employee with a stake in the outcome. As such, it can be deemed unreliable (an exception to the business records exception). Therefore, Handy's report is not admissible under the regularly kept business records exception to the hearsay rule.

Finally, choice (D) is incorrect because Handy's availability as a witness is not relevant to the admissibility of his report. Three hearsay exceptions require the unavailability of a witness: former testimony, statements upon belief of impending death, and statements against interest. Clearly, the first two of those exceptions are inapplicable in this case. In addition, Handy's report does not constitute a statement against interest. The report generally exonerates Mart from any liability. Therefore, the availability of Handy to testify is not a relevant concern in this case.

Because none of the exceptions to the hearsay rule, listed or unlisted among the answer choices, apply in this case, the correct answer is choice (C).

Question 110
Answer: A

This question tests the law of relevancy and character evidence. Evidence is factually relevant if it possesses any tendency to make the existence of any fact that is of consequence to the determination of the action more probable or less probable than it would be without the evidence. Under FRE 403, factually relevant evidence may be excluded when its probative value is substantially outweighed by the dangers of (1) unfair prejudice, (2) confusion of the issues, (3) misleading the jury, (4) undue delay, or (5) cumulative evidence. Here, evidence as to whether or not Dann is a peaceful, law-abiding, and nonviolent person is factually relevant to the assault charge brought against him, and this evidence's probative value is not outweighed by one of the five issues listed above.

FRE 404(a) provides in part that evidence of a person's character or character trait is usually inadmissible to show that the person acted in conformity therewith on a particular occasion. FRE 404(a)(1)-(3) provide exceptions to that rule. The exception pertinent to Dann's case is FRE 404(a)(1), which in a criminal case allows the accused to bring forth a pertinent trait of character. The evidence in this situation is admissible because Dann is the accused and is using the evidence to prove his own good character.

Question 111
Answer: B

This question tests the law of character evidence on cross-examination. If a defendant produces evidence of a pertinent trait of the defendant's character that is inconsistent with a charged offense, or to prove his or her innocence, then under FRE 404(a)(1) a prosecutor may rebut that evidence by cross-examining a defendant's character witness as to the witness's knowledge of certain instances of the defendant's prior conduct pursuant to FRE 405(a). Under FRE 405(a), specific instances of relevant conduct and rumors and reports thereof may be brought out on cross-examination. The reputation or opinion witness may be asked either "if he knows" or "has he heard" of such matters. Because Dann called his employer to provide character evidence pertaining to the assault charge, the prosecutor has the right to cross-examine the employer in order to test his knowledge of Dann's character using past specific instances under FRE 405(a).

Question 112
Answer: A

This question tests the law of character evidence relevant to a defense raised by the defendant. FRE 404(a)(2) permits a criminal defendant to present opinion or reputation evidence regarding an alleged victim's pertinent trait of character if that evidence is relevant to a defense that the defendant raised to a prosecutor's charge. Evidence of specific acts is not admissible for the purpose of showing character; proof must be by reputation or opinion. For example, a victim's reputation for violence is admissible to prove that a defendant acted reasonably to protect himself from harm by the victim. Because Dann is claiming self-defense to the assault charge filed against him, Frank's testimony about Smith is admissible because it relates to Smith's reputation as an aggressive person.

Question 113
Answer: D

This question tests offers to settle. Although the evidence in this question is a relevant admission and seems suitable for trial, the courts exclude this type of evidence because it discourages settlement negotiations. If this type of evidence was allowed, people would be hesitant to settle out of court due to their fear of admitting responsibility or liability. This type of evidence is prohibited by FRE 408 on account of public policy and thus is inadmissible.

Question 114
Answer: C

This question tests the law of hearsay. Under FRE 801(c), hearsay is a statement, other than one made by the declarant while testifying at the trial or hearing, offered in evidence to prove the truth of the matter asserted. If a statement is hearsay it must fall under one of the hearsay exceptions in order to be admissible. Because the Sheriff (witness) is testifying to what Walter Passenger (declarant) said at the scene of the crime to prove the truth of the matter asserted (everyone in the car had been drinking) the evidence is inadmissible as hearsay.

Choice (A) is incorrect because Walter Passenger is not a party to the lawsuit.

Choice (B) is incorrect because it is not a statement against interest. Under FRE 804(b)(3) a statement against interest is a statement which was at the time of its making so far contrary to the declarant's pecuniary and proprietary interest that a reasonable person would not have made the statement unless he believed it to be true. The declarant in this situation was Walter Passenger, not Carr, so Walter's statement is not contrary to his own pecuniary or proprietary interest.

Choice (D) is incorrect because leading the court into non-essential side issues does not automatically bar admission of the evidence.

Question 115
Answer: A

This question tests the law of refreshing recollection. If a testifying witness cannot clearly remember something or an event about which the witness is questioned, then an examining attorney may present an item to the witness for review. Under FRE 612, the writing itself need not be admissible in evidence; all that is required is for the witness to state the facts from his own present recollection after inspecting it. An adverse party is entitled to have the writing produced at the hearing, to inspect it, to cross-examine the witness thereon, and to introduce in evidence those portions which relate to the testimony of the witness. In this case, Walter Passenger may review the letter that he wrote to his sister to refresh his recollection.

Question 116
Answer: C

This question tests the law of expert testimony. In order to admit expert testimony under FRE 702, (1) the testimony must be based upon sufficient facts or data; (2) the testimony must be the product of reliable principles and methods; and (3) the witness has applied the principles and methods reliably to the facts of the case. Under FRE 703, the facts or data in the particular case upon which an expert bases an opinion or inference may be those perceived by or made known to the expert at or before the hearing. In this case, Dr. Wolfe is a board certified pathologist who conducted a scientific experiment in accord with good practice in her specialty. Therefore, the evidence has been properly admitted.

Choice (A) is incorrect. Under the common law, expert witnesses were prohibited from testifying regarding an ultimate issue of fact. FRE 704 departs from the common law and generally permits an expert witness to testify about an ultimate issue of fact unless it concerns a criminal defendant's mental state while committing an alleged offense.

Choice (B) is incorrect. If the facts or data are of a type reasonably relied upon by experts in the particular field in forming opinions or inferences upon the subject, the facts or data need not be admissible in evidence in order for the opinion or inference to be admitted. The microphotographic slides studied by Dr. Wolfe do not need to be admitted into evidence.

Choice (D) is incorrect because Dr. Wolfe's opinion is not based upon matters observed pursuant to a duty imposed by law.

Question 117
Answer: B

This question tests the law of the right to cross-examine. Cross-examination is conducted by the party who did not call a witness to testify. Cross-examination is an absolute right. A defendant possesses a right granted to them under the Sixth Amendment of the U.S. Constitution to confront any witness that testifies against the defendant in criminal proceedings. In this case, if Waite refuses to answer questions on cross-examination, the defendant Davis will be deprived of his constitutional right to confront a witness testifying against him and Waite's direct-examination should be stricken.

Question 118
Answer: B

This question tests the law of authentication and identification. Authentication is a legal requirement of establishing a foundation that evidence is genuinely what it purports to be. Identification is a prerequisite to admissibility that informs a party-opponent and a fact finder what is the nature and essence of each item of proffered evidence. The requirement of authentication or identification as a condition precedent to admissibility is satisfied by evidence sufficient to support a finding that the matter in question is what its proponent claims. Davidson pleaded guilty to driving while intoxicated and the record was properly authenticated. Therefore, the evidence should be admitted as proof of Davidson's intoxication because it is exactly what Pugh purports it to be.

Question 119
Answer: C

This question tests the law of subsequent remedial measures. Under FRE 407, when after an injury or harm allegedly caused by an event, measures are taken that, if taken previously, would have made the injury or harm less likely to occur, evidence of the subsequent measure is not admissible to prove negligence, culpable conduct, a defect in a product, a defect in a product's design, or a need for a warning or instruction. But, this rule does not require the exclusion of evidence of subsequent measures when offered for another purpose, such as proving ownership, control, or feasibility of precautionary measures. Because Pitt, the plaintiff, is bringing the subsequent conduct of Dow, the defendant, into evidence to prove ownership of the tree, instead of using the conduct to prove that the tree was dangerous, the evidence will be allowed under the rule.

Question 120
Answer: A

This question tests the law of former testimony. An unavailable witness's testimony may be used if former testimony was given by that witness at another hearing of the same or a different proceeding, or in a deposition taken in compliance with law in the course of the same or another proceeding, if the party against whom the testimony is now offered had an opportunity and similar motive to develop the testimony by direct, cross, or redirect examination. The defendant, Dean, and her attorney were present at the preliminary examination for the prosecution of Dean. During her preliminary hearing, the defendant had a motive to examine White because White was testifying against her. The defendant also then had the opportunity to develop White's testimony through direct, cross, and redirect examination. Therefore, White's testimony is admissible at Dean's trial even though White refuses to testify at this trial.

Question 121
Answer: B

This question tests the law of first-hand knowledge. According to FRE 602, a witness may not testify to a matter unless evidence is introduced sufficient to support a finding that the witness has personal knowledge of the matter. An ordinary witness must limit his testimony to facts of which he has first-hand knowledge. In this case, Potts personally supervised all of the work and is testifying to various amounts of material and man hours spent on the job. The fact that Dennis, the defendant, is claiming that Potts recorded all of this information actually gives Potts more credibility on the stand and strengthens the argument that he has first-hand knowledge of the testimony that he seeks to provide.

Choice (A) is incorrect because nothing in the problem says that the reports written by Potts were kept in the course of regularly conducted business activity or if it was regular practice for Potts to write the report.

Choice (C) is incorrect because the witness is not testifying to what the document said but is instead testifying to his own personal knowledge. For the Best Evidence Rule to be used, the witness must be testifying about what a document says without being able to produce that document.

Choice (D) is incorrect because the witness is not summarizing the writing.

Question 122
Answer: B

This law tests the law of use immunity. Use immunity is given to a defendant to protect the defendant against the direct or indirect use of testimony given by him in subsequent prosecution. For example, if a defendant granted use immunity testifies that he filed a false insurance claim, that testimony cannot be used against him in later prosecution. The defendant (i.e., witness) is even protected from indirect use of his testimony in ways that lead to information or witnesses, focus the prosecution, or in any other way. In this case, the prosecution used Taylor's testimony to indict Simmons as well as gain testimony regarding Taylor. Because Taylor's testimony indirectly led to his later prosecution, the objection should be sustained.

Question 123
Answer: B

This question tests the law of the probative value of evidence. FRE 403 allows for evidence to be excluded if its probative value is substantially outweighed by the danger of unfair prejudice, confusion of the issues, or misleading the jury. In this situation, the probative value of the video of the defendant is not substantially outweighed by the danger of unfair prejudice, confusion of the issues, or misleading the jury. Unfair prejudice is an undue tendency to suggest a decision on an improper basis. The defendant was arrested for driving while intoxicated, and the video shows an unsteady defendant slurring his words. Therefore, admitting the video as evidence would not create a tendency to suggest a decision on an improper basis.

Question 124
Answer: A

This question tests the law of prior bad acts not resulting in conviction. Evidence of specific instances of conduct, such as prior bad acts not resulting in conviction, may be admitted to impeach a witness under certain circumstances. Prior bad acts are specific instances of misconduct by a witness that do not result in criminal conviction. FRE 608(b) limits an attorney's questions on cross-examination to the prior bad acts of a witness that are probative of truthfulness only, and extrinsic evidence in the form of witness testimony is not permitted. In this case, the defendant's lawyer can use FRE 608(b) to question the witness about the false insurance claim even though there was no criminal conviction because the prior bad act is related to truthfulness.

Question 125
Answer: C

This question tests the law of hearsay. Hearsay is a statement, other than one made by the declarant while testifying at the trial or hearing, offered in evidence to prove the truth of the matter asserted. A statement is an oral or written assertion and the declarant is the person who makes a statement. In this case, the driver who stopped the police officer is the declarant who made the statement at issue. The plaintiff wants Williams, the police officer, to testify about the out-of-court statement made by the driver to prove the truth of the matter asserted—that the driver saw a hit and run accident. This is clearly hearsay not within any exception.

Question 126

Answer: D

This question tests offers to settle. Although the evidence in this question is a relevant admission and seems suitable for trial, the courts exclude this type of evidence because it discourages settlement negotiations. If this type of evidence was allowed, people would be hesitant to settle out of court due to their fear of admitting responsibility or liability. This type of evidence is prohibited by FRE 408 on account of public policy and thus is inadmissible.

Question 127
Answer: A

This question tests the law of the probative value of evidence. FRE 403 provides evidence may be excluded if its probative value is substantially outweighed by the danger of unfair prejudice, confusion of the issues, or misleading the jury, or by the considerations of undue delay, waste of time, or needless presentation of cumulative evidence. Here, the court would conduct a balancing test in order to find out whether or not the probative value is outweighed by any prejudice brought out by the evidence. An important factor to remember is that such prejudice must substantially outweigh the probative value of the evidence and not the other way around. Under a FRE 403 balancing test, a presumption is made that the evidence has more probative value than prejudice, therefore prejudice must be proven.

Question 128
Answer: B

This question tests the law of expert testimony. FRE 703 provides the facts or data in the particular case upon which an expert bases an opinion or inference may be those perceived by or made known to the expert at or before the hearing. In this case, the expert witness heard all the evidence about the plaintiff's symptoms and conditions at trial and then gave her opinion. Rule 703 clearly allows for this procedure.

Question 129
Answer: D

This question tests the law of evidence of character. Under FRE 608(b), specific instances of the conduct of a witness, for the purpose of attacking or supporting the witness' character for truthfulness, other than conviction of crime as provided in FRE 609, may not be proved by extrinsic evidence. When attacking the character of a witness for truthfulness, evidence must be used in the form of opinion or reputation only. Here, witness Weld is using a specific instance to prove that Fisher is an untruthful person. Such an attack on the character of a witness is not allowed under the Federal Rules of Evidence.

Question 130
Answer: A

This question tests the law of spousal immunity. Under the doctrine of spousal immunity or incompetency, under most circumstances, a person may not be called to testify against his or her spouse in any criminal prosecution. The privilege covers testimony regarding events occurring at any time, even before the marriage. Under federal law, the witness, not the party spouse, holds the privilege of spousal immunity. Therefore, under federal law, Wanda may waive the privilege and testify.

Question 131
Answer: A

This question tests the law of relevancy. According to FRE 401, relevant evidence means evidence having any tendency to make the existence of any fact that is of consequence to the determination of the action more probable or less probable than it would be without the evidence. Evidence is relevant if it relates to, and possesses value regarding, an event, people, or time, at issue in litigation.

Once evidence is deemed factually relevant, as Wall's failed chemistry tests would be, the court must also consider whether it is legally relevant under FRE 403. Under FRE 403, factually relevant evidence may be excluded when its probative value is substantially outweighed by the dangers of unfair prejudice, confusion, misleading the jury, considerations of undue delay, waste of time, or needless presentation of cumulative evidence. Evidence of Wall's failed chemistry tests has strong probative value because he is a chemist testifying as an expert witness. It is very unlikely that this evidence's probative value will be substantially outweighed by any of the factors listed in Rule 403 given the circumstances of the case.

Question 132
Answer: A

This question tests the law of authentication. Authentication is a legal requirement of establishing a foundation that evidence is genuinely what it purports to be. The issue in this case is the authentication of a signature. FRE 901(b)(2) clearly states that a signature can be authenticated by non-expert opinion as to the genuineness of the handwriting based upon familiarity with the handwriting, which is not acquired for purposes of the litigation. Because the non-expert was preparing for trial when he familiarized himself with the defendant's signature, the Federal Rules of Evidence forbid the admission of his testimony.

Question 133
Answer: B

This question tests the admissibility of impeachment by contradiction evidence. Generally, a party may not impeach a witness by contradiction on a collateral matter with extrinsic evidence. In this case, the number of years that a roofing company employed Walters is a collateral matter because it has no bearing on the material fact of whether Daly signed the note. Rather, the evidence is only being offered to undercut the credibility of Walters by showing that he incorrectly thought that the roofing company employed him for seven years, and, therefore, must have remembered other facts wrong as well. Furthermore, Wilson's testimony constitutes extrinsic evidence because it is not being offered by Walters, the witness who is being impeached. Therefore, choice (B) is correct because the evidence is inadmissible. Additionally, making a mistake regarding the number of years of employment arguably has some, albeit little, bearing on the capacity of Walters to recollect and identify the handwriting on the note as that of Daly.

Question 134
Answer: C

This question tests the law of prior identification of a witness. FRE 801(d)(1)(C) provides that a witness's prior identification of a witness that occurred out of court is admissible to prove its truth when the witness is presently testifying and is not hearsay. Here, Wall's testimony would be admissible under FRE 801(d)(1)(C) because she had previously identified Dray in the photographs.

Question 135
Answer: D

This question tests the law of character evidence. FRE 404(a) provides that evidence of a person's character or a trait of character is not admissible for the purpose of proving action in conformity therewith on a particular occasion. An exception is made for the accused under 404(a)(1) in that evidence of a pertinent trait of character may be admissible. The key words in this rule are "pertinent trait." In this case, Duncan is trying to bolster his character with opinion evidence that he is a truthful person. Such evidence is not pertinent to assault, the crime for which he is charged. If Duncan were offering opinion evidence that he is a peaceful person the evidence would most likely be admissible.

Question 136
Answer: B

This question tests the law of hearsay exceptions. FRE 803(4) provides that a declarant's statement of a past or present mental, emotional, or physical condition is only admissible if it was made for the purpose of treatment or diagnosis by a physician. Under this rule the declarant is usually a patient and the person who heard the statement and testified about it would be the witness. That witness normally is a physician or another person who is involved with diagnosing or treating the patient. Here, the witness is Parker's physician, who was told by Parker that before the accident he had been working full time without pain or limitation of motion. This evidence is admissible under this hearsay exception.

Answer (A) is not the best answer because Parker's statements to his physician were not spontaneous and impromptu. He was relating a past experience. An existing physical condition does not include a statement of memory or belief to prove the fact remembered.

Question 137
Answer: B

This question tests the law of refreshing recollection. Under FRE 612, if a testifying witness cannot clearly remember something or an event about which the witness is questioned, then an examining attorney may present an item to the witness for review. Items that may be used for that purpose and examined by a witness include documents, tangible objects, sounds, and smells. In this case, West's recollection was properly refreshed by the handwritten notes.

Question 138
Answer: A

This question tests the law of admissions by a party-opponent. A statement is not hearsay if it is an admission by a party-opponent. A party-opponent is an adverse party in a lawsuit. The Federal Rules of Evidence provide that a party-opponent's out-of-court statement may be admitted in the lawsuit if the statement is offered by another party against the party-opponent, and the party-opponent's position is inconsistent with the out-of-court statement. The party-opponent himself need not be the one to make the statement. It will additionally be attributed to the party-opponent in several different circumstances, including an adoptive admission. According to FRE 801(d)(2)(B), an adoptive admission is a statement of which the party has manifested an adoption or belief in its truth.

Here, in response to the plaintiff's interrogatories asking for information concerning the sales of the defendants, the defendants responded by referring the plaintiff to the Annual Journal for the information. The statement the plaintiff is trying to offer as evidence is the information obtained from the Annual Journal regarding the sales. The defendants manifested a belief in the truth of the information found in the Annual Journal by telling the plaintiff to look there for the information sought in the interrogatories. Therefore, the information is admissible as evidence under the rule of adoptive admission.

Question 139
Answer: B

This question tests the law of impeaching a witness. The Federal Rules of Evidence lack an express provision that expressly addresses bias and interest as grounds for impeachment of a witness. Nonetheless, in civil or criminal proceedings that are subject to either the common law or the Federal Rules of Evidence, a witness may always be asked questions that would reveal a bias or an interest of the witness. Specifically, a party-opponent may try to impeach the credibility of a witness on cross-examination by inquiring about partiality, bias, interest, or motivation.

Generally, a witness's testimony may be influenced by an improper motive that results from: (1) a relationship between the witness and another party, (2) the witness' interest in the results of a trial, or (3) feelings or emotions regarding parties or issues in a case. Extrinsic and direct evidence of bias and interest may be produced if a proper evidentiary foundation is laid. In this case, the extrinsic evidence of the gambling operation offered by Parmott was proper in an attempt to show Wade's possible bias towards Dexter.

Question 140
Answer: A

This question tests the law of attorney-client privilege. If a communication is made by a person or an entity to an attorney to obtain legal representation or advice, it is confidential and therefore legally privileged from disclosure. Information about the number of hours an attorney billed on a certain date does not fall within this privilege. The number of hours billed does not involve any kind of confidential communication between attorney and client.

Choice (B) is incorrect because an attorney does have the right to invoke his clients' privilege without instruction. An attorney is obligated to assert the privilege to protect a client who cannot assert it for a valid reason such as incapacity or death.

Choice (C) is incorrect. Work product is an attorney's mental impressions, conclusions, opinions, or legal theories regarding litigation, none of which cover the number of hours billed.

Choice (D) is incorrect because permission is not needed from the clients to reveal the number of hours that Able, the attorney, billed on a given day because the number of hours billed is not protected by the attorney-client privilege.

Question 141
Answer: B

This question tests the law of hearsay exceptions. Although the listing of births in the Bible would be considered hearsay under FRE 801, it fits neatly into one of the hearsay exceptions listed in FRE 803. FRE 803(13) provides for the admissibility of statements of fact concerning personal or family history contained in family Bibles, genealogies, charts, engravings on rights, inscriptions on family portraits, engravings on urns, crypts, or tombstones, or the like. Baggs' Bible is clearly admissible as a family record because of its list of the births of his family members.

Question 142
Answer: C

This question tests the law of authentication. At first glance, choice (A) seems to be a good answer. FRE 901(b)(6) states that telephone conversations, by evidence that a call was made to the number assigned at the time by the telephone company to a particular person or business are authenticated if "(A) in the case of a person, circumstances, including self-identification, show the person answering to be the one called or (B) in the case of a business, the call was made to a place of business and the conversation was related to business reasonably transacted over the" phone. This is not the strongest argument because the plaintiff was the one receiving the call instead of making it. For this rule to have teeth, the plaintiff would have had to make the call to an assigned number and the defendant would have had to identify himself. This rules out choices (A) and (B). Although the defendant identified himself, self-identification alone is not enough, which also rules out choice (D).

Choice (C) is the best answer. According to 901(b)(5), identification of a voice, whether heard firsthand or through mechanical or electronic transmission, by opinion based upon hearing the voice at any time under circumstances connecting it with the alleged speaker is enough to authenticate the conversation. Because the plaintiff recognized the defendant's voice in the judge's chambers as the same voice heard during the telephone conversation, the evidence may be authenticated.

Question 143
Answer: A

This question tests the law of using specific instances of conduct as a method of proving character. Even though character evidence is generally not allowed under the Federal Rules of Evidence, FRE 405(b) provides that in cases in which character or a trait of character of a person is an essential element of a charge, claim, or defense, proof may be made of specific instances of that person's conduct. Because the defendant is being sued for slander, and one of the elements that must be shown to prove slander is that the defendant made a false statement concerning the plaintiff, the defendant's character is an essential element of the claim and he may use specific instances of conduct to rebut the charge against him. Essentially, the defendant is being charged with lying, which is a direct attack on his character. So, FRE 405(b) allows the defendant to show the court that he is not a liar by using specific instances of conduct. In this case, the defendant will be allowed to offer evidence that the plaintiff stole the ring from the jewelry store to prove he did not make a false statement. Also, truth is a defense to a claim of slander, and evidence that plaintiff stole the ring tends to show that defendant made a true statement about plaintiff.

Question 144
Answer: B

This question tests the law of impeachment with hearsay evidence. If impeachment evidence is not being offered to prove its truth, hearsay evidence may be used for the purpose of impeaching a witness. When using a verbal statement to impeach a witness, the testimony of a second witness may be used to establish that a first witness made statements prior to testifying that were inconsistent with the first witness's trial testimony. The testimony about the prior inconsistent verbal statement may be used to impeach the first witness, but it may not be used as substantive evidence in the case. In this case, because the police officer's testimony is being used to impeach Minter and not to prove the truth of the matter asserted, it may be admissible as evidence.

Question 145
Answer: A

This question tests the law of impeachment by evidence of conviction of crime. Choice (C) is incorrect because the defendant's prior conviction was for a crime involving a false statement and FRE 609(a)(2) provides that it may be introduced as evidence regardless of whether it was a misdemeanor or felony. The same reasoning is attributable to choice (B) due to the fact that crimes involving dishonesty may be admitted regardless of punishment. FRE 609(e) provides that the pendency of an appeal does not render evidence of a conviction inadmissible, making choice (D) incorrect. Under FRE 609(b), evidence of a conviction under this rule is not admissible if a period of more than 10 years has elapsed since the release of the witness from the confinement imposed for that conviction, unless the court determines, in the interests of justice, that the probative value of the conviction supported by specific facts and circumstances substantially outweighs its prejudicial effect. Although the defendant was released from prison more than 10 years ago, the court can still determine that the probative value of the conviction is more probative than prejudicial. This makes choice (A) the best answer.

Question 146
Answer: B

This question tests the law of witness impeachment and the scope of cross-examination. Under FRE 611(b), because the defendant already raised the issue of self-defense on direct examination the prosecution can bring forth evidence on cross-examination relating to the issue of self-defense. Not only may the evidence be used to impeach the defendant, but it may also be used as substantive evidence. When using a verbal statement to impeach a witness, the testimony of a second witness may be used to establish that a first witness made statements prior to testifying that were inconsistent with the first witness's trial testimony. In this case, the defendant has raised the issue of self-defense on direct examination allowing for the officer to testify on cross-examination that the defendant stated to him that the gun had accidentally gone off.

Question 147
Answer: D

This question tests the law of legal relevance—the Rule 403 balancing test. According to FRE 403, relevant evidence may be excluded if its probative value is substantially outweighed by the danger of unfair prejudice, confusion of the issues, or misleading the jury, or by considerations of undue delay, waste of time, or needless presentation of cumulative evidence. Here, the court would weigh the probative value of the evidence against its prejudicial nature. In this case, the prosecution's claim that the defendant had robbed two other stores in the past year is so prejudicial to the defense of the defendant that it substantially outweighs its probative value. If this evidence were admitted the case at hand would clearly be tainted and therefore the court would rule it inadmissible.

Question 148
Answer: C

This question is an issue of public policy. If a first party pays for, or offers or promises to pay for, an injured second party's medical expenses, those facts are not admissible under FRE 409 to prove the first party's responsibility for an incident that resulted in the second party's injury. Certain material evidence having probative value may be excluded under FRE 409 on the basis of important social policies, such as encouraging the prompt payment of medical expenses. In this case the defendant said she would pay for the plaintiff's hospital bills, evidence that clearly falls under FRE 409.

Question 149
Answer: B

This question tests the law of hearsay. Choice (D) is incorrect because statements that are made regarding the cause of, or who is at fault for, an injury may be admitted only insofar as reasonably pertinent to medical diagnosis or treatment. Naming Dabney as the person responsible for the injury is not pertinent to Payne's treatment.

Choice (C) is also incorrect because such statements are inadmissible under the exception for records of regularly conducted activity for two reasons. First, despite a physician's administrative duty to record the cause of an injury, he or she normally obtains that information from a patient who lacks that duty. Further, a patient's statements regarding fault for an injury are usually considered to be beyond a reporter's duty to record. Because the statement must be pertinent to medical diagnosis or treatment, choice (A) fails as well.

This leaves choice (B) which is hearsay without an exception. Hearsay is a statement, other than one made by the declarant while testifying at the trial or hearing, offered in evidence to prove the truth of the matter asserted. Here, the notation on the medical record is the out-of-court statement made by someone other than the declarant, used to prove the truth of the matter asserted, that the patient was attacked by Dabney. The evidence is inadmissible as hearsay.

Question 150
Answer: C

(C) is the correct response to this evidence law question. The Fifth Amendment provides that no witness may be compelled to testify in criminal proceedings when doing that would incriminate the witness. This provision applies to grand jury proceedings, but it is subject to certain exceptions. One of these exceptions is part of the rules regarding attorney-client privilege.

If a communication is made from a client to an attorney to obtain legal representation or advice, it is confidential and thus generally privileged from disclosure. The client usually holds, and may exercise, that privilege by preventing anyone from disclosing to any third party, or testifying about, the confidential communication. The privilege does not apply, however, to the attorney's services that were requested to assist in planning or committing a future crime or fraud. When this exception renders the privilege inapplicable, the attorney may, and in some instances must, disclose the confidential information regardless of the client's concerns.

Production of the letter by the attorney to the grand jury should be required because the "crime or fraud" exception applies to the Fifth Amendment privilege against self-incrimination as well as the attorney-client privilege.

The letter expressly requests that the attorney back-date a deed for the purpose of avoiding certain tax consequences. Based on that fact, in light of the investigation of the client for the criminal offense of tax fraud, the letter is a statement made in furtherance of a crime or fraud. Thus, the client is not protected from disclosure to the grand jury and the attorney must release the letter to it.

Answer (A) is incorrect because the attorney-client privilege does not apply to the letter seeking legal assistance in furtherance of a crime or fraud.

Answer (B) is incorrect because the constitutional privilege against self-incrimination does not apply to the Defendant's letter to the attorney that was made to obtain assistance in perpetrating a crime or fraud.

Answer (D) is wrong in its statement of the law. Although generally a client holds the attorney-client privilege, in some instances, an attorney may assert it.

Question 151
Answer: A

(A) is the correct response to this evidence law question. Prior bad acts are specific instances of misconduct by a witness that do not result in a criminal conviction. They reflect negatively on a witness' truthfulness. FRE 608(b) provides that these acts may only be the subject of questioning during the cross-examination. On cross-examination, an attorney may question a witness about prior bad acts that did not result in a criminal conviction. FRE 608(b) limits an attorney's questions on cross-examination to the prior bad acts of a witness that are probative of truthfulness. Extrinsic evidence in the form of witness testimony is not permitted.

Defendant is entitled to cross-examine Expert Witness regarding his testimony on direct examination. Also, FRE 608(b) allows Defendant to question Expert Witness for impeachment purposes with respect to the allegedly false testimony that he provided in his divorce case. Such questions would be permissible for three reasons. First, they concern the character for truthfulness of Expert Witness and could undermine the credibility of his answers in the direct examination. Second, even if he did provide false testimony in his divorce case, he did not receive a perjury conviction for that testimony that would be subject to FRE 609. Third, any answers that Expert Witness provides on cross-examination regarding his testimony in the divorce case would not constitute extrinsic evidence that is precluded by FRE 608(b).

The correct answer is (A) because the impeachment evidence is only admissible if it is obtained from Expert Witness on cross-examination.

Answer (B) is incorrect. This type of evidence may only be elicited on cross-examination. Under these facts, extrinsic evidence is not permitted.

Answer (C) is incorrect. The information that Defendant seeks to elicit on cross-examination is intended to impeach Expert Witness's veracity, which is not a collateral issue.

Answer (D) is incorrect. Defendant seeks to impeach Expert Witness's veracity with Expert Witness's own testimony, not with character evidence about Expert Witness from another witness.

Question 152

Answer: B

(B) is the correct response to this evidence question. FRE 607 states that: "The credibility of a witness may be attacked by any party, including the party calling the witness." FRE 613(b) applies when a witness's prior statement is inconsistent with another statement of the witness. FRE 613 provides a party-opponent an opportunity to question the witness about the statement. Because impeachment evidence is not being directly offered to prove its truth, hearsay evidence may be used for the purpose of impeaching the witness.

Plaintiff may impeach Witness on direct examination pursuant to FRE 607. Witness's statement on the tape recording contradicts Witness's testimony on direct examination. Plaintiff seeks to use the tape recording to show that Witness made a prior statement that is inconsistent with his testimony at trial. Plaintiff seeks to impeach the credibility of Witness with his tape recorded prior inconsistent statement about Defendant's grounds for terminating Plaintiff.

The tape recording constitutes hearsay evidence because it is an out-of-court statement by Witness. Plaintiff is not precluded from using the tape recording as impeachment evidence because it is not being offered to prove the truth of the matter asserted—that Defendant admitted to terminating Plaintiff based on an improper racial motivation. Instead, it is being offered to prove that Witness is not a truthful witness.

The correct answer is (B) because the tape recording is admissible to impeach Witness's testimony.

Answer (A) is incorrect. The tape recording is only admissible for impeachment purposes. It is not admissible as substantive evidence of Defendant's racial motivation.

Answer (C) is incorrect. The tape recording, although it is hearsay evidence, is admissible for impeachment purposes.

Answer (D) is incorrect. The tape recording is admissible to impeach Witness's testimony despite having been secretly made because Witness lacks a reasonable expectation of privacy in the statements that he made at the meeting.

Question 153
Answer: A

(A) is the correct response to this evidence law question. Hearsay is an out-of court statement offered in evidence to prove the truth of the matter asserted. FRE 803(5) is an exception to the hearsay rule which applies if the following two circumstances exist:

(1) A witness states that the witness does not recollect recorded information; and
(2) Presentation of the document does not refresh the witness's recollection.

In that event the document may be read, or the recording may be played, into evidence when these four conditions exist:

(1) A witness possessed personal, firsthand knowledge at the time of the document or recording's creation before the witness testifies;

(2) The document or recording is the witness's knowledge at that time;

(3) The witness made a timely statement when the writing or recording was created; and

(4) The witness testifies to the writing's or recording's reliability.

The exception of FRE 803(5) to the hearsay rule applies because Mr. Wong stated that he did not recollect the license number that he read to Mrs. Wong. The document may be played for four reasons.

(1) Mr. Wong possessed personal knowledge at the time of the recording;

(2) The recording was based on his knowledge then;

(3) Mr. Wong made a timely statement when the recording was created; and

(4) He testified to the writing's or recording's reliability.

The correct answer is (A) because the tape recording is a recorded recollection.

Answer (B) is incorrect. The tape recording does not fall under the hearsay rule exception for public records or reports.

Answer (C) is incorrect because, although the recording is hearsay, it falls under the recorded recollection exception for hearsay.

Answer (D) is incorrect. Mr. Wong possessed firsthand knowledge of the license number.

Question 154
Answer: D

(D) is the correct response to this evidence law question. FRE 801(c) states that: "Hearsay is a statement, other than one made by the declarant while testifying at the trial or hearing, offered in evidence to prove the truth of the matter asserted." FRE 803 describes exceptions to the hearsay rule that do not apply unless a declarant is not available as a witness at a criminal or civil proceeding. Unavailability occurs when a declarant who, through no malfeasance of the evidence's proponent, cannot testify due to a refusal to testify or other grounds. If a presently unavailable declarant testified under oath in a former trial, hearing, proceeding, or deposition, that testimony is admissible in a subsequent proceeding when it:

(1) concerns the same topic as does the present trial, hearing, proceeding, or deposition; and

(2) one of the parties had an opportunity and similar motive to obtain the former testimony by direct, redirect, or cross-examination.

Under FRE 801(c), the Guard's transcribed testimony constitutes a statement that was not made during the civil trial and which is being offered in evidence to prove the truth regarding the director's instruction. As such, this testimony is inadmissible unless it falls under an exception to the hearsay rule.

The former testimony exception would not apply to these facts. Guard is unavailable because he refused to testify due to the appeal of his manslaughter conviction. Guard testified under oath in his former criminal trial. Plaintiff would argue that Guard's former testimony is admissible in the civil trial because it concerns the same topic as does the Plaintiff's civil trial. But Defendant would prevail because it lacked an opportunity and similar motive to obtain the former testimony by direct, redirect, or cross-examination. In fact, Defendant was not involved in the criminal case at all. Moreover, the prosecutor's interests do not align with those of Defendant, and therefore, the prosecutor also had no similar motive to obtain the testimony.

Thus, answer (C) is incorrect, and the correct answer is (D) because the evidence is hearsay that does not fall under any exception.

Answer (A) is incorrect. The statement was made after Guard was no longer employed by Stores.

Answer (B) is incorrect. The instruction is hearsay because the director made it out-of-court as an assertion of the truth of the matter.

Question 155
Answer: D

(D) is the correct response to this evidence law question. FRE 801(c) states that: "Hearsay is a statement, other than one made by the declarant while testifying at the trial or hearing, offered in evidence to prove the truth of the matter asserted."

A declarant's words that express the declarant's state of mind are not hearsay under FRE 803(3). A declarant's statement of a current state of mind or intent to do something in the near future is admissible. An example of such words is a declarant's announcement of feeling fearful when it is presented in support of the affirmative defense of self-defense.

This problem presents a double-hearsay situation. The two statements involved are (1) the statement from Mr. Pence to Mrs. Pence, and (2) the statement from Duarte to Mr. Pence. Mrs. Pence's testimony is hearsay because it is her husband's statement, not one that he made while testifying at the trial, that she offered to prove the truth of—that Duarte threatened to kill him.

The state of mind exception does not apply to Mr. Pence's statement because it does not express his state of mind. The testimony instead purports to express Duarte's state of mind.

The correct answer is (D) because the statement is hearsay that is not within any exception.

Answer (A) is incorrect for the reason set forth above.

Answer (B) is incorrect. Mrs. Pence's testimony is not admissible under FRE 801(d)(2) because it involves an out-of-court statement by Mr. Pence, not one by her party-opponent Duarte.

Answer (C) is incorrect. Mrs. Pence's testimony would be given on direct examination, whereas the prior bad acts rule limits the scope of questions on cross-examination.

Question 156
Answer: B

(B) is the correct response to this evidence law question. FRE 801(c) states that: "Hearsay is a statement, other than one made by the declarant while testifying at the trial or hearing, offered in evidence to prove the truth of the matter asserted."

A declarant's words that express the declarant's state of mind are not hearsay under FRE 803(3). A declarant's statement of a current state of mind or intent to do something in the near future is admissible. FRE 803(1) provides that a declarant's sudden and extemporaneous statement that describes an event when it occurs, or soon afterwards, is admissible.

Witness' proposed testimony is admissible under the state of mind exception because Defendant's statement described her intended plan for future conduct.

The correct answer is (B) because Defendant's statement of her travel plans falls under the hearsay exception for then-existing state of mind.

Answer (A) is incorrect. Witness' proposed testimony is not admissible under the present sense impression exception of FRE 803(1). Defendant did not make a sudden and extemporaneous statement about an event when it occurred or afterwards.

Answer (C) is incorrect. No specific hearsay exception exists for an alibi.

Answer (D) is incorrect because the state of mind exception applies to Witness' hearsay testimony.

Question 157
Answer: B

(B) is the correct response to this evidence law question. FRE 801(c) states that: "Hearsay is a statement, other than one made by the declarant while testifying at the trial or hearing, offered in evidence to prove the truth of the matter asserted." Verbal acts are not hearsay because they state operable facts that not offered to prove the truth of an asserted matter. Verbal acts are facts that possess independent legal significance and are not inadmissible under the hearsay rule. These are facts that are of legal consequence.

Words of offer or acceptance in contracts litigation are verbal acts because they are explanatory words that relate to and give character to a transaction. As such, they may operate with "independent legal effect" upon another person and should be admitted as not hearsay. They are admissible to prove that the statement was made because its independent legal significance and its truthfulness are not at issue.

Under FRE 801(c), Paul's testimony could be hearsay regarding Joan's statement because she did not make it while testifying at the trial, and if he is proffering it to prove the truth of her acceptance of his offer on Donna's behalf. Paul's testimony about Joan's statement is not, however, hearsay because it states operable facts that were offered to prove the effect of Donna's statement–to form a contract between Paul and Donna. Consequently, those facts possess independent legal significance and the statement is admissible as a verbal act.

Joan's alleged words of acceptance are a verbal act because they relate to and give character to the transaction of Paul and Donna. As such, they may operate with "independent legal effect" upon Donna and should be admitted as not hearsay. They are admissible evidence to prove that the statement was made because of its independent legal significance. The statement's truthfulness is not at issue. The issue is whether Joan possessed authority to make the statement to render the contract binding upon Donna.

The correct answer is (B) because the statement is admissible as not hearsay if a foundation is laid for its admissibility showing that Joan had authority to act for Donna.

Answer (A) incorrect. A showing of Joan's authority does not need to be made by a preponderance of the evidence by the court, prior to introduction of the evidence.

Answer (C) is incorrect. No hearsay exception for an unavailable witness applies here.

Answer (D) is incorrect. The statement is not hearsay.

Question 158
Answer: C

(C) is the correct response to this evidence law question. In a criminal case under FRE 404(b), a prosecutor cannot use evidence of specific instances of a criminal defendant's prior wrongful conduct to prove the defendant's bad character. Evidence of prior bad acts is not admissible for a prosecutor to assert that a defendant had a propensity or predisposition to commit a charged offense that is similar to the defendant's prior offenses. The exceptions to FRE 404(b) allow certain evidence of prior wrongful acts and past crimes to be used to establish:

    (1) an element of a charged criminal offense, or
    (2) an affirmative defense to a charge such as the defendant's good character.

Evidence of the prior wrongful acts and past crimes is admissible if it possesses independent relevance and is not being used to prove character. This evidence may be used to prove: motive, intent, absence of mistake, identity, and common plan or scheme.

The exception in FRE 404(b) applies and will allow the prosecutor to use Witness' testimony as evidence of Defendant's prior wrongful acts. Those two instances of Defendant beating his father can be used to establish the element of intent for murder.

Answer (A) is incorrect. The evidence at issue concerns Defendant's conduct, not his character.

Answer (B) is incorrect because Witness must only possess firsthand knowledge of Defendant's previous conduct towards his father.

Answer (D) is incorrect because the evidence may only be used to show prior bad acts, not Defendant's propensity for violence.

This question is a good example of how to avoid common mistakes on questions testing evidence. The admissibility of specific items of evidence cannot be analyzed without asking one key question–for what purpose is the evidence being admitted? An item of evidence may be wholly inadmissible if offered for one purpose, but clearly admissible if offered for another purpose.

Question 159
Answer: C

(C) is the correct response to this evidence law question.

If a first party pays for, or offers or promises to pay for, an injured second party's medical expenses, those facts are not admissible under FRE 409 to prove the first party's responsibility for an incident that resulted in the second party's injury.

Thus, Doctor's offer to pay for Plaintiff's hospital expenses is not admissible under FRE 409 to prove Doctor's medical malpractice liability for prescribing an incorrect medicine that caused Plaintiff's substantial hospitalization.

Question 160
Answer: A

(A) is the correct response to this evidence law question.

Circumstantial evidence, even if it is believed, is evidence that will not resolve an issue without the use of additional reasoning or evidence. Evidence may not be excluded simply on the basis that is it circumstantial. Circumstantial evidence is admissible if it is relevant under FRE 401, has probative value, and not subject to exclusion on any other basis.

The wife's intoxication is circumstantial evidence because the ultimate issue of the accident's cause will not be resolved without additional reasoning or evidence. This evidence is admissible, however, because it is relevant, has probative value, and is not otherwise excludable.

Answer (B) is incorrect because the testimony about intoxication is not admissible evidence to show the wife's character. FRE 405(b) only allows for the admission of evidence of the wife's conduct if character is an ultimate issue in the case. The cause of the accident, not the wife's character, is the ultimate issue.

Answer (C) is incorrect because FRE 405(b) provides that "proof may also be made of specific instances of that person's conduct" if character is the ultimate issue in a case.

Answer (D) is incorrect because the probative effect of the testimony does not outweigh its probative value under FRE 403 with respect to the ultimate issue. The probative value of the wife's intoxication would be significant.

Question 161
Answer: B

(B) is the correct response to this evidence law question. The hearsay rule does not preclude the admission of evidence when a statement is not being offered to prove its truth. A declarant's out-of-court statement is admissible to prove its effect on a reader or hearer instead of the statement's truth or falsity. A declarant's out-of-court statement is admissible to prove that it provided notice of some information (e.g., fact or event) to a reader or a hearer. In that event, the statement is not being presented to establish the statement's truth or falsity.

Evidence that an individual or an entity consistently and predictably acts in a certain way is admissible to prove that the individual or entity's act on a specific occasion conformed to any previous acts. This is called habit evidence. Similarly, an entity's routine practice is admissible to prove the occurrence of a particular event that resulted from that practice. It is not necessary for a party that seeks to prove the existence of a habit to present eyewitnesses to corroborate the occurrence of particular acts or practices.

The hearsay rule will not exclude the letter copy from evidence because it is not being offered to prove the truth of its contents. The letter is Plaintiff's out-of-court statement that is admissible to prove its effect on Defendant as its reader or hearer, but not its truth or falsity. Plaintiff's letter copy is admissible to prove that it provided notice of a cost overrun to Defendant.

Because the letter copy is not hearsay, it falls under the routine practice rule. The facts show that Plaintiff consistently and predictably sent out cost overrun notices. Plaintiff's general manager may testify that Plaintiff's letter copy to Defendant conformed with the previous instances of sending out notices.

Answer (A) is incorrect because the letter copy is not hearsay because it is not offered to prove its truth, but rather to demonstrate notice.

Answer (C) is incorrect because the letter copy is not hearsay.

Answer (D) is incorrect because the Best Evidence Rule includes an exception allowing for the use of a copy.

Question 162
Answer: D

(D) is the correct response to this evidence law question. The hearsay rule does not preclude the admission of evidence when a statement is not being offered to prove its truth. A declarant's out-of-court statement is admissible to prove its effect on a reader or hearer instead of the statement's truth or falsity. A declarant's out-of-court statement is admissible to prove that it provided notice of some information (e.g., fact or event) to a reader or a hearer. In that event, the statement is not being presented to establish the statement's truth or falsity.

Defendant's testimony is not hearsay because Employer's statement is not being offered to prove its truth. The statement is admissible to show that it tended to cause Defendant to believe that Plaintiff could not handle the open job. Defendant is not proffering the evidence to establish as truth that Plaintiff could not work productively for more than four hours a day. The statement afforded Defendant notice regarding Plaintiff's ability to work.

Question 163
Answer: B

(B) is the correct response to this evidence law question. FRE 801(c) states that: "Hearsay is a statement, other than one made by the declarant while testifying at the trial or hearing, offered in evidence to prove the truth of the matter asserted." Under FRE 803(2), the excited utterance rule, a declarant's spontaneous and unprompted statement, which is made under the stress of an exciting or startling event and relates to that event, is admissible.

Alternatively, under the dying declaration exception, a presently unavailable declarant's statement is admissible if it was made:

(1) under a certain expectation of impending death (regardless of if death occurred), and
(2) regarding the circumstances or cause of that expectation.

The correct answer is (B). Smith is offering it in evidence to prove the truth of what Parker said. Thus, Parker's statement is inadmissible as hearsay, and no exception applies.

Answer (A) is incorrect. The statement's probative value is not outweighed by its prejudicial effect under FRE 403.

Answer (C) is incorrect. Parker's statement is not admissible as an excited utterance. Although it was spontaneous, unprompted, and made under the stress of the exciting or startling event of the accident, it did not relate to this event.

Answer (D) is incorrect. Parker's statement is not admissible as a statement made under belief of impending death. Although Parker is unavailable to testify, his statement is inadmissible because, while it was made with a certain expectation of impending death, the statement did not concern the circumstances or cause of this expectation.

Question 164
Answer: B

(B) is the correct response to this evidence law question. FRE 601 deems all witnesses competent unless another provision of the FRE states otherwise. The FRE provide that witnesses, excluding a trial judge and jurors who may be called as witnesses, are only incompetent to testify on two grounds:

(1) lack of personal knowledge of a matter about which the witness may testify as required by FRE 602, and
(2) inability or refusal to solemnly swear (by affirmation or oath) to tell the truth under FRE 603. Inability may result from a lack of understanding.

FRE 602 requires that witnesses provide testimony based on their personal knowledge. Personal knowledge includes any knowledge that witnesses have gained though personal observations that they are recounting when they provide testimony.

The son is deemed a competent witness unless he is proven to be incompetent. The son will not be found incompetent to testify for two reasons. First, he possesses personal knowledge regarding Defendant's shooting as a victim of the shooting. Second, he may be able to understand what it means to, and will probably agree to, tell the truth under FRE 603. The son's proffered testimony about the incident will be based on his firsthand observation of it as an eyewitness.

Answer (A) is incorrect because the prosecutor lacks a burden of proof due to the presumption of competency. Competency is presumed unless proven otherwise.

Answer (C) is incorrect because an honest firsthand account of the criminal act will be highly probative.

Answer (D) is incorrect because truthful testimony by the son should be probative as an eyewitness's recollection of the incident.

Question 165
Answer: D

(D) is the correct response to this evidence law question. An ultimate issue is one upon which a decision by a trier of fact will be outcome determinative in a civil or criminal proceeding. Neither a lay witness nor an expert witness may testify about an ultimate issue of law or assert what the outcome of any proceeding should be. FRE 704 generally permits an expert witness to testify about an ultimate issue of fact, unless it concerns a criminal defendant's mental state while committing an alleged offense.

Whether Defendant felt fear for her life when she killed her husband is an ultimate issue because a decision by a trier of fact regarding her state of mind will factor into a determination of her criminal liability. FRE 704 will not allow the admission of Expert's testimony about Defendant's mental state at the time of the killing because it is an ultimate issue of fact.

Answer (A) is incorrect. Expert's opinion about Defendant's truthful speaking cannot overcome the bar of FRE 704.

Answer (B) is incorrect. FRE 801(d)(1)(B) applies to a witness's prior consistent statement that is offered to rebut an allegation of "recent fabrication or improper influence or motive" if that statement was made before the motive to fabricate existed.

Answer (C) is incorrect because information tainted by hypnosis is not necessarily per se unconstitutional and may be admissible.

Question 166
Answer: B

(B) is the correct response to this evidence law question. FRE 602 requires that witnesses provide testimony based on their personal knowledge. Personal knowledge includes any knowledge that witnesses have gained though personal observations that they are recounting when they provide testimony.

The correct answer is (B) because plaintiff's proposed testimony about the shoe will be based on his personal knowledge that he obtained by looking at it before its disappearance.

Answer (A) is an incorrect conclusion based on a statement that the facts do not support.

Answer (C) is a incorrect. It relies upon an irrelevant basis because Plaintiff could testify about the brake shoe's condition based on personal knowledge even if no settlement conference had occurred.

Answer (D) is incorrect because the shoe is not subject to the Best Evidence Rule that applies to a writing, recording, or photograph.

Question 167
Answer: B

(B) is the correct response to this evidence law question. Real evidence is physical evidence that was involved in or was a part of an incident or situation that gave rise to civil or criminal legal proceedings. Examples of real evidence include pictorial evidence. A prerequisite to the admission of real evidence is authentication and identification.

Pictorial evidence is admissible without any supporting testimony from a witness who observed the person or event that was photographed. This approach allows for the pictorial evidence to "speak for itself." To authenticate pictorial evidence, however, foundational testimony is required from a witness that the technological process used to obtain it is reliable. The types of pictorial evidence that may be authenticated in this manner include films, x-rays, and images captured by automated devices (e.g., surveillance camera videos or pictures).

In this case, the photograph is admissible real evidence because it allegedly depicts Defendant in owner's warehouse. Whether Defendant in fact was there is at issue in his criminal trial. The photograph explains that owner monitored the warehouse for intruders and recorded the image of one. The photograph will enable the jury to determine if Defendant was the intruder. The picture is admissible without any supporting testimony from a witness who observed Defendant being photographed because it speaks for itself.

Answer (A) is incorrect. An expert witness is not required to address any physical similarities between a live person and a photograph of a person. The trier of fact can make its own conclusion.

Answer (C) is incorrect. Eyewitness testimony is not required to authenticate photographic evidence under the majority rule.

Answer (D) is incorrect because a photograph is not a witness whom Defendant is entitled to confront.

Question 168
Answer: D

(D) is the correct response to this evidence law question. The trier of fact must determine what weight to give evidence that is admitted into evidence.

Victim's testimony is not hearsay because it does not concern the contents of an out-of-court statement. Victim seeks to testify from firsthand knowledge about the caller's accent and its similarity to Defendant's accent. The evidence is admissible for that purpose. In light of victim's uncertainty regarding the caller's identity, the trier of fact will determine what weight to accord Victim's testimony.

Answer (A) is incorrect because Victim does not need to identify the caller when no tape recording of the call is offered into evidence.

Answer (B) is incorrect. Best evidence is required to prove the contents of a recording. The testimony is not being offered to prove its contents. It is the identification of the caller that is the issue.

Answer (C) is incorrect. The Best Evidence Rule is not waived by a failure to subpoena a tape.

Question 169
Answer: C

(C) is the correct response to this evidence law question. FRE 704 generally permits an expert witness to testify about an ultimate issue of fact, unless it concerns a criminal defendant's mental state while committing an alleged offense.

The correct answer is (C) because the experienced police accident investigator is an expert witness whom FRE 704 permits to testify about the train's speed, which is an ultimate issue of fact.

Answer (A) is incorrect because expert and lay opinion may be offered regarding the same issue of fact.

Answer (B) is incorrect because the degree of scientific certainty of the investigator's testimony is an issue for the trier of fact to weigh.

Answer (D) is incorrect. The testimony by the investigator is proper regardless of whether Plaintiff first introduced evidence as to speed.

Question 170
Answer: C

(C) is the correct response to this evidence law question. FRE 608(b) generally follows the common law, but limits an attorney's questions on cross-examination to the prior bad acts of a witness that are probative of truthfulness. Prior bad acts are specific instances of misconduct by a witness that do not result in a criminal conviction. These must be for acts that reflect negatively on a witness's truthfulness, such as lying on a credit card application.

FRE 608(b) provides that these acts may only be the subject of questioning during the cross-examination. Extrinsic evidence in the form of witness testimony is not permitted.

In this case, pursuant to FRE 608(b), the prosecutor properly questioned Jaron on cross-examination regarding an alleged prior bad act of making a false statement in a credit card application because it was probative of Jaron's truthfulness. This false statement was a prior bad act that did not result in a criminal conviction. It reflected poorly on Jaron's credibility.

However, the prosecutor may not introduce extrinsic evidence of Wilcox's testimony regarding Jaron's prior bad act. The prosecutor's proffered testimony from Wilcox would exceed the limitation of FRE 608(b) by making the prior bad act a subject of questioning of another witness beyond Jaron's cross-examination. This is impermissible extrinsic evidence of the prior bad act.

Answer (A) is incorrect because Jaron's credibility is not a fact of major consequence. It only affects the weight of his testimony.

Answer (B) is incorrect because Jaron's denial of making a false statement did not "open the door" to the introduction of extrinsic evidence. The examining party must live with the response received by the witness.

Answer (D) is incorrect. Whether there was a misunderstanding would not exclude the evidence. If it were permissible evidence, which it is not, then the witness would have an opportunity to explain the misunderstanding.

Question 171
Answer: D

(D) is the correct response to this evidence law question. FRE 411 provides that evidence about whether a person carried liability insurance is generally inadmissible regarding if the person engaged in negligent or wrongful conduct. However, evidence regarding whether a person possesses liability insurance may only be admitted for the following reasons:

      (1) to show that a witness is biased or prejudiced, or
      (2) to show control, agency, or ownership.

Pursuant to FRE 411, Witness's testimony regarding his sale of a liability insurance policy to Defendant is inadmissible regarding if Defendant negligently failed to maintain the plane. Witness's testimony, however, is admissible to prove that Defendant carried liability insurance to establish that Defendant owned the plane.

Answer (A) is incorrect because the Best Evidence Rule does not apply here because Plaintiff is not seeking to prove the contents of the policy.

Answer (B) is incorrect because FRE 411 is not limited by its terms to cases in which proof of insurance is at issue.

Answer (C) is incorrect because FRE 411 would not permit the evidence's admission to show Defendant's lack of motivation to maintain the plane. This would go directly to the issue of Defendant's negligence, for which evidence of insurance coverage is impermissible.

Question 172
Answer: D

(D) is the correct response to this evidence law question. FRE 104(a) provides that a trial judge may determine preliminary questions including the admissibility of evidence. In deciding issues of this type, a trial judge is only limited by the FRE with respect to determining testimonial privileges. Accordingly, a trial judge could consider hearsay evidence when deciding on the admissibility of other types of evidence.

According to FRE 104 and FRE 103, the issue of admissibility of hearsay evidence is a question for a trial judge to decide. Such a determination should occur in the jury's absence. FRE 801(c) states that: "Hearsay is a statement, other than one made by the declarant while testifying at the trial or hearing, offered in evidence to prove the truth of the matter asserted."

Pursuant to FRE 104(a) the court may consider Doctor's affidavit to determine the preliminary issue of the admissibility of Pedestrian's statement. The affidavit constitutes hearsay because it is an out-of-court statement by Doctor about Pedestrian's statements concerning his expectation of dying.

Pursuant to FRE 104 and FRE 103, only the court may decide the admissibility of Pedestrian's statement to Nurse because it could be hearsay evidence when he made it out of court and her in-court testimony could prove the truth that the car ran the red light.

Answer (A) is incorrect because, even if the affidavit is hearsay, the court may consider it in determining preliminary issues of admissibility. Of course, the court can only do so outside of the presence of the jury.

Answer (B) is incorrect. If the affidavit were irrelevant, that would not prevent the court from considering it as a preliminary matter regarding the admissibility of the Nurse's statement. The affidavit could not be irrelevant for the reason given because dying declarations are admissible in all civil proceedings, not only in criminal prosecutions for homicide.

Answer (C) is a correct conclusion premised on a less than optimal reason. If the affidavit fell under the hearsay rule exception of for statements of then-existing mental condition, this would not be the reason why the judge could consider it. The judge can consider any hearsay evidence when determining preliminary questions of admissibility.

Question 173
Answer: D

(D) is the correct response to this evidence law question.

This question requires you to know and apply several rules of evidence law.

Leading questions are a generally allowed type of inquiry on cross-examination. A leading question suggests to a witness the answer that is sought. Such questions attempt to limit the scope of answer to a "yes" or a "no." Leading questions are usually not allowed when the witness is being cross-examined by the attorney who called the witness, unless this witness is a "hostile" witness.

FRE 611(b) restricts the scope of cross-examination to those issues that were testified to on direct examination, subject to a trial judge's discretion. The credibility of a witness is subject to attack on cross-examination. The questions regarding credibility are not limited to the scope of the testimony on direct examination.

Witnesses may be excluded from the courtroom during part or all of a judicial proceeding. Sequestration is a term that is used to describe their exclusion. Other than the exclusion of a witness for incompetence, FRE 615 authorizes the sequestration of witnesses by a trial judge. The trial judge may exercise that discretionary power of exclusion with respect to any or all witnesses at a trial. The purpose of that exclusion is to prevent the testimony of a witness from influencing or affecting the subsequent testimony of another witness.

Answer (D) is correct because the judge abused his discretion by failing to grant Defendant's request to exclude witnesses and permitting Plaintiff's eyewitnesses to stay in the courtroom after testifying. The judge's erroneous decision contradicts the objective of sequestration by allowing the eyewitness to be influenced by other testimony while waiting to be recalled for cross-examination.

Answer (A) does not involve error by the judge because the scope of cross-examination of Defendant could exceed the scope of Defendant's direct examination when Plaintiff is an adverse witness. The judge may properly exercise discretion by allowing this expanded scope of questioning in that situation.

Answer (B) does not show an error by the judge because a party's attorney cannot cross-examine the party with leading questions unless the party was a hostile witness.

Answer (C) includes no error by the judge because the credibility of a witness is always a legitimate subject of cross-examination regardless of whether this subject was raised in the direct examination.

Question 174
Answer: A

(A) is the correct response to this evidence law question. The Federal Rules of Evidence lack a specific rule that expressly addresses bias and interest as grounds for impeachment of a witness. In civil or criminal proceedings that are subject to either the common law or the Federal Rules of Evidence, a witness may always be asked questions that would reveal a bias or an interest of the witness. Specifically, a party-opponent may try to impeach the credibility of a witness on cross-examination by inquiring about partiality, bias, interest, or motivation.

Even though Frank is not testifying directly, a party has the right to impeach a hearsay declarant to the same extent as a person testifying in the case.

Thus, Dennis may ask Wanda the impeaching question because it seeks to expose a bias of Frank against Dennis. If Frank physically attacked Dennis prior to the accident, then he would have a reason to make his derogatory statement to Wanda about Dennis's driving.

Answer (B) is incorrect. Dennis may not ask Wanda the impeaching question in order to prove character. Under these facts, it may only be asked to show bias.

Answer (C) is incorrect because FRE 613 does not apply to Dennis's evidence to impeach Frank by questioning Wanda. FRE 613 would only apply if Dennis was asking Wanda about a prior inconsistent statement.

Answer (D) is incorrect. It is an incorrect statement of law. Specific instances of prior bad acts that do not result in a criminal conviction may be used for impeachment if they negatively reflect on a witness's truthfulness. In order to be used for impeachment, these acts must be the subject of questioning during cross-examination of the witness.

Question 175
Answer: B

(B) is the correct response to this evidence law question.

In a criminal case under FRE 404(b), a prosecutor cannot use evidence of specific instances of a criminal defendant's prior wrongful conduct to prove the defendant's bad character. Evidence of prior bad acts is not admissible for a prosecutor to assert that a defendant had a propensity or predisposition to commit a charged offense that is similar to the defendant's prior offenses.

However, two exceptions apply. First, proof may be made of specific instances of that person's conduct if the evidence is offered to prove the person's character with respect to an "essential element of a charge, claim, or defense" that is being adjudicated. Second, evidence of prior wrongful acts and past crimes is admissible if they possess independent relevance and are not being used to prove character. This evidence may be used to prove: motive, intent, absence of mistake, identity, and common plan or scheme.

Answer (B) is correct under FRE 405(b) because the prosecutor seeks to introduce inadmissible character evidence. Those specific instances of Defendant's conduct do not satisfy the exceptions' requirement that they concern an "essential element of" the murder charge, or that they may demonstrate identity or common plan. His past shooting of a gun into a house is very different from shooting one into a car. Also, Defendant's pointing of a handgun at a driver while they were operating their vehicles is different from Defendant's waiting in ambush to shoot Victim. Thus, the evidence does not fall under an exception to the general rule barring character evidence.

Answer (A) is incorrect. The prosecutor's evidence of Defendant's prior bad acts bearing on truthfulness could only be the subject of questioning during his cross-examination.

Answer (C) is incorrect because the general rule is that evidence of a prior crime cannot be used to show Defendant's propensity to be violent.

Answer (D) is incorrect because Defendant's previous acts are not sufficiently similar in nature to the charge against Defendant.

Question 176
Answer: A

(A) is the correct response to this evidence law question. FRE 404(a) provides in part that evidence of a person's character or character trait is usually inadmissible to show that the person "acted in conformity therewith on a particular occasion." FRE 404(a)(1)-(3) provide exceptions to that rule. The exceptions in FRE 404(a)(1)-(2) apply to criminal proceedings. FRE 404(a)(1) provides that evidence of a "pertinent trait of character" is admissible if a defendant uses it to prove his or her good character and innocence.

FRE 405(a) provides that both reputation evidence and opinion evidence are admissible in any case "in which evidence of character or a trait of character of a person is admissible." In other words, under certain circumstances, character evidence may be admissible under FRE 405(a) regarding the reputation or opinion of parties and Witness.

FRE 405(b) applies when a defendant's character is an "essential element" of a prosecutor's charge in, or a defense to that charge, in a criminal proceeding. In that instance, FRE 405(a) makes admissible reputation evidence regarding defendant's character.

Witness's testimony about Defendant's character trait of peacefulness may be used to show that Defendant acted in conformity therewith with respect to the alleged murder victim. Defendant's peacefulness is evidence of a "pertinent trait of character" to the offense of murder that is admissible to prove his innocence.

Witness's testimony about Defendant's character trait of truthfulness, however, may not be used to show that he acted in conformity therewith. This is because truthfulness is not relevant as to whether Defendant committed murder. Thus, evidence of truthfulness is inadmissible to prove his good character. Only Witness's testimony about Defendant's reputation for peaceableness is admissible under FRE 405(a) because evidence of this character trait is admissible under 404(a)(1). Defendant's character for peaceableness is an "essential element" of his defense to the murder charge under FRE 405(b).

Question 177
Answer: D

(D) is the correct response to this evidence law question. FRE 201, the rule regarding judicial notice, provides that adjudicative facts must be beyond "reasonable dispute" and that such a status of certitude may be attained because the fact is "capable of accurate and ready determination" through "sources whose accuracy cannot reasonably be questioned."

FRE 803(22) provides that a criminal defendant's prior felony conviction is admissible as substantive evidence of the facts that were necessary to support that conviction if that conviction resulted from a trial or a guilty plea, rather than a plea of nolo contendere.

Answer (D) is correct because judicial notice under FRE 201 is the least effective of the four methods of proving Defendant's prior conviction.

Answer (A) is incorrect because a certified copy of the judgment of conviction under FRE 803(22), offered as a self-authenticating document, would be the best method of proof.

Answer (B) is incorrect because Plaintiff's firsthand account of Defendant's sentencing would be admissible based on his personal knowledge and it is not hearsay.

Answer (C) is incorrect because the witness' testimony about Defendant's oral disclosure would be admissible as an admission by a party-opponent under FRE 801(d)(2).

Question 178
Answer: D

(D) is the correct response to this evidence law question. FRE 803(6) makes business records admissible as an exception to the hearsay rule if they were: made contemporaneously or around the time when an act, condition, or event that the records concern occurred; made by a person possessing personal knowledge of that occurrence; made in the normal course of regularly conducted business activity; and maintained in the normal course of regularly conducted business activity.

The above factors must be established by testimony of a witness who either was the person who possesses personal knowledge of the occurrence; or is the custodian of the business's records.

The person with personal knowledge about an occurrence and who records it does not have to be the one who enters it into the business record. That person and others who create the record which is proffered as evidence must be acting under a business duty.

Plaintiff's hospital record is admissible evidence of a regularly recorded business activity under FRE 803(6). The hospital records custodian could testify that:

(1) Intern's entry of Plaintiff's physical condition was made when Doctor's diagnosis occurred;
(2) Doctor and Intern possessed personal knowledge of that occurrence;
(3) Intern made the entry in the normal course of regularly conducted hospital activity; and
(4) The custodian maintained Plaintiff's record in the normal course of regularly conducted business activity.

Answer (A) is incorrect because Doctor is not testifying as an expert witness.

Answer (B) is incorrect because Doctor is not testifying about his opinion.

Answer (C) is incorrect because the record is not Plaintiff's statement about Plaintiff's physical condition.

Question 179
Answer: D

(D) is the correct response to this evidence law question. An adoptive admission occurs when a party fails to respond to a statement or an act (in the nature of a provocative accusation or event), which may constitute an admission if:

(1) The party-opponent, against whom such evidence is proffered, heard, comprehended, and had the ability to respond to the statement; and

(2) A reasonable person in a party-opponent's position could have responded by refuting that statement or act.

Witness's testimony is admissible as Defendant's adoption of Seller's statement. Defendant made an adoptive admission by failing to respond to the statement. His shaking of Witness's hand might also be construed as an act of adoptive admission.

(1) Defendant heard, comprehended, and had the ability to respond to the statement and act; and

(2) A reasonable person in Defendant's position could have responded by refuting that statement and act.

Answer (A) is incorrect based Seller did not need authorization to speak, in this manner, for Defendant.

Answer (B) is incorrect because Seller's statement is not inadmissible hearsay.

Answer (C) is incorrect because, although Seller's statement is against Defendant's penal interest, Defendant is not unavailable as a witness.

Question 180
Answer: C

(C) is the correct response to this evidence law question. FRE 801(c) states that: "Hearsay is a statement, other than one made by the declarant while testifying at the trial or hearing, offered in evidence to prove the truth of the matter asserted." The Federal Rules provide that a witness's prior identification of a witness that occurred out of court is admissible to prove its truth when the witness is presently testifying. It is not classified as hearsay evidence. It constitutes substantive evidence. However, a witness who made a declaration of identification must personally testify in court in order for the identification to be classified as non-hearsay.

Officer's proposed testimony is hearsay under FRE 801(c). It is a statement by Witness that he is not making while testifying at Defendant's trial or hearing, which the government offered in evidence to prove the truth of Witness's prior out-of-court identification of Defendant. Furthermore, Officer may not testify about what Witness said pursuant to the non-hearsay classification for prior identifications made by a testifying witness. The non-hearsay classification of FRE 801(d)(1)(C) does not apply because Witness refused to testify.

Question 181
Answer: A

(A) is the correct response to this evidence law question. FRE 803(10) is an exception to the hearsay rule which allows hearsay evidence to show the: "Absence of public record or entry. To prove the absence of a record, report, statement, or data compilation, in any form, or the nonoccurrence or nonexistence of a matter of which a record, report, statement, or data compilation, in any form, was regularly made and preserved by a public office or agency, evidence in the form of a certification in accordance with rule 902, or testimony, that diligent search failed to disclose the record, report, statement, or data compilation, or entry."

FRE 803(10) applies to the government's proffered testimony from Witness because it falls under the hearsay rule exception for the absence of a public record or entry. Thus, this hearsay testimony could be used to show the nonoccurrence of Defendant's incarceration based on the lack of any jail record despite a diligent search for them by Witness.

Answer (B) is incorrect because it is based on an inapplicable exception to the hearsay rule.

Answer (C) is incorrect because the hearsay testimony is subject to an exception for the absence of a public record.

Answer (D) is incorrect because the missing records neither need to be, nor can be, produced.

Question 182
Answer: A

(A) is the correct response to this evidence question. Circumstantial evidence will not resolve an issue without the use of additional reasoning or evidence. Evidence may not be excluded simply on the basis that is it circumstantial. Circumstantial evidence is only admissible if it is relevant and not subject to exclusion on any other basis. Circumstantial evidence is evidence of a collateral fact based on which a fact finder could infer the existence of a relevant fact. That inference may be drawn only from the collateral fact or that fact when viewed in combination with other evidence.

Davidson's testimony about his annual salary amount constituted circumstantial evidence that supported his denial of the embezzlement accusation. Its relevance is in showing that Davidson only received a certain amount of funds from Pullco. Witt's testimony indicated that Davidson's account contained $100,000 more than the $150,000 amount representing two years worth of salary. Thus, Witt's testimony constituted circumstantial evidence that Davidson's account contained more funds than his salary income. Witt's testimony is relevant to the claim of embezzlement because the amount of account funds in excess of Davidson's salary could have been wrongfully obtained from Pullco. This circumstantial evidence is probative of the fact that Davidson had possession of more funds than he had earned from Pullco.

The testimony of Davidson and Witt may give rise to an inference that Davidson's embezzled Pullco funds because his account value exceeded his salary income for two years. Additional collateral facts, however, would be needed to prove that the excess amount constituted funds that Davidson embezzled from Pullco.

The correct answer is (A) because Witt's testimony provides circumstantial evidence that tends to establish Davidson's culpability for embezzlement.

Answer (B) is incorrect. It reaches an accurate conclusion for the wrong reason. Witt's testimony is relevant circumstantial evidence and would be admissible regardless of whether Davidson testified.

Answer (C) is incorrect. Witt's testimony is admissible circumstantial evidence with probative value that would have a minimal, if any, prejudicial effect upon Davidson.

Answer (D) is incorrect. The fact that the deposits could have come from legitimate sources is not a valid reason to exclude the evidence. After all, the issue is ultimately one for the trier of fact to weigh. Davidson possesses the full and fair opportunity to explain the source of the funds.

Question 183
Answer: A

The correct answer is (A). An attorney may hire a third party, such as a consultant, to interview the attorney's client regarding a matter in which the attorney is representing the client. The content of the communications between the consultant and the client, and between the consultant and the attorney about those communications, are subject to the attorney-client privilege because the consultant acted as the attorney's agent. This rule applies to other relationships between a client and a third-party that may or may not otherwise be privileged, such as a between a physician and the client as a patient.

The motion should be denied because the content of the communications between the consultant and the client are subject to the attorney-client privilege when the consultant acted as the attorney's agent.

Answer (B) is incorrect because the probable cause standard does not apply regarding whether the interview generated relevant evidence.

Answer (C) is incorrect because the consultant does not need to be an attorney for the privilege to apply to her as the attorney's agent.

AMERIBAR BAR REVIEW

Multistate Bar Examination – Answers to Questions – Section 7

REAL PROPERTY

Question 1
Answer: D

The correct answer is choice (D). This question tests the law of the delivery requirement for a valid deed. A deed is not effective until it is "delivered." In order to properly deliver a deed, there must be evidence that the grantor intended for the deed to be transferred immediately to the grantee. Delivery is a question of fact. In most states, delivery will be presumed if the deed is recorded or if the grantee has physical possession of the deed. Sweeney v. Sweeney, 11 A.2d 806. In this case, because the lawyer properly recorded the deed at the land record office, courts will most likely find a rebuttable presumption of delivery.

Thus, choice (B) is incorrect because a showing that Bernard's estate is listed on the tax rolls as the owner of Blackacre is unnecessary to create a valid conveyance if the deed has previously been properly delivered.

Choice (A) is also incorrect. Although Anna's gift satisfies all the elements for a gift inter vivos (intent, delivery, and acceptance), her expectation of imminent death creates a gift causa mortis. The gift causa mortis is often seen as an emergency substitute for a will and is revocable while a gift inter vivos is not. Thus, because Anna created a gift causa mortis, if this issue was raised in court, Bernard's estate and the cult would not prevail.

Choice (C) is also incorrect. The deed did not mention any negative covenant concerning the use of the land or prohibiting the land from being transferred to the cult. According to the Restatement (Third) of Property, a contract or conveyance creates a servitude if "(1) the parties intend it to do so; (2) it complies with the Statute of Frauds; and (3) the servitude is not illegal, unconstitutional, or violative of public policy." Because there is no evidence that the parties intended to agree that Blackacre was not to be conveyed to a religious cult, a servitude does not exist here.

Question 2
Answer: D

The correct answer is (D). This question tests the law of contracts for the sale of real property. Problems with written contracts encompass all of these options: the Parol Evidence Rule, construction of the contract as to time of performance, as well as Bert's ability to perform.

The Parol Evidence Rule states that when parties have entered into a written agreement that is final and complete, all prior or contemporaneous oral or written manifestations are excluded. In this case, because the previous oral agreement differed from the later written agreement, Bert should raise the issue of the Parol Evidence Rule because the written agreement is more favorable to his case.

The construction of the contract as to time of performance will also be relevant to a decision in favor of Bert. Although the written agreement does not state a time period, even assuming that the written agreement also had the provision that Bert must have the $20,000 within one month, as long as Bert acted in good faith in securing a loan from the bank his ability to perform will also be relevant to a decision in his favor. Each party's performance is an implied condition of the other party's obligation to perform. Once an agreement is valid, each party must show that they have an intention to enforce the agreement. Here, Bert was able and willing to raise the $20,000 within a month. If he had not been, the agreement could be found to be invalid. However, in this case I, II, and III will all be relevant to a favorable decision for Bert.

Question 3
Answer: C

The correct answer is choice (C). This question relates to the law of implied easements, quasi-easements and the rights of easement holders to improve, maintain, or repair that easement.

A quasi-easement arises when an owner of an entire tract of land or two or more adjoining parcels of land uses a part thereof, so that one part of the tract derives a benefit from the other. In the absence of an express agreement to the contrary, the conveyance or transfer imparts a grant in the property with all the benefits and burdens which existed at the time of the conveyance, even though such grant is not reserved or specified in the deed. The correct answer is choice (C).

This question relates to the law of implied easements, quasi-easements and the rights of easement holders to improve, maintain or repair that easement. A quasi-easement arises when an owner of an entire tract of land or two or more adjoining parcels of land uses a part thereof so that one part of the tract derives a benefit from the other. In the absence of an express agreement to the contrary, the conveyance or transfer imparts a grant in the property with all the benefits and burdens which existed at the time of the conveyance, even though such grant is not reserved or specified in the deed.

The creation of an easement from a pre-existing use requires: (1) common ownership of the claimed dominant and servient parcels and a subsequent conveyance or transfer separating that ownership; (2) before the conveyance or transfer severing the unity of title, the common owner used part of the united parcel for the benefit of another part and this was apparent and obvious, continuous, and permanent; and (3) the claimed easement is necessary and beneficial to the enjoyment of the parcel conveyed or retained by the grantor or transferor.

This test is clearly satisfied here. Two years passed where the occupants of both buildings used the stairway in an apparent, obvious, continuous, and permanent manner. Both parcels were previously owned by one person. Access to the second floor of each building was reached by the common stairway located entirely within Building 1, making the use necessary and beneficial. Once the easement was created, Dennis had a right to make improvements on the stairway. Common law states that an easement holder has the right to make improvements on easements as long as the improvements promote the use of the easement within the scope of the easement and do not unreasonably burden the easement or the servient estates owner's use or enjoyment of their property. Dennis was repairing the stairway because it was unsafe and no fact suggests that this interfered with Edward's use and enjoyment of his property. Thus, Dennis' easement in the stairway also created an implied right to keep the stairway in repair.

Question 4
Answer: B

The correct answer is choice (B). This question tests the requirements for an enforceable contract. The Rule Against Perpetuities (Rule) is designed to invalidate certain contingent interests that might vest too late. In applying the Rule, the only facts considered are those existing when the future interest becomes effective. To comply with the Rule, is must be logically provable that within a period equal to the length of one life plus 21 years, a covered interest will vest or forever fail to vest. If there is any possibility that a covered interest might remain contingent after this specified time limit expires, the interest is void. A five-step approach is helpful in applying the rule: (1) determine if the Rule applies to a future interest at issue, (2) decide when the perpetuities period begins, (3) determine what must happen for the interest to vest forever or fail to vest, (4) identify the persons who can affect vesting, and (5) test each relevant life to determine if any one validates the interest. Because Baker's heirs could determine to sell the property more than 21 years after the deaths of both Baker and Aris, the clause in the deed does not satisfy the rule, and Aris' interest in re-purchasing the land is void.

Answer choices (A) and (C) are incorrect because the Parol Evidence Rule here is not dispositive to Aris' claim. Because Aris' interest is void according to the Rule Against Perpetuities, the clause in the written instrument, although construed to embody the complete agreement between the parties, is void. The oral offer from Baker's daughter to Baker would not affect Aris' interest.

Answer choice (D) is also incorrect because even if the deed of Aris to Baker did raise a Statute of Frauds issue, the court will fill in any gaps with reasonable terms customarily used in similar transactions. Also, the type of recording statue will not be dispositive because Aris had constructive notice of the sale. Therefore, the only issue that will determine whether Aris will prevail is the Rule Against Perpetuities. In this case, his interest is void because his interest in re-purchase would fail to vest within the specified period.

Question 5
Answer: A

The correct answer is choice (A). This question deals with the creation of a prescriptive easement. The elements required for a prescriptive easement vary somewhat from state to state. The most common formula requires that the claimant's use be open and notorious, adverse and under a claim of right, and continuous and uninterrupted for the statutory period. Although Len conveyed Lot 1 to Tenny, after Tenny had leased the property for 15 years, by a deed that stated "together with all appurtenances," the right to use the driveway on Lot 2 was not transferred. Because Len owned both Lot 1 and Lot 2 until 8 years ago, Tenny's use has been adverse to the owner (Owen) for only eight years. Therefore, the ten year requisite period of time has not been fulfilled.

Choice (B) is incorrect because the availability of an alternate route does not defeat a claim of prescriptive easement.

Answer choice (C) is incorrect because, although mere use does not constitute adverse possession, here all the elements of adverse possession over the easement are satisfied except the fulfillment of the statutory period.

And answer choice (D) is incorrect because no easement needs to be mentioned in the deed from Len to Owen. The doctrine of prescriptive easements specifically deals with cases where easements are not mentioned in deeds.

Question 6
Answer: A

The correct answer is choice (A). This question tests the law of joint tenancy. A joint tenancy exists when at least two co-tenants own a parcel of land subject to a right of survivorship. To create a joint tenancy at common law, four unities must be present: time, title, interest, and possession. A joint tenant may destroy the joint tenancy at any time by conveyance of the joint tenant's interest. In so doing, the concurrent owners will subsequently possess a tenancy in common, where no right of survivorship exists. Arnold severed his joint tenancy with Beverly when he conveyed his interest in Blackacre to his wife because the unities of time and title were missing. Thus, the interests each held became those of tenants in common.

Choice (B) is incorrect because although joint tenancy was severed, it was at the time Arnold conveyed his interest to Alice and not because of his will.

Choice (C) is incorrect. Alice's reconveyance of the property to Arnold does not reestablish joint tenancy because the unity requirements are not met.

Finally, choice (D) is also not correct because generally, co-tenants do not owe each other fiduciary duties, unless they are voluntarily assumed.

Question 7
Answer: B

The correct answer is choice (B). This question tests the common law of freehold estates. Test's duly probated will devised Blackacre to Arthur for the life of Baker, then to Casper and gave "all the rest, residue and remainder, both real and personal," to Fanny. The words "to Arthur for the life of Baker" create a life estate in Arthur, lasting as long as Baker remained alive, with a remainder in Casper. This is a life estate per autre vie, where the duration of a life estate is measured by the life of a person other that the estate holder. Casper holds a future possessory interest in Blackacre. Because Baker died a week before Test did, the property passes to Casper.

Choice (A) is incorrect because Arthur's life estate was extinguished at the death of Baker, the measuring life.

Choice (C) is incorrect because when Test died, he was testate (with a valid will). Thus, his property will be transferred according to the provisions of his will. Unfortunately, Sonny is not mentioned in the will so no interest in Blackacre can pass to him.

Finally, choice (D) is not correct. Fanny is entitled to "the rest, residue and remainder" of Test's estate, but Casper took Blackacre in fee simple because Baker had passed.

Question 8
Answer: C

The correct answer is choice (C). This question deals with the problem of conflicting title claims and issues of bona fide purchasers. Recording acts vary by state. There are three basic types of recording acts: notice, race-notice, and race. This jurisdiction has a race-notice act, which provides that an unrecorded deed or conveyance shall not be good against a subsequent bona fide purchaser without notice, who first records. A bona fide purchaser is a subsequent good faith purchaser for value who lacks knowledge of a previous interest in the property. Because the conveyance of Greenacre to Maria was properly recorded on January 18, Allen cannot make a case that he is a bona fide purchaser as he would have both record and constructive notice of the prior conveyance to Maria.

Choice (A) is incorrect because in order to prevail under this theory, Barnes must be a bona fide purchaser to claim an exception to the first in time rule. A bona fide purchaser is one who gives valuable consideration to purchase the property and is without notice of a prior unrecorded conveyance. However, this only protects purchasers to the extent that they are the first to record without notice of the prior conveyance. Here, Maria recorded the conveyance before Barnes, so he would have notice of the conveyance.

Choice (B) is incorrect because the delay in recording would only be dispositive if Maria did not record first.

Choice (D) is also incorrect. A person who sells property that is subject to a mortgage often requires that the purchaser either assume or be subject to the mortgage debt. In this case, Barnes, the purchaser of the property, could not have agreed it be subject to or to assume the seller's mortgage debt because he did not know of the mortgage. The purchaser's agreement to assume or be subject to the mortgage is necessary if intent cannot be shown

Question 9
Answer: D

The correct answer is choice (D). This question tests the law of easement by grant. An easement by grant is created by a conveyance of deed from a grantor to a grantee that allows the grantee to use the property. The elements of an easement by grant are that the easement (1) be in writing, (2) be executed by the grantor, (3) express the grantor's intent to provide the easement, (4) adequately describe the land and easement being conveyed, and (5) identify both parties. Frank created an easement by grant when he conveyed Blackacre because the conveyance was written and executed by Frank, contained both his and Sam's names, and both expressed intent and described the land. Because the easement was attached to Blackacre, it would be considered an appurtenant easement and would be conveyable.

Choice (A) is incorrect. If the easement holder also acquired title to the servient estate, the easement is extinguished because an easement only exists in land owned by somebody else. In this case, although Sam owns Blackacre and Whiteacre, Doris holds a future interest in Whiteacre. Thus, the doctrine of merger cannot apply. The easement holder must acquire the entire servient estate for merger to extinguish the easement.

Choice (B) is also incorrect because Joe has not overburdened the easement. He enlarged the hotel by a mere 2 units. The "no increased burden" rule aims to prevent easement holders from placing a burden on the servient estate that is beyond what was initially contemplated. Frank, the original owner, first constructed the 10-unit motel. Adding 2 units cannot be deemed to have substantially increased the burden on the land.

Choice (C) is also incorrect because an easement is implied by necessity only when a common owner divides his property in such a way that one of the resulting parcels is left without access to a public roadway. Joe cannot claim an easement by necessity because of the existence of the "poor public road."

Question 10
Answer: B

The correct answer is (B). This question tests the law of adverse possession and specifically the hostility element of adverse possession. To acquire title by adverse possession, the adverse possessor must prove that their possession is actual, exclusive, open and notorious, adverse (or hostile) to the true owner's interest and under a claim of right, and continuous for the statutory period. Once the adverse possessor has satisfied all the elements of adverse possession for the limitations period, he acquires title to the occupied property. A possessor who enters property under color of title is one who has a defective deed or other writing that purports to transfer title to the possessor, but which the possessor does not know to be invalid.

A claimant with color of title who has actual possession of part of the land described in the faulty deed is deemed to be in constructive possession of the entire parcel. In this case, because Buyer only "occasionally" hunted rabbits on Whiteacre, his possession cannot be said to be continuous. Furthermore, because Buyer's acts were not so visible and obvious that a reasonable owner who inspected the land would receive notice of an adverse title claim, Buyer cannot be said to have adversely possessed Whiteacre. Thus, Buyer's lawyer would properly advise that Buyer would probably not obtain title to Whiteacre.

However, the special problem of boundary disputes raises different issues. Most jurisdictions approach boundary disputes by applying an objective test of hostility. Under this test, the state of mind of the occupier is essentially irrelevant. Instead courts focus on two things: lack of permission and whether the occupier's acts and statements objectively appear to be acts of ownership. If the encroaching owner's actions appear to be those of a true owner, she occupies adversely to her possessor. Here, Buyer planted a row of evergreens and erected a fence. This would satisfy the objective test of hostility because Buyer was conducting himself as a true owner. Buyer actually entered and took exclusive possession of the 10-foot strip of Greenacre. Buyer did so adversely under a claim of right. Buyer's use was open, notorious, and continuous for the 15-year limitations period. Thus, although Buyer cannot claim title to Whiteacre, Buyer satisfies the elements of adverse possession concerning the 10-foot strip of Greenacre.

Question 11
Answer: D

The correct answer is choice (D). This question addresses the termination of concurrent estates by partition. Even though partition by judicial sale is not favored by courts, it is one of the most common methods of partition. After a partition by sale the net proceeds are divided among the co-owners in proportion to their ownership interests. In the absence of clear evidence of unequal shares, courts employ a rebuttable presumption that each co-owner is entitled to an equal share of the proceeds. Partition by judicial sale ends the co-tenancy, distributes the property among the former co-tenants as solely-owned property, and provides a final accounting among them.

In this case, after the partition by judicial sale, Joe would be due a portion of the proceeds in accordance with his share of the property and John would be due the rest. Thus, choices (A) and (C) are incorrect because the proceeds must be split according to each owner's relative interest. Choice (B) is incorrect because, although Joe did possess a half interest in Blackacre, after the partition, the interests are sold. Therefore, Ken's judgment for the pre-partition debt will be a lien on the portion of the proceeds of the sale due to Joe.

Question 12
Answer: C

The correct answer is (C). This question tests the common law doctrine of estoppel by deed (after-acquired title). Estoppel by deed may arise when a seller does not have title at the time he purports to transfer property. If the seller subsequently acquires title to that property, he is estopped from then denying the previous title and transferring it as originally represented. Put another way, if a grantor conveys an interest in property that he does not own to an innocent grantee and later acquires title to the land, it automatically passes directly and immediately to the grantee or the successors in his interest. In this case, Adam had no title to Blackacre at the time he purported to convey it to Betsy, and thus no authority to convey it to another party. However, when he acquired title and refused to close with Betsy even thought she was ready, willing, and able to close pursuant to the contract; he was estopped from selling to a higher bidder. Betsy should be awarded a judgment for specific performance because Adam subsequently acquired title.

Question 13
Answer: B

The correct answer is choice (B). This question tests the requirements of enforcing covenants. An initial promisee and promisor may enforce a restrictive covenant. In this case, the conveyance of Oneacre did not terminate or alter Eatco's leasehold because Jones took the property subject to the lease; however, he did not agree to take on the obligations inherent in the lease. Therefore, Eatco still has a present interest in the land subject to the covenants contained in the lease agreement. Because the original promisee is attempting to enforce the lease against the original promisor, which retains its leasehold interest, the judgment should be in favor of Leaseco.

Choice (A) is incorrect because Eatco had more than an implied obligation to pay its share of expenses. They signed a lease that did not terminate at the time Jones acquired Oneacre.

Choice (C) is incorrect because the standard for vertical privity in these cases is greatly relaxed. Furthermore, the benefit of a covenant will run to a successor of some interest in the benefited estate. Just about any interest will do. Restatement Property Section 547.

Choice (D) is also incorrect. Jones, as Eatco's landlord, does have responsibilities as a landlord, but these do not extend to off-site improvement costs that Eatco already agreed to pay for.

Question 14
Answer: B

The correct answer is (B). This question tests the extent of a seller's duty to disclose defects. The traditional common law rule is that under caveat emptor, a seller of property has no duty to disclose latent defects to the buyer absent unusual circumstances (i.e., a fiduciary relationship between the seller and the buyer). The rule of caveat emptor was premised on the theory that buyers ought to use diligence and due care to inspect the property themselves. By including an "as is" clause the seller was giving "official notice" and opportunity to the buyer to notice any defects in the property; and the Seller is transferring the duty of finding and then accepting those defects to the Buyer. Under the caveat emptor doctrine, the seller's agent, like the seller, was not obligated to disclose. However, it is important to note that now, as a result of court decisions and newly enacted statutes, most jurisdictions are beginning to impose an affirmative duty on a seller to disclose all latent material defects in the condition of the property to the buyer. The trend towards mandating disclosure by the seller has produced a similar movement towards imposing the same disclosure duty on the seller's agent. The vast majority of states, however, still follow the traditional rule, imposing no such duty. Here, the "as is" clause in combination with Paul's inspection of the dwelling, relieve Sally of responsibility. Furthermore, Paul never asked about the condition of the dwelling.

Choice (C) is incorrect because Bill never became the agent of Paul.

Choice (A) is incorrect because Sally's duty to disclose is to the buyer and not to her agent.

The seller does have a duty to refrain from intentional misrepresentation or active concealment of a known defect, thus (D) is incorrect.

Question 15
Answer: D

The correct answer is choice (D). This question tests the termination of joint tenancies. A joint tenancy is a co-tenancy subject to the right of survival that is created through the existence of four unities of interest (interest, title, time, and possession). At common law, if one joint tenant leased his interest the joint tenancy was severed. Most jurisdictions today do not regard joint tenancy as severed by one joint tenant's lease of his interest. The survivorship right continues. Thus, upon Hal's death, his property interest evaporated by operation of the law, creating a fee simple, now held solely by Wan. Tent's lien gave him a legal interest in Hal's portion of Blackacre, so that when the joint tenancy was severed by Hal's death, Hal's interest in Blackacre was terminated.

Choice (A) is incorrect because although both Hal and Wan were entitled to receive a portion of the profits from Tent's rental, Tent was a tenant of Hal's, residing in Hal's portion of the property. Absent a prior agreement, a co-tenant cannot be forced to assume the costs incurred by the other co-tenant.

Choice (B) is incorrect. Although the lien against Hal's interest in the property was filed before Hal's death, the lien was attached to Hal's portion of the property.

Choice (C) is incorrect because Wan did not need actual notice of the lien, as it was attached to Hal's interest in the property and not his own.

Question 16
Answer: D

The correct answer is choice (D). This question tests the law of assumption of the mortgage in the context of a remainder. A vested remainder is a future interest that is created in a living ascertainable person and is not subject to any condition subsequent. If an individual "assumes" a mortgage, rather than being "subject to" it, they become personally liable for the mortgage debt. An assumption agreement is an agreement under which one person assumes the obligations already owed by another to a third party. Thus, the mortgagee is a creditor beneficiary of the purchaser's promise. Therefore, in the event of default, both the purchaser and the original mortgagor are personally liable for the full mortgage debt. In this case, Wilma is the owner of the property because she assumed the mortgage. All three children hold vested remainders. Because her mother currently owns the property and Clara has only a future interest, she cannot be compelled to pay. However, her share in the remainder would be lost if the mortgage is not paid because the property would be sold in a foreclosure sale.

Choice (A) is incorrect because a future interest is a presently existing interest but it confers only a future right to possession.

Choice (B) is incorrect because Wilma cannot be compelled to pay the mortgage. She is within her right to allow the lender to sell the property and have the lender apply the proceeds of the sale to the payment of the loan if she so chooses. Any proceeds left over would go to her.

Choice (C) is incorrect because Clara cannot be held personally liable for the mortgage. Because her mother currently owns the property and Clara has only a future interest, she cannot be compelled to pay.

Question 17
Answer: A, B, C, and D

Technically, all of the above answers were given credit. Although one answer was originally designated as the correct answer, when the exam was scored a large percentage of the exam takers must have chosen the other choices. In such situations, the examiners may give credit for all of the answers.

Choice (A) could be correct because while Barbara was joint owner of his accounts, the deed conveyed Blackacre to Bob only. Therefore, the property would devise according to Bob's will, which leaves the property to First Church.

Choice (B) could be correct. The argument could be made that because Barbara was joint owner of the accounts, and when she purchased the property she could have been doing so with her portion of the money. This answer is the weakest of the four because it is the most illogical.

Choice (C) could be correct because a deed to a grantee who does not exist is void. Bob was dead at the time of the conveyance, and had been for a week, so he technically did not exist, and Adam would retain the property. The problem with this answer is that he was paid valuable consideration for the property, which he would not be allowed to retain.

Choice (D) appears to be the most correct answer. As explained above, the deed to Bob would most likely be void because he was dead at the time of conveyance, but because Barbara had paid $20,000 for the property, it would be unjust for Adam to keep the property free and clear. Therefore, his property would likely be subject to a lien for that amount.

Question 18
Answer: B

The correct answer is choice (B). This question deals with the law of priority among mortgages. A single property can be encumbered by multiple mortgages and other liens. Except in those few states in the United States that adhere to the title theory of mortgages, either a mortgage or a deed of trust will create a mortgage lien upon the title to the real property being mortgaged. The lien attaches to the title when the mortgage is signed by the mortgagor and delivered to the mortgagee and the mortgagor receives the funds whose repayment the mortgage secures. Subject to the requirements of the recording laws of the state in which the land is located, this attachment establishes the priority of the mortgage lien with respect to other liens on the property's title. Liens that have attached to the title before the mortgage lien are said to be senior to, or prior to, the mortgage lien. Those attaching afterward are junior or subordinate. Mortgagees are considered buyers under recording acts and will therefore be subject to the priorities of the recording acts. In this case, Rohan has legal title until a foreclosure occurs. Because Acme sold the same interest twice, first to XYZ and second to Peterson, the priority would be established, without any statute to the contrary, in order of recording.

Choice (A) is incorrect because XYZ Bank recorded the mortgage first.

Choice (C) is also incorrect because although Peterson is in possession of the note, the actual valid mortgage belongs to XYZ bank, with the note being part of that mortgage.

Choice (D) is incorrect also. XYZ Bank receives priority among mortgages in this fact pattern. If, on the other hand, Acme had conveyed the promissory note, the mortgage, and the assignment to Peterson, he would have a purchase money mortgage, which would receive priority over any other competing claims against the real property that secured the mortgage.

Question 19
Answer: D

The correct answer is choice (D). This question tests priority among mortgages. A prior properly recorded interest is senior to later properly recorded interests. Once the prior mortgage is discharged, the next most-senior mortgage takes priority. In the absence of any countervailing equities, one who makes a loan in innocent reliance upon an invalid real estate mortgage is entitled to subrogation for the existing valid liens. Where a loan has been obtained by means of an invalid mortgage and the proceeds used to pay off existing encumbrances against the property, the courts have, without exception, held that the mortgagee under the invalid mortgage is entitled to be subrogated to the right of the prior mortgagee. If a party completely pays the obligation that a mortgage secures, they obtain the right of subrogation.

When Fritsh became owner of the property, he became responsible for the previous mortgages in order of priority. Thus, when Zorn paid off the previous mortgage, she was entitled to be subrogated to the position of Ulrich as senior mortgagee. When Fritsh paid the $100,000 received from Zorn to Ulrich, Ulrich's interest in the land was terminated. At this point, Zorn became entitled to have Ulrich's mortgage revived for her benefit and Zorn is entitled to be subrogated to the position of original mortgagee. Because Ulrich's mortgage was senior, priority passed to Martin. Countervailing equities in favor of Martin would give Martin an exception to the normal hierarchy of priority. Since there are no countervailing equities in his favor, Zorn's mortgage is entitled to priority over Martin's mortgage. Thus, I, II, and III are all necessary to determine Zorn's priority.

Question 20
Answer: A

The correct answer is choice (A). This question tests the formal requirements for the conveyance of deeds. In order for a deed to be valid, a grantor must specifically identify a grantee. Ordinarily in a deed, a grantee is described clearly and specifically. However, a grantee can be described without reference to a specific person, as long as the description is sufficient to identify an actual person. Otherwise, the deed is not valid because of uncertainty of ownership or inability to deliver the deed to a nonexistent grantee. In this case, the fact that the defendants consist of every current Protestant church in the county makes it impossible to determine the identity of grantees because the leaders could have changed.

Choice (B) is incorrect because although there is a presumption of delivery, if the deed is invalid (by reason of inadequate information), delivery of it becomes moot. Furthermore, Olin clearly expressed his intention to transfer the interest and it was properly recorded.

Choices (C) and (D) are also incorrect because the identity of the grantee is too indefinite to be valid.

Question 21
Answer: A

The correct answer is choice (A). This question focuses on the validity of equitable servitudes. Notice is a requirement for the benefit or burden of a covenant to run to successors. If a servitude is anywhere in the chain of title, the buyer will have constructive notice of the servitude. Also, in cases of common development schemes, the development must be uniform in character and recognizable as such by purchasers to constitute effective notice. Here, no constructive notice existed. Because there was no uniform character of this land compared to the subdivision and the covenant was not recorded in the chain of title, Dart should win his case.

Choice (C) is incorrect. In fact, many states permit negative equitable covenants to be created by implication in a situation like this, where there is a common scheme of residential development. If a developer manifests a common plan to impose uniform restrictions on a subdivision, most courts conclude that an equitable servitude will be implied in equity. The common scheme is viewed as an implied promise by the developer to impose the same restrictions on all the lots. In this case, the courts would probably not find a common plan. Because Dart owns nearly one fifth of the entire tract of land, it is possible that the court would decline to find a common scheme. This is not always the case though. The disparity in acreage is only one factor the courts consider. Thus, choice (B) is also incorrect. Although covenants can be deemed illegal restrains on alienation, if the covenant is reasonable and desirable, it is almost always allowed.

Question 22
Answer: B

The correct answer is choice (B). This question tests the transferability of interests. Whenever a life estate is created a future interest also arises. The future interest is either a remainder, which vests to a third person, or a reversion, which vests back to the grantor. A remainder is a future interest created in a transferee that is capable of becoming a possessory estate upon the natural termination of a prior estate created by the same instrument. In this case, by conveying Greenacre to Lafe for life and then to Rem, her heirs and assigns, a remainder was created. As soon as Owen conveyed the property, it belonged to Lafe until Lafe's death. Upon Lafe's death, the property would transfer to Rem. Although Rem died before taking possession of Greenacre, her future interest survived, and passed to her "heirs and assigns." An heir is defined as a person who is designated to receive ownership of real property upon an intestate's death. In our case, Rem did not die intestate and instead devised all her estate (including the future interest in

Greenacre) to Dan. The common law doctrine of destructibility of contingent remainders held that a legal contingent remainder in real property was extinguished if it failed to vest when the preceding freehold estate ended. In our case, the remainder never failed to vest because Lafe held a possessory interest in the estate. The estate never ended. Furthermore, the doctrine is now almost completely abolished in the United States through statute or decisional law. Therefore, Dan would hold title to Greenacre.

Thus, (A) is incorrect because Owen never held a reversion in the land and upon conveyance gave up an interest in the property

Choice (C) is incorrect then because although Hannah is Rem's heir, the vested remainder in Rem was transferred to Dan by Rem's will.

Choice (D) is incorrect because the contingent remainder vested before the end of the freehold estate.

Question 23
Answer: B

The correct answer to this question is choice (B). This question deals with a landowner's right to subjacent support. Every landowner has a common law right to have the land in its natural condition supported by the earth below. If a neighbor's excavation causes the landowner's land to cave in, the neighbor will be strictly liable for damage to buildings on the landowner's property if the landowner can show that the weight of the buildings did not contribute to the collapse of the land. If the landowner is unable to make such a showing, the neighbor must be shown to have been negligent for the landowner to recover any damages. In fact, many courts impose liability for undermining subjacent support only when negligence can be shown due to difficulties in proving that the weight of the building did not cause the land to collapse.

Accordingly, most states use negligence principles in these cases. Thus, Dora can only be held liable if she failed to use due care to avoid injury to Pam's property.

Question 24
Answer: D

The correct answer is choice (D). This question tests the nuisance doctrine as applied to light. The vast majority of courts in the United States would hold that, in the absence of an agreement to the contrary, property owners have absolute rights to develop their property without liability for any interference with their neighbor's interests in light and air. This is often expressed by saying that no easement for light and air exists unless a contract creates it. Prah v. Maretti, 321 N.W.2d 182 (Wis. 1982). Furthermore, courts are even more reluctant to recognize a right to sunlight when the plaintiff's building is located in an urban area, where buildings often buttresses and blocks the sides of adjacent structures. Absent an express easement for light and air, property owners cannot bring suit against their neighbors for interfering with their enjoyment of property because of changes which affect the flow of light and air to their property. Pam and Dora had no such agreement. Therefore, Pam has no cause of action in this case.

Question 25
Answer: A

The correct answer is choice (A). This question deals with the enforceability of restrictive covenants by successors. In order for a covenant to "run with the land" and thereby bind the promisor's successors, American law traditionally requires that several elements be established: (1) the covenant must be in writing; (2) the original parties must intend to bind their successors; (3) the covenant must "touch and concern" the land; and (4) the successor must have notice of the covenant. Baker clearly intended for the benefit of the covenant to run to successors. Dodd can trace his title to Able, the person who imposed the covenant. Thus, Dodd may enforce its benefit.

Choice (B) is incorrect. The doctrine of negative reciprocal covenants requires sufficient evidence to indicate that the necessary intent exists to bind successors. In this case, none of the deeds that were recorded referred to the restrictive covenant. Thus, not enough evidence exists of Able's intent for Dodd to invoke the doctrine of reciprocal negative covenants.

In the same vein, (D) is incorrect because "constructive notice of the possibility" of the covenant is not sufficient to show the requisite intent.

Choice (C) is incorrect. Business-related restrictive covenants are not favored because they decrease alienability.

Question 26
Answer: C

The correct answer is choice (C). This questions tests the requirements for marketability of title. Every contract for the sale of realty contains an implied duty of the seller to deliver marketable title to the buyer. Any defect in title must be substantial and likely to result in injury to the buyer. One common defect in title is a breach of covenant against encumbrances. This covenant is breached if the title is encumbered at the time of delivery of the deed, whether or not the grantor is aware of the encumbrance. An encumbrance almost always makes a title unmarketable. An encumbrance is a burden on the title, such as mortgages, judgments liens, easements, or covenants. Also, by expressly making the time of performance an essential term of the agreement, a party able and willing to perform on the closing date is relieved of and future obligations under the sale contract if the other party fails to perform on the required closing date.

In this case, the contract required Owen to provide evidence of marketable title. Owen's title was not marketable because it was encumbered by Alice's one-eighth interest in Vacantacre. Because of this, Owen was unable to convey the title to Perry within the specified time period.

Choice (B) is incorrect because the covenant against encumbrances was not fulfilled. Thus, the warranty deed did not provide Perry with adequate interim protection.

Choice (A) is incorrect. Although the transfer was made within a reasonable period of time, in this case time was "of the essence" and Owen could not provide a marketable title within that period.

Choice (D) is also incorrect. Excessiveness of an amount of earnest money comes into play only when the buyer fails to complete performance of the contract. If a seller retains the amount given in the earnest money deposit, courts will then examine the amount tendered. If the amount retained by the seller is enough to constitute a penalty, the seller may not be permitted to keep the deposit. If, on the other hand, the amount of the down payment is reasonably related to the seller's actual damages, courts normally allow the grantor to keep the money.

Question 27
Answer: D

The correct answer is choice (D). This question tests the law of classification of estates, divestment, and assignment. A fee simple subject to a condition subsequent is created when the words of a grant support the conclusion that the grantor intends to convey a fee simple "absolute" but has attached a string to the grant so that if a specified future event does or does not happen, the grantor gets his fee simple absolute back. Therefore, the grantor has conveyed a fee simple for forever but has added a condition that will enable him to get it back. The instrument by which Owen conveyed Greenacre to Able created a fee simple subject to condition precedent. Because that condition precedent had not occurred (Able has not graduate college), the property has not been conveyed to Able, and Owen retains ownership. Because Owen retained ownership, Baker is his tenant, Able cannot oust him.

Choice (A) is incorrect. When the grantor has parted with less than a fee simple absolute, the grantor necessarily retains an interest. Thus, Owen still has an interest in the land which he conveyed to Able and remains landlord of the property. Baker therefore is a tenant of Owen and not of Able.

Choice (B) is also incorrect because Owen's conveyance did not terminate Baker's tenancy due to the fact that Owen retained an interest in the land.

Choice (C) is also incorrect. Here, Able has assigned part of the leasehold to Baker. Owen and Baker are thus in privity of estate with respect to Greenacre, and Baker and Owen have the relationship of landlord and tenant.

Question 28
Answer: C

The correct answer to this question is choice (C). This question tests the law of illegal conversion and the rules for marketable title. The title to a piece of real estate must be reasonably free from risk of litigation over possible defects. While the title may not be perfect, it is free from plausible or reasonable objections, and is one that a court of law would order the buyer to accept. As a general rule, a title is unmarketable if the seller's title is subject to any encumbrance. However, while all jurisdictions agree that the mere existence of zoning, building, and land use regulations does not make the title unmarketable, the violation of a zoning ordinance does render title unmarketable. Although a buyer should expect the existence of zoning regulations, the buyer would not reasonably expect that the property currently violates the law. The violation of a law is not an "encumbrance" in the traditional sense of the term, but courts have extended the scope of marketable title doctrine to protect the unwary buyer. If the buyer purchased the land, the buyer would be subject to the risk of civil or criminal litigation. Illegal conversion occurred when Owens converted the single-family home to a structure that contained three separate apartments in an area zoned for single-family residential uses only.

Because Peters learned that Whiteacre did not conform to the zoning ordinance before the closing, Owens would lose his action for specific performance. Thus, choice (A) is incorrect because the title was not in fact marketable.

Choice (B) is incorrect because Peters normally would not be charged with the knowledge of the zoning ordinance, even under the caveat emptor doctrine. Courts have extended the scope of the marketable title doctrine to protect an unwary buyer for situations just like the one presented here. It is not reasonable to expect that the property currently violates the law.

Finally, choice (D) is incorrect because, even if the illegal conversion had occurred previously to Owens taking possession of the title to the land, a marketable title would still not exist for Owens to convey to Peters.

Question 29
Answer: A

The correct answer is choice (A). This question tests the Statute of Frauds. The Statute of Frauds provides that agreements for the sale of property "shall not be enforced unless they are in writing and signed by the vendor." As interpreted in case law, the Statute of Frauds imposes three requirements: (1) the essential terms of the sales contract (2) must be contained in a memorandum or other writing (3) that is signed by the party against whom the enforcement is sought. Courts gradually created two equitable exceptions to the Statute of Frauds which apply where a buyer or seller seeks specific performance of the sales contract, not in an action for damages. These two exceptions are the doctrines of past performance and equitable estoppel. Past performance generally requires that the purchaser take possession of the property, pay all or part of the purchase price and/or improve the property in some way. Equitable estoppel requires that the purchaser reasonably and detrimentally rely on a transfer insufficient to meet the requirements of the Statute of Frauds. This often means that there must be some, albeit insufficient, writing, and that the purchaser pays some money to incur some liability in reliance on the documents validity. Here, the agreement was oral and neither of the exceptions is fulfilled. Thus, the agreement is unenforceable.

Question 30
Answer: C

The correct answer is choice (C). This question tests the conveyance of a fee simple subject to a condition subsequent. A fee simple subject to a condition subsequent is created when the word of a grant supports the conclusion that the grantor intends to convey a fee simple "absolute" but has attached a string to the grant so that if a specified future event does or does not happen, the grantor gets his fee simple absolute back. A fee simple subject to condition subsequent is a defeasible fee estate that does not end automatically upon the happening of a condition specified in the conveyance. The future interest in the estate, a reverter, must be claimed by the holder of the interest. This interest retained by the grantor when a fee simple subject to condition subsequent is created is called right of entry or power of termination. Such conditions are subject to the Rule Against Perpetuities, which requires that the condition vest or fail within 21 years after the death of a life in being at the time of the initial conveyance.

Here, Test retained an interest in Blackacre when he conveyed it to School District. Thus, when Blackacre ceased to be used for school purposes, the property reverted to Test. Test died before that reversion occurred and left all his estate to his friend Fanny. The estate, which Fanny now owns, included that future interest in Blackacre for 21 years after Test's death. Should the condition not be fulfilled, Fanny possesses the right of reverter. Thus, as soon as the land was not used for school purposes, and Test was dead, the title passed to Fanny.

Choice (D) is incorrect because Owner's interest in the estate was automatically terminated when Blackacre ceased to be used as a school.

Choice (B) is incorrect because Test died testate, so his property passes to whomever he chose to name in his will. Had he died intestate, title would pass to Sonny.

Lastly, choice (A) is incorrect. School District was not able to convey title to Owner because as soon as they stopped using Blackacre for school purposes, their interest was terminated since it happened within 21 years of Test's death. Therefore, Fanny now holds valid title to Blackacre.

Question 31
Answer: C

The correct answer is choice (C). This question tests the principles of joint tenancy. Under common law, all tenants must take their interests (1) at the same time, (2) under the same instrument, (3) with the same interests, and (4) with the same right to possession of the entire property. If the four unities are not satisfied, a tenancy in common results. If a joint tenant conveys his interest to a third party or to another joint tenancy, the joint tenancy is severed as to that interest, and the joint tenant creates a tenancy in common instead. Severance occurs at the moment a contract for conveyance is made. Here, when Beth conveyed her interest to Eugenio by warranty deed, Christine and Eugenio became tenants in common. Tenants in common own separate but undivided interests in the same interest in property. Each tenant owns the entire property, but must necessarily share with the other tenants in common. A tenancy in common interest may be alienated, devised, or inherited separately from the other tenancy in common interests. Thus, when Christine conveyed her interest to Darin by warranty deed, Darin and Eugenio both owned Blackacre as tenants in common.

Question 32
Answer: D

The correct answer is choice (D). This question deals with the requirements for transfer of a leasehold interest. An assignment is the transfer of the tenant's existing lease to a third party. A sublease, in contrast, is a wholly new lease between the original tenant and a third party. An assignment places the assignee in privity of estate with the other original party, and the assignee is therefore obligated to perform all the lease covenants that "run with the estate." The clear majority of states employ an objective test to decide if a transfer is a sublease or an assignment. If the tenant transfers the right of possession for the entire remaining term of the lease, the transfer is an assignment. However, if only part of the remaining term is transferred, a sublease arises. An option, like a real estate purchase agreement, is a personal right that is assignable. State courts have split on the issue of whether options to purchase contained in a lease can be assigned separately from the lease. In this case, if the applicable jurisdiction uses the rule which forbids this kind of transfer, Lanny would likely win his action for specific performance because Jones would be forced to close and accept the title with the outstanding option assigned to Oscar.

Choice (A), although accurate, would not result in a favorable decision for Lanny. If the court decided to apply this rule, Lanny would have to convey the interest free of the option.

Choice (B) is incorrect. The doctrine of marketable title requires that the interest being transferred is free from any encumbrances. Thus, any outstanding option that has not yet been exercised burdens the interest in such a way that the doctrine of marketable title would not be satisfied. Here, Teri recorded the instrument of assignment including the outstanding option.

Choice (C) is incorrect. It is true that options to purchase by lessees are subject to the Rule Against Perpetuities, but here the option must be exercised during the lease, which would of necessity occur within 21 years of the death of any lives in being.

Question 33
Answer: C

The correct answer is choice (C). This question tests the laws which regulate the termination of easements. Easements last forever unless terminated by (1) abandonment, (2) release, (3) adverse possession, (4) destruction of a servient estate, (5) condemnation, (6) the end of the necessity for an easement, (7) estoppel, or (8) merger of the dominant and servient estate.

Misuse of an easement does not usually terminate the easement, but may give rise to claims for legal or equitable remedies. Three issues arise in determining whether the owner of an easement is misusing it by going beyond the scope of activities contemplated by the grantor: (1) whether the use is of a kind contemplated by the grantor, (2) whether the use is so heavy that it constitutes an unreasonable burden on the servient estate not contemplated by the grantor, and (3) whether the easement can be subdivided.

Furthermore, determining whether an activity constitutes an unreasonable additional burden on the servient estate beyond that contemplated at the time the easement was created depends on the grantor's intent. Most courts interpret easements broadly and hold that a general right-of-way may be used for any reasonable purpose as long as it does not substantially interfere with the rights of the servient owner.

In this case, the expanded use of the easement is reasonable in the context of the public way leading to the previously erected large residential building. Expanded use of an easement, absent evidence of substantial interference, does not terminate the easement. Thus, choices (A) and (B) are incorrect. Choice (D) is also incorrect. Sally's use of self-help would not deny her the right to pursue equitable relief in court. It would merely be a factor to be considered if and when equitable relief was granted.

Question 34
Answer:

The correct answer is choice (D). This question tests the law of remedies for a breach of contract in the context of real estate transaction that involves a contract containing a liquidated damages provision. A liquidated damages provision may allow a seller of real estate to retain the potential buyer's earnest money deposit in the event of a breach of their contract. The enforceability of such a provision depends on whether the court finds it to be a valid liquidated damages provision or a penalty. If the court determines that the amount retained is a penalty, it is not enforceable and the innocent party is limited to whatever actual damages they can prove.

In this case, because Bert agreed in writing to buy Sam's house, Bert has breached the contract by not completing the sale. Due to this breach, Sam may retain the earnest money deposit because it is only a small fraction of the purchase price and not large enough to constitute a penalty.

Choice (A) is incorrect because Sam's inability to carry out the contract does not negate a breach.

Choice (B) is also incorrect because Bert was not legally justified in not completing the contract.

Choice (C) is incorrect because of the liquidated damages provision. Sam's actual damages were only $2,000, but the $5,000 was a reasonable estimate of damages. Thus, Sam will be permitted to keep the deposit as liquidated damages.

Question 35
Answer: B

The correct answer is choice (B). This question tests the law of requirements for a valid contract. All types of contracts must satisfy the same minimum requirements of offer, acceptance, consideration, reasonably certain terms, and so forth. Like any other contract, a real property sales contract must meet these requirements. However, a contract for sale of an estate or interest in real property is enforceable only if it is also evidenced in a writing whose terms satisfy the Statute of Frauds. Implied in any contract to convey real property is an obligation of good faith and timely performance.

Here, Baker and Able entered into a valid contract which bound both parties to perform. Even though there was no earnest money down payment, they are both still bound to perform because they exchanged one promise (to pay the purchase price) for another (the house). Once an offer to purchase is accepted the parties have a binding contract, regardless of whether the buyer pays the earnest money, and the buyer cannot unilaterally withdraw the offer. Failure to pay the earnest money does not release or relieve the buyer from her contractual obligations.

Choice (A) is incorrect because the mere parking of his car does not constitute part performance on Baker's part. Part performance would require that a party do at least two of the following three things: (1) take possession of the property, (2) pay all or part of the purchase price, and (3) make improvements on the property. Thus, without further action by Able, he has not satisfied the part performance exception.
Choice (C) is also incorrect. Under the common law doctrine of equitable conversion, the buyer is deemed to be the equitable owner of the land until close of escrow unless the contract specifies otherwise. This binds the equitable owner to purchase the land at a later time and places the risk of loss on the buyer. This is a rule that applies to fortuitous loss, not one for which a party to the contract is responsible. Therefore, it does not apply here.

Choice (D) is incorrect. Although it is true that in order to have a valid deed, it must be properly recorded, recording alone does not make a complete case for compelling specific performance. Here, the best answer is choice (B).

Question 36
Answer: C

The correct answer to this question is choice (C). This question deals with landlord liability for personal injury. This issue is a specialized application of the ordinary tort doctrine of negligence. Barring a few exceptions, the common law rule provided that landlords had no duty to make the leased premises safe for tenants or their guests. Today, the duty of landlords to maintain leased premises in a fashion that avoids foreseeable injury to others is increasing. The common law recognized the following exceptions to the general rule that a landlord had no tort liability to the tenant or his guests for dangerous conditions existing on the premises at the inception of the lease: latent defects and public use. In terms of latent defects, because only the landlord would know of a concealed defect, common law imposed on the landlord a duty to warn the tenant of their existence and the specifics of the defects. Under current practice, landlords are liable to tenants for injuries arising out of the landlord's negligence, including negligent failure to comply with housing codes or the implied warranty of habitability. A landlord is liable for harms to tenants only if he has acted negligently. This means that the landlord may be relieved of liability if the injury is caused by a latent defect of which the landlord could not reasonably have been aware. In this case, Les knew of the danger of the latent defect but failed to warn Tom. This is clearly negligent in view of his duty to warn. Thus, Tom should recover because Les negligently failed to comply with the implied warranty of habitability.

Question 37
Answer: B

The correct answer is choice (B). This question tests the problem of conflicting title claims. The traditional common law rule is that the person whose interest is first delivered prevails over anyone who acquires an interest later. All states have modified this general rule through legislation known as recording acts. The recording acts in almost all states create a major exception to the rule: in a title dispute between a first-in-time claimant and a later bona fide purchaser for value, the bona fide purchaser prevails. In general, a bona fide purchaser is one who purchases an interest in land for valuable consideration without notice of an interest already held by a third party. The precise requirements for bona fide purchaser status are spelled out in the recording act of each state.

The two pertinent statutes mentioned in the question signify that this is a notice jurisdiction. In notice jurisdictions, the general bona fide purchaser definition described above is applied. Smollett is a "subsequent purchaser" because the term encompasses almost any person who acquires any interest in the land, including judgment liens. However, because Smollett did not give any new value in return for his lien, he is not considered a purchaser for value. Therefore, Smollett is not a purchaser for value and is not protected by the recording acts.

Choice (D) is incorrect because absent bona fide purchaser status, it does not matter of Smollett did or did not have notice. Furthermore, notice here could found through inquiry or by imputed notice.

Choice (C) is incorrect because the majority of recording acts would not protect a creditor's lien interest over that of a third party. In the majority of states, a judgment lien lacks priority as compared to the grantee of real property. Most recording acts also do not consider a judgment creditor to be a bona fide purchaser for value. Thus, a judgment lien may only be applied against property that the debtor owned when the judgment was entered, excluding any recorded or unrecorded conveyances, unless a recording act afford special protection to judgment liens. Thus, choice (A) is also incorrect.

Although Able's warranty of title does defeat Smollett's claim, it does so because he is not a bona fide purchaser. Therefore, (B) is the best answer.

Question 38
Answer: B

The correct answer is choice (B). This question tests the law of transferability of easements. The transferability of easements depends on the type of easement. An easement appurtenant benefits the easement holder in using the dominant land. By definition, an easement appurtenant exists only when there is both dominant and servient land. Conversely, an easement in gross is personal to the holder. It benefits the holder in a personal sense, whether or not he owns any other parcels of land. Thus, it is attached to the holder, not the land. The easement in gross involves only servient land; by definition, no dominant land exists. An easement appurtenant is automatically transferred when the estate is transferred, while an easement in gross remains with the holder. Any transfer of title also automatically transfers the benefit of the easement, unless there is a contrary agreement. Here, there is both dominant and servient land. The easement only benefits the owner of the back forty acres if someone owns that land. Therefore, it is an easement appurtenant. Any transfer of title to the dominant land transfers the benefit of the easement. Thus, choices (A), (C), and (D) are incorrect.

Question 39
Answer: D

The correct answer to this question is choice (D). This question tests the identification and transferability of life estates. By definition, whenever a life estate is created a future interest arises. In this problem, Louis receives a life estate. Louis' widow holds an indefeasibly vested remainder. The terminology "then to Louis' child or children in equal shares" creates contingent remainder in fee simple absolute. Thus, when Louis died, the title vested in Zelda for life. Without more, a bare reference to "Louis' widow" is construed to refer to the unknown person who answers that description upon Louis' death. This is known as the "unborn widow" rule, one of the two classic traps of the Rule Against Perpetuities. The Rule Against Perpetuities presumes the possibility that aged men and women might substitute younger mates for more elderly ones— even so young that they were not born at the time of the grant. However, the contingent remainder vested in "Louis' widow" is valid because the uncertainty as to the identity of the widow will be resolved at Louis' death.

The same uncertainty as to "Louis' child or children" will also be resolved upon Louis' death as he will have no more children after that. Thus, measured by Louis, this grant does not violate the Rule Against Perpetuities. This is because the interest is certain to vest within 21 years of Louis' death. Therefore, the interest vests to Zelda upon Louis' death. The contingency of the remainder created in "Louis' child or children" is destroyed upon the birth of Norman and the death of Louis. Norman held a remainder in the estate, which was part of his estate when he died. This future interest then passed to the American Red Cross, to whom Norman left his entire estate. Therefore, the title to Greenacre is vested in Zelda for life with the remainder belonging to the American Red Cross.

Question 40
Answer: D

The correct answer is choice (D). This question tests the requirements for a valid contract. All contracts must satisfy the same minimum requirements of offer, acceptance, consideration, reasonably certain terms, etc. However, a contract for the sale of an estate or interest in real property is enforceable only if it is also evidenced by a writing whose terms satisfy the Statute of Frauds.

The Parol Evidence Rule provides that parol evidence will not be admitted to vary, add to, or contradict a written contract that constitutes an integration. A written contract constitutes an integration if the parties to the contract intended the writing to be the final and complete expression of their agreement. Today, most courts hold that a writing is deemed to be an integration only if the parties intended it to be. A contract must be in writing for the Parol Evidence Rule to apply. If the Parol Evidence Rule does apply, and the contract is fully integrated, then Able cannot introduce evidence that the parties intended for time to be of the essence.

In an action for damages for nonperformance of a contract, as Able has here, a call for closing on a certain date is sufficient to make damages available from the party not ready to close on that date. Further, the use of the phrase "time is of the essence" in a contract means that each action required in the contract's provisions must be performed promptly at the date or time specified. However, time is not of the essence unless the contract specifically stipulates this or necessarily implies it. Thus a failure to perform or close on a stipulated date is not, per se, an actionable breach of contract. If no time is set for the closing, a reasonable amount of time is implied. The reason for nonperformance is for the trial judge to determine in view of its reasonableness.

Specific performance is also relevant in advising Able of his legal position. Courts grant specific performance when the plaintiff can show: (1) a contract of sale, binding and enforceable between the parties to it, (2) that the plaintiff was capable of tendering performance, (3) that there is no reason why equity should not enforce the contract, and (4) that the plaintiff does not have an adequate remedy at law. Because real property is unique in that damages are difficult to measure, specific performance became the preferred remedy. The vendor of property must be counseled to keep the title marketable and be ready to tender a satisfactory deed to the property. Depending on the state, Able may not be able to sue for specific performance, forcing him to resell and then sue for damages. Therefore, all four choices are relevant to fully advise Able of his legal position.

Question 41
Answer: C

The correct answer is choice (C). This question tests the priority of security interests in personal property. In the United States, under Article 9 of the Uniform Commercial Code, a security interest is a proprietary right in a debtor's property that secures payment or performance of an obligation. A security interest is created by a security agreement, under which the debtor grants a security interest in the debtor's property as collateral for a loan or other obligation. A security interest grants the holder a right to take remedial action with respect to the property that is subject to the security interest upon the occurrence of certain events, almost always the non-payment of a loan. The holder may take possession of such property in satisfaction of the underlying obligation. However, more commonly, the holder will sell such property and apply the proceeds of such sale to the underlying obligation. To the extent that the proceeds of the sale exceed the amount of the underlying obligation, the debtor is entitled to the excess. To the extent that the proceeds of the sale do not exceed the amount of the underlying obligation, the holder of the security interest is entitled to a deficiency judgment pursuant to which the holder can institute additional legal proceedings aimed at recovering the full amount of the underlying obligation from the debtor. Article 9 of the Uniform Commercial Code governs these conflicts between mortgages on real property and other security interests. Here, because the windows are removable, the court is enabled to return Blackacre to the condition it was in prior to the replacement of the windows as well as allow Vend to recover its products.

Question 42
Answer: C

The correct choice is answer (C). This question tests the marketable title requirement. The purchase and sale agreement ordinarily requires the seller to be able to deliver marketable title at the date set for closing. The seller's inability to do so will excuse the buyer from the deal. However, because Owen offered to arrange for the payment and discharge of the mortgage at closing from the proceeds of the closing, he could have been able to complete his obligation to deliver marketable title at closing. Title is not rendered unmarketable by unpaid liens or mortgages on the real property if the seller gives the buyer reasonable assurances that any encumbrances on title will be discharged when it is tendered.

Choice (A) is incorrect. Priority of mortgages normally becomes pertinent when there are several mortgages and the property is foreclosed upon. The mortgage's existence is important because it is an encumbrance on the title.

Choice (B) is incorrect. Under the common law doctrine of equitable conversion, the buyer is deemed the equitable owner of the land until close of escrow unless the contract specifies otherwise. This would place the "risk of loss" (usually physical destruction) on the buyer, Newton. However, there has been no destruction of the property in this case.

Choice (D) is also incorrect. Newton's real reasons for refusing to close are immaterial as long as she was able to close and did not. This is an intentional breach of contract.

Question 43
Answer: C

The correct answer is choice (C). This question deals with the problem of conflicting title claims. The traditional common law rule is that the person whose interest is first delivered prevails over anyone who acquires an interest later. However, in a title dispute between a first-in-time claimant and a later bona fide purchaser for value, the bona fide purchaser prevails. A bona fide purchaser is one who purchases an interest in land for valuable consideration without notice of an interest already held by a third party. A purchaser may receive notice in four different ways: (1) actual notice, (2) record notice, (3) inquiry notice and (4) imputed notice. Furthermore, the purchaser is obligated to make a reasonable inspection of the land before purchase. If a person other than the grantor is in possession, the purchaser is usually obligated to inquire about the possessor's rights.

Here, the state appears to have adopted a race-notice recording act, which protects subsequent bona fide purchasers who record first without notice of previous claims. Fred neglected to inspect the land at purchase, and thus failed to discover Sam's possession. He is therefore charged with inquiry notice of any interest Sam may have held in Blackacre.

Choice (A) is incorrect. Although it is true that a warranty deed provides more title protection than a quitclaim deed, Sam acquired his interest in Blackacre first, thus giving him priority over Fred.

Choice (B) is also incorrect. Orben's subsequent conveyance to Fred would revoke the gift to Sam if Fred had been a bona fide purchaser. However, since he is not, the general rule applies and the law vests title in Sam.

Choice (D) is incorrect because even assuming the equities favor Sam, this does not necessarily preclude a court from vesting title in Fred.

Question 44
Answer: A

The correct answer to this question is choice (A). This question deals with the requirements for a valid adverse possession claim. To acquire title by adverse possession the adverse possessor must prove four elements. The possessor must (1) actually enter and take exclusive possession that is (2) open and notorious, (3) adverse or hostile to the true owner's interest and claim of right, and (4) continuous for the limitations period.

Here, Agency did actually enter and take exclusive possession of the land. Their use was open and notorious and was hostile to Brown and Silas' property rights. Finally, the requirement that the adverse possessor's use be continuous does not mean that Agency has to be on the property 24 hours a day. Depending on the type of property in question, even extended absences by the adverse possessor may not defeat an adverse possession claim. The continuity requirement is normally interpreted to mean that the adverse possessor must exercise control over the property in the ways customarily pursued by owners of that type of property. Here, Blackacre was undeveloped land, so the customary use rule sets a very low bar. Therefore, because the facts here constitute adverse possession, title to the portion of Blackacre concerned has vested in Agency.

Choice (B) is incorrect because as long as the use is open and notorious, Brown is charged with notice of the use. Here, the piles of waste and Agency's use of the portion of Blackacre were readily visible to any inspector of the property, constituting notice.

Choices (C) and (D) are incorrect. Even if the state had the power of eminent domain here, Silas' claim would not be moot. Silas would be entitled to the fair market value of the taken property or severance damages. The interest of the public would also entitle Silas to an equitable remedy.

Question 45
Answer: A

The correct answer is choice (A). This question tests the classification and transferability of estates and the correlating rights of each. A life estate is a possessory estate that expires upon the death of a specified person. A life estate is always followed by some future interest–either a reversion in the grantor or a remainder in a third party. Here, Ogle holds a reversion and Lilly owns a life estate measured by her life, not Ogle's life. No subsequent act of Ogle, including his death, affects that life estate. Ogle's will makes Mina the beneficiary to whom he devised a life estate in Greenacre. Here, Mina has inherited Ogle's reversion so that upon the death of Lilly (but not until then), she may receive the life estate. Rex simply holds a reversionary future interest in Greenacre. Upon Mina's death, Rex's future interest may become possessory. Therefore, Lilly should be adjudged to have the right to immediate possession as the present life tenant of Greenacre, subject to the respective future interests of Mina and Rex.

Question 46
Answer: B

The correct answer is choice (B). This question tests marketable title and judgment liens. Every contract for the sale of realty contains an implied duty of the seller to deliver marketable title to the buyer. Any defect in title must be substantial and likely to result in injury to the buyer. One common defect in title is a breach of covenant against encumbrances. This covenant is breached if the title is encumbered at the time of delivery of the deed, whether or not the grantor is aware of the encumbrance. An encumbrance almost always makes a title unmarketable. An encumbrance is a burden on the title, such as mortgages, judgments liens, easements, or covenants.

Here, once the binding contract concerning the marketable title was recorded, it became a part of the chain of title, and equitable title passed pursuant to the doctrine of equitable conversion. The jurisdiction at issue permits recording of contracts, which would protect the buyer from an subsequent encumbrance or lien attaching after the recording of the contract. Able and Baker entered into and recorded their contract before Charlie obtained and properly filed the judgment. Even though legal title would pass after Charlie records the judgment, Baker would be insulated against claims attaching after the recording of the contract. Therefore, the title would be marketable at the time of the closing.

Choice (D) is incorrect. A judgment creditor is a party who prevails in a civil action seeking damages from a judgment debtor. The majority of recording acts would not protect a creditor's lien interest over that of a third party. In most states, a judgment creditor lacks priority as compared to a grantee of real property before the judgment is entered.

Choice (A) is incorrect. A purchaser in fact takes on the lien when they purchase the property.

Choice (C) is also incorrect. Recordation of a deed is irrelevant to its validity. An unrecorded deed is normally fully effective and binding. The law presumes that a grantee is accepting a beneficial conveyance. Usually recordation of a deed benefits the grantee and thus a prudent grantee will immediately record his title. This is to protect his title against later claimants such as a bona fide purchaser. If in fact the instrument conveying the interest is later found to be invalid, the recordation does not make it valid.

Question 47
Answer: D

The correct answer is choice (D). This question tests the requirements for a burden and a benefit of a real covenant to run. When a promisee's successor seeks to enforce a covenant against a promisor's successor, the burden and the benefit must both run in order for the covenant to be binding. In order for the burden of a real covenant to "run with the land" and thereby bind the promisor's successors, American law traditionally requires that six elements be established: (1) the covenant must be in writing; (2) the original parties must intend to bind their successors; (3) the covenant must "touch and concern" the land; (4) horizontal privity must exist; (5) vertical privity must exist, and (6) the successor must have notice of the covenant. In order for the benefit of a real covenant to run to successors, only four elements are required: (1) the covenant must be in writing; (2) the original parties must intend to benefit successors; (3) the benefit of the covenant must "touch and concern" the land, and (4) vertical privity must be present.

Here, the covenant is in writing and expressly stipulates that the parties intend for the covenant to run with the land. The burden and the benefit both relate to the use of the land the therefore the "touch and concern" requirement is met. Horizontal privity is normally found when a covenant is created in a transaction involving the conveyance of and interest in land between the covenanting parties. Thus, the horizontal privity requirement is met in this case. Vertical privity concerns the relationship between the original covenanting party and his successors. If the successor succeeds to the entire estate in land held by the original covenanting party, vertical privity exists. The notice requirement is satisfied by actual, record, inquiry, or imputed notice. Here, Oker's deed to Frank was not recorded, so record notice is not satisfied. Inquiry notice, however, is satisfied to the extent that Tim obtained all the original deeds and discovered the covenant in Oker's deed to Frank. Therefore, in this case, the burden and the benefit of the covenant do run with the land. However, the covenant stipulates that the expenses incurred must be reasonable and Tim has not shown his expenditures to be reasonable or customary. If judgment is for Henry, it will be because the $3,500 Tim spent on the retaining wall has not been proven to be in accordance with the covenant.

Question 48
Answer: C

The correct choice is answer (C). This question tests the law of fraud in the context of a tenancy in common. Tenants in common own separate but undivided interests in the same interest in property. Conceptually, each tenant in common owns the entire property, but must necessarily share that ownership with the other tenants in common. There are no survivorship rights among tenants in common. A forged deed is completely void. It conveys nothing to the grantee or any subsequent grantee in the chain of title, including any later bona fide purchaser. If fraud or deceit is employed to procure the initial certificate of title, it can be set aside by the true owner. Or, alternatively, the registered owner will be held to hold it in constructive trust for the true owner. A deed induced by the grantee's fraud is voidable in an action brought by the true owner against the grantee. Here, because Anna and Donald hold separate interests in Blackacre, Donald's fraud voids his interest, but Anna's interest is still valid. However, because the conveyance to Donald was void, Jones retains her interest in Blackacre less the valid conveyance to Anna. Therefore, Anna holds a one-half interest in Blackacre and Jones holds the other half interest.

Question 49
Answer: A

The correct answer is choice (A). This question tests the law which requires disclosure of latent material defects. The emerging rule today is that a seller must reveal all latent material defects. A latent material defect is a defect that (1) materially affects the value or desirability of the property, (2) is known to the seller (or only accessible to the seller), and is (3) neither known to or "within the reach of the diligent attention and observations of the buyer." Most states use an objective standard to assess materiality. Some states require disclosure if a reasonable person would consider the defect an important factor in the decision to purchase. Other states mandate disclosure if the defect has a significant effect on the property's market value. In this case, although there is no intentional misrepresentation, the doctrine of caveat emptor is no longer widely used. However, the sewage seeping into the basement materially affects the value and desirability of the property.

Choice (B) is incorrect because, although Baker did make a proper inspection, the defect is latent and not easily discovered even by an inspection.

Choice (C) is incorrect. The fact that the situation constitutes a health hazard is not always enough to establish a cause of action. However, an owner who innocently purchases "contaminated" property, without actual knowledge of the contamination or any reason to know about it after conducting a diligent, pre-purchase investigation, will qualify for the "innocent purchaser" defense if he later discovers that the land is contaminated. And, accordingly, the owner will not be held strictly liable for cleanup costs. In this case, the fact that the situation constitutes a health hazard reinforces the materiality of the defect.

Choice (D) is also incorrect. The implied warranty of habitability and fitness for purpose is normally used only in landlord-tenant law. Furthermore, without a proper inspection and the other elements of material defect, Baker would have no cause of action.

Question 50
Answer: D

The correct answer is choice (D). This question tests the nuisance doctrine as applied to light. The vast majority of courts in the United States would hold that, in the absence of an agreement to the contrary, property owners have absolute rights to develop their property without liability for any interference with their neighbor's interests in light and air. This is often expressed by saying that no easement for light and air exists unless a contract creates it. Prah v. Maretti, 321 N.W.2d 182 (Wis. 1982). Furthermore, courts are even more reluctant to recognize a right to sunlight when the plaintiff's building is located in an urban area, where buildings often buttress and block the sides of adjacent structures. Absent an express easement for light and air, property owners cannot bring suit against their neighbors for interfering with their enjoyment of property because of changes which affect the flow of light and air to their property. Just because a party has enjoyed the free flow of light and air to their property for years, this will not create an easement for light or air from their neighbor. Since there is no legal right to the free flow of light and air from the adjoining land, where a structure serves a useful and beneficial purpose, it does not give rise to a cause of action for either damages or an injunction, even though it causes injury to another by cutting off light or air or interfering with the view. Therefore, here, the court should grant judgment for Doris because Pauline has no legal right to have sunshine continue to reach the windows of her building.

Question 51
Answer: A

The correct answer is choice (A). This question tests the law of misrepresentation. To be actionable as an intentional/fraudulent, negligent, or innocent misrepresentation, a representation of fact must be one (1) that the seller knows (in some sense) to be false, (2) which is material to a buyer's transaction, (3) that is made with the intention that the buyer will act in reasonable reliance on its truth, and (4) causes the buyer injury.

The materiality of a fact is crucial to a cause of action for misrepresentation, which often involves the distinction between alleged patent and latent defects. A patent defect is subject to inspection, and the risk of its presence is allocated to the purchaser. The underlying premise is that, if the purchaser could see the patent defect, the purchaser adjusted her bargaining over and price of the property to take account of it. A latent defect is by definition not subject to inspection and not bargained over, but it is actionable on that account. All states recognize an action for some type of misrepresentation. Not all states recognize an action for each type. An intentional misrepresentation is the most widely accepted.

Here, Seller, the defendant, has actual knowledge of the falsity of the representation. A misrepresentation can either be an action or some silence or inaction when there is a duty to act or speak. Here, Seller had a duty to inform Buyer that the loading docks could not continue to be used because this fact substantially reduced the value of Blackacre. Because Seller affirmatively concealed the fact from Buyer, he may be held liable for misrepresentation.

Choice (B) is incorrect. Technically, the covenant of warranty is not a promise that the grantor has good title to convey. Rather, it is the grantor's promise to defend the grantee's title against other claimants. The covenant of warranty is breached only when someone holding superior title actually or constructively evicts the grantee from the land.

Choice (C) is incorrect. Buyer provided substantial consideration to Seller.

Choice (D) is incorrect because the mistake was not mutual, it was one sided. Therefore, Buyer's action should be based upon a claim of misrepresentation.

Question 52
Answer: C

The correct answer to this question is choice (C). This question tests the laws of life estates. A life estate is a possessory estate that expires upon the death of a specified person. A life estate is always followed by some future interest–either a reversion in the grantor or a remainder in a third party. A remainder may only be created in a transferee. A life estate is freely transferable during life, but the transferee receives the transferor's life estate. In other words, a life tenant may transfer what he or she has–possession of the land for the duration of the life estate–nothing more. Thus, while a life tenant in theory might lease, mortgage, or even convey his or her interest, the land is bound by these transfers only for so long as the life estate endures. In this case, Ody conveyed a life estate to Leon with remainder in Ralph. Leon conveyed his life estate in Profitacre to Mona. This did not interfere with Ralph's future possessory interest in the property. He still holds the remainder interest. As the current owner of the land, Mona is entitled to all income generated by the property and must pay real estate taxes on it. Mona holds a life estate for the length of the life of Leon. Ralph owns the remainder interest.

Question 53
Answer: B

The correct answer is choice (B). This question tests the agreed boundary line doctrine and the rights of tenants in common. The agreed boundary line doctrine requires: (1) initial uncertainty about the location of the boundary, (2) an express or implied agreement, written or oral, between adjacent owners to treat a particular line as the boundary, and (3) in some states, possession by the parties up to the agreed line.

Neighbors can always agree on a new boundary, reduce the agreement to writing, and record a conveyance to carry it out. If neighbors orally agree on a new boundary when there is genuine uncertainty about the boundary, the oral agreement is a binding method of locating the boundary. The oral agreement is not a conveyance, because that would violate the Statute of Frauds, but it has all the effect of a conveyance. Tenants in common own separate interests in the same property. For example, two people who own a parcel of land as tenants in common each own a fraction of the entire parcel of land, and they are each entitled to use it, but they cannot prevent the other from doing so. By agreeing to a boundary line without consulting Homer, Ethel interfered with Homer's interest in the tenancy in common. One tenant in common cannot bind another tenant in common to a boundary line agreement.

Question 54
Answer: B

The correct answer is choice (B). This question tests sales or transfers by the mortgagor. By taking title subject to the mortgage the buyer incurs no personal liability on the mortgage. In the event of a default, the mortgagee can foreclose and sell the property, but if the foreclosure sale proceeds do not extinguish the debt the mortgagee (i.e., lender) has no further recourse against the owner who has acquired title subject to the mortgage.

The lender can, however, obtain a personal judgment against the original mortgagor for the deficiency, except to the extent that states prohibit deficiency judgments. If a new buyer assumes an existing mortgage, she becomes personally liable for the mortgage loan. The lender can obtain a deficiency judgment against the assuming buyer as well as the original mortgagee (unless the lender has released the original mortgagee). In most states, the lender has option of a suit to collect the debt or to foreclose and cause a sale of the property to satisfy the debt. A few states require the lender first to foreclose and sell before seeking to enforce the debt personally by obtaining a deficiency judgment. The fact that the sale price at foreclosure is inadequate will not by itself void the foreclosure sale. In this case, when Aston conveyed Woodsedge to Beam,

Beam assumed to mortgage and thus became personally liable for the mortgage loan. Beam then conveyed Woodsedge to Carter "subject to the existing mortgage to First Bank." Therefore, Beam and the original owner are liable for the mortgage payments, but Carter is not.

Question 55
Answer: D

The correct answer is (D). This question tests the law of absolute deeds as security. An absolute deed as security occurs when the sell and buy contract, instead of including a mortgage, provides as security a deed in absolute form, which the parties may orally agree to reconvey after the mortgage is paid. This arrangement is not subject to the Parol Evidence Rule or the Statute of Frauds, so such arrangements may be considered mortgages. In this case, Len agreed to lend Oliver money in exchange for the absolute deed to Blackacre. Because Len essentially provided Oliver with a mortgage, he has the right to bring a foreclosure proceeding against Oliver to recover his money.

Answer choice (A) is incorrect. Neither the Parol Evidence Rule nor the Statute of Frauds precludes the admission of evidence that the parties intended to enter into a sell and buy contract with the security deed in absolute form and with the intent to reconvey the property.

Answer choice (B) is incorrect. Prior to the foreclosure, Oliver has the right to pay the delinquent amount and get current on the amount.

Answer choice (C) is incorrect because Len and Oliver entered into an absolute deed as security, which is a valid means of conveying property.

Question 56
Answer: B

The correct answer is choice (B). This question tests the problem of conflicting title claims. The traditional common law rule is that the person whose interest is first delivered prevails over anyone who acquires an interest later. All states have modified this general rule through legislation known as recording acts. The recording acts in almost all states create a major exception to the rule: in a title dispute between a first-in-time claimant and a later bona fide purchaser for value, the bona fide purchaser prevails. In general, a bona fide purchaser is one who purchases an interest in land for valuable consideration without notice of an interest already held by a third party. The precise requirements for bona fide purchaser status are spelled out in the recording act of each state.

The statute mentioned in the question indicates that this is a race-notice jurisdiction. In race-notice jurisdictions, the general bona fide purchaser definition described above is applied plus an additional requirement that the bona fide purchaser must also be the first to record their deed. Recording provides constructive notice to the world of a conveyance. Even if a later purchaser fails to consult the record, he is charged with knowledge of its contents. In a race-notice jurisdiction, recordation cuts off the possibility that either a prior unrecorded purchaser or a later purchaser could prevail. Here, Ann neglected to record her deed. Belle purchased Greenacre for valuable consideration and knew nothing of Ann's claim. She also promptly and properly recorded her deed. Ann is a bona fide purchaser, and thus Belle's purchase cut off Ann's rights. Therefore, the court will hold for Cal who later received the deed to Greenacre from Belle.

Question 57
Answer: A

The correct choice is answer (A). This question tests the law of fee simple subject to condition subsequent. It is sometimes difficult to distinguish between fee simple determinable and fee simple subject to condition subsequent. In general, the hallmark of a fee simple determinable is language of time or duration. Here, there is no language suggesting that a fee simple estate will continue only for the duration of a specified state of affairs. A fee simple subject to condition subsequent, on the other had, does not end automatically, but when created the grantor must provide language containing the right of reentry upon the happening of the specified event. In this case, although there appears to be a condition subsequent, Test did not provide language allowing for reentry. Because the grant was neither of a fee simple determinable or subject to condition subsequent, it would most likely be found to be a fee simple absolute. As a holder of a fee simple absolute, Church has the right to transfer the property, and neither Sonny nor Fanny have a valid claim to the property.

Question 58
Answer: B

The correct answer is choice (B). This question tests the law of life estates. A life estate is a possessory estate that expires upon the death of a specified person. A life estate is always followed by some future interest–either a reversion in the grantor or a remainder in a third party. A remainder may only be created in a transferee. A life estate is freely transferable during life, but the transferee receives the transferor's life estate. In other words, a life tenant may transfer what he or she has–possession of the land for the duration of the life estate–nothing more. Thus, while a life tenant in theory might lease, mortgage, or even convey his or her interest, the land is bound by these transfers only for so long as the life estate endures. Inherent in a life estate is the idea that the life tenant gets to use the property for life, thus deriving the economic value of possession. This use must be consistent with the facts that the property will be handed over to the remainderman at the life tenant's death. Waste is the term used to describe actions of the life tenant that permanently impair the property's value or the interest of the future holders. While a life estate is freely alienable during life, the transferee receives only the transferor's life estate.

Here, Paul cannot sell Eastgate to Acme in order for them to demolish the building, pay off the mortgage, and construct a 30-story office building. This would severely interfere with Richard's interest in the land by reducing the value of Richard's future interest. Therefore, because the proposed demolition of the building constitutes waste, Paul and Acme should be enjoined from carrying out the proposed changes to Eastgate.

Choice (A) is incorrect because life estates (and the corresponding future interests) are freely assignable.

Choice (D) is incorrect. The fact that Richard plans to turn Eastgate into a park is irrelevant. Paul is free to use the land as he sees fit during his lifetime as long as he does not commit waste.

Choice (C) is also incorrect. Although Richard paid the principal portion of each mortgage payment, and is therefore likely subrogate to the mortgagee's rights, this does not mean that he is free to do with Eastgate whatever he wishes. Paul's assignment of the life estate is not necessarily barred by this. Paul is simply barred from unreasonably interfering with Richard's future interest in Eastgate.

Question 59
Answer: D

The correct answer is choice (D). This question tests the law of life estates. Whenever a life estate is created a future interest also arises. The future interest is either a remainder, which vests to a third person, or a reversion, which vests back to the grantor. A remainder is a future interest created in a transferee that is capable of becoming a possessory estate upon the natural termination of a prior estate created by the same instrument.

Here, Cynthia, Cam, and Camelia all have indefeasibly vested remainders in fee simple absolute. These three children are certain to obtain possession following the expiration of Wen's life. Because Cam died prior to obtaining his interest in Purpleacre, his indefeasibly vested remainder is not divested; it has simply expired in accordance with its natural and inherent limits. Therefore, choice (C) is incorrect because Cam's remainder died with him.

This also leads to choices (A) and (B) being incorrect. Cam did not have any interest in Purpleacre to devise to David through his will. Although we do not have sufficient information to determine whether the provision requiring the survival of the children violates the Rule Against Perpetuities, David cannot claim title to Purpleacre either way. Thus, Cynthia and Camelia hold title to Purpleacre as tenants in common because the remainders were contingent upon surviving the life tenant and Cam's interest expired upon his death.

Question 60
Answer: A

The correct answer is choice (A). This question tests the law of prescriptive easements. Easements are not possessory interests so an easement cannot be acquired by adverse possession, but adverse use for a sufficient period of time can ripen into an easement by prescription. Virtually the same elements are needed to establish prescriptive use that are needed to establish adverse possession: (1) adverse use under claim of right that is (2) open and notorious and (3) continuous for the prescriptive period. In this question, Daniel has established a prescriptive easement over Beach's old road.

Generally, easements not acquired by prescription or necessity have language which fixes the duty to repair and maintain the easement. In most states, absent any controlling language, the servient estate has no duty to maintain or repair the property. When Beach conveyed a portion of Blackacre to Carrol, he also granted her an easement over the old road. Carrol made substantial repairs to the road but had no duty to do so. Her grant also lacked any controlling language concerning her duty to repair. Therefore, she will be unable to collect any contribution from Beach or Daniel for her voluntary repairs to the road. In the remainder of states, easement owners have a duty to keep the easement in good repair. Because Carrol has the only express easement, she would still be responsible for the repairs to the road.

Question 61
Answer: C

The correct answer is (C). This question tests the law of easements by prescription. In order to acquire an easement by prescription, and thus a legal right to use the estate of another, a non-owner must be in possession of the owner's estate and his use must be: (1) open, (2) hostile, (3) notorious, (4) continuous, (5) exclusive, (6) and uninterrupted for (7) the legally-required period of time, which varies by jurisdiction. Here, the non-owner's use was not hostile because he had the owner's permission to use the road for ingress and egress for the entirety of the legally-required time. It was not until after the statutory period had passed that the owner revoked the non-owner's right to use the road, at which point the non-owner's use became hostile. Without satisfying all of the elements, Eric will lose.

Answer choice (A) is incorrect because Amos was not the owner of the estate at any point during Eric's use. Although Amos was in adverse possession of the estate for a portion of Eric's use, he did not remain so long enough to acquire title to the estate through adverse possession. Thus, while Eric's use was adverse to Amos, it was not adverse to Oxnard, the owner of the estate.

Answer choice (B) is incorrect because Oxnard was the owner of the estate for the entire period in question and had granted Eric permission to use the driveway. Since Eric never sought permission from Amos, and Amos never had title to the land and thus lacked the right to grant the use, Eric did not need to renew his permission with Oxnard once Amos vacated the property.

Answer choice (D) is incorrect because the statutory period begins to run from the moment that the non-owner begins using the property, regardless of who holds title to the property. In this situation, Oxnard held title to the property throughout the statutory period, and the facts indicate that Eric's use was both continuous and uninterrupted from the point of gaining permission to the revocation.

Question 62
Answer: B

Answer (B) is the correct answer. This question tests the law of joint tenancy. In order for a joint tenancy to be created, four unities must exist at the time of the conveyance: (1) the unity of title, (2) the unity of interest, (3) the unity of time, (4) and the unity of possession. Additionally, if one of the parties to a joint tenancy acts inconsistently with the existence of the joint tenancy, the joint tenancy may be terminated. Here, the unity of possession was likely destroyed during Bruce's lifetime, which would have created a tenancy in common and destroyed Sharon's right of survivorship.

In order to have unity of possession, all of the joint tenants must have the right to possess the entire parcel without the right to exclude the others. Sharon and Bruce orally agreed to divide the land between them, and each did as he or she wished with his or her portion without interference by the other for the remainder of Bruce's lifetime. When Sharon permitted the Audubon Society to use her portion as a nature preserve, she effectively conveyed her interest to a stranger and barred Bruce from possessing that portion. This use of the land is inconsistent with an intent that the joint tenancy remain in force because it makes possession of the entirety impossible.

Answer (A) is incorrect because the Statute of Frauds would apply regardless of the relationship between Sharon and Bruce because the agreement involves the transfer of an interest in real property.

Answer (C) is incorrect because the oral agreement between the two did not necessitate that both would not still be able to possess the entire portion. It was not until Sharon reached the agreement with the Audubon Society that Bruce's ability to posses the southern portion was destroyed.

Answer (D) is incorrect because Sharon would be allowed to assert her claim. If she had chosen to serve as the executrix, she may have been removed from the position of executrix because of the conflict.

Question 63
Answer: A

The correct answer is (A). This question tests the application of the Statute of Frauds to conveyances of real property. The Statute of Frauds requires that the conveyance of an interest in land must be (1) in writing, (2) signed by the party to be charged, and (3) contain all of the essential terms of the agreement in order to be enforceable. Here, Sarah's agreement with Bruce to divide the property was made orally, but because it transferred an interest in land, it needed to be in writing to be valid. Additionally, Sarah's agreement to convey her interest in the southern portion of the property to the Audubon Society was merely an oral agreement and so would not be legally binding without satisfaction of two of the three conditions of partial performance. Although the Audubon Society presumably took possession of the property, there is no indication that it paid part, or the entire price of conveyance, or made substantial improvements to the property. The same would be true if this agreement were for a long-term periodic tenancy. Because there is no exception for part performance, the oral agreement falls under the Statute of Frauds, and proof of it would be inadmissible.

Answer (B) is incorrect because joint tenants can unilaterally sever a joint tenancy through either a mortgage or conveyance to a stranger without consent of the other tenant(s).

Answer (C) is incorrect. While it is true that Sarah would still be able to assert her claim if she is executrix of the will, if the joint tenancy had been severed through Sarah's actions during Bruce's life, then the right of survivorship would have been destroyed. In that case, Bruce would have had the legal right to devise the property to his son.

Answer (D) is incorrect because the severance of a joint tenancy through mortgage or conveyance will automatically change the tenancy to one in common.

Question 64
Answer: B

The correct answer is (B). This question tests the law of licenses. A license may be oral or written, and has several general characteristics: (1) a specified or uncertain duration, (2) a particular or general area to which it applies, (3) a payment of minimal consideration by the licensee to obtain access, (4) an inability on the part of the licensee to control an interest by improvements or repairs, and (5) the ability of the owner to terminate the agreement at will, unless it is irrevocable. In this fact pattern, Purcell has provided in the purchase contract that Homer may remain on the property for 30 days, thus satisfying both the duration and area requirements. Homer did tender a rental payment to Purcell, and although Purcell rejected it, it could satisfy the requirement of consideration. If Homer is a licensee, then Purcell has the right, as owner, to terminate the license at will and thus take immediate possession of the property.

Answer (A) is incorrect. Trespass ab initio occurs when a person is initially permitted, by law, not a person, to enter another's property, and that person exceeds the permission granted. One of the elements to determine a trespasser ab initio is that the right to enter not be granted by an individual. Here, the permission to remain on the property for the 30 days was granted by Purcell, not by law.

Answer (C) is incorrect because the agreement between Purcell and Homer is not a lease. A tenant at sufferance occupies a landlord's premises beyond the expiration of a leasehold interest. Because Homer never had a tenancy agreement with Purcell, he cannot be a tenant at sufferance.

Answer (D) is incorrect because, although the parties have agreed that Homer will be allowed to remain on the premises for 30 days, the agreement did not stipulate an amount for rent or a period for rent and therefore did not create a month-to-month periodic tenancy.

Question 65
Answer: A

The correct answer is (A). This question tests the law of equitable servitudes. In order to enforce the equitable servitude, Sarah would need to show that the burden runs with the land, which requires satisfaction of four elements: (1) The promise regarding the use of the land must be in writing; (2) The initial parties to the promise must have intended for the promise to be enforceable; (3) The promise must touch and concern the land; and (4) The successors to the promisee/promisor must have notice of the promise.

In this fact pattern, the 10-acre tract is recorded in the plan as the designated location for the future school. The original 50 deeds to individual purchasers and the deed to Max all referred to the original plan. The continued referral to the plan, as well as the brochure's emphasis of tract's proximity to the other lots, indicate that Oscar intended the promise of the tract's use as a school to be enforceable. And, it is likely that the first 50 purchasers bought their land in reliance on that representation. The promise relates to the land because it is a restriction on the use. Finally, the successors to the promisor, Max and Pete, should have had notice of the restriction. Constructive notice of prior restrictions would satisfy this requirement, and the original plan for the subdivision as well as the subsequent deed to Max both record the reference to the plan and are in Pete's immediate chain of title.

Answer (B) is incorrect because the city has yet to accept the property for use as a public school, and the facts indicate that the land was not to be purchased with taxpayer funding.

Answer (C) is incorrect because Sarah is not a creditor beneficiary. Black's Law Dictionary defines "creditor beneficiary" as a "third-party beneficiary of a contract who is owed a debt that is to be satisfied by another party's performance under the contract." Sarah is not owed a debt as a third-party beneficiary to a contract.

Answer (D) is incorrect. While it is true that Pete was not a bona fide purchaser because he had at least constructive notice of the restriction on the land, and thus would not have the protection of a notice recording act, the stronger argument for Sarah's case is that there is a recorded restriction that runs with the land.

Question 66
Answer: A

The correct answer is (A). This question tests the law of implied reciprocal equitable servitudes, specifically whether a benefit and burden run with the land. To establish that a benefit runs with the land, (1) the covenant creating the benefit must be in writing; (2) the initial parties to the promise must have intended for the promise to be enforceable; and (3) the promise must touch and concern the land. To establish that a burden runs with the land, all of the above must be met and the successors in interest must have notice of the promise.

Here, the restriction barring mobile homes is recorded in the first 50 deeds conveyed by Oscar to individual purchasers and in the deed conveying the remaining 40 lots to Max. The recording of the restriction in all of the deeds from Oscar to the individual purchasers indicates that both parties intended for the restriction to be enforceable, and this is reinforced by the presence of the restriction in the later deed to Max. Additionally, the promise relates to the land because it restricts the type of dwelling that is permitted to be placed on the property. Finally, Joe would have had constructive notice of the restriction had he adequately researched the chain of title, thus satisfying the notice requirement. Because all of the elements are met, both the benefit and the burden run with the land. Additionally, if the subsequent deeds in a restricted subdivision do not contain the restrictions, the other owners are entitled to seek injunctive relief; therefore, Sarah can enforce the restriction.

Answer (B) is incorrect. While Sarah's concern for the decrease in property value is valid and may have impacted her decision to purchase a restricted lot, the fact that the burden runs with the land is sufficient to enable her to enforce it without referring to the property value.

Answer (C) is incorrect because successive buyers are considered to be on constructive notice if the restriction was recorded in their chain of title. Since the deed to Max came directly from Oscar and contained the restriction, the restriction on Joe is enforceable. He would also be on record notice because a reasonable review of public records would show that his property and the surrounding properties were burdened by the restriction. Additionally, the common scheme doctrine could allow Sarah to enforce the restriction.

Answer (d) is incorrect because there is vertical privity with Joe and Oscar and thus he is not a remote grantee.

Question 67
Answer: D

The correct answer is (D). This answer tests the law of conveyance by dedication. Private property owners can give property to the public through an offer, formal or informal, of dedication on their part and a formal acceptance by the public. When the property in question was platted, the 10-acre plot was designated as "Future Public School," and the brochure promoting the subdivision indicated that the school district would not have to expend funds to acquire the land. Both of the above qualify as offers. The vote by the school board satisfies the requirement that the acceptance be affirmative. Because there was both an offer and acceptance, the dedication was valid, and the original plan and subsequent deed refer to the offer, Pete's claim would be defeated.

Answer (A) is incorrect. Estoppel by laches occurs when a claimant seeking equitable relief is denied such because he has caused unreasonably delayed, or has been negligent in asserting, a claim. The public entity must accept within a reasonable time after the offer is made. The reasonable time requirement has been interpreted to include some long time periods. Here, it is unlikely that a court would find a delay of seven years to be unreasonable when a school board is considering constructing a new school on the land.

Answer (B) is incorrect because the subdivision plan is in Pete's immediate chain of title, and he could have discovered the plan through a title search.

Answer (C) is incorrect because, without acceptance, the offer of dedication is not binding, and the owner of the land can withdraw his offer at any time prior to dedication.

Question 68
Answer: C

Answer (C) is the correct answer. This question tests the law of easements. A valid easement by grant must (1) be written, (2) be executed by the grantor, (3) express the grantor's intent to provide an easement to the grantee, (4) adequately describe the land that is being conveyed, and (5) identify the grantor and the grantee.

It is the duty of a holder of an express easement to maintain the easement, which entails a right to enter the property to make repairs and conversely restricts the owner of the servient estate from prohibiting the repairs. In this situation, the deed lists both parties to the easement, expressly states that the grantor is conveying an easement, adequately identifies the land, and is executed by the grantor. The Water District, as holder of the easement, has a duty to maintain the easement and doing so requires that it be able to enter the land and excavate the pipelines to make inspections and necessary repairs. Because this is part of the Water District's obligation, Peterson cannot prohibit the repairs through the sought injunctive relief.

Answer (A) is incorrect because notice is not a requirement for the continuation of the easement on the servient estate, and Peterson could have searched the title to determine that the easement is present.

Answer (B) is incorrect. The surface of the easement may not have been used for a period of years, but the Water District had continued to use the underground main and had not demonstrated intent to abandon the easement by removing the pipes from the ground.

Answer (D) is incorrect because the nature of the Water District's plan is irrelevant in light of the fact that the easement granted it the right to enter the property to maintain, inspect, repair, and replace the pipes installed on the property.

Question 69
Answer: D

Answer (D) is correct. This question tests the law of easements. The holder of an easement is under a duty to maintain the easement and cannot be sued for damages for unavoidable or necessary harm that arises in the course of making repairs that are within the scope of the easement. Nothing in the facts indicates that the damage to Peterson's property was unnecessary or unavoidable since excavation of the property was required to reach the buried pipeline. Accordingly, Peterson cannot succeed in a suit for damages.

Answer (A) is incorrect because the easement did not have to be mentioned in the deed to apply to the servient estate, particularly since the deed for the easement itself was recorded.

Answer (B) is incorrect because the right to recover for restoration of the servient estate is only applicable when the harm from the repairs is unreasonable. There is no indication in the facts that the Water District's actions qualify as unreasonable.

Answer (C) is incorrect. Although the interest in maintaining a continuous water supply may be great, it has no bearing on the enforcement of the easement or the rights of the servient estate to recover damages.

Question 70
Answer: C

The correct answer is (C). This question tests the law of deeds, specifically land description. Generally the grantor will supply the description of the land to be conveyed, but the grantee is allowed to do so if given the authority by the grantor. If the description is unambiguous, it will stand in the face of parol evidence to the contrary. Here, Devlin specifically authorized Parnell to fill in his choice of lot, and Parnell supplied the lot number on the deed. Although the lot conveyed was neither of the two lots agreed upon, the description in the deed is sufficiently clear that the land can be easily identified. Because there is a lack of ambiguity, evidence of the oral understanding regarding the lot to be conveyed cannot be introduced, and Devlin would lose.

Answer choice (A) is incorrect. While it is true that Devlin's casual attitude toward the completion of the deed did allow Parnell the opportunity to record a different lot, the lax business practices cannot, in themselves, be a basis for excluding evidence of the understanding between the parties.

Answer choice (B) is incorrect. Despite the desire that the recording systems provide certainty, courts will consider cases that involve ambiguous deed provisions even after they are recorded.

Answer choice (D) is incorrect. Courts will undertake interpretation of ambiguous deeds even after they are recorded.

Question 71
Answer: C

The correct answer is (C). This question tests the scope of coverage for recording acts, specifically with regard to a fraudulent conveyance. While an owner may void a fraudulent conveyance in an action against the original purchaser if the grantee induced the conveyance through misrepresentation, false financial statement, or a bad check, he will not prevail in a civil action against a bona fide purchaser to void the conveyance. A bona fide purchaser is one who has paid valuable consideration for property without notice of another person's prior deed that affects the title to the same real estate.

Here, Caruso paid $6,000 for the property, and his attorney's search of the title revealed it to be good and marketable. Thus, because Caruso qualifies as a bona fide purchaser from the original grantee, Devlin will not succeed in voiding the conveyance.

Answer choice (A) is less likely to be correct. Generally, oral modifications of real estate contracts are not valid. The reasoning for the rule is that these modifications essentially create new contracts. However, exceptions are permitted for estoppel and part performance. Here, the written contract supersedes any claims that Devlin has to the agreement regarding Lots 40 and 41. This is unimportant for the case with Caruso, though, because Devlin cannot succeed in voiding a conveyance to a subsequent bona fide purchaser.

Answer choice (B) is incorrect. The recording of a deed does not guarantee that it was not obtained through fraudulent inducement or forgery.

Answer choice (D) is incorrect because Devlin did not violate any equitable principles in his dealings with either Parnell or Caruso, and the clean hands doctrine only bars a party from seeking equitable relief if they have done so. Black's Law Dictionary, 268 (8th ed. 2004).

Question 72
Answer: D

The correct answer is (D). This question tests the Rule Against Perpetuities. Under the common law, contingent interests in property that will not vest within 21 years of the death of a life in being at the time of the conveyance are considered void as against the Rule Against Perpetuities (Rule). Here, if one of Sallie's children were to die within four years of giving birth, it would be possible that the child would not reach 25 years of age within the 21 years required by the Rule. Since it is possible that one or more of the grandchildren might mortgage or sell their property, the condition precedent cannot be upheld. The remainders without the provisions are valid, however, because the death of the child named in the provision of the will precludes the birth of any more grandchildren. Therefore, for example, at Ben's death the contingent remainder in his children is vested because he can have no more children, and thus the remainder is valid.

Answer (A) is incorrect because the contingent remainders in the grandchildren will vest at the death of their parents and thus within the 21 years required by the Rule Against Perpetuities.

Answer (B) is incorrect because, although generally disfavored, reasonable restraints on alienation are allowed for legitimate purposes, which have included keeping property within a family. Here, the purpose of the conveyance seems to be to keep the property within the family itself, at least until the grandchildren reach a reasonable age. Additionally, the prohibition does not extend indefinitely. Even if the provisions against sale or mortgage are valid, the grandchildren can sell their interests upon reaching the age of 25.

Answer (C) is incorrect because the possibility that one of the grandchildren may not reach 25 years of age within 21 years of the death of his or her parent invalidates the provision under the Rule Against Perpetuities.

Question 73
Answer: A

The correct answer is (A). This question tests the application of the Statue of Frauds. Generally, the Statute of Frauds requires that an agreement to convey an interest in land must (1) be in writing, (2) signed by the party to be charged, and (3) contain all of the essential terms of the agreement. Some states, however, allow for an exception for part performance of the contract. This exception requires that there be an oral agreement and at least two of the following three conditions: (1) substantial improvements to the property by the grantee, (2) open and notorious possession of the property by the grantee, and (3) payment, partial or full, of the purchase price. This fact pattern provides an oral agreement between Seth and Jim to convey the property to Jim upon Seth's death in return for Jim's care and operation of the farm.

It is clear that Jim's possession was notorious since he operated the farm as his own and lived in the house with Seth. The facts are less clear regarding improvements, but presumably Jim did make some in the course of his operation of the farm. Key, though, is that Jim sold his business and moved 50 miles in reliance on the promise that the property would come to him. Therefore, the court would likely find for Jim.

Answer (B) is incorrect because there was no contract, and the part performance exception to the Statute of Frauds does not require that the performance refer to a contract.

Answer (C) is incorrect because the "clean hands" doctrine does not apply in this case. Sol did not violate any equitable principles. Black's Law Dictionary, 268 (8th ed. 2004).

Answer (D) is incorrect because the relationship of the parties to a conveyance of property has no bearing on the writing requirement of the Statute of Frauds.

Question 74
Answer: D

The correct answer is (D). This question tests the law of tenancy by the entirety. To create a tenancy by the entirety, a parcel must be conveyed to a married couple. In a state that recognized common-law marriage, the purchase of this property by the Sloans would likely create a tenancy by the entirety. However, the state in which the Sloans reside does not recognize that they are a married and therefore the deed created either a tenancy in common or a joint tenancy. The remedy of partition is available to both tenants in common and joint tenants, and thus the prayer should be granted.

Answer choice (A) is incorrect. Although a tenancy by the entirety cannot be partitioned, the co-tenancy created is either a tenancy in common or joint tenancy, in either of which the tenants can seek partition.

Answer choice (B) is incorrect. Although a tenancy by the entirety was not created, both Wade and Mary were listed in the deed and signed the note and mortgage and were therefore both owners of the property.

Answer choice (C) is incorrect. A tenancy by the entirety was not created because the Sloans were not legally married and so the tenancy could not be severed.

Question 75
Answer: B

The correct answer is (B). This question tests the Statute of Frauds with regard to conveyances of property and the part performance exception to the Statute. The Statute of Frauds requires that agreements to convey an interest in land must be (1) in writing, (2) signed by the party to be charged, and (3) contain all essential terms of the agreement in order to be valid. Here, the agreement for Terrence to purchase the property was merely an oral arrangement, and without conduct sufficient to establish part performance the oral agreement would not be binding.

For the part performance exception to be applicable, there must be an oral agreement between the parties, and the buyer must fulfill at least two of three conditions so that his conduct demonstrates the existence of an agreement. The buyer must (1) make substantial improvements, (2) be in open and notorious possession of the property, or (3) pay part, or all, of the purchase price.

Terrence was in open possession of the property for over five years. He had paid half of the purchase price and had obtained a mortgage for the rest, and had made improvements to the property, although it is unclear if those improvements are substantial or not. These actions do not satisfy the requirements of the part performance exception, though, because all but two are as consistent with Terrence continuing as a tenant as with him purchasing the property. His monthly payments were $200 both when he was a tenant and when he was attempting to purchase, and as a tenant he would have been obligated to make such payments.

As already noted, the improvements may or may not have been substantial, but a tenant is obligated, when the lease is silent, to make necessary repairs to the property. Finally, although Terrence had paid half of the agreed purchase price, that amount would have been paid in that period regardless due to monthly rental payments. Thus, because his actions could be interpreted either way, Terrence did not fulfill the conditions of the part performance exception.

Answer choice (A) is incorrect because the courts recognize a part performance exception to the Statute of Frauds, whereby a conveyance can be valid if there is an oral agreement and two of three conditions are met (substantial improvements, possession, or payment of part or all of the purchase price).

Answer choice (C) is incorrect. If an agreement existed regarding Terrence's purchase of the property, then substantial improvements to the property, with or without the consent of the grantor, would be needed to establish part performance.

Answer choice (D) is incorrect. If the improvements have increased the value of the property, and the payments were truly made in anticipation of purchasing the property, then it would be unconscionable for Olga to benefit from Terrence's expenditures and thus Terrence could likely recover.

Question 76
Answer: B

The correct answer is (B). This question tests the application of the Rule Against Perpetuities to executory interests. An executory interest is an interest in a third party that follows a fee simple determinable interest in the original grantee. Executory interests are subject to the Rule Against Perpetuities (Rule), which at common law requires that contingent interest in property vest no later than 21 years after the death of a life in being at the time of the original conveyance. When an executory interest is voided under the Rule, the estate is considered a fee simple determinable with an implied possibility of reverter back to the grantor or his successors.

In this situation, Barbara's heirs might use the property for something other than farm or residential purposes well beyond 21 years after the deaths of both Barbara and Charles. Because this condition might not come to pass within 21 years of the death of a life in being, the executory interest in Charles and his heirs is destroyed, and the estate becomes a fee simple determinable with a possibility of reverter to Alice or Alice's heirs.

Answer choice (A) is incorrect because the Rule Against Perpetuities destroys only the executory interest in Charles and his heirs and not the fee simple determinable in Barbara or the possibility of reverter to Alice.

Answer choice (C) is incorrect because the occurrence of the condition, the use of the property for purpose other than those stated, automatically terminates the estate in Barbara. The grantor does not have to take affirmative steps to regain possession, as is required by a right of reentry.

Answer choice (D) is incorrect because a reversion is created only when the grantor conveys something less than a fee simple interest to the grantee. Here, Alice conveys a fee simple defeasible to Barbara and thus cannot retain a reversion.

Question 77
Answer: B

The correct answer is (B). This question tests the law of co-tenancies and the right of survivorship. Both joint tenancies and tenancies by the entirety provide a right of survivorship, but only a tenancy by the entirety, and thus its right of survivorship, cannot be destroyed by a conveyance. If Celeste and Donald had created a tenancy by the entirety, then Celeste's transfer to Paul would have no effect on the tenancy, and upon her death Donald would obtain ownership of the entire property.

Answer choice (A) is incorrect because it is unclear whether Donald is the sole owner. If the tenancy is a tenancy by the entirety, then the conveyance would not destroy the right of survivorship and Donald would indeed be the sole owner. If, however, the tenancy is a joint tenancy, the conveyance would have destroyed the right of survivorship, and he would not be the sole owner.

Answer choice (C) is incorrect because a conveyance by a joint tenant to a stranger destroys the joint tenancy and transforms it into a tenancy in common, regardless of whether the other tenants know of the conveyance.

Answer choice (D) is incorrect because a tenancy in common would only have been created if the original tenancy was a joint tenancy and not a tenancy by the entirety.

Question 78
Answer: B

The correct answer is (B). This question tests the law of landlord and tenant and the implied warranty of habitability. In jurisdictions that have codified such warranties, provisions also prohibit retaliatory eviction for reporting such problems, including raising the rent. In this situation, Tess was within her rights when she organized the other tenants, and she had a right to complain that her rent was being raised in retaliation for her actions. Unless Len can show that he evicted Tess for a legitimate, non-retaliatory reason, the eviction will not be allowed to stand.

Answer choice (A) is incorrect. Even if a periodic tenancy had been created by implication, the required notice to terminate a month to month tenancy is only one month, and Len complied with the statutory notice requirement.

Answer choice (C) is incorrect because landlords are allowed to charge varying rents in their properties, and there is no implied agreement that the landlord will charge the same for all.

Answer choice (D) is incorrect. An actual tenancy for years is created by express agreement and thus is not implied by law. However, where "parties enter into a lease of no stated duration and periodic rent is reserved or paid, a periodic tenancy is presumed." 49 Am. Jur. 2d Landlord and Tenant § 115 (2002).

Question 79
Answer: A

The correct answer is (A). This question tests the law of easements, particularly implied easements. Implied easements arise from a non-owner's ongoing, permitted, and lawful use of an owner's estate. There is no indication in the facts that White ever used the area of Black's land now designated as College Avenue as his means of access to the property, nor that Black every permitted such use. Because Breyer lacks evidence of such ongoing permissive use, he would not be able to establish that an implied easement had arisen.

Answer choice (B) is incorrect because Breyer would be permitted to introduce evidence to show that he had no other way in or out of his property. He need not show proof of pre-existing use nor does the easement itself need to be in writing.

Answer choice (C) is incorrect because Breyer could also assert his right to use the land as a future public street. Depending on the municipal ordinances, the submission of a subdivision plan designating public areas, including streets, may constitute a dedication.

Answer choice (D) is incorrect. If Breyer has no other means to access his property, then granting him an easement would not unjustly enrich him at Black's expense. Additionally, once completed, College Ave. will be a public way from which no one can unjustly benefit.

Question 80
Answer: D

The correct answer is (D). This question tests both the law of easements and the law of conveyance by dedication. The acceptance of a plat for a subdivision that includes areas designated as public streets can be considered an acceptance of a dedication of that property. Here, Black had submitted his proposed plan, which all necessary governmental agencies approved. Because the streets were designated as public, and the plan was approved, Breyer could assert that the streets had been dedicated and that as a citizen he has a right to use them.

Answer choice (A) is incorrect because Whiteacre does not appear to have been severed from Black's property, and Breyer has another, albeit inconvenient, means of accessing a public road.

Answer choice (B) is incorrect. While it is true that a deed for a lot within the subdivision will by implication include a private easement to use the roads within the subdivision, that is an exception to the general rule regarding implied easements. While Breyer may have a right to use any dedicated public streets within the plan, he does not own a lot within the subdivision and thus does not have a right to use all of the roads contained therein.

Answer choice (C) is incorrect because Breyer does not own a lot within the subdivision. It is true that sale of lots in a subdivision by reference to the plan creates private easements to use streets that access that lot, but Breyer's unrelated property does not contain such easements.

Question 81
Answer: C

The correct answer is (C). This question tests the law of restrictive covenants. A restraint that discriminates against a person based on a constitutionally protected classification will generally not be enforced. Restrictions based on age, though, have been enforced by courts when fulfilling a legitimate public need. Thus, the court would need to determine if the restrictions do indeed fulfill such a need in order to determine if they violate the Equal Protection Clause.

Answer choice (A) is incorrect. The restriction as recorded applies to the lot that was purchased, not the home that was placed upon it, and so whether the mobile home is real property or personal property is not determinative.

Answer choice (B) is incorrect. Common law prohibits restraints on alienation unless reasonable and for a legitimate purpose. Age restrictions have been found to fulfill a legitimate public need.

Answer choice (D) is incorrect. Regardless of whether the restriction is reproduced verbatim in Dawson's deed, if such a restriction is unconstitutional, then it will not be enforced.

Question 82
Answer: D

The correct answer is (D). This question tests the law of condemnation of premises in a landlord/tenant relationship. If the government obtains only a portion of a tenant's leased premises through condemnation, the lease will not be cancelled and the landlord does not have to abate the rent. Here, the government only condemned 20 out of the 30 acres that Tanner leased. Because he retained the ability to occupy the remaining 10 acres, his duties to his landlord were not affected by the condemnation, and he was still required to pay rent.

Answer choice (A) is incorrect because, even though Tanner's purpose was frustrated, the condemnation of the property was through a government action and therefore the landlord/tenant relationship is not affected.

Answer choice (B) is incorrect. In order to succeed in an action for violation of the covenant of quiet enjoyment, the tenant must demonstrate that a constructive eviction resulted from the landlord's actions and not those of a third party. In this case, the constructive eviction resulted from the actions of the government.

Answer choice (C) is incorrect. Although a tenant is required to repair any damage that occurs on the premises as a result of his or his invitees' actions, the property was not damaged but rather condemned by the government and thus the loss was beyond the tenant's control.

Question 83
Answer: A

The correct answer is (A). This question tests the law of easements and the duty of the dominant estate to maintain the easement. The holder of an express easement has a duty to maintain that easement and may have tort liability for any damages that occur to the servient estate as a result of its negligent failure to maintain the easement. Maria conveyed the easement to Reliable in an express written agreement and so Reliable has a duty to maintain its easement (i.e., the electric line). Because it failed to make the necessary repairs, and because Maria did not hinder its ability to do so, Reliable is responsible for the damage to Maria's property that resulted from the dilapidated state of the easement.

Answer choice (B) is incorrect because the holder of an easement is only liable in tort if he negligently breaches his duty to maintain the easement or unreasonably damages the servient estate while repairing the easement.

Answer choice (C) is incorrect because the duty to maintain an easement falls solely on the easement holder, and the owner of the servient estate has no duty to report defective conditions.

Answer choice (D) is incorrect. It is true that the easement holder has no obligation to maintain the easement for the owner of the servient estate. However, the easement holder does have a duty to repair the easement and to maintain it so that there is no additional burden on the servient estate.

Question 84
Answer: D

The correct answer is (D). This question tests the law of conveyance by gift and the law of deeds. In order to convey real property as a gift, the donor must execute a deed and fulfill the elements of a gift: (1) donative intent, (2) delivery, and (3) acceptance. Key, for both conveyances for consideration and conveyances by gift, is that once the elements of the conveyance are satisfied, the original owner can only regain ownership if the new owner executes a new deed conveying the property. The destruction of a deed does not affect the grantee's title. The facts of this situation show that Metterly intended to convey the property to her daughter without consideration, the deed was delivered to Doris, and Doris accepted the deed. With all of the elements satisfied, the conveyance was complete, and destruction of the deed, which was mere evidence of her valid title, does not change the fact that Doris has title to the property. She would have needed to execute a new deed in order to have transferred the property back to Metterly.

Answer choice (A) is incorrect because a gift of real property needs a deed to succeed, but no specific type of deed is required.

Answer choice (B) is incorrect because destruction of a valid deed does not reconvey title to the property to the original owner. A new valid deed is required for a title to be reconveyed.

Answer choice (C) is incorrect. Since destruction of the deed does not affect the status of the title, the possibility of undue influence does not change the outcome of the determination.

Question 85
Answer: B

The correct answer is (B). This question tests the duty owed to a social guest. The law recognizes that a guest in an individual's home is a licensee, despite being invited, to whom the owner owes only the duty to not injure by active negligence. Because Guest was a social guest in Dotty's home, the duty owed by Dotty to Guest is to refrain from injuring him through negligence, and unless Dotty was negligent in purchasing and serving the tuna from the damaged cans, she will not be liable for the resulting illness.

Answer choice (A) is incorrect. Homeowners are not held strictly liable for injuries caused to social visitors to their homes. There must be at least some negligent action on the part of the homeowner in order to establish liability.

Answer choice (C) is incorrect because a homeowner need only be negligent in her actions toward a social guest in order to be held liable. She need not satisfy the higher culpability standard of recklessness.

Answer choice (D) is incorrect. A social visitor assumes the designation of a licensee and the homeowner has the duty to refrain from injuring that person through his negligence.

Question 86
Answer: C

The correct answer is (C). This question tests the law of buy and sell contracts, as well as the doctrine of merger. The doctrine of merger provides that a buyer's claims that arise from title defect issues, such as encumbrances, are limited to those that may be asserted pursuant to the deed's title covenants. Any covenants of title in the sell and buy contract are subsumed by the deed's covenants of title.

Although Owens and Painter had contracted to sell the property by general warranty deed, which would have included covenants of title, Painter accepted a quitclaim deed, which contains no covenants of title. Because Painter accepted the deed, he can only sue on the covenants contained in his deed. And, since the quitclaim deed did not contain a covenant against encumbrances, Painter would have a weaker case and Owen would likely succeed. Here, the easement for a highway across Overlea constitutes an encumbrance upon Overlea.

Answer choice (A) is incorrect. The existence of the encumbrance would violate the contract if the contract contained a covenant against encumbrances, but Painter accepted the deed and thus the covenants of the contract are subsumed.

Answer choice (B) is incorrect. If the action were based on the contract, then the encumbrance could be a violation of a covenant against encumbrances in the contract; however, the action here must be based on the deed pursuant to the doctrine of merger.

Answer choice (D) is incorrect. Rescission is a possible remedy for a breach of sell and buy contract, but Painter must pursue a cause of action based on the deed and not the contract.

Question 87
Answer: A

The correct answer is (A). This question tests the law of assignment and subleasing in landlord/tenant relationships. The law permits landlords to restrict the tenant's right to assign or sublease the leasehold, but courts will construe such prohibitions strictly because they are restraints on the alienation of land. The lease's restrictive clause listed only subletting as restricted. Since assignment was not listed, and the courts will construe the prohibition narrowly, Taylor would be permitted to assign his interest.

Answer choice (B) is incorrect. A disabling restraint on alienation is a provision that causes a subsequent conveyance to be invalidated. Restraining Taylor from assigning or subletting his leasehold would not void subsequent conveyances.

Answer choice (C) is incorrect because the terms refer to transfers of two different types of interest and so are not used interchangeably. Since the restrictions are construed narrowly, a landlord must include both terms to prohibit both, and here only subletting is included.

Answer choice (D) is incorrect because, absent an express prohibition, a tenant may assign his interest without the landlord's permission.

Question 88
Answer: A

The correct answer is (A). This question tests the law of joint tenancy. A joint tenancy is created when real property is conveyed to at least two co-tenants and the four unities of interest (Title, Time, Possession, and Interest) are satisfied. The distinguishing characteristic of a joint tenancy is the right of survivorship, which stipulates that a joint tenant's ownership automatically passes upon his death to the surviving joint tenants. Here, the four unities of interest are satisfied because Oleg conveyed his interest to Bob and Bill in the same document, at the same time, with both being able to possess the entire property for the same duration.

Since the right of survivorship was created, Bob's interest in the property automatically transferred to Bill upon his death, despite Bob's attempt to devise it to his child. Because the joint tenancy was destroyed when Bill obtained sole ownership, he had the right to devise the interest as he chose. Therefore, Frank had an undivided interest in the property, which he properly conveyed to Paul who has the right to alienate the fee simple. Charles and his devisees/heirs have no claim to the property and thus do not have to be joined.

Answer choice (B) is incorrect. Paul does not have to seek joinder of Charles, Sam, or Sam's child because they never acquired an interest in the property.

Answer choice (C) is incorrect because Charles, and thus his son Sam, never acquired an interest in the property.

Answer choice (D) is incorrect. A quitclaim deed may be unmerchantable if the title it conveys is encumbered, but conversely the title may be fully marketable, and the quitclaim deed would be fully merchantable.

Question 89
Answer: B

The correct answer is (B). This question tests the law of implied reciprocal servitudes. Implied reciprocal servitudes arise when a builder subdivides a large parcel of land into equally-sized lots and sells the lots with deeds that contain restrictive covenants.

Purchasers of restricted lots can seek injunctive relief against purchasers of later lots whose deeds do not contain the restrictions if (1) the later lot was originally part of a parcel held in common ownership; (2) the lot was subject to a common building plan or scheme involving a use restriction; and (3) the buyer possessed inquiry notice of the use restriction. In this situation, the first and third conditions are met. All of the lots involved were originally owned by Oscar, and inquiry notice is satisfied by the fact that the first 140 lots only contain single-family homes, and their recorded deeds contain the restriction. The facts are silent, though, on the common plan. If the subdivision was developed on a common scheme, then Payne can receive injunctive relief. If there was no common scheme, then the latter lots may not be subject to the restriction.

Answer choice (A) is incorrect because the provision may bind both parties if there is a representation, in the conduct or conversations of the grantor, that indicates that the grantor intended for the restriction to benefit the land that he retained and thus, that he intended a common scheme.

Answer choice (C) is incorrect because the enforceability of a common scheme of a subdivision is not dependent upon the composition of the rest of the municipality.

Answer choice (D) is incorrect. Even though ambiguities in the deed are generally resolved against the drafter, the question here does not involve an ambiguous provision but rather a lack of a provision indicating that the grantor promises that the remaining lots will be similarly restricted.

Question 90
Answer: D

The correct answer is (D). This question tests the law of implied reciprocal servitudes. The three elements necessary to establish that an implied reciprocal servitude is enforceable are that (1) the lot was originally part of a parcel held in common ownership; (2) the lot was subject to a common building plan or scheme involving a use restriction; and (3) the buyer of a deed to the lot possessed inquiry notice of the use restriction. Here, the facts establish that the lots were originally held in common ownership by Oscar and that nearly half of the lots contained single-family homes each with a recorded deed containing the restriction. Key for Doyle, though, is that the facts do not establish that Oscar had established a common scheme with the use restriction. He had merely obtained permission to build a subdivision and had inserted the restriction into 140 lots without any mention of a common scheme. The remaining 185 lots did not contain restrictions. Without evidence of a common scheme, Pringle lacks an essential element to establish enforceability, and thus this would be Doyle's strongest defense.

Answer choice (A) is incorrect because it is a weaker defense. Courts may infer that a common scheme, even an implied one, has been abandoned, if the omission of restrictions from subsequent deeds combined with other circumstances, such as the inability to sell the properties, indicates this. However, this approach implies that a common scheme could be inferred from the previous 140 restricted deeds, which strengthens Pringle's case.

Answer choice (B) is incorrect. The general rule is that restraints on use, even if they decrease the number of buyers, are generally not unreasonable restraints on alienation.

Answer choice (C) is incorrect. Pringle does not have to establish the danger of monetary loss to his property in order to enforce an implied equitable servitude. Pringle must only establish the three factors listed above.

Question 91
Answer: B

The correct answer is (B). This question tests the Rule Against Perpetuities. The common law rule is that an interest in land must vest, if at all, within 21 years of the death of a life in being at the time of the interest's creation. Here, Farley is a life in being at the creation of the interest and thus the interest will either vest within his lifetime, with him being alive 30 years later, or will be destroyed by his death.

Answer choice (A) is incorrect because Farley's interest is not a reversion, but rather a shifting executory interest.

Answer choice (C) is incorrect because Farley's interest is an executory interest. Pike's interest is vested subject to divestment because his fee simple can divest to Farley if Farley is still living 30 years later.

Answer choice (D) is incorrect because the Rule Against Perpetuities will not operate to invalidate an interest that will vest within 21 years of the death of a life in being.

Question 92
Answer: C

The correct answer is (C). This question tests the law of present and future estates. As a general rule, absent contrary provision in the conveyance, a life tenant possesses the duty to pay the carrying costs of the property. Carrying costs include mortgage interest. Because the facts do not indicate that the conveyance contained any other provisions, Wanda, as a life tenant, is only responsible for the interest payments on the mortgage.

Answer choice (A) is incorrect. Life tenants are not required to make full mortgage payments unless the conveyance so stipulates.

Answer choice (B) is incorrect. An apportionment may occur in the event of a default, in order to preserve the interests of the holder of the life estate and the remainderman. However, there was no default here.

Answer choice (D) is incorrect. The holder of the remainder possesses the duty to pay the mortgage principal.

Question 93
Answer: B

The correct answer is (B). This question tests the law of contracts as applicable to the sale of real property. A contract for the sale of property, as with any contract, is formed when there is an offer and acceptance. Any invalid attempted oral modification of an existing, written contract, will generally not impact the enforcement of the original contract, unless the court allows an exception for waiver or part performance. In this example, Ohner and Byer were already bound by a contract for the sale of lot 101 for $5,000 through the offer by Ohner to sell the lots for $5,000 and Byer's acceptance with regard to lot 101. The attempt to change the price of lot 101 was an oral modification of the earlier agreement and therefore would not be enforced. However, because there was no formalized contract regarding the remaining lots, and the offeror can modify his offer prior to acceptance, Byer's later telegraph that he would accept the offer of $6,000 for each lot with regard to the rest of the lots binds him to the higher price.

Answer choice (A) is incorrect because there were two contracts, one for the sale of lot 101 and one for the sale of the remaining lots. The price of $5,000 was binding on the first contract, but the modified offer of $6,000 was binding on the second.

Answer choice (C) is incorrect because there were two contracts, one for the sale of lot 101 and one for the sale of the remaining lots. The price of $5,000 was binding on the first contract, but the modified offer of $6,000 was binding on the second.

Answer choice (D) is incorrect because the oral modification of the price did not change the agreement that was already reached regarding lot 101. The modification did, however, change the offer price for the remaining lots and bound Byer to the higher price for them.

Question 94
Answer: B

The correct answer is (B). This question tests the law of priorities and recording. By using time of recording the controlling factor in fixing priority of title, the jurisdiction would be following essentially a pure race recording act, where the first buyer who records his title acquires priority interest over any other buyers. This approach would allow the first to record to prevail, regardless of whether or not he had notice of a prior, unrecorded deed.

Answer choice (A) is incorrect because a witness to a deed simply verifies authenticity and has little impact on the priorities of recorded deeds. Eliminating the requirement of witnesses would still leave the question of which deed was first recorded in the public record.

Answer choice (C) is incorrect. Both the initial and subsequent purchasers may have paid valuable consideration for the property, or no consideration may have been paid at all if the conveyance was a gift. However, that payment does not affect the public record and who had recorded ownership first.

Answer choice (D) is incorrect. Making protection of bona fide purchasers the controlling factor could potentially undermine the public record, as a bona fide purchaser might be allowed priority over an initial purchaser who had recorded his deed prior to the later conveyance.

Question 95
Answer: C

The correct answer is (C). This question tests the law of takings. It is generally true that a government may, through regulation or the use of eminent domain, appropriate all types of private property interests as long as it pays just compensation to the owner of that interest. Property owners who suffer a taking have the constitutional right to seek legal or equitable relief.

Sovereign immunity would not be a consideration in drafting legislation that amounts in a taking because an individual whose property is taken generally has the constitutional right to bring civil action against the government to recover damages or to seek an injunction against the taking. The state cannot claim sovereign immunity in such situations.

Answer choice (A) is incorrect because the U.S. Constitution provides that citizens shall not be deprived of property without just compensation, and therefore compensation would be a significant consideration.

Answer choice (B) is incorrect because the U.S. Constitution prohibits laws that impair the obligations of contracts, and thus impairment of contract would be a main consideration. Indeed, legislation rendering unenforceable all land use restrictions imposed by deeds could, and likely would, effect contractual agreements between individuals and businesses.

Answer choice (D) is incorrect because legislation rendering unenforceable all land use restrictions imposed by deeds would constitute a taking, and the legislature would be concerned with whether the contemplated legislation constituted a valid use of the state's police power.

Question 96
Answer: A

The correct answer is (A). This question tests the application of the Rule Against Perpetuities (Rule). Under the common law Rule, a contingent remainder must vest within 21 years after the death of a life in being at the time of the initial conveyance in order to be valid. A life in being may be someone who is alive at the time of the conveyance, even if that person is not expressly mentioned in the conveyance. Trease had three children who were alive at the time of his conveyance. By implication, these children may serve as the lives in being, because when the last one dies, no more grandchildren will be born and presumably all of them would reach the age of 21 within 21 years of the death of their parents. Therefore, the conveyance would be considered valid.

Answer choice (B) is incorrect. "Under the rule of convenience, a class will close to afterborn members as soon as the first distribution of principal is no longer postponed by the terms of the will." Future Interests – Determination of Classes – "Rule of Convenience" Closes Class When First Member Reaches Twenty-One, Although No Member Alive at Termination of Previous Interest, 65 Harv. L. Rev. 1068, 1069 (1952). Although this rule would be applicable and would ensure that the interest would vest with the oldest grandchild, it would not ensure that the devise was valid as to the entire class.

Answer choice (C) is incorrect because the conveyance clearly demonstrates that Trease intended for the conveyance to be all of the grandchildren born, both in the wording "whenever born" and the use of his children as lives in being.

Answer choice (D) is incorrect. While it is true that if it is possible to construe a document so that it does not violate the Rule and invalidate the interest, the document should be so construed, the conveyance here does not violate the Rule and so would not need to be interpreted so as to conform.

Question 97
Answer: C

The correct answer is (C). This question tests the Rule Against Perpetuities (Rule). Under the common law Rule, a contingent remainder must vest within 21 years after the death of a life in being at the time of the initial conveyance in order to be valid. Because an inter vivos conveyance occurs during the grantor's life, the lives in being to be considered are not all of Trease's children, but merely those alive at the time of the conveyance. It is possible that Trease could have more children after the conveyance. Therefore, there is uncertainty as to whether the interest will vest within 21 years after the death of the last life in being, as a later child could have children after the death of his or her siblings, and such uncertainty violates the Rule.

Answer choice (A) is incorrect. Presumably, Trease's posthumous child was in gestation on the date of his death, and for purposes of the Rule Against Perpetuities, a child in gestation is a life in being.

Answer choice (B) is incorrect because, based on the facts as given, Trease had three living children at his death, and at the death of those children the interest of the grandchildren will vest as no more children can be born.

Answer choice (D) is incorrect because the measuring lives are those of his children, and as long as those grandchildren that are born reach the age of 21 within 21 years of the death of the last measuring life their interest will vest.

Question 98
Answer: C

The correct answer is (C). This question tests the doctrine of equitable conversion.

Under this doctrine, once a buyer and seller enter into an enforceable sell and buy contract, the seller retains a legal interest in the real property and receives a right in personal interest in personal property to obtain the purchase price while the buyer obtains an equitable interest in the real property and a right in realty to a conveyance of that property. When a seller dies, the doctrine stipulates that his interest is considered personal property secured by a lien. Therefore, as Perry inherited the Seller's personal property, he inherits the right to the proceeds of the sale.

Answer choice (A) is incorrect because the doctrine of equitable conversion applies to the distribution of property under both testate and intestate succession.

Answer choice (B) is incorrect because the doctrine of equitable conversion does apply, and she does not have an interest in the personal property, which includes the Seller's interest in the real property in question.

Answer choice (D) is incorrect because a title becomes unmarketable when a reasonable person would not purchase it. The death of Seller does not necessarily cause doubt about the title's validity nor any threats of or actual litigation relating to the title.

Question 99
Answer: A

The correct answer is (A). This question tests the doctrine of equitable conversion.

Under this doctrine, once a buyer and seller enter into an enforceable sell and buy contract, the seller retains a legal interest in the real property and receives a right in personal interest in personal property to obtain the purchase price while the buyer obtains an equitable interest in the real property and a right in realty to a conveyance of that property. The doctrine applies to the distribution of property, and in the event of the death of a buyer prior to closing, his interest is considered real property. Because his heir inherited an interest in real property, he or she would have the right to seek specific enforcement of the agreement.

Answer choice (B) is incorrect because rescission is generally a remedy for a breach of the contract, and there has been no breach in this situation.

Answer choice (C) is incorrect because the doctrine of equitable conversion does not provide for the termination of the contract upon the death of either party but rather provides for the respective interests to be devised to the heirs.

Answer choice (D) is incorrect because at Buyer's death his interest in the property transfers to his heirs, and this action does not raise a situation where a reasonable person would not purchase the property.

Question 100
Answer: A

The correct answer is (A). This question tests the law of covenants. A restrictive covenant is a legal obligation imposed in a deed by the grantor upon the grantee of real estate to do or not to do something. In this case, the grantor wishes to require that all lot owners pay annual dues. By placing a covenant in the deed to that effect, the grantor can implement his requirement. If the covenant runs with the land, then it can be enforced by successors in interest.

Answer choice (B) is incorrect because an easement is a limited right to use or access the real property of another. Although arguably the right to use the club and courses are easements, granting an easement does not ensure that non-users will contribute to the upkeep.

Answer choice (C) is incorrect. A mortgage is "a lien against property that is granted to secure an obligation (such as a debt) and that is extinguished upon payment or performance, according to stipulated terms." Black's Law Dictionary, 1031 (8th ed. 2004). Because the owners would be required to pay the dues for as long as they owned the property, they would never be released from the mortgage.

Answer choice (D) is incorrect. While a personal contractual obligation would secure the payments from the original purchaser, there would be nothing to make the obligation binding upon subsequent purchasers.

Question 101
Answer: D

The correct answer is (D). This question tests the law of covenants. A restrictive covenant is a legal obligation imposed in a deed by the grantor upon the grantee of real estate to do or not to do something. Covenants may be personal, and not binding on future owners, or they may run with the land and be binding on future owners. In order for a burden to run with the land, (1) the covenant must be in writing, (2) the original parties must have intended for the burden to run with the land, (3) the covenant must touch and concern the land, and (4) there must be horizontal and vertical privity. Courts have been reluctant to recognize indefinite money payments as running with the land because they do not touch and concern the land. Raintree Corp. v. Rowe, 248 S.E.2d 904 (N.C. Ct. App. 1978). The court in *Raintree* held that "the performance...of this covenant is not connected with the use of [the] land." Id. at 907-08. Since courts are likely to find this type of covenant to be personal, establishing such a scheme would be difficult.

Answer choice (A) is incorrect. The Fourteenth Amendment provides protection from deprivation of property by the state, including through state action, without due process. This fact pattern does not demonstrate a deprivation of property by enforcing the requirement of dues.

Answer choice (B) is incorrect because although covenants can reduce the marketability of property, one such as this does not necessarily render the title completely unmarketable. Here, in fact, the covenant might be viewed as beneficial because it ensures the continued operation of the club and course which could in turn increase the value of the burdened property.

Answer choice (C) is incorrect because common scheme restrictions do not unreasonably restrain alienation, and the third provision explicitly provides that all owners have the right to transfer the lot. While the requirement of dues might deter some prospective buyers, it is unlikely that the owner would be unable to find anyone to purchase.

Question 102
Answer: D

The correct answer is (D). This question tests the law of conveyance by deed. An individual may authorize an agent to sell his real estate, but such an agent is limited in what he may do by the words of the authorization. A power to sell is not always construed as granting the power to conclude a contract of sale, and a power to convey is likewise narrowly construed. Additionally, an agent who is authorized to sell or to sell and convey may or may not be authorized to include the usual covenants for title and thus execute a general warranty deed. Therefore, the validity of the transfer and the success of the suit for breach of covenant depend on the extent of authority given by the authorization to "sell and convey."

Answer choice (A) is incorrect because quitclaim deeds are an effective means of conveying realty.

Answer choice (B) is incorrect because the validity of covenants for title is not determined by whether they are personal or run with the land.

Answer choice (C) is incorrect. Although a bona fide purchaser usually acquires valid title if the deed is voidable, it is not an absolute guarantee, and a determination must first be made as to whether the deed is voidable for breach of fiduciary duty.

Question 103
Answer: C

The correct answer is (C). This question tests the law of vested remainders subject to open. A vested remainder subject to open, also called a vested remainder subject to partial defeasance, occurs when a specified class of persons holds a remainder, since the number of class members may increase or decrease until all of the members have been ascertained. In this case, the number of members of the class of Selden's children, which at the time of conveyance included two adult children, could fluctuate until Selden's death. The Rule Against Perpetuities would not apply here because the remainder would completely vest at Selden's death.

Answer choice (A) is incorrect. An indefeasibly vested remainder cannot be subject to a condition precedent or subsequent. Here, the remainder is to all of Selden's children, and the contingency exists that more children will be born.

Answer choice (B) is partially incorrect. Selden's living children possess a vested remainder subject to open in the farm. His potential unborn children, though, possess remainders contingent upon them being born.

Answer choice (D) is incorrect because Selden's death does not eliminate his adult children's remainders.

Question 104
Answer: C

The correct answer is (C). This question tests the law regarding tenancy in common and partition. A tenancy in common is a concurrent estate in which each tenant owns separate and distinct shares of their joint property. A tenancy in common does not include a right of survivorship, and each interest can be conveyed. Co-tenants can seek a partition of their joint property, either through voluntary agreement or by judicial proceedings, by which they divide the property between themselves. Here, Allen and Barker are concerned about the possibility of a future, new co-tenant partitioning. If Allen and Barker voluntarily partition the property, they can also chose to execute an indenture granting the cross-easement that can be construed as binding. Because the cross-easement would be granted after the partition occurs, it would not be subject to partitioning.

Answer choice (A) is incorrect. Although such a covenant would normally be void as an unreasonable restraint on alienation, a court may permit such a covenant if it is limited to a reasonable time. By creating such a covenant, though, Allen and Baker run the risk of a challenge to, and possible invalidation of, the covenant.

Answer choice (B) is incorrect because easements are also subject to partition. If a subsequent owner were to seek a partition of the property, the easement could be divided and the purpose of it frustrated.

Answer choice (D) is incorrect. The establishment of a trust brings up the issue of a beneficiary. There may be problems with designating an ascertainable beneficiary or class of beneficiaries if the property is conveyed.

Question 105
Answer: B

The correct answer is (B). This question tests priorities and recording systems. A race-notice recording system provides that a subsequent buyer who is a bona fide purchaser, or one who acted in good faith and purchased property for value, who recorded first without notice of the other conveyance will prevail over the initial purchaser.

This jurisdiction has a race-recording system, as demonstrated by the good faith and value requirements. Crider acted in good faith as he apparently had no notice of Price's claim, which was not recorded, and Crider relied on the warranty deed. However, to succeed in defeating Price's valid title by recording first, the statute requires that he pay valuable consideration. The determination, then, will rest on whether the loan to Crider for $35,000 satisfies the requirement of consideration.

Answer choice (A) is incorrect. If Crider does not satisfy the elements and good faith, Price's claim would succeed regardless of whether he was a bona fide purchaser.

Answer choice (C) is incorrect. If Crider satisfies the elements of the recording statute then he will succeed over any unrecorded prior conveyance, regardless of whether the first buyer paid consideration. The valuable consideration helps to establish bona fide purchaser status.

Answer choice (D) is incorrect. If Price can demonstrate that Crider did not act in good faith, had notice of the prior conveyance, or did not pay valuable consideration, then his title will prevail.

Question 106
Answer: D

The correct answer is (D). This question tests the law of nuisance. In order to receive equitable relief for a claim of nuisance, a plaintiff must establish that he suffered some sort of injury by pleading personal injuries or special damages. The courts will balance such injuries against the utility of the activity giving rise to the nuisance to make their determination. The facts here indicate that Fred had suffered no personal injury at the time that he made his claim; therefore, he must assert a claim for special damage in order to prevail. His only claim, however, was for a violation of the ordinance. Because there was no claim for damages, the court would likely weigh in favor of the utility of presenting wares.

Answer choice (A) is incorrect. Fred may have come to the nuisance, but that defense is not absolute, and a renter is not barred from seeking relief because he does not vacate the premises.

Answer choice (B) is incorrect. An isolated violation of an ordinance does not constitute a nuisance. However, a nuisance may exist through repeated violations of an ordinance. Hank violated the ordinance on multiple occasions, and multiple infractions would be unreasonable.

Answer choice (C) is incorrect because Fred had asked Hank to refrain from placing items on the sidewalk and had sought police help, and the nuisance had continued.

Question 107
Answer: A

The correct answer is (A). This question tests the requirement of land description in deeds. The law requires that a deed contain an accurate legal description of the land that is sufficient to facilitate specific performance. Here, the deed contained the description of the land in question as that at 44 Main Street. Although the acreage was off by one eighth, and there was an unmentioned right-of -way, the fact that Pat owned no other property on the street means that the physical address and approximate size are sufficient to allow for specific performance to be rendered. Additionally, such an error can be corrected by the courts by reference to the prior deeds.

Answer choice (B) is incorrect. Although the use of metes and bounds is one method for describing the property in question, the grantor is not required to use it, and the description will be sufficient if the court can identify the property described.

Answer choice (C) is incorrect. While the acreage is incorrect and could lead to a challenge, it is not so incorrect as to make specific performance impossible when the other descriptive evidence, like the location of the property, which would likely refer to a government plat, can be used to resolve the discrepancy.

Answer choice (D) is incorrect. A grantor cannot convey more than he or she owns. A mistake as to the amount of land being conveyed does not necessarily render the deed void. Rather, deeds purporting to convey more than a grantor owns may be subject to equitable remedies.

Question 108
Answer: D

The correct answer is (D). This question tests the law of land description in deeds. The description of land to be conveyed must be sufficiently descriptive so as to allow identification of the land for specific performance. Here, the description is not specific enough to allow the property to be identified. Pat purports to convey only a portion of his farm and the only reference to identify it is that the southeast corner is somewhere in the north line of one piece of property. Had the southeast corner of the property been designated by a specific landmark, boundaries could have been ascertained by measuring a 200-foot square from that point. However, without a starting point there is no way to do so.

Answer choice (A) is incorrect because payment of consideration does not impact whether the description in the deed is sufficient.

Answer choice (B) is incorrect because it could be argued that the lack of clarity in the description constitutes an ambiguity on the face of the deed. Regardless, if the description is not sufficient, then the deed will not be enforceable.

Answer choice (C) is incorrect. It is not disputed that Pat owns the estate that is purported to be conveyed. The problem with this deed is the vagueness of the description of the land.

Question 109
Answer: C

The correct answer is (C). This question tests the law of restrictive covenants and implied reciprocal servitudes. Owners of restricted lots in a subdivision are entitled to enforce those restrictions against other owners in the subdivision if all of the lots contain restrictive deeds or if such restrictions can be implied from a common scheme of development.

Here, all of the lots were conveyed with the restriction, and the restrictions are not discriminatory or unreasonable. Additionally, the deed expressly grants the right of enforcement to the owners of the lots against other owners. Because of the validity of the restrictions, any present owner of a restricted lot would be entitled to enforcement of that restriction against other owners.

Answer choice (A) is incorrect. State action is in conflict with the U.S. Constitution when it is enforcing discriminatory behavior against a protected class. A restriction to single-family dwellings does not discriminate against such a protected class. Therefore, judicial enforcement of the restriction would not be unconstitutional state action.

Answer choice (B) is incorrect because the remaining 100 acres have not been platted and thus are not part of a common scheme.

Answer choice (D) is incorrect. Restrictive covenants are enforceable first through equitable relief. Although the courts would likely permit any use that was consistent with zoning laws, the remedy that they would initially attempt would be injunctive relief.

Question 110
Answer: D

The correct answer is (D). This question tests the law of implied reciprocal servitudes.

Owners of restricted lots in a subdivision are entitled to enforce those restrictions against other owners in the subdivision if all of the lots contain restrictive deeds or if such restrictions can be implied from a common scheme of development. The problem posed by these facts is that the 100 acres was not platted at the same time as the 200 acre subdivision, and yet the developer wants owners in the first subdivision to be able to enforce building restrictions against the second subdivision. If the court determines that the identical restrictions and zoning are indicative of a common scheme of development encompassing both subdivisions, the restrictions will be enforceable by owners in the first subdivision. If there is no common scheme, then the restrictions will not be enforceable.

Answer choice (A) is incorrect because developers of subdivisions can impose restrictions beyond those imposed by zoning, including, but not limited to, restrictions to single-family use.

Answer choice (B) is incorrect. The designation of 200 acres for commercial purposes does not impact the ability to designate the remaining 100 acres for residential.

Answer choice (C) is incorrect. Lots in subdivisions are most often restricted to residential purposes, and such restrictions are enforceable by the developer (while he retains property) and by other lot owners.

Question 111
Answer: D

The correct answer is choice (D). This question tests the law concerning termination of easements. Easements can be terminated in five principal ways: (1) expiration, (2) merger, (3) some act of the easement holder, (4) complete cessation of purpose, or (5) some act of the servient estate owner. Once an easement is extinguished it cannot be revived, it must be created anew. Here, Akers and Bell hold express reciprocal easements over the common driveway. The removal of the need for the easement can terminate only easements implied from necessity. Because this is an express easement, the new public street does not affect Bell's right to use the driveway. Thus, Akers will be enjoined from interfering with Bell's continued use of the common driveway.

Choice (A) is incorrect. Termination of the necessity for the easement would terminate an easement if that easement was created by the necessity. Here, Akers and Bell created an express easement so the cessation of the necessity does not affect the easement holders' rights.

Choice (B) is also incorrect. Although courts do sometimes terminate easements because of frustration of purpose or changed conditions, the purpose of the easement must have completely ceased for the easement to be extinguished. Easements that are terminated by changed conditions will not be enforced only if conditions have changed so drastically that enforcement will be of no substantial benefit to the dominant estate. It is covenants, and not easements, that were traditionally subject to termination in those very specific cases of changed conditions leading to cessation of purpose.

Choice (C) is incorrect. An incorporeal hereditament is simply a right which is attached to property and is inheritable. Easements are one type and as previously discussed, there are several ways for easements to be terminated without a formal writing.

Question 112
Answer: D

The correct answer is choice (D). This question tests the nuisance doctrine as applied to light. The vast majority of courts in the United States would hold that, in the absence of an agreement to the contrary, property owners have absolute rights to develop their property without liability for any interference with their neighbor's interests in light and air. This is often expressed by saying that no easement for light and air exists unless a contract creates it. Prah v. Maretti, 321 N.W.2d 182 (Wis. 1982). Furthermore, courts are even more reluctant to recognize a right to sunlight when the plaintiff's building is located in a more urban area, where buildings often buttress and block the sides of adjacent structures. Absent an express easement for light and air, property owners cannot bring suit against their neighbors for interfering with their enjoyment of property because of changes which affect the flow of light and air to their property. The fact that a party has enjoyed the free flow of light and air to her property for years will not create an easement for light or air from the party's neighbor. Since there is no legal right to the free flow of light and air from the adjoining land, where a structure serves a useful and beneficial purpose, it does not give rise to a cause of action for either damages or an injunction, even though it causes injury to another by cutting off light or air or interfering with the view. Therefore, because Bell has no right to an easement for light, air, or view, Bell has no cause of action.

Question 113
Answer: A

The correct answer is choice (A). This question tests transfers of a mortgage. When a mortgagor transfers his title to property securing the mortgage, the grantee-transferee may take the title of the mortgagor-vendor subject to the outstanding lien of the pre-existing mortgage. Taking title subject to the mortgage does not oblige the purchaser to pay the debt evidenced in the note, but the property he receives may nonetheless be called on to secure repayment of that debt through a sale by foreclosure, which will extinguish the purchaser's rights in the property.

Here, however, Perez did not purchase the property but instead received a life estate in Greenacre with remainder to Rowan. A life estate is freely transferable during life, but the transferee receives the transferor's life estate. In other words, a life tenant may transfer what he or she has—possession of the land for the duration of the life estate–nothing more. Thus, while a life tenant in theory might lease, mortgage, or even convey his or her interest, the land is bound by these transfers only for so long as the life estate endures. Inherent in a life estate is the idea that the life tenant gets to use the property for life, thus deriving the economic value of possession. This use must be consistent with the facts that the property will be handed over to the remainderman at the life tenant's death. The life tenant is entitled to the use and enjoyment of the land, including any rents and profits its produces. However, if there is an existing mortgage on the house, the life tenant is responsible for mortgage interest and the remainderman is responsible for the principal portion of that debt. Therefore, in this case, Rowan must pay the principal payment, and Perez must pay the interest to First Bank.

Question 114
Answer: C

The correct answer is choice (C). This question tests the requirements for a defeasible fee simple. A defeasible fee simple is an estate in land in which the holder possesses a fee simple title, but the title is subject to being divested upon the occurrence of a certain condition. Thus, a conveyance of a defeasible fee simple includes language that may limit its duration. This durational language must be clear and unequivocal. When conveyances include language explaining the purpose of the transfer, the vast majority of courts will hold the language as precatory—not intended to have any legal significance—and will interpret the conveyance to have transferred all the interests the grantor owned. If the grantors owned a fee simple, the courts presume that is what they intended to convey. This result follows from the presumption against forfeitures and protects the interests of the grantee, placing the burden on the grantors to be clear if they intend to retain a future interest in the property.

Here, the conveyance lacks any durational language. Although it appears to be a defeasible estate, the language in the deed created only a contractual obligation, and did not provide for retention of a property interest by Anders.

Question 115
Answer: C

The correct answer is choice (C). This question tests the law of subleases and assignments. An assignment is the transfer of the party's entire interest under the lease. If a tenant retains any interest it is a sublease. A sublease occurs when the lessee transfers anything less than his entire interest in the leasehold, thereby retaining a reversion. Unless a lease expressly limits or prohibits assignment or sublease, a tenant is free to transfer the leasehold by either method. However, most leases do contain such restrictions. The typical landlord insists on such a restriction to avoid an irresponsible or undesirable successor tenant. Of course, even when an express restriction does apply the landlord may consent to transfer. Furthermore, courts will not enforce a lease's covenant against assignments or subleases when: (1) an initial landlord provides consent to an assignment, which serves as consent to subsequent assignments; or (2) an initial landlord waives the covenant by allowing an assignee or sublessee to pay rent.

Here, Andrews agreed to pay part of the rent to Lane, the landlord, who did not object to this arrangement. Because a provision restraining subleases and assignments is meant to benefit the landlord, only the landlord has the ability to waive that lease covenant.

Question 116
Answer: A

The correct answer is choice (A). This question tests the law of abstractor's liability. An abstractor today is generally liable not only to the party for whom the abstract is prepared, but also to those who did in fact or who would foreseeably rely on the abstract. An abstract of title is the result of the title search, so those abstracts prepared negligently create a cause of action for negligent misrepresentation. Any title searcher is obligated to exercise reasonable diligence in performing the search. A searcher is liable for a negligent search that results in damage to the buyer if the search results are provided to the buyer.

One of the protected classes of people are third party beneficiaries of the abstract. A third-party beneficiary is a person who may have the right to sue on a contract, despite not having originally been a party to the contract. This right arises where the third party is the intended beneficiary of the contract, as opposed to an incidental beneficiary. It vests when the third party relies on or assents to the relationship, and gives the third party the right to sue either the promisor or the promisee of the contract, depending on the circumstances under which the relationship was created. The buyer is universally treated as the third party beneficiary of the search and it is obviously foreseeable that a buyer might rely on any title search.

Here, even though not a party to the contract between Abstract Company and Sloan to furnish an abstract of title, Jones is a named, third-party beneficiary of it and so he has a direct cause of action against Abstract Company.

Question 117
Answer: B

The correct answer is choice (B). This question tests the law of marketability of title. Every contract for the sale of realty contains an implied duty of the seller to deliver marketable title to the buyer. Any defect in title must be substantial and likely to result in injury to the buyer. If one of the title covenants is breached, the grantee may recover damages from the grantor. One common defect in title is a breach of the covenant against encumbrances. This covenant is breached if the title is encumbered at the time of delivery of the deed, whether or not the grantor is aware of the encumbrance. An encumbrance almost always makes a title unmarketable. An encumbrance is a burden on the title, such as mortgages, judgments liens, easements, or covenants. Here, the deed included a covenant against encumbrances and Newacre was subject to right-of-way deed in favor of the power company.
In this case, the deed also included a covenant of general warranty. Technically, the covenant of warranty is not a promise that the grantor has good title to convey. Rather, it is the grantor's promise to defend the grantee's title against other claimants. The covenant of warranty is breached only when someone holding superior title actually or constructively evicts the grantee from the land.

In this case, the property conveyed was clearly burdened by an encumbrance. Newacre's title is thus defective. It is irrelevant that Sloan was without knowledge of the defects. Thus, choices (C) and (D) are both incorrect. Choice (A) is incorrect because Sloan was not negligent. It was Abstract Company who owed a duty of fully researching the chain of title.

Question 118
Answer: D

The correct answer is choice (D). This question tests the Rule Against Perpetuities. The Rule Against Perpetuities invalidates future interest that may vest too far into the future. Future interest are invalid unless they are certain to vest or fail to fest within the lifetime of someone who is alive at the creation of the interest or no later than 21 years after her death. This is known as the "unborn widow" rule, one of the two classic traps of the Rule Against Perpetuities (Rule).

The Rule presumes the possibility that aged men and women might substitute younger mates for more elderly ones—even so young that they were not born at the time of the grant.

However, the contingent remainder vested in Hubert's surviving widow is valid because the uncertainty as to the identity of the widow will be resolved upon Hubert's death. The same uncertainty as to the remainder Hubert left to "such of my children as shall live to attain the age of 30 years" will also be resolved upon Herbert's death as he will clearly have no more children after that. At the time of the creation of the will in 1965, Hubert had two living children. However, this class, "my children," is still open. More children may be born. The third child, Carter, was born within 21 years of the creation of the grant. Thus, measured by Allan and Beth, this grant does not violate the Rule Against Perpetuities. This is because the interests are certain to vest within 21 years of Hubert's death. Therefore, in a jurisdiction which recognizes the common law Rule Against Perpetuities unmodified by statute, the result of the application of the Rule is that the remainder property interest belongs to the children and the substitutionary gift to the grandchildren is valid.

Question 119
Answer: D

The correct answer is choice (D). This question deals with recording acts and chain of title problems. Incorporated into the recording act (of any type) are the practices of the local abstractors or searchers of titles. They search the public records by first chaining the title and then searching for conveyances from the owners forming the chain. Chaining the title involves a search backward in time. A title searcher's objective is to identify all the past title transactions pertinent to a particular parcel, in order to determine the present state of the title. Recording provides constructive notice to the world of a conveyance. Even if a later purchaser fails to consult the record, he is charged with knowledge of its contents. In a race or race-notice jurisdiction, recordation cuts off the possibility that either a prior unrecorded purchaser of a later purchaser could prevail. In a notice jurisdiction, recordation provides constructive notice, thus also preventing later purchasers from prevailing.

Here, Vine purportedly conveyed Lot 1 to Purvis by a deed when Vine did not own Lot 1 because Ogawa then held title to Lot 1 in fee simple. Purvis recorded the deed before Ogawa conveyed Lot 1 to Vine by deed. Vine subsequently conveyed Lot 1 to Rand by deed. The deed from Vine to Purvis and the deed from Vine to Rand would each be indexed under Vine's name. If Purvis' deed is deemed recorded in Rand's chain of title, Purvis holds title to Lot 1. If on the other hand Purvis' deed is not deemed recorded in Rand's chain of title, title would belong to Rand.

Question 120
Answer: C

The correct answer is choice (C). This question tests the law of the rights and obligations of concurrent owners, specifically tenants in common. Tenants in common own separate but undivided interests in the same interest in property. Each tenant owns the entire property, but must necessarily share with the other tenants in common. A tenancy in common interest may be alienated, devised, or inherited separately from the other tenancy in common interests. Each co-owner has the right to possess the entire property and no co-owner may exclude his fellow co-owners. Because each co-owner has a right to possess all of the property, exclusive possession by one co-owner is presumptively valid. If it is pursuant to agreement of all co-owners it is conclusively valid. If not by agreement the co-tenant in exclusive possession has a number of obligations to his co-tenants. For example, one co-tenant cannot obtain adverse possession against another unless the possessing tenant makes clear to the nonpossessory tenant that he is asserting full ownership rights in the property to the exclusion of the other co-tenants. Courts generally require some affirmative act by which the nonpossessory tenant is put on notice that her co-owner is claiming adversely to the non-possessory tenant's interests. Ouster refers to an explicit act by which one co-owner wrongfully excludes others from the jointly owned property. Sole possession of the property does not violate the property rights of the other owners and thus does not constitute trespass. Nonpossessory owners therefore are not put on notice that the possessing owner is intending to claim his interest by adverse possession. Because here there is no evidence that Arthur has performed sufficient acts to constitute Celia's ouster, he cannot claim the expanded title to Goodacre.

Question 121
Answer: C

The correct answer is choice (C). This question tests the law of conveyance of one joint tenant's interest. A joint tenant may destroy the joint tenancy at any time by severing the joint tenancy, usually by conveyance. A tenancy in common results. Because the "four unities" were necessary to create a joint tenancy at common law, the destruction of any of those unities would operate to sever joint tenancy. Jurisdictions differ as to whether a joint tenancy is severed by the act of one joint tenant mortgaging his interest. Resolution of the issue traditionally depended upon whether the jurisdiction adhered to the lien theory or the title theory of mortgages. The title theory holds that a mortgage effects a transfer of legal title, subject to an equitable right of the mortgagor to reclaim title by paying off the loan secured by the mortgage. This was the common law theory of mortgages. As a result, a mortgage by one joint tenant had the effect of severing joint tenancy because the unity of interest was destroyed. The joint tenancy could not be restored because the unities of time and title would not be present. After the mortgage, the former joint tenants would become tenants in common.

Many jurisdictions today, however, follow the lien theory of mortgages. The lien theory of mortgages holds that the mortgagee only has a lien against the property. On this view, a mortgage by one joint tenant makes no alteration to title and thus does not sever joint tenancy. Upon the death of the mortgaging tenant while the loan in unpaid, the surviving tenant takes an interest free and clear of the mortgage.

Therefore, in this case, because the jurisdiction recognizes the title theory of mortgages, Johnson's mortgage severed the joint tenancy, resulting in a tenancy in common. His half was subject to the mortgage while Tenniel's half was not. Upon Johnson's death, Stokes received the encumbered half interest in Brownacre via intestate succession. The court should determine that title to Brownacre is thus vested half in Tenniel, free and clear of the mortgage and half in Stokes, subject to Johnson's mortgage.

Question 122
Answer: C

The correct answer is choice (C). This question deals with the law of marketability of title. Every contract for the sale of realty contains an implied duty of the seller to deliver marketable title to the buyer. Any defect in title must be substantial and likely to result in injury to the buyer. If one of the title covenants is breached, the grantee may recover damages from the grantor. One common defect in title is a breach of covenant against encumbrances. This covenant is breached if the title is encumbered at the time of delivery of the deed, whether or not the grantor is aware of the encumbrance. An encumbrance almost always makes a title unmarketable. An encumbrance is a burden on the title, such as mortgages, judgments liens, easements, or covenants. Also, the chain of title may have a faulty or nonexistent link. If there is no record evidence of a deed passing from one party to another in the chain of title, the title is unmarketable. Because a chain is only as good as its weakest link, such defects make the title unmarketable unless there is adequate proof of adverse possession sufficient to create a new, valid, and marketable title.

Here, the title is not marketable because of these problems. If Simmons obtained an order compelling specific performance by Boyd, most likely Boyd would be forced to bring suit against Olsen, the actual owner of Wideacre, in order to make him tender title to Wideacre. Even though Boyd is likely to win in a suit against Olsen, he cannot be required to buy a lawsuit from Simmons.

Question 123
Answer: A

The correct answer is choice (A). This question tests the classification of future interests and the Rule Against Perpetuities. A remainder is a future interest created in a grantee that will become possessory upon the natural expiration of the preceeding possessory estate. Remainders are classified as either vested or contingent. A remainder is vested if it is created in a known person and possession is not subject to any condition subsequent. As a result, a vested remainder must necessarily become possessory whenever the prior possessory estate expires. A contingent remainder is a remainder created in an unknown person or that has a condition precedent to ultimate possession. Contingent remainders have no certainty of becoming possessory, but that is also true of vested remainders subject to divestment.

Here, Ana Maria has no children, so her unborn children must be born in order to retain possession in Ranchacre. Therefore, Ana Maria's unborn children hold a contingent remainder at the time of the conveyance. Because this interest is certain to vest or certain not to vest within 21 years of Enrique's death, this conveyance does not violate the Rule Against Perpetuities. Thus, choice (D) is incorrect.

Choice (C) is incorrect because Martinez has not granted an executory interest. Springing uses stem from a future interest created in a grantee that divests the grantor at some future time after the conveyance.

Choice (B) is incorrect also. Because the remainder is not created in a known person and is subject to a condition precedent, Anna Maria's unborn children cannot hold a vested remainder subject to divestment.

Question 124
Answer: B

The correct answer is choice (B). This question tests the law of profits a prendre. A license is simply permission to enter the licensor's land. Licenses may be oral or written and are revocable at any time unless the licensor makes the license irrevocable, either expressly or by his conduct. A profit is the right to take a natural resource or crop from one land to another. Typical profits include the right to take minerals, timber, fish, game, or crops. Common law courts preferred to construe profits as in gross rather than appurtenant. It makes economic sense to treat profits as easements in gross because the right conferred has substantial economic value by itself and thus is most efficiently utilized if it is easily transferable by title, rather than as an adjunct to some unrelated property. For that reason, profits are freely assignable. Profits are generally governed by the same rules that apply to easements. The final clause of the Fifth Amendment, the Takings Clause, applies only when private property is taken. It imposes two restrictions on the eminent domain power. Government may take private property only for public use and must pay compensation to the owner. Any type of private property may be acquired through eminent domain. The vast majority of cases involve the condemnation of a possessory estate in land, almost always fee simple absolute. All possessory estates, both freehold and non-freehold, and other interests including easements and future interests in real property may be similarly condemned. Thus, Miner is entitled to compensation for the state's condemnation of Stoneacre. He has a profit a prendre, which is a property right protected by the Due Process Clause.

Question 125
Answer: B

The correct answer is choice (B). This question tests the law of preemptive option contracts. In a preemptive option contract, the seller grants the buyer the right of first refusal to purchase the seller's interest in the property. Here, Amato granted Barton the right to purchase her property if ever it is offered for sale or, if Amato retains the property, within 60 days of her death, which does not violate the Rule Against Perpetuities. The general rule is that a restraint on alienation must be for a reasonable purpose and limited in duration in order to be valid. Here, the restraint is for the reasonable purpose of allowing the life tenant to purchase the property and he must do so within a limited period of time. Therefore, Barton's right to purchase is not an unreasonable restraint on alienation.

Question 126
Answer: A

The correct answer is choice (A). This question tests the Rule Against Perpetuities. The Rule Against Perpetuities (Rule) is designed to invalidate certain contingent interests that might vest too late. In applying the Rule, the only facts considered are those existing when the future interest becomes effective. To comply with the Rule, is must be logically provable that within a period equal to the length of one life plus 21 years, a covered interest will vest or forever fail to vest. If there is any possibility that a covered interest might remain contingent after this specified time limit expires, the interest is void. A five-step approach is helpful in applying the Rule: (1) determine if the Rule applies to a future interest at issue; (2) decide when the perpetuities period begins; (3) identify the determine what must happen for the interest to vest forever or fail to vest; (4) identify the persons who can affect vesting; and (5) test each relevant life to determine if any one validates the interest. The validity of future interests under the Rule is tested when they are created. If you can prove any single scenario, no matter how improbable of actual occurrence, in which uncertainty of vesting will continue until after expiration of the permitted period, the interest is void. Here, it is possible that Bogatz, her heirs and assigns could use Applewood Farm for 100 years and then convert the property to something else. Cohen's interest may fail to vest or may vest within the statutory period. Thus, Cohen's interest in Applewood farms is void and amounts to nothing.

Question 127
Answer: D

The correct answer is choice (D). This question tests the law of marketability of title. Every contract for the sale of realty contains an implied duty of the seller to deliver marketable title to the buyer. Any defect in title must be substantial and likely to result in injury to the buyer. One common defect in title is a breach of covenant against encumbrances. This covenant is breached if the title is encumbered at the time of delivery of the deed, whether or not the grantor is aware of the encumbrance. An encumbrance almost always makes a title unmarketable. An encumbrance is a burden on the title, such as mortgages, judgments liens, easements, or covenants. The covenant against encumbrances is a present covenant. Present covenants are representations of presently existing facts. The covenant is either breached when it was made or can never be breached at all. Thus, the grantor must warrant that there are no liens, mortgages, easements, covenants restriction use, or other encumbrances upon title to the property at the time of the conveyance.

If a developer manifests a common plan or common scheme to impose uniform restrictions on a subdivision, most courts conclude that an equitable servitude will be implied in equity. The common plan or scheme is viewed as an implied promise by the developer to impose the same restrictions on all the retained lots. Under this approach, every lot in the subdivision is both benefited and burdened by the restriction. No lot owner may violate the restriction, and any lot owner can enforce the restriction against another. The development must be of uniform character and recognizable as such by purchasers. Otherwise, there is no basis for concluding that purchasers were relying on reciprocal covenants burdening everyone's use in order to produce a development of uniform character. Because of the uncertainty as to the restrictions imposed on the rest of the subdivision in terms of the unnumbered lot, Diaz is unable to warranty an unencumbered title. A court may find the title to be burdened by the same restrictions, or may not. Thus, title to the parcel is not marketable at the time of the conveyance.

Question 128
Answer: A

The correct answer is choice (A). This question tests the requirements that must be met in order for the burden of an equitable servitude to run to successors to the original estate. Covenants are promises to use or not to use one's own land in a certain way. When an injunction is sought for enforcement by or against successors in interest the covenant is called an equitable servitude. In order for the burden of an equitable servitude to bind the promisor's successors, American law generally requires that four elements be satisfied: (1) the promise must be in writing or impled from a "common development scheme"; (2) the original parties must impliedly or expressly intend to bind successors; (3) the promise must "touch and concern" the land; and (4) the successor must have actual or constructive notice of the promise. In order for either the benefit or the burden of an equitable servitude to run to successors in interest the substance of the covenant must touch and concern the land. Courts typically state that this means that the burden of the covenant must relate to use of the land. As one court summarized, "the promise must exercise direct influence on the occupation, use or enjoyment of the premises." Caullett v. Stanley Stilwell & Sons, Inc. 170 A.2d 52, 54. The traditional view is that covenants to pay money—here, to Gaint's power plant—do not touch and concern.

Choice (B) is incorrect because even if the court held that the residential development had a common development scheme, the touch and concern requirement is still not met. Choice (C) is incorrect because the covenant does not affect the alienability of the property. Page's power to dispose or deal with her real property is untouched by the covenant. Choice (D) is also incorrect. Neither horizontal nor vertical privity is required for the burden of an equitable servitude to bind the promisor's successors.

Question 129
Answer: C

The correct answer is choice (C). This question tests the law of quitclaim deeds. The quitclaim deed contains no title covenants. By its use, the grantor does not warrant that he owns the property or—if he has any title—that the title is good. A quitclaim deed merely conveys whatever right, title, or interest the grantor may have in the property. The quitclaim conveyance grew out of the release and came to mean that the transfer is an "as is" transaction in which the transferor says in effect "I'm not sure what I have, but whatever it is, I give it to the transferee." When Luis quitclaimed all interest in Blackacre to Jose, he transferred his future interest in the property. Thus, when Eugenia died and was survived by her husband Jose, but no children, Luis' contingent remainder became a fee simple in Blackacre belonging to Jose. By quitclaiming his interest, Luis effectively conveyed his entire interest in Blackacre to Jose. Thus, choice (B) is incorrect. Choices (A) and (D) are incorrect because the doctrine of after-acquired title applies only when a grantor conveys an interest in property that he does not own. Here, because Luis conveyed a valid future interest by quitclaim deed to Jose, the doctrine of after-acquired title is not relevant.

Question 130
Answer: A

The correct answer is choice (A). This question tests the law of adverse possession. To acquire title by adverse possession, the adverse possessor must prove that their possession is actual, exclusive, open and notorious, adverse (or hostile) to the true owner's interest and under a claim of right, and continuous for the statutory period. Once the adverse possessor has satisfied all the elements of adverse possession for the limitations period, the adverse possessor acquire titles to the occupied property. The adverse possessor must physically occupy the property. The owner's cause of action accrues at that moment and the clock on the limitations period starts to run at the moment of actual entry. The possession must not be shared with either the true owner or the general public. Yet, absolute exclusivity is not required. The claimant's possession must be as exclusive as would characterize an owner's normal use for such land. In order to interrupt the claimant's exclusive possession, the owner must retake possession of the property. The acts of possession must be so visible and obvious that a reasonable owner who inspects the land will receive notice of an adverse title claim. The adverseness requirement means that the use is nonpermissive. A showing that the true owner has permitted the use will defeat the claim. Lastly, the requisite period for adverse possession must be met.

Here, Hull acquired title to Brownacre through adverse possession. He occupied Brownacre through the construction of the dam as a user would, and the facts do not indicate that he shared the property at that time with Orris. Hull did not have permission, and he occupied the property for 12 years, 2 years beyond the statutory period. When Hull purported to transfer this interest to Burns, he did so by a document that was insufficient as a deed to transfer real property. Burns then entered into a lease with Orris. Orris subsequently conveyed Brownacre by quitclaim deed to Powell. However, because Orris did not retain an interest in the land after Hull acquired title by adverse possession, title to Brownacre remains in Hull.

Question 131
Answer: A

The correct answer to this question is choice (A). This questions deals with the law of accession. When one person uses labor or materials to attach chattel to the property of another, the doctrine of accession determines that the landowner is entitled to ownership of the chattel. However, title to personal property can also be acquired by adverse possession. Under the traditional view, one whose possession of a chattel is actual, adverse, hostile, exclusive, open and notorious, and continuous for the appropriate statute of limitations period obtains title to it. Hull constructed a dam on Brownacre that increased the value of the property. Upon his receipt of the title to Brownacre, the dam became part of the property interest included in the title. Thus, the title to the earthen dam was in whoever then held title to Brownacre in fee simple.

Question 132
Answer: D

The correct answer is choice (D). This question tests the formal requirements for a valid deed. The basic requirements for a valid deed are simple. In general a deed must (1) be in writing, (2) be signed by the grantor, (3) identify the grantor and grantee, (4) contain words of conveyance, and (5) describe the property. The first two elements stem from the Statute of Frauds. In general, a conveyance of any interest in real property must be memorialized in a writing that is signed by the grantor. The standard exceptions to the Statute of Frauds, notably part performance and estoppel, may obviate the need for a writing. Furthermore, a deed is not effective until it is delivered. A deed must be delivered by the grantor in order to be effective to transfer and interest in land. Delivery means that the grantor has said or done things that demonstrate the grantor's intent to transfer immediately an interest in land to the grantee. Delivery does not necessarily require the physical act of handing over the paper deed to the grantee. The deed must also be accepted by the grantee. Courts generally presume acceptance of a beneficial deed, but the presumption can be rebutted through a grantee's conduct and statements to the contrary.

Here, there was not effective acceptance because Simon emphatically decline to accept. Because Simon did not accept, Marsh would be determined to hold the title. Choice (C) is incorrect because Simon never accepted the property, he could not reconvey it. Choice (B) is incorrect because delivery is presumed in the three circumstances above. The grantee's knowledge of the recording of the deed is not necessary. Finally, choice (A) is incorrect because constructive trusts can be imposed only in cases where one party has been wrongfully deprived of some right, benefit, or title to property by mistake, fraud, or some other breach of faith or confidence. In order to prevent unjust enrichment of the legal holder, the wronged party is deemed to hold the property as a trustee for the beneficial use of that party. This is done regardless of the grantor's intent.

Question 133
Answer: D

The correct answer is choice (D). This question deals with the conveyance of the interests of joint tenants. Joint tenancy differs from other types of concurrent estates in that each joint tenant has the right of survivorship. Joint tenants are seen as both a unit that owned the entire estate and individuals who each owned an undivided fractional share in the estate. Joint tenants own an equal share in all of the property, so that when one tenant dies nothing passes to the other joint tenants. The death of one of two joint tenants merely extinguishes the deceased tenant's interest in the estate while the surviving tenant then holds a fee simple absolute in the property. If both joint tenants die simultaneously, for example in an airplane or car crash, the joint tenancy is normally treated like a tenancy in common, with no right of survivorship. The joint tenants are each deemed to own a half interest in the property that passes to their respective heirs. However, the applicable statute in the jurisdiction mandates that when "there is insufficient evidence that the persons have died otherwise than simultaneously, the property of each person shall be disposed of as if he had survived. Therefore, Susan and Henry's heirs will acquire their respective interests. However, Susan also owns an interest in Greenacre.

The most persistently troublesome delivery cases involve the "deed in a box." If a party executes a deed conveying the party's property to another and places it in a safe deposit box where it is discovered after the grantor party's death, courts agree that the requisite intent for delivery has not been met. However, courts are much more likely to find delivery where the grantee is a close relative, on the theory that the conveyance is consistent with prudent estate planning. Thus, the deed to Susan's which was held in a safe-deposit box without being recorded will be deemed to have been delivered. Therefore, Susan rightly holds an undivided one-half interest in Greenacre. When Susan died intestate, this interest passed to her heirs. The title to Greenacre is one-half in the heirs of Susan, one quarter in the heirs of Henry, and one quarter in the heirs of Audrey.

Question 134
Answer: B

The correct answer is choice (B). This question tests the law of subsurface rights. The ownership of land has both horizontal and vertical dimensions. If a party owns a fee simple absolute, their ownership includes the land surface of the property, the air space above the surface that is reasonably necessary for the use and enjoyment of the property, and everything underneath the land surface down to the "center of the earth." In theory then, that party's property includes a column of soil and rock that extends downward from the surface thousands of miles below the property to a point precisely in the middle of the planet. Ownership of gold, coal, and other hard minerals is governed by that general common law rule. Whoever owns the land surface also owns the minerals in place under the surface. Of course, it is possible—and quite common—to split off minerals from surface ownership. Oil and natural gas do not fit neatly into the absolute ownership model because they are both "fugitive" minerals. They can move through porous underground strata, unlike hard minerals.

In this case, Andy discovered and mined a considerable quantity of valuable ore. Although Jane and Bob have future interests in the property, as long as Andy has not acted in bad faith or committed waste on the property, the mineral rights belong to him. The right to take minerals is an incident of a fee simple, and thus the court will decide for Andy.

Question 135
Answer: D

The correct answer is choice (D). This question deals with the types of concurrent ownership. A tenancy in common is a concurrent estate when at least two co-tenants possess an ownership interest in the same parcel of real property. There is no right of survivorship for a tenancy in common; rather, the interest is descendible to the co-tenant's heirs. In this case, Taylor and Scott were co-tenants, and as such their interests devised to their heirs, Mark and Martha.

The Statute of Frauds requires that unless there is some exception available, a contract for the sale or transfer of land must be in writing and must be signed by the party against whom it is sought to be enforced. Therefore, Taylor and Scott's intentions to create a joint tenancy through their oral agreement are irrelevant. Thus, choice (B) is incorrect because the verbal agreement cannot lead to reformation of the deed.

Choice (A) is also incorrect. Estoppel is applicable where one party has been induced by the other to substantially change position in justifiable reliance on and oral contract and serious or irreparable injury would result from refusing specific performance of the contract. Neither Taylor nor Scott substantially changed their position in reliance on the oral contract.

Finally, choice (C) is incorrect. The joint tenancy Taylor and Scott intended to create never materialized. They instead held a tenancy in common. If they had held a joint tenancy and Taylor and Scott had died simultaneously, Mark and Martha would each hold divided one half interests in the property. Since they instead had a tenancy in common, each of their heirs own a one–half interest in the property.

Question 136
Answer: B

The correct answer is choice (B). This question tests the law concerning the scope of easements. The scope of an easement may evolve over time as the manner, frequency, and intensity of use change. Broadly speaking, the scope of the easement depends on the intent of the original parties. Courts consider a number of factors in determining this intent, including: (1) the circumstances surrounding the creation of the easement, (2) whether the easement is express, implied, or prescriptive, and (3) the purpose of the easement. Because it is usually difficult to ascertain the parties' actual intent, the law relies heavily on what might be called presumed intent. In general, the law presumes that the parties to an express or implied easement intended that the easement holder would be entitled to do anything that is reasonably necessary for the full enjoyment of the easement, absent evidence to the contrary. Accordingly, reasonable changes in the manner, frequency, or intensity of use to accommodate normal development of the dominant land are permitted, even if this somewhat increases the burden on the servient land. On the other hand, the easement holder cannot change the scope of the easement so as to impose an unreasonable burden on the servient land.

Here, Oaks expressly conveyed the right-of-way to United Utility. Courts look to prior use of the easement to determine the proper scope of the easement. In this case, the easement granted a right-of-way in a specific location agreed to by the parties, and installing another three feet away would go beyond the scope of the original right-of-way. Thus, if Oaks prevails it will be because the scope of the easement was defined by the original installation by United Utility.

Choice (A) is incorrect because a right implied to expand the original use of a right-of-way does not necessarily create an interest that would violate the Rule Against Perpetuities. In fact, courts regularly allow an expansion of a right-of-way as long as the use is reasonable.

Choice (C) is incorrect because Oaks did not need to expressly agree to the location of the right-of-way. Here, he acquiesced to the original placement of the pipeline after granting the easement. Because he did not object to the placement, he cannot object to it.

Lastly, choice (D) is also incorrect. "Inverse condemnation" is a term used to describe a situation where the government has so greatly damaged the use of a parcel of real property that it is the equivalent of condemnation of the entire property. In the United States, the owner of such property is entitled to compensation for this taking under the Fifth Amendment to the U.S. Constitution. This clearly does not apply here.

Question 137
Answer: D

The correct answer is choice (D). This questions tests the categories of easements. An easement appurtenant benefits the easement holder in using the dominant land. Thus, it benefits the holder of the easement as the owner of the dominant land. An easement appurtenant is automatically transferred when the dominant estate is transferred. Frank granted Sam an easement that touched and concerned the land because it concerned the use of the land, and thus is an appurtenant easement. Because of this, when Sam conveyed the interest to Joe, the easement passed to Joe, and Doris cannot enjoin his use.

Easements are severed in five main ways: (1) expiration, (2) merger, (3) some act of the easement holder, (4) complete cessation of purpose, or (5) some act of the servient estate owner. Choice (A) is incorrect. If the easement holder also acquires title to the servient estate, the easement is extinguished because an easement only exists in land owned by somebody else. In this case, although Sam owns Blackacre and Whiteacre, Doris holds a future interest in Whiteacre. Thus, the doctrine of merger cannot apply. The easement holder must acquire the entire servient estate for merger to extinguish the easement.

(B) is also incorrect because Joe has not overburdened the easement. He enlarged the hotel by a mere 2 units. The "no increased burden" rule aims to prevent easement holders from placing a burden on the servient estate that is beyond what was initially contemplated. Frank, the original owner, first constructed the 10-unit motel. Adding 2 units cannot be deemed to have substantially increased the burden on the land.

(C) is also incorrect because an easement is implied by necessity only when a common owner divides his property in such a way that one of the resulting parcels is left without access to a public roadway. Joe cannot claim an easement by necessity because of the existence of the "poor public road."

Question 138
Answer: D

The correct answer is choice (D). This question tests the law of assumption of the mortgage in the context of a remainder. A vested remainder is a future interest that is created in a living ascertainable person and is not subject to any condition subsequent. If an individual "assumes" a mortgage, rather than being "subject to" it, the individual becomes personally liable for the mortgage debt. An assumption agreement is an agreement under which one person assumes the obligations already owed by another to a third party. Thus, the mortgagee is a creditor beneficiary of the purchaser's promise. Therefore, in the event of default, both the purchaser and the original mortgagor are personally liable for the full mortgage debt. In this case, Wilma is the owner of the property because she assumed the mortgage. All three children hold vested remainders. Because her mother currently owns the property and Clara has only a future interest, she cannot be compelled to pay. However, her share in the remainder would be lost if the mortgage is not paid because the property would be sold in foreclosure sale.

Choice (A) is incorrect because a future interest is a presently existing interest but it confers only a future right to possession.

Choice (B) is incorrect because Wilma cannot be compelled to pay the mortgage. She is within her right to allow the lender to sell the property and have the lender apply the proceeds of the sale to the payment of the loan if she so chooses. Any proceeds left over would go to her.

Choice (C) is incorrect because she cannot be held personally liable for the mortgage. Because her mother currently owns the property and Clara has only a future interest, she cannot be compelled to pay.

Question 139
Answer: B

The correct answer is choice (B). This question deals with the law of priority among mortgages. A single property can be encumbered by multiple mortgages and other liens. Except in those few states in the United States that adhere to the title theory of mortgages, either a mortgage or a deed of trust will create a mortgage lien upon the title to the real property being mortgaged. The lien attaches to the title when the mortgage is signed by the mortgagor and delivered to the mortgagee and the mortgagor receives the funds whose repayment the mortgage secures. Subject to the requirements of the recording laws of the state in which the land is located, this attachment establishes the priority of the mortgage lien with respect to other liens on the property's title. Liens that have attached to the title before the mortgage lien are said to be senior to, or prior to, the mortgage lien. Those attaching afterward are junior or subordinate. Mortgagees are considered buyers under recording acts and will therefore be subject to the priorities of the recording acts. In this case, Rohan has legal title until a foreclosure occurs. Because Acme assigned and sold the same interest twice, first to XYZ and second to Peterson, the priority would be established, without any statute to the contrary, in order of recording.

Choice (A) is incorrect because XYZ Bank recorded the mortgage first.

Choice (C) is also incorrect because although Peterson is in possession of the note, the actual valid mortgage belongs to XYZ bank, with the note being part of that mortgage.

Choice (D) is incorrect also. XYZ Bank receives priority among mortgages in this fact pattern. If, on the other hand, Acme had conveyed the promissory note, the mortgage, and the assignment to Peterson, he would have a purchase money mortgage, which would receive priority over any other competing claims against the real property that secured the mortgage.

Question 140

The correct answer is choice (B). This question tests the transferability of interests. Whenever a life estate is created a future interest also arises. The future interest is either a remainder, which vests to a third person, or a reversion, which vests back to the grantor. A remainder is a future interest created in a transferee that is capable of becoming a possessory estate upon the natural termination of a prior estate created by the same instrument.

In this case, by conveying Greenacre to Lafe for life and then to Rem, her heirs and assigns, a remainder was created. As soon as Owen conveyed the property, it belonged to Lafe until Lafe's death. Upon Lafe's death, the property would transfer to Rem. Although Rem died before taking possession of Greenacre, her future interest survived, and passed to her "heirs and assigns." An heir is a person who is designated to receive ownership of real property upon an intestate's death. In our case, Rem did not die intestate and instead devised all her estate (including the future interest in Greenacre) to Dan.

The common law doctrine of destructibility of contingent remainders held that a legal contingent remainder in real property was extinguished if it failed to vest when the preceding freehold estate ended. In our case, the remainder never failed to vest because Lafe held a possessory interest in the estate. The estate never ended. Furthermore, the doctrine is now almost completely abolished in the United States through statute or decisional law. Therefore, Dan would hold title to Greenacre.

Thus (A) is incorrect because Owen never held a reversion in the land and upon conveyance gave up an interest in the property

Choice (C) is incorrect then because, although Hannah is Rem's heir, the vested remainder in Rem was transferred to Dan by Rem's will.

Choice (D) is incorrect because the contingent remainder vested before the end of the freehold estate.

Question 141
Answer: C

The correct answer is (C). This question tests the law of bona fide purchaser status. A bona fide purchaser is a buyer of an interest in real property who: (1) has received an instrument of conveyance after giving valuable consideration to a seller, (2) in good faith, and (3) without notice of a third party's prior deed that affects title to the same real property. A buyer of real property may qualify for bona fide status if an instrument reflecting an interest in real property was not recorded, and such status protects the purchaser from prior interest holders whose interests do not appear in the chain of title.

Ted received and recorded a warranty deed for a fee simple interest in Goldacre from Susan. He also executed and performed under the Trust Agreement ("Trust") before selling Goldacre. Assuming that the Trust remained valid when Ted sold Goldacre to Patricia, she lacked any type of notice of the Trust. She did not receive actual notice of it by any communication from Ted, Susan, or Benton. She could not receive constructive or record notice of it from the public record because the Trust was not recorded. No reason existed for her to obtain inquiry notice or to have received imputed notice of the Trust. The lack of notice to Patricia of the Trust and her giving of fair market value to Ted to acquire Goldacre rendered her a good faith purchaser. This status entitled her to take possession of the real property without any liability to Benton under the Trust.

Answer (A) is incorrect. Benton will not prevail because, although Patricia was Ted's successor in title, she did not take title to Goldacre subject to the Trust when she lacked any notice of the Trust's existence.

Answer (B) is not correct because equitable interests are subject to a recording act if they are property recorded pursuant to the act. Here, Benton will not prevail because his equitable interest of the Trust was not recorded.

Answer (D) is wrong because, although Patricia will prevail, the facts indicate the creation of a valid trust when only a week transpired between Susan's conveyance of Goldacre to Ted and the execution of the Trust. Moreover, the Trust's creation indicates that both Susan and Ted consented to placing Goldacre into the corpus of the Trust.

Question 142
Answer: D

The correct answer is (D). This question tests the law of recording acts and bona fide purchaser status. An easement by grant may be established by a conveyance of a deed of easement from a grantor to a grantee that allows a grantee to use certain property. A notice recording act provides that regardless of which of multiple buyers for value first records, a subsequent bona fide purchaser for value of an interest in real property will have priority over prior purchasers and grantees if that purchaser lacked notice of the other buyers' prior interests. Bank could have obtained inquiry notice of Anna's use of the easement. The fact that Bank could have obtained notice of the easement prevents Bank from being obtaining the status of good faith subsequent purchaser for value as required by the jurisdiction's recording act, and Anna's interest remains intact.

Answer (A) is incorrect. The fact that Anna recorded the deed of easement before Bank filed its foreclosure action does not protect her rights under the jurisdiction's recording act. Rather, to fully protect her rights under this act she should have recorded the deed before Bank recorded the mortgage.

Answer (B) is incorrect because the fact that the easement provides access to Blackacre from a public street is not outcome determinative. Anna could have accessed a public street by a route other than the easement that only existed on Whiteacre.

Answer (C) is incorrect because, although it correctly describes the easement as appurtenant, this fact would not protect the easement if Bank were a bona fide purchaser.

Question 143
Answer: C

The correct answer is (C). This question tests the law of fixtures in leasehold estates. When a leasehold estate tenant attaches a chattel to the estate property, the courts generally do not consider that attachment permanent for most purposes. The courts usually only allow the tenant to remove such a "fixture" during the tenancy period. Removal of an attached chattel may not occur if the removal would result in (1) substantial injury to property to which it is attached or (2) substantial destruction of the attached chattel.

Tina reasonably and properly exercised her rights under the agreement by adding and taking away "certain necessary or useful items." The law support's Tina's removal of those items because they would not be considered permanently attached to the house, she exercised her legal right to remove her chattels during the tenancy period, and the removal would neither cause substantial injury to the house nor substantial destruction of the attached chattel. Clearly, the lease memorialized its parties' intent that Tina could remove the chattels during her tenancy.

The correct answer is (D) because the lease and the law authorized Tina to remove all of the items other than the carpet because the carpet could be damaged or destroyed by removal.

Answers (A), (B), and (D) are incorrect because, except for the carpet, Tina could remove any or all of the other items without damaging either the items or the property.

Question 144
Answer: B

The correct answer is (B). This question tests the law of conveyance by deed. For a deed to operate as a valid conveyance, a grantor needs to (1) show intent to immediately transfer an interest in real property and (2) engage in conduct or cause one to engage in conduct conveying a deed. A deed must be unconditionally delivered. Therefore, a grantor's delivery of a deed to a grantee cannot be conditioned upon the occurrence of a future event. A presumption exists that that no valid delivery of a deed was made if a grantor fails to transfer the deed to a grantee.

Olivia did not deliver her deed to Grant. The fact that there was no physical delivery is not outcome determinative because physical transfer is not a requirement. Olivia conditioned the conveyance of the deed on Grant's reaching the age of 21 and receiving a degree. These conditions indicate that Olivia lacked effective present intent. Without the intent to convey, there was no delivery, and Grant did not receive a valid conveyance. Because Grant did not have title to the property, he had no interest to convey to Bonnie. Therefore, Olivia would still retain title to the property.

Answer (A) is incorrect. The reason that Grant's deed to Bonnie was void is his lack of title, not the amount of consideration that Bonnie provided. One dollar is adequate consideration.

Answer (C) is not correct. The conveyance to Grant was not valid because it was conditional and lacked intent, and fulfilling the conditions cannot validate the conveyance.

Answer (D) is incorrect. Bonnie should not prevail despite the recording of the deed to her because that deed did not convey title to her.

Question 145
Answer: C

The correct answer is (C). This question tests the law of tenancy in common. A tenancy in common is a concurrent estate in which each owner is regarded as owning separate and distinct shares. Partition occurs when co-tenants seek to divide property between them. Co-tenants may seek and obtain an involuntary partition through judicial proceedings with an accounting of their respective financial share relative to their ownership interest. If one of the co-tenants is in exclusive possession of their estate, then the other co-tenants possess no right to receive rental payments from the one co-tenant. Each of the co-tenants, however, may be separately assessed their ownership interest in the property maintenance expenses, insurance, and taxes. When Alex refused to voluntarily partition the property, Betty had the right to seek an involuntary judicial partition, and since Alex had not met the statutory requirements for adverse possession, the court should partition the property and account for any interests.

Answer (A) is incorrect. Alex cannot prevail in a counterclaim against Betty alleging adverse possession because the fact that both of them own the estate as co-tenants precludes Alex from obtaining this type of remedy. Even if Alex could maintain that counterclaim, he only occupied the premises as a co-owner for 7 years, instead of the minimum 10-year period of the jurisdiction's adverse possession statute.

Answer (B) is incorrect because there is no legal basis for reaffirming the tenancy in the face of a partition proceeding.

Answer (D) is not correct because it although Betty and Alex may receive a partition as equal owners, an accounting should also occur.

Question 146
Answer: B

The correct answer is (B). This is question of license. A property owner may grant a license which enables a non-owner of a property to access the property for a particular reason and duration. A mere license is revocable earlier than anticipated at the will of a property owner, either by verbal or written means. If a license is coupled with an interest it is irrevocable for a reasonable duration.

ABC granted Janet a license that allowed her to access Central Arena for all Scorpion's hockey games during a season. Janet's conduct of soliciting signatures for her petition to terminate the Scorpion's coach exceeded the scope of her rights under the license because it violated ABC's posted policy against solicitation and ABC's verbal notices to her that she cease and desist from any solicitation. Additionally, Janet informed ABC at the fourth home game that she intended to disobey both the posted and verbal notices. Because Janet's license was not coupled with an interest, nor had she expended money or labor in reliance on it, it was revocable at the will of the property owner through written means.

Answer (A) is incorrect because the right and duty to control the activities would not permit the revocation of a license if the license is irrevocable.

Answer (C) is incorrect. Paying value for the ticket is precondition for access that all licensees must fulfill. This precondition, however, is not a special interest that renders a license irrevocable.

Answer (D) is incorrect because Janet did not have to commit a nuisance in order for ABC to be entitled to revoke her license.

Question 147
Answer: A

The correct answer is (A). This question tests the law of transfers of mortgaged property. The personal liability of a mortgagor to a mortgagee usually continues after a transfer of the mortgage to a third party. If a transferor conveys real property to a transferee that is "subject to" a mortgage, the transferee does not become personally liable for the mortgage debt.

Bart, the mortgagor, is a transferor of the mortgage as a result of his agreement with Pam, a transferee. Because Pam agreed to buy Goldacre subject to the mortgage to Mort, she will not be personally liable for the mortgage debt. Bart violated the mortgage by transferring it to Pam because the mortgage expressly required Mort's consent for Bart to do this. The law renders Bart personally liable to Mort for the debt that the mortgage secures. That personal liability continued after the transfer.

Answer (B) is incorrect. Although Pam is not liable to Mort, her lack of privity of estate with Mort is not the reason that she is not liable to him. She is not liable to him based on other facts and the law.

Answer (C) is incorrect. Mort will not prevail because, although Bart's deed to Pam violated the due on sale clause, she was not personally liable for the mortgage debt.

Answer (D) is not correct. Mort will not prevail because Pam took the property subject to the mortgage, which does not impute liability.

Question 148
Answer: D

The correct answer is (D). This question tests the law of priority. In the majority of states, a judgment creditor lacks priority as compared to a grantee of real property before the judgment is entered. Barbara and Corp. performed their valid written contract that resulted in the conveyance of Blackacre to her by a proper form of deed. Although George obtained his judgment against Corp. before Barbara recorded her deed to Blackacre, George only subsequently recorded his money judgment against Corp. Further, the statute of the jurisdiction provides for a judgment lien upon the property "then owned or subsequently acquired by any person against whom the judgment is rendered." Consequently, George's recorded judgment is not a lien on Blackacre because Corp. provided the deed to Barbara before George obtained the judgment. Thus, Corp. did not own the property at that time. Moreover, Barbara recorded her deed to Blackacre before George recorded the judgment.

Answer (A) is incorrect. Corp. did not own the property when the judgment was entered, so the judgment could not attach to the property.

Answer (B) is incorrect because George's filed judgment is not a threat of litigation as it was against Corp., not Barbara.

Answer (C) is incorrect because the fact that Barbara recorded her deed before George filed the judgment is not dispositive. In a minority of jurisdictions, recording acts do not protect a third party's interest over that of a creditor.

Question 149
Answer: C

The correct answer is (C). This question tests the law of power of appointment. The donee of a general power of appointment receives all rights to appoint the property to herself, her creditors, or any others. A power of appointment is considered general unless it is limited by the terms of its creation in an instrument of conveyance.

Arthur's trust instrument granted a general power of appointment to Alice because she could exercise it to benefit others under her will. The instrument provided that if Alice's will did not appoint a distributee of net trust estate, then it would go to Charles by default. Alice's will made Marie her sole beneficiary and intentionally disinherited Charles. As such, Marie could argue that Alice's will exercised the power of appointment and that she should receive the net trust estate and Charles should receive nothing. The correct answer is (C) because if Marie is entitled to the net trust estate, it will be because the jurisdiction deems "entire estate" in the will to be a reference to Blackacre or Alice's general power of appointment.

Answer (A) is incorrect. Alice's life estate and general power of appointment cannot merge because the former property interest only exists during her lifetime and latter one only applies upon her decease.

Answer (B) is incorrect because the facts and law provide that the Rule Against Perpetuities would apply to Alice's general power of appointment.

Answer (D) is incorrect. The dispositive provision in Alice's will may be construed as her exercise of the general power of appointment to Marie. That provision is more significant and controlling than her affirmative disinheritance of Charles.

Question 150
Answer: B

The correct answer is (B). This question tests the law of implied reciprocal servitudes. An implied reciprocal servitude exists under the common scheme doctrine. It occurs when a builder of property or real estate developer subdivides a parcel of land into equally-sized lots. Those lots are initially sold and conveyed using a deed containing a restrictive covenant limiting use of the lots for single-family dwellings. If a subsequent buyer receives such a deed that lacks the restrictive covenant language, then the other owners may seek and obtain injunctive relief against the building of anything other than a single-family dwelling on the lot. The test to determine if an implied reciprocal servitude is enforceable is if: (1) A lot was originally part of a parcel held in common ownership; (2) The lot was subject to a common building plan or scheme involving a use restriction; and (3) A buyer of a deed to the lot possessed inquiry notice of the use restriction.

Lots 2 and 4 were both originally owned by Sal, Sal conveyed Lot 2 to Peter by a deed containing a restrictive covenant limiting its use, and that of Lot 4, to a single-family dwelling, thus establishing a common building scheme for those lots. Betty possessed inquiry notice of the restrictive covenant language in Peter's deed because it was referenced in the title report that her lawyer reviewed. Because the other lots were sold prior to Lots 2 and 4, and their deeds did not contain restrictive language, the owners do not have the right to enforce the restriction. The elements of implied reciprocal servitude are satisfied as to Peter, though, so he may recover.

Answer (A) is incorrect because Sal only expressly provided for a common development scheme in one deed with respect to two of five lots.

Answer (C) is incorrect because the facts do not indicate that Betty's construction of a two-family residence would result in decreasing the market value of their single-family homes, and an injunction would be an appropriate remedy for Peter's complaint.

Answer (D) is incorrect because the zoning does not preempt any private scheme of covenants that is consistent with the zoning rules, and none of the lots violated the zoning.

Question 151
Answer: C

The correct answer is (C). This question tests the part performance exception to the Statute of Frauds. The Statute of Frauds generally requires that, in order to be enforceable, an agreement conveying an interest in land must be in writing, signed by the party to be charged, and contain all essential terms of the parties' agreement. Part performance of a contract is an exception to the Statute of Fraud's requirement of a writing that applies when the parties only have a verbal agreement and at least two or more of the following conditions are fulfilled: (1) A buyer makes substantial improvements to the property; (2) A buyer is in open and notorious possession of a seller's property; and (3) A buyer pays the purchase price in part or in full.

The Statute of Frauds applies to the parties' agreement because it conveys an interest in land between them. Because the agreement is oral, Betty can only prevail if her conduct fulfills the part performance exception. First, the structural modifications that Betty made constitute substantial improvements to Blackacre. Second, Betty has exercised open and notorious possession of Abel's property since the formation of their agreement. Third, Betty paid him $25,000 towards the purchase price. Accordingly, a court would grant Betty specific performance of their agreement because of her part performance that would not have occurred but for the agreement's existence.

Answer (A) is incorrect because the part performance doctrine applies.

Answer (B) is incorrect because the $25,000 was consideration for the agreement that ended the tenancy.

Answer (D) is incorrect because the Statute of Frauds does apply to oral purchase and sale agreements between landlords and tenants in possession but is here alleviated by the part performance doctrine.

Question 152
Answer: B

The correct answer is (B). This question tests the law of redemption of a mortgage debt. Redemption is the right of a mortgagor to purchase the real property by fully paying the mortgage debt within a certain time before the date of foreclosure. Both Alex and Brenda are mortgagors of Greenacre. Brenda's payment of one-half of the balance due on the mortgage did not redeem it because it could not be redeemed without a full payment of the balance due.

Answer (A) is incorrect. The warranty that Marge received valid title to Greenacre is not a reason why Brenda should lose.

Answer (C) is an incorrect conclusion because marshalling applies when there are multiple creditors and properties, and one of the creditors cannot access one of those properties to satisfy the debts. It does not apply here.

Answer (D) is incorrect conclusion because the nature of the parties' cotenancy is not dispositive. Had they entered a joint mortgage as either joint tenants or tenants in common they both would have been liable for the entire mortgage debt.

Question 153
Answer: D

The correct answer is (D). This question tests the law of permissive waste. A reversionary interest holder, or remainderman, is entitled to receive a parcel in essentially the same condition that a life tenant found it upon taking possession of it. Accordingly, a life tenant possesses a duty not to commit waste that would unreasonably impair the value of the parcel when a reversionary interest holder takes possession of it. Permissive waste results from a life tenant's failure to fulfill legal duties. Those duties include maintaining the parcel with its structures and making property tax and mortgage payments. Those payments are limited to the degree of profits or income from the parcel, or if none, then in the amount of the parcel's reasonable rental value.

Lena, a life tenant, is obligated not to commit permissive waste that would unreasonably impair the Lots' value when Rose, the remainderwoman, takes possession of it. Although Lena failed to fulfill her legal duty of paying taxes, Rose is not entitled to repayment because the Lots were vacant and consequently produced no profits or income. Moreover, because they were unimproved they lacked any reasonable rental value.

Answer (A) is incorrect because Lena lacked a duty to pay current charges when the lots produced no profits, income, and had no rental value.

Answer (B) is incorrect because the controlling law would not allow for such an equitable remedy.

Answer (C) is incorrect because her duty to pay taxes was conditioned on the income of the lot, not her possession.

Question 154
Answer: A

The correct answer is (A). This question tests the law of subletting in a landlord/tenant agreement. A sublease occurs when a third party and a tenant enter into their own agreement that does not include all of the interests reflected in the lease. The third party becomes a sublessee for a duration that is less than the full term of the tenancy. With respect to a sublease, a tenant and a landlord stay in privity of contract, and a tenant remains liable for the rent and may be sued for breach of contract if neither he nor the subletting tenant fulfill this duty.

Tenn and Agrit entered into a sublease agreement by which Agrit was entitled to possession of Blackacre for the second of the lease's three-year terms. Tenn and Oner remained in privity under this arrangement, so Tenn continued to be liable for the rental payments if Agrit did not pay. Agrit was not liable to Oner in the breach of contract suit because there was no privity between them, but Tenn may be able to recover against Agrit.

Answers (B), (C), and (D) are incorrect because Agrit is not liable to Oner

Question 155
Answer: C

The correct answer is (C). This question tests the law of adverse possession. Adverse possession is a doctrine that allows a non-owner of a real property estate who is in possession of that estate to obtain a legal right of title to own and use its owner's estate under certain conditions. In order to prevail on an adverse possession claim, the non-owner's use must be (1) open and notorious, (2) actual, (3) hostile or adverse, (4) continuous and uninterrupted, and (5) exclusive (6) for the legally-required period The statutory period for adverse possession commences when a non-owner makes a hostile entry onto the premises.

The court should decide that Ron has fee simple title to Blackacre through adverse possession by Trent because the facts satisfy the doctrine's elements. Trent's use of Blackacre was open, notorious, actual, continuous, exclusive and uninterrupted, for the jurisdiction's 10-year period. The 10-year period for adverse possession began when Lois died. During the next 11 years

Olive did not assert her reversionary interest, Trent occupied the premises without Olive's consent, and Ron accepted Trent's rent payments as the successor in interest of Lois.

Answer (A) is an incorrect because Olive failed to assert her reversion interest against Ron during Trent's occupancy.

Answer (B) is incorrect because Lois, as a life tenant, had the right to convey whatever interest she possessed during her life, and therefore the lease was not adverse as to Olive.

Answer (D) is incorrect because Trent did not possess the property as adverse to Olive but rather with the mistaken belief that Ron was the property owner.

Question 156
Answer: D

The correct answer is (D). This question tests the law of recording acts and priority. Most recording acts charge a subsequent purchaser of a real property interest with constructive notice that another buyer previously recorded an instrument of conveyance for the same interest, but such instrument must be properly registered and entered in the appropriate governmental office. The previously recorded instrument must exist within the chain of title, and subsequent buyers are not charged with notice of such "wild deeds" and may be eligible for bona fide purchaser status.

In this case, the chain of title descends from Olivia to Dawn by will and then to Carl through deed. Because Dawn did not own the property when she purported to convey it to Bruce, his title to the property would not be indexed under Olivia. Carl would therefore not be charged with constructive notice of this prior claim, and since the jurisdiction's recording act protects subsequent purchasers for value without notice, Carl's interest would have priority over Bruce's interest.

Answer (A), although a correct statement of fact, is not the basis upon which Carl will win because Bruce recorded his deed and Bruce could have an ownership interest in Blackacre based on the after acquired title doctrine.

Answer (B) is a wrong statement because the facts do not support it.

Answer (C) is a correct statement of a fact that cannot legally establish title in Carl.

Question 157
Answer: B

The correct answer is (B). This question tests the law of conveyance of real property by deed. For a deed to be a valid instrument and thus convey valid title, it must at a minimum set forth in writing (1) the parties' names, (2) an accurate legal description of the land, (3) language indicating an intention to convey the land, and (4) the grantor's signature.

Owner conveyed a proper form of deed to Purchaser. It may be presumed that the deed satisfied the elements of a valid deed, but because consideration is not a prerequisite for a valid deed, it cannot serve as a basis to invalidate the deed.

Answer (A) is incorrect because the deed was valid once it was delivered and accepted, which removes any right Owner might have had to revoke the transfer.

Answer (C) is incorrect because the inclusion of a recitation of consideration does not affect the validity of the deed if the consideration has not been paid.

Answer (D) is incorrect because the deed was valid, so recordation does not affect the outcome.

Question 158
Answer: A

The correct answer is (A). This question tests the law of earnest money deposits. The parties' sell and buy contract may require a buyer to pay funds, called an earnest money deposit, to a seller or a third party that normally will be applied towards the purchase price of the interest in real property. A sell and buy contract may allow a seller to retain a down payment of earnest money if a buyer fails to complete performance of the contract. Such a provision is unenforceable if the amount retained is sufficient to constitute a penalty. Such a provision is enforceable if the amount of down payment is reasonably related to the seller's actual damages.

Ven is not entitled to retain the down payment of deposit pursuant to the contract's liquidated damages provision. The provision is unenforceable because the amount of half the purchase price is enough to constitute an unenforceable penalty. The deposit's amount is not reasonably related to the seller's actual damages from the contract's breach.

Answer (B) is incorrect because Pur's death did not terminate the contract under the equitable conversion doctrine.

Answer (C) is incorrect because, although the contract is generally enforceable, the excessive liquidated damages provision is not.

Answer (D) is incorrect. The doctrine of equitable conversion would prevent termination, but the liquidated damages are still excessive and unenforceable.

Question 159
Answer: B

The correct answer is (B). This question tests the law of recording acts and priority. A judgment creditor is a party who prevails in a civil action seeking damages from a judgment debtor. In the majority of jurisdictions, a judgment creditor lacks priority as compared to a grantee of real property before the judgment is entered. The statute in this jurisdiction allows for judgments to be liens on "real property then owned ... by any person against whom the judgment is rendered." Owen did not own Blackacre when Cred's judgment was entered because he had already delivered, and Bryer had already accepted, the valid deed to the property. The fact that Bryer had not recorded the deed does not affect the validity of the conveyance. Because a judgment creditor is not a bona fide purchaser, the recording act does not protect Cred's priority.

Answer (A) is incorrect because the equitable conversion doctrine does not apply.

Answer (C) is incorrect because Owen's continued possession after the completed transaction with Bryer could not provide Cred constructive notice of Bryer's interest.

Answer (D) is incorrect Bryer would be protected as against Cred because Cred lacks bona fide purchaser status.

Question 160
Answer: D

The correct answer is (D). This question tests the law of co-tenancies. A tenancy in common is a concurrent estate in which owner owns a separate and distinct share of the property. There is no right of survivorship, so a co-tenant's interest is descendible to his or her heirs. Title to a parcel of real property that is subject to a cotenancy may become outstanding as a result of either a foreclosure proceeding or tax sale. One co-tenant may acquire title to the parcel and other co-tenants may assert and regain their interest. A co-tenant that acquires title to the parcel in a tax sale may recover from each co-tenant their ownership share of the tax debt. Likewise, the co-tenants may recover their ownership share by reimbursing the purchasing co-tenant.

Because there is no right of survivorship in a tenancy in common, Alpha's death did not terminate the tenancy in common, and her interest descended to Hera, her heir. Beta paid for her and Hera's ownership share of the property taxes in the tax sale and acquired sole ownership interest in the property. The sale terminated the tenancy in common, and Hera may only recover her ownership share in Greenacre by reimbursing the purchasing co-tenant for one half of the sum that Beta paid to the governmental authority.

Answer (A) is incorrect because there is no right of survivorship in a tenancy in common.

Answer (B) is incorrect because defaulting on such an obligation does not automatically terminate a tenancy in common.

Answer (C) is incorrect because Hera must pay only one half of the amount Beta paid for the tax deed.

Question 161
Answer: D

The correct answer is (D). This question tests the law of real property mortgages. In both title and lien theory states, a discharge occurs when the entire mortgage debt is paid in full, such that a mortgagor and his or her transferee are released from any further payment obligation to a mortgagee. Opal properly received a discharge from Bank on Lot 2 because she fully paid its mortgage debt. Opal fraudulently altered the instrument of release to include Lot 5 because she had not paid its mortgage debt. The fraudulent alteration rendered this part of the release null and void such that it did not discharge the mortgage debt for Lot 5.

Answer (A) is an incorrect conclusion because Bank lacked a legal duty to check on the recorded release for an alteration.

Answer (B) is incorrect because a recorded document may still be voided if it is fraudulently executed.

Answer (C) is incorrect the altered release was void regardless of whether Eva could have discovered the alteration.

Question 162
Answer: A

The correct answer is (A). This question tests the law of real property mortgages and foreclosure sales. If a lawful forfeiture results in a sale of a mortgaged interest in real property, then at least three results could occur. First, if the amount that a buyer paid is equal to the balance that is due on the mortgage, then the mortgagee receives a full recovery. Second, if the amount that the buyer paid is less than the mortgage balance that is due, then a deficiency remains due to the mortgagee. In that event, the mortgagor remains liable to pay that balance due. Third, if the buyer pays an amount that is greater than the remaining mortgage balance, then a surplus exists. The surplus is first paid to the junior lienholders and any residue will be paid to the mortgagor.

Because Lender One is a junior lienholder on the parking garage, by virtue of its judgment lien, it would have priority over surplus proceeds in a foreclosure sale of the property. The sale of the hotel resulted in a $100,000 deficiency, which is satisfied by distributing $100,000 of the proceeds from the parking garage. The remaining $100,000 would go to Owner as the mortgagor.

Choice (B) is incorrect because Lender Two's balance was satisfied in the sale, and the junior lienholder would be entitled to the $100,000.

Choice (C) is incorrect because Lender Two is not entitled to the surplus.

Choice (D) is incorrect because the junior lienholder's interest must be satisfied before surplus is distributed to the mortgagor.

Question 163
Answer: A

The correct answer is (A). This question tests the law of conveyance of property and real property mortgages. An installment contract, otherwise known as a contract of deed or a land contract, is an agreement pertaining to a purchase of real property and the financing of that purchase. Often an installment contract requires that a buyer provide a specified down payment and make periodic payments for a particular duration. After the buyer fulfills those payment obligations, then the buyer will receive a deed for that interest in real property. A seller who does not deliver marketable title at the mutually agreed upon time and/or place breaches a covenant in the sell and buy contract that marketable title will be tendered. This breach involves the failure of a constructive condition which discharges a buyer from performing further and provides certain remedies.

Pursuant to the parties' installment agreement, Purchaser needed to make 290 more periodic payments in order to receive a warranty deed to Greenacre from Vendor. Neither the agreement nor the law required Vendor to possess marketable title during the agreement's term. The agreement required Vendor to deliver a warranty deed, which guarantees marketable title, upon receipt of Purchaser's final installment payment. Only if the mortgage on Greenacre existed at the time of closing could Purchaser properly file a lawsuit alleging that Vendor breached the contract and seeking the requested remedy.

Answer (B) is incorrect because Purchaser would have the right to seek damages if marketable title is not delivered at the end of the contract, but the time is not ripe for such a claim.

Answer (C) is incorrect because Vendor's implied obligation to deliver marketable title would not exist until Purchaser completed his payment obligation, and in any event the contract stipulates that he will deliver a warranty deed that would be sufficient to convey marketable title.

Answer (D) is incorrect because Purchaser does assume the risk that, in the event of his nonpayment, that Vendor will retain payments made, but that does not impact the determination that there has been no breach by Vendor.

Question 164
Answer: A

The correct answer is (A). This question tests the law of appurtenant easements. Appurtenant easements are subject to, and included with, a conveyance of a dominant estate. They also are usually conveyed with a servient estate unless its buyer lacks notice of the easement and buys the premises in good faith. A property owner of a servient estate is entitled to use the land in a manner that does not unreasonably or unduly interfere with an easement. The holder of an easement is not necessarily entitled to an exclusive right to use the area that is subject to the easement. That area may be subject to concurrent use.

Able, a servient estate owner, provided a written conveyance of an appurtenant easement to Baker, a dominant estate owner, which extended to assigns such as Dorcas. This easement is subject to, and included with, the conveyance of the dominant estate from Baker, grantor, to Dorcas, grantee. The succession of ownership in Greenacre from Able to Charlie was subject to the conveyance of the appurtenant easement because Charlie possessed actual notice of its existence due to its use by Dorcas.

Although reasonable modifications may be made to express rights of easement that are generally described, 23 three years of continuous use by Baker established a set location for the easement.

Because Charlie has notice that the easement is now set in a specific location, first through Baker's use and then Dorcas's use, reasonable modifications are no longer appropriate, and attempts to modify would likely be seen as unreasonable interference with Dorcas's easement.

Answer (B) is incorrect because the location was fixed by grant, not prescription.

Answer (C) is incorrect because Dorcas was not obligated to suggest alternative locations.

Answer (D) is incorrect. While modifications may be made to easements that are generally described, the easement in this case has acquired specificity.

Question 165
Answer: C

The correct answer is (C). This question tests the law of warranty deeds. A warranty deed usually includes six covenants unless they are explicitly excluded by the terms of that deed. These covenants are divided into the two categories of present covenants and future covenants. The three future covenants of title are of warranty, quiet enjoyment, and further assurances. They are promises that a grantee will not be disturbed in possession and are not actionable until the grantee suffers an eviction.

Answer (C) is correct because Art owned an undisputed fee simple interest in Blackacre and conveyed valid title to Bea, rendering her the owner of Blackacre who possessed sole responsibility to pay the cost of defending her title. Art provided Bea with a warranty deed that included a future covenant of warranty. The future covenants applied once Bea received the deed of title. None of the future covenants were violated by Celia's unsuccessful lawsuit because it did not result in disturbing Bea's possession by means of an eviction from Blackacre. Thus, Bea is not entitled to recover from Art her costs from Celia's lawsuit.

Answer (A) is incorrect because Art's conveyance to Bea of the deed transferred Blackacre's title to her.

Answer (B) is incorrect because no violation of the covenant of warranty occurred when Celia did not prevail in her lawsuit.

Answer (D) is incorrect because Celia lacked a valid basis to sue Art because he effectively transferred title to Bea.

Question 166
Answer: D

The correct answer is (D). This question tests the law of equitable servitude. Equitable servitudes are promises and/or agreements regarding the use of real property that bind an initial promisor and promisee and their successors. Whether these successors may enforce the servitude depends on if its covenant(s) run with the land that is conveyed from the initial promisee and promisor to their successors. If the covenant runs with the land, it may be considered a cloud or "burden" on the title to the land. The following elements must be satisfied for a burden to run with the land: (1) A promise that is in writing; (2) The initial promisee and promisor must have intended for the promise to be enforceable; (3) The promise must relate to, or touch and concern, the land; and (5) The successors of the promisee and the promisor must have notice of the promise.

The court will enforce the quoted restriction in Abel's conveyance because it is valid equitable servitude. Ollie made, and Abel and Betty accepted, an agreement restricting their use of real property that bound them and their successors. The conveyance's covenants run with the land as a "burden" on the land's title. First, they are in writing. Second, Ollie, Abel, and Betty, all intended the conveyance to be enforceable. Third, the agreements in the conveyance touch and concern, the land. Finally, Able and Betty were the original grantees, they had notice of the restriction, and because all of the elements are satisfied, the equitable servitude will be enforced.

Answer (A) is incorrect because the change in circumstances exception does not apply to these facts.

Answer (B) is incorrect because an equitable servitude may be more restrictive than, or conflict with, the applicable zoning.

Answer (C) is incorrect because the equitable servitude is not limited in application to the original grantees if their successors have notice of it.

Question 167
Answer: A

The correct answer is (A). This question tests the law of the Rule Against Perpetuities. The Rule Against Perpetuities provides that an interest must vest, if at all, within 21 years of the death of a life in being at the time of the interest's creation. If there is any possibility, no matter how remote, that the interest will not vest within the time period, then a future interest will fail. The Rule is applicable options to purchase land.

Adam's deed to Betty provided him a right to repurchase Blackacre if she failed to use it for residential purposes. The provision created an option contract that violates the Rule Against Perpetuities because it does not necessarily vest, if at all, within 21 years of the death of Adam or Betty. Betty's heirs or their heirs may use the property for nonresidential purposes well after the 21 year mark.

Answer (B) is incorrect because the Bank lacked any privity of contract with Adam and Betty with respect to their option contract.

Answer (C) is incorrect because, even if Adam's rights under the option contract were subordinated to the Bank's right as a mortgagee, the Rule Against Perpetuities rendered Adam's rights null and void.

Answer (D) is incorrect because the law recognizes even smaller amounts than $1,000 as valid consideration to enforce an agreement.

Question 168
Answer: C

The correct answer is (C). This question tests the law of life estates and future interests. A grantor who wishes to make a conveyance effective upon his or her decease must use a testamentary instrument, rather than a deed, to fulfill that purpose. A life estate is a possessory interest in a parcel of real property that lasts for the life of some person. A life estate creates a future interest that becomes effective upon the end of a measuring lifetime. That future interest may either be a reversion or a remainder.

Theresa's will took effect upon her decease and the court would properly construe its operative effect as implying a condition that remaindermen survive Della. The court reasonably construed the will as providing Della a possessory interest in Blueacre during her lifetime as a life estate holder or life tenant. Della's life estate included a future interest that would become effective at the end of her lifetime. The court correctly construed the will as implying a future interest of a remainder in Theresa's "descendants per stirpes" because Theresa's death prevented her from receiving a reversion of Blueacre upon Della's death. The "per stirpes" designation ensures that if Seth dies before Della, his interest in Blueacre will devise to his heirs, so the remaindermen must survive Della. Because it is not known who will be alive at Della's death, the remainder is contingent. This construction would fulfill Theresa's intent, avoid any failure of the bequest, and ensure that Della's death created a remainder interest for any remaindermen.

Answers (A) and (B) are incorrect because, although Theresa's will created a remainder, not all vesting related to when she executed the will because it was subject to open and her descendants could not be ascertained until after Della's decease.

Answer (D) is incorrect because the facts do not support it. Theresa granted Della a life estate.

Question 169
Answer: B

The correct answer is (B). This question tests the law of present estates. A fee simple absolute is the most substantial type of property interest. It neither involves, nor is subject to, a future interest. The usual language that creates a fee simple absolute may state either "from a grantor to a grantee" or "from a grantor to a grantee and her heirs." That language is neither qualified in any way nor limited by any other interest. The grantee of a fee simple absolute has the exclusive rights of possession and use.

Oscar effectively conveyed his fee simple absolute to Albert. Thus, Albert's interest in Blackacre was not subject to a future interest in Donna. The statement in Oscar's warranty deed of "to Albert and his heirs" is the functional equivalent of "to Albert." The statute in the jurisdiction supports this construction of Oscar's warranty deed. Albert, as Oscar's sole grantee of a fee simple absolute, exercised his exclusive rights of possession and use by conveying

Blackacre to Bea. Because Donna had no future interest, Bea owned Blackacre in fee simple absolute pursuant to the deed.

Answer (A) is incorrect because Bea received a fee simple interest in Blackacre.

Answer (C) is incorrect because Albert and Donna were not tenants in common, and Albert conveyed a fee simple interest to Bea.

Answer (D) is incorrect because Albert conveyed a fee simple interest to Bea.

Question 170
Answer: B

(B) is the correct response to this real property law question. A mortgagee may obtain possession of a parcel of real estate that secures the mortgage during its existence. This may occur if a mortgagor is in default of a mortgage or abandons the mortgaged parcel. The mortgagee need not occupy a parcel in order to be in possession of it. The mortgagee needs to exercise some "dominion and control" of the parcel to be in possession of it. A mortgagee in possession is personally liable in tort for injuries attributable to its use of the property or lack of performing legally required duties as a landowner.

Instead of occupying Martin's abandoned premises, Marie used employees to care for it and harvest its crops. This action is an exercise of "dominion and control" that indicates Marie's possession. As a mortgagee in possession, Marie will be personally liable in tort for Paul's injuries arising from his use of the property as a business invitee.

Answer (A) is incorrect because regardless of whether this was a title or lein theory jurisdiction, Marie did take possession of the property and therefore became personally liable.

Answer (C) is incorrect because she did not act as Martin's agent; rather, she acted as the mortgagee in possession.

Answer (D) would only be a correct conclusion in a lien theory state where the mortgage needed to authorize Marie's taking possession to protect her security interest in Orchardacres.

Question 171
Answer: A

The correct answer is (A). This question tests the law of assignment and subleasing. An assignment occurs when a third party receives a tenant's interest in a lease, including its remaining duration, and becomes an assignee. A sublease occurs when a third party and a tenant enter into their own agreement that does not include all of the interests reflected in the lease and is for less than the duration of the lease. Absent an explicit provision that prohibits assignment or subletting, the parties to a lease may assign or sublet it by means of a writing that satisfies the Statute of Frauds.

Bertha sublet a part of the lease to Charles because their written agreement provided him with an interest in using the garage for two of its three-year duration in return for consideration. Bertha violated the lease provision prohibiting subletting. The agreement with Doris did not violate the lease provision because, unlike with Charles, Bertha retained an interest in the field.

Answers (B) and (C) are incorrect because Bertha's agreement with Doris did not violate the lease.

Answer (D) is incorrect because Bertha's sublease violated the lease.

Question 172
Answer: A

The correct answer is (A). This question tests the law of the scope and extent of real property. The right of lateral support from adjacent land and under the ground's vertical surface is absolute. Absolute liability arises from a violation of this right. Lateral support protects real property and/or structures on that property from excavation, erosion, or other harms that are caused by acts or omissions of an owner of adjacent real property. Lateral support is not an absolute right, however, if a structure that is built upon the land artificially places weight upon the natural forces that hold the ground intact.

Due to the exception, Bill possesses an absolute right of lateral support from Gail if the building that he constructed on Lot 1 did not place any artificial weight upon the ground along the common boundary of Lot 2.

Answer (B) is incorrect because the wall of Bill's building did not occupy Lot 2. Thus, none of the elements of adverse possession exist.

Answer (C) is incorrect based on an irrelevant and incorrect explanation.

Answer (D) is an incorrect response because the legality of Gail's construction and use of her building would not be a valid defense that could shield her from liability.

AMERIBAR BAR REVIEW

Multistate Bar Examination – Answers to Questions – Section 8

TORTS

Question 1
Answer: D

The correct answer is choice (D). This question tests the law of design defect in connection with products liability. In a design defect case, the plaintiff will not prevail if the defendant can show that the benefits of the design outweigh the risks of the design and the feasibility of a safer design. In this case, a chemistry set is of great benefit for educational purposes. A chemistry set could be not created to completely avoid harm without the destroying the benefit of the product, but the risks can be greatly diminished with reasonable care.

Choice (A) is incorrect because a defendant is liable only for harm that results from foreseeable uses of a product if the product is inherently dangerous and failure to inform the user of a non-obvious danger. A plaintiff cannot recover on the basis of strict products liability if the plaintiff's misuse of the product was not reasonably foreseeable. The classmates were misusing the chemistry set to make a bomb at the time of the injury to Peter, a misuse of the product that is not reasonably foreseeable.

Choice (B) is incorrect because an abnormally dangerous activity must pose a substantial risk of serious harm to persons or property regardless of the degree of care that is exercised in carrying out that activity. The production or use of the chemistry set falls under this definition because any harm that the chemistry set poses is decreased with the degree of care that is exercised in its normal production or use.

Choice (C) is incorrect because it states that the reason Peter would not prevail is that Walter's negligence was a cause in fact of the injury. In order to find negligence on the part of Walter you must find that he proximately caused the injury which includes a determination of reasonable foreseeability as well as cause in fact.

Question 2
Answer: A

The correct answer is choice (A). This question tests the law of products liability. In order to recover under the confines of products liability claim, the plaintiff must be able to show causation. If a warning on the product would not have prevented the injury asserted, then a judgment cannot be taken against the defendant for failure to provide such warning. Thus, if a warning that the wine stopper may suddenly shoot out after opening a wine bottle would not have prevented Paul's eye injury, then he cannot recover from Winery, Inc. merely because the wine bottle lacked a warning.

Question 3
Answer: D

The correct answer is choice (D). This question tests the law of defamation. To prevail on a defamation claim, a communication must involve publication to a least one third party who understood it. Even though Able's accusation may have been heard by third persons, if it was not understood by anyone, it does not fall under the confines of a defamation claim. Thus, Baker cannot prevail on a defamation claim against Able unless one of the third persons who heard the statement actually understood Russian.

Choice (A) is incorrect because in order to have a claim for slander per se the communication must involve a publication that was heard and understood by a third party.

Choice (B) is incorrect because even though the comment was made in front of third persons, if it was not understood by anyone because they did not understand Russian, then the statement is not defamatory.

Choice (C) is incorrect because this answer speaks to the malice standard used to determine fault with regard to a defamatory statement. In order to have a defamatory statement, Able did not have to make the statement with malice, but may be held liable if the statement was negligently made, as long as it was published and understood by a third party.

Question 4
Answer: D

The correct answer is choice (D). This question tests the law of defamation of public officials. In order for a public official to prevail in a defamation action, the official must prove with clear and convincing evidence that a defendant published a defamatory communication with actual malice. Actual malice is a knowledge of the falsity of the statement or a reckless disregard as to the truth or falsity of the statement.

If the only reasonable interpretation of the sign was that "murderer" meant someone who would sign a death warrant, then the statement of Able and Baker would be held to convey the truth that Doe had signed the death warrant and allowed the death proceedings to continue against Rend. Thus, XYZ Corporation's production of Able and Baker's statement was not made with actual malice, as the statement would be truthful and not made with reckless disregard.

Choice (A) is incorrect because in order to hold XYZ Corporation liable for causing people to hold Doe in lower esteem, it must be first proven that XYZ Corporation acted with actual malice.

Choice (B) is not correct, because the word "murderer" is subject to interpretation and does not necessarily mean one actually committed homicide. In light of the signed death warrant by Doe, it is reasonable to interpret the signage to relate to the act of signing the death warrant and allowing the death proceedings to continue against Rend. Thus, XYZ Corporation did not publish the sign with knowledge of its falsity or with reckless disregard.

Choice (C) is incorrect because in order to hold XYZ Corporation for a pecuniary loss, it must be first proven that XYZ Corporation acted with actual malice.

Question 5
Answer: D

The correct answer is choice (D). This question tests the law of intentional infliction of emotional distress. If the plaintiff is a public figure, actual malice must be demonstrated for a cause of action for intentional infliction of emotional distress to succeed. Actual malice is knowledge of the falsity of the statement or a reckless disregard as to the truth or falsity of the statement.

In light of the signed death warrant by Doe, it is reasonable to interpret the signage to relate to the act of signing the death warrant and allowing the death proceedings to continue against Rend, which is truthful depiction of the circumstances. Thus, XYZ Corporation has not acted with knowledge of the falsity or with reckless disregard for the truth.

Choice (A) is incorrect because in order to hold XYZ Corporation liable for causing severe emotional distress, it must be first proven that XYZ Corporation acted with actual malice.

Choice (B) is incorrect because in addition to showing that that signs were extreme and outrageous, Doe could only recover if it was also proven that XYZ Corporation acted with malice.

Choice (C) is incorrect because even if Doe suffered physical harm, in order to hold XYZ Corporation liable, it must be first proven that XYZ Corporation acted with actual malice.

Question 6
Answer: B

The correct answer is choice (B). This question tests the law of misrepresentation. A material misrepresentation is a defendant's false statement that a reasonable person would find of significant importance under the circumstances and on which he relied to his detriment.

The specific statements made in the brochure were false but they were relied upon by Powell and induced him into purchasing the product. If the product had not stated that it would renew all antique furniture and would not damage the original oil finishes, then Powell would not have purchased the product and it would not have damaged his original finish and diminished the value of the antique. Alternatively, if the statements in the brochure were true, the antique cabinet would not have suffered damage and would have actually increased the value of the antique. Thus the misrepresentation made by Restorall, Inc. was the cause of Powell's injury.

Choice (A) is incorrect because other removal techniques have no bearing on the misrepresentation made by Restorall, Inc. It is the false statements made by Restorall, Inc. in its own brochure that makes it liable under the principles of misrepresentation.

Choice (C) is incorrect because the product does not have to be defective in order to recover on a claim for misrepresentation.

Choice (D) is incorrect because the product does not have be dangerous in order to recover on a claim for misrepresentation.

Question 7
Answer: D

The correct choice is (D). This question tests the law of strict products liability. In a claim for strict products liability for a design defect, the plaintiff must show that an injury in fact resulted from a condition of the product, that condition existed when the product left the defendant's hands, and that the product was not materially altered before the injury occurred. The damages available for strict products liability include personal injury and property damages. The personal injury damages encompass claims for emotional distress.

Thus, in order for Palko to recover emotional distress damages under the theory of strict products liability, Palko merely has to show that the asbestos caused him an injury in fact, which in his case is the abnormal chest condition, and he will be able recover for his emotional distress that has been caused from his asbestos exposure.

Choice (A) is incorrect because this choice states the principle for recovery under negligent infliction of emotional distress. The question states that Palko sued under a strict products liability claim under which he can recover his emotional distress damages arising from his bodily harm caused by his exposure to asbestos.

Choice (B) is incorrect because the injury in fact is his asbestosis, an abnormal chest condition that has formed in his body due to his exposure to asbestos. The physical harm does not have to rise to the level of being cancerous to be actionable.

Choice (C) is not the best choice, because certain conditions have to be met before a supplier is found to be strictly liable for a dangerous product, one of which being that it caused an injury in fact. Thus, choice (D) is a better statement of the law in light of the circumstances presented in this question.

Question 8
Answer: D

The correct answer is choice (D). This question tests the law of res ipsa loquitur. The law allows an inference of negligence on a party when an event would have not otherwise occurred unless someone was negligent. In this case, the pedestrian was hit while walking on the shoulder of the highway, a place where cars are not normally driven in the absence of negligence. Since the evidence presented shows that Driver was driving the car that struck Walker, it can be inferred that hitting a pedestrian on the shoulder of the road was a result of negligent operation of the vehicle by Driver.

Question 9
Answer: D

The correct answer is choice (D). The question is testing the law of a parent's liability for the commission of an intentional tort by their child. Normally parents are not held personally responsible for their child's intentional torts. An exception to that rule, however, is when a parent has reason to know or does know of dangerous propensities of the child and fails to exercise reasonable care. In this case, Dent is not the parent of Camden, but this jurisdiction holds that a person having custody of a child has the same duties and responsibilities that he would have if he was the parent of the child. Thus, since Camden's assault is an intentional tort, Dent would not be responsible for its commission, unless Dent knew or had reason to know that Camden had a propensity to attack younger children.

Question 10
Answer: D

The correct answer is choice (D). This question tests the law of res ipsa loquitur. The law allows an inference of negligence on a party when an event would have not otherwise occurred unless someone was negligent. In this case, even though a flower pot falling from a building would probably not have otherwise occurred without the negligence of someone, we have been presented with no evidence as to the identity of that someone who may have been negligent. There was no evidence presented that Landco had any connection with the flower pot that fell from the building. Thus, though it may be inferred that someone was negligent in this circumstance, there is no evidence to show that the negligent party was Landco, and thus the court must grant the directed verdict.

Choice (A) is appealing, but is incorrect because a landowner must exercise reasonable care to protect pedestrians and others on a public street from injuries that arise from dangerous artificial conditions that are located on the landowner's real property. A flower pot located in an apartment building owned by Landco, without additional evidence, is not a dangerous artificial condition for which Landco could be held liable.

Question 11
Answer: A

The correct answer is choice (A). This question tests the law of the rescue doctrine. An original wrongdoer will be held liable for the reasonably foreseeable events that occur in connection with the immediate consequences of the wrongdoer's actions. An attempt to aid a person injured by the original wrongdoer is considered to be a foreseeable course of events. The circumstances surrounding a rescue attempt of a party who has been injured by a wrongdoer does not supersede the liability of the original wrongdoer who caused the original injury.

Donald knew that the cake would be harmful to Peter and served it to him anyway, so that he would eat it and get sick. As intended by Donald, the cake made Peter ill, which caused Peter to have go to the hospital, and set in motion the events that led to Peter's ultimate injury. Thus, Peter's trip to the hospital was a foreseeable event that occurred in connection with the immediate consequences of Donald's actions. Since the ambulance driver was attempting to aid Peter when the car accident occurred, his negligence, if any, would not supersede the liability of Donald for Peter's broken leg.

Question 12
Answer: D

The correct answer is choice (D). This question tests the law of premises liability. A person is an invitee if he or she is on a landowner's real property (1) by invitation of the landowner, and (2) for a purpose connected with the landowner's use of the property. The invitee may receive an express or implied invitation to enter onto the land. A patron of a grocery store would be considered to be an invitee, as they have been invited to shop for groceries on the premises.

Landowners possess a duty of reasonable care to an invitee. They only have a duty to warn the invitee of a dangerous condition on their real property of which they are aware, if that condition presents an unreasonable risk of harm to the invitee. The only duty the grocery store has to its invitee Peterson is to warn of a dangerous condition if it presents an unreasonable risk of harm to its customers. If the store can show that a supervised child pushing a cart does not pose an unreasonable risk to its customers, then it has not breached its duty to Peterson, and cannot be held liable for his injuries.

Question 13
Answer: D

The correct answer is choice (D). This question tests the law of negligent parent supervision. Parents have a general duty to control the behavior of their children. In a claim for negligent parental supervision, the standard of care for a parent is that of a reasonably prudent parent. If Dora's mother did not act as reasonably prudent parent in her supervision of Dora, she may be held liable for negligence, which would allow Peterson to recover from her for his injuries.

Question 14
Answer: A

The correct answer is choice (A). This question tests the law of negligence of a child. A child can be subject to tort liability, even if supervised, if they act in a negligent manner. To determine whether a child has acted negligently, the court looks to the standard of care for a child, which is that of an ordinary child of similar age, education, intelligence, and experience. Thus, if Dora was able to prove that she exercised care commensurate with her age, intelligence, and experience, then Peterson will not be able to show that she was negligent and will not be able to recover from her.

Question 15
Answer: A

The correct answer is choice (A). This question tests the law of intentional infliction of emotional distress. Intentional infliction of emotional distress is defined as extreme and outrageous conduct, made intentionally or recklessly, that causes severe emotional distress to another. To be deemed extreme and outrageous, a defendant's act or words must exceed the ordinary bounds of behavior that are permitted in a decent society. Outrageous acts or words might arise from a defendant's abuse of a relation with a plaintiff that affords the defendant power to damage the plaintiff's interests. Additionally, a person may be held liable if he knew that the plaintiff was particularly susceptible to emotional distress.

In this situation, Dayton has been previously made aware of Pratt's health condition, inability to work, and willingness to pay when able. Under the circumstances, his behavior and threats toward her, knowing that Pratt in her condition was particularly susceptible to emotional distress, would be deemed to exceed the ordinary bounds of behavior that are permitted in a decent society.

Choice (B) is incorrect because the validity of the bill is not defense to extreme and outrageous conduct that causes an individual severe emotional distress.

Choices (C) and (D) are incorrect because under a claim for intentional infliction of emotional distress, the plaintiff does not have to show physical harm, unlike the principles of its counterpart negligent infliction of emotional distress.

Question16
Answer: A

The correct answer is choice (A). The question is testing the law of trespass to land. In order to recover on a claim for trespass onto land, a land possessor must prove that the entry onto the land was intentional. A land owner can recover for an intentional trespass, even if the damages are nominal. Thus, the only allegation that would provide a sufficient basis for a claim against Dan would be that he intentionally drove his car onto Peter's land. Peter would not have to additionally show that Dan's car actually damaged Peter's land.

Question 17
Answer: B

The correct answer is choice (B). The question is testing the law of private nuisance. A private nuisance occurs when a defendant substantially and unreasonably disturbs the right to use and enjoy the land of a real property owner or lessee. The various types of actionable disturbances may include disruptive noises and vibrations, as well as physical harms to a landowner's real property and the structures and chattel on that property. A viable basis for bringing a private nuisance action is a decrease in the use and value of the plaintiff's property due to the defendant's adverse conditions or activities.

The stone-crushing machine has created such a continuous and intense noise as to constitute a substantial and unreasonable disturbance of Palmco's right to use and enjoy its land, as evidenced by the fact that the noise is so disturbing that the hotel guests are canceling their reservations. Additionally, the operation of the machinery has caused a decrease in the use and value of the Palmco's property, as its guests are canceling their reservations in order to avoid having to endure the noise.

Choice (A) is incorrect. An abnormally dangerous activity is one that presents a substantial risk of serious harm to persons or property regardless of the degree of care that is exercised in carrying out that activity. The stone crushing machine may be an abnormally dangerous activity. However, it has caused no physical harm to Palmco or its customers.

Choice (C) is incorrect, as this question does not allege any facts that would show that Dredgeco has operated the machinery in a negligent manner.

Choice (D) is incorrect because Dredgeco is operating the machinery on public property owned by City with the permission of City, and thus, it cannot be considered to constitute a trespass.

Question18
Answer: B

The correct answer is choice (B). The question is testing the laws of assault and battery. A person is liable for assault if he acts intending to cause an imminent apprehension of a harmful or offensive contact and causes an imminent apprehension of a harmful or offensive contact. After hearing Patty say that she had realized she had made a mistake and thought she was on public property, the property owner cursed at her and approached her with a stick intending to cause apprehension of a harmful contact. His actions did cause Patty the intended apprehension that the she would be struck and/or fall off the horse and thus the property owner's actions constitute an assault.

Battery is defined as an act intentionally causing either a harmful or offensive contact or immediate apprehension of a harmful or offensive contact with the person of another and actually causing such contact. The term "person of another" includes intentional and impermissible contact upon any part of the body, anything that is attached to the body, and anything that is reasonably connected to it. When the owner intentionally struck the horse with the stick, he made a harmful contact with Patty who, while riding at the time, was reasonably connected to the horse.

Choice (A) is incorrect because in order to recover for a trespass to chattel, a wrongdoer's act must result in an interference with an owner's right of possession and also must result in actual damages of the chattel. In this case, the owner's strike to the horse did not interfere with Patty's possession of the horse and there is no indication in the fact pattern that it suffered actual damages.

Choice (C) is incorrect because in order to recover for an assault or battery, a person does not have to suffer physical harm.

Choice (D) is incorrect because a defendant must advise a plaintiff to leave his premises before the defendant may use non-deadly force to defend his property interests. If the plaintiff fails to leave in response to that warning, then the defendant can only use a reasonable means of defense. Patty's response to the property owner indicated that she had realized she had made a mistake and gave no indication of an intent to be disrespectful to the property owner and his wishes for her to leave the property or posed a threat to him. Thus, the property owner's actions towards Patty would not be considered a reasonable means of defense of his property.

Question 19
Answer: D

The correct answer is choice (D). The question is testing the laws of comparative negligence and contribution. When a plaintiff and defendant, or multiple defendants, are each partially negligent, the amount of damages that are awarded to the plaintiff is subject to a reduction in the amount of the plaintiff's liability. In a pure comparative negligence jurisdiction, the allocation of liability for damages is assessed in proportion to each party's fault, despite the fact that a plaintiff's degree of fault may exceed that of a defendant. In this question, Plaintiff was held to be 40 percent liable, and thus his percentage of liability will be deducted from the damages awarded, leaving him with an amount of $60,000 for which D-1 and D-2 are jointly and severally liable.

When a plaintiff is entitled to recover damages on the basis of joint and several liability in a comparative negligence jurisdiction, the plaintiff may recover the entire award of damages from any of the defendants. Thus, Plaintiff can collect the full sum of $60,000 from D-1 who will then have to himself collect the $30,000 owed in contribution from D-2 in accordance with the apportioned percentages of fault.

Question 20
Answer: C

The correct answer is choice (C). This question tests the law of the rescue doctrine. An independent duty of care is owed to a rescuer by a tortfeasor and the tortfeasor will be held liable to any subsequent parties that are injured in the course of a rescue attempt that occurs in connection with the tortfeasor's actions.

If Desmond's peril arose from his own failure to exercise reasonable care, Desmond would be considered to be the tortfeasor. If that were the case, then Desmond's estate would be liable to Pearson for the injuries sustained in the attempted rescue of Desmond.

Question 21
Answer: D

The correct answer is choice (D). The question is testing the law of strict liability. An abnormally dangerous activity is one that presents a substantial risk of serious harm to persons or property regardless of the degree of care that is exercised in carrying out that activity and is subject to the principles of strict liability. The elements of a strict liability claim are (1) a defendant's absolute duty to make a something safe; (2) the defendant's breach of that duty (which in most states is only owed to a foreseeable plaintiff); and (3) the defendant proximately caused injury to a plaintiff's person or property. The law imposes an absolute duty on whoever engages in an abnormally dangerous activity to safely perform it.

The production of nuclear power would be considered to be an abnormally dangerous activity, and thus the exposed persons would proceed with a claim for strict liability. Therefore, the negligence of the power plant is not a factor in the determination of whether the exposed individuals will prevail against NPP in a strict liability action. Choices (A), (B), and (C) encompass the factors that will be analyzed in a determination of NPP's liability to the exposed persons under the theory of strict liability.

Question 22
Answer: D

The correct answer is choice (D). This question tests the laws of the rescue doctrine and strict products liability. An original tortfeasor will be held liable for the reasonably foreseeable events that occur in connection with the immediate consequences of the tortfeasor's actions. An attempt to aid a person injured by the tortfeasor is considered to be a foreseeable course of events. Under a strict products liability theory, any commercial supplier (i.e., middleman, supplier, dealer, or retailer) may be held strictly liable for a plaintiff's injuries from a commercial product if the product is dangerously defective.

In this question, the retailer will be held to be strictly liable as the tortfeasor for the manufacturing defect, even though it may not have manufactured the safety device. Therefore, as the tortfeasor, Outfitters, Inc. will be liable for the foreseeable events that occurred in connection with the defective safety harness, including the injuries to Rollins, the rescuer who attempted to aid Alper.

Question 23
Answer: A

The correct answer is choice (A). The question is testing the laws of joint and several liability and apportionment. The doctrine of joint and several liability provides that when there is more than one defendant whose concurrent negligence results in harm to a plaintiff, they may each be found liable for the entire amount of damages that they caused by their indivisible wrongful conduct. It is in the plaintiff's best interest to have defendants who are jointly and severally liable, as it increases the chances of actual recovery of the award. Thus, once the plaintiff has brought forth evidence of both parties' wrongdoing, it should be the duty of the multiple wrongdoers to then bear the burden of trying to apportion the damages between themselves, as it is in their best interest to try to avoid joint and several liability to the plaintiff.

Question 24
Answer: A

The correct answer is choice (A). The question is testing the law of strict products liability. Under a strict products liability theory, any commercial supplier (i.e., middleman, supplier, dealer, or retailer) may be held strictly liable for a plaintiff's injuries from a commercial product if the product is dangerously defective. The fact that a supplier and/or installer did not act in a negligent manner has no bearing on the analysis. Thus, because the engine that was installed by Airco on the plane was dangerously defective, Airco will be held strictly liable to Flyer for full compensation for all of the damages caused in connection with the defective engine, including the damage to Landers' property.

Question 25
Answer: C

The correct answer is choice (C). The question is testing the law of causation. A tortfeasor will be held liable for the reasonably foreseeable events that occur in connection with the immediate consequences of the tortfeasor's actions.

In this question, it was Dant's negligence that caused the original car accident. A reasonably foreseeable event that occurred in connection with the original car accident was a passerby slowing down to see if aid was needed, which could (and did) cause additional traffic accidents. Thus, the jury could find that Page's injury arose from a risk that was a continuing consequence of Dant's negligence, and Dant could be held liable for her damages.

Question 26
Answer: B

The correct answer is choice (B). Assault requires placing a person in fear of an immediate harmful or offensive bodily contact. By providing Pocket with 10 minutes to leave, the threatened harm was not immediate.

Choice (A) is incorrect because actual contact is not a required to prevail in a claim for assault.

Choice (C) is incorrect because intending to cause severe emotional distress is not the standard required in order to prevail in a claim for assault. Additionally, even if Dudd intended to cause emotional distress, in order to prevail on a claim for assault, he must prove that the threatened contact was imminent.

Choice (D) is incorrect because even though Pocket was threatened with a harmful or offensive bodily contact, Dudd will escape liability for assault because his threat was not imminent.

Question 27
Answer: C

The correct answer is choice (C). The question is testing the law of battery. In order to prevail on claim for battery, the plaintiff must show that the defendant committed an act intentionally causing a harmful or offensive contact or immediate apprehension of a harmful or offensive contact with the person of another and actually caused such contact.

In this case, the jury does not have to find that Dooley intended to actually hit Patricia, but merely that he intentionally meant to cause the hecklers fear of being hit by the ball. It does not matter that Dooley could not foresee the ball going through the mesh fence or that he did not intend for the ball to actually strike someone. Dooley can be held liable for battery merely for the intent to put the hecklers in apprehension of being hit and the fact that such contact actually occurred.

Question 28
Answer: A

The correct answer is choice (A). The question is testing the law of vicarious liability. An employee's intentional torts are generally considered to have occurred outside of the scope of employment, unless the employee committed them in furtherance of the employer's business activities. In other words, if the employee entirely or partially uses force to advance the employer's goals, even inadvertently, that use of force will fall under the scope of employment. It will result in the employer being vicariously liable to a plaintiff who is harmed as a result of the employee's conduct.

In this question, a jury could find that Dooley's behavior on the baseball field was in furtherance of the City Robins' business activities and to advance the baseball team's goals, and hold the City Robins vicariously liable for the intentional tort of Dooley. For example, the publicity from the event would attract attention to the baseball team and potentially draw new fans to the stadium creating additional exposure and revenue for the team.

Question 29
Answer: D

The correct answer is choice (D). The question is testing the law of negligence per se. In order to prevail on a claim of negligence per se, the plaintiff must show that the defendant's conduct violated the reason for the ordinance. If prevention of traffic accidents was not a purpose of the city's parking ordinance, then Dieter cannot be held to be liable for Grove's injuries on a claim based on Dieter's violation of the ordinance.

Question 30
Answer: B

The correct answer is choice (B). The question is testing the law of strict liability. An owner of a domestic or inherently non-dangerous animal is generally not strictly liable for the injuries that it causes. However, the owner's liability attaches if the owner knows of, or has reason to know about, a domestic animal's particularly dangerous propensities. In this question, the propensity of a dog to chase after cars is dangerous, not only to the dog, but potentially to drivers as well. Thus, if Dorfman knew or had reason to know of his dog's propensity to chase cars and did not restrain the dog, then he could be liable for Peterson's injuries.

Question 31
Answer: A

The correct answer is choice (A). The question is testing the law of conversion. A claim for conversion addresses a wrongdoer's interference with an owner's goods that is significant enough to justify a forced judicial sale of the goods to the wrongdoer. Conversion may result from the wrongdoer's unauthorized taking and/or destruction of the goods. Conversion occurs if a possessor's conduct substantially goes beyond the scope of possession and use that an owner has authorized.

In this question, Dower has intentionally and substantially gone beyond the scope of possession and use that Puder has authorized, which culminated in the destruction of Puder's car, and thus Puder will prevail on a claim for conversion. A conversion claim forces a judicial sale of the goods to Dower. Thus, Puder is entitled to recover $12,000 from Dower, the market value of the car at the time of the conversion.

Question 32
Answer: C

The correct answer is choice (C). The question is testing the laws of negligence per se and comparative negligence. A plaintiff will prevail on a claim for negligence per se if (1) the plaintiff is within the class of individuals that a statute is designed to protect; (2) a defendant's conduct violated the statute; (3) the defendant's conduct violated the reason for the statute; (4) that conduct constitutes the type of risk that the statute covers; and (5) the conduct is not excused. In a pure comparative negligence jurisdiction, the allocation of liability for damages is assessed in proportion to each party's fault, despite the fact that a plaintiff's degree of fault may exceed that of a defendant.

In this question, Deland violated the statute prohibiting parking too close to a street intersection, a law that's purpose is to prevent automobile accidents and injuries occurring therefrom. Thus, Pilcher is in the class of individuals the statute is intended to protect, and Deland's conduct is the type of risk that the statute covers. Therefore, Pilcher can recover his losses from Deland for negligence per se, reduced by a percentage that reflects the negligence attributable to Pilcher.

Question 33
Answer: B

The correct answer is choice (B). The question is testing the law of vicarious liability. In certain instances, an employer's business activities and his relationship to a plaintiff impose upon him a duty that cannot be delegated to an independent contractor. In such a case, the employer cannot be relieved of liability by hiring the independent contractor to perform those nondelegable duties. Consequently, an employer will be liable for the torts that an independent contractor commits while performing a nondelegable duty for the employer. Thus, Bruce can be held liable for his independent contractor's negligence, if Chase's actions were a breach of a nondelegable duty owed by Bruce to Anson.

Question 34
Answer: D

The correct answer is choice (D). The question is testing the law of causation. A tortfeasor will be held liable for the reasonably foreseeable events that occur in connection with the immediate consequences of the tortfeasor's actions.

The cancellation of the soap opera and subsequent firing of Penn, a co-worker of Star, is not a reasonably foreseeable event that occurred in connection with the immediate consequences of a car accident caused by Danton and to which Penn was not even involved. Thus, Danton's liability does not extend to an economic loss to Penn that arises solely from the physical harm Danton's actions caused to Star.

Question 35
Answer: C

The correct answer is choice (C). The question is testing the law of negligent infliction of emotional distress. A plaintiff who suffers no physical harm or impact may only prevail in a claim of negligent infliction of emotional distress under rare circumstances which guarantee that the claim is not illegitimate. In these types of fact patterns, a plaintiff need not prove physical harm or impact.

The circumstances described in this question are of the type that would be so horrific to a mother that it guarantees that her claim for emotional distress is not illegitimate. If the mausoleum was negligent in its failure to use reasonable care to safeguard the body, Ann would be able to recover for negligent infliction of emotional distress from the mausoleum without the necessity of proving physical harm.

Question 36
Answer: D

The correct answer is choice (D). The question is testing the law of premises liability. A landowner and its agents have a duty to warn known trespassers of dangerous artificial conditions on the property. Prad would be considered to be a trespasser because of the signage designating the space as an area for employees only. After Prad was seen by a store employee who did not vacate him from the area, he became a known trespasser. Thus, the clerk had a duty to warn him of the existence of the open shaft, a dangerous artificial condition on the premises.

Question 37
Answer: C

The correct answer is choice (D). The question is testing the law of battery. Even though the doctrine of transferred intent could make someone liable for harming an unintended target, self-defense is an available defense to any battery action. Thus, if Guard fired the weapon reasonably in his own defense, then Plaintiff cannot prevail on a claim of battery against Guard.

Question 38
Answer: C

The correct answer is choice (C). The question is testing the law of defamation. In order for a plaintiff to prevail in a claim for defamation, the plaintiff must show that the publication of the statement to a third party was at least negligently made. Thus, unless Jones knew or should have reasonably foreseen that the statement would be published to a third party, Jones will not be held liable to Smith for defamation.

Question 39
Answer: C

The correct answer is choice (C). The question is testing the law of private nuisance. A private nuisance occurs when a defendant substantially and unreasonably disturbs the right to use and enjoy the land of a real property owner or lessee. The standard to determine whether a nuisance is substantial and unreasonable is the reasonable person standard. Thus, the Pinners could not prevail on a nuisance action against the Darleys, unless they could show that the noise constituted a substantial and unreasonable disturbance to persons of normal sensibilities.

Question 40
Answer: C

The correct answer is choice (C). The question is testing the laws of joint and several liability and comparative negligence. The doctrine of joint and several liability provides that when there is more than one defendant whose concurrent negligence results in harm to a plaintiff, they may each be found liable for the entire amount of damages that they caused by their indivisible wrongful conduct. Additionally, in a pure comparative negligence jurisdiction, the allocation of liability for damages is assessed in proportion to each party's fault, including the plaintiff's, despite the fact that a plaintiff's degree of fault may exceed that of a defendant.

In this question, Davis and Jones will be held jointly and severally liable for their negligence in connection with Peters' injury because they were concurrently negligent and their wrongdoing is indivisible. If Davis had not negligently parked his car in the street, even though Jones was driving negligently, the car may not have been hit. Alternatively, if Jones had not been driving negligently, he would have been able to avoid hitting Davis' car negligently parked in the street. Further, since this a pure comparative negligence jurisdiction, any amount of damages awarded to Peters will be reduced by the percentage of the total negligence that is attributed to his actions.

Question 41
Answer: C

The correct answer is choice (C). This question is testing the law of battery. In order for a battery claim to prevail, the plaintiff must show that the defendant intentionally caused a harmful or offensive contact to the person of another. If Dorwin did not know that he was striking a person, then it was not his intent to cause a harmful contact with a person of another, and he cannot be held liable for battery. Choices (A) and (B) are incorrect, as they are not relevant to whether the elements of battery are satisfied. Choice (D) is incorrect because in a majority of jurisdictions, a defendant claiming self-defense must show that he acted reasonably.

Question 42
Answer: A

The correct answer is choice (A). This question is testing the law of trespass to land. In order to prevail on a claim for trespass to land, a land possessor must prove that the entry onto the land by the trespasser was intentional. A land possessor does not, however, need to prove that the wrongdoer knew that the land belonged to another. Further, nominal damages are available for trespass to land actions when actual damages have not been suffered.

In this question, Drury intentionally used the channel as a shortcut to the lake, and thus Penstock will be able to prevail in his claim for trespass to land. The fact that Drury thought that it was a public waterway has no bearing on the analysis, because in order to prevail, Penstock does not have to show that Drury knew the land belonged to another person. Since there was no harm from the trespass to Penstock, he will only be allowed to recover nominal damages from Drury.

Question 43

Answer: C

The correct answer is choice (C). This question is testing the law of trespass to land. In order to prevail on a claim for trespass to land, a land possessor must prove that the entry onto the land by the trespasser was intentional. A land possessor does not, however, need to prove that the wrongdoer knew that the land belonged to another.

In this question, David intentionally built his garage in a specific location that happened to encroach on Prudence's property, and thus Prudence will be able to prevail in a claim for trespass to land. The fact that David did not know that the garage was encroaching on Prudence's property line when he built it has no bearing on the analysis, because in order to prevail, Prudence does not have to show that David knew the land encroached upon belonged to another person.

Question 44
Answer: B

The correct answer is choice (B). This question is testing the law of the firefighter's rule. The firefighter's rule provides that public servants, including police officers, at risk of injury by the perils that they have been employed to confront assume all ordinary and inherent risks of their highly dangerous employment. As a result, they may not sue in common law when those dangers result in injury.

In this question, Officer will not be able to recover damages from Daniel based on a claim of common law negligence, as Officer has assumed all ordinary and inherent risks of employment as a police officer. Such risks would include suffering injury from breaking up a fight in the normal scope of his duty as a police officer.

Question 45
Answer: A

The correct answer is choice (A). This question is testing the law of premises liability. Landowners possess a duty of reasonable care to an invitee, which cannot be disclaimed. They not only have a duty to warn the invitee of a dangerous condition on their property of which they are aware, but also possess a duty to make reasonable inspections of their property to identify any dangerous conditions that might exist on that property and to repair them.

In this question, Lorner is an invitee of the supermarket. The supermarket has complied with requirement that it warn its invitees about the dangerous condition of the muggers and pickpockets in the area. Yet, knowing that the area is prone to pickpockets and muggers (a dangerous condition of the property), if it has failed to take reasonable steps to protect customers against criminal attacks in its parking lot, then it will have breached its duty of reasonable care to its shoppers and will be held liable for Lorner's damages.

Question 46
Answer: C

The correct answer is choice (C). This question is testing the law of strict products liability and comparative negligence. A supplier of a product is liable to foreseeable users for harm that results from foreseeable uses of the product if the product is inherently dangerous and the supplier fails to inform the user of the danger. In a pure comparative negligence jurisdiction, the allocation of liability for damages is assessed in proportion to each party's fault, despite the fact that a plaintiff's degree of fault may exceed that of a defendant.

In this question, the manufacturer of the car had a duty to adequately warn Peter of any inherent danger of high speed driving on the tires mounted on the car, which is a foreseeable use of the vehicle. Further, in a pure comparative negligence jurisdiction, Peter may recover even if he was also negligent, as his recovery from the car manufacturer will merely be reduced by the percentage of fault allocated to him.

Choice (A) is an attractive answer, but it is incorrect because in order for misuse to be a defense in a products liability case, the misuse has to not be reasonably foreseeable by the manufacturer. In this case, driving with excessive speed is a reasonably foreseeable misuse of a high-powered sports car.

Question 47
Answer: C

The correct answer is choice (C). The question is testing the law of private nuisance. A private nuisance occurs when a defendant substantially and unreasonably disturbs the right to use and enjoy the land of a real property owner or lessee. Unless Electco actually caused a substantial and unreasonable interference with Paul's business located on the real property, Paul will not be able to meet the requirements to show that Electco's activity constitutes a private nuisance and will not prevail against same.

Question 48
Answer: B

The correct answer is choice (B). The question is testing the law of negligence. In order to recover on a claim for negligence, the plaintiff must be foreseeable. Foreseeable plaintiffs are those individuals or entities to whom a defendant could have reasonably expected to be harmed or put at risk of harm as a result of the defendant's act or omission. A defendant has a duty to avoid reasonable risks of harm created by his own negligent behavior.

In this question, Doe will be held liable to any person he could have reasonably expected to be injured or put at risk for injury in connection with his negligence. Sunshine burning his neighbor's trees is not a risk of harm that is reasonably foreseeable as a consequence of Doe negligently burning down his own house, and thus Doe did not have a duty to protect Peter from such damage. Therefore, Doe's best argument in support of his motion to dismiss is that his duty to avoid the risks created by a fire did not encompass the risk that sunshine would damage Peter's trees.

Question 49
Answer: C

The correct answer is choice (C). The question is testing the law of a parent's liability for the commission of a negligent act by their child. Normally parents are not held personally responsible for their child's negligent acts. An exception to that rule, however, is when a parent has reason to know or does know of dangerous propensities of the child and fails to exercise reasonable care. If Dan's parents knew that he had the propensity to drive into the highway, and took no steps to prevent it, they may be held liable for damages caused to Peter as a result of Dan's negligence.

Question 50
Answer: D

The correct answer is choice (D). The question is testing the law of a negligent infliction of emotional distress. In order to prevail on a claim of negligent infliction of emotional distress, the plaintiff must show that the defendant negligently engaged in conduct which caused the plaintiff severe emotional distress and it was foreseeable that it would do so.

The issue that will ultimately determine whether Hill can recover from Weber is the unsettled question of whether a person can recover damages for harm resulting from shock solely from an unrelated person's peril or injury and for which the plaintiff was not in the zone of danger.

Question 51
Answer: C

The correct answer is choice (C). This question is testing the law of res ipsa loquitur. The law allows an inference of negligence on a party when an event would have not otherwise occurred unless someone was negligent.

In this case, even though a car rolling down the hill would probably not have otherwise occurred without the negligence of someone, there was no evidence produced that Defendant was the one who was actually negligent. In fact, the opposite is true, as Defendant has produced evidence to show that she behaved in a reasonably prudent manner and provided the jury with a reasonable alternative party that was likely to be the one whose negligence caused the accident and resulting damage. Thus, the jury was not required to draw an inference of negligence from the circumstances of the accident, as other evidence was presented by Defendant to rebut such an inference.

Question 52
Answer: A

The correct answer is choice (A). This question is testing the law of indemnity. The doctrine of indemnification requires one or more defendants to fully reimburse another defendant who discharged their mutual liability. Indemnity may be available when one defendant's culpability level is much higher than the other defendant's in connection with the harm caused to the plaintiff.

In this question, Mark had a significantly higher culpability level in connection with the damages caused to the plaintiff, as he shot Paul intentionally. David, even though he may have been negligent, did not intend for Paul to get shot with his gun nor knew of Mark's intent to use his gun in that manner. Thus, David can seek indemnity for the full amount of the judgment from Mark, because he is substantially less culpable than Mark with regard to the damages caused to Paul.

Question 53
Answer: B

The correct answer is choice (B). This question is testing the law of trespass to land. A land possessor has an actionable trespass claim if a wrongdoer has caused harmful liquids to enter upon the land possessor's property. Since the harmful chemical leaked from Chemco's property onto the property of Farmer, Chemco will be liable to Farmer for his damages.

Question 54
Answer: C

The correct answer is choice (C). This question is testing the law of battery. In order to prevail on a claim for battery, the plaintiff must be able to show that the defendant intended to cause a harmful or offensive contact or the immediate apprehension of such a contact to the plaintiff. Unless Daring actually intended to cause an impermissible contact between the horses or intended to cause an apprehension of such contact, Daring will not be held liable for battery.

Question 55
Answer: B

The correct answer is choice (B). This question is testing the law of defamation. In order to prevail on a claim for defamation of a private figure, the plaintiff must show that the defendant was negligent with regard to the truth (or falsity) of the statement. If no evidence was presented as to the Daily Sun's negligence as to the truth or falsity of the charges of embezzlement at the time of its publication, then it cannot be held liable for defamation.

Question 56
Answer: D

The correct answer is choice (D). This question is testing the law of wrongful conception. A plaintiff can prevail on a claim for wrongful conception from the improper performance of a contraceptive procedure. In this case, Surgeon improperly performed the sterilization procedure, which culminated in the birth of a baby who happened to have a severe birth defect. Thus, Patient will be able to recover damages in connection with its claim of wrongful conception, such as those relating to labor and delivery. But, the availability of recovery for the baby's future medical expenses for a birth defect not caused by the negligence of Surgeon is controversial and will depend on the particular court and its jurisdiction.

Question 57
Answer: B

The correct answer is choice (B). This question is testing the law of defamation. In order for a plaintiff to prevail in a claim for defamation, the plaintiff must show that the publication of the statement to a third party was at least negligently made by the defendant. Thus, if Drew should have reasonably foreseen that the statement would be overheard by other employees, Drew will be held liable to Pat for defamation.

Question 58
Answer: A, C

The correct answers to this question are choices (A) and (C). The examiners of the MBE counted both choices to this question as correct answers. This question tests the law of res ipsa loquitur. The law allows an inference of negligence on a party when an event would have not otherwise occurred unless someone was negligent. In this question, the presence of a horse on a highway is an event that probably would not have occurred unless someone was negligent. Depending on the evidence that is presented to the court by Rancher showing his reasonably prudent behavior, the inference may be rebutted that the Rancher was the one who actually negligent.

Question 59
Answer: D

The correct answer is choice (D). This question is testing the law of causation. In a negligence action, in order for a plaintiff to recover all of his losses from a defendant, a plaintiff merely has to show that such defendant was a proximate cause of all of his damages. Proximate cause includes a finding of actual cause ("but for" the defendant's conduct, the plaintiff's injury would have been avoided) and a finding that the damages were reasonably foreseeable. There can be more than one proximate cause.

In this question, Railroad negligently maintained its storm drain, and a reasonably foreseeable consequence of such a failure to maintain is a flooding of the ravine and damages caused therefrom. Further, but for the storm drain being negligently maintained by Railroad, the manufacturing plant would not have flooded (even if City had also negligently maintained its storm drain). Thus, since Railroad's negligence was a proximate cause of Penkov's damages, he will be entitled to recover all of his losses from Railroad.

Question 60
Answer: B

The correct answer is choice (B). This question is testing the law of false imprisonment. False imprisonment is the intentional confinement or restraint of a person to a contained space without justification. With regard to shoplifting, a storekeeper has the privilege to detain a suspect who it has a reasonable belief may have shoplifted, but may only confine the suspect for a reasonable time period and in a reasonable manner.

In this question, the store's best defense would be that it is not liable to Paula for false imprisonment, because the manager was reasonable in his belief that she may have stolen the scarf and his method of detainment was not overly aggressive. Further, the length of the detention was just long enough to conduct a reasonable investigation of the facts. Also, when Paula's innocence was brought to light, Paula was immediately released from confinement.

Question 61
Answer: A

The correct answer is choice (A). The question is testing the law of negligent infliction of emotional distress. A plaintiff who suffers no physical harm or impact may only prevail in a claim of negligent infliction of emotional distress under rare circumstances which guarantee that the claim is not illegitimate.

The circumstances described in this question are of the type that would be so horrific, in light of the sensitivity a son would have regarding his deceased father's body, that it guarantees that John's claim for emotional distress is not illegitimate. Thus, since Hospital was negligent in allowing the amputated leg to get into Jeremiah's drawer, John would be able to recover for negligent infliction of emotional distress from Hospital without the necessity of proving physical harm or impact.

Question 62
Answer: D

The correct answer is choice (D). The question is testing the law of negligence damages. A plaintiff who suffers a physical injury or incapacity resulting from a defendant's negligence can recover compensatory damages for pain and suffering, medical expenses, and other adverse pecuniary consequences resulting from the injury or incapacity. The available damages also include recovery for the aggravation of pre-existing conditions or disabilities of a plaintiff. The type of damage sustained by a plaintiff does not have to be foreseeable by the defendant, as defendants must take plaintiffs as they find them, with all of their physical qualities, susceptibilities, and disabilities.

Thus, in light of Acme's negligence, Prudence can recover for all damages she sustained in connection with the falling elevator, including the aggravation of her pre-existing disability.

Question 63
Answer: A

The correct answer is choice (A). The question is testing the law of trespass to land. A trespass to land is an act of an intentional physical invasion of the land of another. Even though necessity is a valid defense to trespass, if the trespass serves to benefit an individual or his property (private necessity), then the person will be held liable for the damages caused by such trespass.

Driver intentionally entered onto the property of Gardner out of necessity, in order to avoid being hit by a falling tree, and such trespass caused damage to Gardner's property. Since Driver benefited from the trespass, Gardner will be able to recover from Driver for the damages caused to his backyard by Driver's golf cart.

Question 64
Answer: C

The correct answer is choice (C). The question is testing the law of intentional infliction of emotional distress. In order to prevail on a claim for intentional infliction of emotional distress, a plaintiff must show that the defendant intentionally or recklessly engaged in extreme and outrageous conduct that caused severe emotional distress to another. If Perkins did not suffer severe emotional distress from the actions of Dumont, she will not be able to recover from him for her emotional distress.

Question 65
Answer: D

The correct answer is choice (D). The question is testing the law of intentional misrepresentation. An intentional misrepresentation is a defendant's false statement of fact with the intent to mislead or deceive another person. In order to recover on a claim for intentional misrepresentation, a plaintiff must show pecuniary loss. In this situation, Perkins did not suffer any pecuniary loss and thus cannot prevail on a claim for misrepresentation against Dumont.

Question 66
Answer: D

The correct answer is choice (D). The question is testing the law of negligence. If a defendant's conduct placed a plaintiff in a situation of danger, then the defendant possesses a duty to assist the plaintiff to either avoid the danger or to be delivered from that dangerous situation. Further, vicarious liability is imposed on an employer for tortious acts of an employee that occur during the course of, and in the scope of, the servant's employment.

By serving Morton so many drinks when he was obviously intoxicated, the flight attendant was putting Perkins in a dangerous situation, though inadvertently, and thus should have perceived the danger and removed Perkins from the situation. Since the flight attendant was in the course and scope of employment when the failure to remove Perkins from the dangerous situation occurred, Perkins will be able to recover from the employer Delval Airlines for negligence through the principle of vicarious liability.

Question 67
Answer: C

The correct answer is choice (C). The question is testing the law of vicarious liability. A party is not vicariously liable for the commission of an intentional tort by a third party, unless such third party was acting as their agent or employee and the act was in furtherance of the master's business activities. Thus, Delval Airlines cannot be held responsible for the actions of Morton, who was not acting as an agent or an employee of Delval Airlines when he struck Perkins.

Question 68
Answer: D

The correct answer is choice (D). The question is testing the law of negligence. A person possesses a general legal duty to act reasonably and with prudence in every situation in order to avoid causing an unreasonable risk of injury to other people.

The jury could find that Grandmother did not act with reasonable prudence by forgetting to lock the gun cabinet before the eight year old boys came over to her house. If Grandmother acted unreasonably with regard to protecting the boys from access to her gun, she will have breached her duty of care to Patrick to avoid causing him an unreasonable risk of injury and Patrick will prevail in his claim against her.

Question 69
Answer: B

The correct answer is choice (B). The question is testing the law of vicarious liability. An employer cannot escape liability for damages caused from an independent contractor performing an inherently dangerous activity. Inherently dangerous activities, such as blasting or fumigating, involve a significant amount of risk relative to the circumstances. Landco will be held vicariously liable to Plaintiff, since Poolco was employed by Landco to engage in an inherently dangerous activity that ultimately caused damage to Plaintiff.

Question 70
Answer: A

The correct answer is choice (A). The question is testing the law of attractive nuisance. A landowner must exercise reasonable care to ensure the safety of trespassing children. If trespassing children would normally be aware of the dangerous condition, understand its risk of danger, and could avoid it, then the landowner lacks a heightened duty to prevent injury to such children. Thus, if children likely to be attracted to the trampoline would normally realize the risk of using it without mats, then Philip cannot recover from Davis for his injuries.

Question 71
Answer: C

The correct answer is choice (C). The question is testing the law of products liability. To prevail on a claim for products liability, the plaintiff must show that the product is defective. A product is dangerously defective if a reasonably foreseeable person would not have expected it to present the danger that resulted in his or her injury.

The product in this question is not defective, because it was designed and sold for protection only against small flying objects, and was not designed to protect consumers from large flying objects. Since the warning label attached to the glasses adequately warned consumers of its intended purpose, an ordinary consumer would have expected the glasses not to protect against large flying objects. Therefore, Grinder will not prevail in an action against Glassco for products liability, as the glasses are not defective.

Question 72
Answer: D

The correct answer is choice (D). The question is testing the law of products liability. In order to prevail on a claim for a manufacturing or design defect, a plaintiff must show that the product is unreasonably dangerous and places people at an unreasonable risk of harm. In order to prevail on a failure to adequately warn claim, the plaintiff merely has to show that the manufacturer failed to adequately warn the consumer of a non-obvious inherent risk of the product.

In this question, the product itself is not unreasonably dangerous and does not place people at an unreasonable risk of harm, as the risk of contracting dermatitis from the product is remote. Thus, the most promising theory of liability for Paul is the Shampoo Company's failure to adequately warn of the non-obvious risk that the product may cause dermatitis by not putting the warning label on the bottle itself and making it non-removable.

Question 73
Answer: D

The correct answer is choice (D). The question is testing the law of strict products liability. In order for misuse to be a defense in a products liability case, the misuse has to not be reasonably foreseeable by the manufacturer. Further, contributory negligence is not a defense to strict liability when the plaintiff's misuse is reasonably foreseeable. In this scenario, Paul's misuse of the shampoo, by using too much of it too often, is a reasonably foreseeable misuse of the product. Thus, neither Paul's misuse of the product nor his contributory negligence will provide a defense for Shampoo Company in a strict products liability action.

Under a strict liability theory, any commercial supplier may be held strictly liable for a plaintiff's injuries from a commercial product if the product is dangerously defective. The plaintiff does not have to be the purchaser of the product nor actually in privity with the manufacturer. Thus, even though Paul was a remote user of the product and not in privity with Shampoo Company, it will not prevent him from being able to recover from Shampoo Company on a claim for strict products liability.

Question 74
Answer: A

The correct answer is choice (A). The question is testing the law of contributory negligence. The rule of contributory negligence requires a plaintiff to exercise due care to avoid an injury. A plaintiff engages in contributory negligence by failing to exercise due care that results in harm from a defendant. Traditionally, under the common law rule, which the facts indicate governs in this jurisdiction, any evidence of contributory negligence on the part of the plaintiff entirely precludes a plaintiff's recovery of damages. Thus, if Paul failed to exercise due care to avoid his injuries, he will be found contributorily negligent and will not be able to recover from Oscar.

Question 75
Answer: B

The correct answer is choice (B). The question is testing the law of negligence. In order to prevail on a negligence claim, a plaintiff must show that a defendant acted unreasonably and that his unreasonable actions were the proximate cause of the plaintiff's injuries. Proximate cause includes a finding of actual cause ("but for" the defendant's conduct, the plaintiff's injuries would have been avoided) and a finding that the damages were reasonably foreseeable.

In this question, Driver was not acting like a reasonably prudent person when he took his eyes off the road and swerved off of the roadway. Further, Driver's unreasonable behavior was the proximate cause of Walker's injuries, because but for Driver swerving off of the roadway, Walker would not have jumped backwards and injured himself. Additionally, it is reasonably foreseeable that taking his eyes off the road could lead Driver to swerve off the roadway and injure someone. Thus, Driver's summary judgment motion should be denied.

Question 76
Answer: B

The correct answer is choice (B). The question is testing the law of contributory negligence and assumption of risk. The rule of contributory negligence requires a plaintiff to exercise due care to avoid an injury. Under the traditional rule, which the examiners indicate governs in this jurisdiction, any evidence of contributory negligence on the part of the plaintiff entirely precludes a plaintiff's recovery of damages. In this question, Paul failed to exercise due care to avoid injury when he did not heed the warnings and proceeded to walk his dog where Diggers was blasting. In a traditional contributory negligence jurisdiction, Paul's negligence bars him from any recovery against Diggers for his injuries.

Further, a plaintiff's recovery can be denied on the basis that the plaintiff voluntarily assumed a risk of harm by knowing the risk existed and voluntarily proceeding with the activity anyway. Paul will also not recover from Diggers based on the fact that he assumed the risk of his injuries when he read the warning signs and voluntarily proceeded into the blasting site despite knowing the risk of harm.

Question 77
Answer: B

The correct answer is choice (B). The question is testing the law of defamation. In order to prevail on a claim for defamation of a private figure, the plaintiff must show that the defendant was negligent with regard to the truth (or falsity) of the statement. If Allen had substantial doubts as to the accuracy of the information he published to a third party, but did so anyway, Bradley would be able to recover from Allen for defamation for Allen's false statements about him to the interviewer.

Question 78
Answer: A

The correct answer is choice (A). The question is testing the laws of joint and several liability, comparative negligence, and contribution. The doctrine of joint and several liability provides that when there is more than one defendant whose concurrent negligence results in harm to a plaintiff, they may each be found liable for the entire amount of damages that they caused by their indivisible wrongful conduct. Drew and Donald's concurrent negligence caused harm to Pat for which they will both be jointly and severally liable.

When a plaintiff and defendant, or multiple defendants, are each partially negligent, the amount of damages that are awarded to the plaintiff is subject to a reduction in the amount of the plaintiff's liability. In pure comparative negligence jurisdiction, the allocation of liability for damages is assessed in proportion to each party's fault, despite the fact that a plaintiff's degree of fault may exceed that of a defendant. In this question Pat was held to be 30 percent liable, and thus that percentage of liability will be deducted from the damages awarded, leaving an amount of $70,000 for which Drew and Donald are jointly and severally liable.

When a plaintiff is entitled to recover damages on the basis of joint and several liability in a comparative negligence jurisdiction, the plaintiff may recover the entire award of damages from any of the defendants. The doctrine of contribution may require one of several defendants to pay his or her respective share to another defendant who paid more than his share of joint and several liability. Thus, Plaintiff can collect the full sum of $70,000 from Donald who will then have to himself collect the $40,000 owed in contribution from Drew in accordance with the apportioned percentages of fault.

Question 79
Answer: C

The correct answer is choice (C). The question is testing the laws of laws of comparative negligence, joint and several liability, and contribution. When a plaintiff and defendant, or multiple defendants, are each partially negligent, the amount of damages that are awarded to the plaintiff is subject to a reduction in the amount of the plaintiff's liability. In a pure comparative negligence jurisdiction, the allocation of liability for damages is assessed in proportion to each party's fault, despite the fact that a plaintiff's degree of fault may exceed that of a defendant.

In this question Pat was held to be 30 percent liable, and thus that percentage of liability will be deducted from the damages awarded, leaving an amount of $70,000. Since there is no joint and several liability in this jurisdiction, Pat will only be able to recover $40,000 from Drew and will only be able to recover $30,000 from Donald. Since neither party will be required to pay more than their allocated share of the damages awarded to Pat, neither Drew nor Donald will have a contribution claim against the other.

Question 80
Answer: B

The correct answer is choice (B). The question is testing the law of negligence. In order to recover on a claim for negligence, a plaintiff must be able to show that he suffered damages from the negligence of the defendant. Otherwise, a plaintiff cannot prevail on a negligence claim against the defendant. The operation on Patten was successful and he suffered no harm from the failure of the Cutter to disclose such risk. Thus, Patten cannot prevail against Cutter on his negligence claim.

Question 81

Answer: C

The correct answer is choice (C). This question is testing the law of assault. Self-defense, defense of others, defense of property, and consent are available defenses to an assault action. If it was apparent that Lender was about to inflict serious bodily injury upon Borrower, Mann's threat of violence against Lender was in defense of another, and thus Lender will not prevail against him in an action for assault.

Question 82
Answer: A

The correct answer is choice (A). This question is testing the law of assault. In order to prevail on a claim for assault, a plaintiff must show that the defendant acted intending to make a harmful or offensive contact, without making such contact, or to cause an imminent apprehension of a harmful or offensive contact and caused such imminent apprehension of a harmful or offensive contact. Proof of actual damage is not required to recover for this tort. A plaintiff may recover at least nominal damages from a defendant.

In this scenario, Carr was in immediate apprehension of a harmful or offensive contact when the two students purposefully surrounded the car. Thus, if Carr can show that the students intended to cause apprehension of such an uninvited contact, Carr will prevail on a claim for assault against the students without having to prove actual damages.

Question 83
Answer: D

The correct answer is choice (D). This question is testing the law of vicarious liability. A party is not vicariously liable for the commission of an intentional tort by a third party, unless such third party was acting as their agent or employee and the act was in furtherance of the master's business activities.

The students in this question performed the experiment without the authorization of the university or any of its professors. In fact, the students were actually told not to perform the experiment without gaining permission from their professor first. Thus, since they were unauthorized to perform the experiment and were not acting as agents or employees of the university, the university cannot be held liable for the intentional torts of these students.

Question 84
Answer: C

The correct answer is choice (C). This question is testing the law of failure to act. A first person lacks a general duty to make affirmative efforts to assist another person that the first person knows is in a situation of danger that the first person did not create. But, the first person cannot leave the other person in worse condition than when the first person originally found him. In this question, Passer had no duty to assist Tom when he found him on the side of the road. Thus, if Passer did not make Tom's situation worse in any way before he left the scene, then Tom will not prevail in action against Passer for damages.

Question 85
Answer: A

The correct answer is choice (A). This question is testing the law of negligence. In order to prevail on a negligence claim, a plaintiff must show that a defendant acted unreasonably and that his unreasonable actions were the proximate cause of the plaintiff's injuries. Proximate cause includes a finding of actual cause ("but for" the defendant's conduct, the plaintiff's injuries would have been avoided) and a finding that the damages were reasonably foreseeable.

In this question, Traveler was not acting like a reasonably prudent person when he was drowsy and inattentive and swerved off of the roadway. Further, Traveler's unreasonable behavior was the proximate cause of Tom's injuries, because but for Traveler swerving off of the roadway, Tom would not have sustained his injuries. Additionally, it is reasonably foreseeable that his drowsiness and inattentiveness could lead Traveler to swerve off the roadway and injure someone. Thus, Tom will be able to prevail against Traveler in a claim for negligence.

Question 86
Answer: B

The correct answer is choice (B). The question is testing the law of negligence. A person possesses a general legal duty to act reasonably and with prudence in every situation in order to avoid causing an unreasonable risk of injury to other people. By leaving the ladder against the side of the house, Roofer did not act like a reasonably prudent person, as he created an unreasonable risk that a person may unlawfully enter the house. Therefore, Orissa will prevail in a claim for negligence against Roofer.

Question 87
Answer: D

The correct answer is choice (D). The question is testing the law of abnormally dangerous activities. An abnormally dangerous activity is one that presents a substantial risk of serious harm to persons or property regardless of the degree of care that is exercised in carrying out that activity. The law imposes strict liability on whoever engages in an abnormally dangerous activity.

The operation of a nuclear power plant is an abnormally dangerous activity, as it poses a substantial risk of serious harm regardless of what degree of care is exercised. Thus, strict liability is imposed on NPP for any damages associated with its nuclear power activities, even in the absence of negligence on the part of NPP.

Question 88
Answer: B

The correct answer is choice (b). The question is testing the law of vicarious liability. An employer cannot escape liability for damages caused from an independent contractor performing an inherently dangerous activity. Inherently dangerous activities involve a significant amount of risk relative to the circumstances.

In this question, House will be held vicariously liable to Driver, if to House's knowledge, Contractor was engaged in a hazardous activity which involved a significant amount of risk and ultimately caused Driver's damages.

Question 89
Answer: C

The correct answer is choice (C). The question is testing the law of negligence. In order to prevail on a negligence claim, a plaintiff must show that a defendant acted unreasonably and that his unreasonable actions were the proximate cause of the plaintiff's injuries. Proximate cause includes a finding of actual cause ("but for" the defendant's conduct, the plaintiff's injuries would have been avoided) and a finding that the damages were reasonably foreseeable.

If Contractor can show that it was not reasonably foreseeable that the tree would fall down, then the damages caused by the falling tree were also not reasonably foreseeable. Thus, Contractor would not be the proximate cause of Driver's damages and Driver would not be able to prevail in a claim against Contractor.

Question 90
Answer: C

The correct answer is choice (C). The question is testing the law of indemnity. If a master is held liable for the tort of an agent, the master will be entitled to indemnification from such agent. Thus, if House is held vicariously liable for the negligent acts of Contractor, he may bring a claim against Contractor for indemnification and recover the monies he was forced to pay in connection with the judgment.

Question 91
Answer: B

The correct answer is choice (B). The question is testing the law of the duties of a tenant for life property owner. A tenant for life is not permitted to take advantage of the natural resources on the real property, as a tenant for life property owner has a duty to avoid injuring the interests of the future interest holders of the property. A violation of this duty can lead to the award of both an injunction and damages to the future interest holders.

The grandchildren will be able to prevail against Church and Darin and obtain both an injunction and damages for their injuries. Church and Darin have taken advantage of the natural resources of the real property and profited from the sand and gravel's removal, decreasing the value of the property for the grandchildren, the future interest holders of the property. But, since their interest will not vest until the future, the damages will be impounded until the grandchildren actually vest in ownership of the property.

Question 92
Answer: D

The correct answer is choice (D). The question is testing the law of negligence. A person possesses a general legal duty to act reasonably and with prudence in every situation in order to avoid causing an unreasonable risk of injury to other people. If it is found that the hotel employees acted reasonably under the circumstances to try to avoid an unreasonable risk of injury to others, then their conduct will not be considered to be negligent, and Smith will not prevail in a claim against Ohner.

Question 93
Answer: D

The correct answer is choice (D). The question is testing the law of defamation. In order to prevail on a claim for defamation of a private figure, the plaintiff must show that the defendant was negligent with regard to the truth (or falsity) of the statement. If News exercised ordinary care in determining whether the story was true or false, then News was not negligent with regard to the truth or falsity of the statement. Therefore, Leader's first wife will not prevail on a claim for defamation against News.

Question 94
Answer: C

The correct answer is choice (C). The question is testing the law of private nuisance. A private nuisance occurs when a defendant substantially and unreasonably disturbs the right to use and enjoy the land of a real property owner or lessee. A basis for bringing a private nuisance action is a decrease in the use and value of the plaintiff's property due to a defendant's adverse conditions or activities. A plaintiff may recover for personal damages within the scope of liability of the defendant.

The gases being emitted from Utility's operations are substantially and unreasonably interfering with Farmer's livelihood from his real property (his crops) and his own personal health. Additionally, there has been a decrease in the ability to use the property for crop growth and a decline in the value of the real property itself. Thus, Farmer would prevail against Utility for private nuisance and be able recover all of his damages associated with such nuisance, including but limited to, his personal injuries.

Question 95
Answer: A

The correct answer is choice (A). The question is testing the law of negligence. A person or entity possesses a general legal duty to act reasonably and with prudence in every situation in order to avoid causing an unreasonable risk of injury to other people.

In this question, it states that Utility built the plant in accordance with the best practicable technology and that the plant is operating in line with industry standards. Since there is no evidence brought forth suggesting that Utility did not act with prudence to avoid causing an unreasonable risk of injury to others, Farmer will not prevail on a claim of negligence against Utility.

Question 96
Answer: A

The correct answer is choice (A). The question is testing the law of attractive nuisance. An attractive nuisance is any inherently dangerous object or condition of property that can be reasonably expected to attract children. A land possessor will be held liable for negligence if the land possessor fails to exercise reasonable care to eliminate the danger or otherwise to protect the children.

Since Sand knew that the children were playing on the chute after hours, Sand owed the children a duty to exercise reasonable care to eliminate the danger to them or to otherwise protect them. If Sand could have eliminated the danger to the children by effectively securing the chute at a reasonable cost and did not do so, Ladd will prevail against Sand on a claim for negligence.

Question 97
Answer: B

The correct answer is choice (B). The question is testing the law of negligence. A person or entity possesses a general legal duty to act reasonably and with prudence in every situation in order to avoid causing an unreasonable risk of injury to other people.

The cause of the accident in this question was the failure of Commuter's brakes and not the negligent driving of Commuter. Thus, Commuter cannot be held to be liable for Ladd's damages due to the brake failure, unless she was negligent in maintaining her brakes properly. Thus, her best defense is that she was not negligent because she used reasonable care in the maintenance of her brakes.

Question 98
Answer: B

The correct answer is choice (B). The question is testing the law of negligence. In order to prevail on a negligence claim, a plaintiff must show that a defendant acted unreasonably and that his unreasonable actions were the proximate cause of the plaintiff's injuries. Proximate cause includes a finding of actual cause ("but for" the defendant's conduct, the plaintiff's injuries would have been avoided) and a finding that the damages were reasonably foreseeable.

If Garage was negligent in inspecting Commuter's brakes, Ladd will prevail against Garage for his damages because Garage's negligence would have been a factual and proximate cause of Ladd's injury. But for the negligent brake inspection, Commuter's brakes would not have failed and Ladd would not have been injured. Further, it is reasonably foreseeable that a faulty inspection may lead to brake failure which subsequently causes an accident where another person is injured.

Question 99
Answer: B

The correct answer is choice (B). The question is testing the law of contributory negligence. The rule of contributory negligence requires a plaintiff to exercise due care to avoid an injury. A plaintiff engages in contributory negligence by failing to exercise due care that results in harm from a defendant. Thus, Ped's failure to exercise due care by not using the crosswalk will be considered by the trier of fact in determining the proportion of liability of Driver in comparison with the proportion of liability of Ped in connection with the cause of Ped's injuries.

Question 100
Answer: B

The correct answer is choice (B). The question is testing the law of negligence per se. A plaintiff will prevail on a claim for negligence per se if (1) the plaintiff is within the class of individuals that a statute is designed to protect; (2) a defendant's conduct violated the statute; (3) the defendant's conduct violated the reason for the statute; (4) that conduct constitutes the type of risk that the statute covers; and (5) the conduct is not excused.

In this question, Trucker was parked in violation of Section 2 of the Vehicle Code of State, the purpose of which is to safeguard pedestrians using the crosswalk. Ped was a pedestrian who was injured while trying to use the crosswalk that Trucker was blocking. Thus, Ped is in the class of individuals that the statute was meant to protect and incurred the type of injury that the statute was trying to protect against. Thus, Trucker will prevail on his claim for damages from Ped under the theory of negligence per se.

Question 101
Answer: A

The correct answer is choice (A). The question is testing the law of battery. A plaintiff will prevail on a claim for battery if a defendant intentionally acted to cause either a harmful or offensive contact or the immediate apprehension of a harmful or offensive contact with the person of another and actually caused such contact.

In this scenario, Grower did not have to intend for the dog to actually bite Wife in order to be held liable for battery. The fact that Grower intended to cause Wife immediate apprehension of a harmful or offensive contact with the dog combined with the fact that the dog actually bit Wife is enough for her to prevail on her battery claim against Grower.

Question 102
Answer: B

The correct answer is choice (B). This question is testing the law of assault. In order to prevail on a claim for assault, a plaintiff must show that the defendant acted intending to cause an imminent apprehension of a harmful or offensive contact and caused such imminent apprehension of a harmful or offensive contact. Proof of actual damage is not required to recover for this tort. A plaintiff may recover at least nominal damages from a defendant.

In this scenario, Grower intended to cause Husband an imminent apprehension of a harmful or offensive contact with the dog. At the time of the incident, if Husband reasonably believed that the dog might bite him, then Grower caused the imminent apprehension of a harmful or offensive contact with the dog. Thus, Husband will prevail against Grower in his claim for assault. Husband does not need to prove actual damages in order to prevail.

Question 103
Answer: A

The correct answer is choice (A). The question is testing the law of trespass to land. A trespass to land is an act of an intentional physical invasion of the land of another. Even though necessity is a valid defense to trespass, if the trespass serves to benefit an individual or his property (private necessity), then the person will be held liable for the damages caused by such trespass.

Husband and Wife intentionally entered onto the property of Grower out of necessity, in order to avoid being attacked by a bull, and such trespass caused damage to Grower's property. Since Husband and Wife benefited from the trespass, Grower will prevail against Husband and Wife for the damages caused to his yard.

Question 104
Answer: D

The correct answer is choice (D). The question is testing the law of strict products liability. In order to recover on a claim against the manufacturer for a defective product, the plaintiff must show that the original product was not materially altered before the injury occurred.

In this case, Storekeeper materially altered the saw, as he disassembled the saw and rebuilt the entire saw himself. Thus, Employee will not prevail against Power Saw Company for strict products liability, as the original product manufactured by Power Saw Company had been materially altered by Shopkeeper.

Question 105
Answer: A

The correct answer is choice (A). The question is testing the law of strict products liability. The majority of courts decline to entertain strict product liability claims alleging only economic losses. Since Purchaser is seeking solely economic losses in this scenario, he will probably not prevail in a claim against Storekeeper.

Question 106
Answer: C

The correct answer is choice (C). The question is testing the law of strict products liability. Under a strict liability theory, any commercial supplier (i.e., middleman, supplier, dealer, or retailer) may be held strictly liable for a plaintiff's injuries from a commercial product if the product is dangerously defective. But, a plaintiff's voluntarily and unreasonable assumption of a known risk precludes the plaintiff from recovering on a strict products liability basis.

Thus, Employee will be able to recover from Storekeeper who is a commercial supplier of a dangerously defective product. But, if Employee knew that the shaft was coming loose and proceeded with using the saw anyway knowing such risk existed, his assumption of the risk will bar his recovery from Storekeeper.

Question 107
Answer: A

The correct answer is choice (A). The question is testing the law of strict products liability. Under a strict liability theory, any commercial supplier (i.e., middleman, supplier, dealer, or retailer) may be held strictly liable for a plaintiff's injuries from a commercial product if the product is dangerously defective. Thus, Employee will be able to recover from Storekeeper who is a commercial supplier of a dangerously defective product, even though Storekeeper did not manufacture the product.

Question 108
Answer: B

The correct answer is choice (B). The question is testing the law of strict products liability. A plaintiff cannot recover on the basis of strict products liability if the plaintiff's misuse of the product was not reasonably foreseeable. The best defense for Saw-Blade Company to the strict liability claim is that Employee was misusing the saw blade, as it is not reasonably foreseeable that someone who was using a saw blade designed specifically to cut plywood would use it to try to cut hard plastic.

Question 109
Answer: A

The correct answer is choice (A). The question is testing the law of defamation. In order to prevail on a claim for defamation of a public figure, the plaintiff must prove with clear and convincing evidence that a defendant published a defamatory communication with actual malice.

Actual malice includes either knowledge of the falsity or a reckless disregard for the truth or falsity of the communication. In order for Player to prevail against Shoe Store for defamation, he will have to prove at the very least that Shoe Store was reckless in accepting Photo's statement that Photo had Player's approval to use the picture.

Question 110
Answer: B

The correct answer is choice (B). The question is testing the law of invasion of privacy. In order to prevail on a claim for invasion of privacy, the plaintiff must prove that the defendant appropriated plaintiff's likeness or identity for the defendant's commercial advantage. Since Shoe Store used Player's picture for commercial advantage without his permission, Player will prevail against Shoe Store on his claim of invasion of privacy.

Question 111
Answer: C

The correct answer is choice (C). The question is testing the law of assumption of risk. A plaintiff's recovery can be denied on the basis that the plaintiff voluntarily assumed a risk of harm by knowing the risk existed and voluntarily proceeding with the activity anyway. But, a plaintiff does not assume the risk if there is no other reasonable alternative than to proceed with the activity.

If it appeared that there was no other practicable way of getting out of the lot before Monday besides climbing the fence, then there was no other reasonable alternative than for Johnson to proceed with his actions in spite of the risk. Thus, the defense of assumption of the risk will not be applicable in an action against Car Company for damages.

Question 112
Answer: D

The correct answer is choice (D). The question is testing the law of false imprisonment. In order for a plaintiff to prevail on a claim for false imprisonment, the defendant must have intended to confine the plaintiff. In this question, unless the security guard knew that someone was in the lot at the time he locked the gate, Johnson will not prevail against Car Company for false imprisonment, because the confinement was not intentional.

Question 113
Answer: A

The correct answer is choice (A). The question is testing the law of public nuisance. A plaintiff cannot bring, as a private individual, an action for a public nuisance unless the plaintiff shows that he or she suffered a different harm that is distinct from the harm that the public sustained or suffered a far greater degree of special damages. Thus, in this case, the plaintiffs will not prevail unless they can show that the damages they have sustained are different from that suffered by the public at large.

Question 114
Answer: A

The correct answer is choice (A). The question is testing the law of private nuisance. A private nuisance occurs when a defendant substantially and unreasonably disturbs the right to use and enjoy the land of a real property owner or lessee.

The magnitude of flies and odors created by the activities of Cattle Company are obnoxious, pose a substantial health risk to plaintiffs, and have decreased plaintiffs' use and enjoyment of their real property. Since Cattle Company has substantially and unreasonably interfered with plaintiffs' use of their property, plaintiffs will prevail against Cattle Company in a claim based on private nuisance.

Question 115
Answer: A

The correct answer is choice (A). The question is testing the law of negligence. In order to prevail on a negligence claim, a plaintiff must show that a defendant acted unreasonably and that his unreasonable actions were the proximate cause of the plaintiff's injuries. Proximate cause includes a finding of actual cause ("but for" the defendant's conduct, the plaintiff's injuries would have been avoided) and a finding that the damages were reasonably foreseeable.

In this case, Cross acted unreasonably by crossing in front of Motorist in violation of the traffic signal. Further, Cross was the proximate cause of the injuries to Motorist, as but for Cross' negligence, the accident would not have occurred. Additionally, it was reasonably foreseeable that crossing in front of Motorist in violation of the traffic signal would result in a collision. Since Motorist did not act unreasonably and was not at fault for his brake failure, he cannot be held to be proportionately liable for his own damages. Thus, Motorist will be able to recover his full amount of damages from Cross.

Question 116
Answer: B

The correct answer is choice (B). The question is testing the law of comparative negligence. When a plaintiff and defendant, or multiple defendants, are each partially negligent, the amount of damages that are awarded to the plaintiff is subject to a reduction in the amount of the plaintiff's liability. In a pure comparative negligence jurisdiction, the allocation of liability for damages is assessed in proportion to each party's fault, despite the fact that a plaintiff's degree of fault may exceed that of a defendant.

Spouse will be able to recover from Cross based on his negligence that contributed to the car accident. But, Spouse's amount of recoverable damages will be reduced by the proportion of fault she is assigned by the trier of fact in connection with the accident for her failure to tell Motorist about the faulty brakes.

Question 117
Answer: A

The correct answer is choice (A). The question is testing the law of negligence. In order to prevail on a negligence claim, a plaintiff must show that a defendant acted unreasonably and that his unreasonable actions were the proximate cause of the plaintiff's injuries. Proof of causation includes a finding of actual cause ("but for" the defendant's conduct, the plaintiff's injuries would have been avoided) and a finding that the damages were reasonably foreseeable (legal cause).

In this question, Owner acted unreasonably by failing to inform Motorist of the faulty brakes. Further, Owner was the proximate cause of the injuries to Motorist, as but for Owner's failure to tell Motorist of the faulty brakes, the accident would not have occurred, as Motorist would not have driven the car. Also, it was reasonably foreseeable that failing to tell Motorist that his brakes were faulty and letting him proceed with driving the vehicle anyway would result in a collision with another vehicle. Thus, Motorist will be able to recover his damages from Owner.

Question 118
Answer: C

The correct answer is choice (C). The question is testing the law of res ipsa loquitur. The law allows an inference of negligence on a party when an event would have not otherwise occurred unless someone was negligent.

In this question, res ipsa loquitur is not applicable because the case of tuna had been compromised by being knocked over by the workmen. The cans of tuna in the same shipment that were not knocked over were not contaminated, but the ones that had been knocked over were unfit for consumption. Thus, it would not be proper to make an inference of negligence on the part of Canco based on solely on the fact that the product was unfit for consumption, as it is as likely that the tuna cans were contaminated by the negligence of the workmen.

Question 119
Answer: B

The correct answer is choice (B). The question is testing the law of negligence. A person or entity possesses a general legal duty to act reasonably and with prudence in every situation in order to avoid causing an unreasonable risk of injury to other people, including social visitors. Further, strict products liability only applies to commercial suppliers.

Dotty will not be held strictly liable for the damages to Guest, as she is not a commercial supplier of the tuna. But, Dotty did owe a duty to Guest to act reasonably and with prudence in order to avoid causing an unreasonable risk of injury to Guest. Thus, the only way that Guest can hold Dotty liable is if she was found to be negligent in serving the contaminated tuna.

Question 120
Answer: B

The correct answer is choice (B). The question is testing the law of strict products liability. Under a strict liability theory, any commercial supplier (i.e., middleman, supplier, dealer, or retailer) may be held strictly liable for a plaintiff's injuries from a commercial product if the product is dangerously defective. The consumer does not have to be in privity with the supplier in order to recover for the damages caused by the defective product.

Guest, as a consumer of the product, will be able to recover from Supermart, a commercial supplier of a dangerously defective product, even though Supermart did not manufacture the product and Guest was not the purchaser of the tuna.

Question 121
Answer: D

The correct answer is choice (D). The question is testing the law of private nuisance. A private nuisance occurs when a defendant substantially and unreasonably disturbs the right to use and enjoy the land of a real property owner or lessee. Circumstances like property owners being present before the institution of the nuisance and legislative authority, such as zoning provisions, may be determining factors in the analysis of a private nuisance. The court will examine the totality of the circumstances to determine whether the actions in question are substantially and unreasonably disruptive.

Thus, the fact that Householders were present in the area before Diner will be evidence, along with other factors such as the unreasonableness of the disturbance and applicable zoning ordinances, in determining whether Diner's actions constitute a private nuisance.

Question 122
Answer: D

The correct answer is choice (D). The question is testing the law of trespass to land. A trespass to land is an act of an intentional physical invasion of the land of another. Even though necessity is a valid defense to trespass, if the trespass serves to benefit an individual or his property (private necessity), then the person will be held liable for the damages caused by such trespass.

If Peter had reasonable grounds to believe his boat might be swamped and sink, then his trespass was due to necessity. Further, in this case, Peter did not benefit from the trespass, as his boat was sent out to sea by the Owner and it sunk with his shoes and parka on board, causing Peter brave the storm with only his swim trunks for protection. Therefore, Peter will be able to assert necessity as a valid defense to his trespass.

Answer choice (A) is incorrect because in order to prevail on a trespass claim, Owner merely has to show that Peter intended to physically invade the property. The property is not required to have any signage indicating that it is private property in order for Owner to prevail on a trespass claim.

Answer choices (B) and (C) are incorrect because in order for Owner to prevail on a claim for trespass, he does not have to prove that Peter knew or should have known that the land was private property.

Question 123
Answer: A

The correct answer is choice (A). The question is testing the law of trespass to land. A defendant must advise a plaintiff to leave his premises before the defendant may use non-deadly force to defend his or her property interests. If the plaintiff fails to leave in response to that warning, then the defendant can only use a reasonable means of defense.

In this question, Peter docked his boat to remove himself and his property from the wrath of an oncoming storm. Peter's boat was merely knocking against the dock's bumper and not causing any other physical damage to Owner's property. Thus, Owner's action of releasing Peter's boat, his only mode of transportation, into the lake and causing it to sink while leaving Peter with only his swim trunks for protection against the storm was an unreasonable means of defending his property. Thus, Owner will be liable to Peter for his damages.

Question 124
Answer: B

The correct answer is choice (B). The question is testing the law of invasion of privacy. Privacy invasion may occur when a defendant publicly discloses private facts about a plaintiff. The fairness and accuracy of the disclosure is a defense in an action alleging public disclosure of private facts.

The announcement Pauline made about the circumstances surrounding the birth of her own child brought this aspect of her private life into the public eye. Since the statements in the article are true, Journal cannot be held liable for invasion of privacy because it fairly and accurately reported on a matter that would typically be private but for Pauline opening the door to it by disclosing issues of her childbirth in a public manner.

Question 125
Answer: C

The correct answer is choice (C). This question is testing the law of negligence. In order to prevail on a negligence claim, a plaintiff must show that a defendant acted unreasonably and that his unreasonable actions were the proximate cause of the plaintiff's injuries. Proximate cause includes that the damages were reasonably foreseeable.

In this question, it is not reasonably foreseeable to a prudent person that parking on the street next to a fire hydrant would cause another car to sideswipe the vehicle turning it onto the hydrant, breaking the hydrant, and thus causing severe injury to the vehicle's passenger. Thus, Ned will not recover for his injuries from Parker because they were not proximately caused by Parker.

Answer choice (A) is an attractive answer but is incorrect because this type of scenario is not reason for which the ordinance was created. This ordinance was created for the purpose of allowing access to the hydrant for firemen, not preventing traffic accidents.

Question 126
Answer: A

The correct answer is choice (A). This question is testing the law of negligence. In order to prevail on a negligence claim, a plaintiff must show that a defendant acted unreasonably and that his unreasonable actions were the proximate cause of the plaintiff's injuries. Proximate cause includes a finding of actual cause ("but for" the defendant's conduct, the plaintiff's injuries would have been avoided) and a finding that the damages were reasonably foreseeable.

In this question, Driver's actions by swerving to miss a non-existent pothole and sideswiping Parker's car were unreasonable and but for his actions, Parker's car would not have been damaged. Additionally, it was reasonably foreseeable that Driver's unreasonable behavior would lead to a car accident that would damage another vehicle. Thus, Parker will be able to recover from Driver for his damages.

Further, Parker will not be found contributorily negligent as matter of law because this type of scenario is not the reason for which the ordinance was created. This ordinance was created for the purpose of allowing access to the hydrant for firemen, not preventing traffic accidents.

Question 127
Answer: A

The correct answer is choice (A). This question is testing the law of negligence. In order to prevail on a negligence claim, a plaintiff must show that a defendant acted unreasonably and that his unreasonable actions were the proximate cause of the plaintiff's injuries. Proximate cause includes a finding of actual cause ("but for" the defendant's conduct, the plaintiff's injuries would have been avoided) and a finding that the damages were reasonably foreseeable.

In this question, Driver's actions by swerving to miss a non-existent pothole and sideswiping Parker's car were unreasonable and but for his actions, the fire hydrant would not have been damaged. Additionally, it was reasonably foreseeable that Driver's unreasonable behavior would lead to a car accident that would damage another vehicle and/or property in close proximity to another vehicle (e.g., the fire hydrant). Thus, City will be able to recover from Driver for negligence, because Driver was the cause in fact and legal cause of City's harm.

Question 128
Answer: D

The correct answer is choice (D). This question is testing the law of attractive nuisance. A land possessor may be held liable for attractive nuisance if the possessor fails to exercise reasonable care to eliminate the danger or otherwise to protect the children. In this scenario, the key inquiry will be whether Macco could have elminated the danger to the children (including Philip) by exercising reasonable care without unduly intefering with its normal business operations.

Question 129
Answer: B

The correct answer is choice (B). This question is testing the law of the rescue doctrine. An original wrongdoer will be held liable for the reasonably foreseeable events that occur in connection with the immediate consequences of the wrongdoer's actions. An attempt to aid a person injured by the wrongdoer's actions, including the wrongdoer, is considered to be a foreseeable course of events.

Rescuer will be able to prevail against Si because Si was at fault in causing the fire. A foreseeable consequence of Si's negligence in creating the fire is a party coming to his aid and suffering burn damages, and thus, Si will be held liable to Rescuer for his injuries.

Question 130
Answer: C

The correct answer is choice (C). This question is testing the laws of negligence and the rescue doctrine. A person or entity possesses a general legal duty to act reasonably and with prudence in every situation in order to avoid causing an unreasonable risk of injury to other people, including social visitors. Only a wrongdoer will be held liable for the reasonably foreseeable events that occur in connection with the immediate consequences of a wrongdoer's actions.

Rescuer will be able to prevail only against Si, the wrongdoer in this situation, because in the absence of any other facts Neighbor apparently acted reasonably and with prudence and did not contribute to the creation of the fire and Rescuer's subsequent injuries. Thus, Rescuer will not be able to prevail against Neighbor for the damages he sustained in connection with the rescue of Si.

Question 131
Answer: C

The correct answer is choice (C). This question is testing the law of negligence. In order to prevail on a negligence claim, a plaintiff must show that a defendant acted unreasonably and that his unreasonable actions were the proximate cause of the plaintiff's injuries. Proximate cause includes a finding of actual cause ("but for" the defendant's conduct, the plaintiff's injuries would have been avoided) and a finding that the damages were reasonably foreseeable.

In this question, Trucker's action of obscuring the traffic light and prohibiting Visitor from being able to see and stop at the light was unreasonable and but for his actions, Driver would not have run into Visitor. Additionally, it was reasonably foreseeable that Trucker's obstruction would lead to a driver not seeing (and thus not being able to obey) the traffic signal and causing a car accident that would damage one or more vehicles. Thus, Driver will be able to recover from Trucker for negligence, because Trucker was both the actual and legal cause of Driver's injuries.

Question 132
Answer: B

The correct answer is choice (B). This question is testing the law of negligence. In order to prevail on a negligence claim, a plaintiff must show that a defendant acted unreasonably and that the defendant's unreasonable actions were the proximate cause of the plaintiff's injuries. Proximate cause includes a finding of actual cause ("but for" the defendant's conduct, the plaintiff's injuries would have been avoided) and a finding that the damages were reasonably foreseeable.

In this question, City's actions of not replacing the broken pole within 72 hours was unreasonable and but for City's actions, Visitor would have known not to proceed through the intersection and the accident with Driver would not have taken place. Additionally, it was reasonably foreseeable that not being timely in replacing a broken street light would cause a car accident that damaged one or more vehicles. Thus, Driver has the best chance of recovery from City for negligence, because City was a proximate cause of Driver's harm.

Question 133
Answer: C

The correct answer is choice (C). This question is testing the law of intentional infliction of emotional distress. Intentional infliction of emotional distress is defined as extreme and outrageous conduct that is made intentionally or recklessly and that causes severe emotional distress to another.

In this question, Henry will be liable to Wanda for damages because his intentional actions were extreme and outrageous and they caused severe emotional distress to Wanda. It does not matter that John was the person who showed her the microphone, as it only matters that Henry placed it there with the intention to cause severe emotional distress to Wanda and such emotional distress was actually caused to her.

Question 134
Answer: B

The correct answer is choice (B). This question is testing the law of liability of parents for their children's intentional torts. Normally, parents are not held personally responsible for their child's intentional torts or negligence. An exception to that rule, however, is when a parent has reason to know or does know of dangerous propensities of the child and fails to exercise reasonable care to warn others or alleviate the situation.

In this scenario, Dave had exhibited a propensity for bullying younger and smaller children. Since Dave's parents knew of his propensity for violence, they had a duty to warn others of his tendencies or to alleviate the situation. Instead, Dave's parents encouraged his aggressive behavior. Thus, they will be held liable to Pete's parents for the damages associated with Pete's injuries. The claim against the parents would be grounded in negligence.

Question 135
Answer: A

The correct answer is choice (A). This question is testing the law of battery. Under the law, all persons have the capacity to commit an intentional tort, even young children, as long as the person intentionally acted to cause either a harmful or offensive contact or the immediate apprehension of a harmful or offensive contact with the person of another and actually caused such contact.

Dave will be held liable for Pete's damages because he acted intentionally to cause a harmful and offensive contact to Pete that resulted in Pete being injured. The fact that he is a minor child has no bearing on his ability to commit an intentional tort and be held responsible for the damages associated with his actions.

Choice (B) is incorrect because it is termed in the language of negligence, not intentional tort.

Choice (C) is incorrect because there is no flat age limitation for intentional torts. This is a common red herring.

Choice (D) is incorrect as a matter of law.

Question 136
Answer: B

The correct answer is choice (B). This question is testing the law of battery. A defendant will be held liable for battery if the defendant intentionally acted to cause either a harmful or offensive contact or the immediate apprehension of a harmful or offensive contact with the person of another and actually caused such contact.

Store installed the chemical spray on the premises in an effort to prevent theft, and thus intended for the spray to make contact with the person of another. However, in order to prevail against Store, Customer must prove that the contact was actually harmful or offensive in order to prevail on a claim for battery.

Question 137
Answer: A

The correct answer is choice (A). This question is testing the law of defamation. Truth is a complete affirmative defense in a defamation action, even if a defendant published the statement with ill will.

If Paul really does wear women's clothes when he is at home, the fact that Dock's statement was true will be an absolute defense to a defamation action against him by Paul. The fact that he may have written the letter with spite or ill will has no bearing on the analysis when the communication published was truthful.

Question 138
Answer: A

The correct answer is choice (A). This question is testing the law of negligence. An original wrongdoer will be held liable for the reasonably foreseeable events that occur in connection with the immediate consequences of the wrongdoer's actions. An attempt to aid a person injured by the wrongdoer's actions is considered to be a foreseeable course of events.

In this question, the action of Construction Company in allowing a large trench to remain uncovered and without any barricades or barriers, especially during a rainstorm, was negligent. Thus, in light of Construction Company's actions, it was reasonably foreseeable that someone may fall into the trench and have to be rescued by a third party. Further, it is reasonable that because of Construction Company's negligence, the walls of the trench were rain soaked and prone to collapse. Therefore, Construction Company will be held liable to Tommy's administrator for Tommy's death, a foreseeable and immediate consequence of Construction Company's negligent actions.

Question 139
Answer: C

The correct answer is choice (C). This question is testing the law of negligence. In order to prevail on a negligence claim, a plaintiff must show that a defendant acted unreasonably and that the defendant's unreasonable actions were the proximate cause of the plaintiff's injuries.

The car accident in this scenario was proximately caused by the defective brakes in Parker's car. It was Parker's unreasonable actions that caused the accident, as he was the one responsible for the maintenance and inspection of his own brakes. Parker was the one in violation of the law. Since the actions of Doctor were not a proximate cause of the accident, and Doctor was not negligent in maintaining the brakes on the car, Parker will not be able to recover from Doctor for his injuries in connection with the accident.

Question 140
Answer: B

The correct answer is choice (B). The question is testing the law of res ipsa loquitur. The law allows an inference of negligence on a party when an event would have not otherwise occurred unless someone was negligent.

In this question, the overhead door which injured Peter was only controlled by two switches located on the premises of Auto Company. At the time of the accident, only the employees of Auto Company were present in the vicinity of these switches. Thus, if all of the mechanisms and switches associated with the overhead door were functioning properly, the only conclusion that can be drawn from the scenario is that door descended as a result of the negligence of one of Auto Company's employees, the only ones with access to the switches at the time of the accident.

Question 141
Answer: A

The correct answer is choice (A). The question is testing the law of strict products liability. Under a strict liability theory, a manufacturer or any commercial supplier (i.e., middleman, supplier, dealer, or retailer) may be held strictly liable for a plaintiff's injuries from a commercial product if the product is dangerously defective. The injured party does not have to be in privity with the manufacturer or be the intended user of the product in order to recover for the damages caused by the defective product.

Since the dishwasher was defectively manufactured, Elex Company will be held strictly liable for Accountant's injuries. Under a strict liability claim, it is of no consequence that Accountant was not in privity with Elex Company nor the intended user of the product.

Question 142
Answer: D

The correct answer is choice (D). The question is testing the law of strict products liability. Under a strict liability theory, a manufacturer or any commercial supplier (i.e., middleman, supplier, dealer, or retailer) may be held strictly liable for a plaintiff's injuries from a commercial product if the product is dangerously defective. Thus, in order for Brenda to prevail on a strict liability claim against Stove Company, she must prove that the stove was defective and unreasonably dangerous to her.

Question 143
Answer: B

The correct answer is choice (B). The question is testing the law of strict products liability. Under a strict liability theory, any commercial supplier (i.e., middleman, supplier, dealer, or retailer) may be held strictly liable for a plaintiff's injuries from a commercial product if the product is dangerously defective and if the product was not materially altered before the injury occurred.

Thus, in order for Brenda to prevail on a strict liability claim against Local Retailer, she must prove that the stove was substantially in the same condition when she was injured as it was when it was purchased from Local Retailer.

Question 144
Answer: D

The correct answer is choice (D). This question is testing the law of liability of a parent her child's negligent acts. Normally parents are not held personally responsible for their child's intentional torts or negligence. An exception to that rule, however, is when a parent has reason to know or does know of dangerous propensities of the child and fails to exercise reasonable care to warn others or alleviate the situation.

Mrs. Dennis had a duty to act reasonably to avoid causing a risk of injury to Robby. Mrs. Dennis acted unreasonably and put Robby at risk when she did not disclose Gala's propensity for not getting along well with others and failed to warn of Gala's lack of babysitting experience. Therefore, Mrs. Dennis will be liable to Robby for his injuries sustained in connection with her negligent behavior.

Question 145
Answer: D

The correct answer is choice (D). The question is testing the law of a failure to act. If a defendant's conduct placed a plaintiff in a situation of danger, then the defendant possesses a duty to assist the plaintiff to either avoid the danger or to be delivered from that dangerous situation. Thus, X will have a duty to render aid to another human being who is in immediate danger of serious harm from X's own non-negligent conduct.

Question 146
Answer: D

The correct answer is choice (D). The question is testing the law of negligence per se. A violation of a statute will not constitute negligence per se if the violator's conduct does not constitute the type of risk that the statute was designed to protect against.

Walker's violation of the statute will not defeat her cause of action against Driver because she was not negligent per se. The risks that the statute was designed to protect against probably did not include an earlier arrival at another point. Thus, Walker will still be able to prevail in her claim against Driver.

Question 147
Answer: B

The correct answer is choice (B). This question is testing the law of negligence. In order to prevail on a negligence claim, a plaintiff must show that a defendant acted unreasonably and that his unreasonable actions were the proximate cause of the plaintiff's injuries.

The unreasonable action that led to the accident in this scenario was Driver's failure to stop at a red light. The fact that he did not have a valid driver's license was not the actual or proximate cause of the accident. Whether or not his driver's license was valid, Driver would have still hit Walker as a consequence of Driver running the red light. Thus, his failure to have a valid driver's license will not furnish a basis for his liability.

Question 148
Answer: D

The correct answer is choice (D). This question is testing the law of negligence. The available damages for a plaintiff in a negligence action include recovery for the aggravation of pre-existing conditions or disabilities. The type of damage sustained by a plaintiff does not have to be foreseeable by the defendant, as defendants must take plaintiffs as they find them, with all of their physical qualities, susceptibilities, and disabilities.

Thus, even though the extent of the injury to Walker was not a foreseeable consequence of the impact, Driver will be liable to Walker for all of her physical injuries associated with the accident caused by Driver.

Question 149
Answer: D

The correct answer is choice (D). The question is testing the law of negligence per se. A violation of a statute will not constitute negligence per se if the violator's conduct did not violate the reason for the statute and/or does not constitute the type of risk that the statute covers.

Walker's injury was caused by Driver who failed to stop at a red light, not the result of a risk that the crosswalk statute was enacted to protect Walker against. Therefore, Walker's violation of the crosswalk statute should not be considered by the jury.

Question 150
Answer: C

The correct answer is choice (C). The question is testing the law of a failure to act. A first person lacks a general duty to make affirmative efforts to assist another person that the first person knows is in a situation of danger that the first person did not create. Thus, Dow, even though he is a physician, had no duty to come the aid of Paulsen because Dow did not create the dangerous situation. Thus, Paulsen will not be able to prevail on a claim against Dow for damages for Paulsen's injuries associated with Dow's failure to render aid.

Question 151
Answer: D

The correct answer is choice (D). The question is testing the law of products liability. In order to recover on a claim for products liability founded on the basis of negligence, a plaintiff must show that the defendant acted unreasonably and such actions were the proximate cause of the plaintiff's injury.

Child must first be able to show that the product was actually defective. Further, Child must also be able to prove that Seller was unreasonable in its actions and such actions caused Child to be injured. In this case, if the defect would have been discovered if Seller had exercised reasonable care in inspecting the system, but Seller did not do so, Child will prevail against Seller for negligence.

This is an interesting question because it illustrates an example of a common tactic used by the examiners – reciting the appropriate standard in the correct answer. Choice (D) is correct because it states the standard for the claim of negligence. In order to avoid negligence, a person must exercise reasonable care. If a person fails to do so, the person will be liable for foreseeable injury resulting from the failure.

Question 152
Answer: A

The correct answer is choice (A). The question is testing the law of strict products liability. Under a strict liability theory, a manufacturer or any commercial supplier (i.e., middleman, supplier, dealer, or retailer) may be held strictly liable for a plaintiff's injuries from a commercial product if the product is dangerously defective.

The heating and cooling systems designed by Heatco and Coolco were not dangerously defective as manufactured, and only became dangerous because of the defective manner in which the ventilating system was designed by Mobilco. Since the heating and cooling systems themselves were not defective, Child will not prevail against Heatco or Coolco for damages. However, because the ventilation system designed by Mobilco was dangerously defective, Child will be able to recover against Mobilco based on a claim of strict products liability.

Question 153
Answer: A

The correct answer is choice (A). The question is testing the law of negligence. A person or entity possesses a general legal duty to act reasonably and with prudence in every situation in order to avoid causing an unreasonable risk of injury to other people.

If Light Company could have taken reasonable steps to prevent the lines from falling when the insulators were destroyed and avoid causing an unreasonable risk of injury to others, then Paul will prevail on his claim and recover his damages from Light Company.

Question 154
Answer: C

The correct answer is choice (C). The question is testing the law of intentional infliction of emotional distress. In order to prevail on a claim for intentional infliction of emotional distress, a plaintiff must show that the defendant acted with the intent to inflict emotional distress upon the plaintiff.

Joplin will not prevail on a claim for intentional infliction of emotional distress against Smythe because Smythe did not know that Joplin was watching from the window in the apartment. Therefore, Smythe could not have intended to cause emotional distress to Joplin in connection with his actions toward Nelson. In order to prevail in a bystander case for intentional infliction of emotional distress, a plaintiff must show that the defendant was aware of the plaintiff's presence.

Question 155
Answer: A

The correct answer is choice (A). The question is testing the law of premises liability. A landowner has a duty to warn known trespassers, or anticipated trespassers, of dangerous artificial conditions on his or her real property. An increased standard of care applies with respect to children trespassers and artificial conditions that are on the property. In such a case, a landowner must exercise reasonable care to prevent injury to the children.

O'Neill knew that children regularly played in the common area, including those did not live in the apartment complex, and he did not object. Thus, the children that did not live in the complex became discovered trespassers, as O'Neill knew of their existence on the property. Therefore, O'Neill had a duty to warn the children, including Peter, of any dangerous artificial conditions on the property and to exercise reasonable care to prevent injury to the children. In this scenario, if the sprinkler head was a hazard that Peter would not have otherwise discovered, O'Neill had a duty to warn Peter of its existence and use reasonable care to try to protect him from injury.

Question 156
Answer: A

The correct answer is choice (A). The question is testing the law of strict products liability. Under a strict liability theory, any commercial supplier (i.e., middleman, supplier, dealer, or retailer) may be held strictly liable for a plaintiff's injuries from a commercial product if the product is dangerously defective.

If Innes can show that the product was dangerously defective when it left the hands of Steel, then Innes will be able to recover from Paint Company as a supplier of a dangerously defective product on a claim of strict products liability.

Question 157
Answer: D

The correct answer is choice (D). The question is testing the law of negligence. A person or entity possesses a general legal duty to act reasonably and with prudence in every situation in order to avoid causing an unreasonable risk of injury to other people.

Since the employees of Glass did not know that there was common duct work for the air conditioners, they had no reason to suspect that the fumes could seep through the ducts and injure Innes. Thus, in light of the limited knowledge the employees possessed regarding the duct, their actions were not unreasonable and Innes will not be able to prevail against Glass for her injuries.

Question 158
Answer: D

The correct answer is choice (D). The question is testing the law of defamation. In the absence of a constitutionally required standard of proving fault, most states use a negligence standard of proof for showing the liability of a defendant. Negligence with regard to the truth or falsity of the communication is needed in order to prevail on a claim for defamation against a private person.

If the hospital reasonably believed that Siddon took the narcotics, then the hospital was not negligent with regard to the truth or falsity of the statement when it was made to Registry. Therefore, Siddon will not be able to recover from Doctors' Hospital on a defamation claim because the statement was not negligently made.

Although choice (B) may seem attractive, it is not the best answer because, even if Siddon did not take the narcotics, the hospital will avoid liability if it can show that it possessed reasonable belief that Siddon took the narcotics. Thus, choice (D) is correct.

Question 159
Answer: A

The correct answer is choice (A). The question is testing the law of indemnity. Indemnity may be available when one defendant's culpability level is much higher than the other defendant's culpability level in connection with the harm caused to the plaintiff.

The Zappo video game was found to be defective because of Ellis' improper design. Thus, because Ellis actually designed the video game, his culpability level with regard to Carla's damages is much higher than that of Tyco, who merely manufactured the game to Ellis' specifications. Since Ellis is responsible for the design of the game and for the injuries Carla sustained, Tyco will be able to recover from Ellis for indemnity.

Question 160
Answer: A

The correct answer is choice (A). The question is testing the law of abnormally dangerous activities. An abnormally dangerous activity is one that presents a substantial risk of serious harm to persons or property regardless of the degree of care that is exercised in carrying out that activity. The law imposes strict liability on whoever engages in an abnormally dangerous activity.

A storage facility where flammable gases are stored in a liquefied form in high pressure tanks is an abnormally dangerous activity, as it poses a substantial risk of serious harm regardless of what degree of care is exercised. Thus, strict liability is imposed on Gasco for any damages associated with its storage activities and Gasco will be liable to Farber for his damages, even if Gasco was not negligent.

Question 161
Answer: D

The correct answer is choice (D). The question is testing the law of negligence. A person or entity possesses a general legal duty to act reasonably and with prudence in every situation in order to avoid causing an unreasonable risk of injury to other people.

In constructing the storage facility for Gasco, Acme Company owed a general duty to act reasonably and with prudence to avoid causing an unreasonable risk of injury to other people. Thus, if the explosion resulted from a defect of which Acme Company was aware, but did nothing about it and/or failed to give a warning of such defect, Farber will prevail against Acme Company for negligence.

Question 162
Answer: C

The correct answer is choice (C). The question is testing the law of negligence. In order to prevail on a negligence claim, a plaintiff must show that a defendant acted unreasonably and that the defendant's unreasonable actions were the proximate cause of the plaintiff's injuries.

In order for Bobby to prevail on a claim against Dugan, he must show that Dugan or his employees acted unreasonably and their actions were the proximate cause of the injuries Bobby sustained. Thus, unless Dugan or his employees failed to exercise reasonable care to assure Bobby's safety in the nursery and such failure actually caused his skull injury, Bobby will not prevail against Dugan for his damages.

Question 163
Answer: D

The correct answer is choice (D). The question is testing the laws of joint and several liability and indemnity. The doctrine of joint and several liability provides that when there is more than one defendant whose concurrent negligence results in harm to a plaintiff, they may each be found liable for the entire amount of damages that they caused by their indivisible wrongful conduct.

Garrison will be held liable for negligence because of his unreasonable actions leading to the car accident. Astin will be held to be negligent per se because of his violation of the statute. Thus, both parties will be held to be concurrently negligent.

When a plaintiff is entitled to recover damages on the basis of joint and several liability, the plaintiff may recover the entire award of damages from any of the defendants. Thus, Placek will be able to recover the $100,000 judgment from either Astin or Garrison.

Indemnity may be available when one defendant's culpability level is much higher than the other defendant's in connection with the harm caused to the plaintiff. Because Garrison actually caused the car accident, he has a much higher culpability level with regard to Placek's damages than Astin, who merely lent him the car to perform repairs on it. Since Garrison is the one truly responsible for the injuries Placek sustained, Astin will be able to recover from Garrison under a claim for indemnity for the amount of money Astin is required to pay to Placek.

Question 164
Answer: A

The correct answer is choice (A). This question is testing the law of negligence. In order to prevail on a negligence claim, a plaintiff must show that a defendant acted unreasonably and that his unreasonable actions were the proximate cause of the plaintiff's injuries. Proximate cause includes a finding of actual cause ("but for" the defendant's conduct, the plaintiff's injuries would have been avoided) and a finding that the damages were reasonably foreseeable.

The proper inquiry to make in this scenario is to what extent Peters' damages were caused by Dever's negligence. But for Dever's negligence, Peters presumably would not have sustained as much damage to his house, as the fire would have been extinguished in a timelier manner. Further, it is reasonably foreseeable that having an accident with a fire truck may cause a delay in aid to a person in need of the fire truck's services and allow the fire to cause additional damage. Therefore, Dever, because of his negligence, will be held responsible for the part of Peters' loss that would have been prevented if the collision had not occurred.

Question 165
Answer: A

The correct answer is choice (A). This question is testing the law of defamation. In the absence of a constitutionally required standard of proving fault, most states use a negligence standard of proof for showing the liability of a defendant. Negligence with regard to the truth or falsity of the communication is necessary in order to prevail on a claim for defamation against a private person.

If Hammond reasonably believed his statement to be true, then the communication was not negligent with regard to its truth or falsity when it was made. Therefore, Miller will not be able to recover from Hammond for defamation because the statement was not negligently made by Hammond.

Question 166
Answer: C

The correct answer is choice (C). This question is testing the law of fraudulent misrepresentation. Fraudulent misrepresentation is a defendant's false statement of fact with the intent to mislead or deceive another person. A statement of fact does not include opinions, judgments, or puffery.

Statements 1 and 2 are factual statements that were made by Daley with the intent to mislead or deceive Purvis and induce him into purchasing the car. Thus, these statements are actionable in a claim for fraudulent misrepresentation. Statement 3 will not support Purvis' claim because it is a statement of opinion and therefore cannot form the basis for a claim of fraudulent misrepresentation against Daley.

Question 167
Answer: D

The correct answer is choice (D). The question is testing the law of joint and several liability. The doctrine of joint and several liability provides that when there is more than one defendant whose concurrent negligence results in harm to a plaintiff, they may each be found liable for the entire amount of damages that they caused by their indivisible wrongful conduct. Since both Acorp and Beeco's negligence concurrently led to Landesmann's damages, they will be jointly and severally liable to him for his injuries.

Question 168
Answer: A

The correct answer is choice (A). The question is testing the law of strict products liability. Under a strict liability theory, any commercial supplier (i.e., middleman, supplier, dealer, or retailer) may be held strictly liable for a plaintiff's injuries from a commercial product if the product is dangerously defective.

If Roth can show that the brake failed because of a defect present when the bicycle left the hands of the manufacturer, Cycle Company, then Roth will be able to recover from Bike Shop on a strict products liability claim, as a supplier of a dangerously defective product.

Question 169
Answer: B

The correct answer is choice (B). A person or entity possesses a general legal duty to act reasonably and with prudence in every situation in order to avoid causing an unreasonable risk of injury to other people.

In manufacturing and distributing the bicycle, Cycle Company owed a general duty to act reasonably and with prudence to avoid causing an unreasonable risk of injury to other people. Thus, if the brake defect could have been discovered through the exercise of reasonable care in order to avoid causing an unreasonable risk of injury to other people, Perez will prevail against Cycle Company on a claim for negligence.

Question 170
Answer: B

The correct answer is choice (B). The question is testing the law of strict products liability. Under a strict liability theory, a manufacturer or any commercial supplier (i.e., middleman, supplier, dealer, or retailer) may be held strictly liable for a plaintiff's injuries from a commercial product if the product is dangerously defective.

Morris will recover from Trailco because Trailco will be strictly liable for the damages caused in connection with the dangerously defective product it manufactured. Dixon's negligence will have no bearing on Trailco's liability, as Trailco will be held to a standard of strict liability for manufacturing a defective product.

Question 171
Answer: A

The correct answer is choice (A). A person or entity possesses a general legal duty to act reasonably and with prudence in every situation in order to avoid causing an unreasonable risk of injury to other people. In order to prevail on a negligence claim, a plaintiff must show that a defendant acted unreasonably and that the defendant's unreasonable actions were the proximate cause of the plaintiff's injuries.

Dixon was aware of the dangerous propensity of the trailer, and thus had a duty to act reasonably in order to avoid any unreasonable risks of injury to other people in connection with the defective trailer. Dixon knew of the existence of the restraining device, and he could have obtained it at a nominal cost. Therefore, Dixon acted unreasonably in not procuring the restraining device, and if it would have prevented the trailer from overturning, Morris will prevail against Dixon for negligence.

Question 172
Answer: D

The correct answer is choice (D). This question is testing the law of defamation. In order to prevail on a claim for defamation by slander, special damages must be proven to have been sustained by the plaintiff. Thus, Poe will not prevail on a claim against Kane for defamation unless Poe suffered some special damage.

Question 173
Answer: A

The correct answer is choice (A). This question is testing the law of intentional infliction of emotional distress. Intentional infliction of emotional distress is defined as extreme and outrageous conduct that is made intentionally or recklessly and that causes severe emotional distress to another.

In this situation, Poe will prevail against Kane for intentional infliction of emotional distress because Kane's intentional actions were extreme and outrageous and caused severe emotional distress to Poe.

Question 174
Answer: B

The correct answer is choice (B). The question is testing the law of battery. A plaintiff will prevail on a claim for battery if a defendant intentionally acted to cause either a harmful or offensive contact or the immediate apprehension of a harmful or offensive contact with the person of another and actually caused such contact. A plaintiff's person is protected from a defendant's intentional and impermissible contact upon any part of the body, anything that is attached to the body, and anything that is reasonably connected to the body.

If Poe knew that the door was substantially certain to strike Kane's bullhorn, then Poe possessed the intent to cause a harmful or offensive contact to the person of another and Kane will prevail against Poe for battery. The bullhorn was reasonably connected to Kane, as he was holding it in his hand, and thus the impermissible contact with the bullhorn will substantiate a claim for battery against Poe.

Question 175
Answer: A

The correct answer is choice (A). This question is testing the law of intentional infliction of emotional distress. If the plaintiff is a public figure, actual malice must be demonstrated for a cause of action for intentional infliction of emotional distress to succeed. Further, the plaintiff does not need to prove that any physical suffering resulted from the emotional distress.

If Devon knew that Plummer was about to sit on the chair, his action of pulling the chair away was malicious, as it was solely intended to embarrass Plummer in front of a large crowd at a political dinner. Plummer does not need to show that he suffered physical harm from the incident, but merely that he suffered severe emotional distress. Since Plummer suffered emotional distress in terms of embarrassment as a consequence of Devon's malicious action, he will be able to prevail against Devon for intentional infliction of emotional distress.

Question 176
Answer: C

The correct answer is choice (C). The question is testing the law of assault. In order to prevail on claim for assault, the plaintiff must show that the defendant placed him in reasonable apprehension of an imminent harmful or offensive contact. Thus, a person may escape liability for assault if he threatens a harmful or offensive contact at some time in the future. Therefore, if Denton took no action that threatened an imminent harmful or offensive contact, but merely threatened future harm, Prout will not recover from Denton for assault.

This is an excellent example of a question testing the elements of a cause of action. Without knowing any of the facts, this question may be answered just by understanding the elements of assault. A threat of immediate physical harm is an element of assault. Therefore, as set forth in choice (C), as a matter of law, Prout will not recover if Denton took no action that threatened immediate physical harm to Prout.

Question 177
Answer: A

The correct answer is choice (A). This question is testing the law of intentional infliction of emotional distress. Intentional infliction of emotional distress is defined as extreme and outrageous conduct that is made intentionally or recklessly and that causes severe emotional distress to another.

If Prout actually suffered severe emotional distress, Prout will recover from Denton on a claim of intentional infliction of emotional distress because Denton's comments were extreme and outrageous and were made intentionally to Prout to dissuade him from selling his house to a minority purchaser.

Question 178
Answer: C

The correct answer is choice (C). This question is testing the law of premises liability. A landowner generally owes no duty of care to an undiscovered trespasser. Since Dwyer had no reason to know or anticipate Page's presence in the cabin, she was an undiscovered trespasser to which Dwyer owed no duty of care. Therefore, Page will not recover from Dwyer for the injuries she sustained at his cabin.

Question 179
Answer: D

The correct answer is choice (D). The question is testing the law of joint and several liability. The doctrine of joint and several liability provides that when there is more than one defendant whose concurrent negligence results in harm to a plaintiff, they may each be found liable for the entire amount of damages that they caused by their indivisible wrongful conduct. Since both Telco and Rhodes' negligence concurrently led to Walker's injuries, they will be jointly and severally liable to Walker for the full amount of his damages.

Question 180
Answer: B

The correct answer is choice (B). The question is testing the law of private nuisance. A private nuisance occurs when a defendant substantially and unreasonably disturbs the right to use and enjoy the land of a real property owner or lessee. Petrone will prevail on a claim for private nuisance against Silo if the cement dust has substantially and unreasonably interfered with Petrone's right to use and enjoy his property.

This is another excellent example of the examiners using the standard of the law in the correct answer. As choice (B) sets forth, "*if* the cement dust interfered unreasonably with the use and enjoyment of Petrone's property," then Petrone will prevail in a claim for private nuisance. As a matter of law, this statement is true, and therefore, must be correct. Conversely, the examiners could just as easily come to a different conclusion. Suppose an answer choice provided: "No, if the cement dust did not interfere unreasonably with the use and enjoyment of Petrone's property." This answer would also be true, and therefore, would have to be correct. Be alert to how the examiners phrase the answers because the examiners can easily interchange conclusions (e.g., prevail or not prevail) by changing only a few words.

Question 181
Answer: D

The correct answer is choice (D). The question is testing the law of strict products liability. Under a strict liability theory, a manufacturer or any commercial supplier (i.e., middleman, supplier, dealer, or retailer) may be held strictly liable for a plaintiff's injuries from a commercial product if the product is dangerously defective.

If the product was manufactured by Abco and was defective, Crane can prevail against Abco for his damages. But, with the six different manufacturers of the drug, it will be impossible to prove that Abco was actually the manufacturer of the drug that Crane's father took. Therefore, the determining question will be whether liability can be imposed against Abco without proving that its pills were taken by Crane's father.

Question 182
Answer: D

The correct answer is choice (D). This question is testing the law of defamation. In the absence of a constitutionally required standard of proving fault, most states use a negligence standard of proof for showing the liability of a defendant. Negligence with regard to the truth or falsity of the communication is necessary in order to prevail on a claim for defamation against a private person.

If Josephs had reasonable grounds to believe his statement about Norris to be true, then his communication was not negligent with regard to its truth or falsity when it was made. Therefore, Norris will not be able to recover from Josephs for defamation because the statement was not negligently made by Josephs.

Question 183
Answer: A

The correct answer is choice (A). The question is testing the law of abnormally dangerous activities. An abnormally dangerous activity is one that presents a substantial risk of serious harm to persons or property regardless of the degree of care that is exercised in carrying out that activity. The law imposes strict liability on whoever engages in an abnormally dangerous activity.

The storage of highly toxic gas is an abnormally dangerous activity, as it poses a substantial risk of serious harm regardless of what degree of care is exercised. Thus, strict liability is imposed on Chemco for any damages associated with its storage activities and Chemco will be liable to Nyman for his damages, even if Chemco was not negligent or the tank was not built in a defective manner.

Question 184
Answer: D

The correct answer is choice (D). The question is testing the law of abnormally dangerous activities. An abnormally dangerous activity is one that presents a substantial risk of serious harm to persons or property regardless of the degree of care that is exercised in carrying out that activity. The law imposes strict liability on whoever engages in an abnormally dangerous activity.

The operation of a nuclear power plant is an abnormally dangerous activity, as it poses a substantial risk of serious harm regardless of what degree of care is exercised. Thus, strict liability is imposed on NPP for any damages associated with its nuclear power activities, even in the absence of negligence on the part of NPP.

Question 185
Answer: D

The correct answer is (D). This question tests the doctrine of negligence per se. In the majority of jurisdictions, a violation of a statute is considered negligence per se, and a plaintiff is permitted to bring a cause of action based upon that statute to recover damages. In order to be entitled to recover under such a doctrine, though, the plaintiff generally must demonstrate that (1) he or she is within the class of persons intended to be protected by the statute and (2) that the injury suffered is within the type of harm the legislature sought to avert by passing the statute. Here, Dieter violated a statute that prohibits motorists from parking their vehicles within 10 feet of a fire hydrant. While the ordinance is meant to protect members of the public, which would place Plaintiff within the protected class, it is far from apparent that the purpose of such a preventative measure is to reduce traffic accidents. If the ordinance was not intended to prevent such an outcome, then Plaintiff would not be able to meet his burden to entitle him to bring a cause of action.

Although any potential cause of action would be brought under the doctrine of negligence per se, Plaintiff here cannot meet the initial hurdles to that claim, and therefore answer choice (A) is incorrect.

It is true that Plaintiff would not have been injured had the car not been parked as it was, but although Plaintiff might be able to bring a negligence claim for the poor parking decision, he cannot bring such a claim under the parking ordinance. Therefore, answer choice (B) is incorrect.

Finally, the success of Plaintiff's action under the parking ordinance would not hinge on whether the parking job was an active or efficient cause of the accident. If the aforementioned requirements are met, then the claim would proceed under negligence pro se. Thus, answer choice (C) is incorrect.

Question 186
Answer: B

(B) is the correct response. The tort of conversion involves a wrongdoer's intentional exercise of dominion or control over an owner's item of personal property. If the wrongdoer seriously interferes with the owner's right of control over the property, then the wrongdoer may be required to pay for part or all of its value. Thus, if the interference is sufficient enough, then the wrongdoer maybe obligated to purchase the personal property. The degree of the interference will determine the extent of the damages that should be awarded.

The word "borrow" is a definite clue regarding Neighbor's state of mind. This word implies that Neighbor only intended to temporarily use and then return the saw to Homeowner. Neighbor apparently planned to return it because he ended up breaking it where he initially obtained it. The degree of Neighbor's interference with Homeowner's right of ownership of the saw, however, constituted an assertion of dominion and control over the saw. The fact that the saw broke while Neighbor operated is a sufficient interference to justify an award of damages.

The breaking of the saw should render Neighbor liable to Homeowner for conversion because that conduct harmed Homeowner's personal property. Although Neighbor probably planned to return the saw to Homeowner, the saw needed to be returned in nearly the same condition as it was when Neighbor borrowed it.

Under the circumstances of Neighbor's ability to access the saw, the fact that he intended to return it to Homeowner, and the fact that he broke it while working for Homeowner's benefit, it is appropriate for Neighbor to pay damages. Those damages should be in the amount of the saw's value at the time that Neighbor borrowed it for two reasons. First, Homeowner purchased it and used it up until that time. Second, the Neighbor subsequently used the saw and is at fault for breaking it.

(B) is the correct answer. Neighbor is liable to pay damages in the amount of the saw's value before he took it and used it.

Answer (A) is wrong because Homeowner is not entitled to recover actual damages. The examiners indicate that the claim is for conversion. Because the interference is substantial (the equipment broke), Homeowner is entitled to the entire value of the saw, as opposed to just the actual damages.

Answer (C) is wrong because for two reasons Neighbor's liability for the conversion and breaking of the saw is not eliminated or mitigated by the fact that he used the saw to benefit Homeowner. First, Neighbor's earlier use of the saw to work on his own trees contributed to breaking the saw. Second, the saw broke while Neighbor used it.

Answer (D) is wrong because Neighbor's liability for the conversion and breaking of the saw is not eliminated or mitigated by the fact that he did not intend to keep it.

Question 187
Answer: A

(A) is the correct response to this torts law question. To prove a defendant's strict liability for a defectively manufactured product, a plaintiff must demonstrate that:

(1) Injury in fact resulted from a condition of the product;
(2) That condition existed when the product left the defendant's hands;
(3) The condition renders the product unreasonably dangerous for its use; and
(4) Its use was foreseeable by a defendant; and
(5) Its misuse was reasonably foreseeable.

The lighter operated in an ordinary manner when the arsonist used it to light the fire. An interval of time occurred between when the arsonist used the lighter, stopped using it, and when it exploded. The explosion occurred without any causation due to starting the fire.

The facts fulfill the analytical criteria of the strict liability rule. First, an injury in fact occurred to the arsonist's leg due to some defective condition of the lighter. Second, the defective condition apparently existed when the product left the manufacturer's factory. Third, the lighter's defective condition rendered the lighter unreasonably dangerous for its use. Fourth, the manufacturer could have foreseen the arsonist's use of lighter in terms of lighting it, turning it off, and placing it into his pocket. Fifth, the manufacturer might have reasonably foreseen that its cigarette lighter might be misused by an arsonist to start a house fire, although such misuse apparently did not cause the explosion. Even if the misuse caused the explosion, the law provides that the manufacturer could be liable for the arsonist's foreseeable misuse of the lighter.

The correct answer is (A). The arsonist will prevail because the lighter exploded due to a manufacturing defect instead of as a result of his unforeseeable misuse of the lighter.

Answer (B) is not correct because his strict liability action does not include the element of proximate cause, which is an element of a negligence tort.

Answer (C) is incorrect because, although the arsonist used the lighter for a purpose that was neither intended nor reasonably foreseeable, a break in the causal chain occurred between his act of arson and the explosion.

Answer (D) is wrong because the law of strict liability does not take into consideration whether the arsonist's injuries occurred in the course of committing a felony or from a device used to commit the felony.

Question 188
Answer: B

(B) is the correct response to this torts law question. Battery can occur if the following elements are established:

(1) A defendant acts with the intent to contact a plaintiff's body;
(2) This contact is offensive or harmful to an ordinary reasonable person; and
(3) The defendant's contact with the plaintiff must result in an injury or harm.

A privilege exists when certain factors justify or excuse a prima facie tort. A privilege allows a defendant to escape tort liability. The law provides a limited privilege of protecting others under certain circumstances. A person may defend a third party from an attack to the same degree that the law would allow the third party to defend himself.

John intentionally pushed Karen's body out of the automobile's way. John's contact was offensive to an ordinary reasonable person, Karen, because she did not permit it. John's contact with Karen resulted in breaking her leg, an actionable injury. Karen is entitled to recover compensatory damages from John for the battery that injured her leg unless he avoids liability pursuant to an applicable defense. John may assert that he possessed a privilege to protect Karen from the approaching automobile that would excuse or justify his contact with her. The law in a majority of jurisdictions provides that John would not succeed with this defense if he should have realized that Karen was not in danger when he pushed her.

The correct answer is (B) because Karen should prevail if John should have realized that Karen was not at risk from the approaching automobile.

Answer (A) is incorrect because it reaches an accurate conclusion for the wrong reason. Although John could have shouted a warning instead of pushing Karen, doing that would have been unnecessary if he had recognized that she was not in danger.

Answer (C) is not correct because it provides the wrong conclusion on an incorrect basis. The facts do not necessarily establish the automobile driver's responsibility for Karen's injury.

Answer (D) is wrong because it is an inaccurate conclusion that is based on an incorrect explanation. Although John's subjective intent might have been to save Karen, in a majority of jurisdictions, this subjective intent must be reasonable.

Question 189
Answer: D

(D) is the correct response to this torts question. Battery may be established with proof of the following elements:

(1) A defendant must act with the intent to contact a plaintiff's body;
(2) This contact is offensive or harmful to an ordinary reasonable person;
(3) A contact is offensive if the plaintiff did not permit it; and
(4) The defendant's contact with the plaintiff must result in an injury or harm.

A contact is offensive if a plaintiff did not permit it. A contact is not permitted if the plaintiff did not consent to it. A determination of whether a contact is unpermitted should consider that contact's factual context.

Consent is a defense to battery that usually precludes a plaintiff from obtaining a recovery from a defendant in an intentional tort action. Consent negates the existence of such a tort because no harm can occur to one who consciously permits a tort to occur. The test is if a reasonable person could imply consent to a tort from a plaintiff's conduct? Consent is not a defense when a defendant has exceeded the consent that a plaintiff has given.

The correct answer is (D) because Perry provided valid consent when Dever's conduct occurred within the players' consent to physical contact while playing basketball. It is likely that Dever acted with intent to contact Perry's body when both parties attempted to obtain a basketball as it rebounded from the backboard. This contact is not offensive because Perry permitted for two reasons: (1) the rough nature of the game; and (2) players including Perry used their elbows against each other to prevent interference.

Perry will not recover compensatory damages from Dever for his injury because Perry consented to the type of harm that he sustained based on Perry's conduct. Perry had liberally used his elbows to discourage interference by other players like Dever.

Answer (A) is incorrect because it reaches an inaccurate conclusion for the wrong reason. Even if Dever intended to strike Perry with his elbow, the defense of consent would avoid liability for the battery.

Answer (B) is not correct because it provides the wrong conclusion on an incorrect basis. Even if Dever intended to cause a harmful or offensive contact with Perry, the defense of consent would avoid liability for the battery.

Answer (C) is wrong because it is an accurate conclusion that is based on an incorrect explanation. Although Perry impliedly consented to rough play, Perry could still prevail in his battery action if Dever intentionally used force that exceeded Perry's consent. Thus, although answer choice (C) is a plausible answer, the best answer is choice (D). This is a great example of a question in which the wording of the answer makes one answer choice the best option. Many students likely selected choice (C), and didn't even read choice (D). Do not make that mistake on the exam.

Question 190
Answer: A

(A) is the correct response to this torts question. False imprisonment involves the intentional confinement of a person, who is aware of the confinement, for any period of time.

However, if the defendant's objective involved the privilege of defending third parties or himself, the defendant may be justified even if his or her conduct resulted from a mistaken belief about the necessity for invoking the privilege.

Owner's false statement that Traveler's car had a broken fan belt resulted in intentionally restraining her at his premises. Confinement existed because Traveler lacked a reasonable means of escape from Owner's situation. Traveler possessed awareness of the confinement because she knew that she could not leave Owner's premises. The delay in Traveler's trip due to Owner's statement is an actionable duration of restraint. Because Owner had the necessary intent for false imprisonment, when examined only under the general rule his reasonably mistaken belief that Traveler was Robber would not provide a viable excuse for his conduct.

The general rule, however, is subject to the privilege exception. Here, Owner possessed a justifiable basis to directly defend himself, and indirectly defend third parties, from someone that reasonably appeared to be Robber. Thus, Owner's objective warrants application of the privilege exception that justifies his reasonably mistaken belief regarding the necessity for confining Traveler.

The correct answer is (A) because Traveler will not prevail if Owner reasonably believed that Traveler was Robber.

Answer (B) is incorrect. The fact that Traveler did not suffer any physical or mental harm will not allow Owner to avoid liability for false imprisonment because he harmed her in terms of the delay and inconvenience that resulted from his false statement.

Answer (C) is incorrect. Although Traveler's reasonable belief that she could not leave Owner's premises fulfills an element of false imprisonment, Owner possesses a valid defense of privilege to liability for this tort.

Answer (D) is incorrect. Although Traveler may be able to present a prima facie case of false imprisonment based in part on Owner's false statement, Owner possesses a valid defense of privilege to liability for this tort.

Question 191
Answer: B

(B) is the correct response to this torts question. This question is testing the role of judge and jury, not necessarily the tort of strict negligence. If you skimmed the call of the question before reading the facts, you would have immediately identified this.

In a jury trial, the jury determines questions of fact. In a bench trial, the court decides questions of fact. In both jury and bench trials, the court determines questions of law. A burden of proof is a question of law. A plaintiff in a civil proceeding possesses the burden of proof.

The correct answer is (B) because it is a question of law. Selection (B) is the only choice addressing a standard of proof that the court, and not the jury, is permitted to decide.

Answer (A) is incorrect because the existence or nonexistence of other safer insulation materials is a question of fact that the jury would decide.

Answer (C) is wrong because the issue of whether the defendant should have known of the risk prior to 1966, although nobody else had discovered it, is a question of fact for the jury to decide.

Answer (D) is not correct because the issue of if the asbestos insulation was inherently dangerous is a question of fact for the jury to decide.

Question 192
Answer: C

(C) is the correct response to this torts question. A plaintiff will prevail in a products liability action against a defendant if a product that the defendant manufactured was unreasonably dangerous. The question is if the product was dangerous beyond the expectations of an ordinary consumer due to a design defect that existed when it was sold. A product is defective in its design if it poses a danger to people or property. In order to prove that a design defect exists, a plaintiff must satisfy the benefits test. Do the benefits of a design outweigh the risk of danger inherent in the design?

Plaintiff will not prevail in her products liability action against Engineer in the absence of proof that the filter system, a product that the Engineer provided, was unreasonably dangerous. Because discovery established that the explosion in Company's processing plant was unrelated to the filter system, the filter was not unreasonably dangerous. The rule applies to the design defect in the plant that Company designed because it constituted a danger to Plaintiff. Plaintiff might be able to satisfy the benefits test with respect to Company's design of the plant. Plaintiff would not, however, be able to fulfill that test with respect to Engineer.

Plaintiff may be able to show that the benefits of the plant's design outweighed the risk of danger inherent in the design. Based on the results of discovery, Plaintiff could establish that Company's design caused the injury. Company would have to prove that the benefits of the design outweighed the risks of the design and the cost of a safer design.

The correct answer is (C) because Engineer lacked a duty to the Plaintiff, to prevent this specific risk of harm, because it resulted from Company's defective plant design, not Engineer's.

Answer (A) is incorrect. Plaintiff will not prevail. Although Engineer signed, sealed, and submitted the blueprint containing a design defect, she did not design that portion of the plant which exploded and injured Plaintiff.

Answer (B) is incorrect. Plaintiff cannot prevail on the basis that all of the plant's designers were jointly and severally liable because this theory of liability apportionment does not apply when Engineer is not at fault.

Answer (D) is incorrect. Although Plaintiff will not prevail against Engineer, it is not because of Engineer's independent contractor status. Engineer is not liable to Plaintiff because her design did not cause the injury.

Question 193
Answer: C

(C) is the correct response to this torts law question. A person is an invitee if he or she is on a landowner's real property (1) by invitation of the landowner, and (2) for a purpose connected with the landowner's use of the property. The invitee may receive an express or implied invitation to enter onto the land.

Landowners possess a duty of reasonable care to an invitee. They have a duty to warn the invitee of a dangerous condition on their real property of which they are aware, if that condition presents an unreasonable risk of harm to the invitee. Landowners have a duty of making reasonable inspections of their property to identify any dangerous condition that might exist on that property.

Mom is an invitee for two reasons. First, she occupied Hospital's real property pursuant to its implied invitation while she accompanied her daughter to the emergency room for treatment of her injuries. Second, Mom occupied the emergency room for a purpose connected with Hospital's use of the property. Specifically, Mom was there while Hospital treated her daughter whose injury needed medical attention. Mom also needed immediate medical care for the accidental injury that she sustained from falling there.

Hospital, through its employees, owed Mom, an invitee, a duty of reasonable care. Thus, they possessed a duty to Mom to inspect the property and to identify its dangerous conditions. They also were obligated to warn Mom of any known dangerous condition on Hospital's premises that posed an unreasonable risk of injury to Mom. Hospital's employees arguably failed to notice and take reasonable steps to eliminate the metal fixture protruding from the emergency room's wall if it was not a necessary item.

Answer (C) is correct because it is based on the negligence standard. Mom will not prevail in her tort action and recover damages unless Hospital's staff failed to take reasonable steps to anticipate and prevent Mom's injury.

Answer (A) is wrong because it reached an inaccurate conclusion for the correct reason. Mom's public invitee status does not necessarily entitle her to prevail against Hospital. Mom must establish all the elements of a negligence tort; particularly that Hospital breached a duty of care.

Answer (B) is incorrect. If the fixture upon which Mom received her injury was "obvious" and "commonly used," then Hospital lacked a duty to warn Mom about it and could not be liable for a breach of its duty to warn her of it. However, this is not the only way to ground liability. Use of the word "unless" is what makes it incorrect.

Answer (D) is wrong because it incorrectly describes the duty of care by Hospital and its personnel. They did owe Mom a duty and she had to prove a breach of that duty.

Question 194
Answer: A

Choice (A) is the correct response to this torts law question. A plaintiff may seek a civil remedy from a defendant for a private nuisance if the defendant unreasonably interferes with the plaintiff's use and enjoyment of the land. The interference must be offensive to a community member of normal sensibilities, rather than to a person of abnormal sensitivity.

Neighbor's dam has created a private nuisance because it eliminated all water flow onto Vacationer's land. Thus, Neighbor's conduct intentionally interfered with Vacationer's right to use and enjoy the land. This interference would be offensive to a community member of normal sensibilities and unreasonably interferes with Vacationer's right to use and enjoy the land.

The correct answer is (A) because the effect of Neighbor's the dam is to unreasonably interfere with Vacationer's right to use and enjoy the real property.

Answer (B) is incorrect. This answer does not address the unreasonableness of the interference.

Answer (C) is incorrect. The fact that Vacationer did not use the stream is irrelevant and not a valid defense.

Answer (D) is incorrect. The fact that the dam was built in conformity with all laws is not a valid defense. A lawful interference can still be unreasonable.

Question 195
Answer: B

(B) is the correct response to this torts law question. Contributory negligence is defined as a plaintiff's conduct that contributed as a legal cause to the plaintiff's injury and which fell below the standard to which the plaintiff should have complied to avoid this harm. In a traditional contributory negligence jurisdiction, the plaintiff is barred from recovering from a defendant when the plaintiff's negligence caused the injury, regardless of how minimal that negligence might have been.

The doctrine of last clear chance is an exception to the general rule of contributory negligence. A plaintiff's contributory negligence will not bar a negligence action when the defendant had the last clear chance to avoid an accident involving those parties. The focus of inquiry should be if the duration between a plaintiff's act of contributory negligence and the plaintiff's injury was sufficient for a defendant to exercise due care to prevent the injury. If the answer is yes, then the defendant possessed the last clear chance to avoid the injury and the plaintiff's contributory negligence will not preclude a recovery of damages.

There is no doubt that Fran's driving of her automobile at an excessive rate of speed constituted contributory negligence. It is a legal cause of her injury because it resulted in her car's sliding into a perpendicular position when she applied the breaks. Driving at an excessive speed fell below the standard of care with which Fran should have complied to avoid finding herself in a position that exposed her to harm.

Fran may prevail in her negligence action against Sid because he had the last clear chance to avoid the parties' accident. Sid negligently operated his automobile at an excessive rate of speed. He failed to take advantage of the opportunity to safely stop his automobile as it approached Fran's automobile. Thus, instead of exercising due care within that interval, Sid forfeited the last clear chance of avoiding the accident resulting from attempting to pass Fran's automobile.

The correct answer is (B) because Fran should recover despite her contributory negligence if Sid had the last clear chance to avoid the accident.

Answer (A) is incorrect. The answer is premised on the inaccurate basis of comparative negligence. The question clearly indicates that the rule of contributory negligence applies.

Answer (C) is incorrect. Whether Fran legally caused the accident is not the dispositive issue.

Answer (D) is incorrect. Whether Fran assumed the risk is not a controlling issue, it is a defense.

Question 196
Answer: A

(A) is the correct response to this torts law question. The other responses are incorrect because they include at least one cause of action for which Applicant would not recover damages from Doctor.

One type of privacy invasion occurs when a defendant publicly discloses private facts about a plaintiff by means of highly objectionable publication. Doctor is not liable for this tort because he did not publicly disclose private facts about Applicant in a highly objectionable publication. The publication required is typically one made to the public at large.

The elements of negligent misrepresentation are as follows:

Business Capacity: A defendant makes a representation in the course of his business, or in a transaction in which the defendant possesses a pecuniary interest.

Breach of Duty: The defendant owed a duty to a foreseeable plaintiff and the defendant did not exercise reasonable care or competence in obtaining or communicating the information.

Causing Damages: A plaintiff suffers a pecuniary loss by justifiably and actually relying on the representation.

Doctor is not liable for negligent misrepresentation because, although he made an inaccurate representation about Applicant while practicing medicine and breached his duty of reasonable care by confusing her file, Applicant did not suffer a pecuniary loss as a result of his wrongful conduct.

To establish a negligent infliction of emotional distress, a plaintiff must prove that the surrounding circumstances and a defendant's negligent conduct both resulted in a particular probability of causing the plaintiff real and significant emotional distress.

The correct answer is (A) because Applicant can prove a negligent infliction of emotional distress. Applicant may prevail by proving that Doctor's negligent confusion of her file with a person who had AIDS resulted in her mental shock that caused her heart attack. Thus, Applicant's physical injury arose from her emotional distress that Doctor induced.

Question 197
Answer: C

(C) is the correct response to this torts law question. Negligence per se may be established in a civil action by invoking a criminal or civil statute that describes a special standard of care for specified conduct. In the majority of states, in order to subject a defendant to tort liability based on negligence per se, a plaintiff must prove that:

(1) A plaintiff is within the class of individuals that a statute is designed to protect; and

(2) A defendant's conduct violated the statute;

(3) The defendant's conduct violated the reason for the statute;

(4) That conduct constitutes the type of risk that the statute covers; and

(5) The conduct is not excused.

The correct answer is (C) because Motorist is entitled to a directed verdict in Child's tort action. Negligence per se applies because the state motor vehicle code provides the standard of care. Child, a pedestrian who lawfully crossed the street, is within the class of individuals that the code provision protects. Motorist violated the code's prohibition of driving through the red light. Motorist's conduct violated the reason for the code, which was to protect pedestrians who were crossing the street. Motorist's conduct presented the risk of collision between vehicles and passengers that the code sought to prevent. Motorist's conduct, however, is excused due to his heart attack that occurred without warning. Moreover, Motorist was driving within the speed limit and had begun to stop.

Answer (A) is an incorrect conclusion because Motorist's violation of the code was excused.

Answer (B) provides a wrong conclusion because the doctrine of res ipsa loquitur does not apply.

Answer (D) is an incorrect conclusion because the ordinary standard of negligence does not apply. The facts indicate that, at "trial it was stipulated that (1) immediately prior to suffering the heart attack, Motorist had been driving within the speed limit, had seen the red light, and had begun to slow his car; (2) Motorist had no history of heart disease and no warning of this attack; (3) while Motorist was unconscious, his car ran the red light." Thus, Motorist did, in fact, act reasonably under the circumstances.

Question 198
Answer: C

(C) is the correct response to this torts law question. A plaintiff who suffers a loss of property resulting from a defendant's negligence can recover damages in the amount of the property loss. The plaintiff may not, however, recover damages for the emotional distress that arises from the property loss.

Owner is only entitled to recover the amount of this property loss as damages because he established that Company's negligence caused the destruction of his restaurant. Owner cannot, however, recover damages for his emotional distress that resulted from the property loss.

Question 199
Answer: C

(C) is the correct response to this torts law question. In order to present a prima facie case and prevail on a cause of action for negligence, a plaintiff must plead and prove the following four elements:

(1) Duty - A defendant owed the plaintiff a legal duty of care;
(2) Breach - The defendant's conduct breached that duty;
(3) Causation - The defendant's conduct proximately caused the plaintiff's injury; and
(4) Damages - The plaintiff suffered harm from the defendant's conduct.

Restaurant's strongest defensive strategy is to allege and show that Patron has failed to establish a prima facie case of negligence. This failure will prevent Patron from recovering damages. Even if he establishes Restaurant's duty of care regarding food preparation and a breach of this duty, Patron will not prevail if he cannot show that the Restaurant's food caused his illness. In that event, he could not recover damages from Restaurant. Therefore, an argument that Restaurant did not cause Patron's infection will be most effective for him.

There are two main factors in the question which tend to favor Restaurant's contention. First, Patron ate three meals after the meal at Restaurant. Second, no employees of Restaurant tested positive for the bacteria. It is far from certain that Restaurant would be successful in asserting these points. Remember, the question is not asking for a winning argument, just the best argument of the four alternatives.

Answer (A) is not the best contention because it goes to the Restaurant's breach of duty and causation is a more crucial element for proving its liability. Additionally, just because no one else complained about stomach discomfort, it does not follow that Restaurant was not negligent in preparing Patron's meal. Therefore, choice (A) is not the best answer.

Answer (B) is a less than optimal argument because it goes to the Restaurant's duty of care and causation is a more critical element for establishing its liability. Additionally, it is an incorrect statement of the law.

Answer (D) is not the most effective assertion because if Restaurant prevents Patron from proving a prima facie case, then a defense to the established case such as assumption of risk will not be needed.

Question 200
Answer: C

(C) is the correct response to this torts law question. A privacy invasion may occur when a defendant publicly discloses private facts about a plaintiff. The plaintiff may make a prima facie case by presenting these elements of proof:

(1) The facts disclosed are private facts;

(2) the defendant disclosed them to the public generally or to a large number of persons; and

(3) the disclosure was in a form of publicity of a highly objectionable kind.

The fairness and accuracy of the disclosure is a defense in an action alleging public disclosure of private facts. No actionable privacy invasion resulted from the newspaper's public disclosure of the private fact of the parent's request for reimbursement for their payment to the psychologist. The newspaper's defense of its disclosure's fairness and accuracy would succeed.

Son's legal representative cannot establish a prima facie case. Although the psychologist's provision of services to Son is private fact regarding a confidential relationship, his parents made a public request for reimbursement. This request did not reveal any privileged information about the evaluation or its results. The reporter's disclosure of the parent's public request and Son's name in the article only could have revealed that an evaluation occurred. It could not have disclosed the results to the public.

The article cannot be considered a highly objectionable form of publicity.

Answer (D) is incorrect. Parents' knowledge of the reporter's presence cannot, of itself, constitute their consent to the publication.

Question 201
Answer: D

(D) is the correct answer to this torts law question. Foreseeability is the most prevalent test of proximate causation. If a plaintiff's injury is foreseeable based on a defendant's conduct, then the defendant may be liable. If a plaintiff's injury is too unforeseeable or remote under the circumstances, then the defendant is not liable.

Mechanic will obtain a judgment if his injury from the gas explosion and fire was a foreseeable result of Basher's conduct of driving his car into Adam's car. The facts indicate that Basher was, in fact, negligent. Therefore, Basher's negligence is a given. If Basher's negligent driving was the proximate cause of Mechanic's injury, it must follow that Basher will be liable to Mechanic. The conditional language of the answer choice is critical.

Answer (A) is incorrect. Basher's knowledge of the gasoline leak is not a prerequisite to his liability.

Answer (B) is incorrect. Even if Adam warned Mechanic of the leak, an explosion and fire still could have occurred.

Answer (C) is incorrect. Even if Mechanic's negligence contributed to his injury, under the comparative negligence rule, which expressly applies to his question, it could only reduce the amount of damages that he could recover.

Question 202
Answer: C

(C) is the correct response to this torts law question. The law determines if a defendant owes a duty of care to a foreseeable plaintiff. A person who engages in an activity has a legal duty to act in accordance with the legal standard of care that applies to that activity. A person who fails to act in accordance with that standard may be liable to a foreseeable plaintiff for such a failure.

Adam owed a duty of care to Mechanic, a foreseeable plaintiff, to disclose the known danger of the leaking gas tank. Informing Mechanic of that fact would have fulfilled the standard of reasonable care for delivering a car with this dangerous condition. Adam failed to act in accordance with this standard. His breach of the duty to disclose this known risk resulted in Mechanic's injuries. Consequently, Mechanic will receive a judgment for damages.

Choice (C) is correct because is conditionally applies the standard for negligence. It is true that, if a reasonable person in Adam's position would have warned Mechanic about the leak, then failing to warn about the leak would be negligent. Conversely, by the same logic, the answer choice could have provided: "No, if a reasonable person in Adam's position would *not* have warned Mechanic about the gas leak." This is how the examiners can use the specific language of the answer choices to reach either conclusion (e.g., Yes or No).

Answer (A) is incorrect. Mechanic's breach of his duty to look for a dangerous condition does not negate Adam's negligence. It only constitutes comparative negligence that could reduce Mechanic's recovery of damages.

Answer (B) is incorrect. Mechanic should prevail if Adam knew of the danger posed by the gasoline leak.

Answer (D) is incorrect. The car was dangerous, but not "unreasonably dangerous."

Question 203
Answer: D

(D) is the correct response to this torts law question. Intentional infliction of emotional distress involves a defendant's act, made intentionally or recklessly, that amounts to extreme and outrageous conduct resulting in severe emotional distress to a plaintiff.

Photographer intentionally took a picture of Mobster, but not Prisoner. Photographer might have recklessly included Prisoner in the photograph. Photographer's conduct of taking a flight over the prison to take pictures of Mobster is extreme, but it was not outrageous conduct as to Prisoner, that caused Prisoner severe emotional distress. Note that Photographer's acts could be considered extreme and outrageous as to Mobster, but that is not what the question asks.

Answer (A) is incorrect. A reasonable person could conclude that Photographer intended to take a picture of Prisoner.

Answer (B) is incorrect. Prisoner did not need to prove any physical injury, an element that instead may be relevant for a negligent infliction of emotional distress.

Answer (C) is incorrect. No privilege applies when Warden prohibited the taking of photographs of Mobster.

Question 204
Answer: B

(B) is the correct response to this torts law question. A landowner generally owes no duty of care to an undiscovered trespasser. A landowner is not obligated to inspect his or her real property to discover a trespasser. However, a landowner may never willfully or wantonly injure a person on his or her land.

Vintner owed no duty of care to Trespasser who was undiscovered because Trespasser entered the vineyard without Vintner's knowledge or consent. Vintner had no duty to discover Trespasser, whom Vintner only accidentally injured as a result of operating a balloon above the vineyard. But once Vintner became aware of Trespasser's presence, then Vintner must not willfully injure Trespasser.

Answer (A) is incorrect. The cause of the crash landing is irrelevant.

Answer (C) is incorrect. Ballooning is not an abnormally dangerous activity.

Answer (D) is incorrect. If Vintner knew that a place was frequented by trespassers, then Vintner would owe trespassers a duty to warn them of dangerous artificial conditions only.

Question 205
Answer: A

(A) is the correct response to this torts law question. A person who keeps animals of a type that may escape, trespass onto another's property, and cause harm, is strictly liable for their harm. The rule applies to wild animals in captivity and livestock.

Thus, Neighbor will prevail because Farmer is strictly liable for the destruction of the crops by his cattle because they escaped, trespassed upon Neighbor's adjacent land, and damaged its crops.

Answer (B) is incorrect. It rests upon an incorrect premise of the minority rule. Under the majority rule, Neighbor does not have to prove that the cattle's escape was reasonably foreseeable when by their combined strength they could break through the fencing.

Answer (C) is an officially accepted correct alternative conclusion because its facts allow Neighbor to make a prima facie case of negligence against Farmer.

Answer (D) is incorrect. "Force of nature" is not an available defense to a strict liability tort.

Question 206
Answer: C

(C) is the correct response to this torts law question. The standard of care for professionals is that they must employ reasonable care and exercise a certain level of special knowledge and ability. Professionals must utilize the knowledge, skill, and care that are ordinarily possessed by others of their profession in good standing.

If a defendant has greater knowledge or expertise than an average person, determine if the defendant acted as a reasonable person by exercising the standard level of knowledge and expertise of someone in good standing of the same or an identical trade or profession as the defendant. An additional requirement applies to medical doctors (e.g., physicians, surgeons), who must perform good medical practice as measured by what is standard and usual in that profession.

The critical element of this question is causation. It is not enough to demonstrate that Surgeon breached a duty to Pat. The breach must be shown to be the proximate cause of death. If the plaintiff cannot show that a cardiologist, had one examined Pat before the operation, would have provided evidence that would change the outcome, then Pat's death would have resulted regardless of whether Surgeon was negligent.

Answer (A) is incorrect. It is not as good of an answer as choice (C). Proof that Surgeon breached his duty of care will not, without evidence of causation, entitle the plaintiff to recover damages.

Answer (B) is incorrect. The wrongful death action's main claim is Surgeon's negligent failure to consult. Whether Surgeon's operation caused the clot is a secondary issue.

Answer (D) is incorrect. From the facts, it appears that Pat was on artificial life-support, meaning that she would have died without the equipment. She also had no hope of recovery. The removal of artificial life support is not a sufficient superseding cause to break the chain of causation.

Question 207
Answer: B

(B) is the correct response to this torts law question. Landowners are liable for harm that someone suffers as a result of unreasonably dangerous conditions on, or structures upon, their real property or adjoining it. A defendant is obligated to use reasonable care to prevent an injury to a plaintiff who is not on the defendant's real property, which is due to unreasonably dangerous artificial conditions that protrude upon or abut adjacent property.

In particular, a landowner must exercise reasonable care to protect pedestrians and others on a public street from injuries that arise from dangerous artificial conditions that are located on the landowner's real property.

Seller may be liable for Pedestrian's injury resulting from the unreasonably dangerous artificial condition of the roof on the house that he sold a day earlier. Pedestrian may establish that Seller failed to exercise reasonable care to prevent the harm to Pedestrian. First, Seller knew that slates did and could fall off and failed to remedy that situation before selling the house. Second, Seller knew of the proximity of the house to the sidewalk where Pedestrian walked when the slate hit him. Seller's breach of his duty of reasonable care to protect Pedestrian from the slate by not repairing the roof before selling the house makes Seller the cause of the injury and liable for damages.

Answer (A) is incorrect. Whether the roof was defective at the time of the sale is irrelevant. All that is relevant in this negligence action is whether Seller knew, or should have known, that the roof posed a risk to pedestrians.

Answer (C) is incorrect. Seller cannot be relieved of liability for foreseeable injury just because he sold the home a day earlier. If a year had passed, then this may no longer be the case.

Answer (D) is incorrect. This answer focuses on assumption of the risk, which would not apply under these circumstances, and does not address the critical element of the roof's unreasonably dangerous condition.

Question 208
Answer: D

(D) is the correct response to this torts law question. The law of negligence determines if a defendant owes a duty of care to a foreseeable plaintiff. A person who engages in an activity has a legal duty to act in accordance with the legal standard of care that applies to that activity. A person who fails to act in accordance with that standard may be liable to a foreseeable plaintiff for such a failure.

Hospital owes a duty of care to Patient as a foreseeable plaintiff because she resided in their custody. Hospital, through its Orderly, engaged in taking care of Patient. As such, its legal duty was to provide reasonable custodial health care, which does not include sexual relations. If, as answer choice (D) requires you to assume, Hospital failed to use reasonable care to protect Patient from such conduct, then Hospital would be directly negligent. This answer choice uses the language for negligence and, therefore, must be correct if assumed to be true.

Answer (A) is incorrect. This may be an accurate statement regarding Hospital's vicarious liability for Orderly's actions, as they exceeded his scope of employment. But the negligence action in this case may be brought directly against Hospital, as is set forth in choice (D).

Answer (B) is incorrect. Patient could not provide valid consent due to her severely retarded condition.

Answer (C) is incorrect. As for choice (A), Hospital could not be vicariously liable.

Question 209
Answer: C

(C) is the correct response to this torts law question. Negligence per se may be established in a civil action by invoking a criminal or civil statute that describes a special standard of care for specified conduct. In order to subject a defendant to tort liability based on negligence per se, a plaintiff must prove that:

(1) A plaintiff is within the class of individuals that a statute is designed to protect;
(2) A defendant's conduct violated the statute;
(3) The defendant's conduct violated the reason for the statute;
(4) That conduct constitutes the type of risk that the statute covers; and
(5) The conduct is not excused.

Representative will not succeed in establishing operator's negligence per se with respect to Passenger's death under the statute requiring its ocean liner to carry certain life boats. Representative may only establish some, but not all, of the requisite elements of negligence per se because Operator's conduct is excused. Operator's conduct is excused because, even if Operator provided lifeboats in compliance with the statute, Passenger could not have used one when the storm's severity prevented their use.

Answer (A) is incorrect. Despite operator's non-compliance with the statute, the storm would have prevented use of the lifeboats.

Answer (B) is incorrect. The circumstances do not support a strict liability tort theory.

Answer (D) is incorrect. Even if Passenger assumed the risk of being swept overboard, which is far from certain, this defense is less dispositive than Passenger's representative's inability to establish a prima facie case of negligence per se.

Question 210
Answer: A

(A) is the correct response to this torts law question. A plaintiff will prevail in a products liability action against a defendant if a product that the defendant manufactured was unreasonably dangerous. The question that is posed is whether the product was dangerous beyond the expectations of an ordinary consumer due to a design defect when it was sold.

A product is defective in its design when it poses a danger to people or property. In order to prove a design defect exists, a plaintiff must satisfy the benefits test. A plaintiff must establish that the design caused the injury. Then a court would inquire whether the benefits of a design outweigh the risk of danger inherent in the design.

The defendant is not entitled to a directed verdict because a jury could conclude that the engine had an unreasonably dangerous defect that caused the collision. The plaintiff presented evidence that a safer alternative engine design could solve the stalling problem which ultimately resulted in her injuries. A jury could find the engine's design to be dangerous beyond the expectations of an ordinary consumer, such as the plaintiff.

The plaintiff's evidence showed the benefits of an alternative design that would eliminate the risk of danger in the defendant's design.

Answer (B) is incorrect. The crashworthiness of the Rapido is not at issue.

Answer (C) is incorrect. Troody's failure to stop was not a superseding cause of the accident, but its cause in fact.

Answer (D) is incorrect. In a strict liability action, the plaintiff's sensitivity is not a valid defense.

Question 211
Answer: C

(C) is the correct response to this torts law question. A plaintiff must prove that the surrounding circumstances and a defendant's negligent conduct both resulted in a particular probability of causing the plaintiff real and significant emotional distress. Owner could show that Driver's negligent operation of the car almost resulted in seriously harming him and the child, which caused Owner to suffer serious emotional distress. In any event, however, in order to recover for the claim of negligent infliction of emotional distress, the plaintiff must show that the defendant was, in fact, negligent.

Answer (A) is an incorrect conclusion. It is based on the wrong tort theory of trespass. Driver's entry upon Owner's driveway was justified by necessity.

Answer (B) is incorrect. It is not as good of an answer as choice (C). At the time this question was written, arguably, a claim for negligent infliction of emotional distress required proof of physical harm in a majority of jurisdictions. Owner did not suffer any physical harm or impact as a consequence of his emotional distress. Therefore, the answer was definitively incorrect. In recent years, the examiners have indicated that the physical impact rule has been abandoned in a majority of jurisdictions.

Answer (D) is incorrect. The child's exercise of reasonable care is not a legal prerequisite for Owner to prevail.

Question 212
Answer: C

(C) is the correct response to this torts law question. Res ipsa loquitur applies under the following circumstances:

(1) It is highly likely that a plaintiff's injury could not have occurred absent a defendant's negligent act;

(2) The instrumentality of harm was within a defendant's exclusive control; and

(3) Neither the plaintiff nor a third party's conduct contributed to the plaintiff's injury.

Proof of those elements of res ipsa loquitur creates an inference of a defendant's negligence from circumstantial evidence. A jury may accept or reject the inference.

The court should deny the motion because the facts would allow a jury to infer that Airline's negligence resulted in the aircraft's crash. Res ipsa loquitur applies to the facts for three reasons. First, it is highly likely that Traveller's death could not have happened but for Airline's negligence because its aircraft collided with a mountain during good flying weather. Second, Airline's employees exclusively controlled its aircraft. Third, no facts indicate that the conduct of Traveller or another party contributed to Traveller's injury.

The jury may accept the above three elements of res ipsa loquitur as creating a sufficient inference of Airline's negligence from the evidence for the representative's case to proceed to trial.

Answer (A) is incorrect. It is based on an inaccurate statement of the law because the representative did not need to proffer evidence of causation regarding the crash.

Answer (B) is incorrect. It rests upon an incorrect statement of the law because the representative did not have to proffer evidence negating the possibility that the crash might have been caused by an unavoidable mechanical failure.

Answer (D) is incorrect. Common carriers are not strictly liable in this situation.

Question 213
Answer: C

(C) is the correct response to this torts law question. Under a strict liability theory, any commercial seller (i.e., middleman, supplier, dealer, or retailer) may be held strictly liable for a plaintiff's injuries from a commercial product. An auctioneer is not a commercial seller.

The plaintiff will not succeed in recovering damages from the defendant because an auctioneer is not a commercial seller that could be subject to strict liability for the plaintiff's injuries attributable to the tractor, a commercial product.

Answers (A) and (B) are incorrect because, although the defendant resold a defective tractor, an auctioneer is not a commercial seller subject to strict liability in tort.

Answer (D) is incorrect. The reason why the defendant will prevail is because auctioneers are not considered commercial sellers. Thus, even if the plaintiff was not negligent, he would not prevail.

Question 214
Answer: B

(B) is the correct response to this torts law question. A private nuisance occurs when a defendant substantially and unreasonably disturbs the right to use and enjoy the land of a real property owner or lessee. The various types of actionable disturbances may include physical harms to a landowner's real property and the structures and chattel on that property. One basis for bringing a private nuisance action would be a decrease in the use and value of the plaintiff's property due to a defendant's adverse conditions or activities.

Answer (B) is correct based on the following analysis. Adam's strongest argument would be that Greenacre's condition poses a danger to Townacre's occupants. This contention best supports his action's claim that Bess's failure to maintain Greenacre substantially and unreasonably disturbs his right to use and enjoy Townacre. Thus, Greenacre's natural condition presents a risk that debris and falling limbs could endanger Townacre's occupants, rather than its structures. A secondary effect of that physical danger could be a decrease in the use and value of Townacre.

Answer (A) is not an optimal argument because economic harm to Townacre's owners is a less significant concern than physical harm to its occupants. Thus, although it is a possible answer, it is not the best answer.

Answer (C) is not the strongest allegation because a violation of community aesthetic standards is a less significant issue than physical injury to Townacre's occupants.

Answer (D) is a weak assertion because the lack of an alternative remedy is not a more significant consideration than the safety of Townacre's occupants.

Question 215
Answer: A

(A) is the correct response to this torts law question because the facts fulfill the elements of a private nuisance. A private nuisance occurs when a defendant substantially and unreasonably disturbs the right to use and enjoy the land of a real property owner or lessee.

Homeowner intentionally interfered with Neighbor's use and enjoyment of his land by erecting and using the spot light every night because it adversely affects Neighbor's view of the lake. Homeowner's conduct resulted in the type of interference with Neighbor's use of his land that Homeowner intended to cause based on the light's purposeful annoyance. Neighbor suffered a substantial interference with his lake view due to Homeowner's use of the light. The interference would be offensive to a community member of normal sensibilities, rather than to a person of abnormal sensitivity. Moreover, the extent of Homeowner's interference constitutes an unreasonable interference with Neighbor's use and enjoyment of the land because it obstructs his lake view.

Answer (B) is incorrect. Neighbor's recovery is not contingent upon any decrease in his property's value.

Answer (C) is incorrect. Neighbor's lake view is unreasonably obstructed by the light when it is on at night.

Answer (D) is incorrect. The facts do not support this answer choice.

Question 216
Answer: B

(B) is the correct response to this torts law question. A defendant's conduct must cause a plaintiff's injury. There are two types of causation that must be demonstrated to show the defendant's liability. First, the defendant's conduct must be the cause in fact or "actual" cause. Second, the conduct must be the legal or "proximate" cause of harm to the plaintiff. "But for" causation is the most commonly used test of actual cause. That test of causation inquires if a plaintiff would not have been injured "but for" a defendant's conduct?

Driver's conduct actually directly caused Pedestrian's broken leg because he negligently drove his car into her. Market's manager's conduct of leaving the banana peel on the floor directly caused Pedestrian's broken arm because she slipped due to non-negligently placing a crutch on a banana peel. Driver's conduct, however, was a proximate cause of her broken arm because Pedestrian would not have fallen if she had stepped on the banana peel without having to use crutches, and this type of injury is reasonably foreseeable after suffering a broken leg. Incidentally, Market is also liable for Pedestrian's broken arm.

Answer (A) is incorrect. Driver proximately caused both of Pedestrian's injuries.

Answer (C) is incorrect. Market did not proximately cause Pedestrian's leg injury.

Answer (D) is incorrect. Driver is not liable for her broken leg only, but also for her broken arm.

Question 217
Answer: A

(A) is the correct response to this torts law question. The tort of battery consists of the following elements:

(1) A defendant must act with the intent to contact a plaintiff's body;
(2) This contact is offensive or harmful to an ordinary reasonable person;
(3) The defendant's contact with the plaintiff must result in an injury or harm.

Answer (A) is correct because the facts fulfill the elements of battery.

(1) Surgeon acted with the intent to contact the Athlete's body;
(2) Surgeon's unauthorized operation would be offensive to an ordinary reasonable person because Athlete did not permit it and only authorized Doctor to perform it;

(3) Although Surgeon successfully performed the operation, Athlete suffered harm because Surgeon lacked permission to do so.

Answer (B) is incorrect. Athlete only provided written consent to Doctor's performance of the operation.

Answer (C) is incorrect. The fact that Surgeon possessed superior skills does not overcome the fact that Athlete did not authorize him to perform the surgery.

Answer (D) is incorrect. The operation's success does not excuse or justify the Surgeon's unpermitted touching of Athlete.

Question 218
Answer: C

(C) is the correct response to this torts law question. The plaintiff may establish a prima facie case of commercial appropriation with the following evidence:

(1) A defendant makes unauthorized use of a plaintiff's likeness (picture or name) or identity (name);
(2) for the defendant's commercial advantage; and
(3) the defendant's conduct proximately caused an invasion of the plaintiff's interest in privacy.

Actor can establish a prima facie case of commercial appropriation.

(1) Vineyard made unauthorized use of his likeness (picture) and identity (name) by using the photograph of Actor in its advertisement;
(2) The advertisement furthered Vineyard's commercial advantage by promoting its product based on Actor's apparent endorsement; and
(3) Actor's conduct proximately caused an invasion of Actor's interest in privacy because his photograph was not taken for the purpose of endorsing or promoting Vineyard's product.

Answer (A) is incorrect. Actor only consented to being photographed by an amateur, not for Vineyard's benefit.

Answer (B) is incorrect. Actor's public figure status does not entitle Vineyard to use his photograph in the manner it did or serve as a valid defense to his tort action.

Answer (D) is incorrect. the fact that Actor enjoyed the Vineyard wine neither entitles Vineyard to use his photograph in the advertisement nor provides a viable defense to his tort action.

Question 219
Answer: A

(A) is the correct response to this torts law question. Proof of the following elements is required to establish battery:

(1) A defendant must act with the intent to contact a plaintiff's body;
(2) This contact is offensive or harmful to an ordinary reasonable person; and
(3) The defendant's contact with the plaintiff must result in an injury or harm.

If Hermit buried the explosive charge intending to contact Seller's body, then Hermit is responsible for the harmful contact to Seller's body.

The fact that Hermit erected a sign warning people to proceed at their own risk does not relieve Hermit of liability for battery. Hermit cannot use any kind of mechanical device or weapon to defend his property. A powerful explosive charge could cause serious bodily injury or death.

Answer (B) is incorrect. Even if Hermit only intended to deter Seller, his intentional conduct caused Seller's injuries and harmed his vehicle.

Answer (C) is incorrect. Seller assumed the risk of prosecution for trespassing, but not the risk that the driveway would explode.

Answer (D) is incorrect. The use of an explosive device in the driveway is not a reasonable way to remedy reasonable fear.

Question 220
Answer: D

(D) is the correct response to this torts law question. The law determines if a defendant owes a duty of care to a foreseeable plaintiff. A person who engages in an activity has a legal duty to act in accordance with the legal standard of care that applies to that activity. A person who fails to act in accordance with that standard may be liable to a foreseeable plaintiff for such a failure.

Justice Cardozo's rule in *Palsgraf v. Long Island Railroad Company*, adopted in a majority of jurisdictions, provides that a defendant only owes a duty to "foreseeable" plaintiffs. Foreseeable plaintiffs are those individuals or entities to whom a defendant could have reasonably expected to be harmed as a result of the defendant's act or omission.

Del does not necessarily owe a duty of care to Paula because she may be an unforeseeable plaintiff. Del's operation of his shop creates a legal duty to act pursuant to the applicable legal standard of care to lock up his shop, and arguably to use a burglar alarm. By failing to activate the burglar alarm, Del may be liable to Paula if it is foreseeable that this negligence could have proximately caused her injury due to the inmate's shooting.

The correct answer is (D) because Paula is a reasonably foreseeable plaintiff if the circumstances suggest a high risk of theft and criminal use of firearms by escaped inmates or others.

Answer (A) is incorrect. Activation of the motion detector would not necessarily have prevented Paula's injury.

Answer (B) is incorrect. Paula might have received the same injuries even if Del had activated the motion detector.

Answer (C) is a correct conclusion based on an accurate, but less than optimal, statement.